Garfield
Fat Cat 3 Pack
VOLUME 2

BY: JIM DAVIS

Ballantine Books • New York

GARFIELD WEIGHS IN: Copyright © 1982 by United Feature Syndicate, Inc.
GARFIELD TAKES THE CAKE Copyright © 1982 by United Feature Syndicate Inc.
GARFIELD EATS HIS HEART OUT Copyright © 1983 by United Feature Syndicate Inc.
GARFIELD Comic Strips Copyright © 1978, 1979 by United Feature Syndicate, Inc.

All rights reserved under International and Pan-American Copyright
Conventions. Published in the United States by Ballantine Books, a
division of Random House, Inc., New York, and simultaneously in
Canada by Random House of Canada Limited, Toronto.

Originally published by Ballantine Books as three separate volumes.

Library of Congress Catalog Card Number: 94-94383

ISBN: 0-345-39192-6

Manufactured in the United States of America

First Edition: September 1994

10 9 8 7 6 5 4 3

Garfield Weighs in

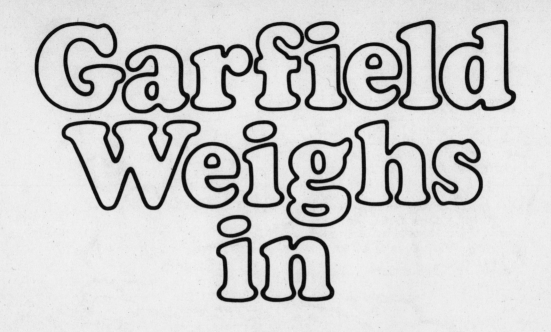

BY: JIM DAVIS

A GARFIELD MORNING

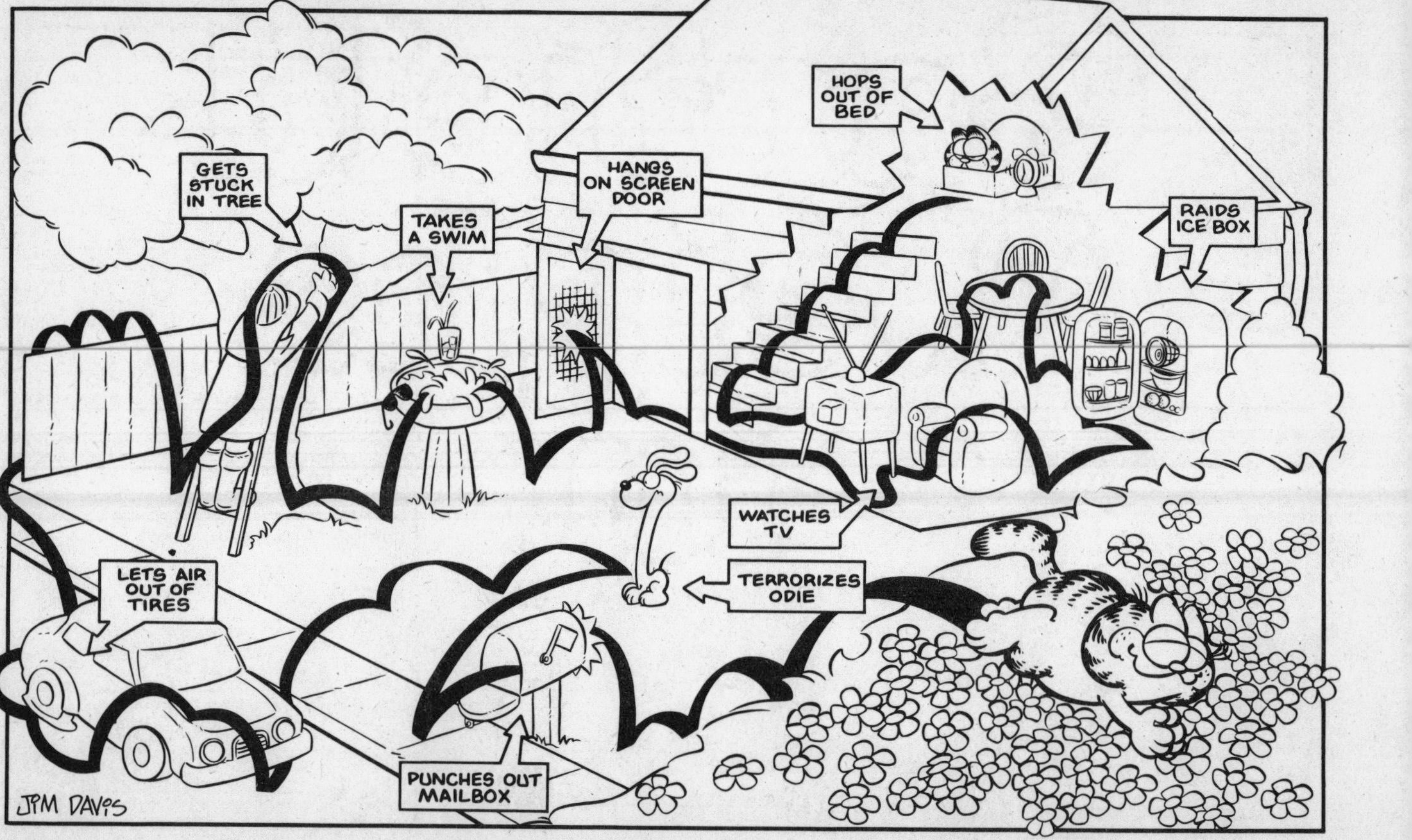

HOPS OUT OF BED
RAIDS ICE BOX
HANGS ON SCREEN DOOR
GETS STUCK IN TREE
TAKES A SWIM
WATCHES TV
TERRORIZES ODIE
LETS AIR OUT OF TIRES
PUNCHES OUT MAILBOX
JIM DAVIS

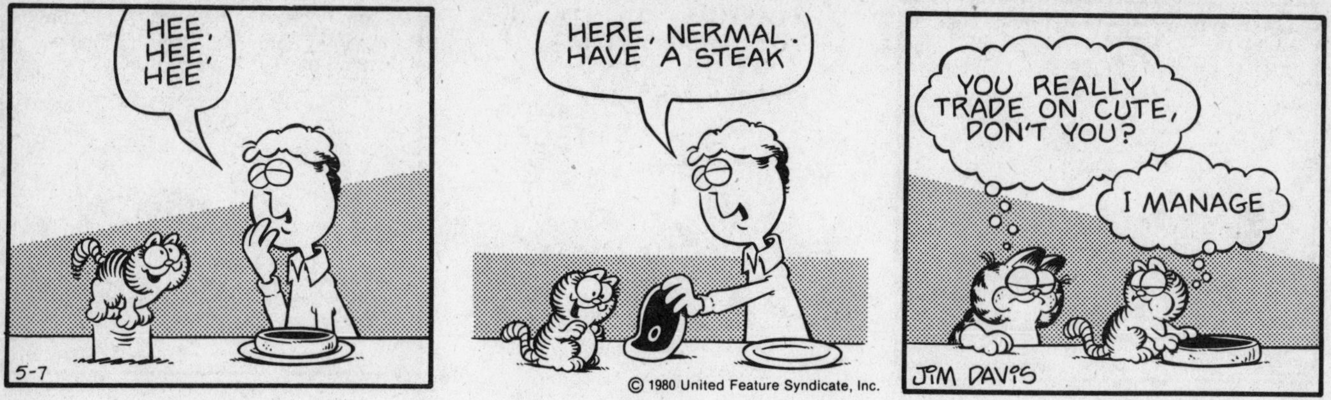
HEE, HEE, HEE
HERE, NERMAL. HAVE A STEAK
YOU REALLY TRADE ON CUTE, DON'T YOU?
I MANAGE
5-7
JIM DAVIS
© 1980 United Feature Syndicate, Inc.

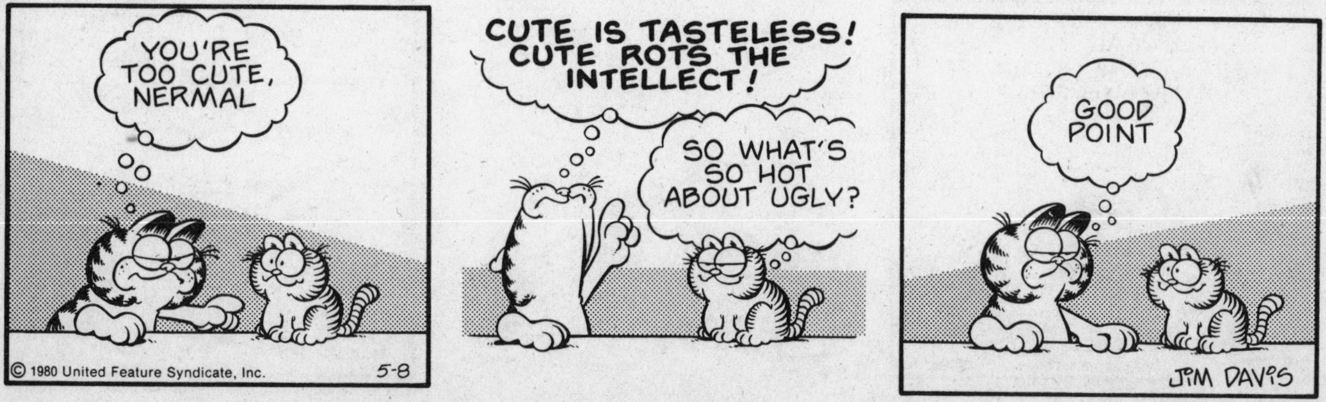
YOU'RE TOO CUTE, NERMAL
CUTE IS TASTELESS! CUTE ROTS THE INTELLECT!
SO WHAT'S SO HOT ABOUT UGLY?
GOOD POINT
© 1980 United Feature Syndicate, Inc.
5-8
JIM DAVIS

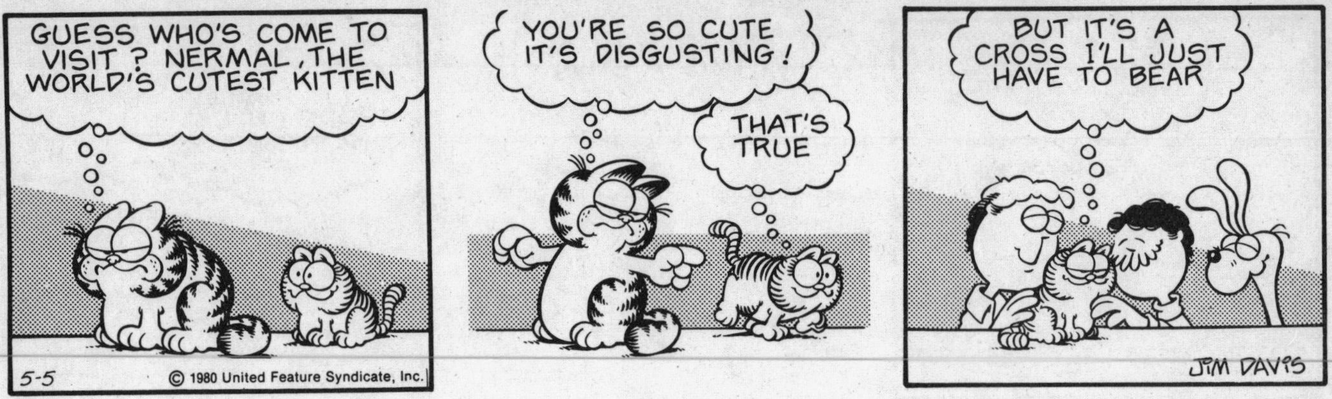
GUESS WHO'S COME TO VISIT ? NERMAL, THE WORLD'S CUTEST KITTEN
YOU'RE SO CUTE IT'S DISGUSTING !
THAT'S TRUE
BUT IT'S A CROSS I'LL JUST HAVE TO BEAR
5-5
© 1980 United Feature Syndicate, Inc.
JIM DAVIS

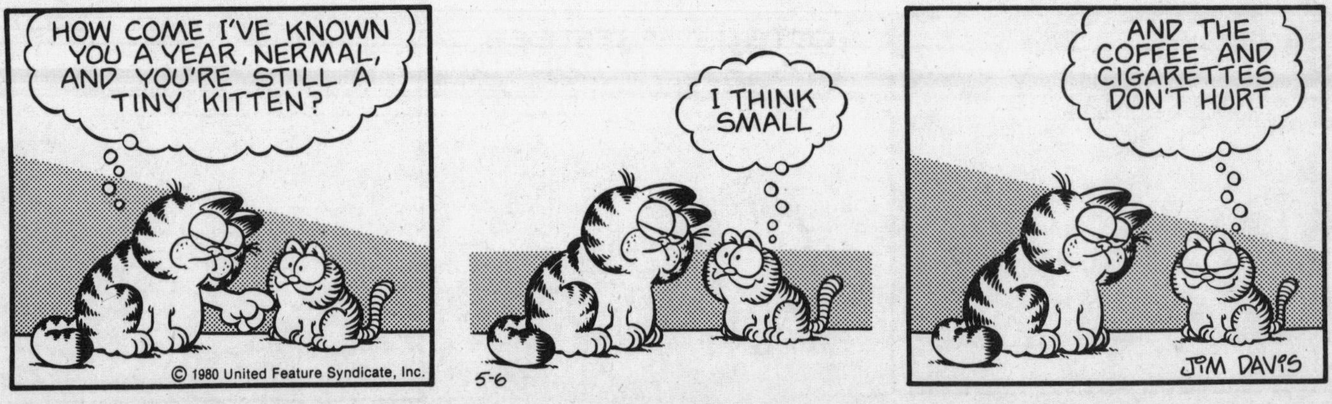
HOW COME I'VE KNOWN YOU A YEAR, NERMAL, AND YOU'RE STILL A TINY KITTEN?
I THINK SMALL
AND THE COFFEE AND CIGARETTES DON'T HURT
© 1980 United Feature Syndicate, Inc.
5-6
JIM DAVIS

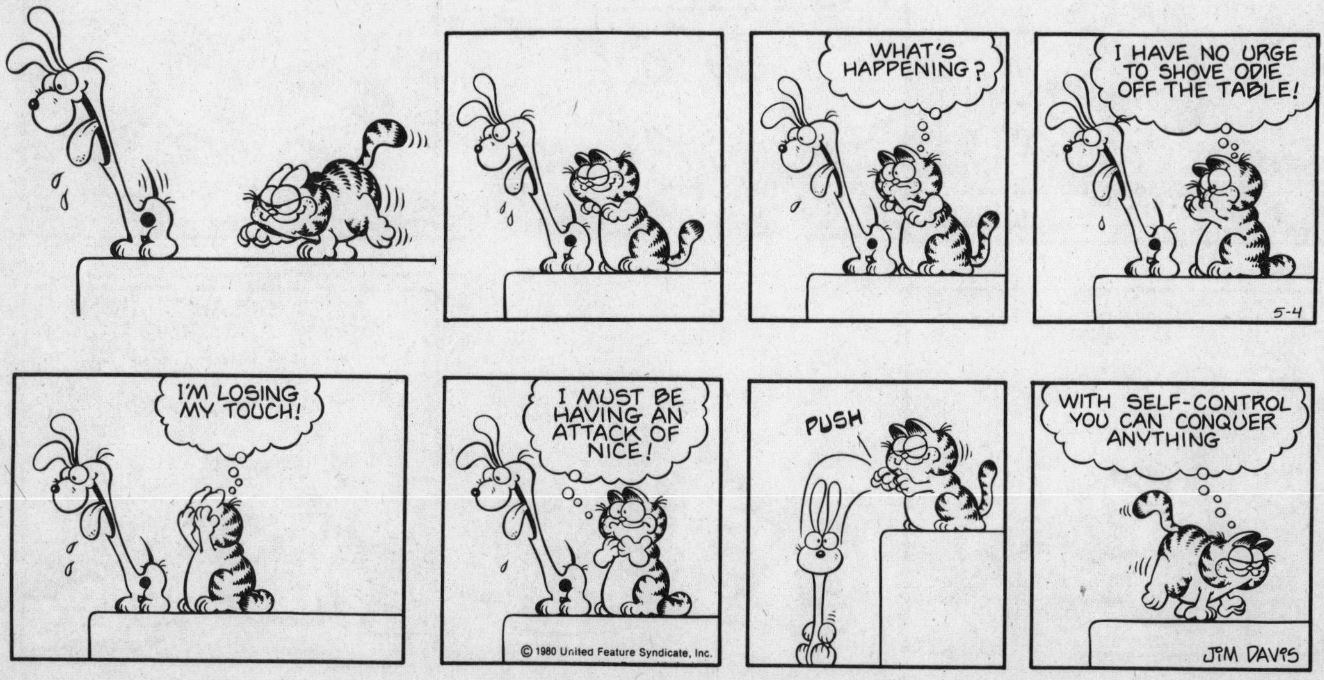
WHAT'S HAPPENING?
I HAVE NO URGE TO SHOVE ODIE OFF THE TABLE!
5-4
I'M LOSING MY TOUCH!
I MUST BE HAVING AN ATTACK OF NICE!
© 1980 United Feature Syndicate, Inc.
PUSH
WITH SELF-CONTROL YOU CAN CONQUER ANYTHING
JIM DAVIS

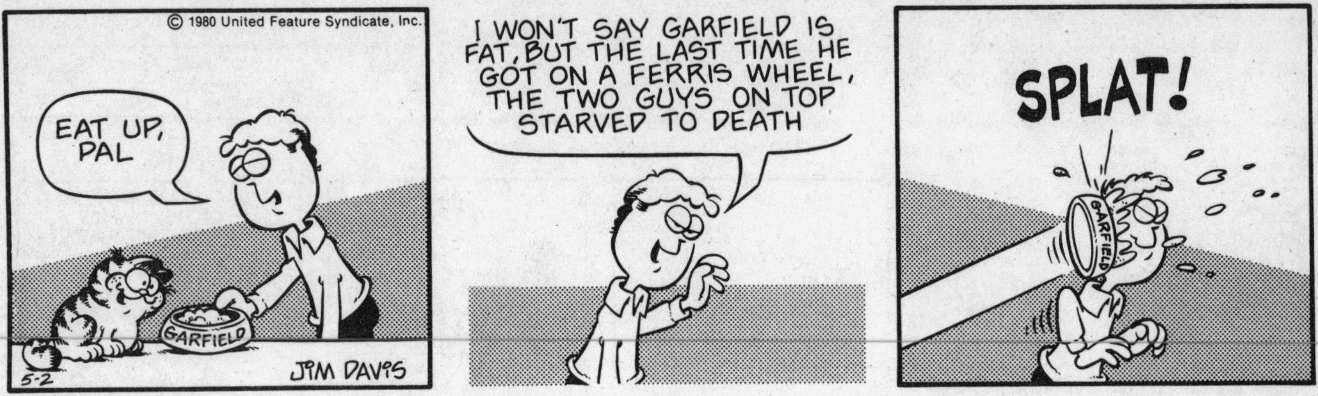
© 1980 United Feature Syndicate, Inc.
EAT UP, PAL
5-2
JIM DAVIS
I WON'T SAY GARFIELD IS FAT, BUT THE LAST TIME HE GOT ON A FERRIS WHEEL, THE TWO GUYS ON TOP STARVED TO DEATH
SPLAT!
GARFIELD

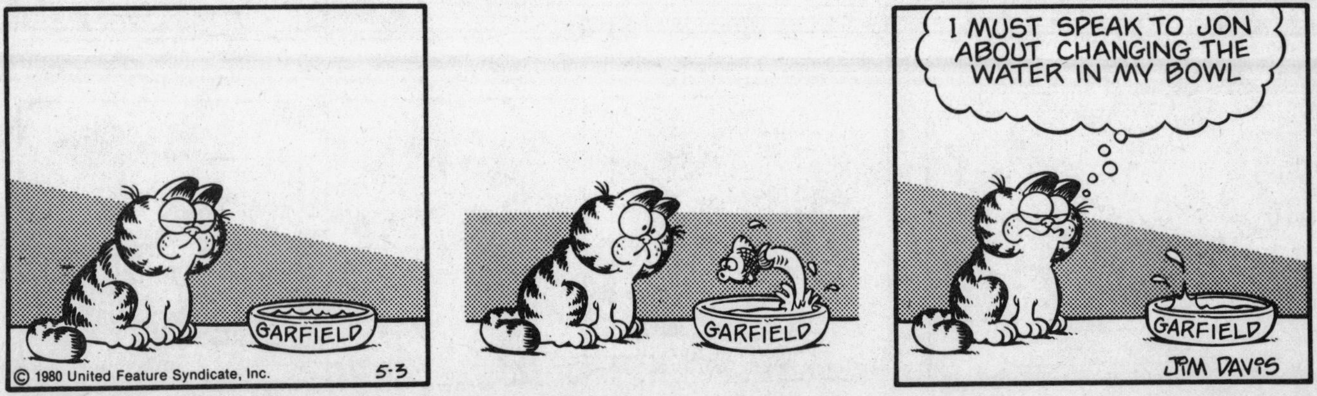
GARFIELD
© 1980 United Feature Syndicate, Inc.
5-3
GARFIELD
I MUST SPEAK TO JON ABOUT CHANGING THE WATER IN MY BOWL
GARFIELD
JIM DAVIS

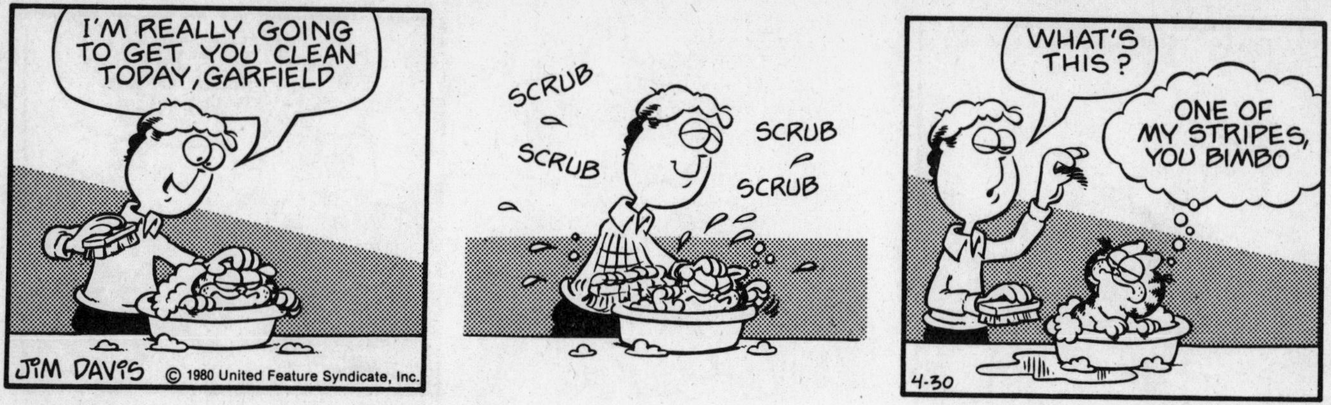
I'M REALLY GOING TO GET YOU CLEAN TODAY, GARFIELD
JIM DAVIS
© 1980 United Feature Syndicate, Inc.
SCRUB
SCRUB
SCRUB
SCRUB
WHAT'S THIS?
ONE OF MY STRIPES, YOU BIMBO
4-30

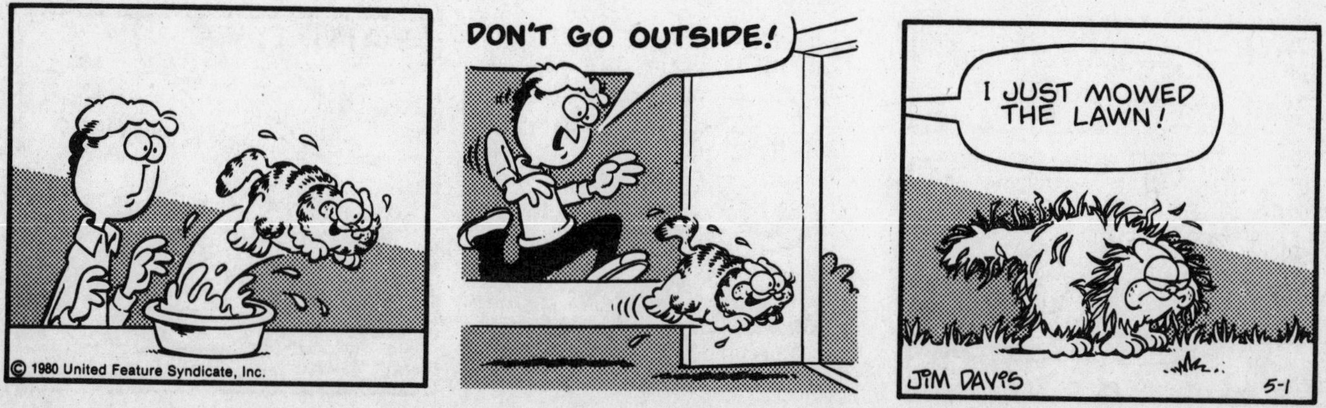
© 1980 United Feature Syndicate, Inc.
DON'T GO OUTSIDE!
I JUST MOWED THE LAWN!
JIM DAVIS
5-1

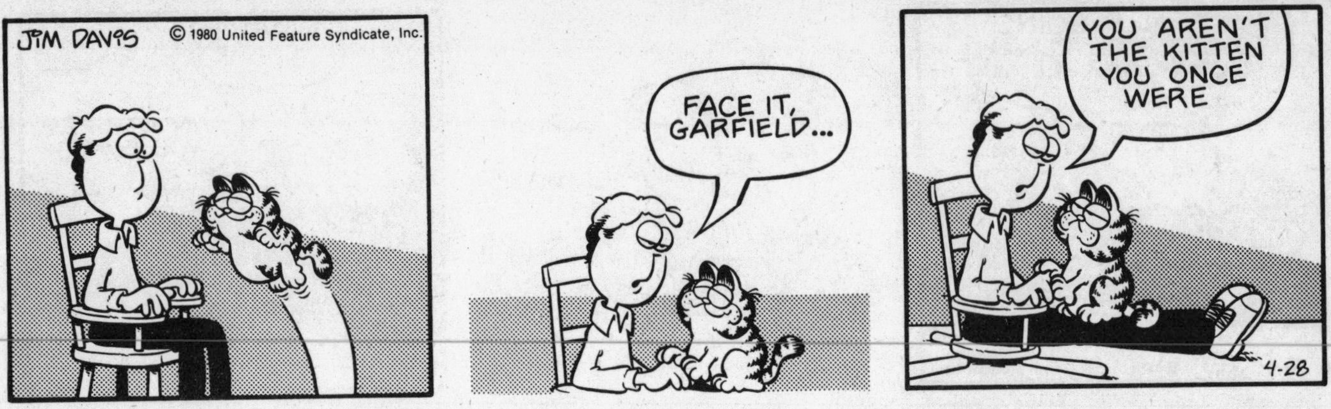
JIM DAVIS
© 1980 United Feature Syndicate, Inc.
FACE IT, GARFIELD...
YOU AREN'T THE KITTEN YOU ONCE WERE
4-28

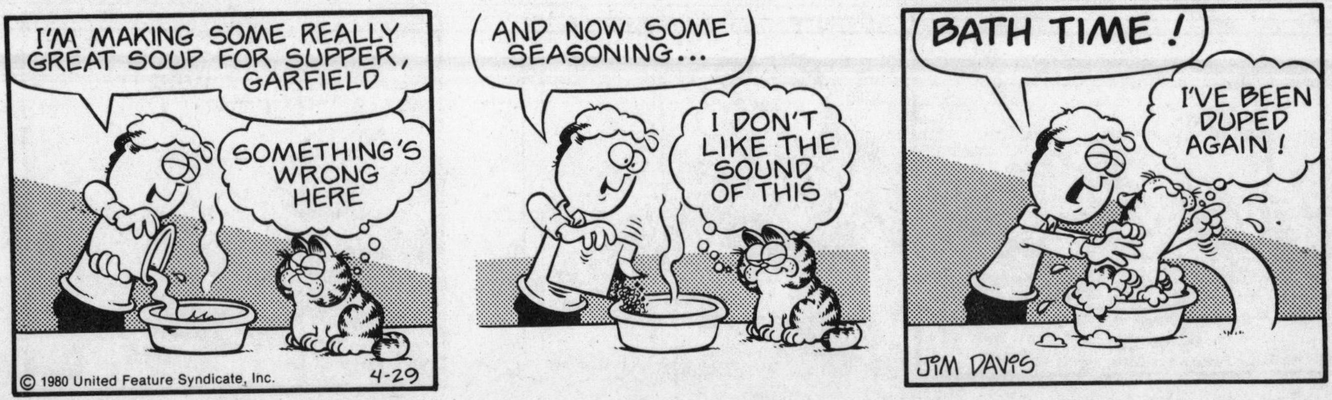
I'M MAKING SOME REALLY GREAT SOUP FOR SUPPER, GARFIELD
SOMETHING'S WRONG HERE
© 1980 United Feature Syndicate, Inc.
4-29
AND NOW SOME SEASONING...
I DON'T LIKE THE SOUND OF THIS
BATH TIME!
I'VE BEEN DUPED AGAIN!
JIM DAVIS

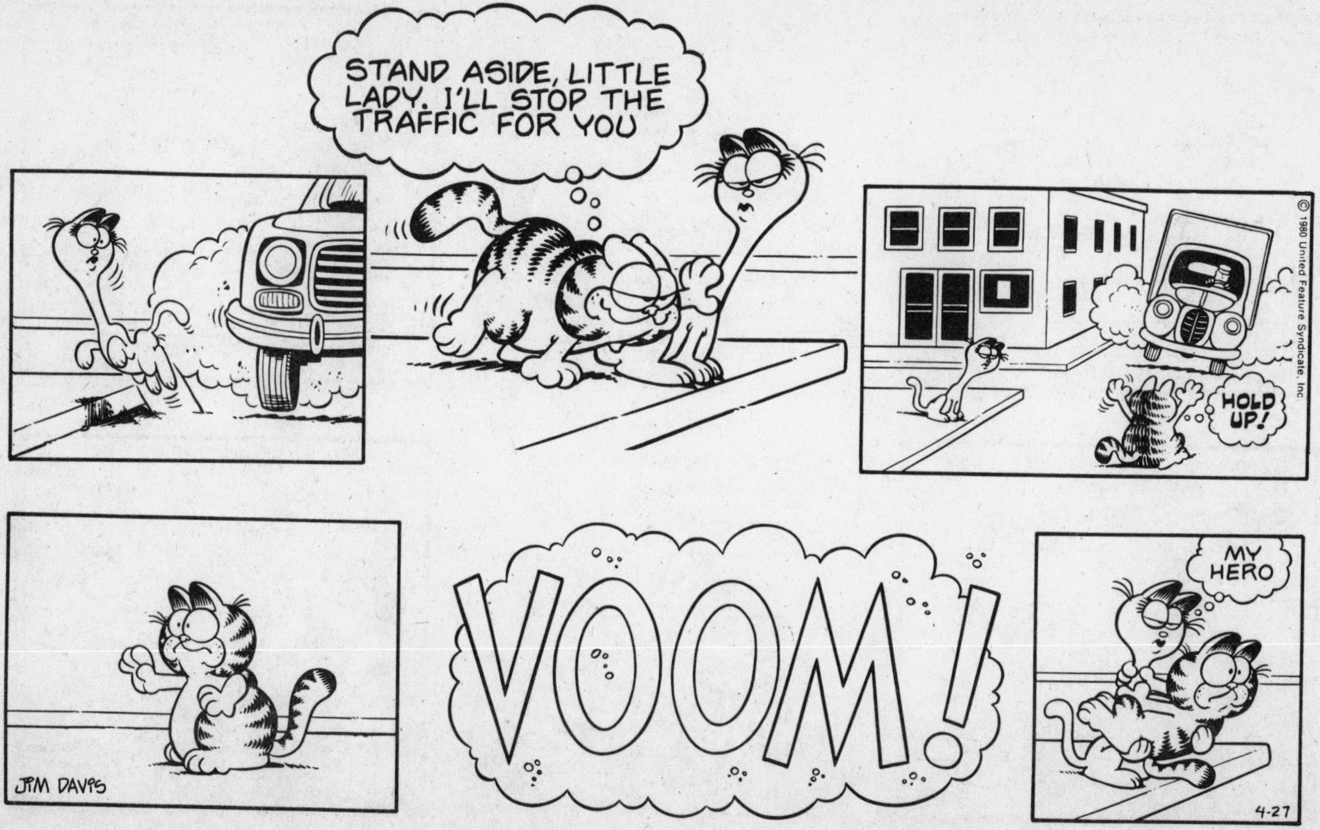
STAND ASIDE, LITTLE LADY. I'LL STOP THE TRAFFIC FOR YOU
HOLD UP!
© 1980 United Feature Syndicate, Inc.
VOOM!
JIM DAVIS
MY HERO
4-27

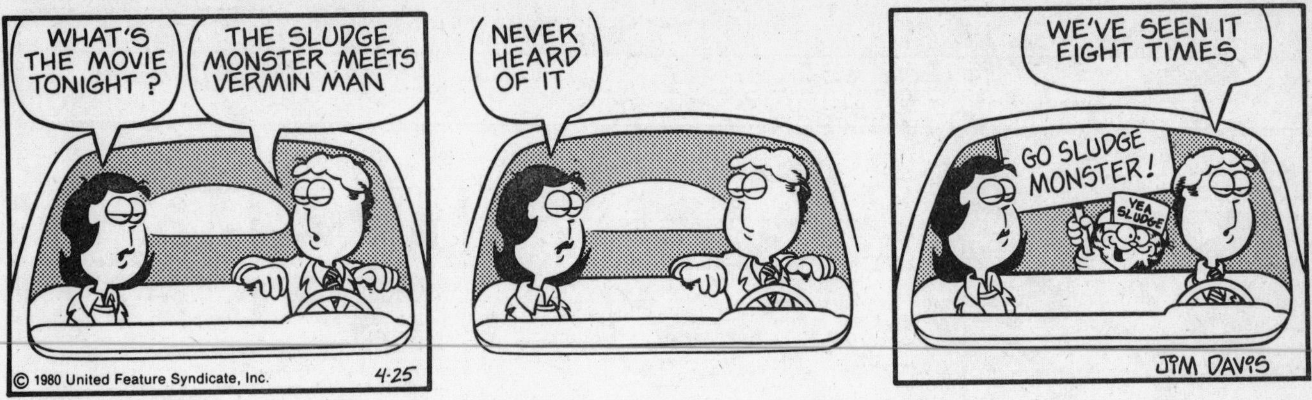
WHAT'S THE MOVIE TONIGHT ?
THE SLUDGE MONSTER MEETS VERMIN MAN
NEVER HEARD OF IT
GO SLUDGE MONSTER!
YEA SLUDGE
WE'VE SEEN IT EIGHT TIMES
© 1980 United Feature Syndicate, Inc.
4-25
JIM DAVIS

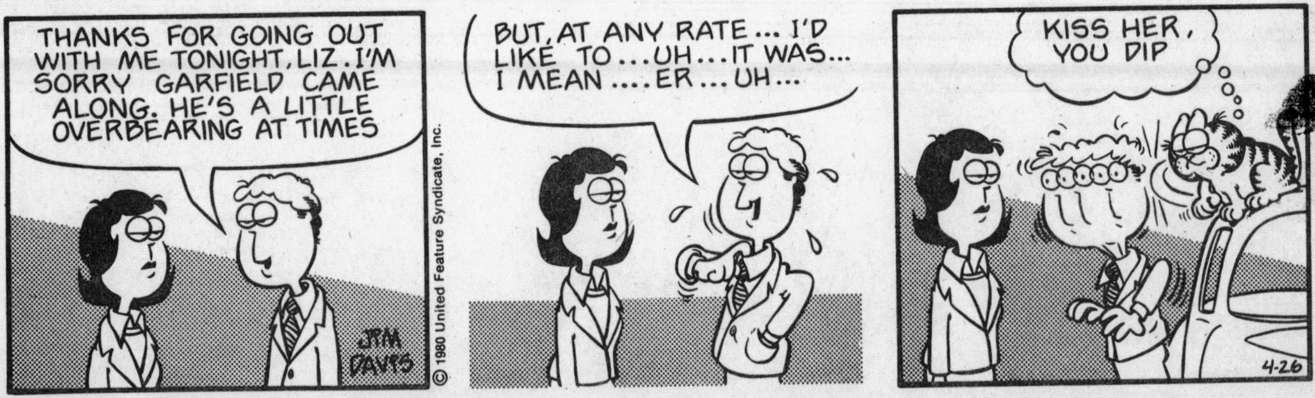
THANKS FOR GOING OUT WITH ME TONIGHT, LIZ. I'M SORRY GARFIELD CAME ALONG. HE'S A LITTLE OVERBEARING AT TIMES
JIM DAVIS
© 1980 United Feature Syndicate, Inc.
BUT, AT ANY RATE ... I'D LIKE TO ... UH ... IT WAS ... I MEAN .... ER ... UH ...
KISS HER, YOU DIP
4-26

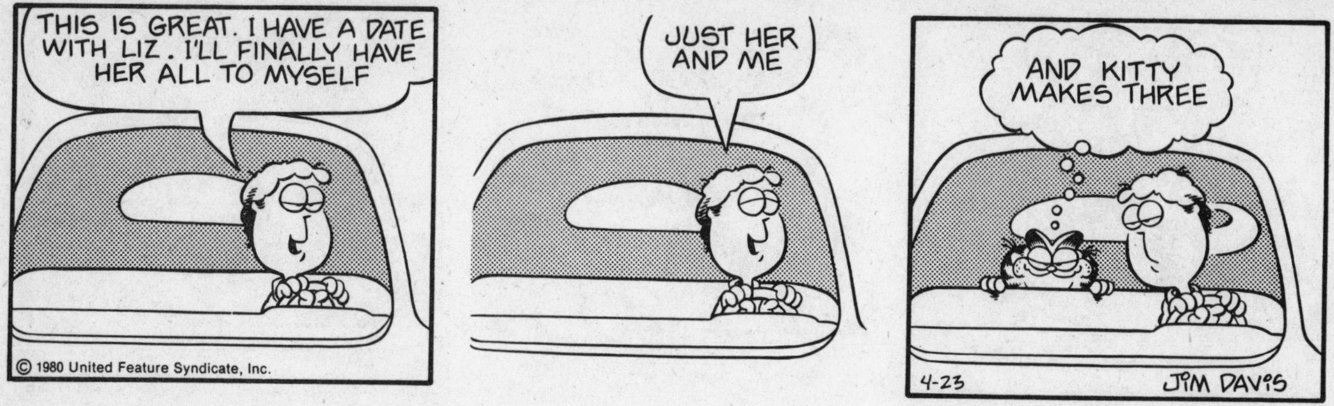
THIS IS GREAT. I HAVE A DATE WITH LIZ. I'LL FINALLY HAVE HER ALL TO MYSELF
© 1980 United Feature Syndicate, Inc.
JUST HER AND ME
AND KITTY MAKES THREE
4-23
JIM DAVIS

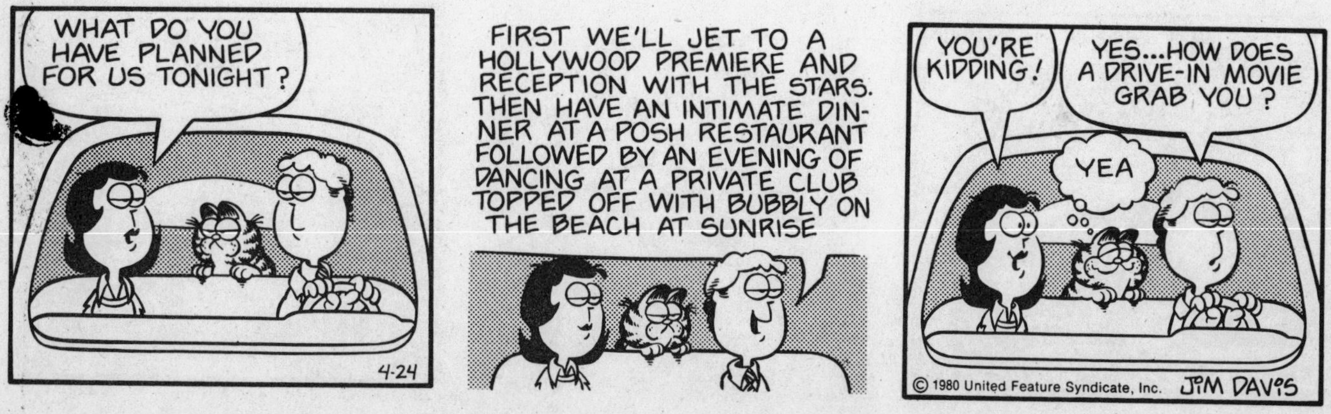
WHAT DO YOU HAVE PLANNED FOR US TONIGHT?
4-24
FIRST WE'LL JET TO A HOLLYWOOD PREMIERE AND RECEPTION WITH THE STARS. THEN HAVE AN INTIMATE DINNER AT A POSH RESTAURANT FOLLOWED BY AN EVENING OF DANCING AT A PRIVATE CLUB TOPPED OFF WITH BUBBLY ON THE BEACH AT SUNRISE
YOU'RE KIDDING!
YES...HOW DOES A DRIVE-IN MOVIE GRAB YOU?
YEA
© 1980 United Feature Syndicate, Inc.
JIM DAVIS

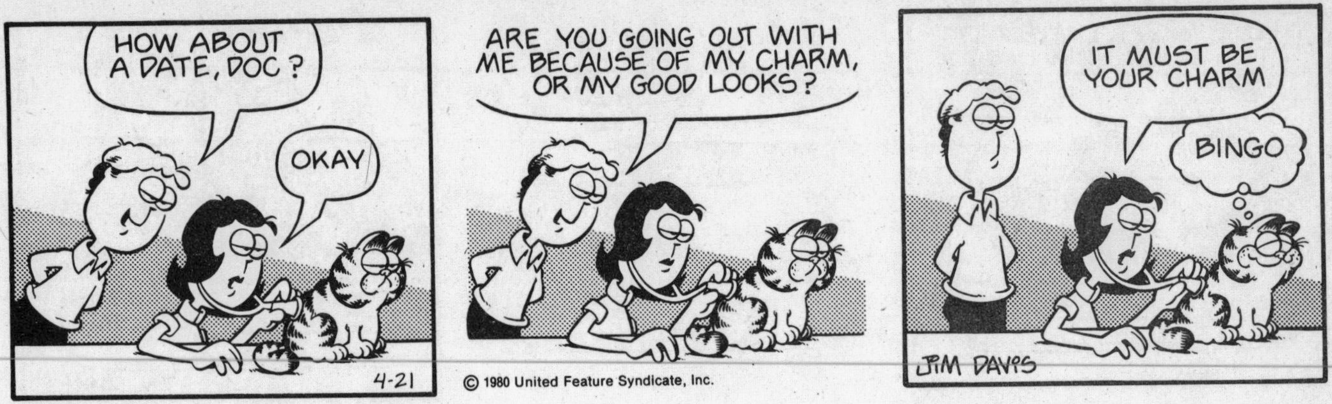
HOW ABOUT A DATE, DOC?
OKAY
ARE YOU GOING OUT WITH ME BECAUSE OF MY CHARM, OR MY GOOD LOOKS?
IT MUST BE YOUR CHARM
BINGO
4-21
© 1980 United Feature Syndicate, Inc.
JIM DAVIS

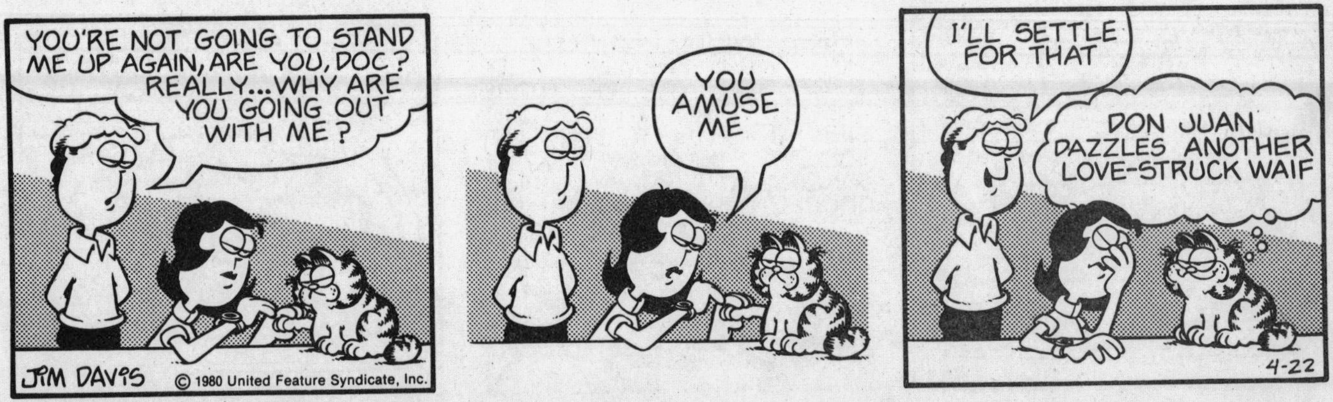
YOU'RE NOT GOING TO STAND ME UP AGAIN, ARE YOU, DOC? REALLY...WHY ARE YOU GOING OUT WITH ME?
JIM DAVIS
© 1980 United Feature Syndicate, Inc.
YOU AMUSE ME
I'LL SETTLE FOR THAT
DON JUAN DAZZLES ANOTHER LOVE-STRUCK WAIF
4-22

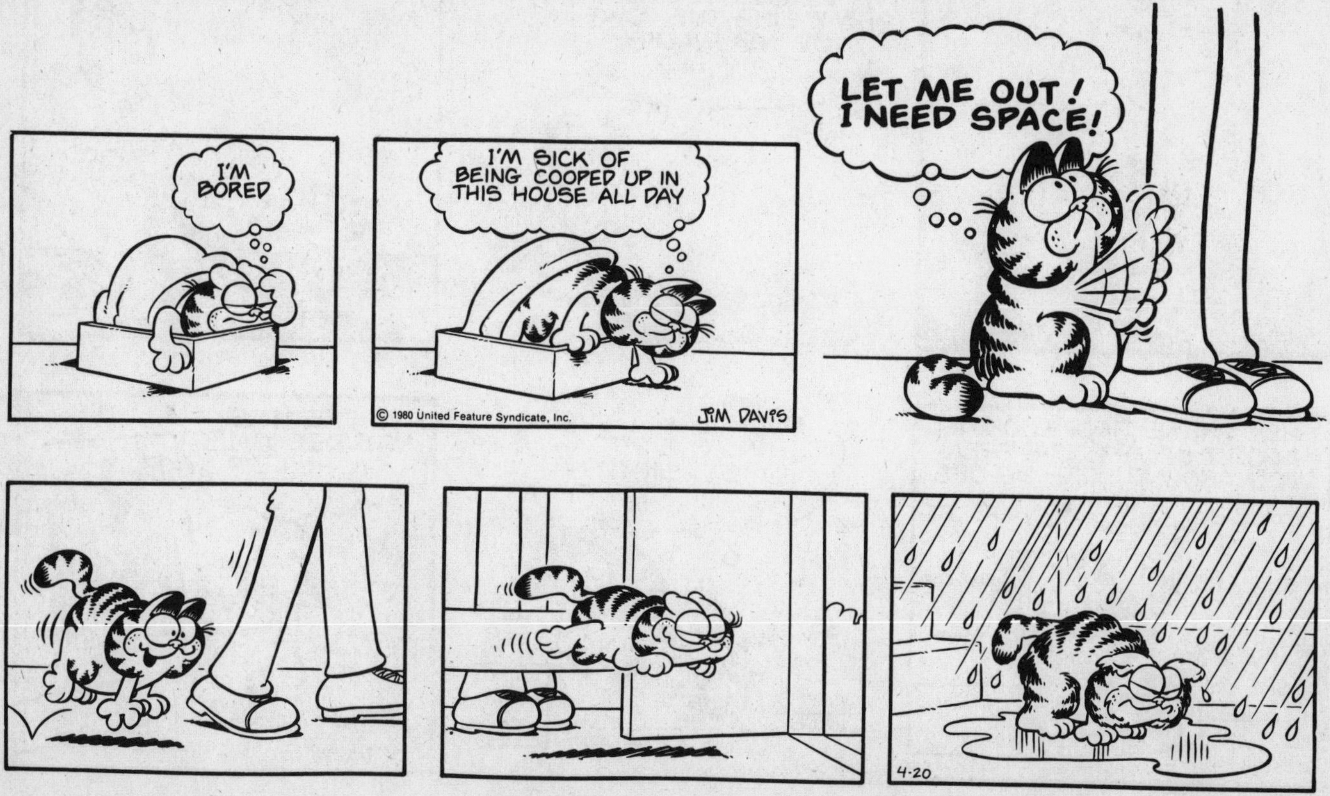
I'M BORED
I'M SICK OF BEING COOPED UP IN THIS HOUSE ALL DAY
© 1980 United Feature Syndicate, Inc.
JIM DAVIS
LET ME OUT! I NEED SPACE!
4-20

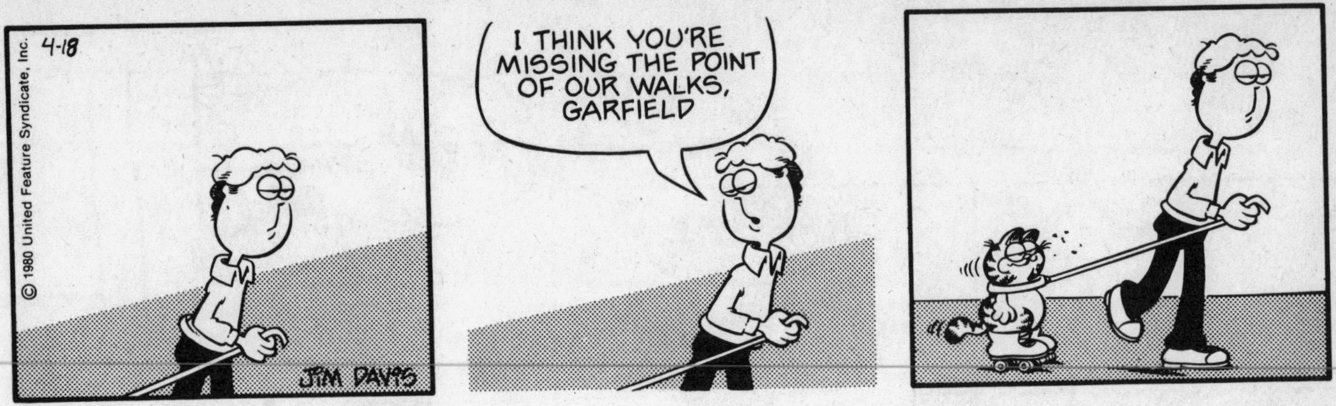
4-18
© 1980 United Feature Syndicate, Inc.
JIM DAVIS
I THINK YOU'RE MISSING THE POINT OF OUR WALKS, GARFIELD

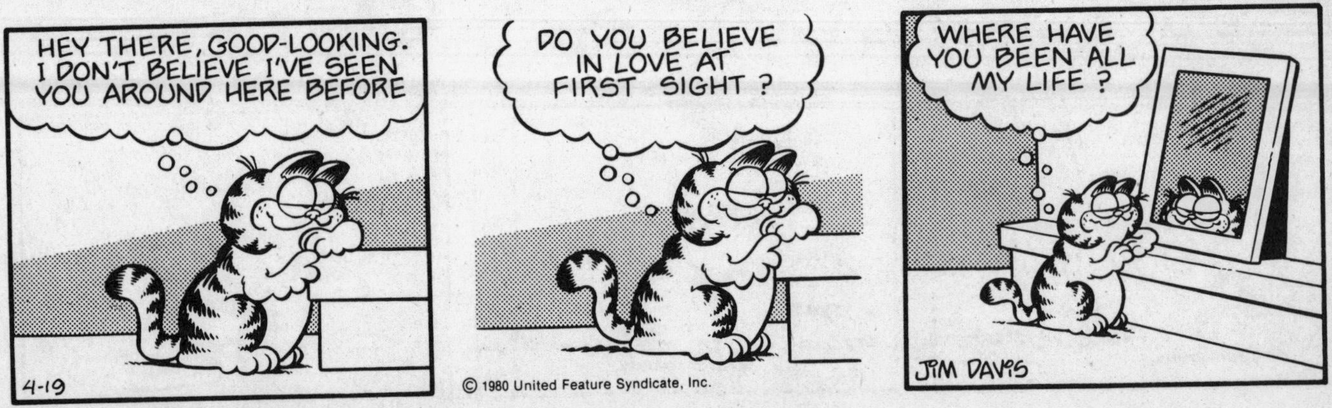
HEY THERE, GOOD-LOOKING. I DON'T BELIEVE I'VE SEEN YOU AROUND HERE BEFORE
4-19
DO YOU BELIEVE IN LOVE AT FIRST SIGHT ?
© 1980 United Feature Syndicate, Inc.
WHERE HAVE YOU BEEN ALL MY LIFE ?
JIM DAVIS

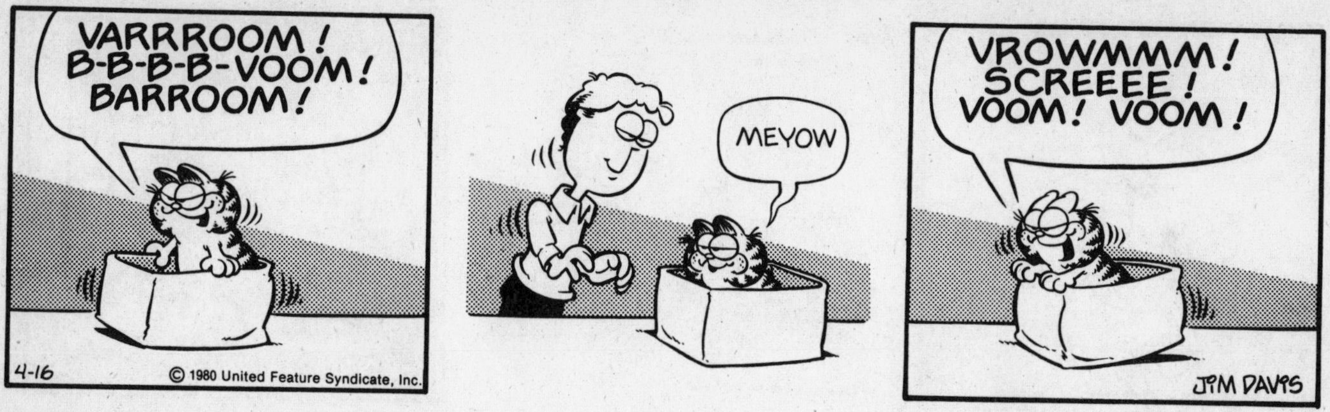
VARRROOM! B-B-B-B-VOOM! BARROOM!
4-16
© 1980 United Feature Syndicate, Inc.
MEYOW
VROWMMM! SCREEEE! VOOM! VOOM!
JIM DAVIS

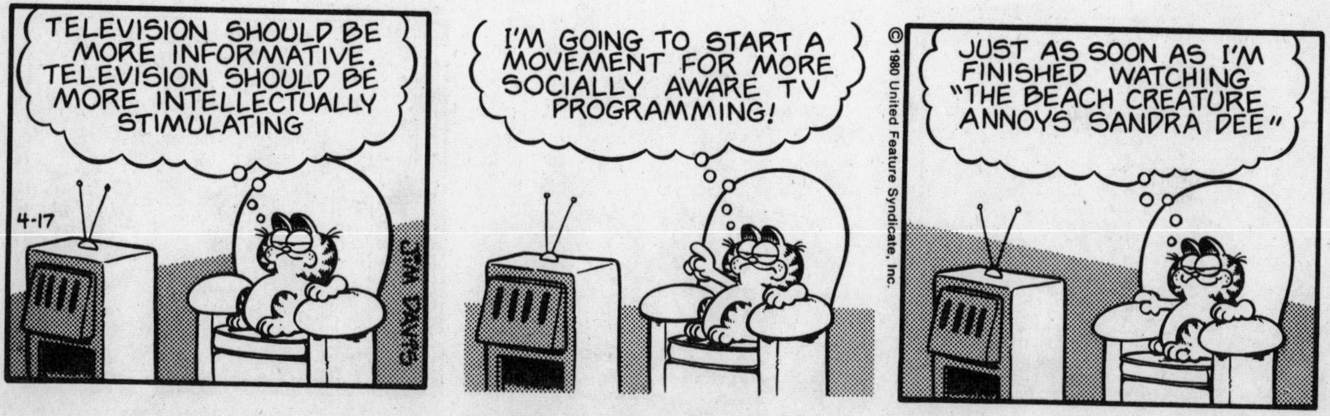
TELEVISION SHOULD BE MORE INFORMATIVE. TELEVISION SHOULD BE MORE INTELLECTUALLY STIMULATING
4-17
JIM DAVIS
I'M GOING TO START A MOVEMENT FOR MORE SOCIALLY AWARE TV PROGRAMMING!
© 1980 United Feature Syndicate, Inc.
JUST AS SOON AS I'M FINISHED WATCHING "THE BEACH CREATURE ANNOYS SANDRA DEE"

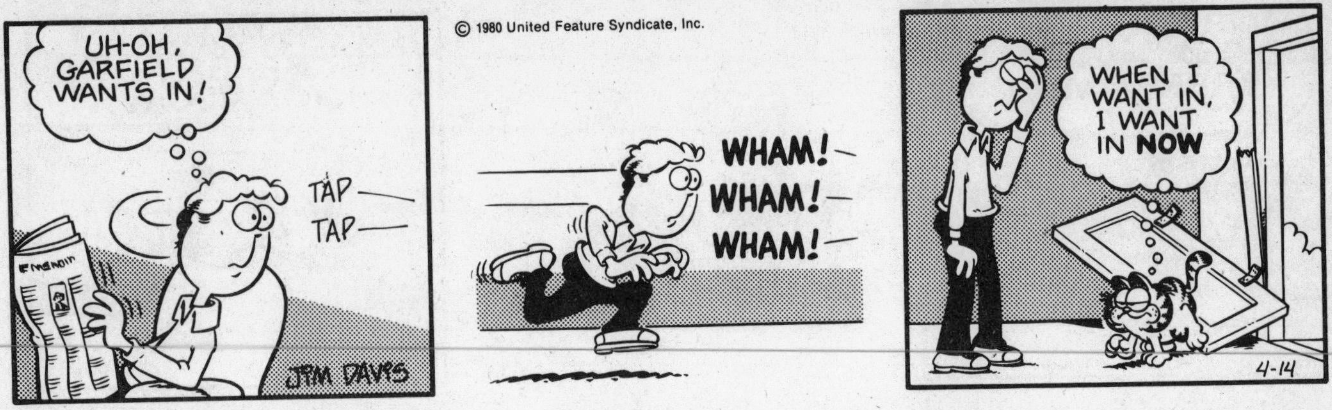

UH-OH, GARFIELD WANTS IN!
TAP
TAP
JIM DAVIS
© 1980 United Feature Syndicate, Inc.
WHAM!
WHAM!
WHAM!
WHEN I WANT IN, I WANT IN **NOW**
4-14

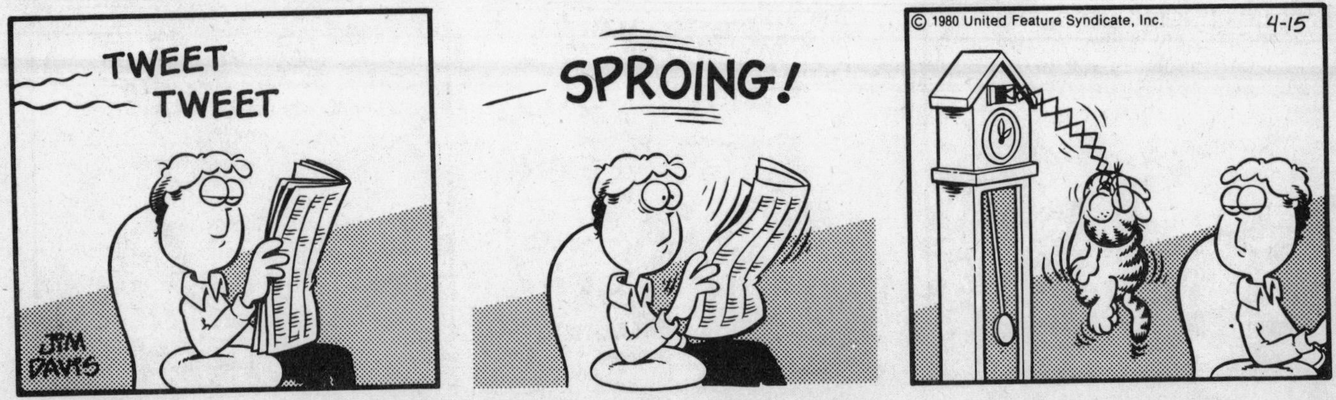

TWEET
TWEET
JIM DAVIS
SPROING!
© 1980 United Feature Syndicate, Inc.
4-15

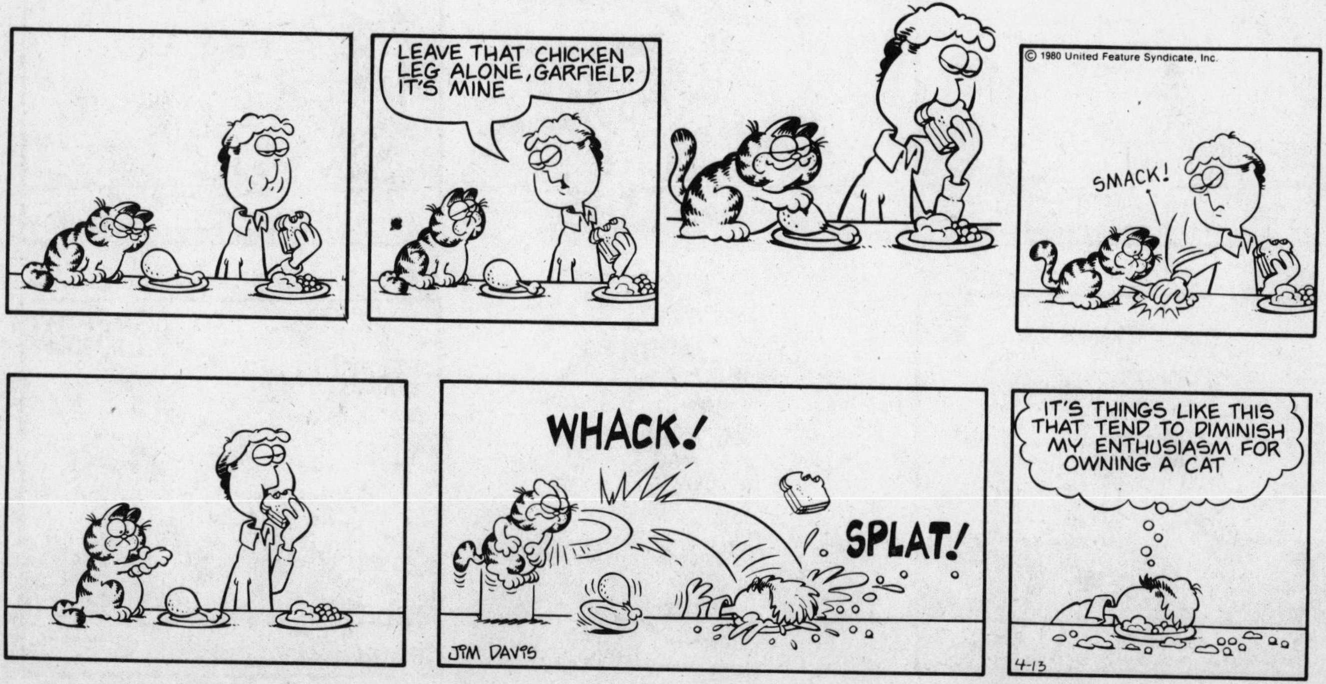

LEAVE THAT CHICKEN LEG ALONE, GARFIELD. IT'S MINE
© 1980 United Feature Syndicate, Inc.
SMACK!
WHACK!
SPLAT!
JIM DAVIS
IT'S THINGS LIKE THIS THAT TEND TO DIMINISH MY ENTHUSIASM FOR OWNING A CAT
4-13

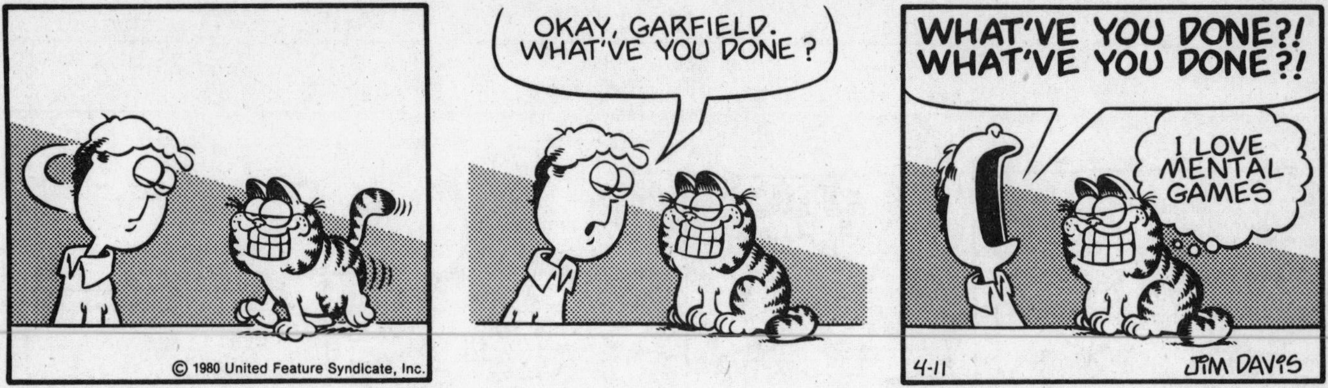
OKAY, GARFIELD.
WHAT'VE YOU DONE ?
WHAT'VE YOU DONE?!
WHAT'VE YOU DONE?!
I LOVE MENTAL GAMES
© 1980 United Feature Syndicate, Inc.
4-11
JIM DAVIS

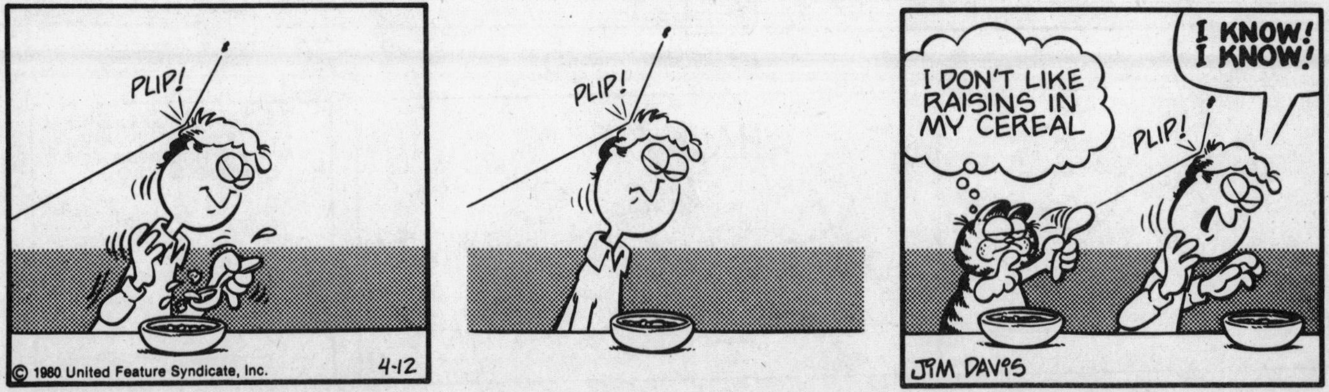
PLIP!
PLIP!
I DON'T LIKE RAISINS IN MY CEREAL
PLIP!
I KNOW! I KNOW!
© 1980 United Feature Syndicate, Inc.
4-12
JIM DAVIS

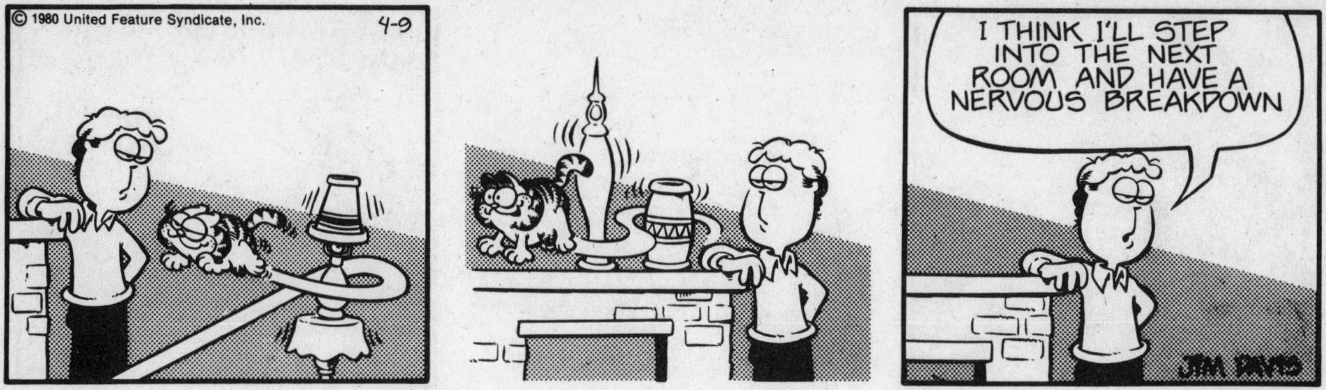
© 1980 United Feature Syndicate, Inc.
4-9
I THINK I'LL STEP INTO THE NEXT ROOM AND HAVE A NERVOUS BREAKDOWN
JIM DAVIS

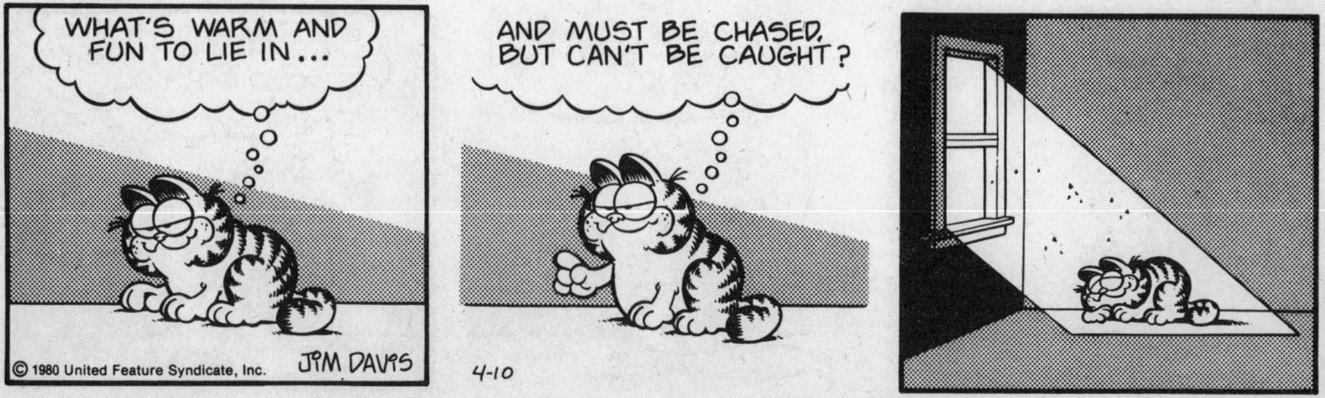
WHAT'S WARM AND FUN TO LIE IN...
© 1980 United Feature Syndicate, Inc.
JIM DAVIS
AND MUST BE CHASED, BUT CAN'T BE CAUGHT?
4-10

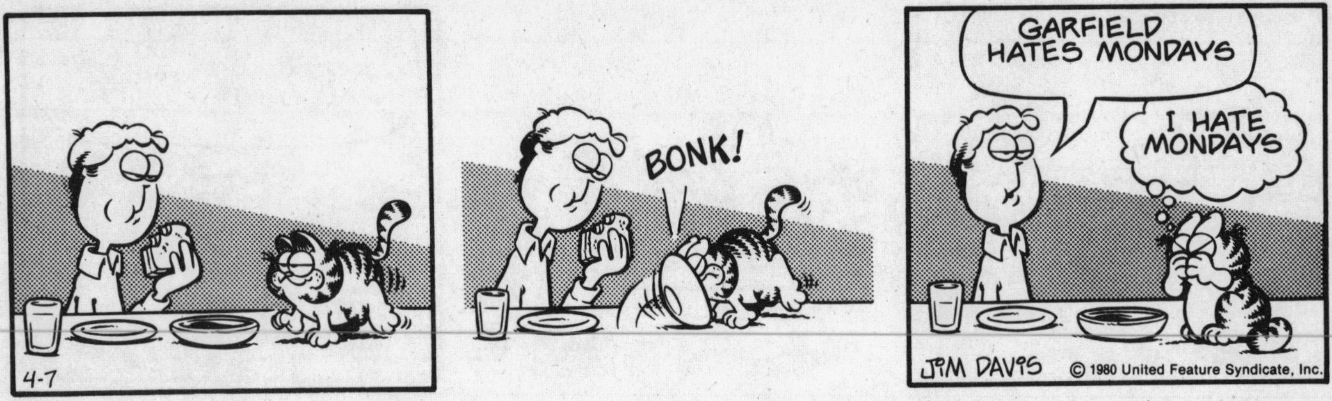

4-7
BONK!
GARFIELD HATES MONDAYS
I HATE MONDAYS
JIM DAVIS
© 1980 United Feature Syndicate, Inc.

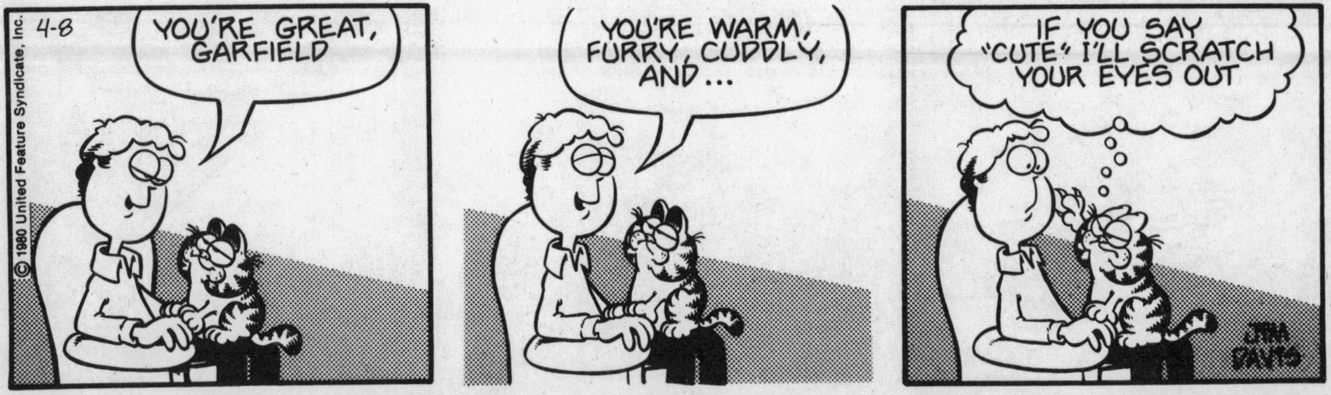

© 1980 United Feature Syndicate, Inc.
4-8
YOU'RE GREAT, GARFIELD
YOU'RE WARM, FURRY, CUDDLY, AND...
IF YOU SAY "CUTE" I'LL SCRATCH YOUR EYES OUT
JIM DAVIS

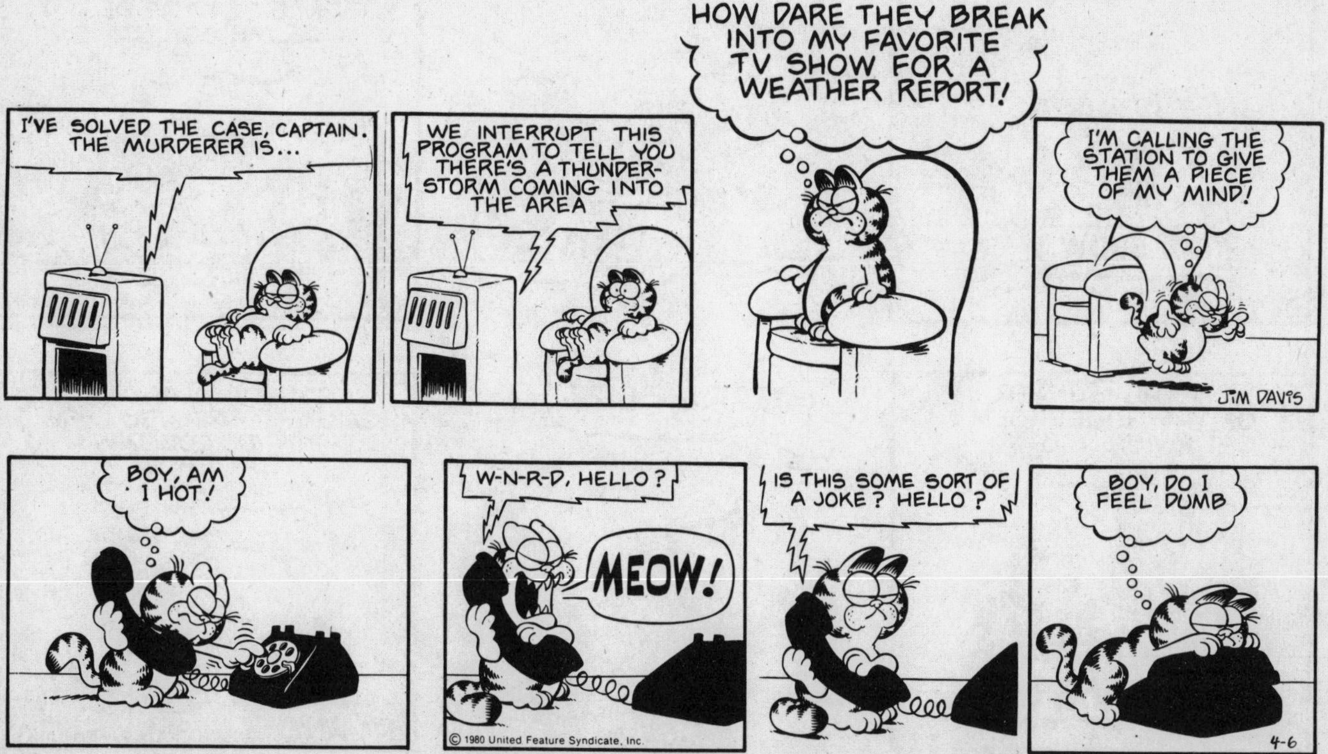
I'VE SOLVED THE CASE, CAPTAIN. THE MURDERER IS...
WE INTERRUPT THIS PROGRAM TO TELL YOU THERE'S A THUNDER-STORM COMING INTO THE AREA
HOW DARE THEY BREAK INTO MY FAVORITE TV SHOW FOR A WEATHER REPORT!
I'M CALLING THE STATION TO GIVE THEM A PIECE OF MY MIND!
JIM DAVIS
BOY, AM I HOT!
W-N-R-D, HELLO?
MEOW!
IS THIS SOME SORT OF A JOKE? HELLO?
BOY, DO I FEEL DUMB
© 1980 United Feature Syndicate, Inc.
4-6

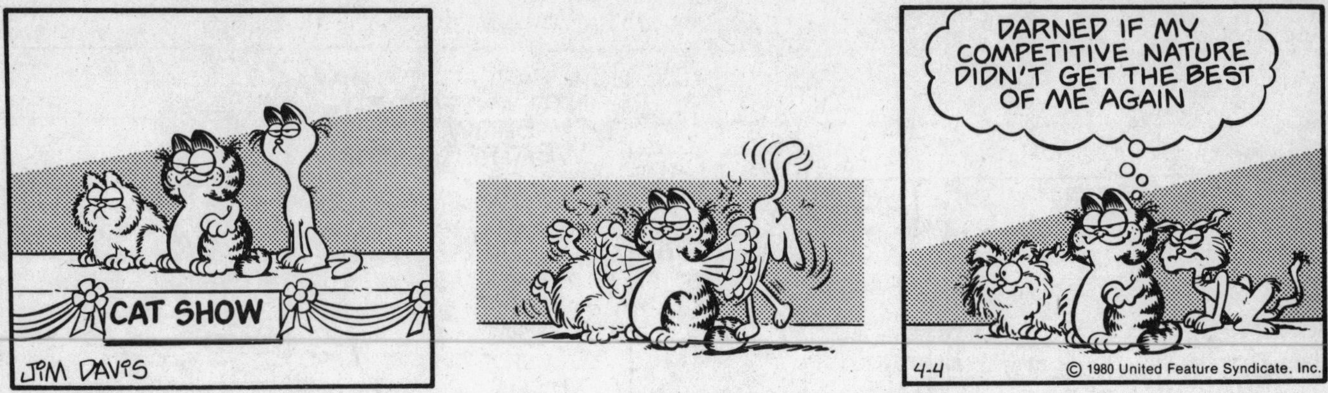
CAT SHOW
JIM DAVIS
DARNED IF MY COMPETITIVE NATURE DIDN'T GET THE BEST OF ME AGAIN
4-4
© 1980 United Feature Syndicate, Inc.

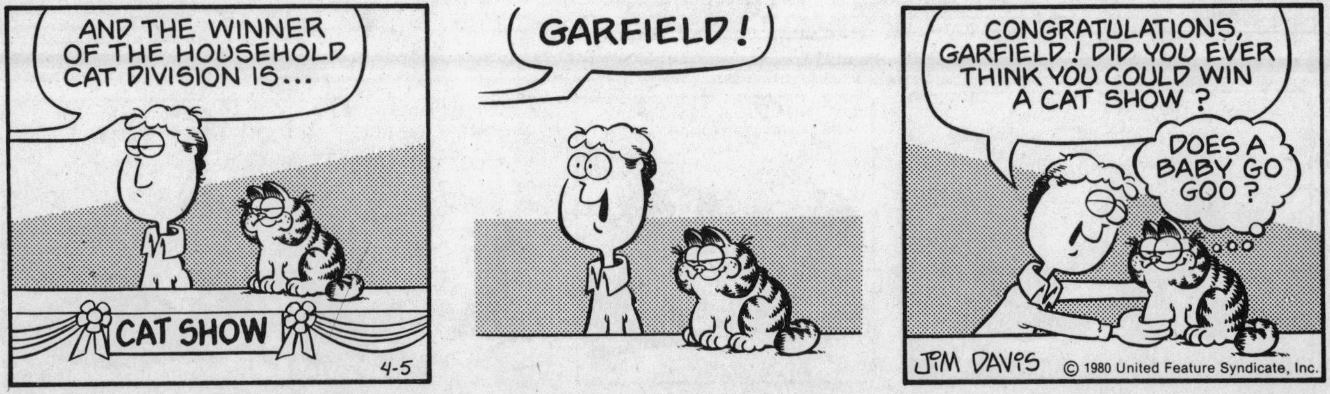
AND THE WINNER OF THE HOUSEHOLD CAT DIVISION IS...
CAT SHOW
4-5
GARFIELD!
CONGRATULATIONS, GARFIELD! DID YOU EVER THINK YOU COULD WIN A CAT SHOW?
DOES A BABY GO GOO?
JIM DAVIS
© 1980 United Feature Syndicate, Inc.

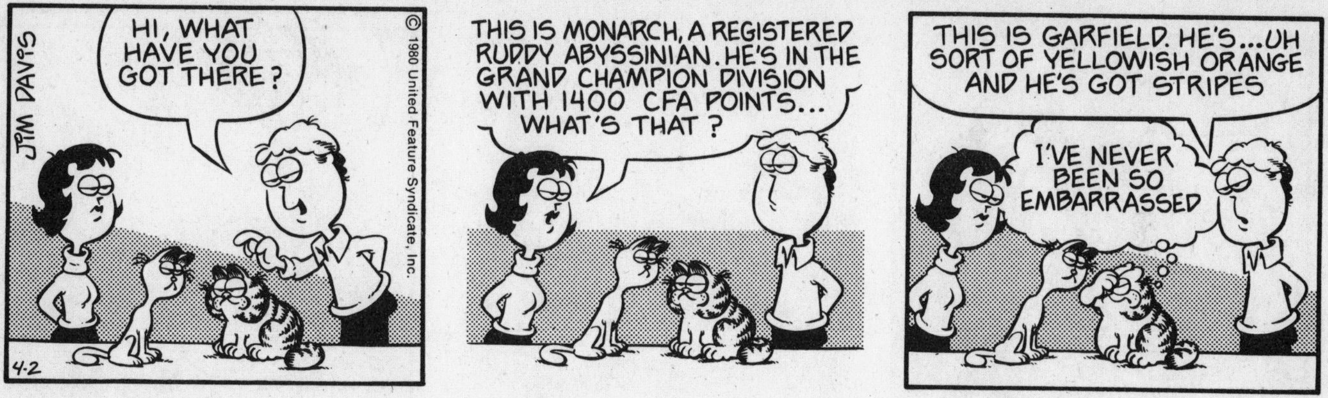
JIM DAVIS
HI, WHAT HAVE YOU GOT THERE?
© 1980 United Feature Syndicate, Inc.
4-2
THIS IS MONARCH, A REGISTERED RUDDY ABYSSINIAN. HE'S IN THE GRAND CHAMPION DIVISION WITH 1400 CFA POINTS... WHAT'S THAT?
THIS IS GARFIELD. HE'S...UH SORT OF YELLOWISH ORANGE AND HE'S GOT STRIPES
I'VE NEVER BEEN SO EMBARRASSED

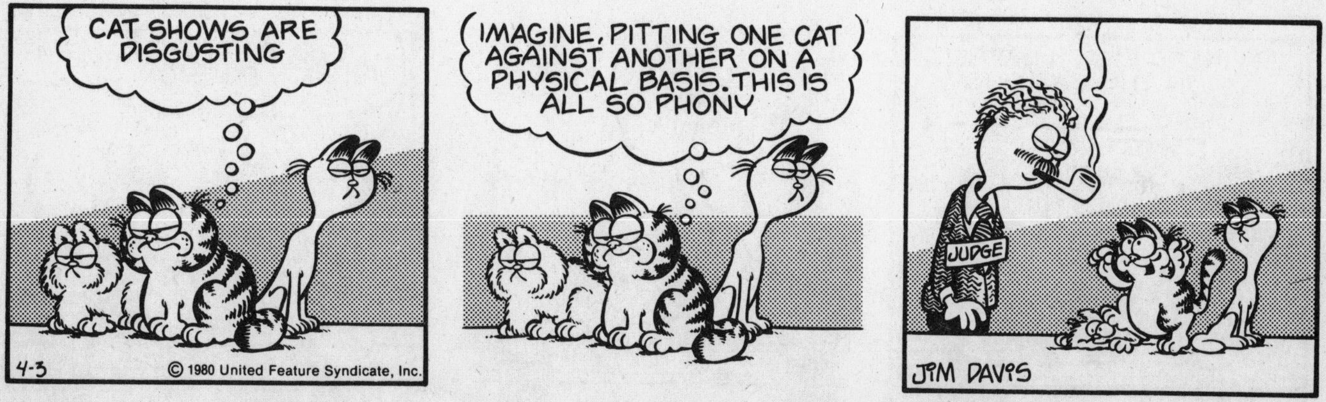
CAT SHOWS ARE DISGUSTING
4-3
© 1980 United Feature Syndicate, Inc.
IMAGINE, PITTING ONE CAT AGAINST ANOTHER ON A PHYSICAL BASIS. THIS IS ALL SO PHONY
JUDGE
JIM DAVIS

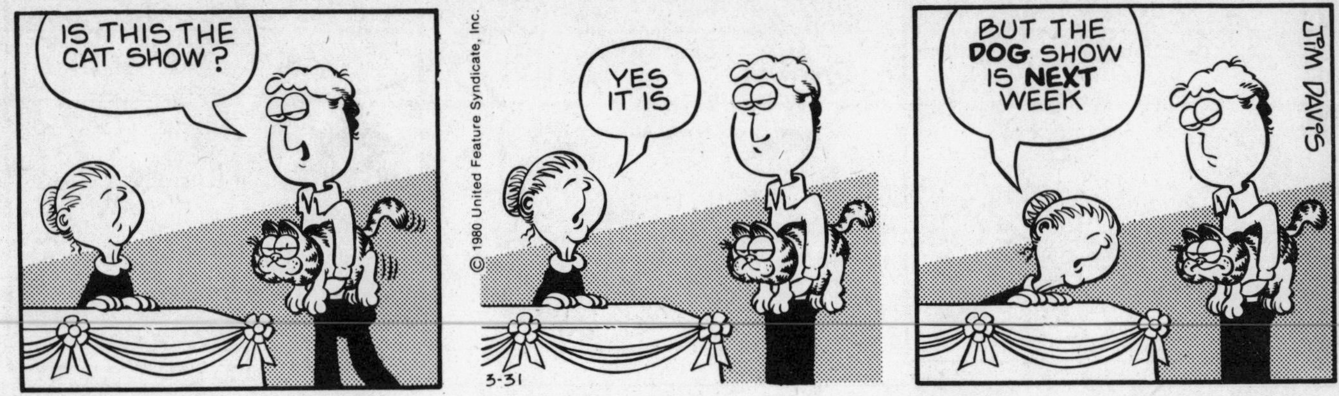
IS THIS THE CAT SHOW?
YES IT IS
BUT THE **DOG** SHOW IS **NEXT** WEEK
JIM DAVIS
© 1980 United Feature Syndicate, Inc.
3-31

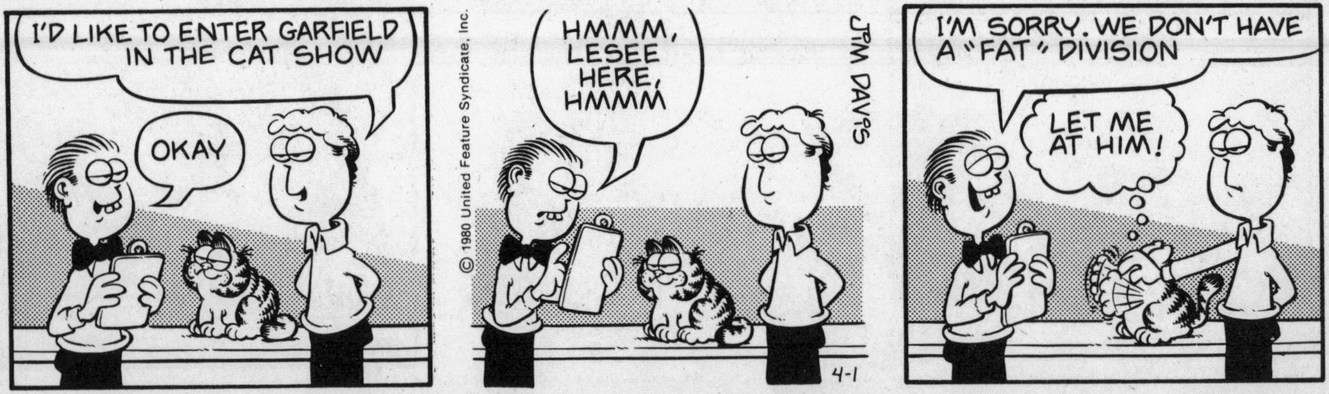
I'D LIKE TO ENTER GARFIELD IN THE CAT SHOW
OKAY
HMMM, LESEE HERE, HMMM
I'M SORRY. WE DON'T HAVE A "FAT" DIVISION
LET ME AT HIM!
JIM DAVIS
© 1980 United Feature Syndicate, Inc.
4-1

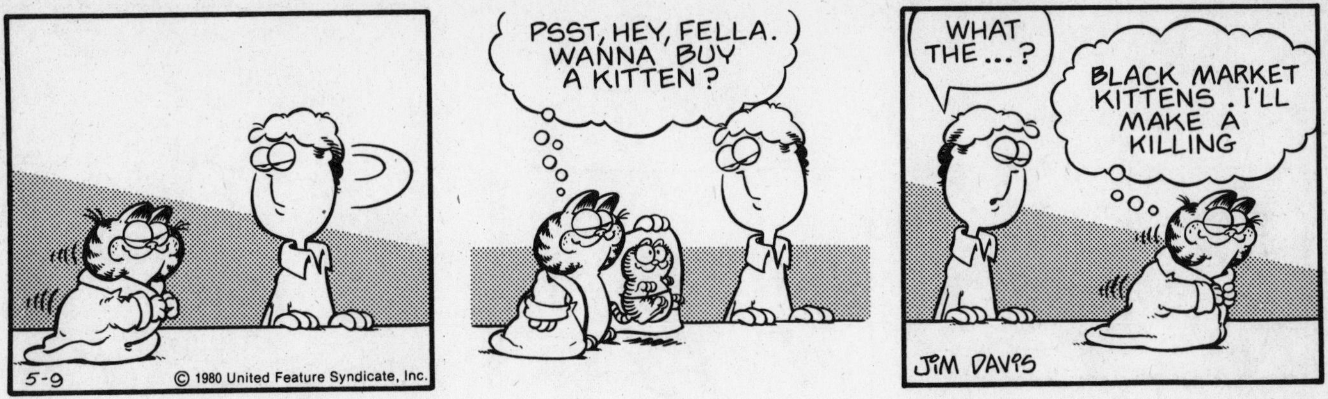
PSST, HEY, FELLA. WANNA BUY A KITTEN?
WHAT THE...?
BLACK MARKET KITTENS. I'LL MAKE A KILLING
5-9
© 1980 United Feature Syndicate, Inc.
JIM DAVIS

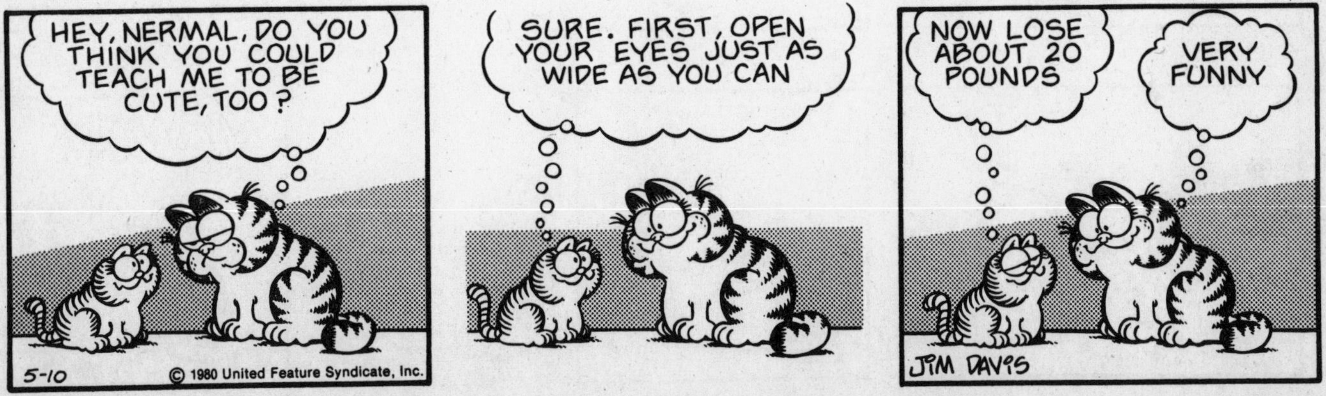
HEY, NERMAL, DO YOU THINK YOU COULD TEACH ME TO BE CUTE, TOO?
SURE. FIRST, OPEN YOUR EYES JUST AS WIDE AS YOU CAN
NOW LOSE ABOUT 20 POUNDS
VERY FUNNY
5-10
© 1980 United Feature Syndicate, Inc.
JIM DAVIS

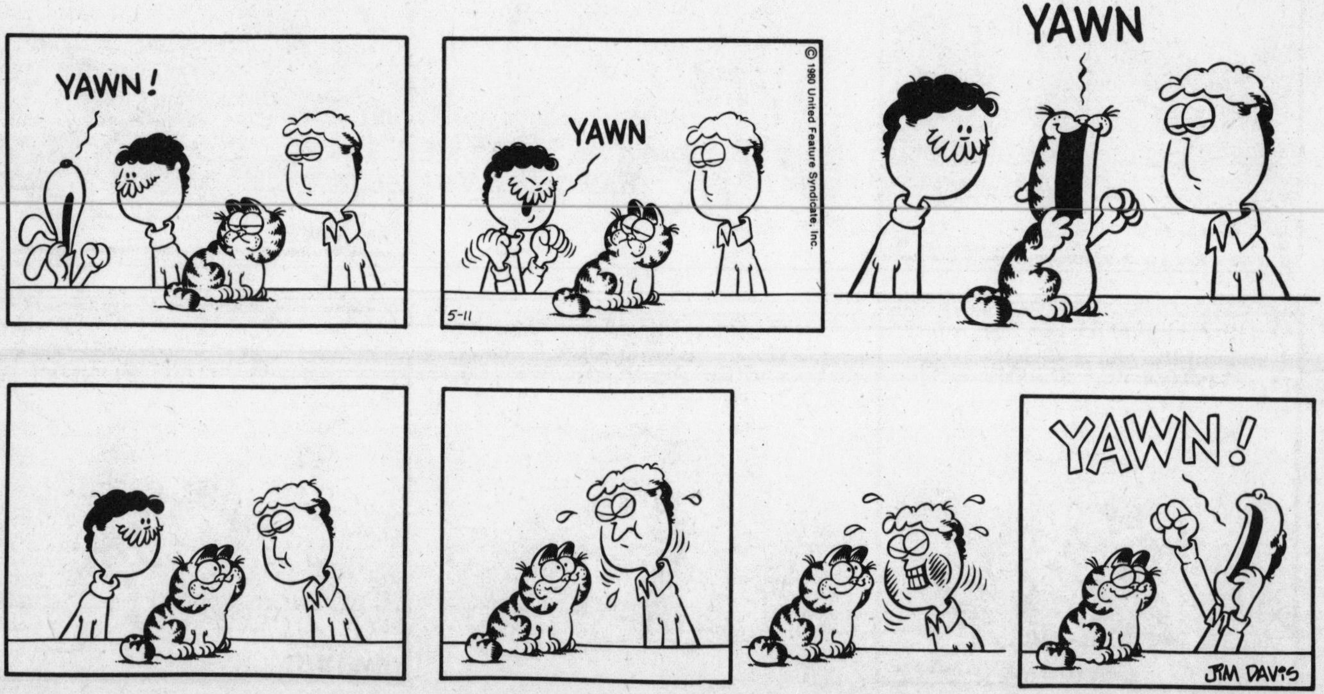
YAWN!
YAWN
© 1980 United Feature Syndicate, Inc.
5-11
YAWN
YAWN!
JIM DAVIS

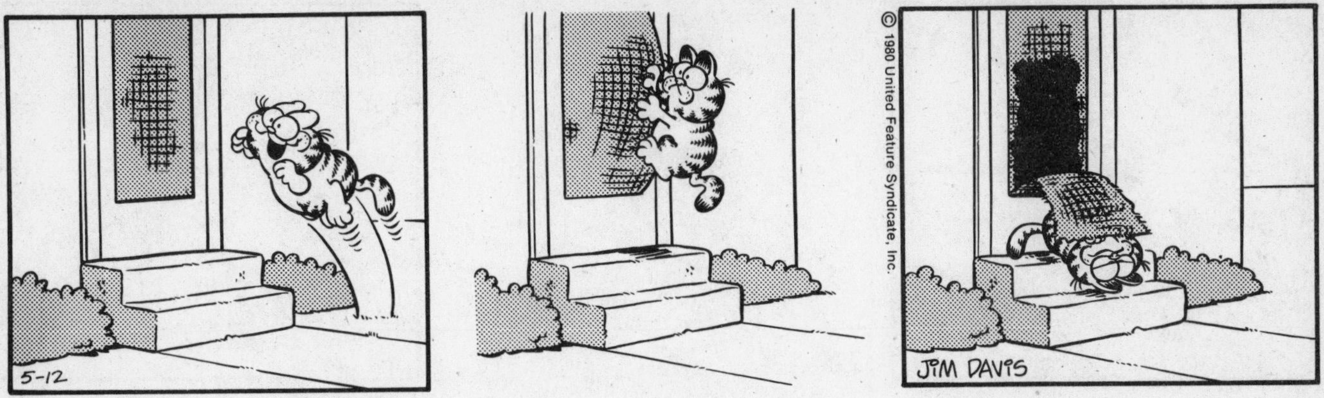
5-12
© 1980 United Feature Syndicate, Inc.
JIM DAVIS

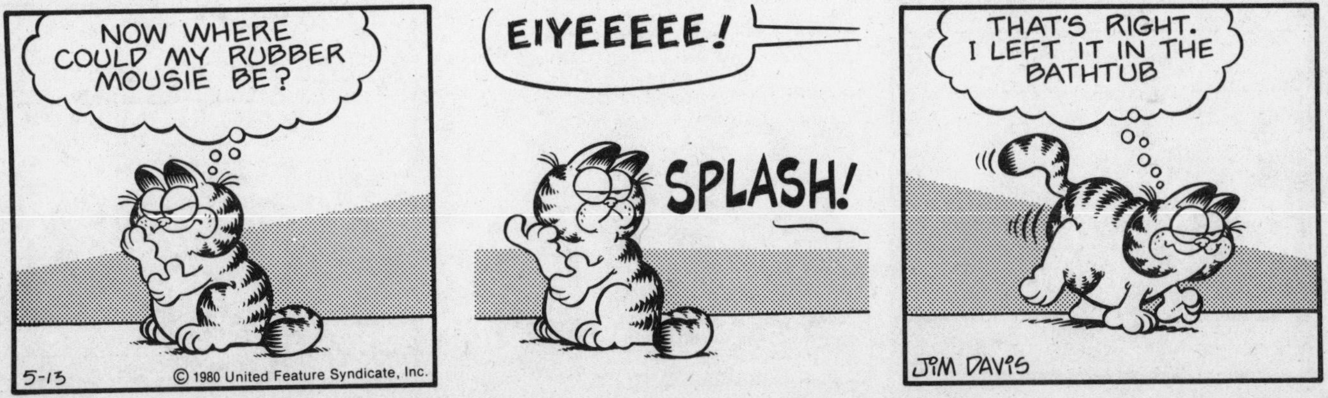
NOW WHERE COULD MY RUBBER MOUSIE BE?
5-13
© 1980 United Feature Syndicate, Inc.
EIYEEEEE!
SPLASH!
THAT'S RIGHT. I LEFT IT IN THE BATHTUB
JIM DAVIS

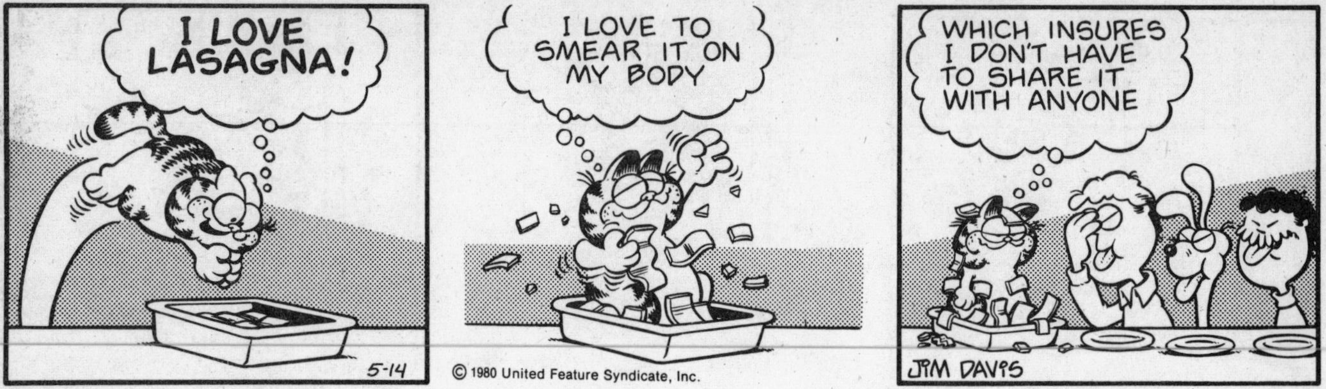
I LOVE LASAGNA!
5-14
I LOVE TO SMEAR IT ON MY BODY
© 1980 United Feature Syndicate, Inc.
WHICH INSURES I DON'T HAVE TO SHARE IT WITH ANYONE
JIM DAVIS

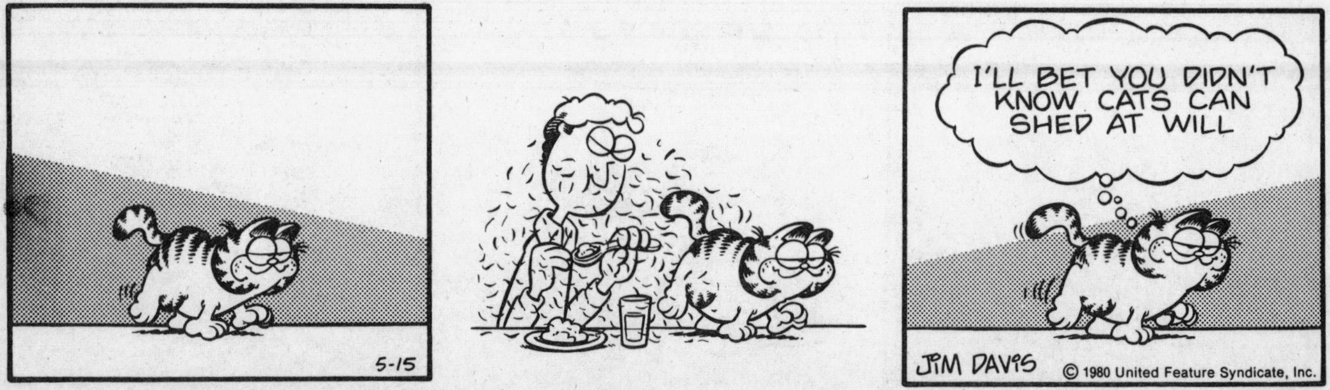
5-15
I'LL BET YOU DIDN'T KNOW CATS CAN SHED AT WILL
JIM DAVIS
© 1980 United Feature Syndicate, Inc.

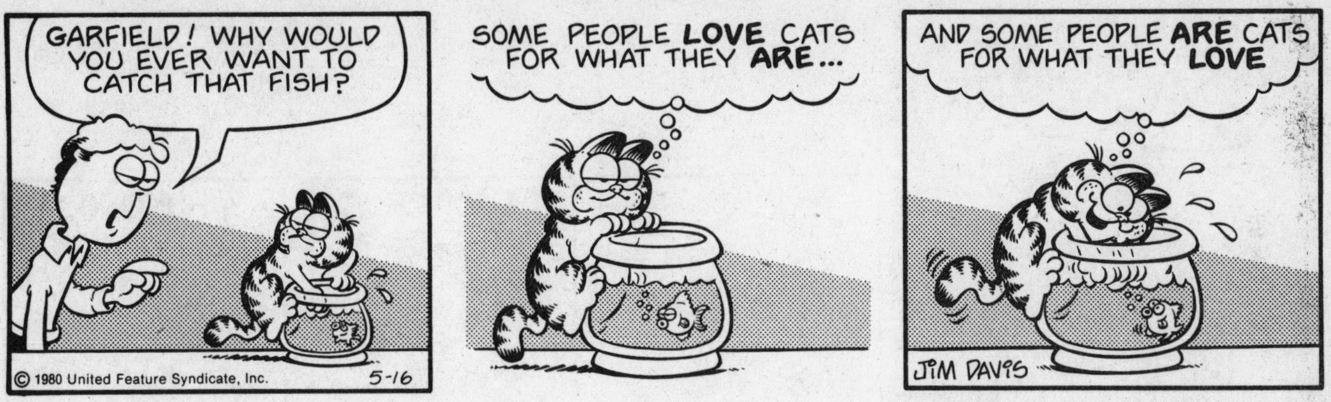
GARFIELD! WHY WOULD YOU EVER WANT TO CATCH THAT FISH?
SOME PEOPLE **LOVE** CATS FOR WHAT THEY **ARE**...
AND SOME PEOPLE **ARE** CATS FOR WHAT THEY **LOVE**
© 1980 United Feature Syndicate, Inc.
5-16
JIM DAVIS

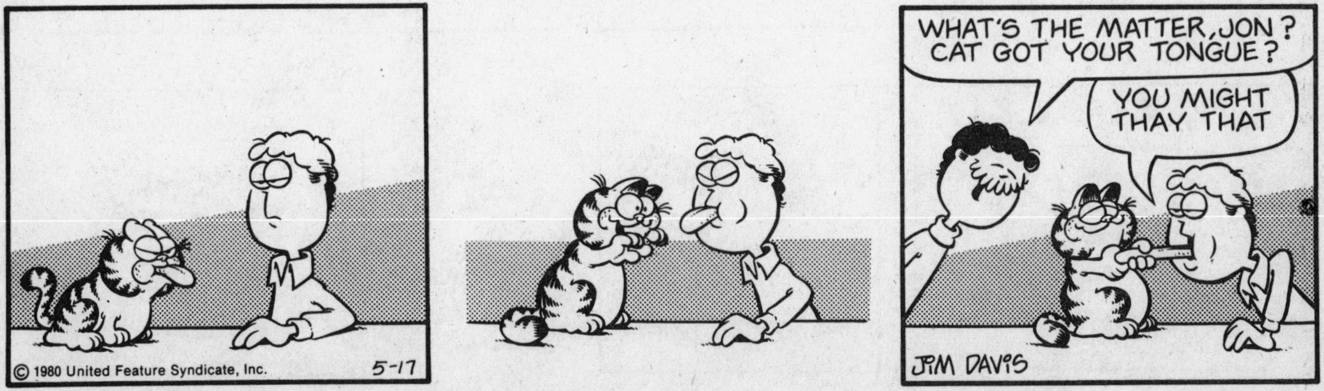
WHAT'S THE MATTER, JON? CAT GOT YOUR TONGUE?
YOU MIGHT THAY THAT
© 1980 United Feature Syndicate, Inc.
5-17
JIM DAVIS

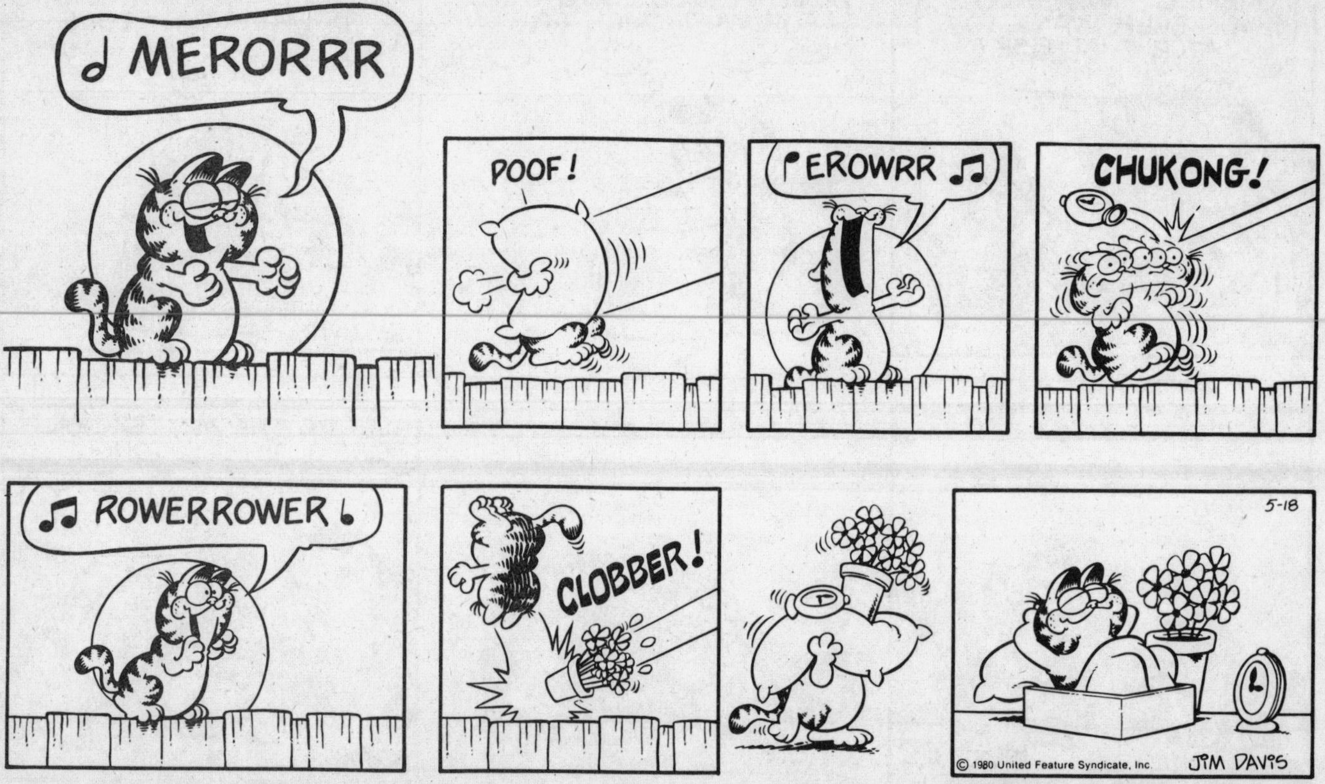

MERORRR
POOF!
EROWRR
CHUKONG!
ROWERROWER
CLOBBER!
5-18
© 1980 United Feature Syndicate, Inc.
JIM DAVIS

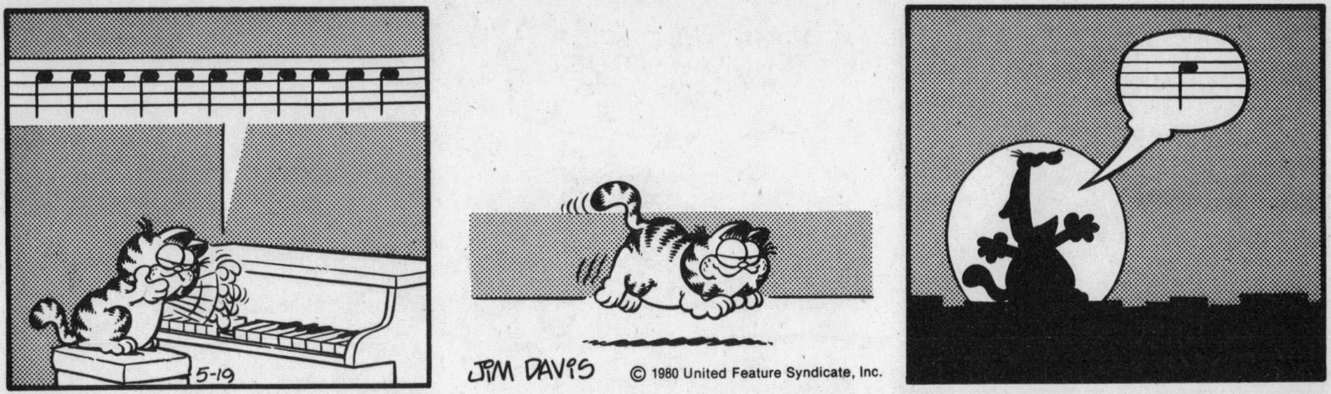
JIM DAVIS
© 1980 United Feature Syndicate, Inc.
5-19

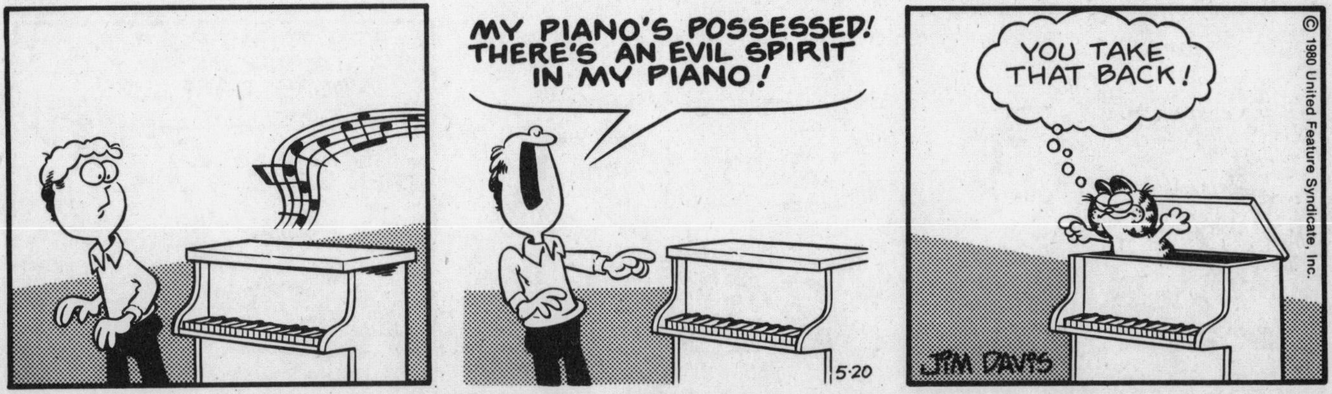
MY PIANO'S POSSESSED! THERE'S AN EVIL SPIRIT IN MY PIANO!
YOU TAKE THAT BACK!
5·20
JIM DAVIS
© 1980 United Feature Syndicate, Inc.

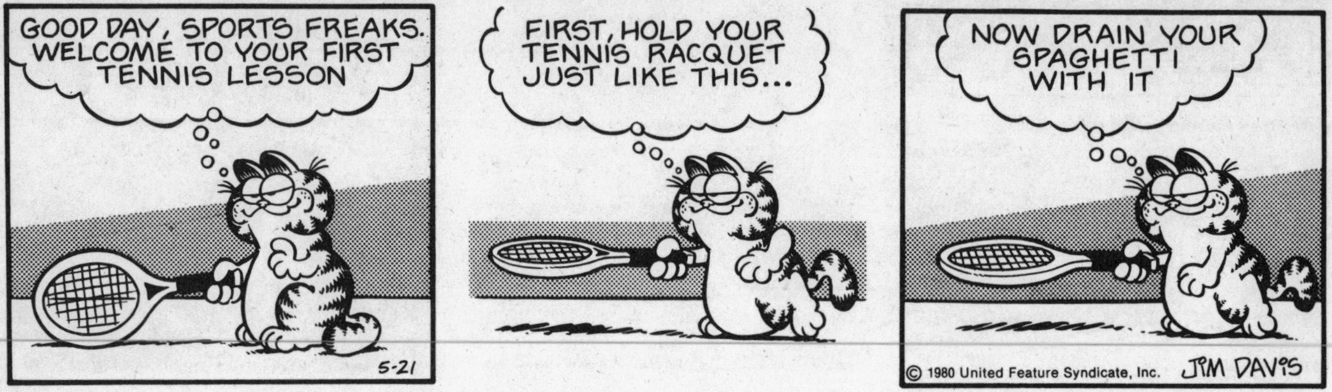
GOOD DAY, SPORTS FREAKS. WELCOME TO YOUR FIRST TENNIS LESSON
5-21
FIRST, HOLD YOUR TENNIS RACQUET JUST LIKE THIS...
NOW DRAIN YOUR SPAGHETTI WITH IT
© 1980 United Feature Syndicate, Inc.
JIM DAVIS

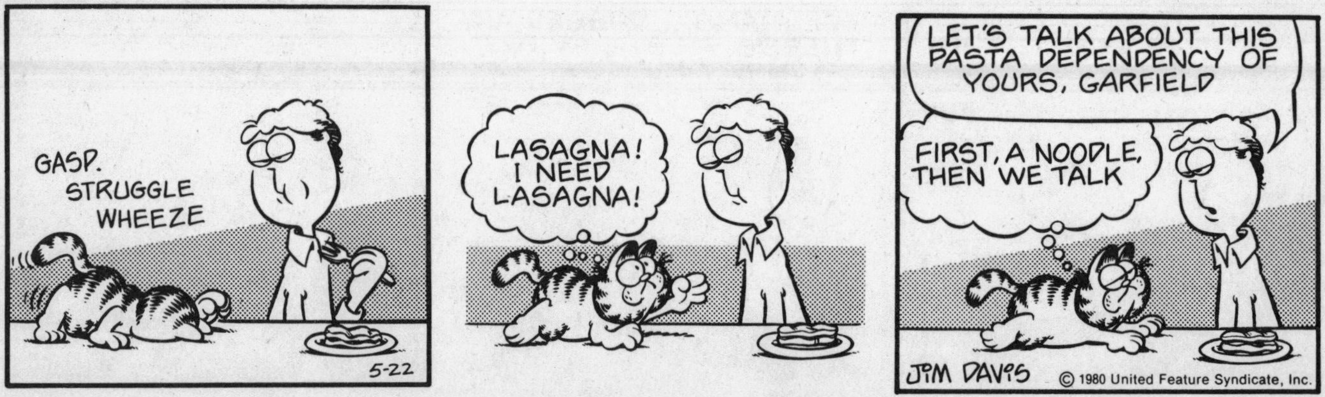
GASP.
STRUGGLE
WHEEZE
5-22
LASAGNA! I NEED LASAGNA!
LET'S TALK ABOUT THIS PASTA DEPENDENCY OF YOURS, GARFIELD
FIRST, A NOODLE, THEN WE TALK
JIM DAVIS
© 1980 United Feature Syndicate, Inc.

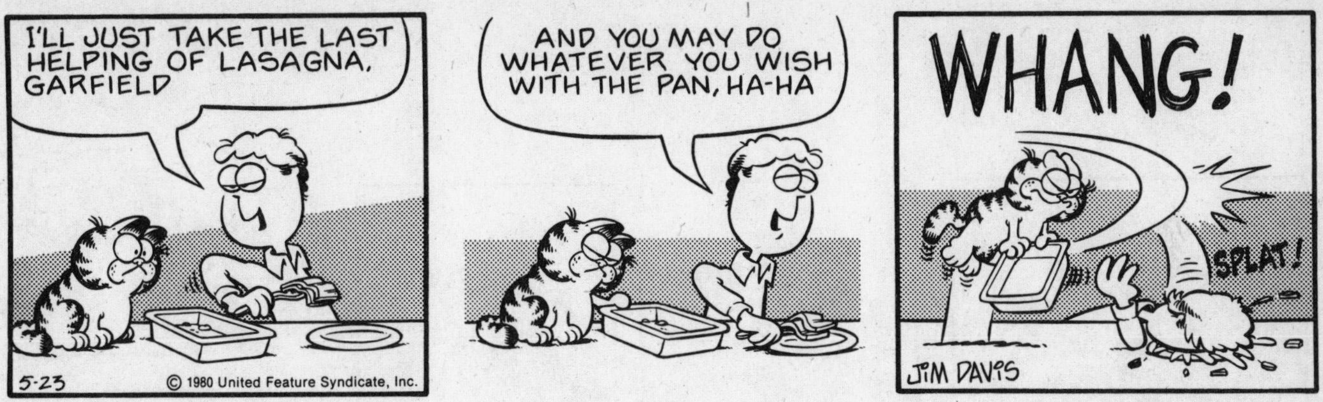

I'LL JUST TAKE THE LAST HELPING OF LASAGNA, GARFIELD
5-23
© 1980 United Feature Syndicate, Inc.
AND YOU MAY DO WHATEVER YOU WISH WITH THE PAN, HA-HA
WHANG!
SPLAT!
JIM DAVIS

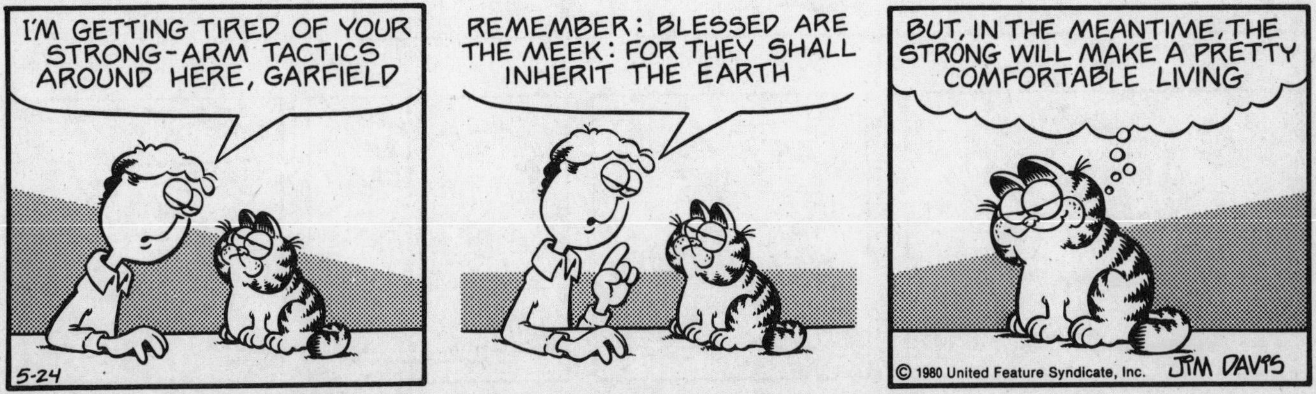

I'M GETTING TIRED OF YOUR STRONG-ARM TACTICS AROUND HERE, GARFIELD
5-24
REMEMBER: BLESSED ARE THE MEEK: FOR THEY SHALL INHERIT THE EARTH
BUT, IN THE MEANTIME, THE STRONG WILL MAKE A PRETTY COMFORTABLE LIVING
© 1980 United Feature Syndicate, Inc.
JIM DAVIS

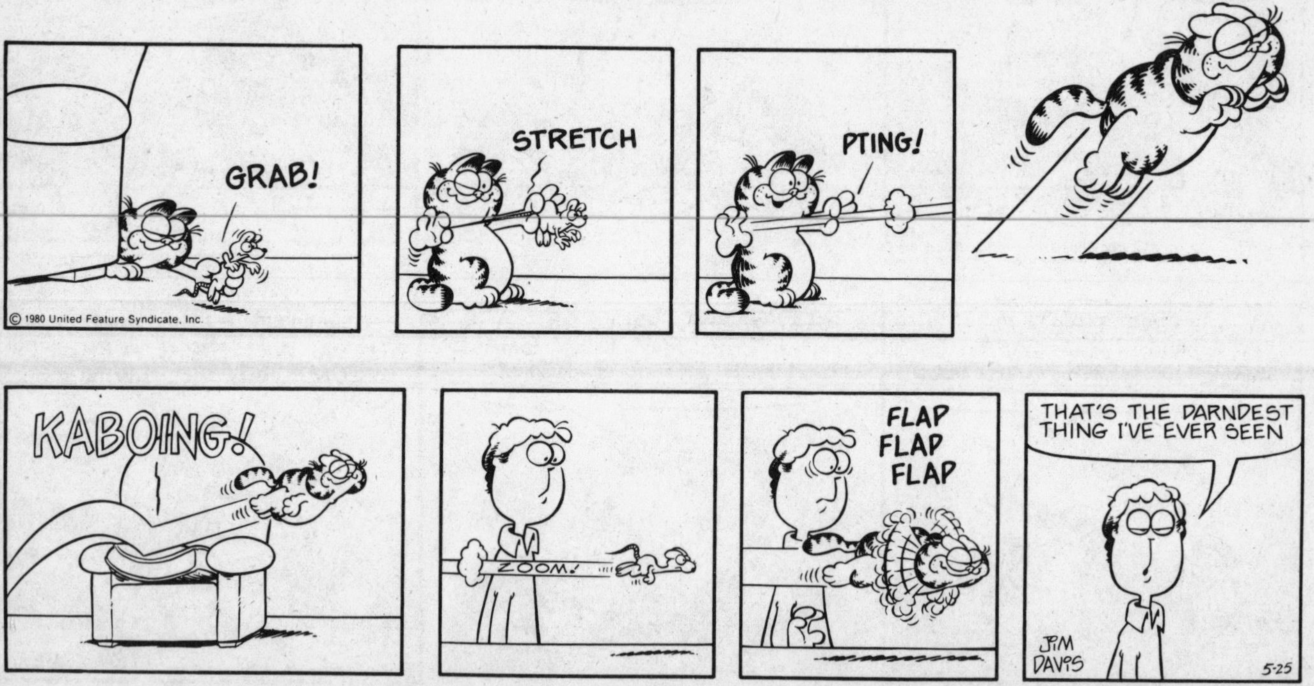
GRAB!
© 1980 United Feature Syndicate, Inc.
STRETCH
PTING!
KABOING!
ZOOM!
FLAP
FLAP
FLAP
THAT'S THE DARNDEST THING I'VE EVER SEEN
JIM DAVIS
5-25

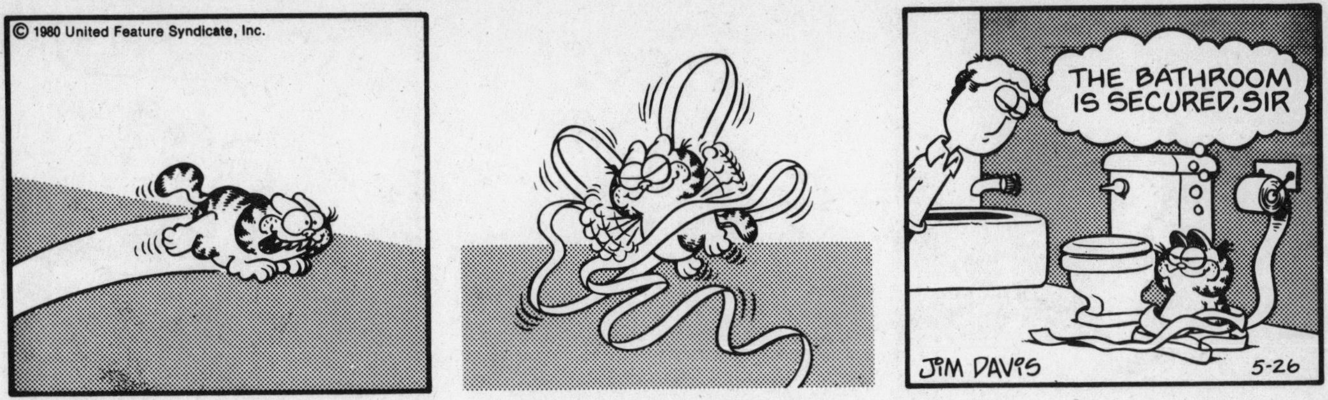
© 1980 United Feature Syndicate, Inc.
THE BATHROOM IS SECURED, SIR
JIM DAVIS
5-26

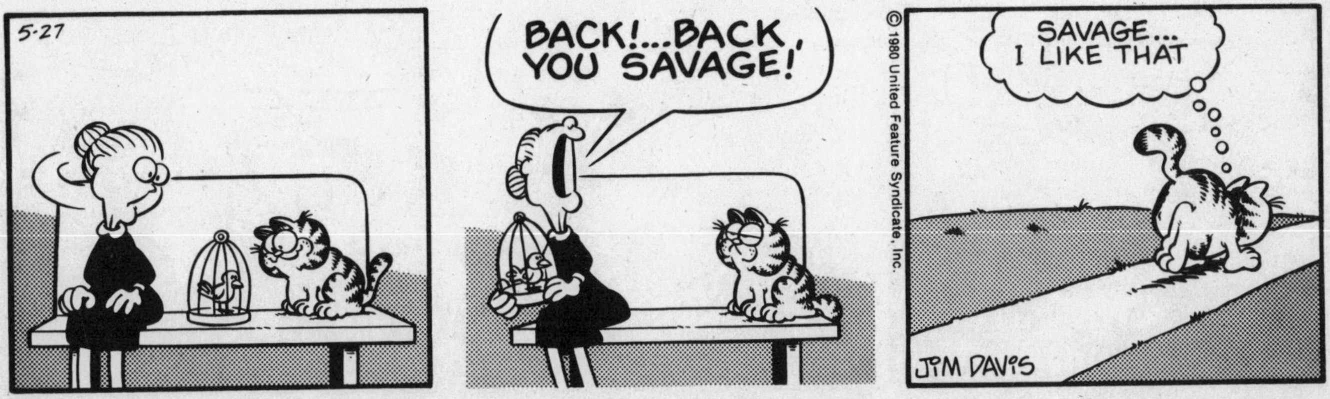
5-27
BACK!...BACK, YOU SAVAGE!
© 1980 United Feature Syndicate, Inc.
SAVAGE... I LIKE THAT
JIM DAVIS

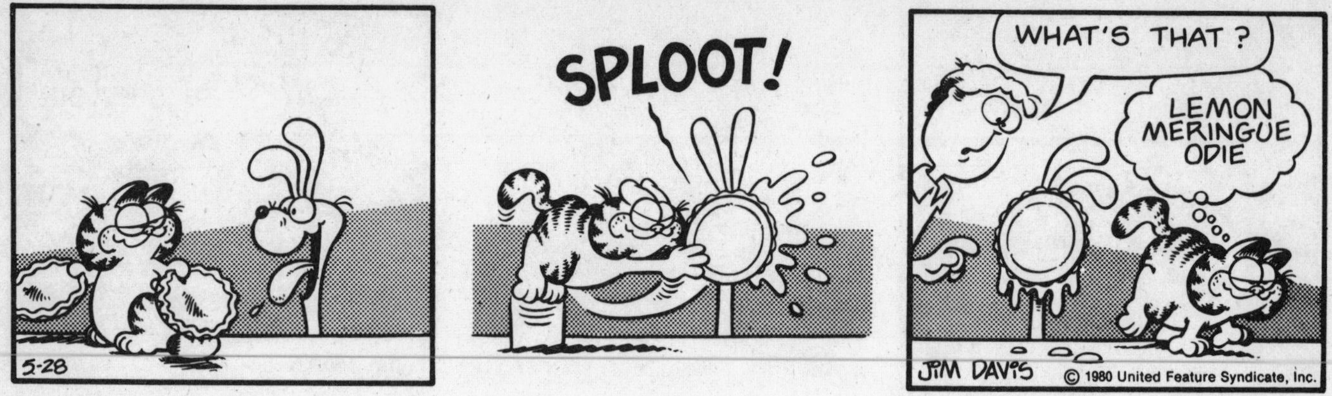
5-28
SPLOOT!
WHAT'S THAT?
LEMON MERINGUE ODIE
JIM DAVIS
© 1980 United Feature Syndicate, Inc.

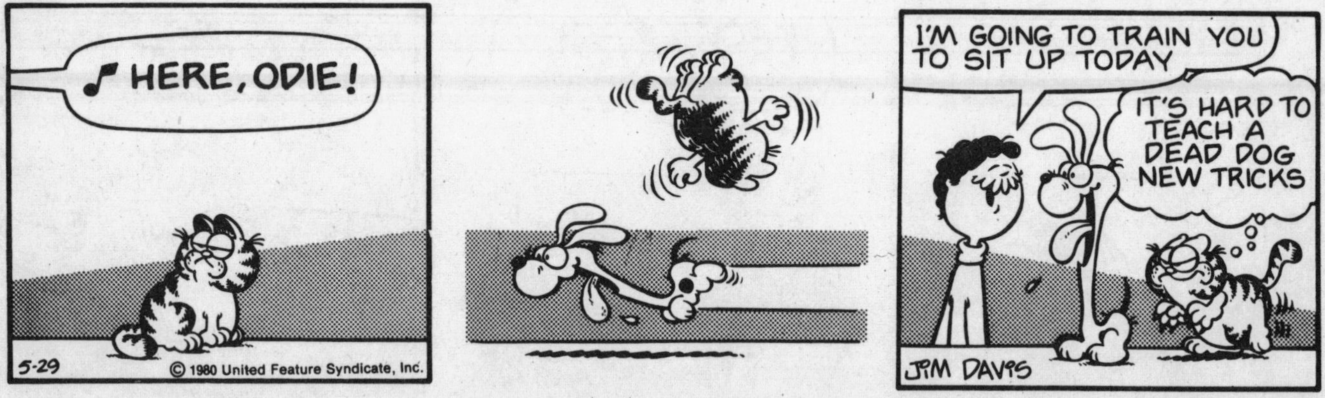
♪ HERE, ODIE!
5-29
© 1980 United Feature Syndicate, Inc.
I'M GOING TO TRAIN YOU TO SIT UP TODAY
IT'S HARD TO TEACH A DEAD DOG NEW TRICKS
JIM DAVIS

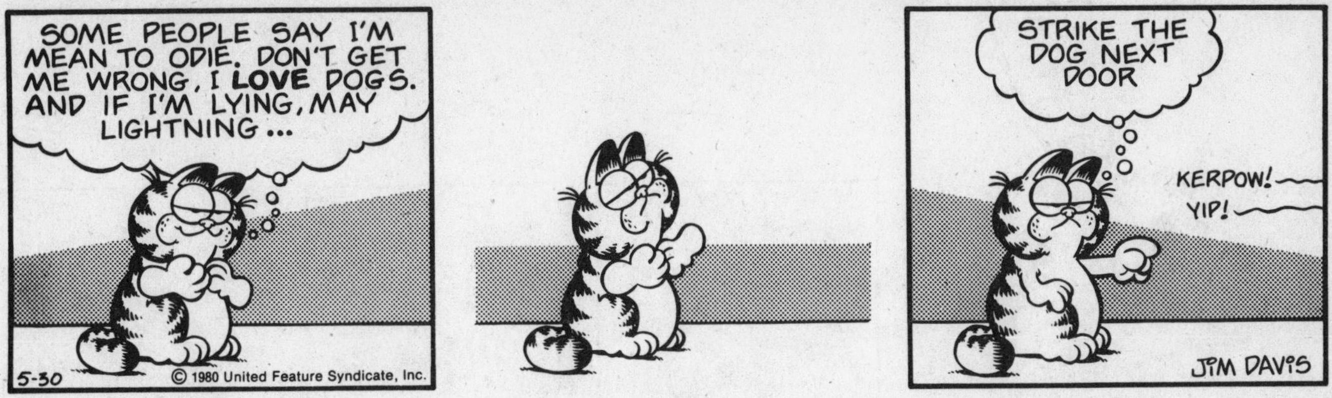
SOME PEOPLE SAY I'M MEAN TO ODIE. DON'T GET ME WRONG, I **LOVE** DOGS. AND IF I'M LYING, MAY LIGHTNING...
STRIKE THE DOG NEXT DOOR
KERPOW!
YIP!
5-30
© 1980 United Feature Syndicate, Inc.
JIM DAVIS

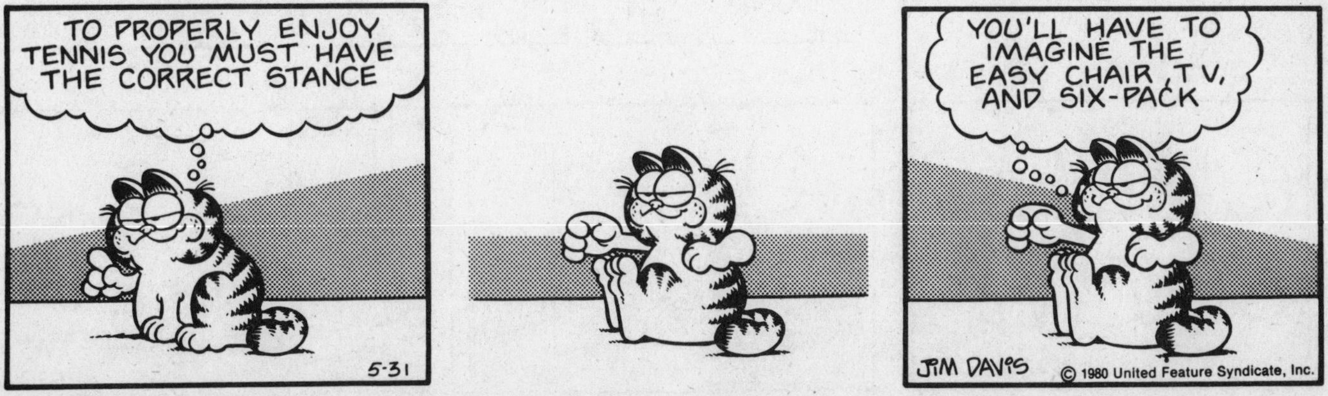
TO PROPERLY ENJOY TENNIS YOU MUST HAVE THE CORRECT STANCE
YOU'LL HAVE TO IMAGINE THE EASY CHAIR, T.V., AND SIX-PACK
5-31
JIM DAVIS
© 1980 United Feature Syndicate, Inc.

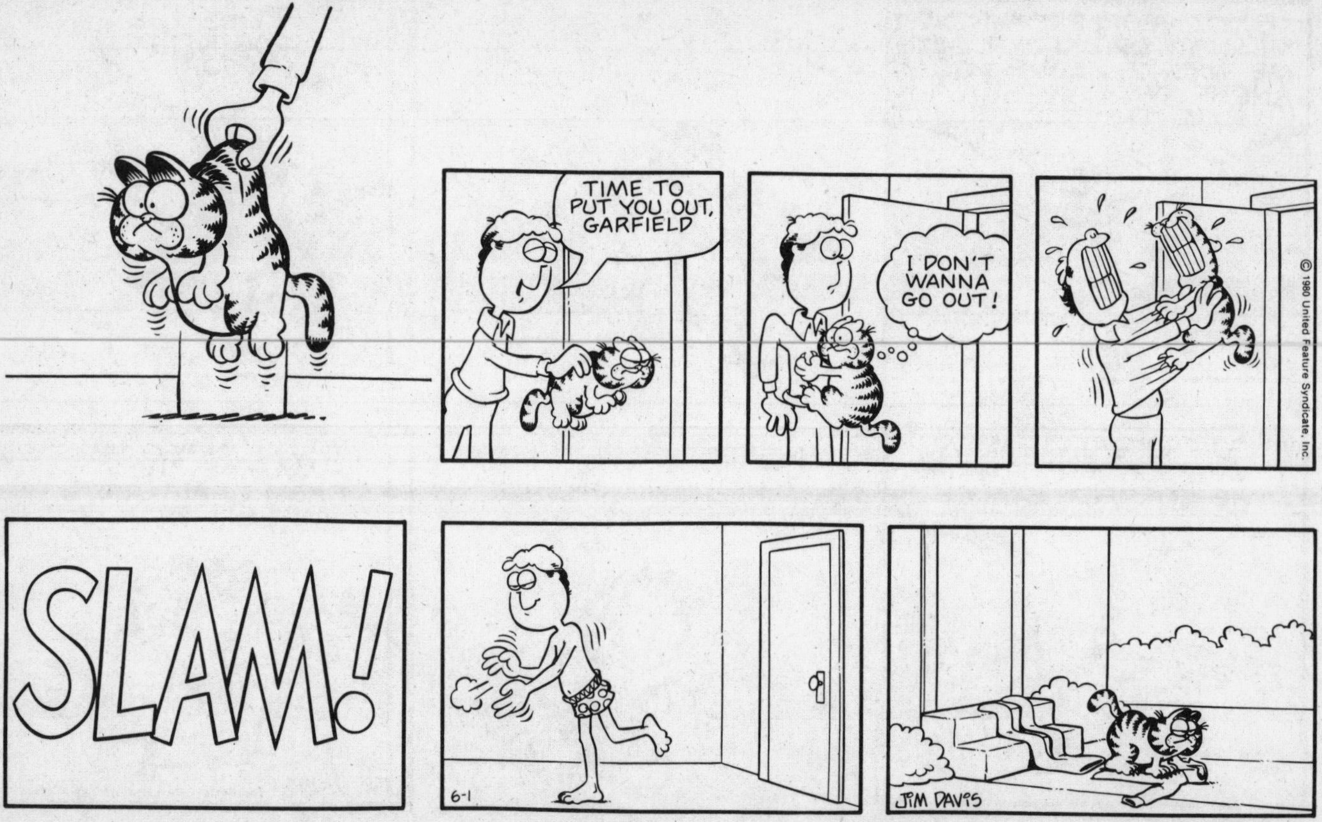
TIME TO PUT YOU OUT, GARFIELD
I DON'T WANNA GO OUT!
© 1980 United Feature Syndicate, Inc.
SLAM!
6-1
JIM DAVIS

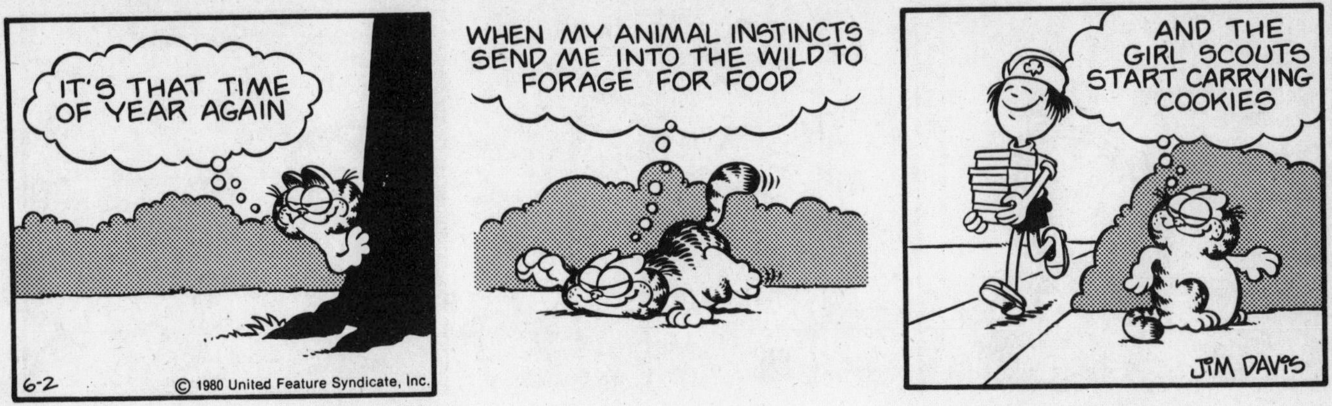
IT'S THAT TIME OF YEAR AGAIN
6-2
© 1980 United Feature Syndicate, Inc.
WHEN MY ANIMAL INSTINCTS SEND ME INTO THE WILD TO FORAGE FOR FOOD
AND THE GIRL SCOUTS START CARRYING COOKIES
JIM DAVIS

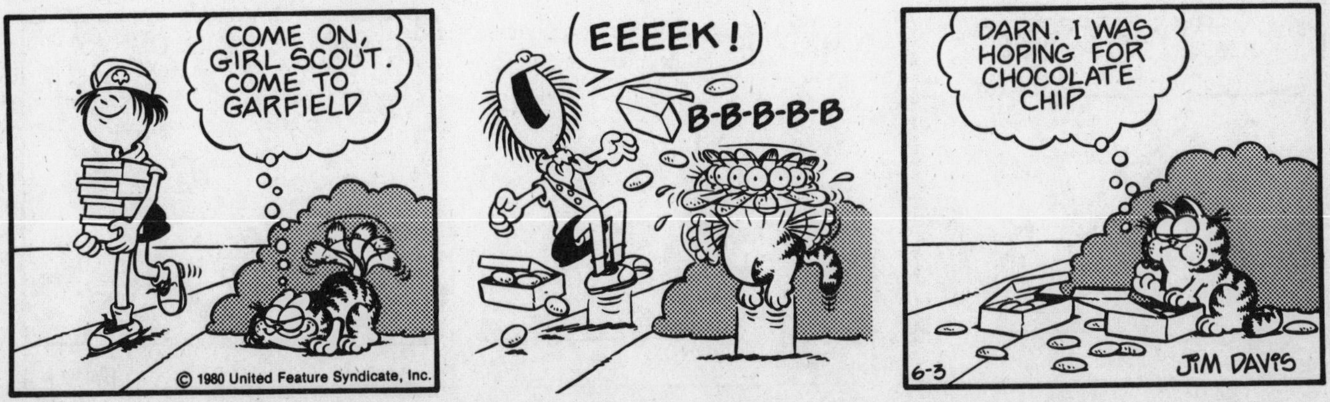
COME ON, GIRL SCOUT. COME TO GARFIELD
© 1980 United Feature Syndicate, Inc.
EEEEK!
B-B-B-B-B
DARN. I WAS HOPING FOR CHOCOLATE CHIP
6-3
JIM DAVIS

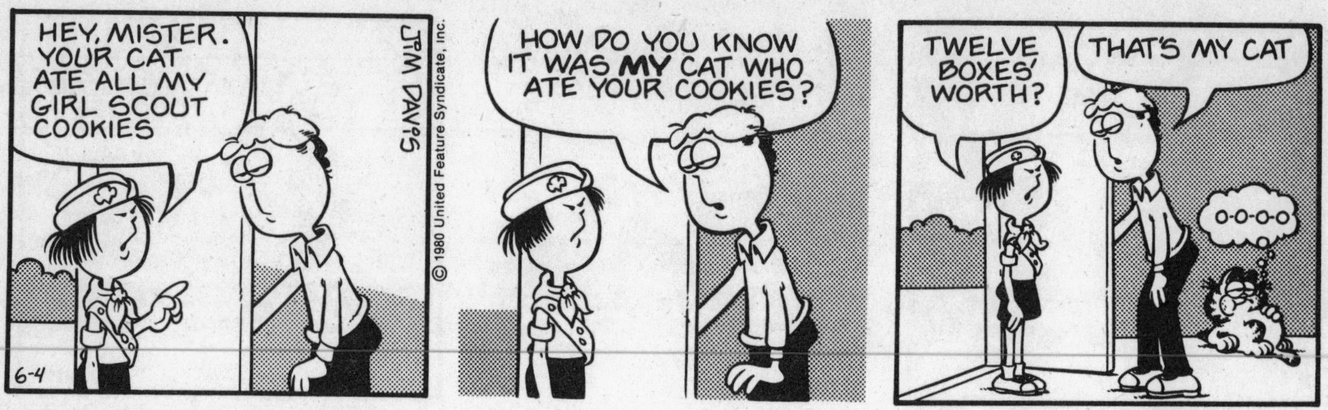
HEY, MISTER. YOUR CAT ATE ALL MY GIRL SCOUT COOKIES
JIM DAVIS
© 1980 United Feature Syndicate, Inc.
6-4
HOW DO YOU KNOW IT WAS MY CAT WHO ATE YOUR COOKIES?
TWELVE BOXES' WORTH?
THAT'S MY CAT
O-O-O-O

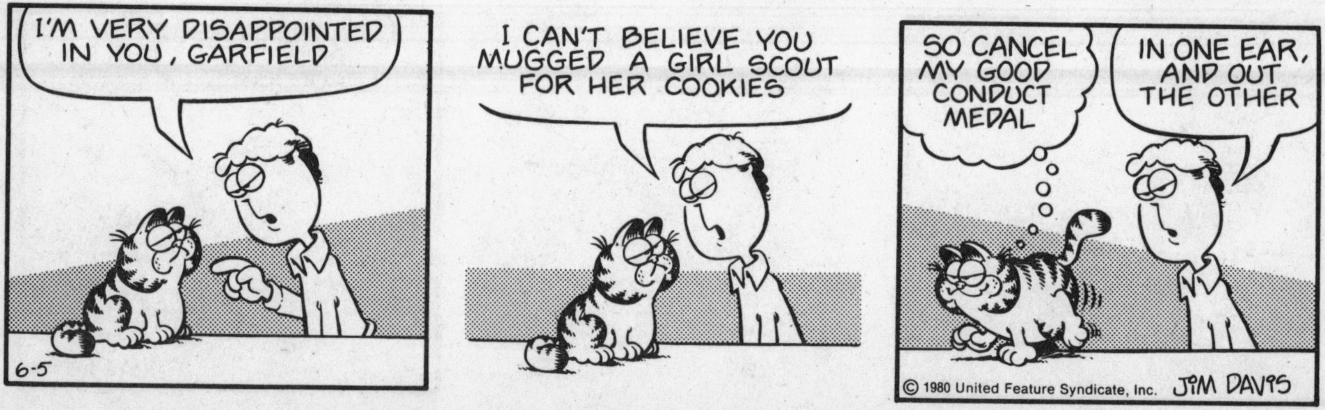
I'M VERY DISAPPOINTED IN YOU, GARFIELD
6-5
I CAN'T BELIEVE YOU MUGGED A GIRL SCOUT FOR HER COOKIES
SO CANCEL MY GOOD CONDUCT MEDAL
IN ONE EAR, AND OUT THE OTHER
© 1980 United Feature Syndicate, Inc.
JIM DAVIS

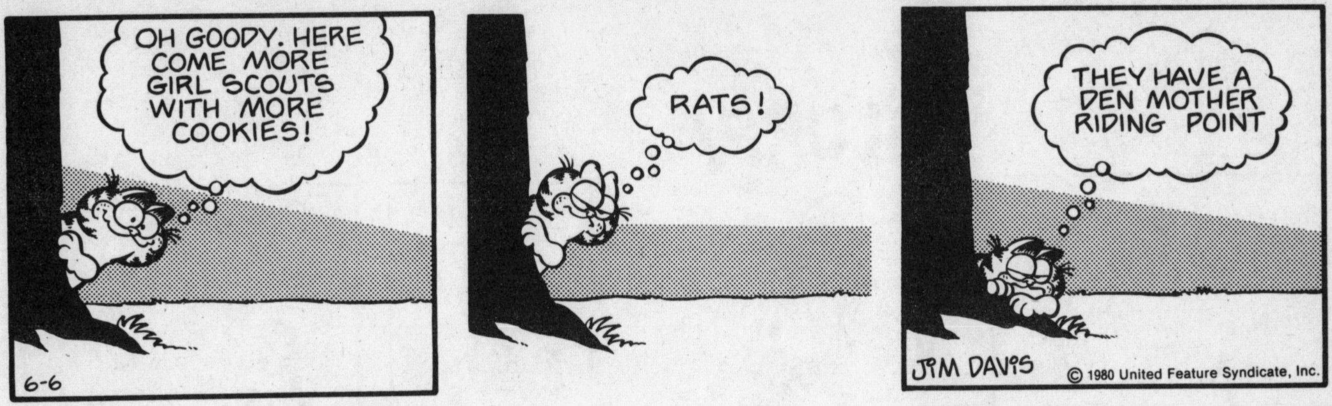
OH GOODY. HERE COME MORE GIRL SCOUTS WITH MORE COOKIES!
6-6
RATS!
THEY HAVE A DEN MOTHER RIDING POINT
JIM DAVIS
© 1980 United Feature Syndicate, Inc.

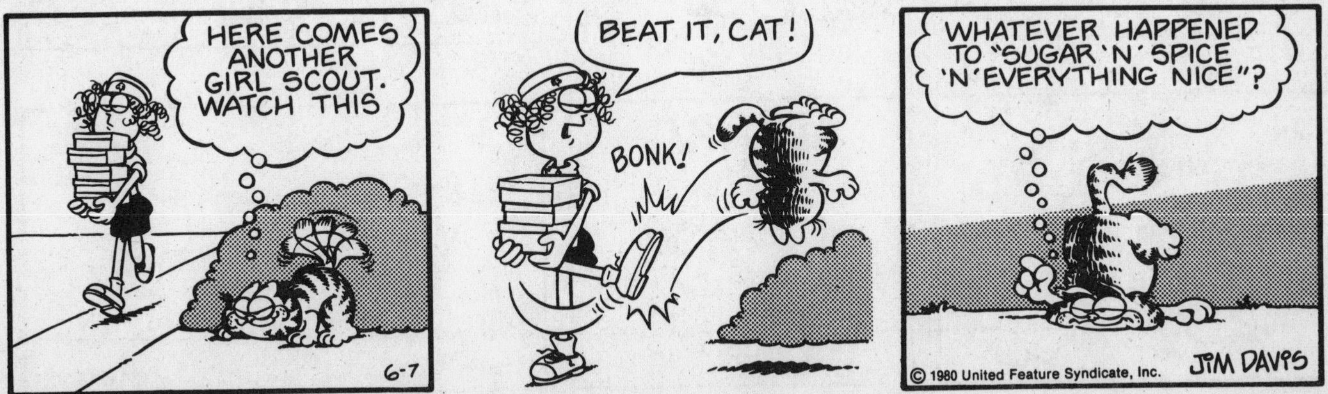
HERE COMES ANOTHER GIRL SCOUT. WATCH THIS
6-7
BEAT IT, CAT!
BONK!
WHATEVER HAPPENED TO "SUGAR 'N' SPICE 'N' EVERYTHING NICE"?
© 1980 United Feature Syndicate, Inc.
JIM DAVIS

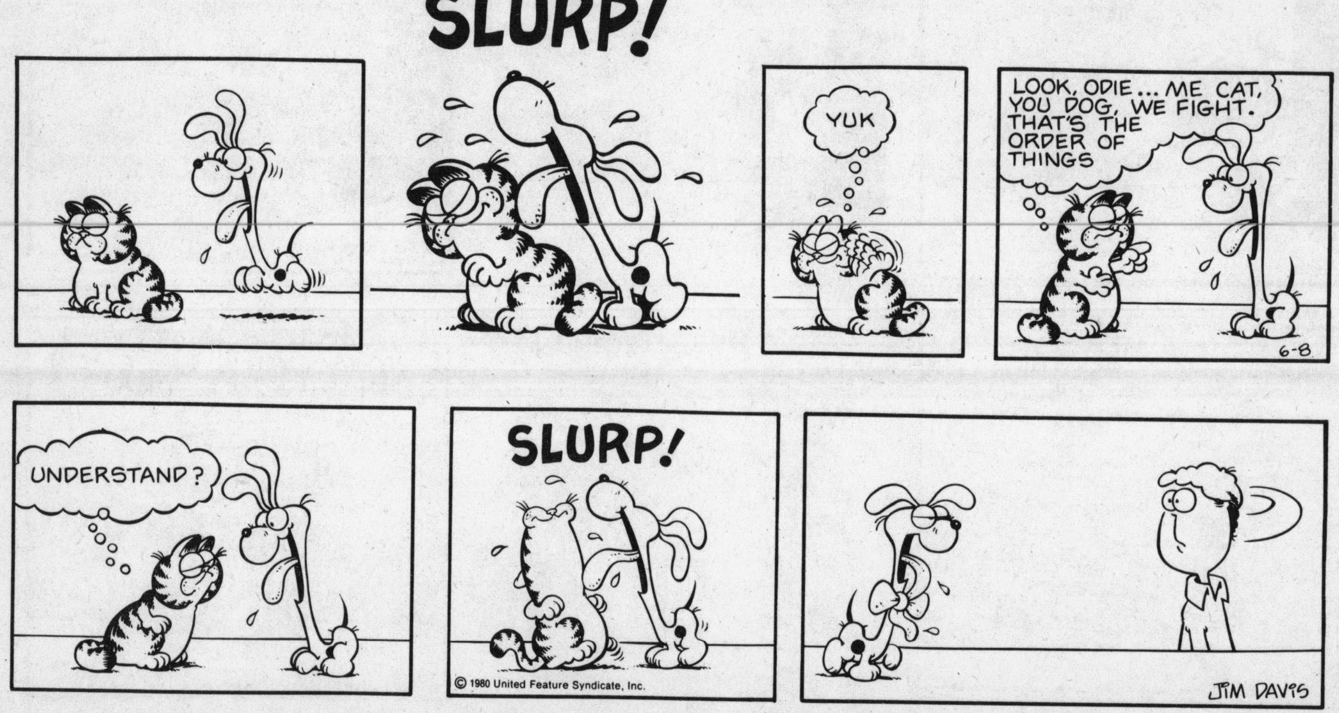
SLURP!
YUK
LOOK, ODIE... ME CAT, YOU DOG, WE FIGHT. THAT'S THE ORDER OF THINGS
6-8
UNDERSTAND?
SLURP!
© 1980 United Feature Syndicate, Inc.
JIM DAVIS

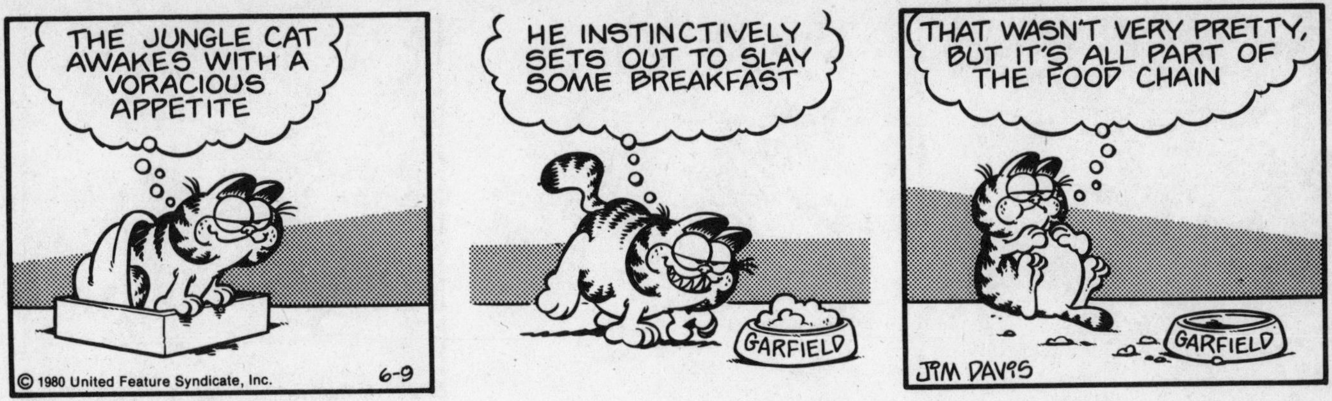
THE JUNGLE CAT AWAKES WITH A VORACIOUS APPETITE
© 1980 United Feature Syndicate, Inc.
6-9
HE INSTINCTIVELY SETS OUT TO SLAY SOME BREAKFAST
GARFIELD
THAT WASN'T VERY PRETTY, BUT IT'S ALL PART OF THE FOOD CHAIN
GARFIELD
JIM DAVIS

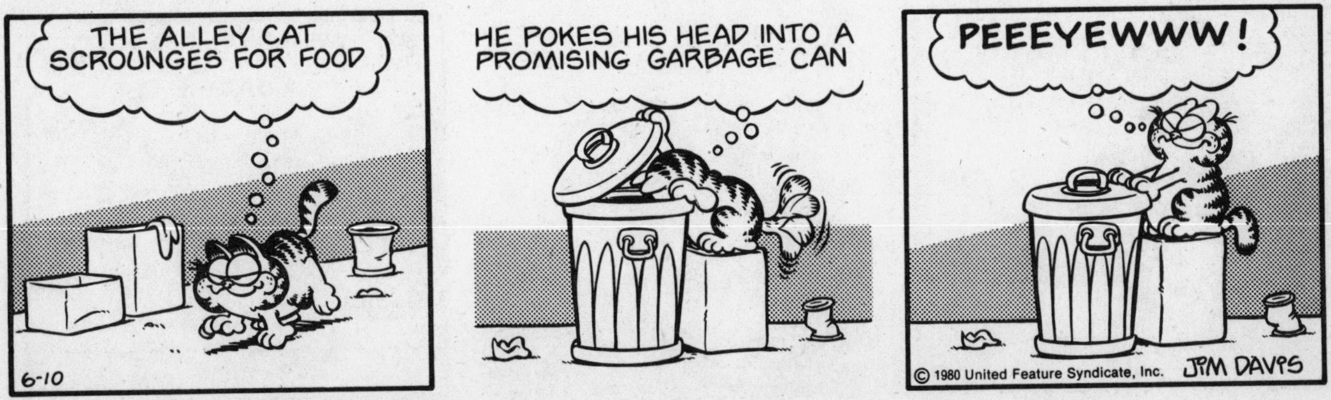
THE ALLEY CAT SCROUNGES FOR FOOD
6-10
HE POKES HIS HEAD INTO A PROMISING GARBAGE CAN
PEEEYEWWW!
© 1980 United Feature Syndicate, Inc.
JIM DAVIS

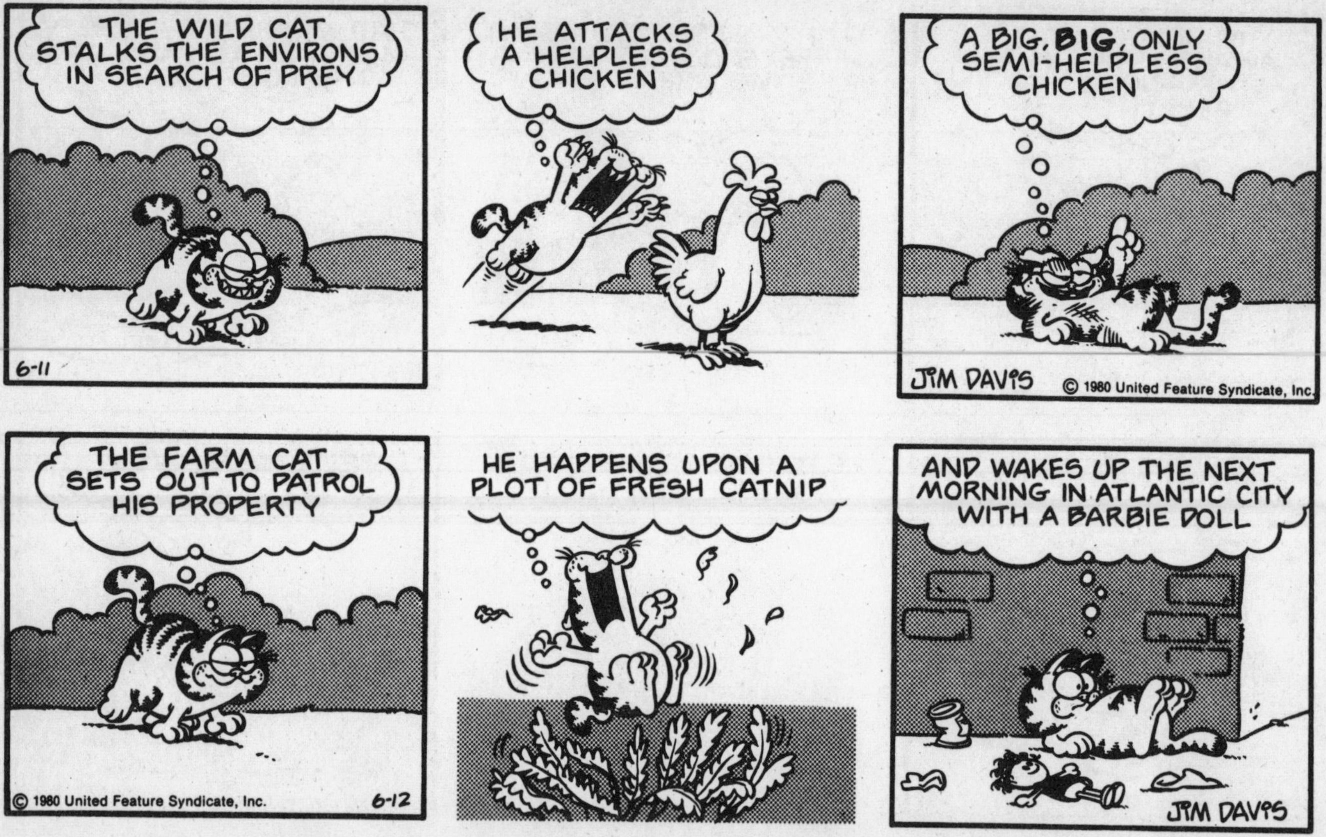
THE WILD CAT STALKS THE ENVIRONS IN SEARCH OF PREY
6-11
HE ATTACKS A HELPLESS CHICKEN
A BIG, BIG, ONLY SEMI-HELPLESS CHICKEN
JIM DAVIS
© 1980 United Feature Syndicate, Inc.
THE FARM CAT SETS OUT TO PATROL HIS PROPERTY
© 1980 United Feature Syndicate, Inc.
6-12
HE HAPPENS UPON A PLOT OF FRESH CATNIP
AND WAKES UP THE NEXT MORNING IN ATLANTIC CITY WITH A BARBIE DOLL
JIM DAVIS

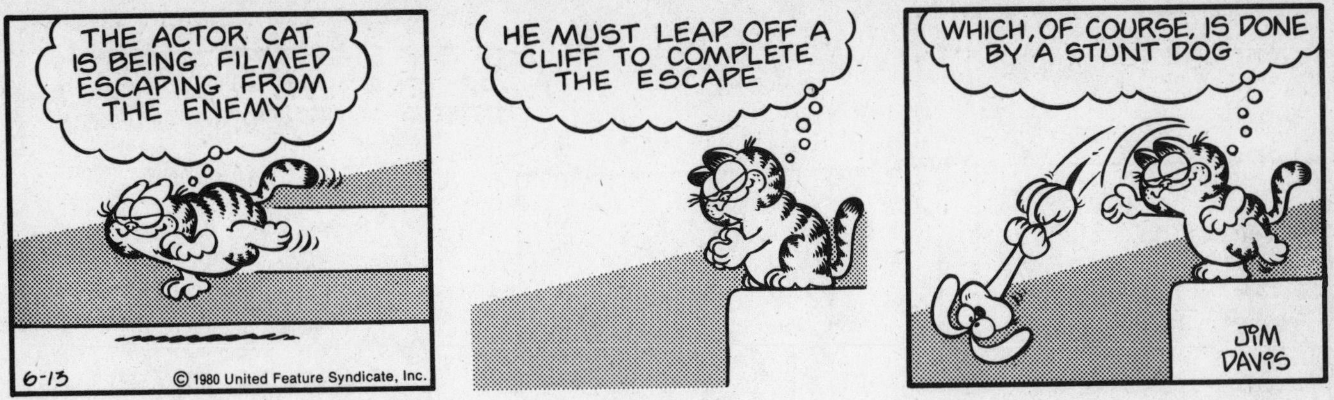
THE ACTOR CAT IS BEING FILMED ESCAPING FROM THE ENEMY
HE MUST LEAP OFF A CLIFF TO COMPLETE THE ESCAPE
WHICH, OF COURSE, IS DONE BY A STUNT DOG
6-13
© 1980 United Feature Syndicate, Inc.
JIM DAVIS

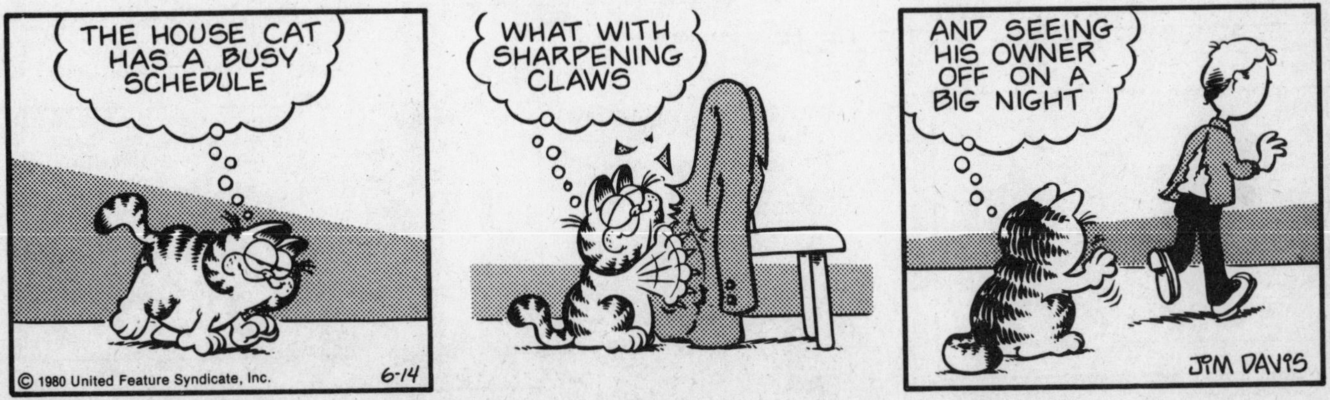
THE HOUSE CAT HAS A BUSY SCHEDULE
WHAT WITH SHARPENING CLAWS
AND SEEING HIS OWNER OFF ON A BIG NIGHT
© 1980 United Feature Syndicate, Inc.
6-14
JIM DAVIS

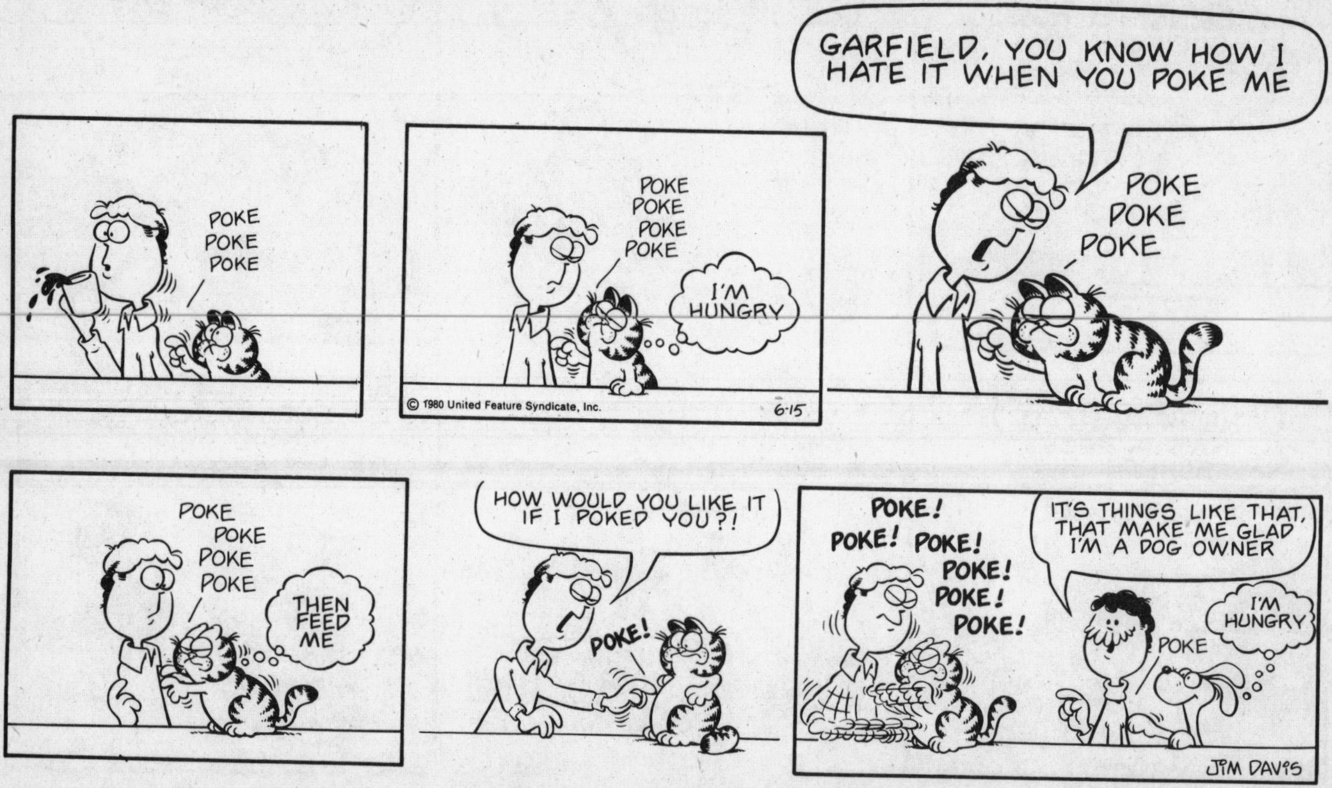
POKE
POKE
POKE
POKE
POKE
POKE
POKE
I'M HUNGRY
© 1980 United Feature Syndicate, Inc.
6-15
GARFIELD, YOU KNOW HOW I HATE IT WHEN YOU POKE ME
POKE
POKE
POKE
POKE
POKE
POKE
POKE
THEN FEED ME
HOW WOULD YOU LIKE IT IF I POKED YOU?!
POKE!
POKE!
POKE! POKE!
POKE!
POKE!
POKE!
IT'S THINGS LIKE THAT, THAT MAKE ME GLAD I'M A DOG OWNER
POKE
I'M HUNGRY
JIM DAVIS

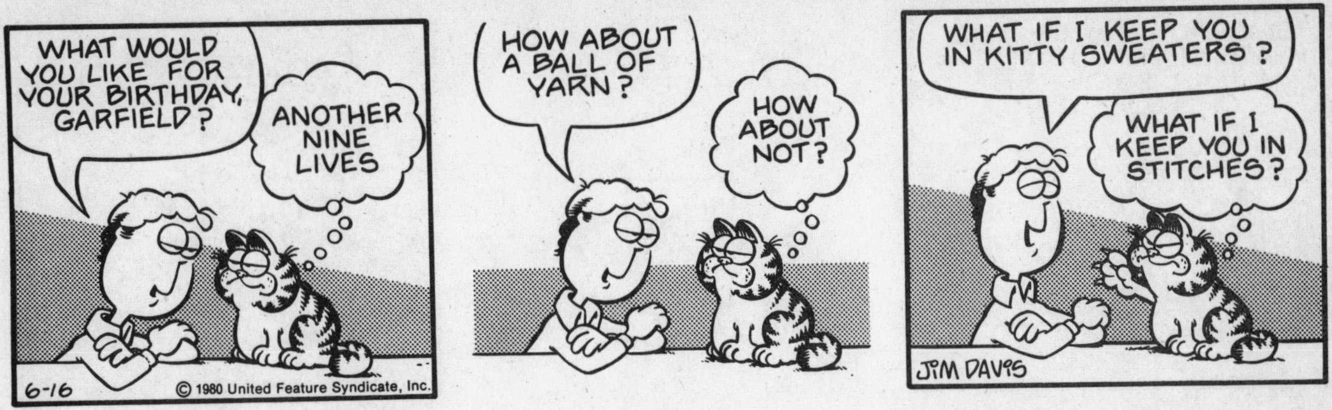
WHAT WOULD YOU LIKE FOR YOUR BIRTHDAY, GARFIELD?
ANOTHER NINE LIVES
HOW ABOUT A BALL OF YARN?
HOW ABOUT NOT?
WHAT IF I KEEP YOU IN KITTY SWEATERS?
WHAT IF I KEEP YOU IN STITCHES?
6-16
© 1980 United Feature Syndicate, Inc.
JIM DAVIS

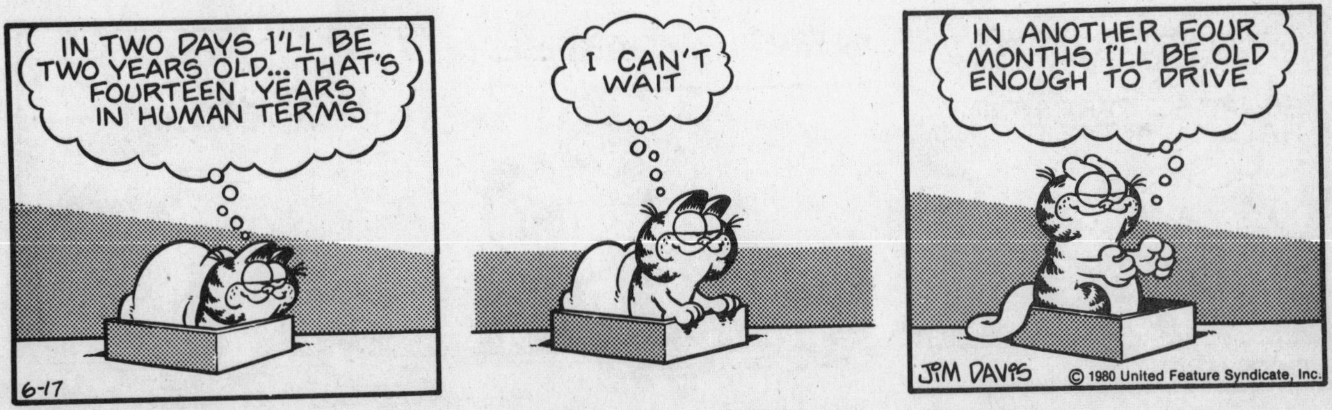
IN TWO DAYS I'LL BE TWO YEARS OLD... THAT'S FOURTEEN YEARS IN HUMAN TERMS
I CAN'T WAIT
IN ANOTHER FOUR MONTHS I'LL BE OLD ENOUGH TO DRIVE
6-17
JIM DAVIS
© 1980 United Feature Syndicate, Inc.

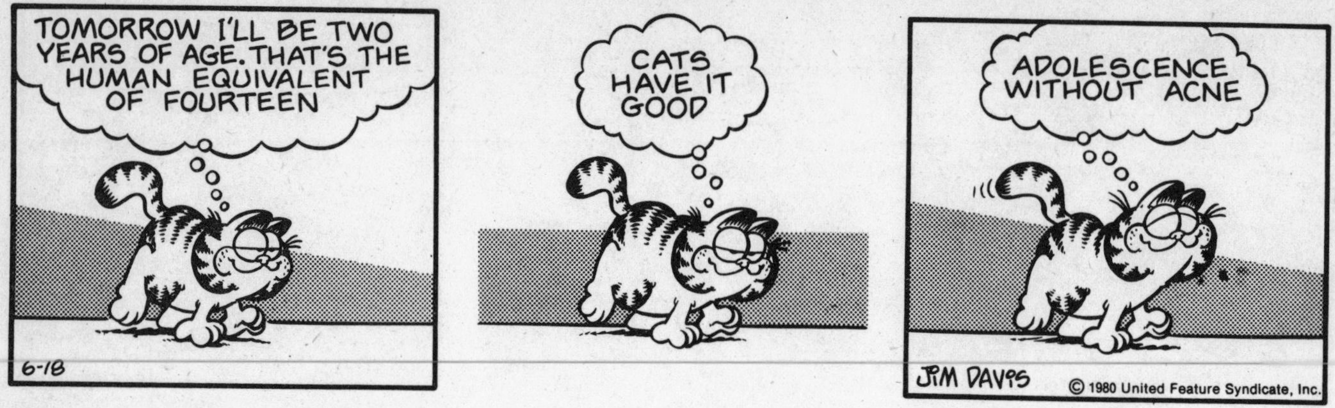
TOMORROW I'LL BE TWO YEARS OF AGE. THAT'S THE HUMAN EQUIVALENT OF FOURTEEN
CATS HAVE IT GOOD
ADOLESCENCE WITHOUT ACNE
6-18
JIM DAVIS
© 1980 United Feature Syndicate, Inc.

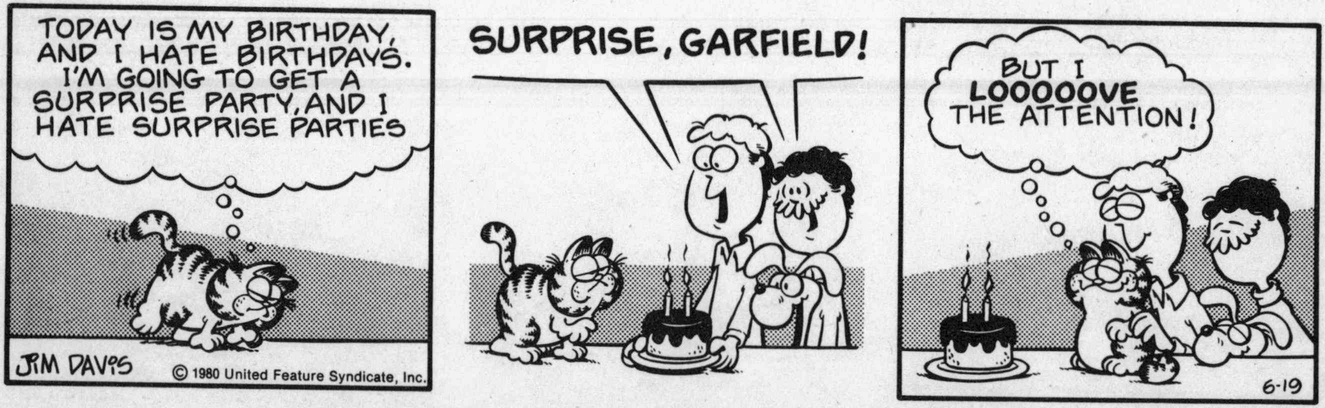
TODAY IS MY BIRTHDAY, AND I HATE BIRTHDAYS. I'M GOING TO GET A SURPRISE PARTY, AND I HATE SURPRISE PARTIES
SURPRISE, GARFIELD!
BUT I **LOOOOOVE** THE ATTENTION!
JIM DAVIS
© 1980 United Feature Syndicate, Inc.
6-19

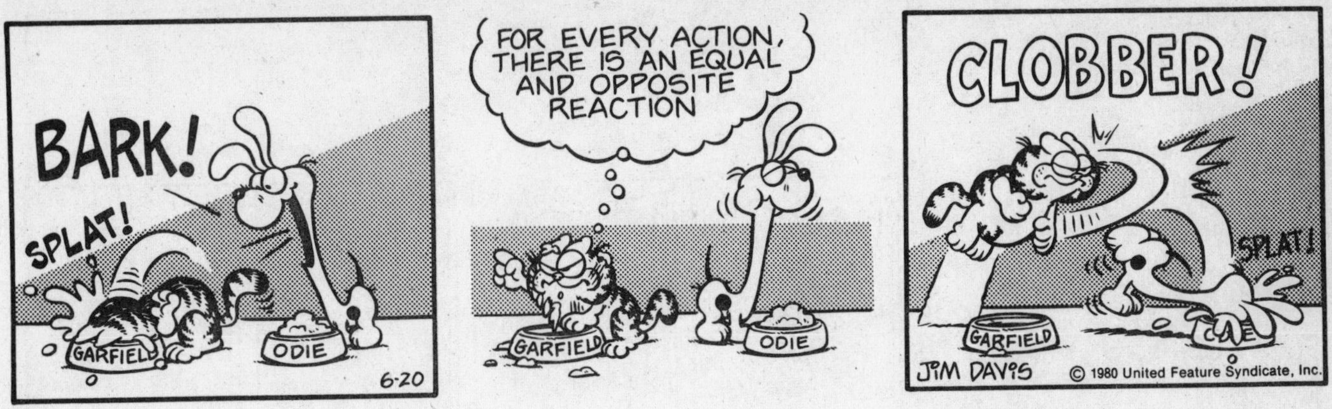
BARK!
SPLAT!
GARFIELD
ODIE
6-20
FOR EVERY ACTION, THERE IS AN EQUAL AND OPPOSITE REACTION
GARFIELD
ODIE
CLOBBER!
SPLAT!
GARFIELD
JIM DAVIS
© 1980 United Feature Syndicate, Inc.

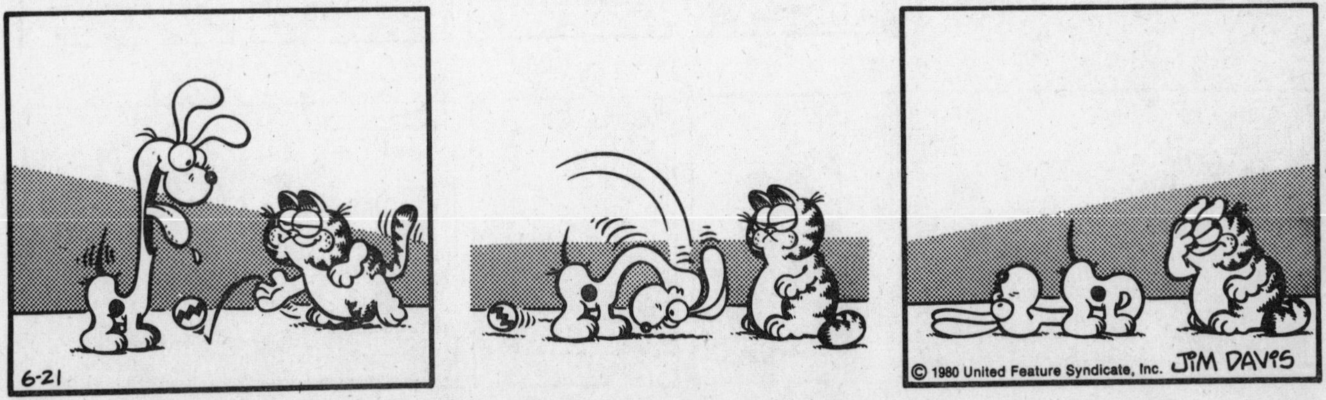
6-21
© 1980 United Feature Syndicate, Inc.
JIM DAVIS

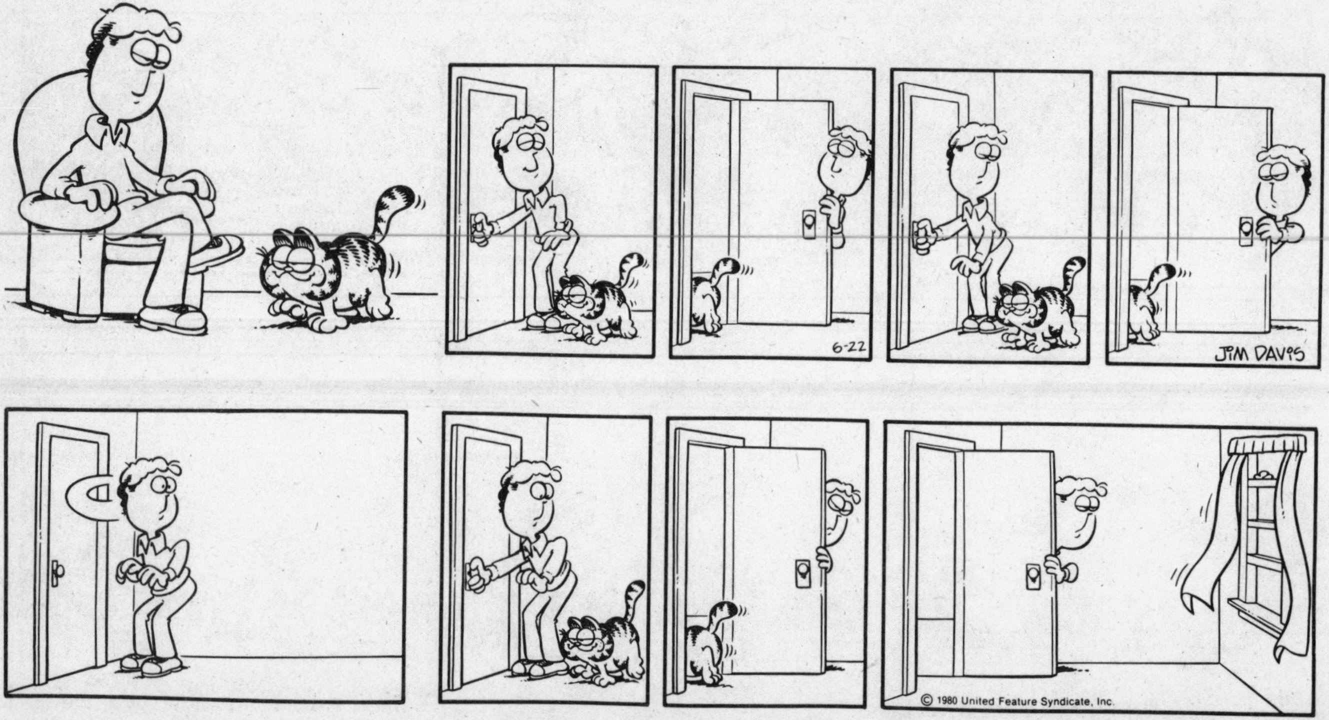
6-22
JIM DAVIS
© 1980 United Feature Syndicate, Inc.

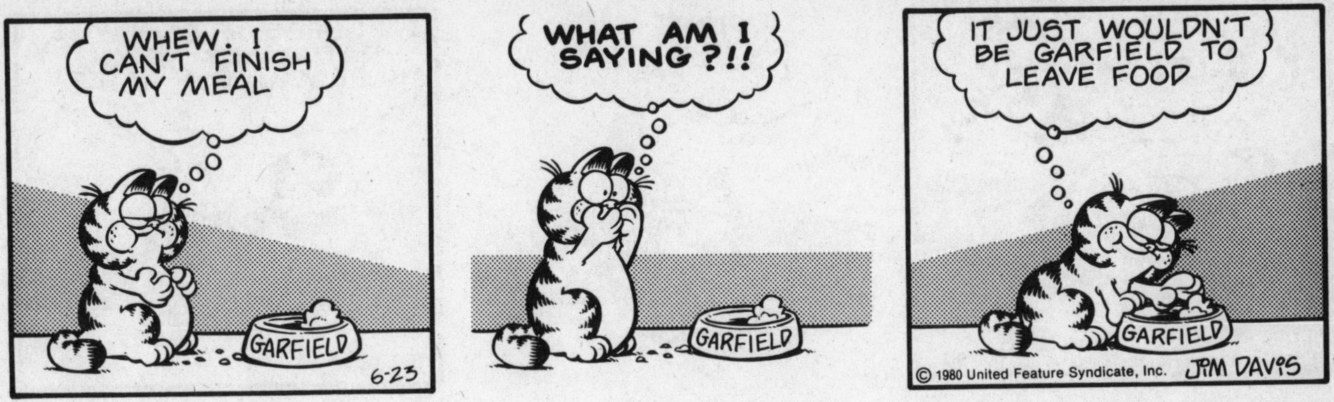

WHEW. I CAN'T FINISH MY MEAL
GARFIELD
6-23
WHAT AM I SAYING?!!
GARFIELD
IT JUST WOULDN'T BE GARFIELD TO LEAVE FOOD
GARFIELD
© 1980 United Feature Syndicate, Inc.
JIM DAVIS

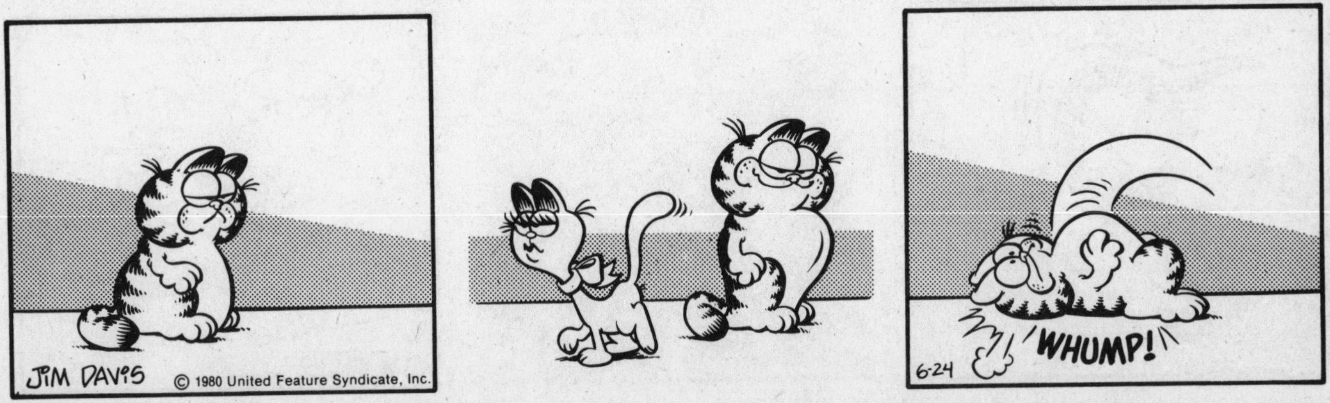

JIM DAVIS
© 1980 United Feature Syndicate, Inc.
WHUMP!
6-24

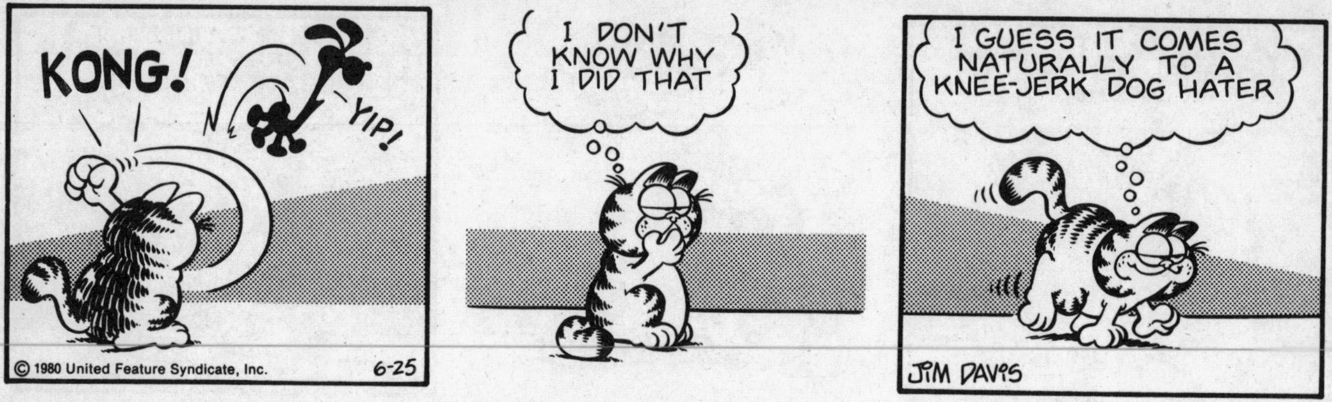
KONG!
YIP!
I DON'T KNOW WHY I DID THAT
I GUESS IT COMES NATURALLY TO A KNEE-JERK DOG HATER
© 1980 United Feature Syndicate, Inc.
6-25
JIM DAVIS

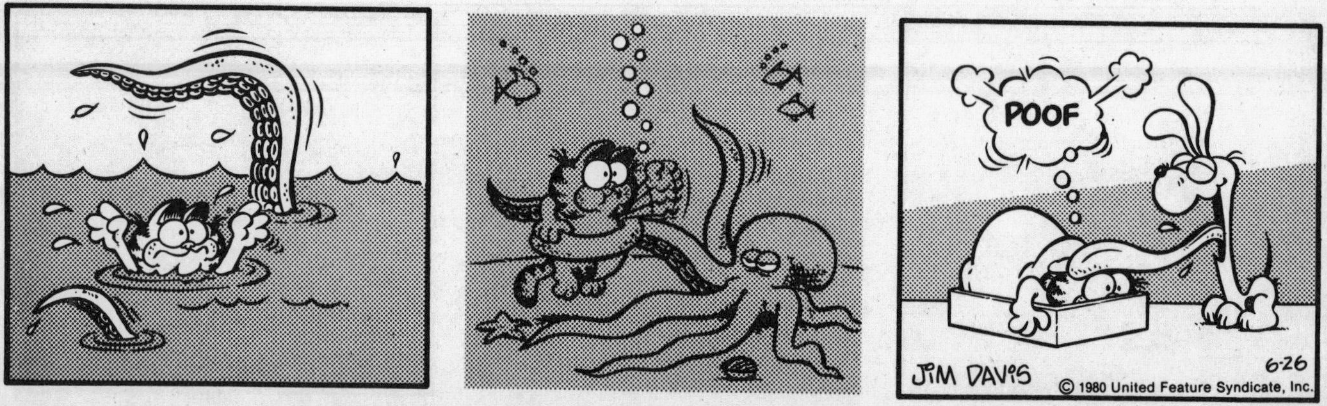
POOF
JIM DAVIS
6-26
© 1980 United Feature Syndicate, Inc.

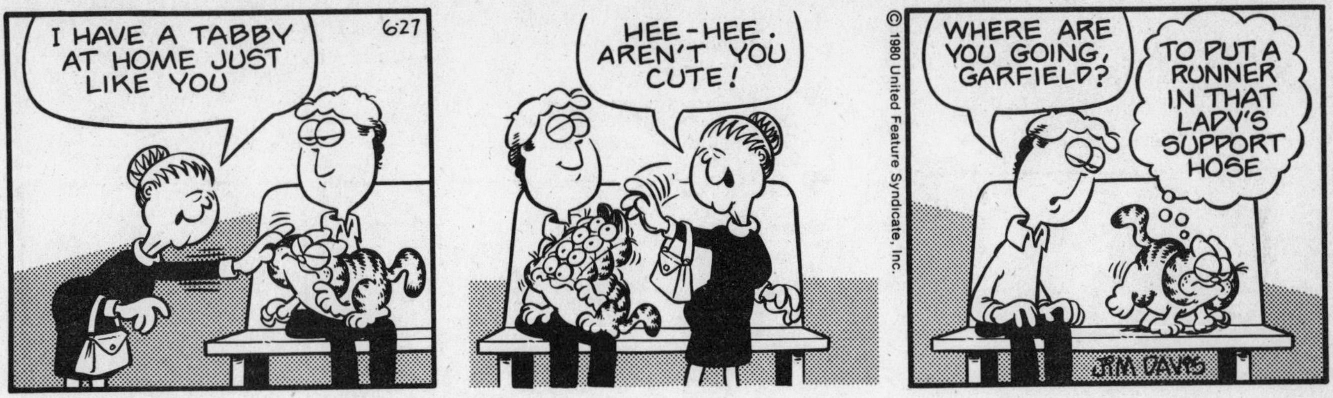
6-27
I HAVE A TABBY AT HOME JUST LIKE YOU
HEE-HEE. AREN'T YOU CUTE!
WHERE ARE YOU GOING, GARFIELD?
TO PUT A RUNNER IN THAT LADY'S SUPPORT HOSE
JIM DAVIS
© 1980 United Feature Syndicate, Inc.

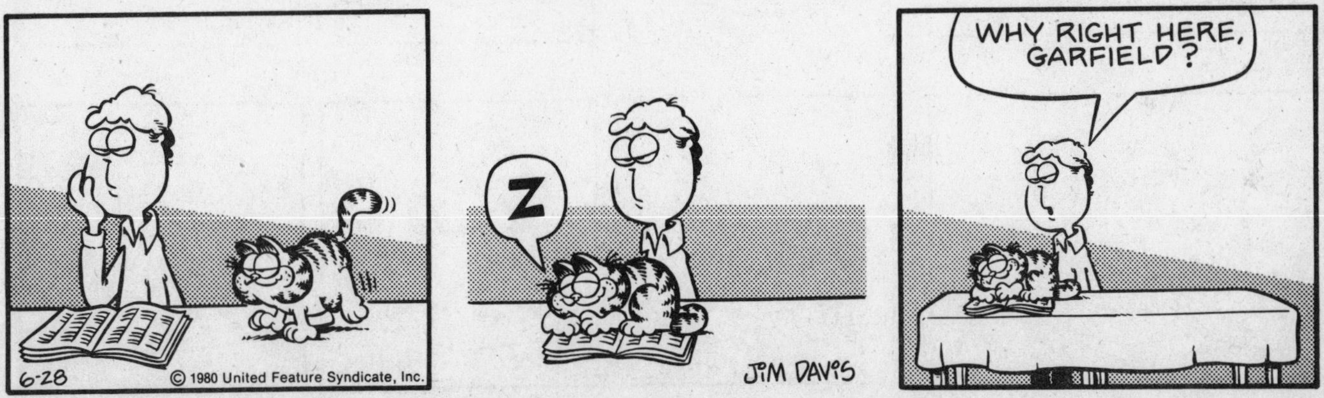
6-28
© 1980 United Feature Syndicate, Inc.
Z
JIM DAVIS
WHY RIGHT HERE, GARFIELD?

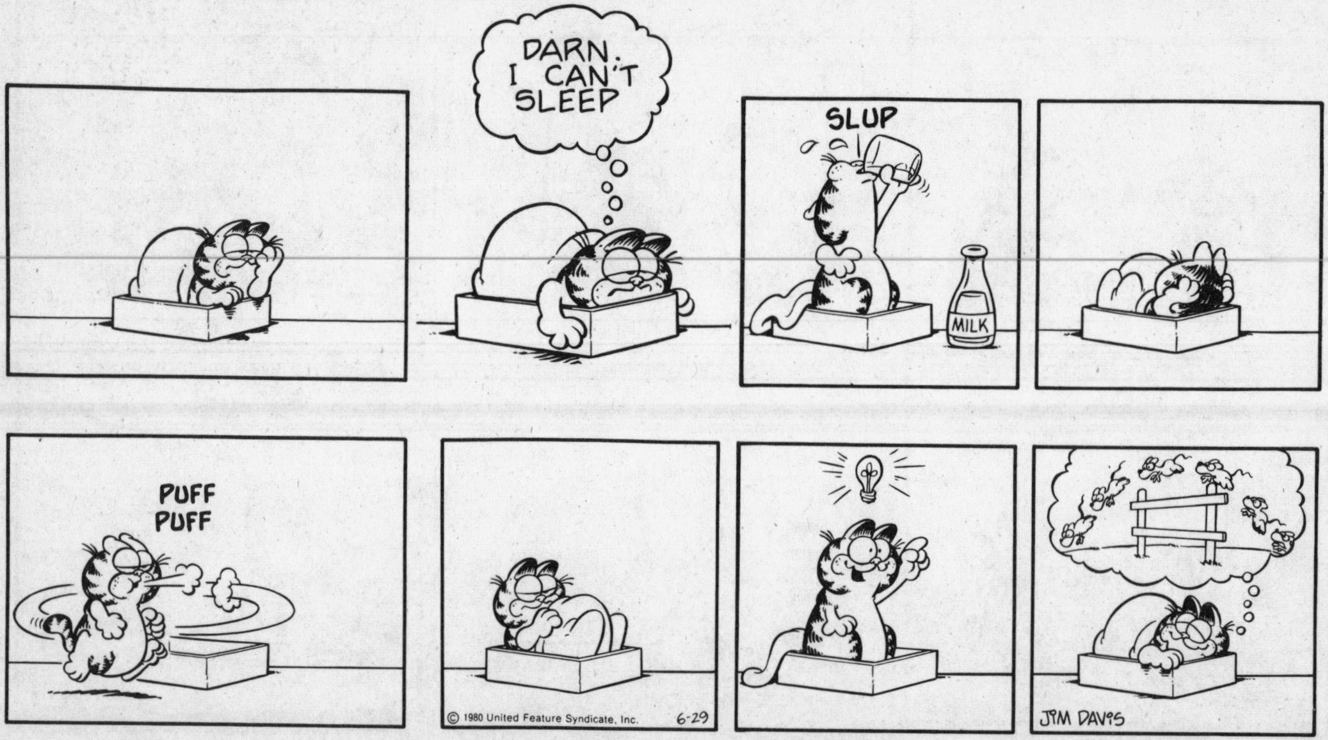
DARN. I CAN'T SLEEP
SLUP
MILK
PUFF PUFF
© 1980 United Feature Syndicate, Inc.
6-29
JIM DAVIS

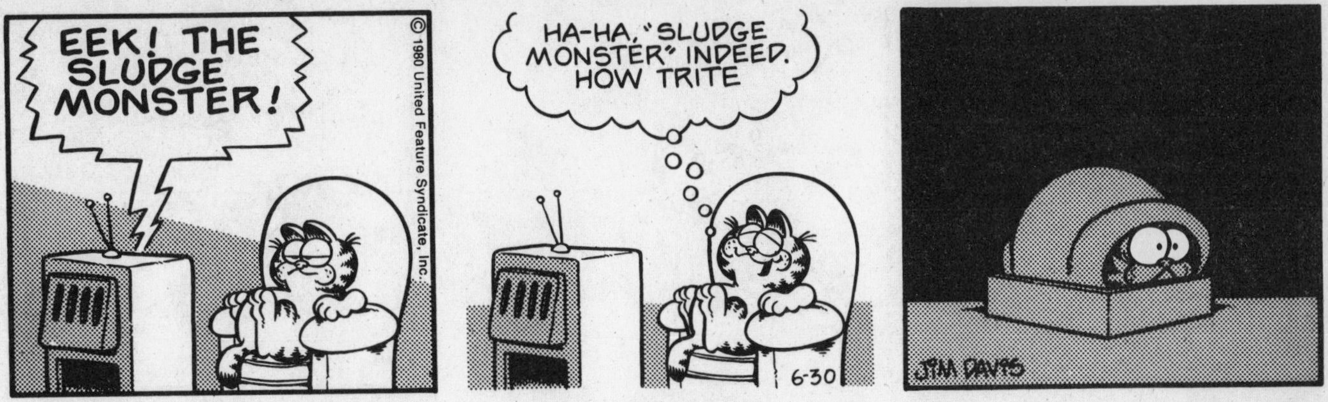
EEK! THE SLUDGE MONSTER!
© 1980 United Feature Syndicate, Inc.
HA-HA, "SLUDGE MONSTER" INDEED. HOW TRITE
6-30
JIM DAVIS

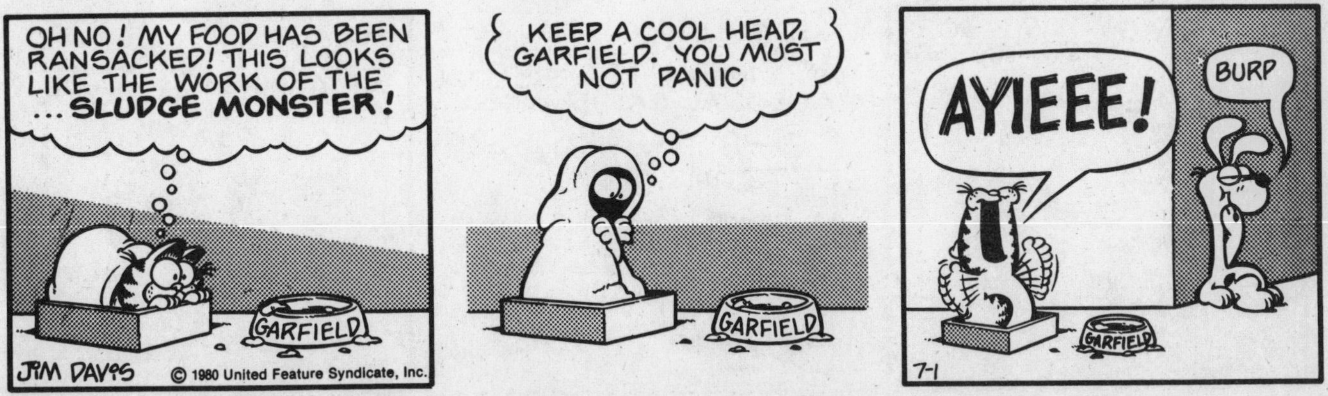
OH NO! MY FOOD HAS BEEN RANSACKED! THIS LOOKS LIKE THE WORK OF THE ...SLUDGE MONSTER!
GARFIELD
JIM DAVIS
© 1980 United Feature Syndicate, Inc.
KEEP A COOL HEAD, GARFIELD. YOU MUST NOT PANIC
GARFIELD
AYIEEE!
BURP
GARFIELD
7-1

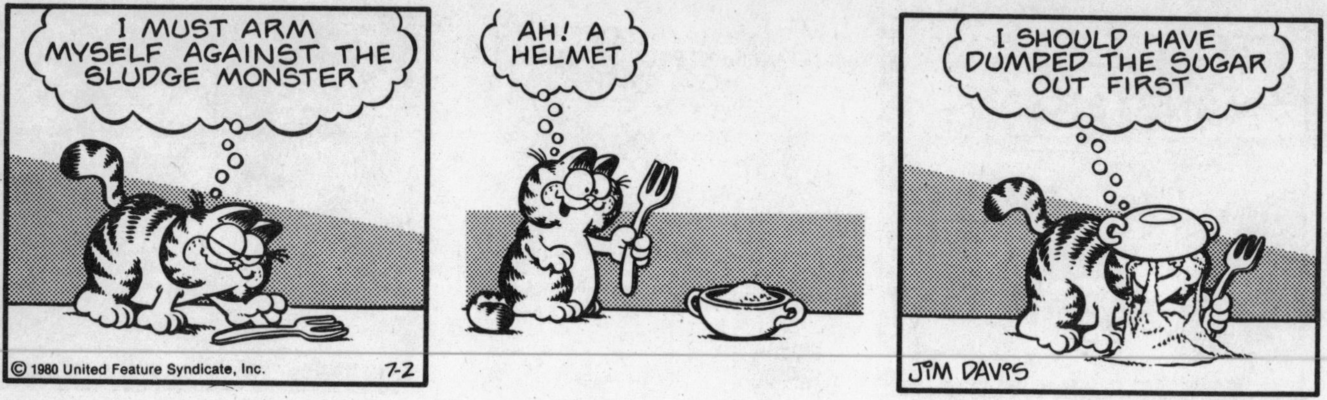
I MUST ARM MYSELF AGAINST THE SLUDGE MONSTER
© 1980 United Feature Syndicate, Inc.
7-2
AH! A HELMET
I SHOULD HAVE DUMPED THE SUGAR OUT FIRST
JIM DAVIS

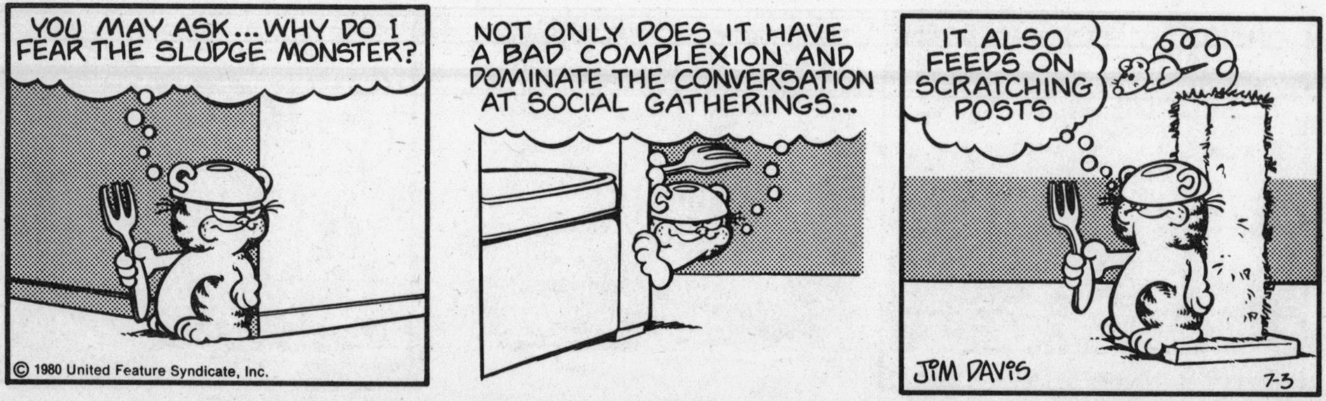
YOU MAY ASK... WHY DO I FEAR THE SLUDGE MONSTER?
© 1980 United Feature Syndicate, Inc.
NOT ONLY DOES IT HAVE A BAD COMPLEXION AND DOMINATE THE CONVERSATION AT SOCIAL GATHERINGS...
IT ALSO FEEDS ON SCRATCHING POSTS
JIM DAVIS
7-3

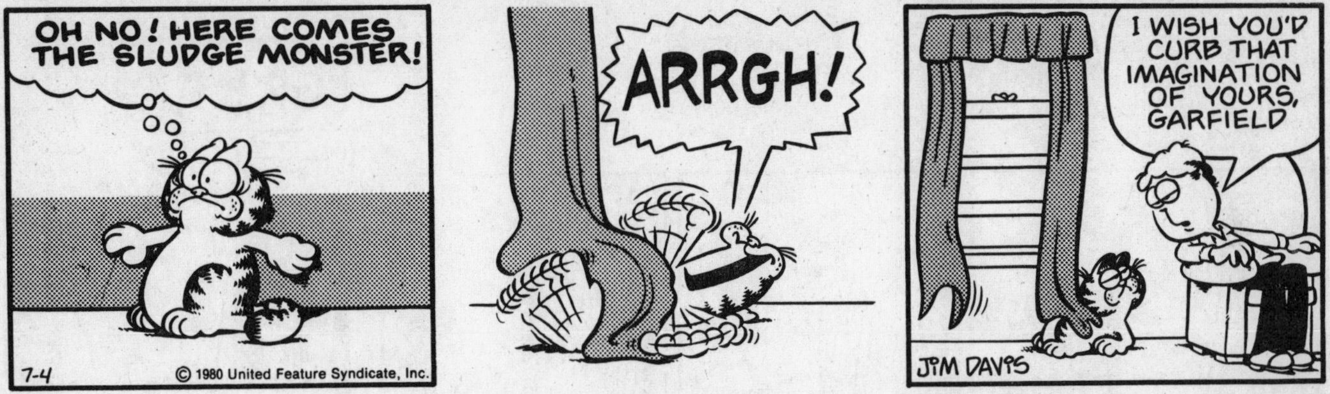
OH NO! HERE COMES THE SLUDGE MONSTER!
ARRGH!
I WISH YOU'D CURB THAT IMAGINATION OF YOURS, GARFIELD
7-4
© 1980 United Feature Syndicate, Inc.
JIM DAVIS

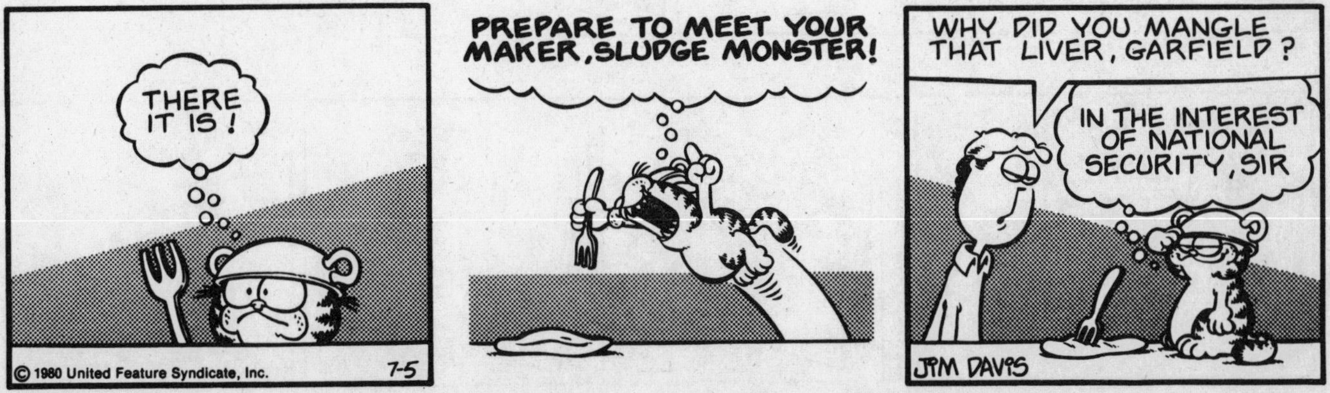
THERE IT IS!
PREPARE TO MEET YOUR MAKER, SLUDGE MONSTER!
WHY DID YOU MANGLE THAT LIVER, GARFIELD?
IN THE INTEREST OF NATIONAL SECURITY, SIR
© 1980 United Feature Syndicate, Inc.
7-5
JIM DAVIS

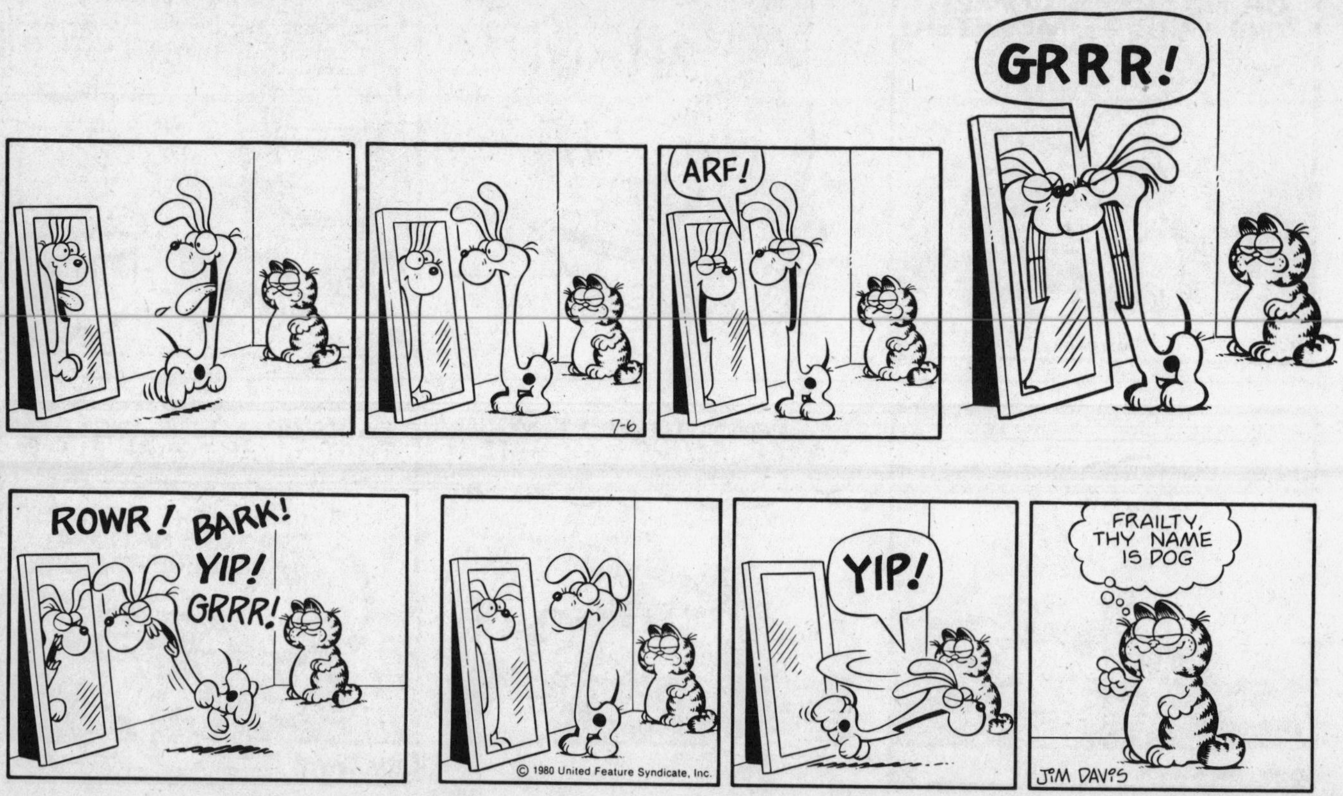
7-6
ARF!
GRRR!
ROWR! BARK! YIP! GRRR!
© 1980 United Feature Syndicate, Inc.
YIP!
FRAILTY, THY NAME IS DOG
JIM DAVIS

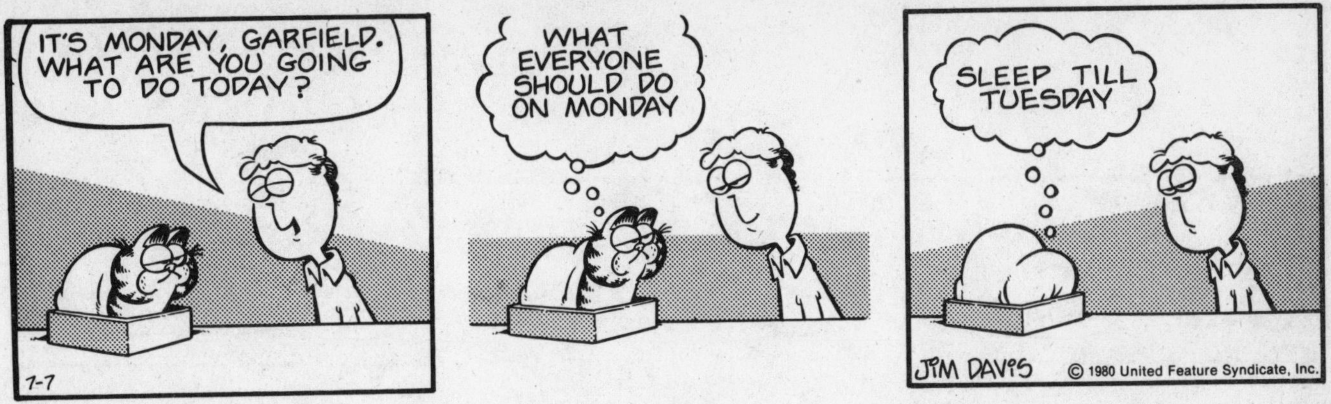
IT'S MONDAY, GARFIELD. WHAT ARE YOU GOING TO DO TODAY?
7-7
WHAT EVERYONE SHOULD DO ON MONDAY
SLEEP TILL TUESDAY
JIM DAVIS
© 1980 United Feature Syndicate, Inc.

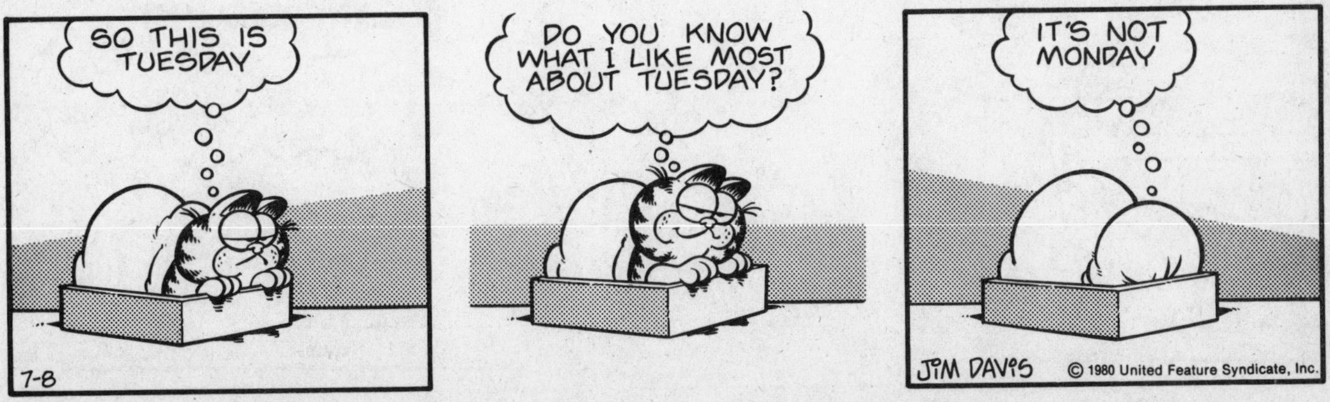
SO THIS IS TUESDAY
7-8
DO YOU KNOW WHAT I LIKE MOST ABOUT TUESDAY?
IT'S NOT MONDAY
JIM DAVIS
© 1980 United Feature Syndicate, Inc.

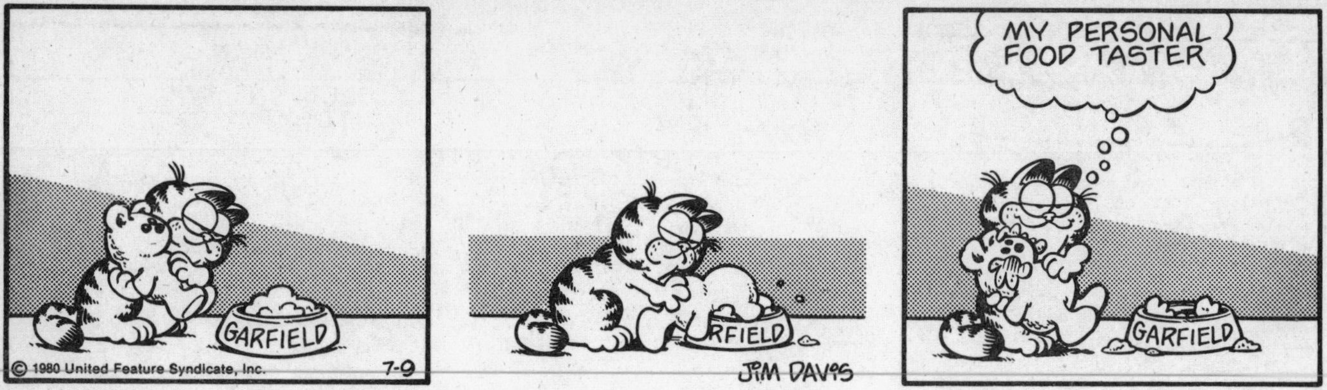
GARFIELD
© 1980 United Feature Syndicate, Inc.
7-9
RFIELD
JIM DAVIS
MY PERSONAL FOOD TASTER
GARFIELD

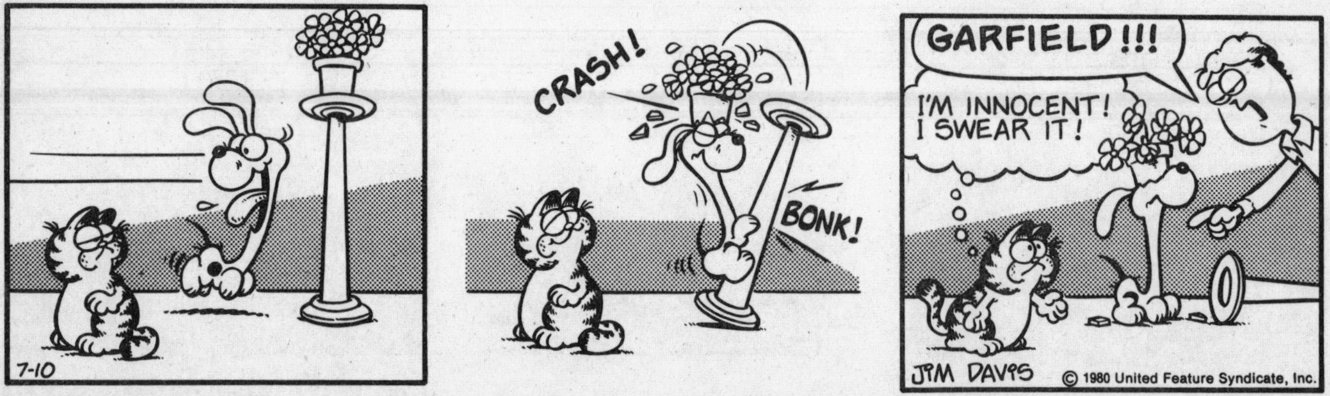
7-10
CRASH!
BONK!
GARFIELD!!!
I'M INNOCENT! I SWEAR IT!
JIM DAVIS
© 1980 United Feature Syndicate, Inc.

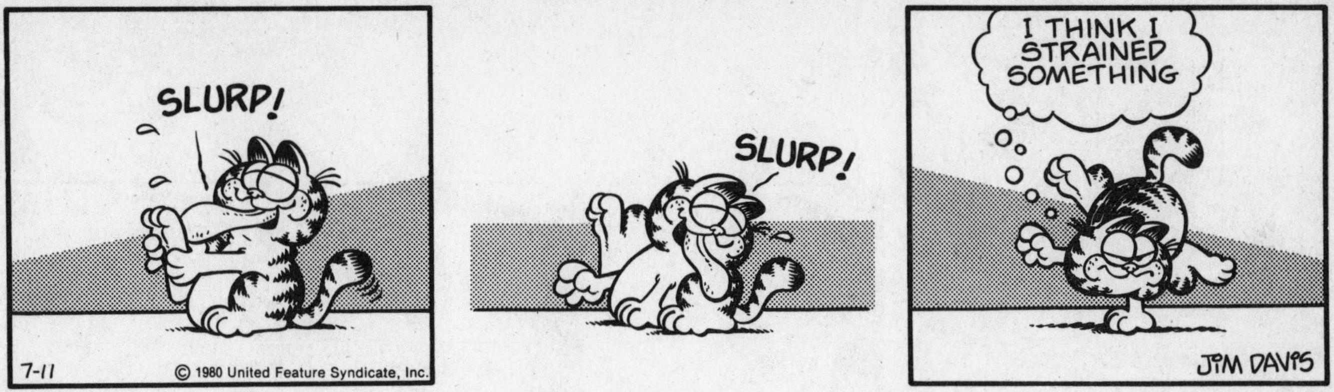
SLURP!
7-11
© 1980 United Feature Syndicate, Inc.
SLURP!
I THINK I STRAINED SOMETHING
JIM DAVIS

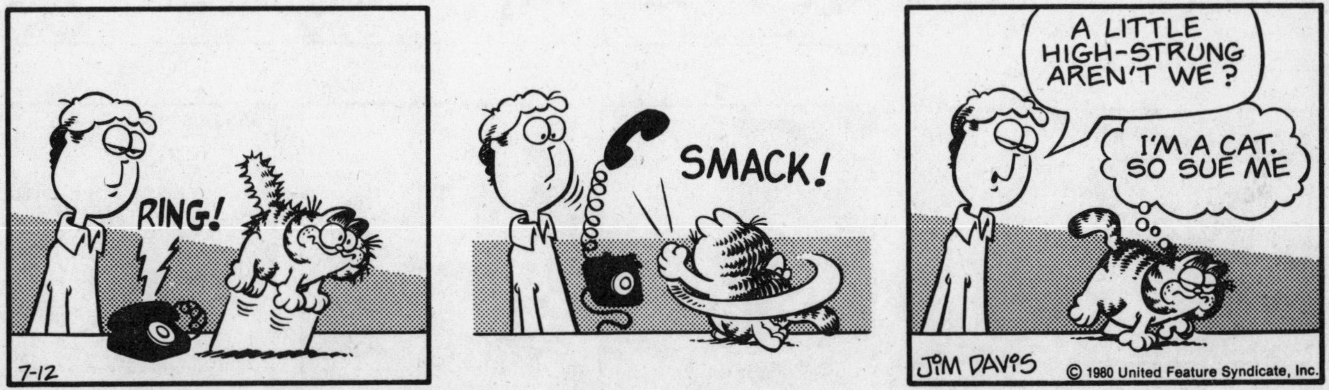
RING!
7-12
SMACK!
A LITTLE HIGH-STRUNG AREN'T WE?
I'M A CAT. SO SUE ME
JIM DAVIS
© 1980 United Feature Syndicate, Inc.

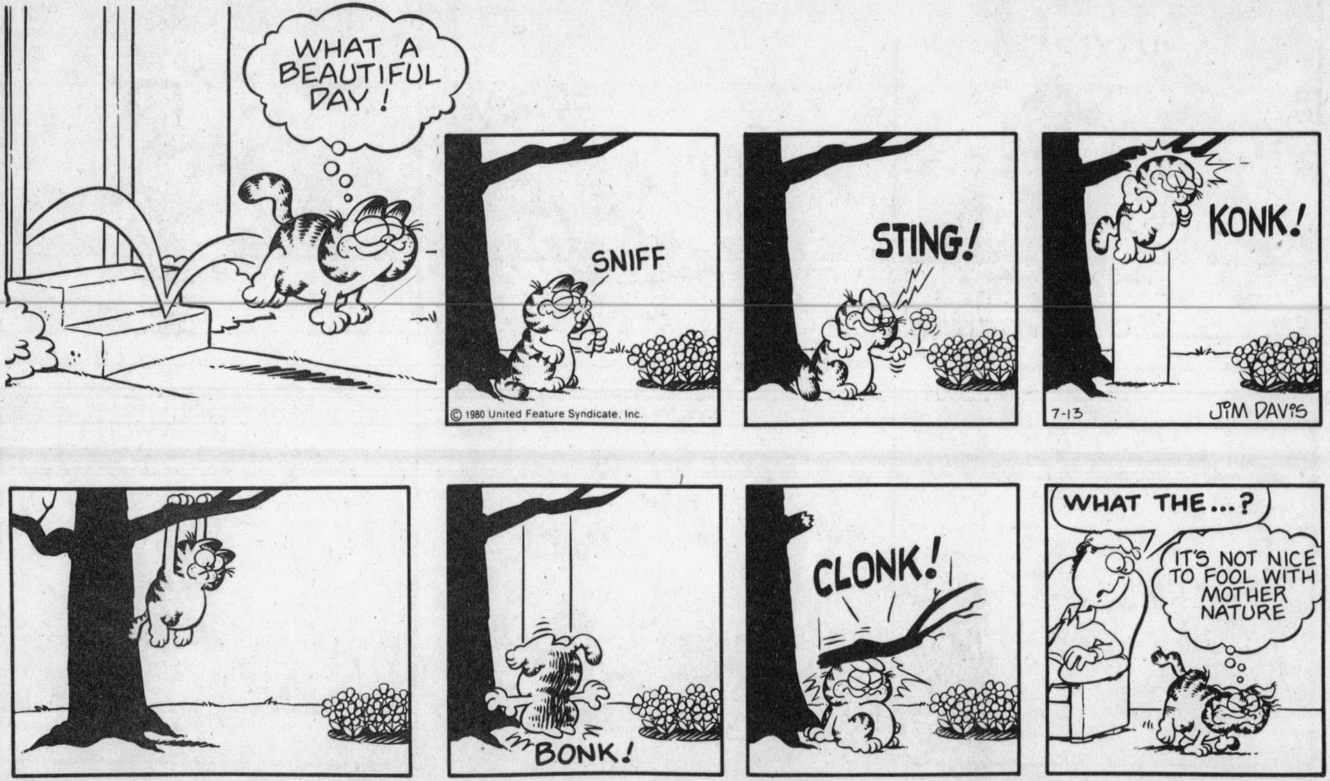
WHAT A BEAUTIFUL DAY!
SNIFF
© 1980 United Feature Syndicate, Inc.
STING!
KONK!
7-13
JIM DAVIS
BONK!
CLONK!
WHAT THE...?
IT'S NOT NICE TO FOOL WITH MOTHER NATURE

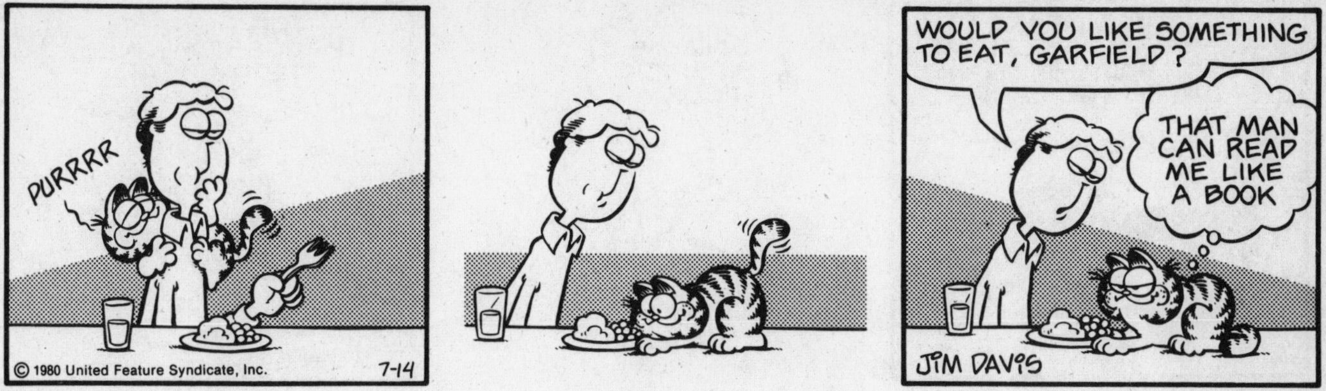
PURRRR
WOULD YOU LIKE SOMETHING TO EAT, GARFIELD?
THAT MAN CAN READ ME LIKE A BOOK
© 1980 United Feature Syndicate, Inc.
7-14
JIM DAVIS

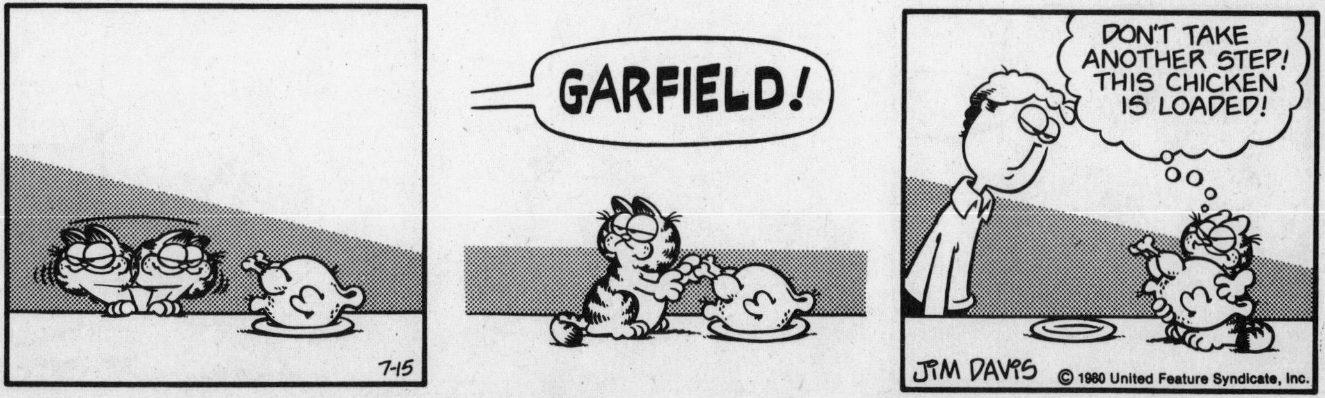
7-15
GARFIELD!
DON'T TAKE ANOTHER STEP! THIS CHICKEN IS LOADED!
JIM DAVIS
© 1980 United Feature Syndicate, Inc.

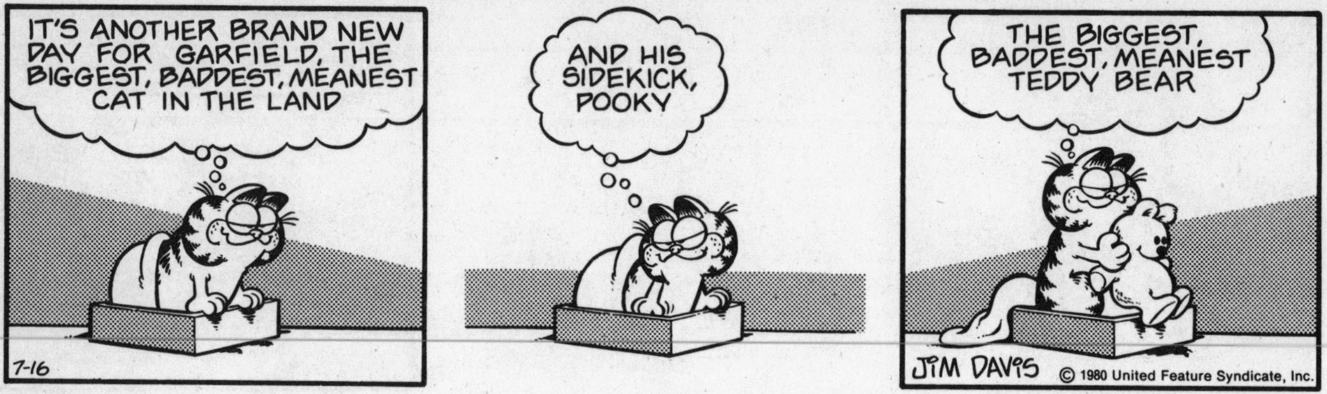
IT'S ANOTHER BRAND NEW DAY FOR GARFIELD, THE BIGGEST, BADDEST, MEANEST CAT IN THE LAND
AND HIS SIDEKICK, POOKY
THE BIGGEST, BADDEST, MEANEST TEDDY BEAR
7-16
JIM DAVIS
© 1980 United Feature Syndicate, Inc.

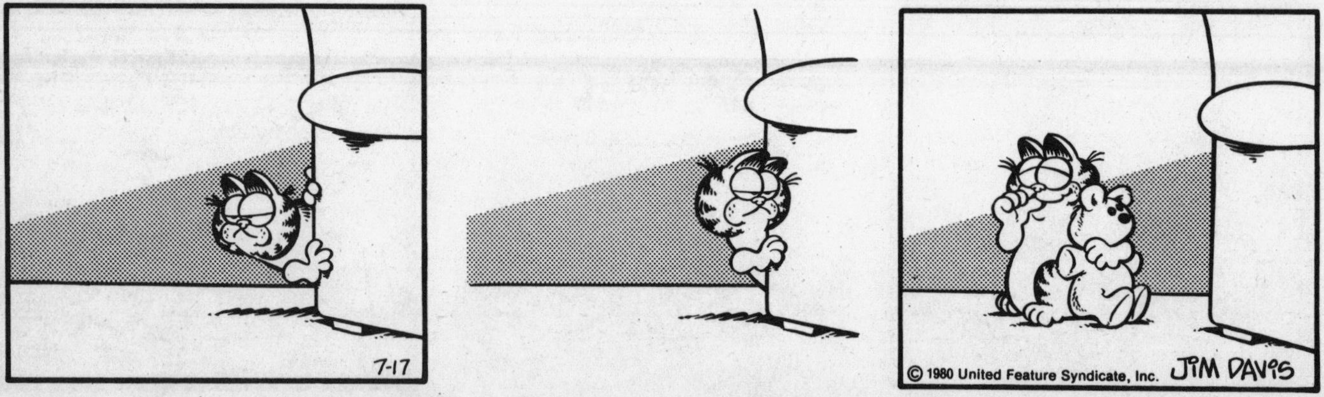
7-17
© 1980 United Feature Syndicate, Inc.
JIM DAVIS

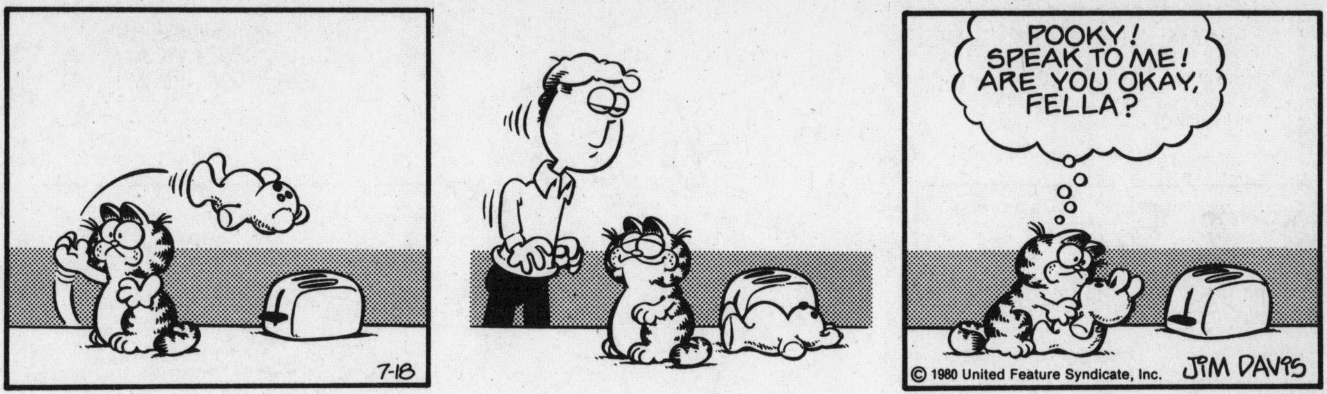
7-18
POOKY! SPEAK TO ME! ARE YOU OKAY, FELLA?
© 1980 United Feature Syndicate, Inc.
JIM DAVIS

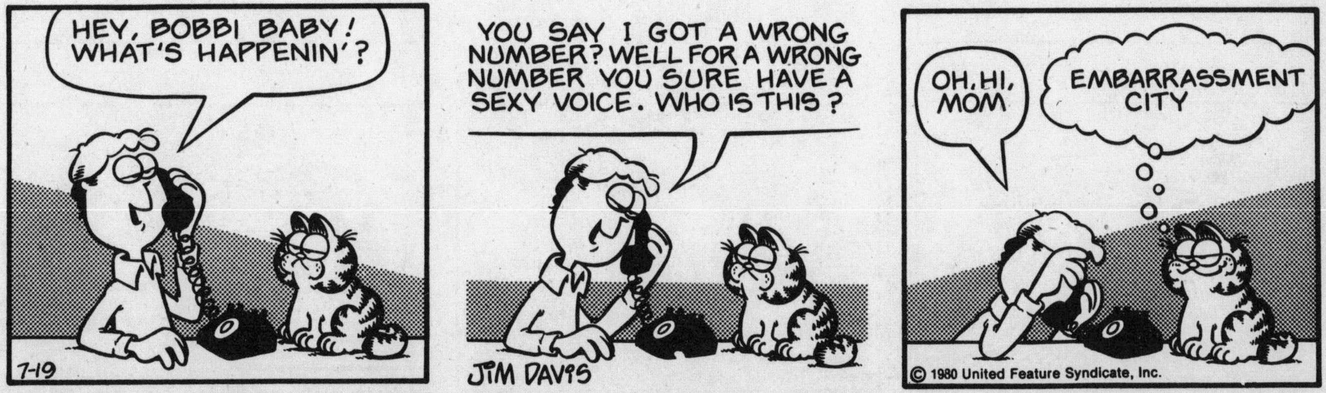
HEY, BOBBI BABY! WHAT'S HAPPENIN'?
7-19
YOU SAY I GOT A WRONG NUMBER? WELL FOR A WRONG NUMBER YOU SURE HAVE A SEXY VOICE. WHO IS THIS?
JIM DAVIS
OH, HI, MOM
EMBARRASSMENT CITY
© 1980 United Feature Syndicate, Inc.

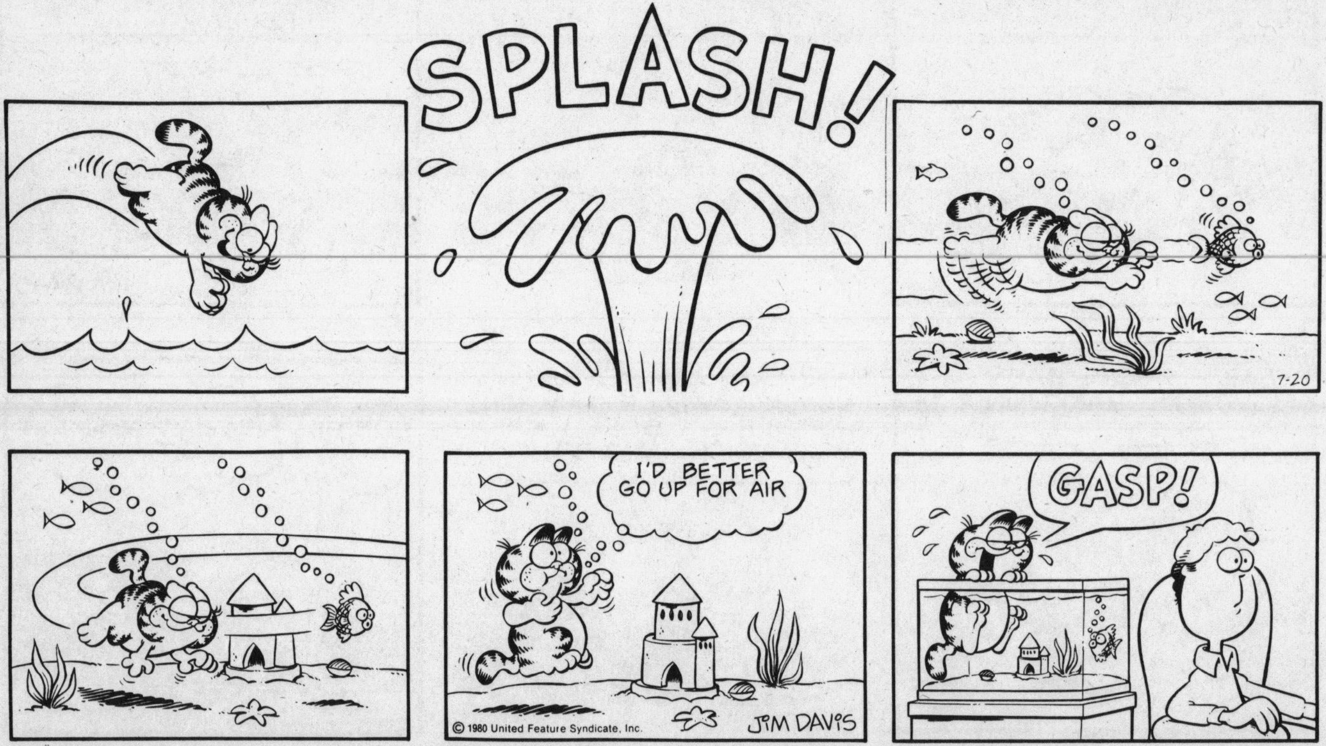
SPLASH!
7-20
I'D BETTER GO UP FOR AIR
© 1980 United Feature Syndicate, Inc.
JIM DAVIS
GASP!

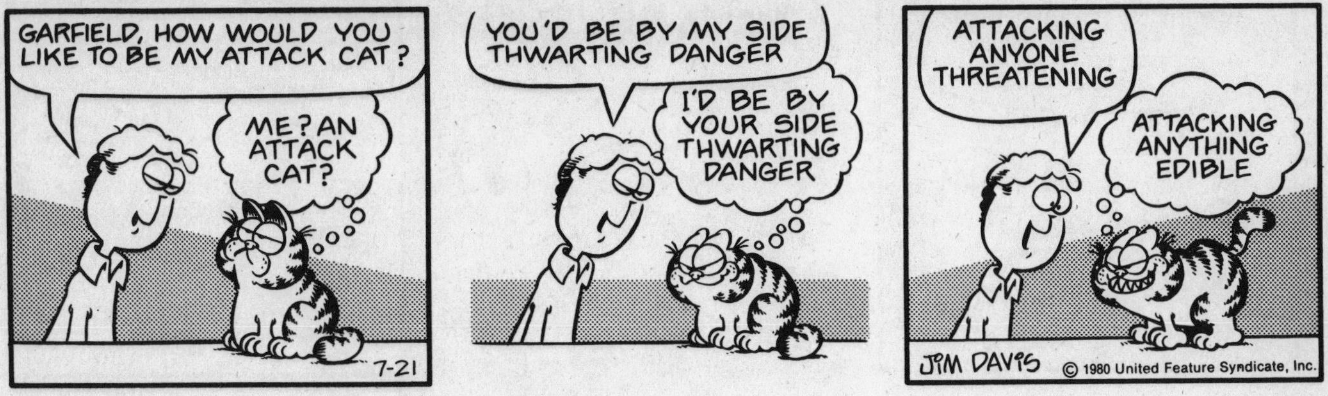
GARFIELD, HOW WOULD YOU LIKE TO BE MY ATTACK CAT?
ME? AN ATTACK CAT?
7-21
YOU'D BE BY MY SIDE THWARTING DANGER
I'D BE BY YOUR SIDE THWARTING DANGER
ATTACKING ANYONE THREATENING
ATTACKING ANYTHING EDIBLE
JIM DAVIS
© 1980 United Feature Syndicate, Inc.

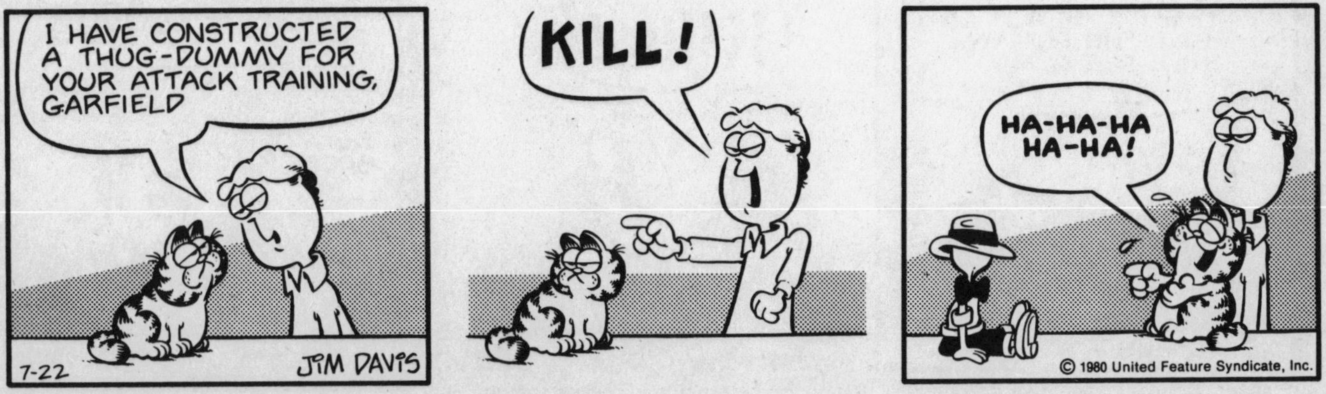
I HAVE CONSTRUCTED A THUG-DUMMY FOR YOUR ATTACK TRAINING, GARFIELD
7-22
JIM DAVIS
KILL!
HA-HA-HA HA-HA!
© 1980 United Feature Syndicate, Inc.

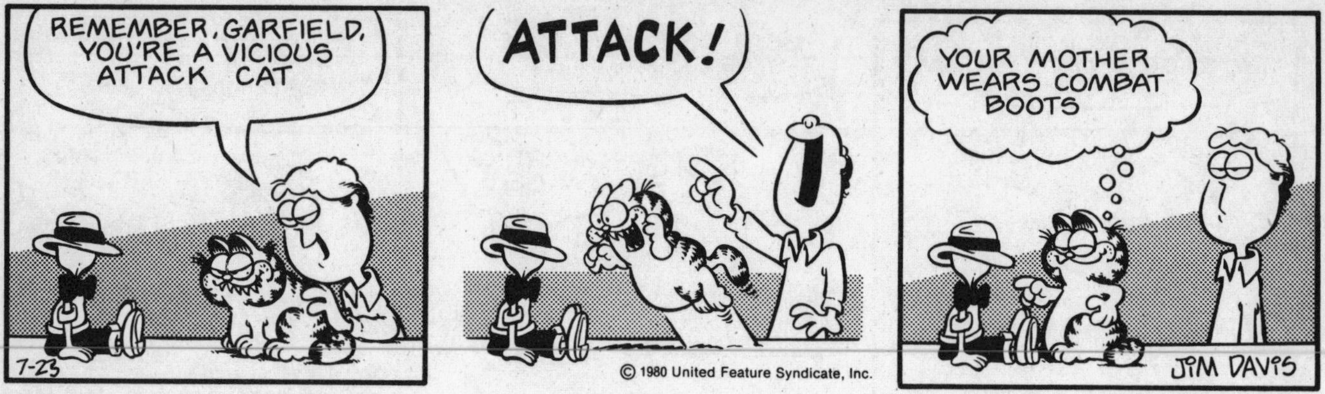
REMEMBER, GARFIELD, YOU'RE A VICIOUS ATTACK CAT
7-23
ATTACK!
© 1980 United Feature Syndicate, Inc.
YOUR MOTHER WEARS COMBAT BOOTS
JIM DAVIS

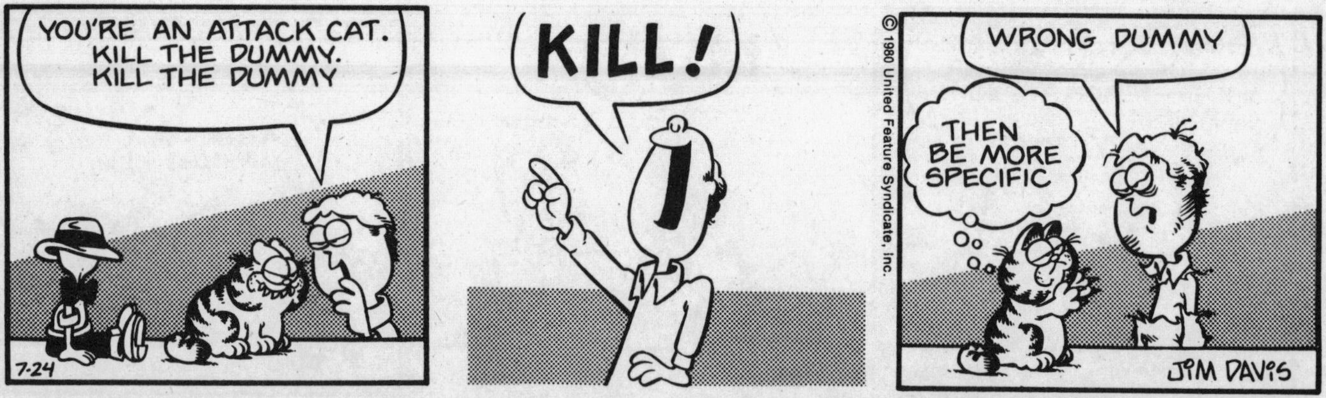
YOU'RE AN ATTACK CAT. KILL THE DUMMY. KILL THE DUMMY
7-24
KILL!
© 1980 United Feature Syndicate, Inc.
WRONG DUMMY
THEN BE MORE SPECIFIC
JIM DAVIS

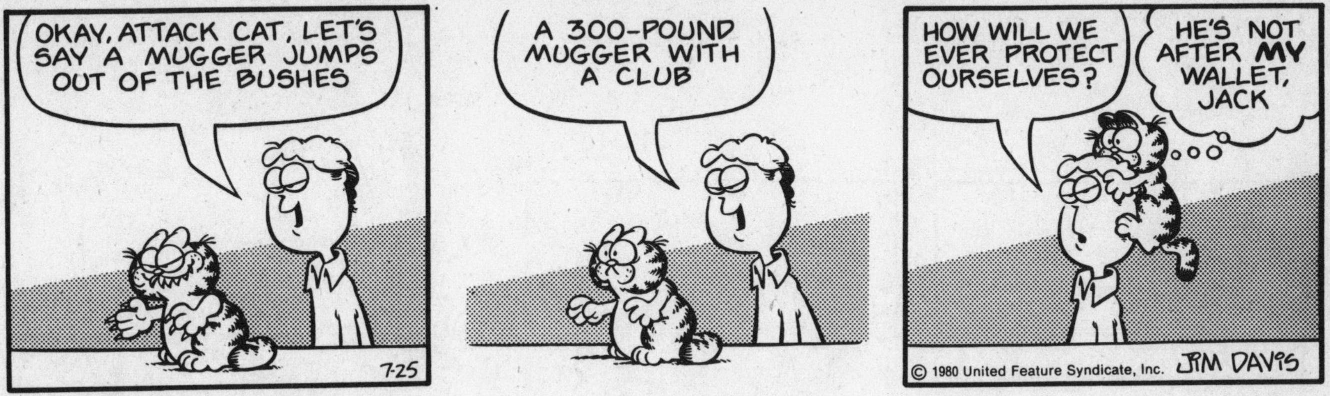
OKAY, ATTACK CAT, LET'S SAY A MUGGER JUMPS OUT OF THE BUSHES
7-25
A 300-POUND MUGGER WITH A CLUB
HOW WILL WE EVER PROTECT OURSELVES?
HE'S NOT AFTER **MY** WALLET, JACK
© 1980 United Feature Syndicate, Inc.
JIM DAVIS

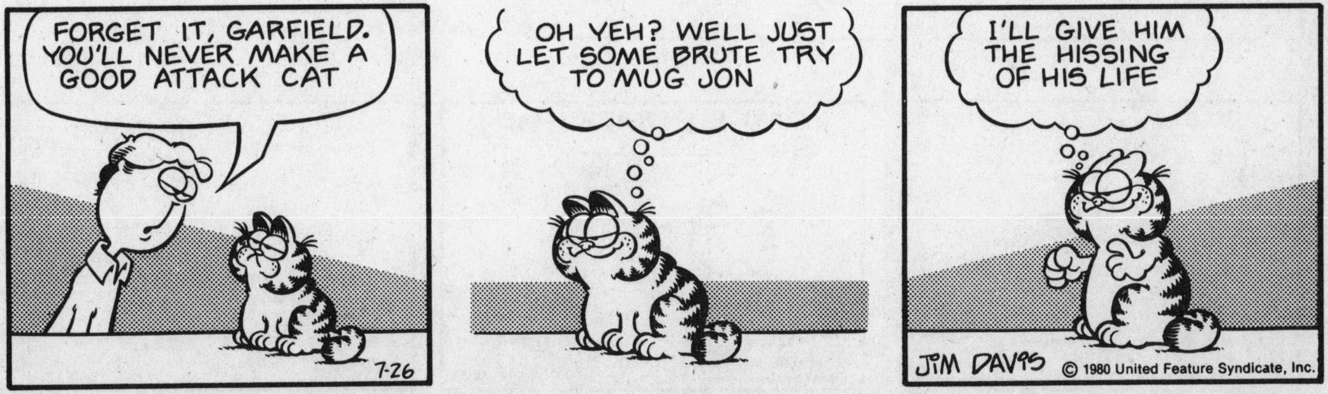
FORGET IT, GARFIELD. YOU'LL NEVER MAKE A GOOD ATTACK CAT
7-26
OH YEH? WELL JUST LET SOME BRUTE TRY TO MUG JON
I'LL GIVE HIM THE HISSING OF HIS LIFE
JIM DAVIS
© 1980 United Feature Syndicate, Inc.

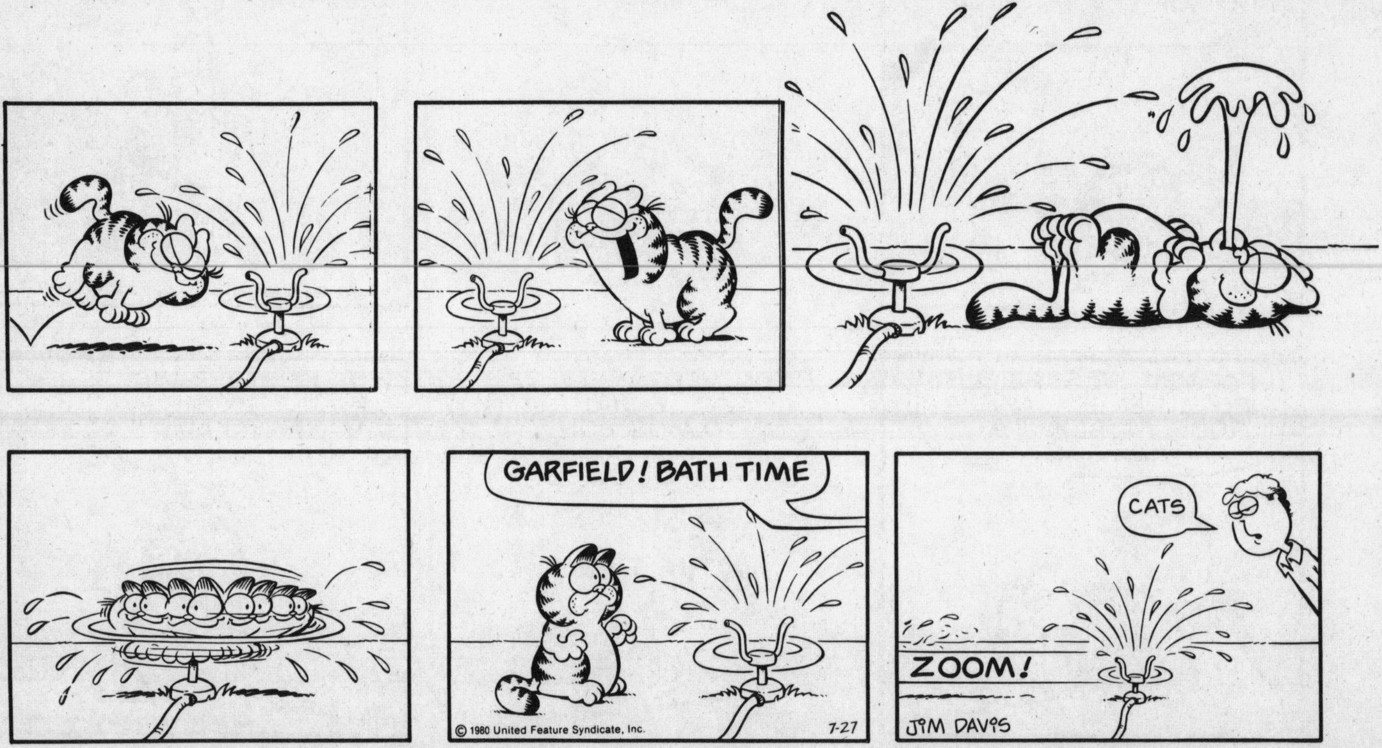
GARFIELD! BATH TIME
© 1980 United Feature Syndicate, Inc.
7-27
CATS
ZOOM!
JIM DAVIS

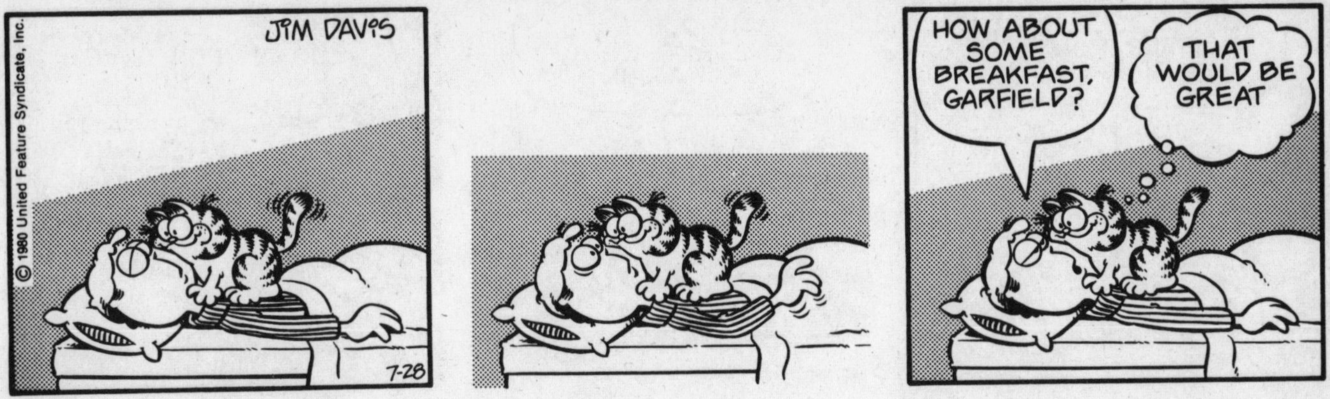
JIM DAVIS
© 1980 United Feature Syndicate, Inc.
7-28
HOW ABOUT SOME BREAKFAST, GARFIELD?
THAT WOULD BE GREAT

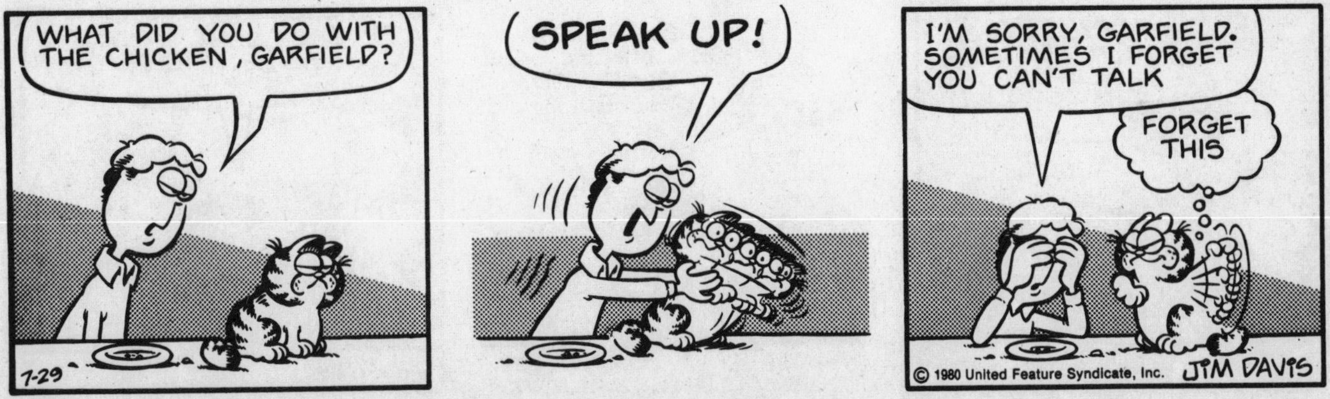
WHAT DID YOU DO WITH THE CHICKEN, GARFIELD?
7-29
SPEAK UP!
I'M SORRY, GARFIELD. SOMETIMES I FORGET YOU CAN'T TALK
FORGET THIS
© 1980 United Feature Syndicate, Inc.
JIM DAVIS

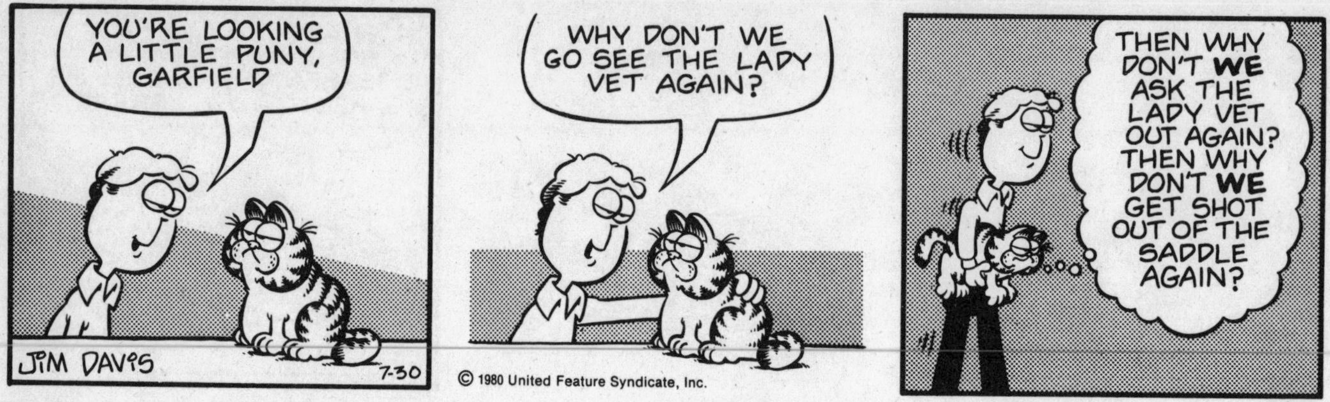
YOU'RE LOOKING A LITTLE PUNY, GARFIELD
JIM DAVIS
7-30
WHY DON'T WE GO SEE THE LADY VET AGAIN?
© 1980 United Feature Syndicate, Inc.
THEN WHY DON'T **WE** ASK THE LADY VET OUT AGAIN? THEN WHY DON'T **WE** GET SHOT OUT OF THE SADDLE AGAIN?

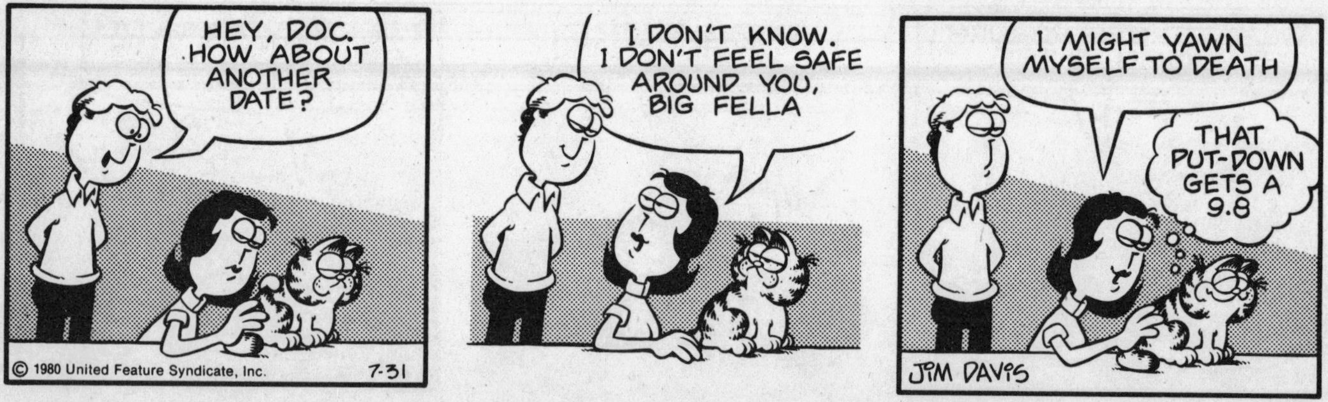
HEY, DOC. HOW ABOUT ANOTHER DATE?
© 1980 United Feature Syndicate, Inc.
7-31
I DON'T KNOW. I DON'T FEEL SAFE AROUND YOU, BIG FELLA
I MIGHT YAWN MYSELF TO DEATH
THAT PUT-DOWN GETS A 9.8
JIM DAVIS

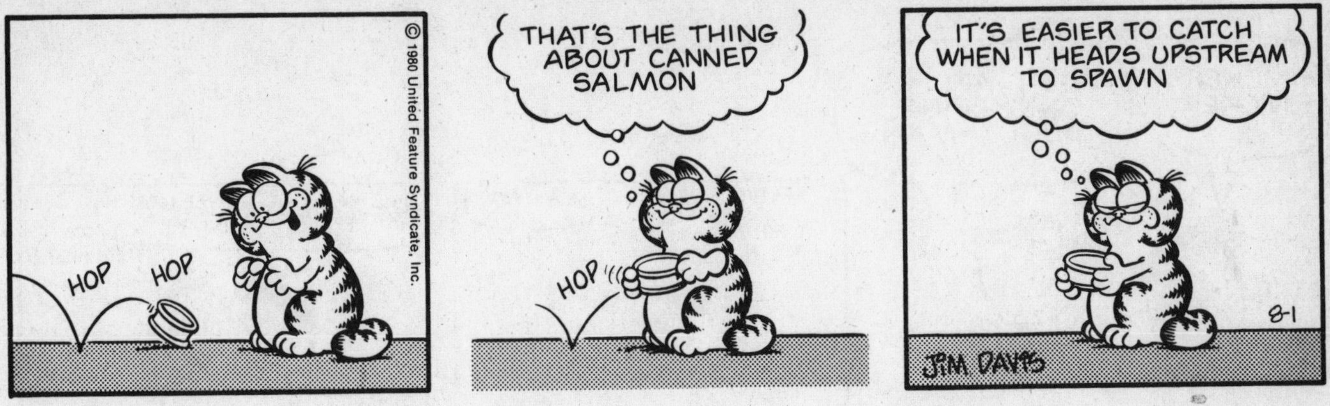
© 1980 United Feature Syndicate, Inc.
HOP HOP
THAT'S THE THING ABOUT CANNED SALMON
HOP
IT'S EASIER TO CATCH WHEN IT HEADS UPSTREAM TO SPAWN
8-1
JIM DAVIS

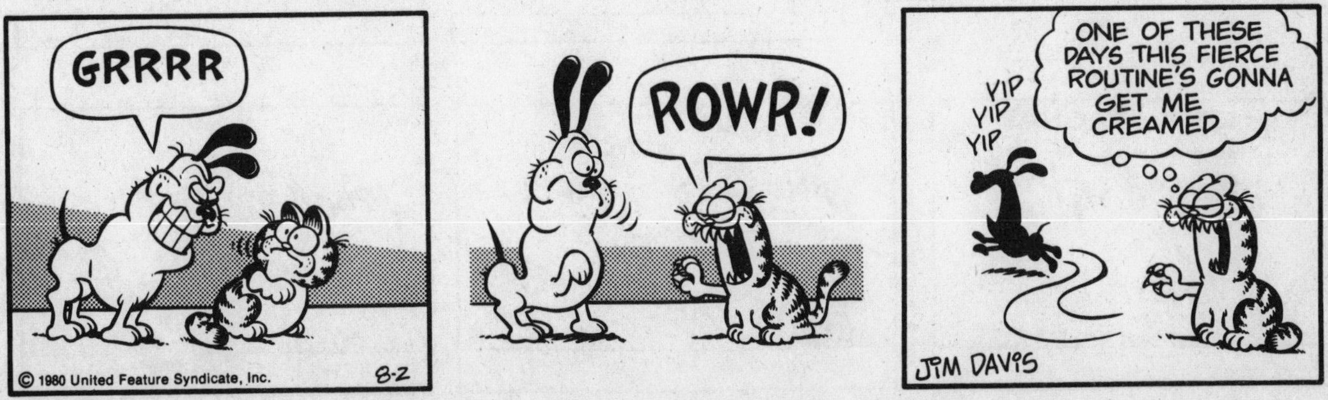
GRRRR
© 1980 United Feature Syndicate, Inc.
8-2
ROWR!
YIP YIP YIP
ONE OF THESE DAYS THIS FIERCE ROUTINE'S GONNA GET ME CREAMED
JIM DAVIS

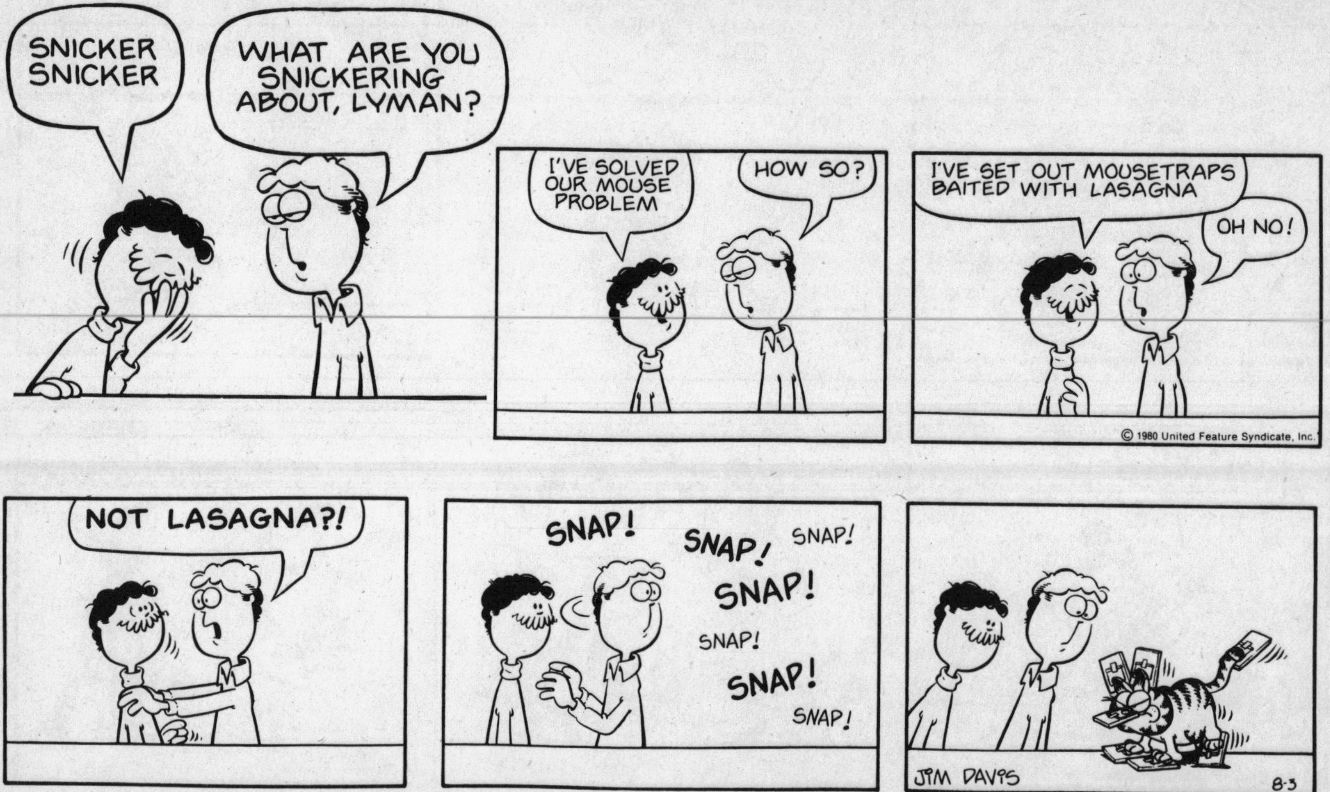
SNICKER SNICKER
WHAT ARE YOU SNICKERING ABOUT, LYMAN?
I'VE SOLVED OUR MOUSE PROBLEM
HOW SO?
I'VE SET OUT MOUSETRAPS BAITED WITH LASAGNA
OH NO!
© 1980 United Feature Syndicate, Inc.
NOT LASAGNA?!
SNAP!
SNAP!
SNAP!
SNAP!
SNAP!
SNAP!
SNAP!
JIM DAVIS
8-3

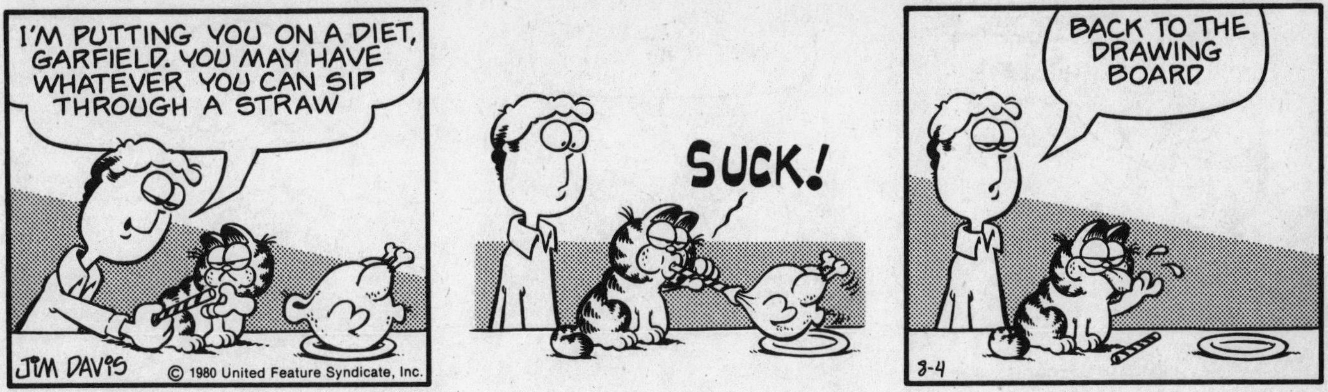
I'M PUTTING YOU ON A DIET, GARFIELD. YOU MAY HAVE WHATEVER YOU CAN SIP THROUGH A STRAW
JIM DAVIS
© 1980 United Feature Syndicate, Inc.
SUCK!
BACK TO THE DRAWING BOARD
8-4

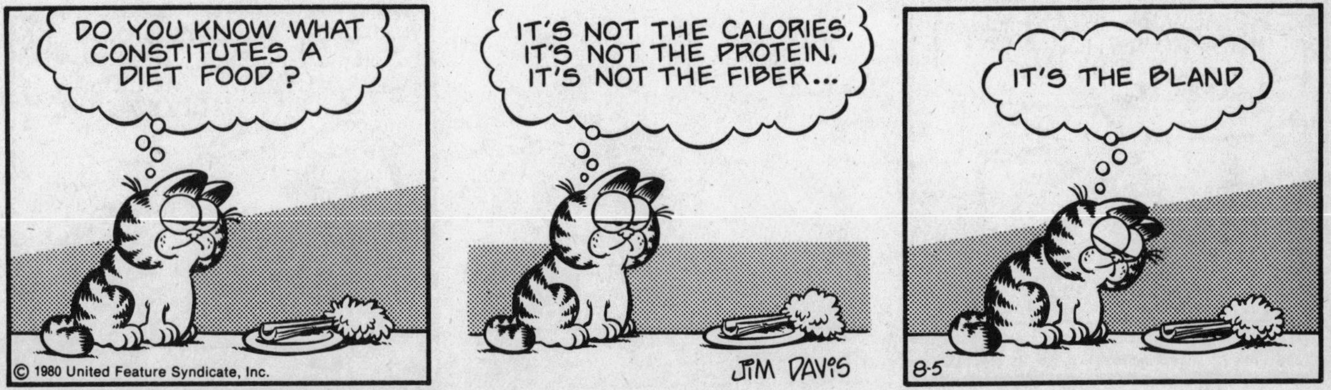
DO YOU KNOW WHAT CONSTITUTES A DIET FOOD ?
© 1980 United Feature Syndicate, Inc.
IT'S NOT THE CALORIES, IT'S NOT THE PROTEIN, IT'S NOT THE FIBER...
JIM DAVIS
IT'S THE BLAND
8-5

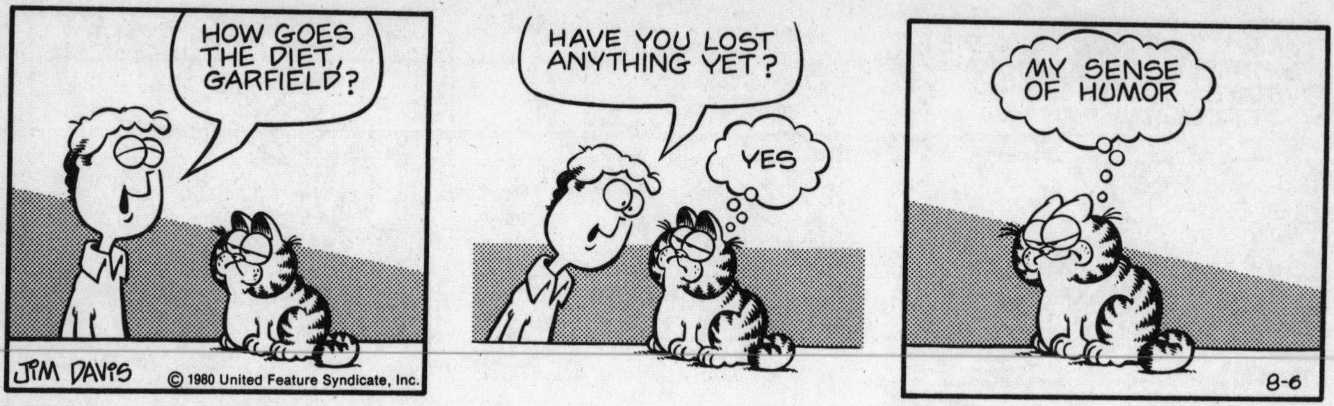
HOW GOES THE DIET, GARFIELD?
HAVE YOU LOST ANYTHING YET?
YES
MY SENSE OF HUMOR
JIM DAVIS
© 1980 United Feature Syndicate, Inc.
8-6

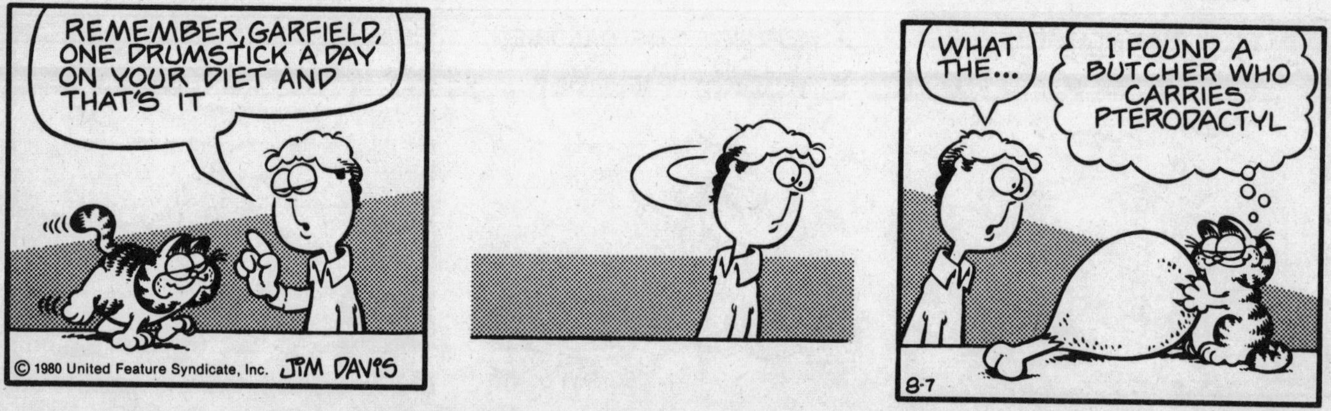
REMEMBER, GARFIELD, ONE DRUMSTICK A DAY ON YOUR DIET AND THAT'S IT
WHAT THE...
I FOUND A BUTCHER WHO CARRIES PTERODACTYL
© 1980 United Feature Syndicate, Inc.
JIM DAVIS
8-7

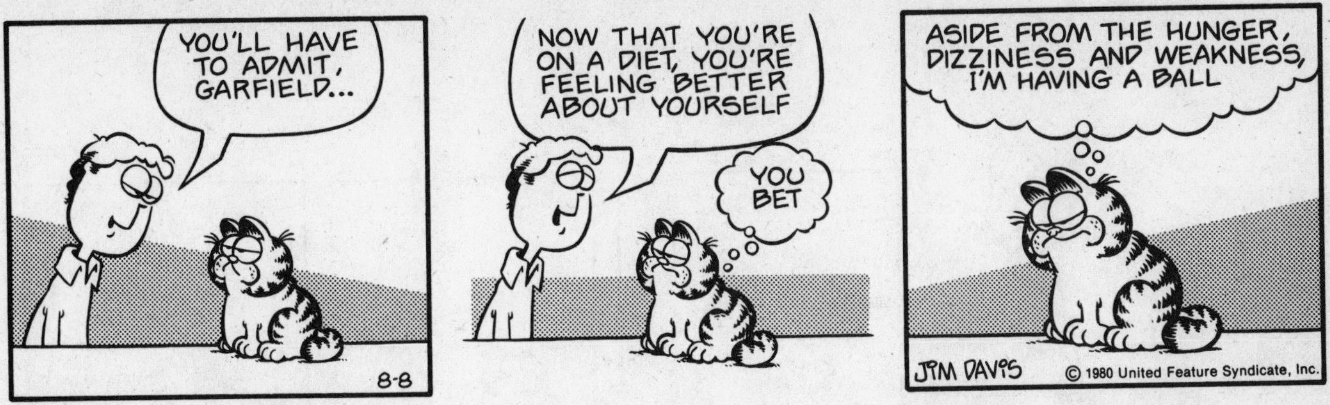
YOU'LL HAVE TO ADMIT, GARFIELD...
8-8
NOW THAT YOU'RE ON A DIET, YOU'RE FEELING BETTER ABOUT YOURSELF
YOU BET
ASIDE FROM THE HUNGER, DIZZINESS AND WEAKNESS, I'M HAVING A BALL
JIM DAVIS
© 1980 United Feature Syndicate, Inc.

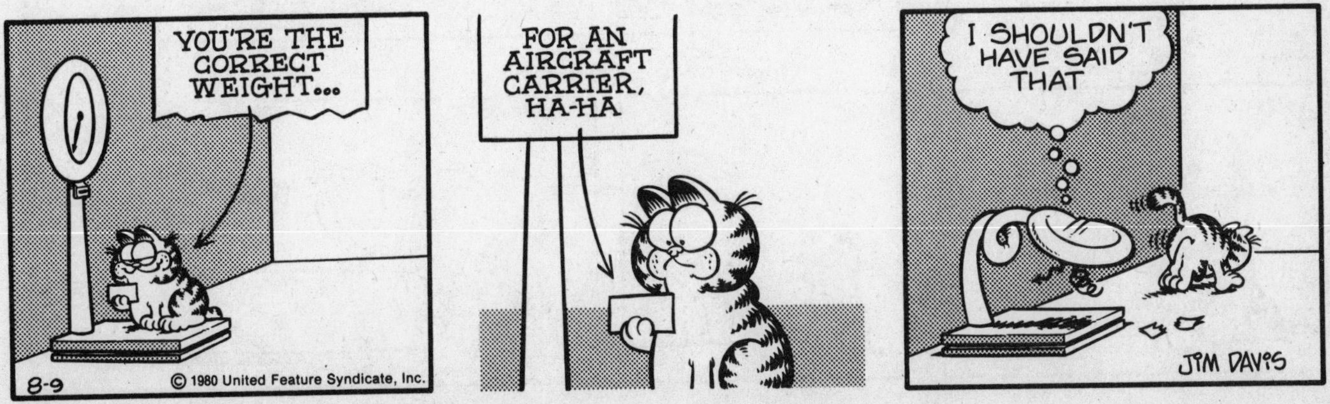
YOU'RE THE CORRECT WEIGHT...
8-9
© 1980 United Feature Syndicate, Inc.
FOR AN AIRCRAFT CARRIER, HA-HA
I SHOULDN'T HAVE SAID THAT
JIM DAVIS

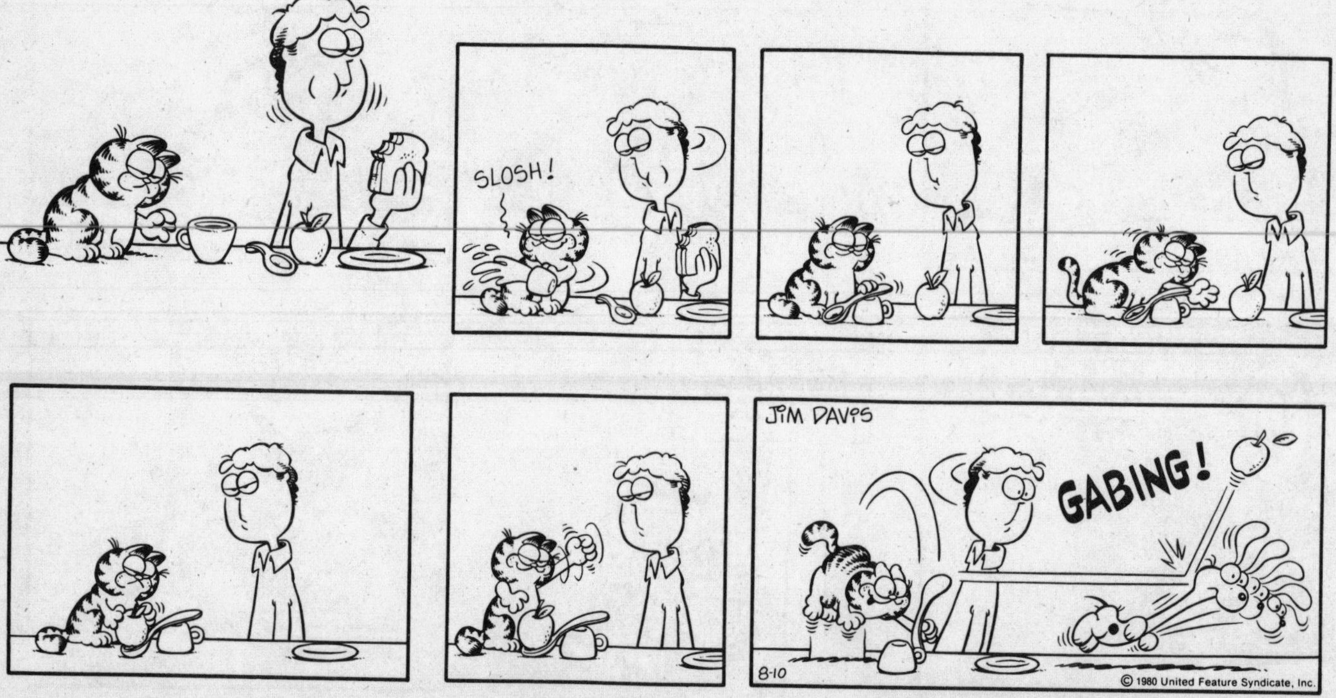
SLOSH!
JIM DAVIS
GABING!
8-10
© 1980 United Feature Syndicate, Inc.

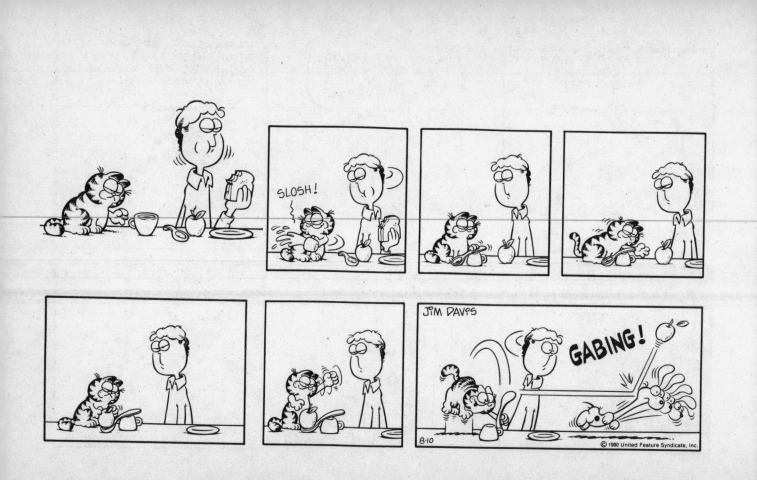

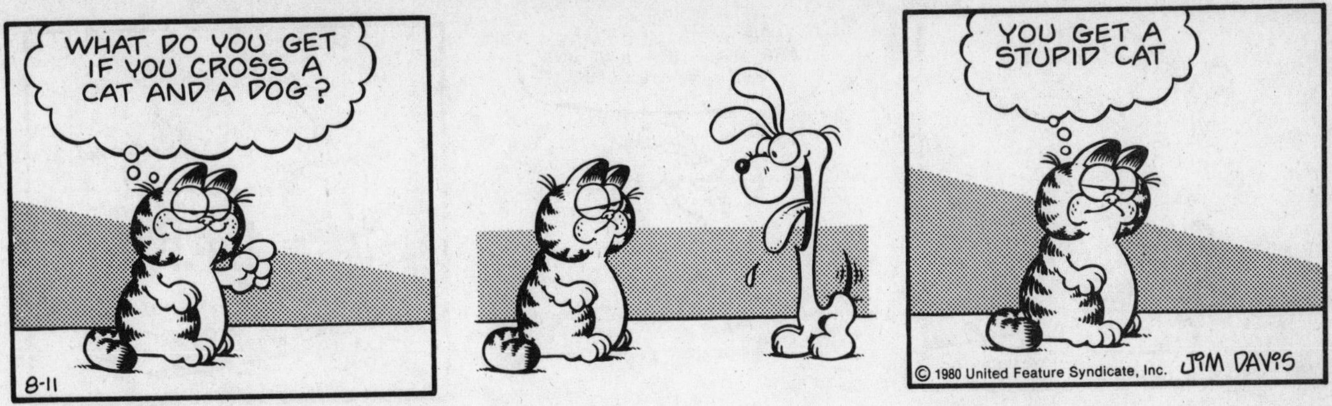
WHAT DO YOU GET IF YOU CROSS A CAT AND A DOG?
8-11
YOU GET A STUPID CAT
© 1980 United Feature Syndicate, Inc.
JIM DAVIS

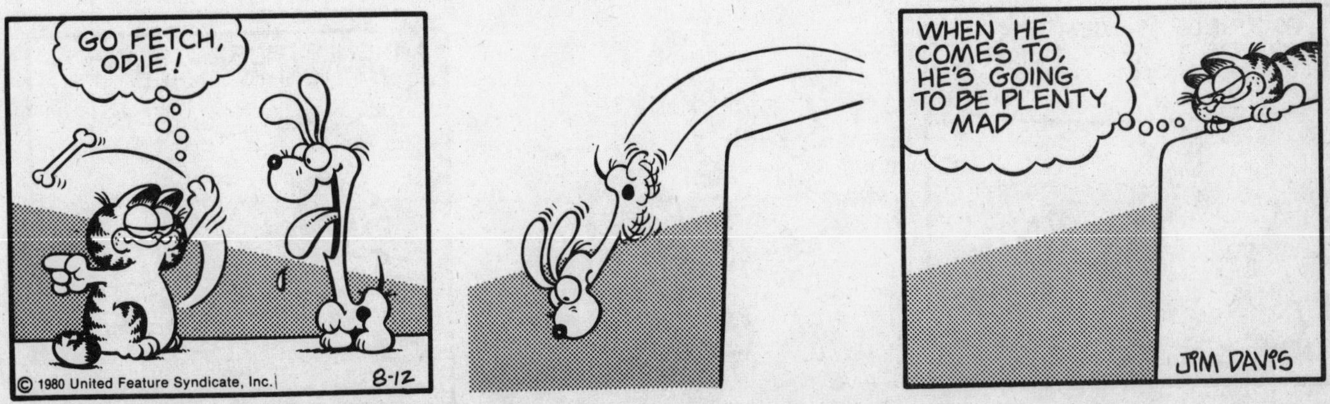
GO FETCH, ODIE!
© 1980 United Feature Syndicate, Inc.
8-12
WHEN HE COMES TO, HE'S GOING TO BE PLENTY MAD
JIM DAVIS

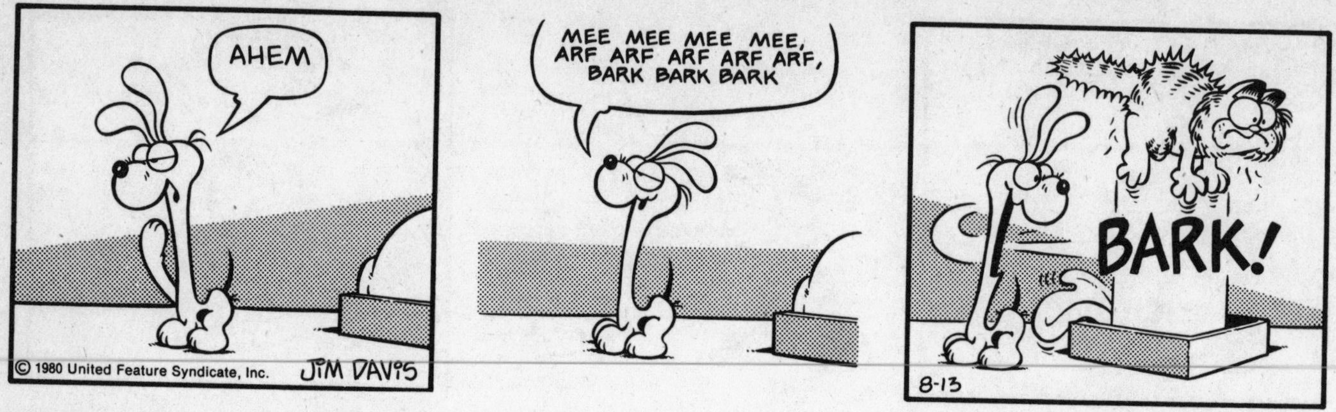
AHEM
MEE MEE MEE MEE, ARF ARF ARF ARF ARF, BARK BARK BARK
BARK!
© 1980 United Feature Syndicate, Inc.
JIM DAVIS
8-13

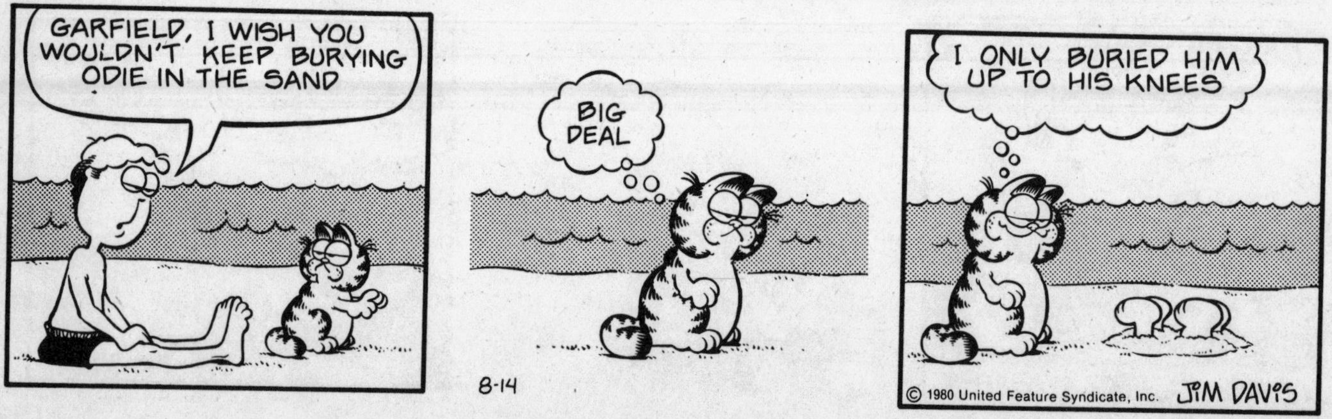
GARFIELD, I WISH YOU WOULDN'T KEEP BURYING ODIE IN THE SAND
BIG DEAL
I ONLY BURIED HIM UP TO HIS KNEES
8-14
© 1980 United Feature Syndicate, Inc.
JIM DAVIS

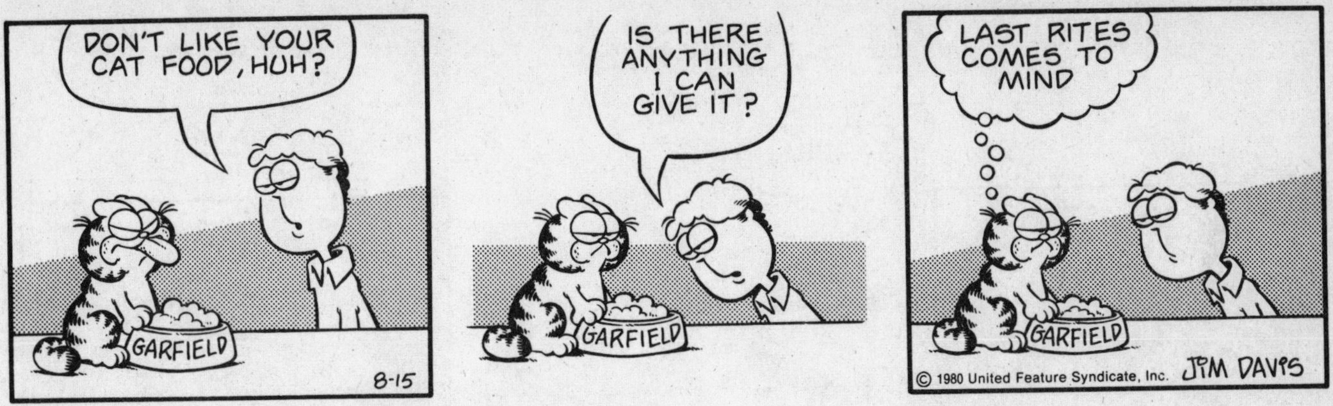
DON'T LIKE YOUR CAT FOOD, HUH?
GARFIELD
8-15
IS THERE ANYTHING I CAN GIVE IT?
GARFIELD
LAST RITES COMES TO MIND
GARFIELD
© 1980 United Feature Syndicate, Inc.
JIM DAVIS

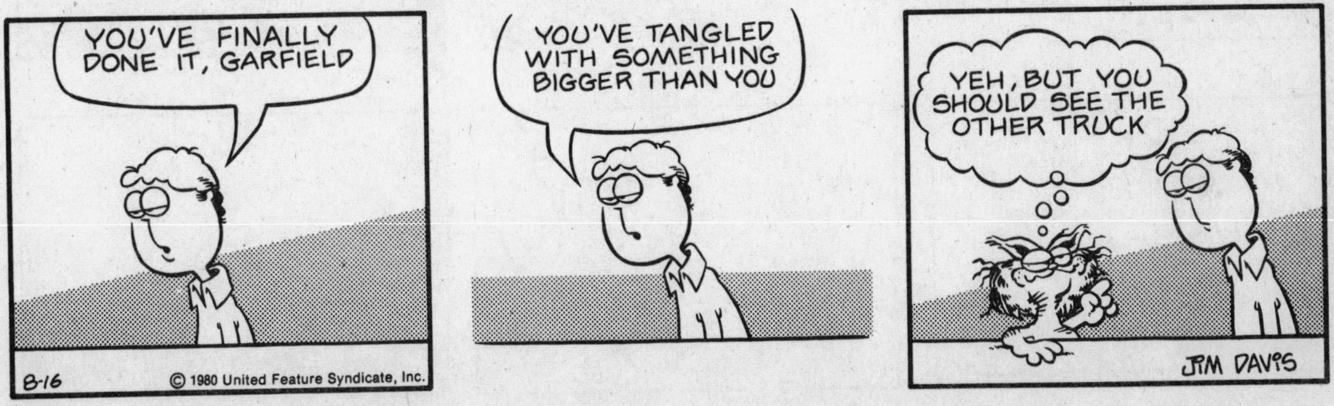
YOU'VE FINALLY DONE IT, GARFIELD
8-16
© 1980 United Feature Syndicate, Inc.
YOU'VE TANGLED WITH SOMETHING BIGGER THAN YOU
YEH, BUT YOU SHOULD SEE THE OTHER TRUCK
JIM DAVIS

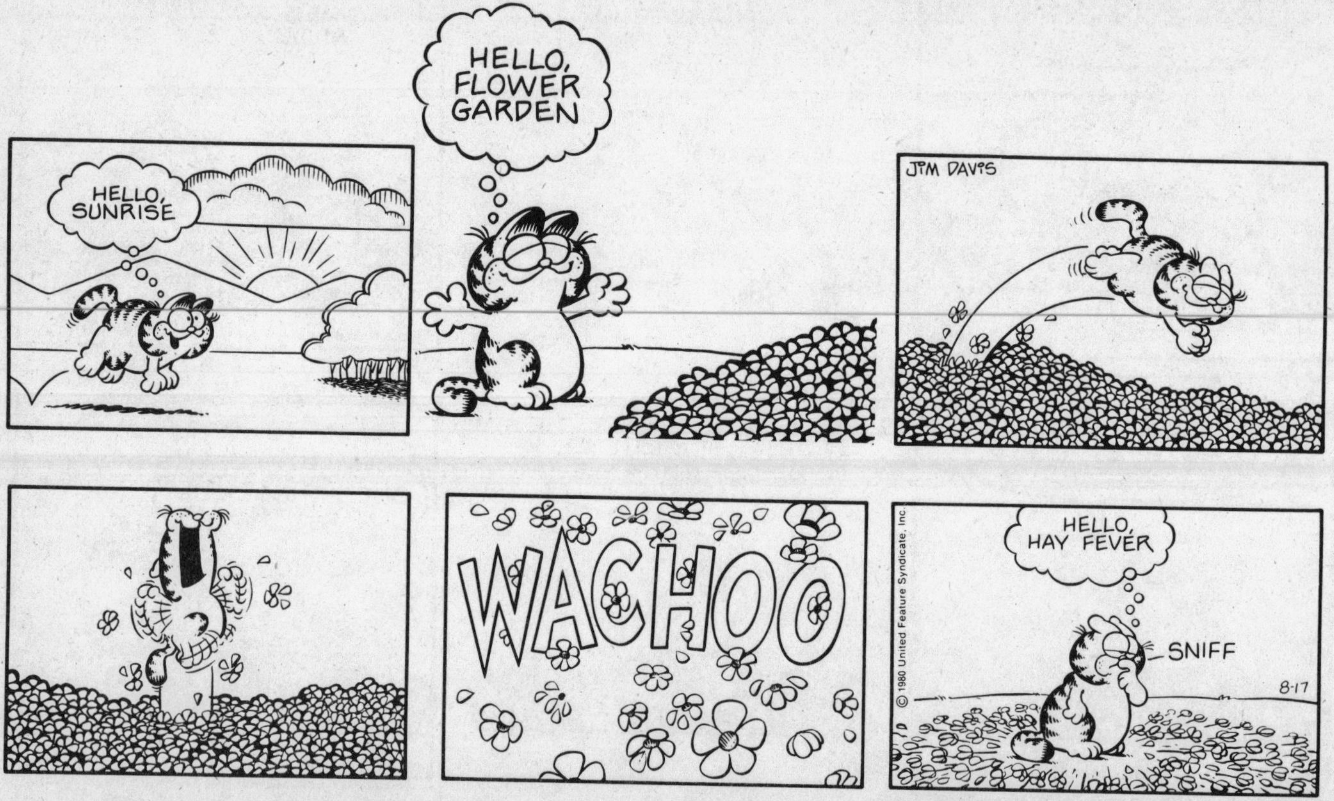
HELLO, SUNRISE
HELLO, FLOWER GARDEN
JIM DAVIS
WACHOO
HELLO, HAY FEVER
SNIFF
8-17
© 1980 United Feature Syndicate, Inc.

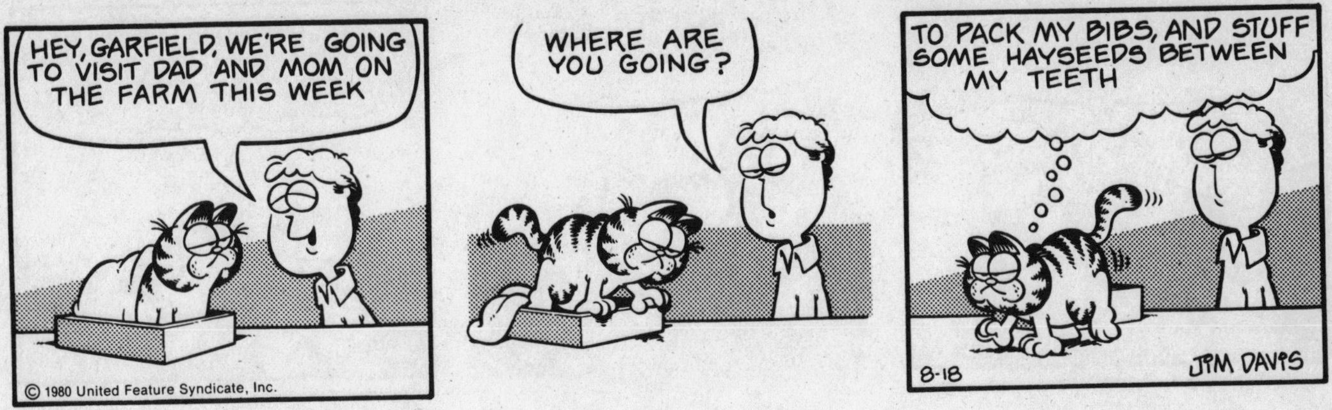
HEY, GARFIELD, WE'RE GOING TO VISIT DAD AND MOM ON THE FARM THIS WEEK
© 1980 United Feature Syndicate, Inc.
WHERE ARE YOU GOING?
TO PACK MY BIBS, AND STUFF SOME HAYSEEDS BETWEEN MY TEETH
8-18
JIM DAVIS

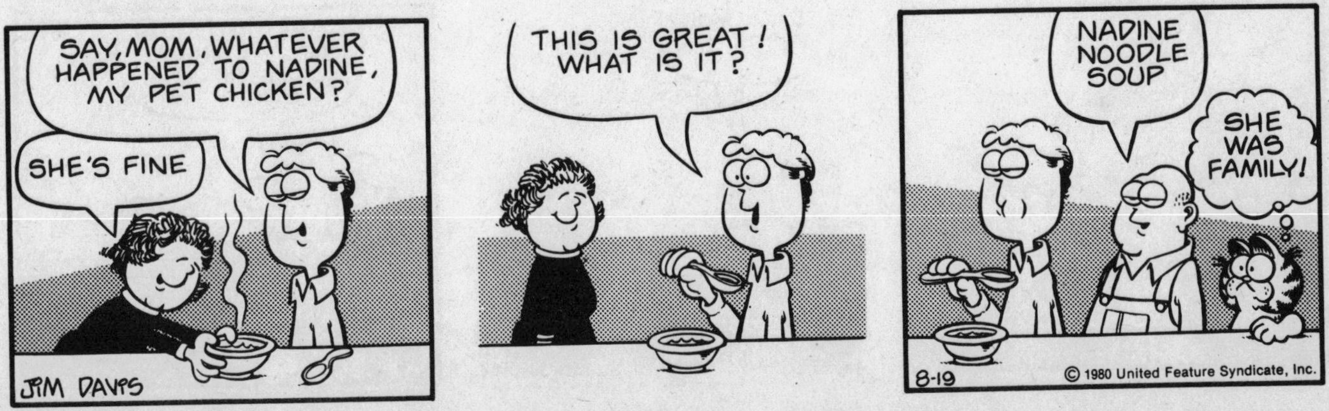
SAY, MOM, WHATEVER HAPPENED TO NADINE, MY PET CHICKEN?
SHE'S FINE
JIM DAVIS
THIS IS GREAT! WHAT IS IT?
NADINE NOODLE SOUP
SHE WAS FAMILY!
8-19
© 1980 United Feature Syndicate, Inc.

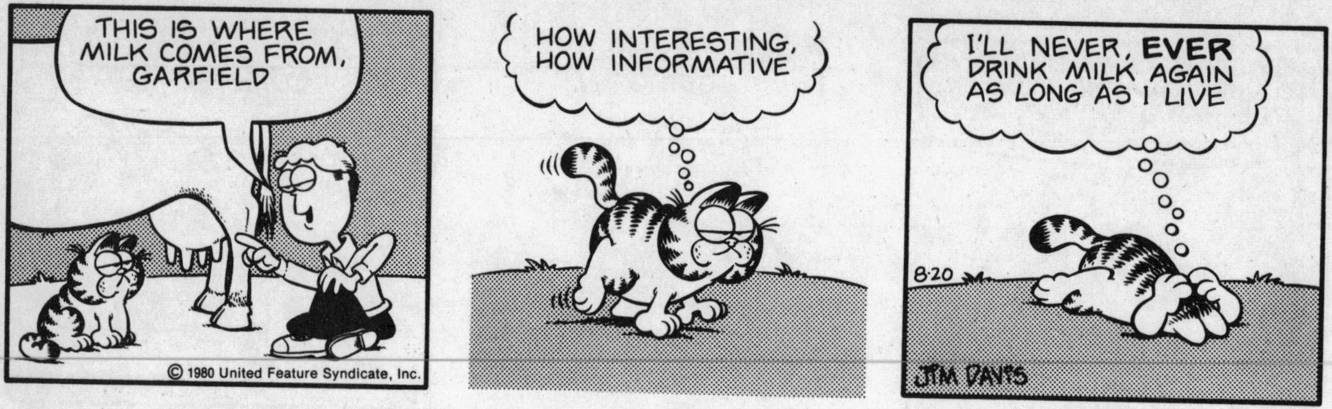
THIS IS WHERE MILK COMES FROM, GARFIELD
© 1980 United Feature Syndicate, Inc.
HOW INTERESTING, HOW INFORMATIVE
I'LL NEVER, **EVER** DRINK MILK AGAIN AS LONG AS I LIVE
8·20
JIM DAVIS

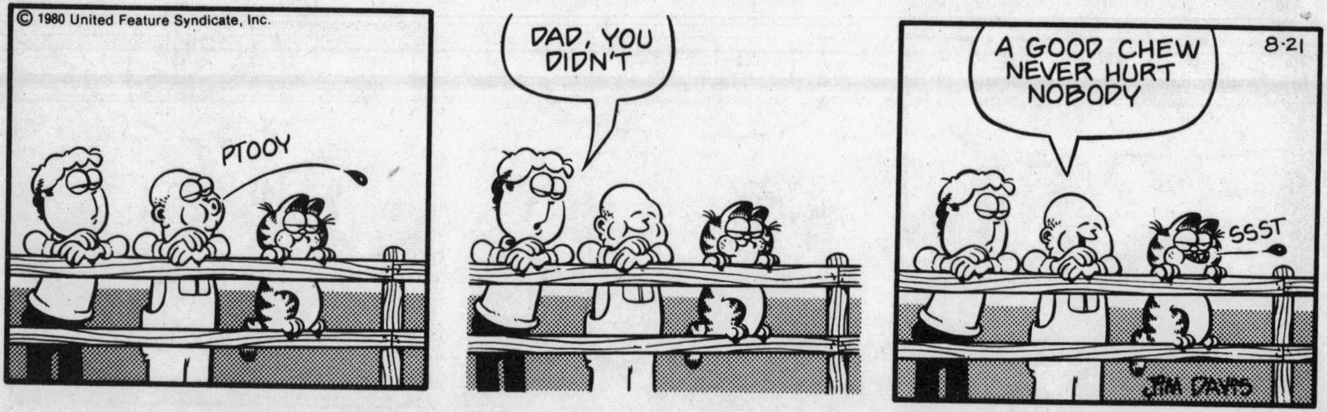
© 1980 United Feature Syndicate, Inc.
PTOOY
DAD, YOU DIDN'T
A GOOD CHEW NEVER HURT NOBODY
8·21
SSST
JIM DAVIS

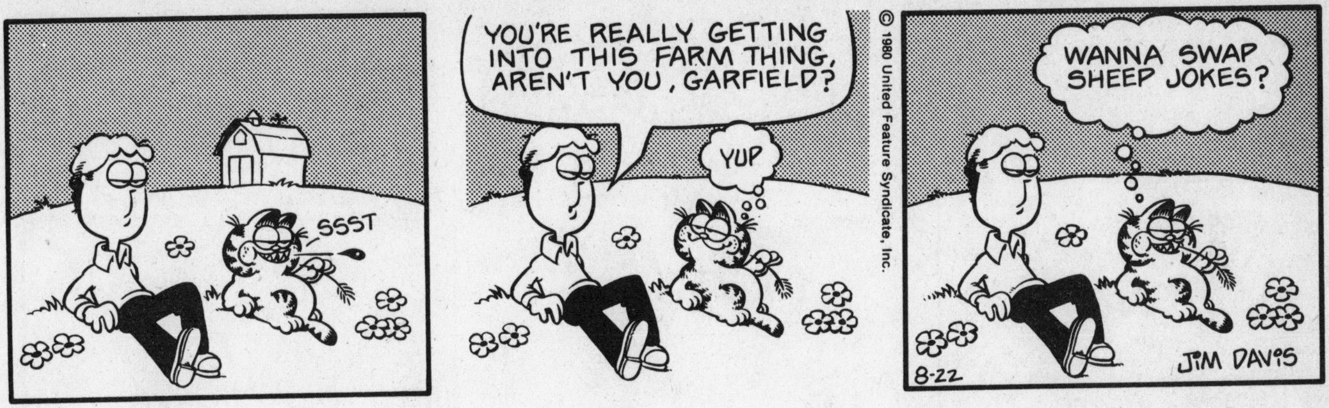
SSST
YOU'RE REALLY GETTING INTO THIS FARM THING, AREN'T YOU, GARFIELD?
YUP
© 1980 United Feature Syndicate, Inc.
WANNA SWAP SHEEP JOKES?
8-22
JIM DAVIS

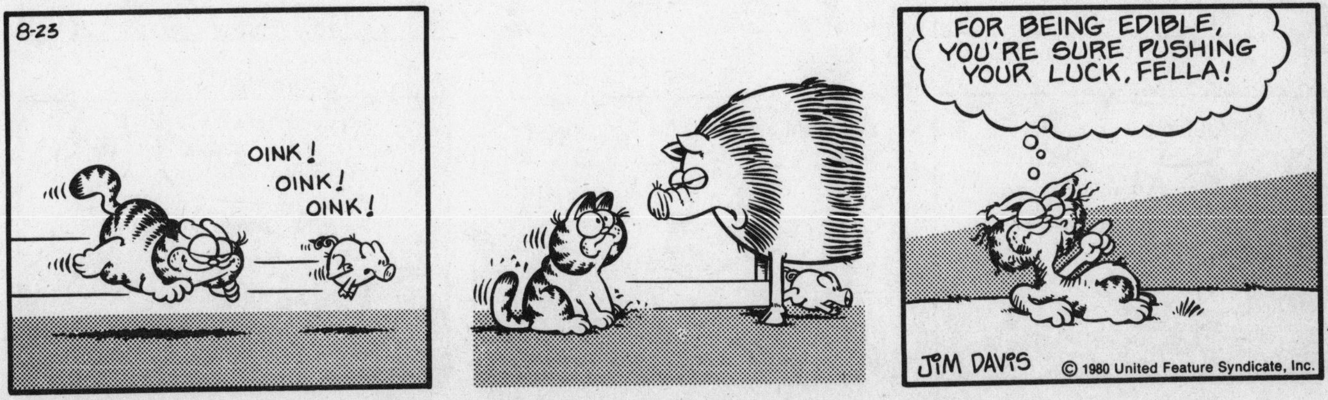
8-23
OINK! OINK! OINK!
FOR BEING EDIBLE, YOU'RE SURE PUSHING YOUR LUCK, FELLA!
JIM DAVIS
© 1980 United Feature Syndicate, Inc.

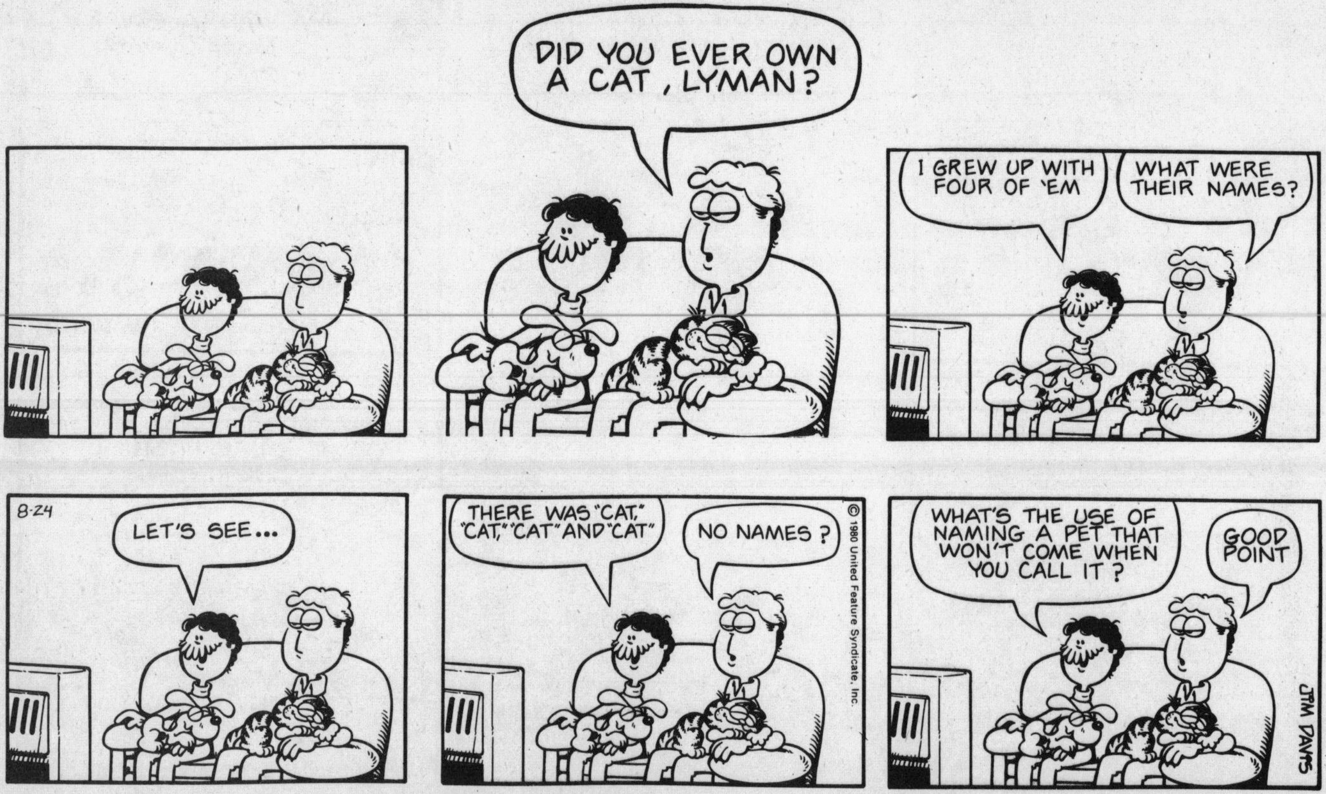
DID YOU EVER OWN A CAT, LYMAN?
I GREW UP WITH FOUR OF 'EM
WHAT WERE THEIR NAMES?
8-24
LET'S SEE...
THERE WAS "CAT," "CAT," "CAT" AND "CAT"
NO NAMES?
© 1980 United Feature Syndicate, Inc.
WHAT'S THE USE OF NAMING A PET THAT WON'T COME WHEN YOU CALL IT?
GOOD POINT
JIM DAVIS

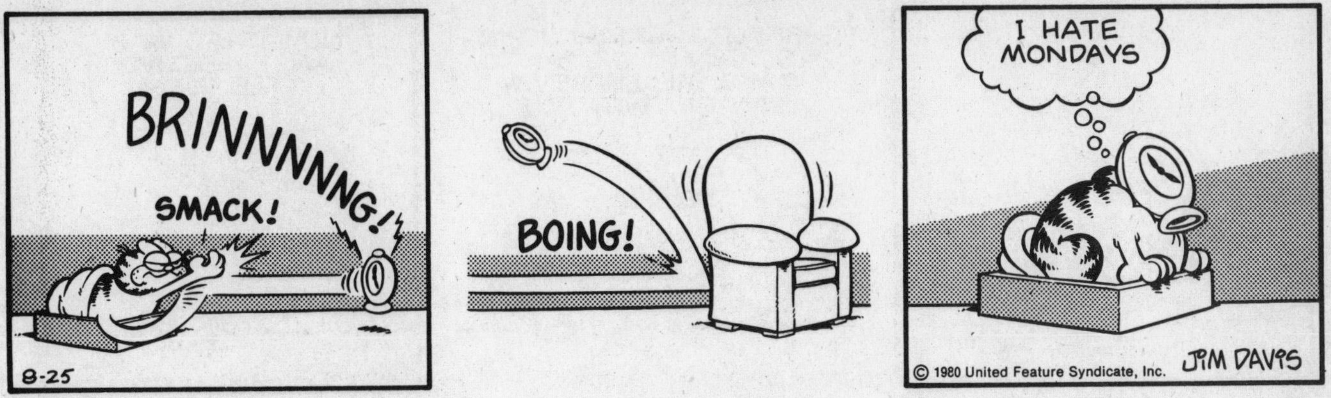
BRINNNNNNG!
SMACK!
8-25
BOING!
I HATE MONDAYS
© 1980 United Feature Syndicate, Inc.
JIM DAVIS

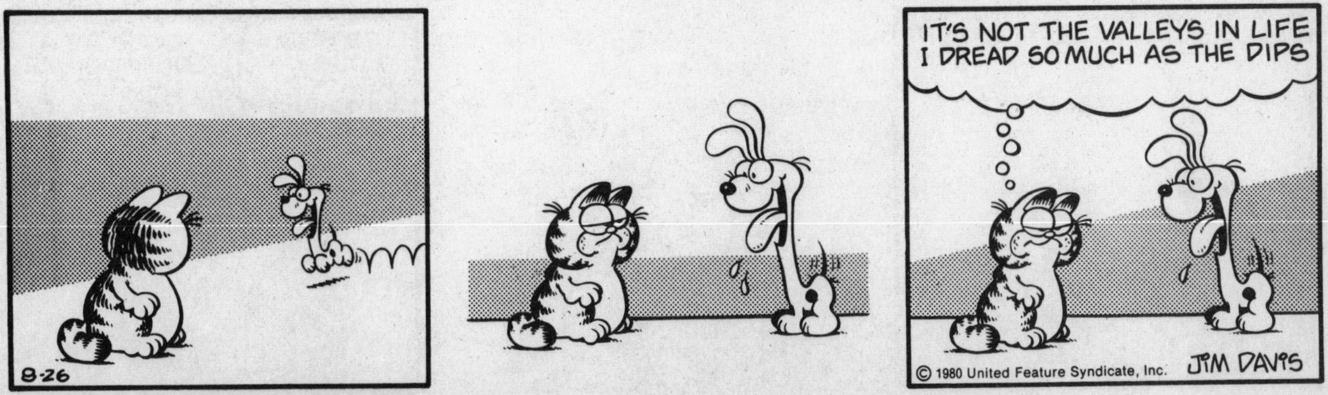
8-26
IT'S NOT THE VALLEYS IN LIFE I DREAD SO MUCH AS THE DIPS
© 1980 United Feature Syndicate, Inc.
JIM DAVIS

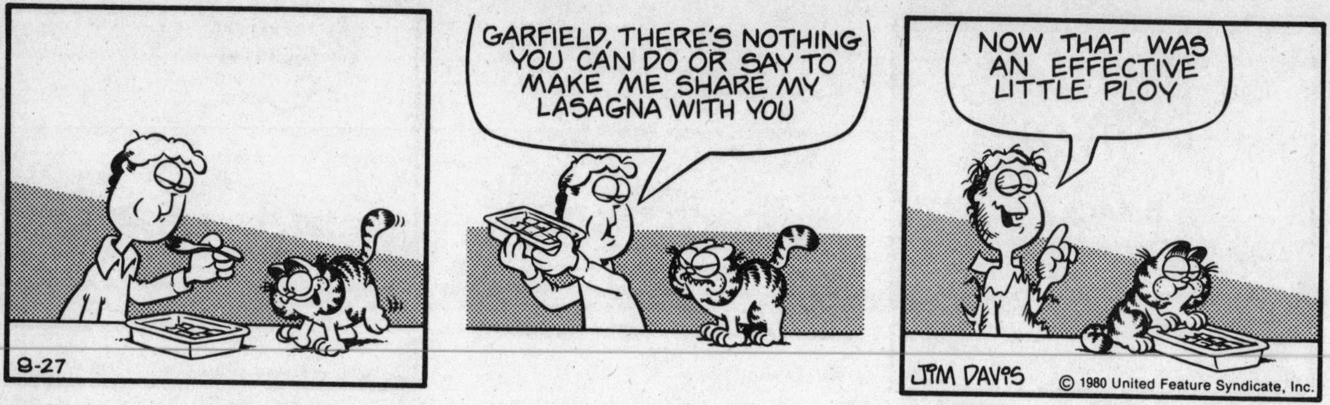
8-27
GARFIELD, THERE'S NOTHING YOU CAN DO OR SAY TO MAKE ME SHARE MY LASAGNA WITH YOU
NOW THAT WAS AN EFFECTIVE LITTLE PLOY
JIM DAVIS
© 1980 United Feature Syndicate, Inc.

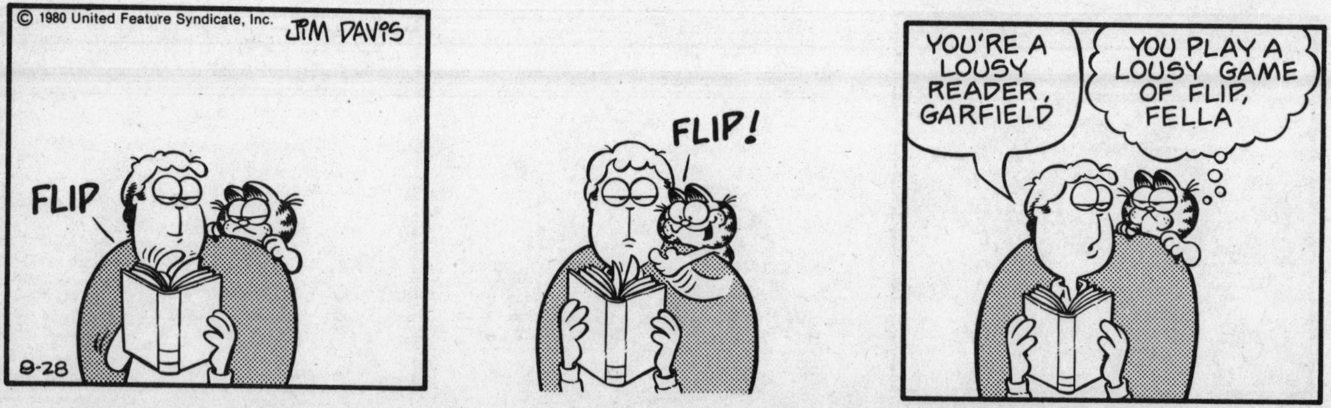
© 1980 United Feature Syndicate, Inc.
JIM DAVIS
FLIP
8-28
FLIP!
YOU'RE A LOUSY READER, GARFIELD
YOU PLAY A LOUSY GAME OF FLIP, FELLA

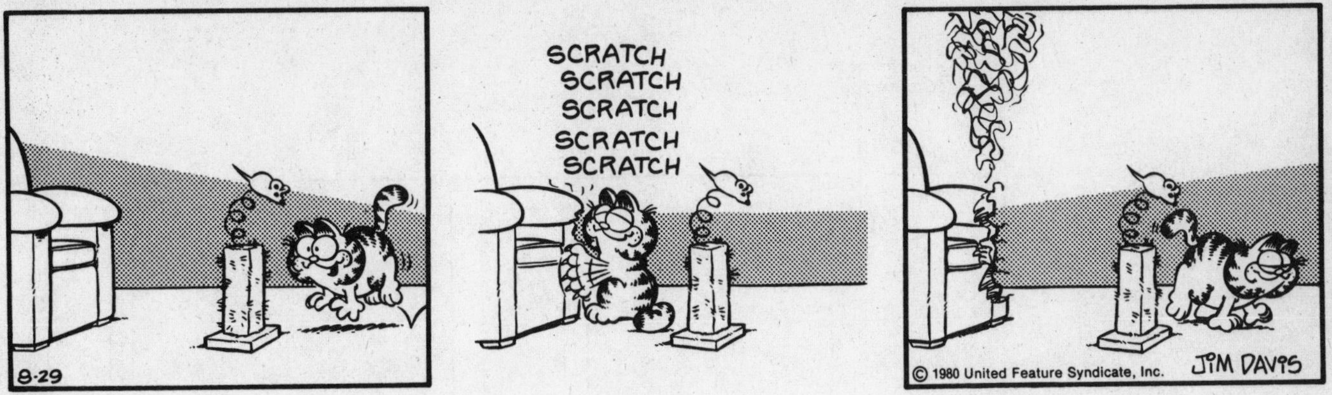
SCRATCH
SCRATCH
SCRATCH
SCRATCH
SCRATCH
8-29
© 1980 United Feature Syndicate, Inc.
JIM DAVIS

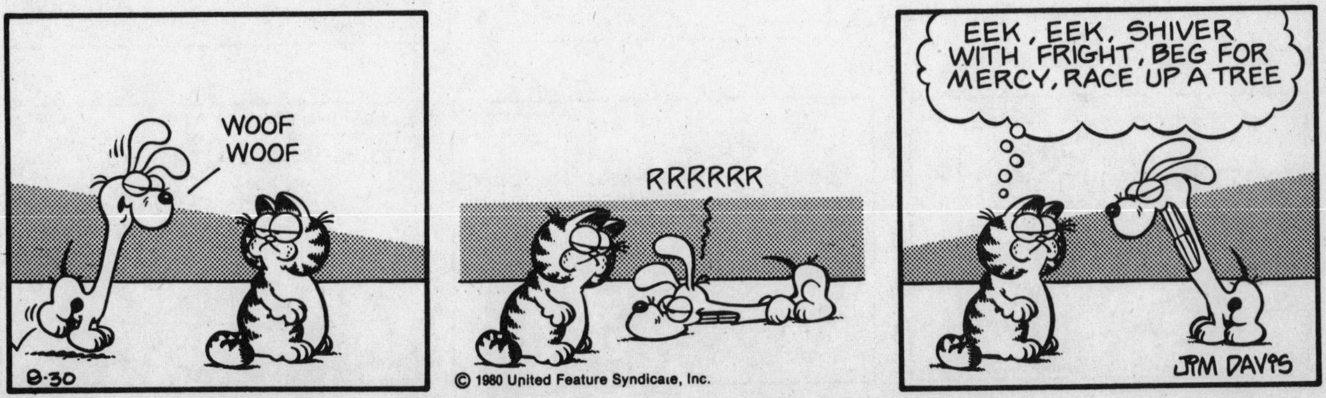
WOOF
WOOF
RRRRRR
EEK, EEK, SHIVER WITH FRIGHT, BEG FOR MERCY, RACE UP A TREE
8-30
© 1980 United Feature Syndicate, Inc.
JIM DAVIS

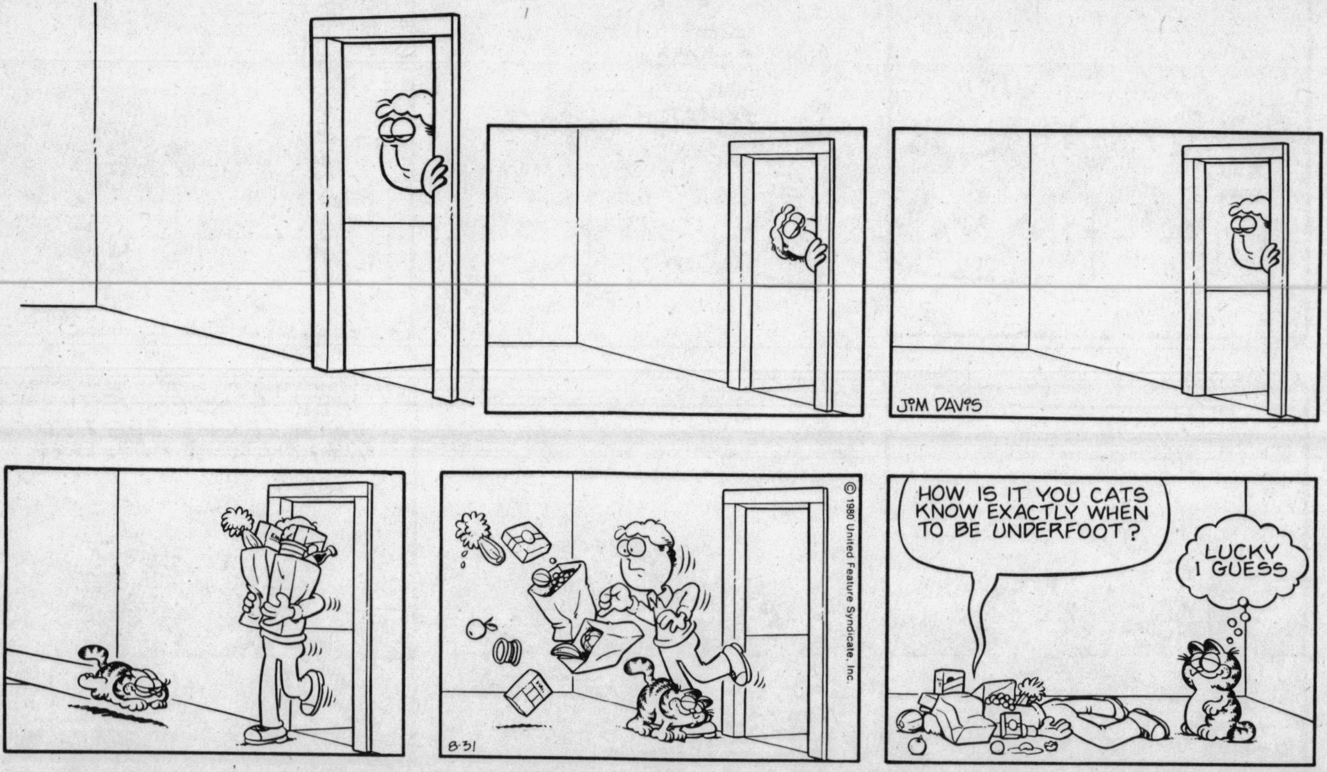
JIM DAVIS
© 1980 United Feature Syndicate, Inc.
8-31
HOW IS IT YOU CATS KNOW EXACTLY WHEN TO BE UNDERFOOT?
LUCKY I GUESS

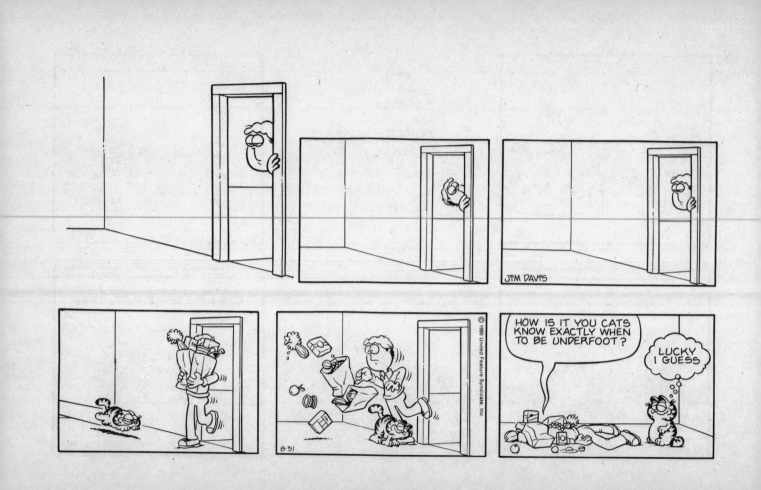

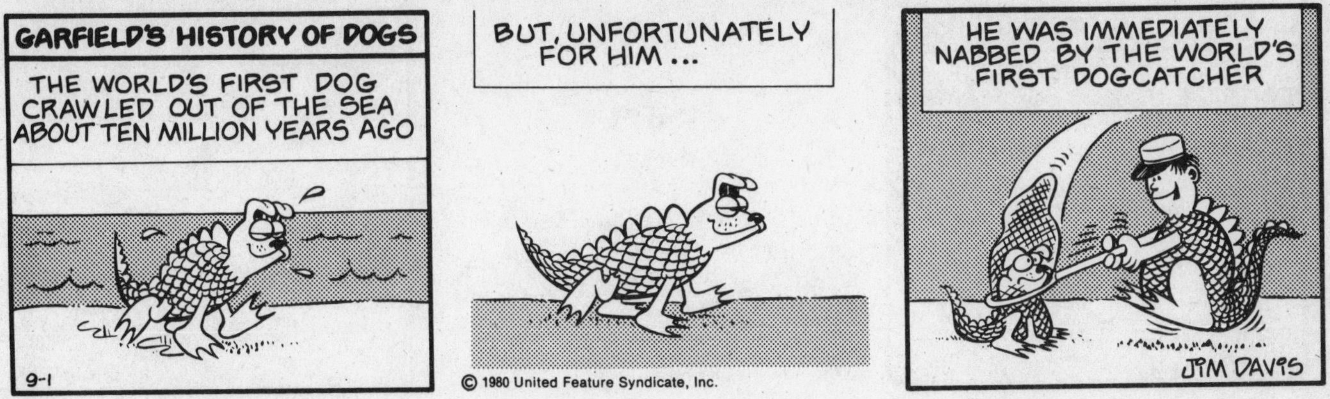
GARFIELD'S HISTORY OF DOGS
THE WORLD'S FIRST DOG CRAWLED OUT OF THE SEA ABOUT TEN MILLION YEARS AGO
9-1
BUT, UNFORTUNATELY FOR HIM ...
© 1980 United Feature Syndicate, Inc.
HE WAS IMMEDIATELY NABBED BY THE WORLD'S FIRST DOGCATCHER
JIM DAVIS

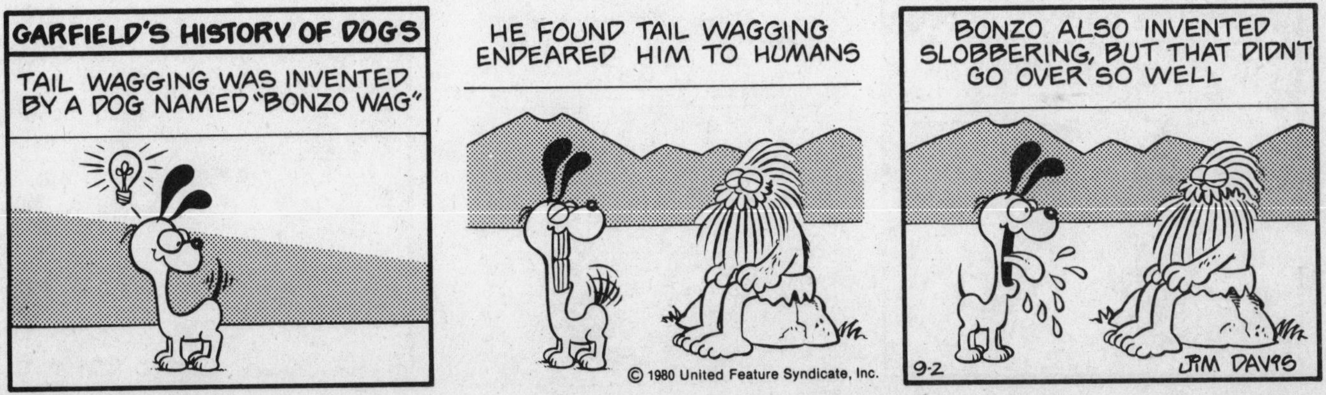
GARFIELD'S HISTORY OF DOGS
TAIL WAGGING WAS INVENTED BY A DOG NAMED "BONZO WAG"
HE FOUND TAIL WAGGING ENDEARED HIM TO HUMANS
© 1980 United Feature Syndicate, Inc.
BONZO ALSO INVENTED SLOBBERING, BUT THAT DIDN'T GO OVER SO WELL
9-2
JIM DAVIS

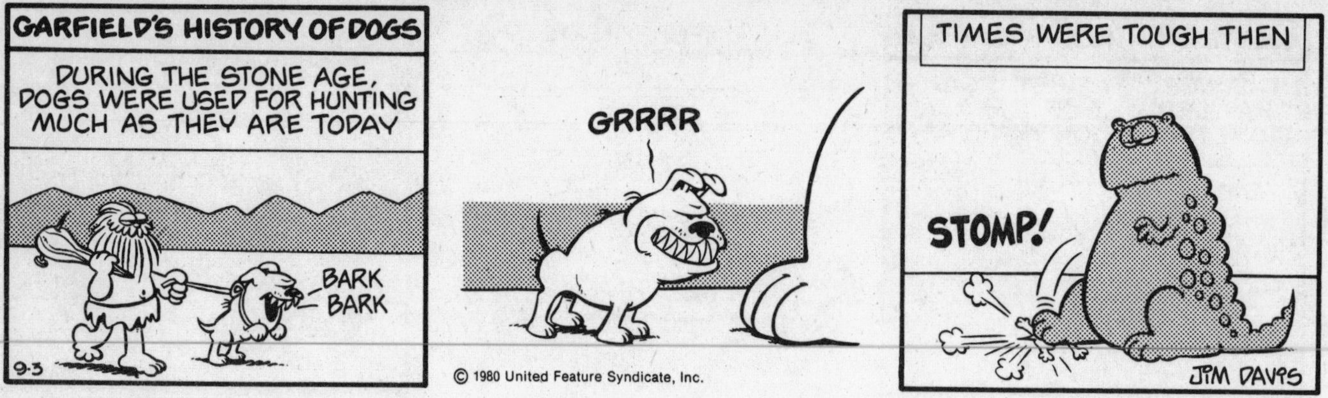
GARFIELD'S HISTORY OF DOGS
DURING THE STONE AGE, DOGS WERE USED FOR HUNTING MUCH AS THEY ARE TODAY
BARK BARK
9-3
GRRRR
© 1980 United Feature Syndicate, Inc.
TIMES WERE TOUGH THEN
STOMP!
JIM DAVIS

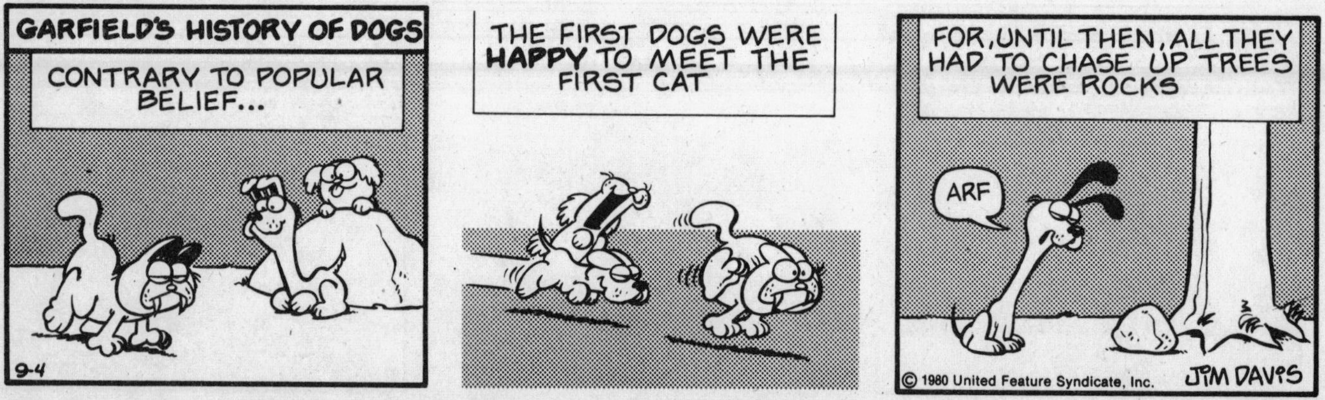
GARFIELD'S HISTORY OF DOGS
CONTRARY TO POPULAR BELIEF...
9-4
THE FIRST DOGS WERE HAPPY TO MEET THE FIRST CAT
FOR, UNTIL THEN, ALL THEY HAD TO CHASE UP TREES WERE ROCKS
ARF
© 1980 United Feature Syndicate, Inc.
JIM DAVIS

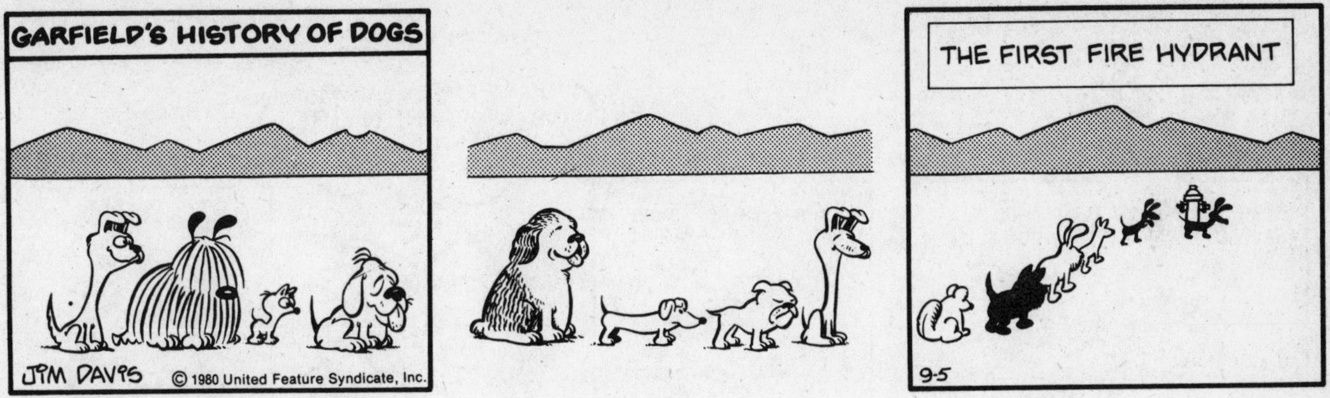
GARFIELD'S HISTORY OF DOGS
JIM DAVIS
© 1980 United Feature Syndicate, Inc.
THE FIRST FIRE HYDRANT
9-5

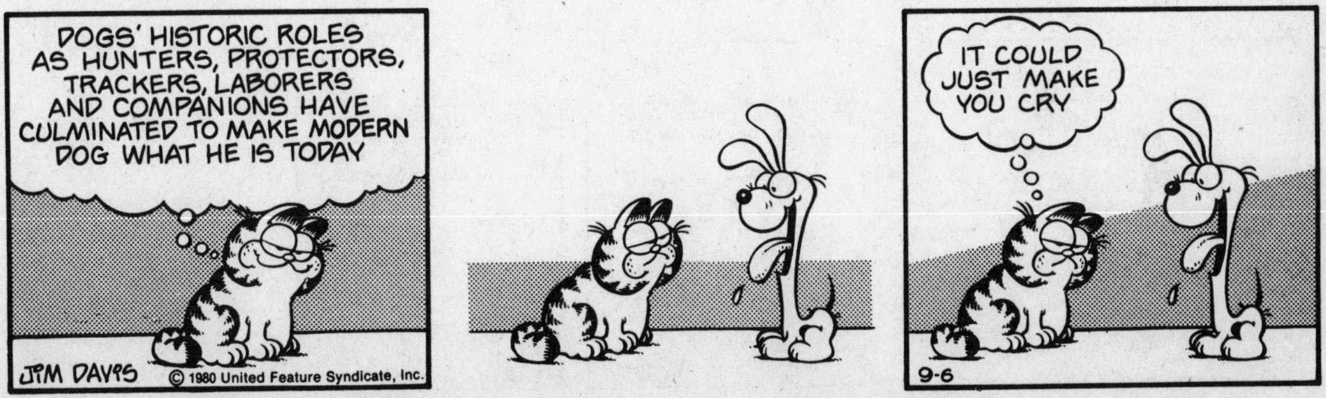
DOGS' HISTORIC ROLES AS HUNTERS, PROTECTORS, TRACKERS, LABORERS AND COMPANIONS HAVE CULMINATED TO MAKE MODERN DOG WHAT HE IS TODAY
JIM DAVIS
© 1980 United Feature Syndicate, Inc.
IT COULD JUST MAKE YOU CRY
9-6

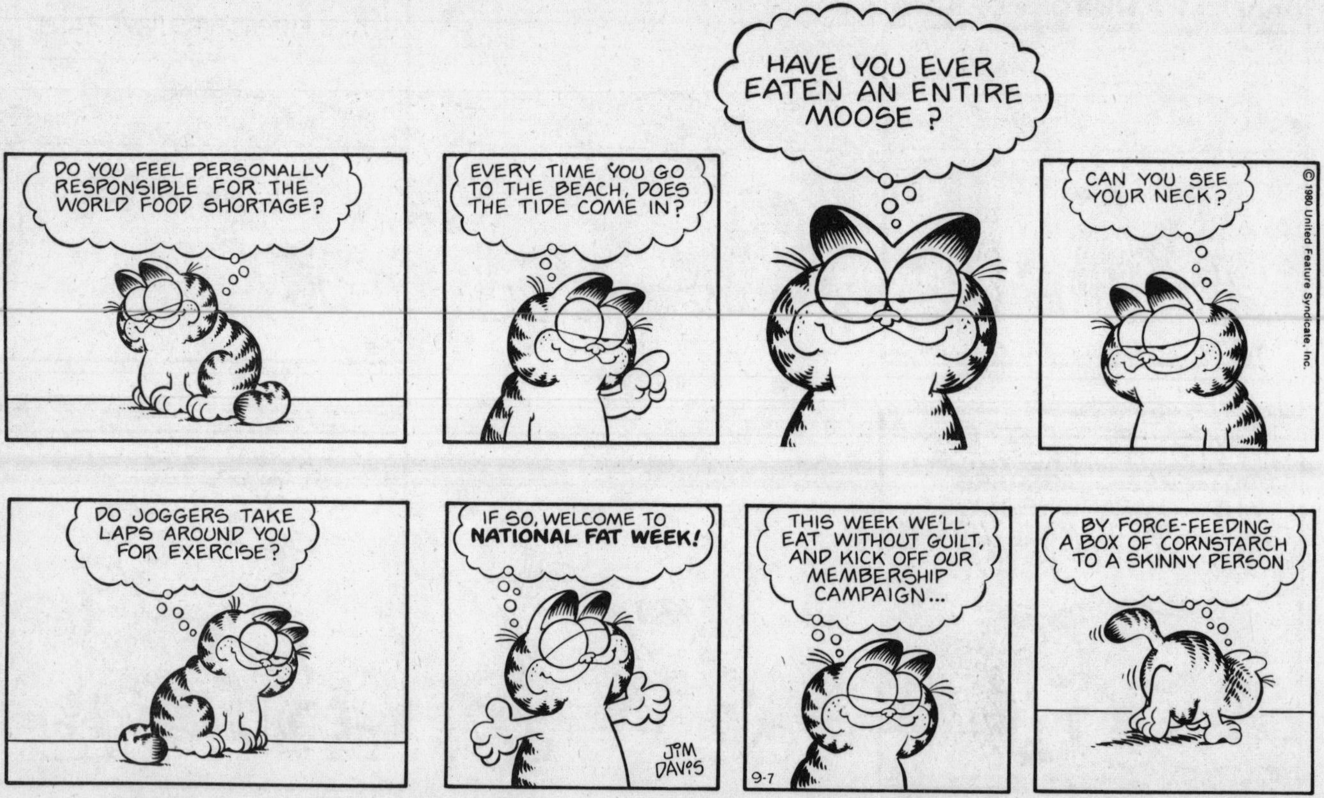
HAVE YOU EVER EATEN AN ENTIRE MOOSE ?
DO YOU FEEL PERSONALLY RESPONSIBLE FOR THE WORLD FOOD SHORTAGE?
EVERY TIME YOU GO TO THE BEACH, DOES THE TIDE COME IN?
CAN YOU SEE YOUR NECK?
© 1980 United Feature Syndicate, Inc.
DO JOGGERS TAKE LAPS AROUND YOU FOR EXERCISE?
IF SO, WELCOME TO **NATIONAL FAT WEEK!**
JIM DAVIS
THIS WEEK WE'LL EAT WITHOUT GUILT, AND KICK OFF OUR MEMBERSHIP CAMPAIGN...
9-7
BY FORCE-FEEDING A BOX OF CORNSTARCH TO A SKINNY PERSON

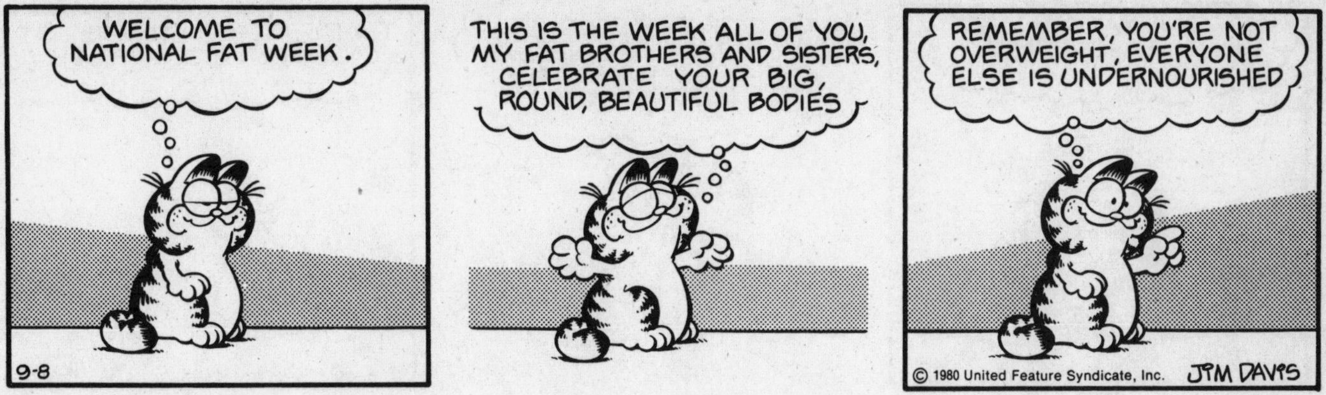
WELCOME TO NATIONAL FAT WEEK.
9-8
THIS IS THE WEEK ALL OF YOU, MY FAT BROTHERS AND SISTERS, CELEBRATE YOUR BIG, ROUND, BEAUTIFUL BODIES
REMEMBER, YOU'RE NOT OVERWEIGHT, EVERYONE ELSE IS UNDERNOURISHED
© 1980 United Feature Syndicate, Inc.
JIM DAVIS

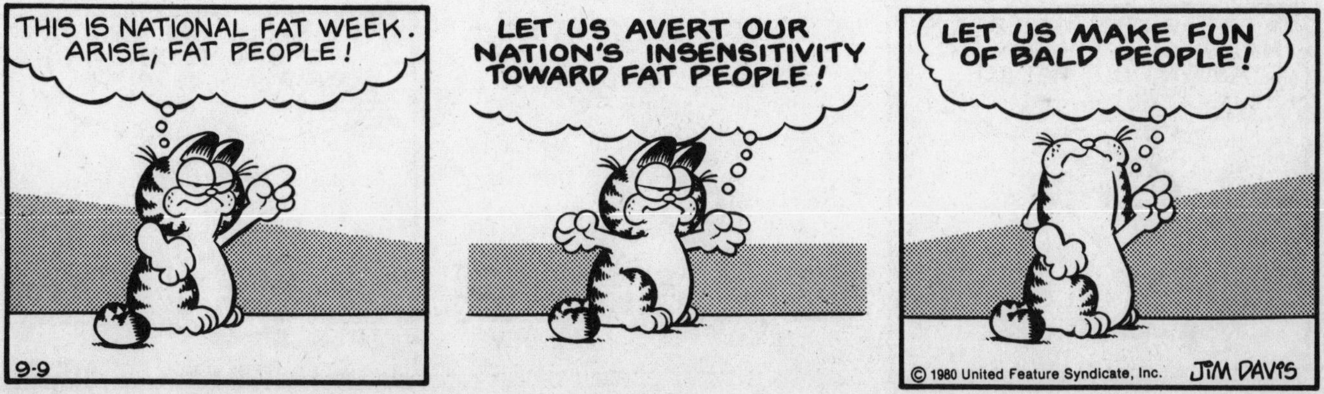
THIS IS NATIONAL FAT WEEK. ARISE, FAT PEOPLE!
9-9
LET US AVERT OUR NATION'S INSENSITIVITY TOWARD FAT PEOPLE!
LET US MAKE FUN OF BALD PEOPLE!
© 1980 United Feature Syndicate, Inc.
JIM DAVIS

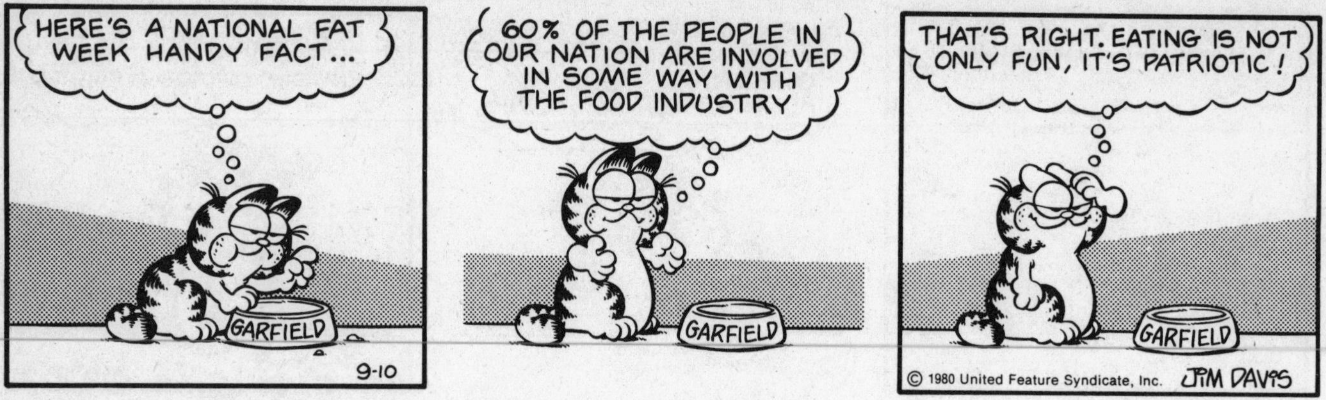
HERE'S A NATIONAL FAT WEEK HANDY FACT...
GARFIELD
9-10
60% OF THE PEOPLE IN OUR NATION ARE INVOLVED IN SOME WAY WITH THE FOOD INDUSTRY
GARFIELD
THAT'S RIGHT. EATING IS NOT ONLY FUN, IT'S PATRIOTIC!
GARFIELD
© 1980 United Feature Syndicate, Inc.
JIM DAVIS

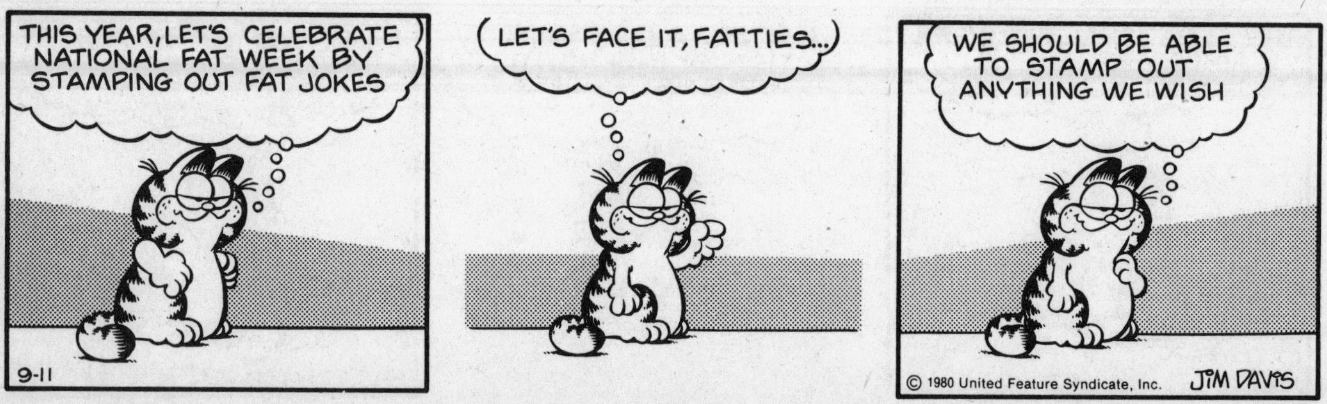
THIS YEAR, LET'S CELEBRATE NATIONAL FAT WEEK BY STAMPING OUT FAT JOKES
9-11
LET'S FACE IT, FATTIES...
WE SHOULD BE ABLE TO STAMP OUT ANYTHING WE WISH
© 1980 United Feature Syndicate, Inc.
JIM DAVIS

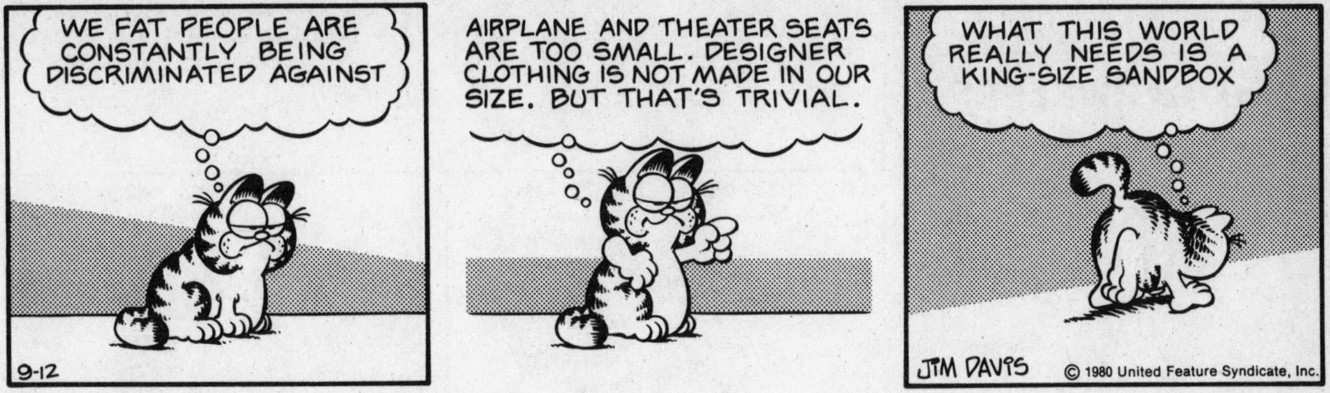
WE FAT PEOPLE ARE CONSTANTLY BEING DISCRIMINATED AGAINST
AIRPLANE AND THEATER SEATS ARE TOO SMALL. DESIGNER CLOTHING IS NOT MADE IN OUR SIZE. BUT THAT'S TRIVIAL.
WHAT THIS WORLD REALLY NEEDS IS A KING-SIZE SANDBOX
9-12
JIM DAVIS
© 1980 United Feature Syndicate, Inc.

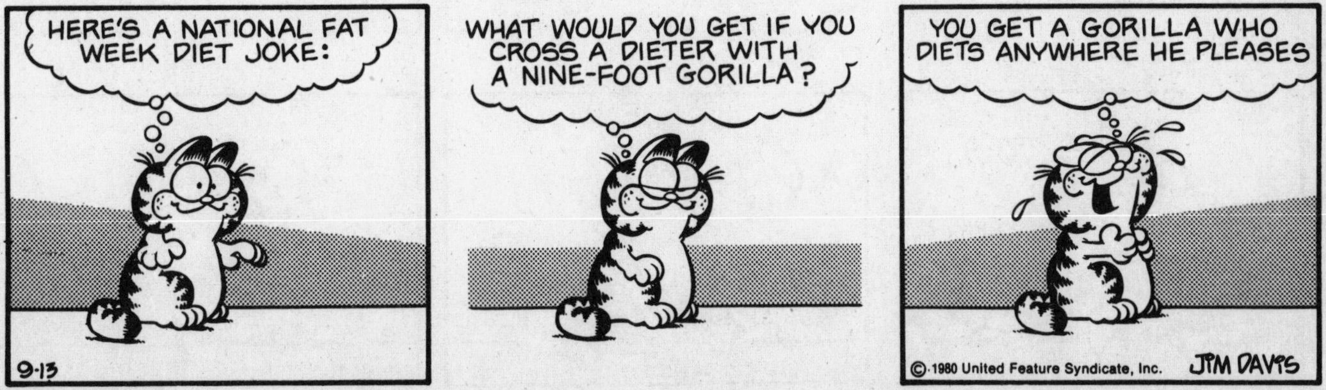
HERE'S A NATIONAL FAT WEEK DIET JOKE:
WHAT WOULD YOU GET IF YOU CROSS A DIETER WITH A NINE-FOOT GORILLA?
YOU GET A GORILLA WHO DIETS ANYWHERE HE PLEASES
9-13
© 1980 United Feature Syndicate, Inc.
JIM DAVIS

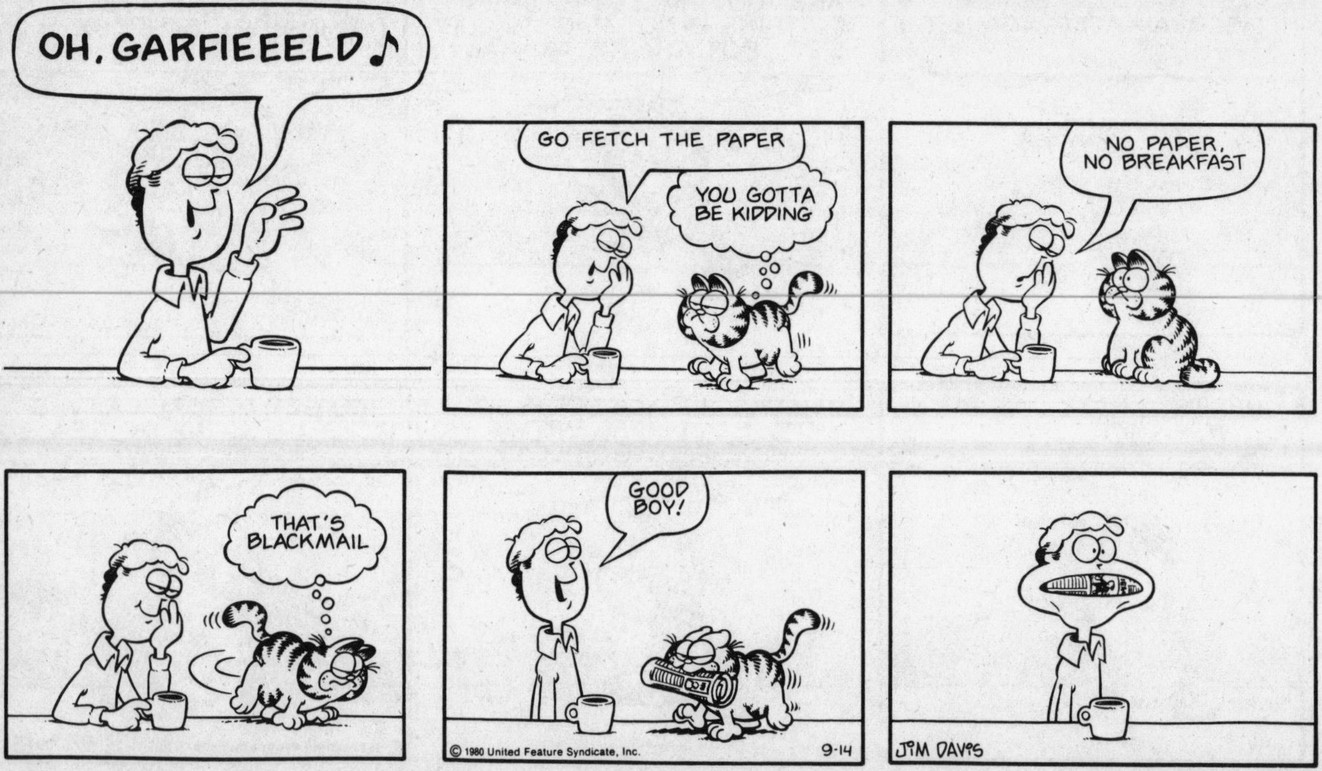

OH, GARFIEEELD ♪
GO FETCH THE PAPER
YOU GOTTA BE KIDDING
NO PAPER, NO BREAKFAST
THAT'S BLACKMAIL
GOOD BOY!
© 1980 United Feature Syndicate, Inc.
9-14
JIM DAVIS

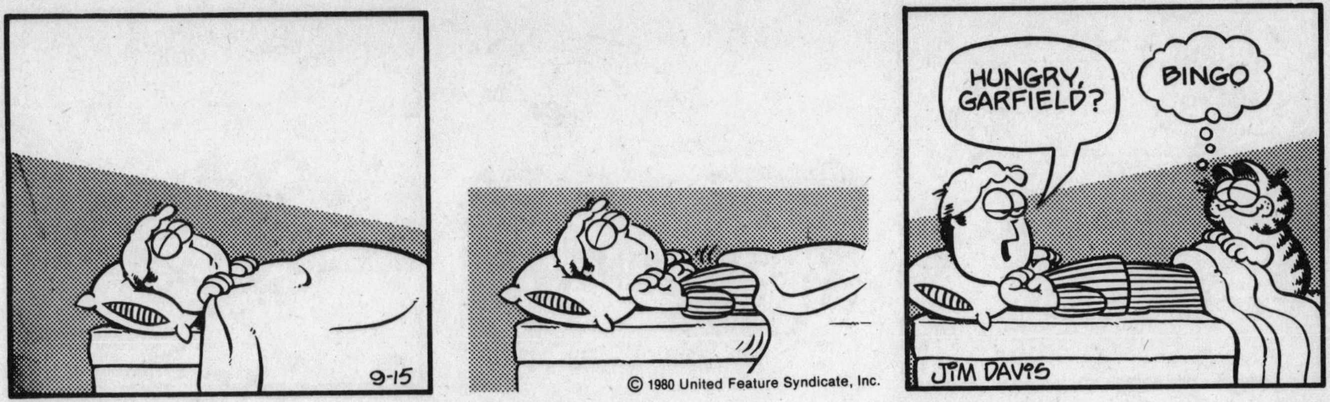
9-15
© 1980 United Feature Syndicate, Inc.
HUNGRY, GARFIELD?
BINGO
JIM DAVIS

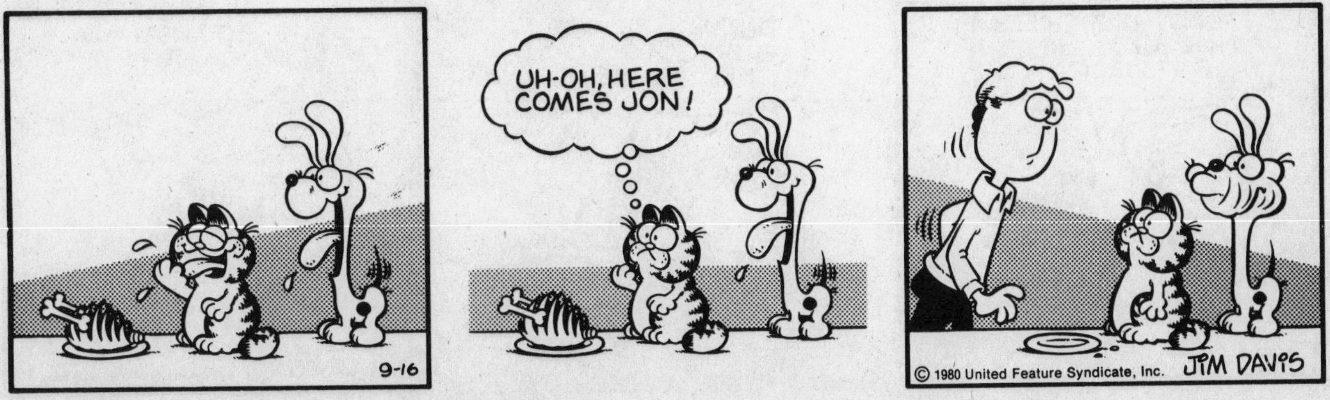
9-16
UH-OH, HERE COMES JON!
© 1980 United Feature Syndicate, Inc.
JIM DAVIS

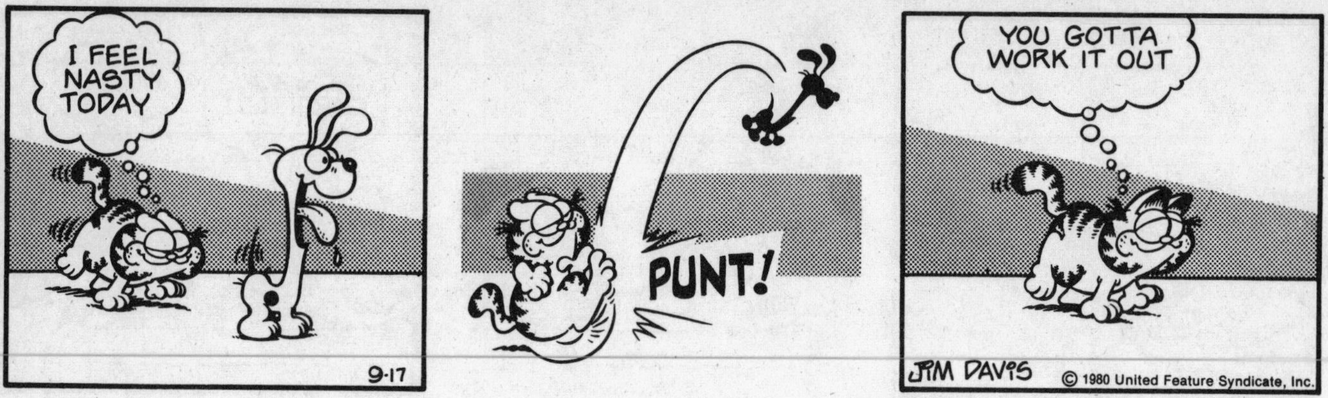
I FEEL NASTY TODAY
9-17
PUNT!
YOU GOTTA WORK IT OUT
JIM DAVIS
© 1980 United Feature Syndicate, Inc.

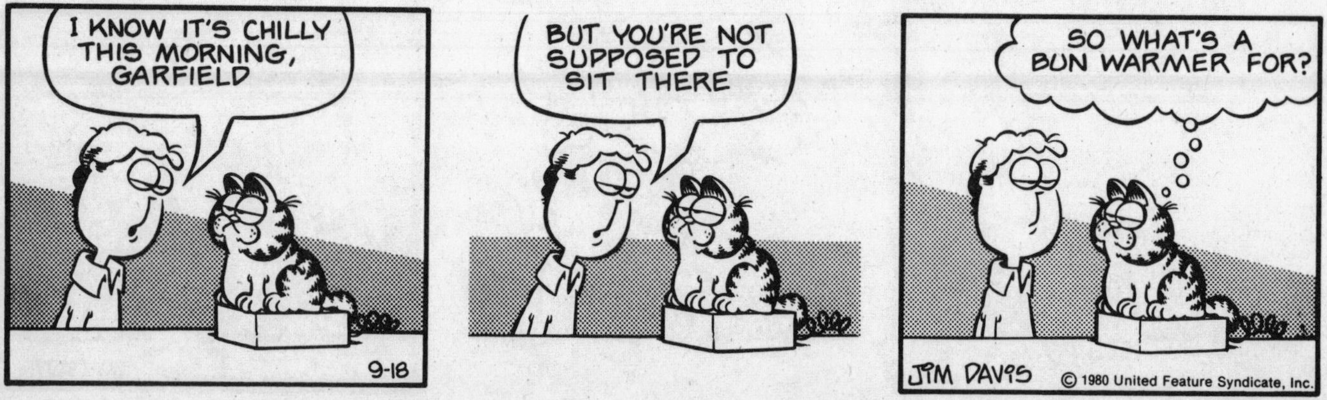
I KNOW IT'S CHILLY THIS MORNING, GARFIELD
9-18
BUT YOU'RE NOT SUPPOSED TO SIT THERE
SO WHAT'S A BUN WARMER FOR?
JIM DAVIS
© 1980 United Feature Syndicate, Inc.

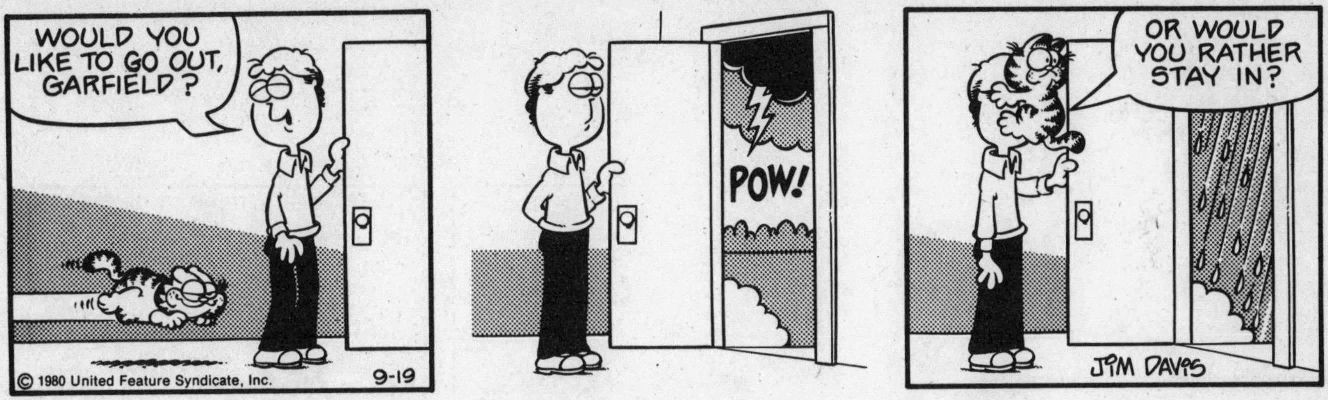
WOULD YOU LIKE TO GO OUT, GARFIELD?
POW!
OR WOULD YOU RATHER STAY IN?
© 1980 United Feature Syndicate, Inc.
9-19
JIM DAVIS

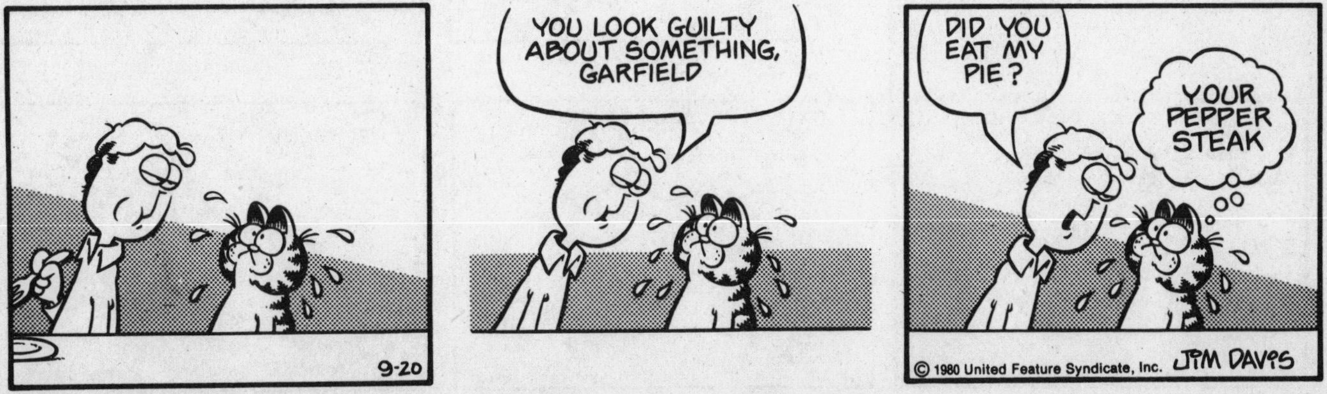
YOU LOOK GUILTY ABOUT SOMETHING, GARFIELD
DID YOU EAT MY PIE?
YOUR PEPPER STEAK
9-20
© 1980 United Feature Syndicate, Inc.
JIM DAVIS

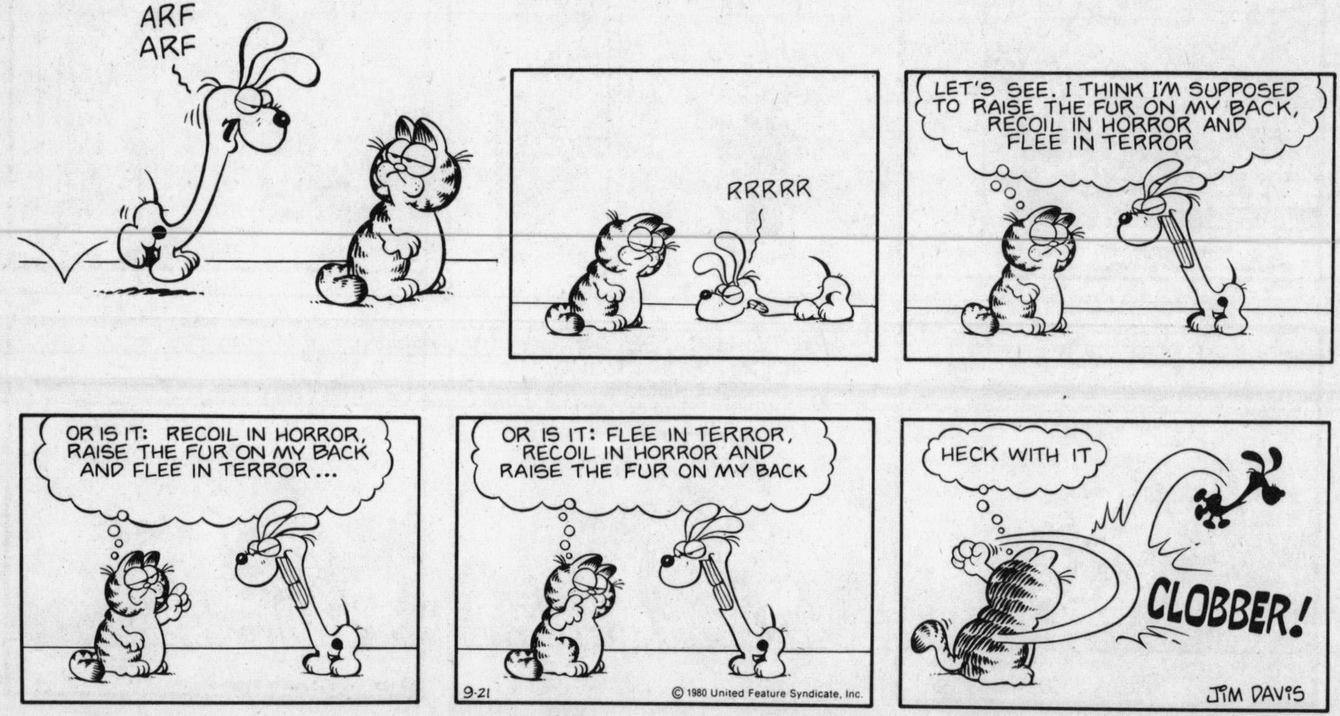

ARF
ARF
RRRRR
LET'S SEE. I THINK I'M SUPPOSED TO RAISE THE FUR ON MY BACK, RECOIL IN HORROR AND FLEE IN TERROR
OR IS IT: RECOIL IN HORROR, RAISE THE FUR ON MY BACK AND FLEE IN TERROR...
OR IS IT: FLEE IN TERROR, RECOIL IN HORROR AND RAISE THE FUR ON MY BACK
9-21
© 1980 United Feature Syndicate, Inc.
HECK WITH IT
CLOBBER!
JIM DAVIS

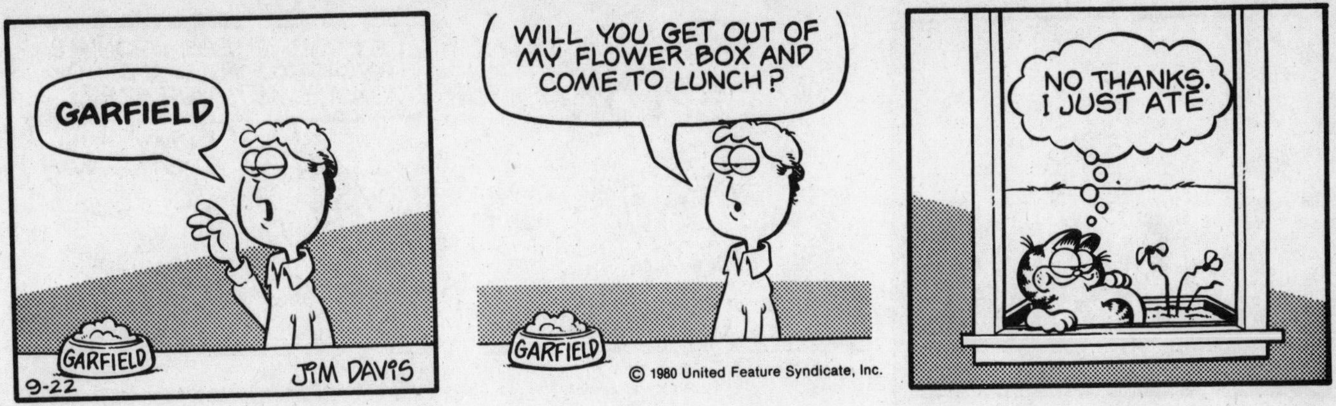
GARFIELD
GARFIELD
JIM DAVIS
9-22
WILL YOU GET OUT OF MY FLOWER BOX AND COME TO LUNCH?
GARFIELD
© 1980 United Feature Syndicate, Inc.
NO THANKS. I JUST ATE

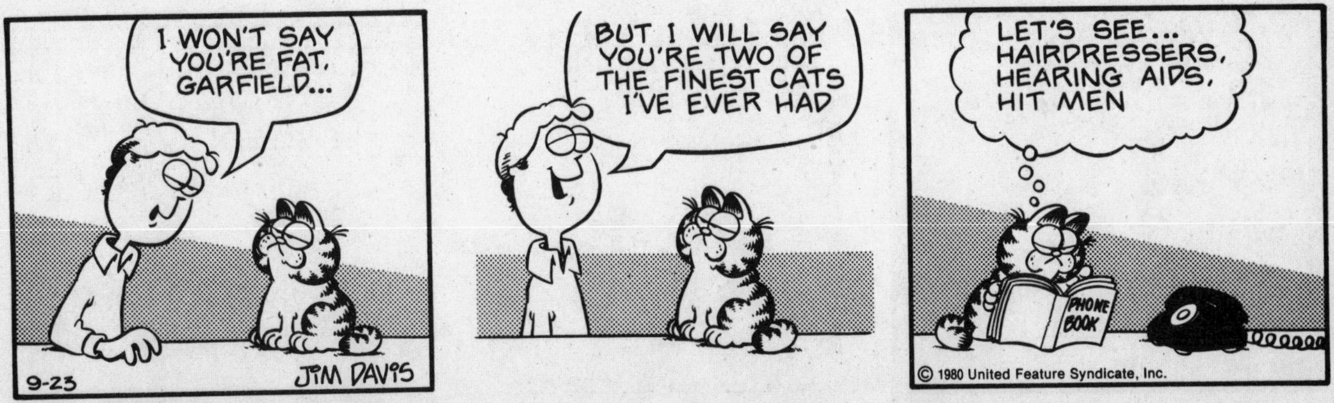
I WON'T SAY YOU'RE FAT, GARFIELD...
JIM DAVIS
9-23
BUT I WILL SAY YOU'RE TWO OF THE FINEST CATS I'VE EVER HAD
LET'S SEE... HAIRDRESSERS, HEARING AIDS, HIT MEN
PHONE BOOK
© 1980 United Feature Syndicate, Inc.

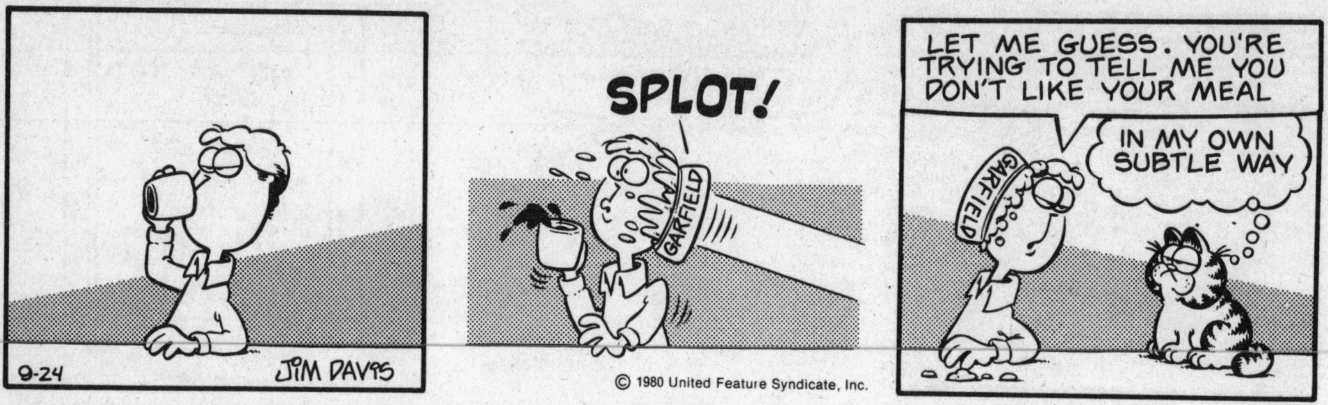
9-24
JIM DAVIS
SPLOT!
GARFIELD
LET ME GUESS. YOU'RE TRYING TO TELL ME YOU DON'T LIKE YOUR MEAL
IN MY OWN SUBTLE WAY

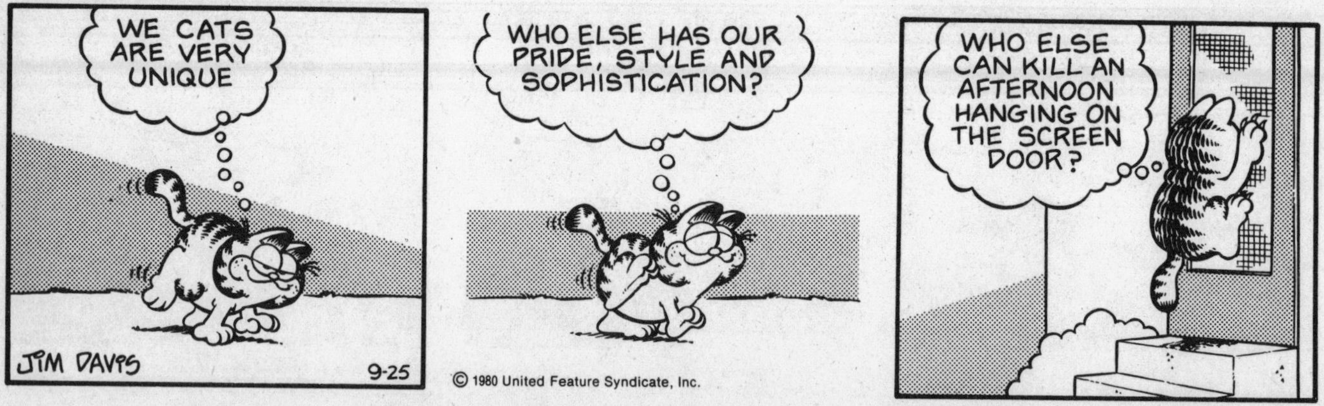
WE CATS ARE VERY UNIQUE
JIM DAVIS
9-25
WHO ELSE HAS OUR PRIDE, STYLE AND SOPHISTICATION?
WHO ELSE CAN KILL AN AFTERNOON HANGING ON THE SCREEN DOOR?

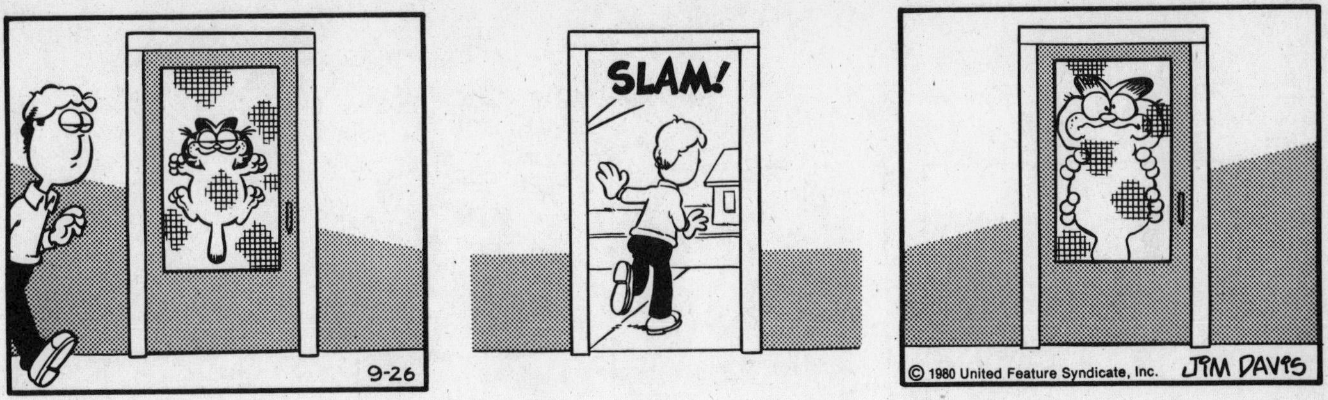
9-26
SLAM!
© 1980 United Feature Syndicate, Inc.
JIM DAVIS

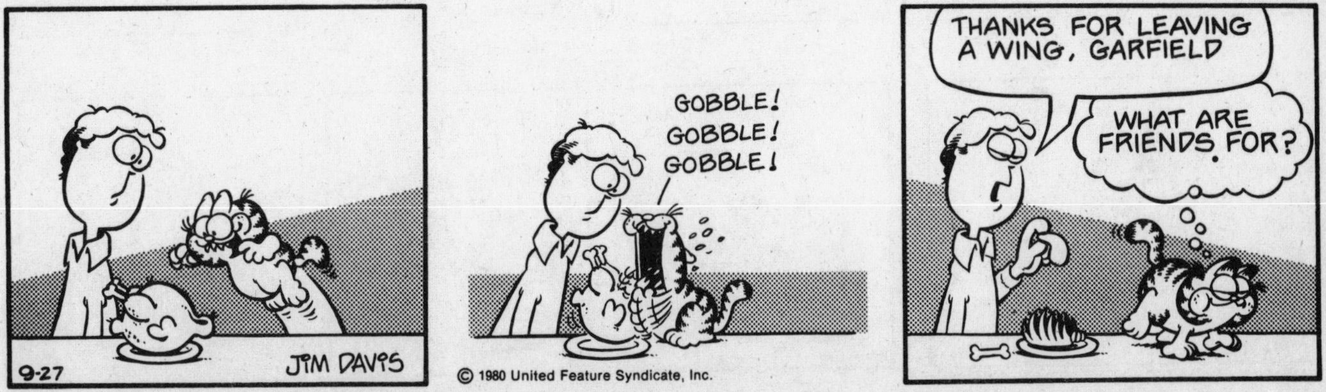
9-27
JIM DAVIS
GOBBLE! GOBBLE! GOBBLE!
© 1980 United Feature Syndicate, Inc.
THANKS FOR LEAVING A WING, GARFIELD
WHAT ARE FRIENDS FOR?

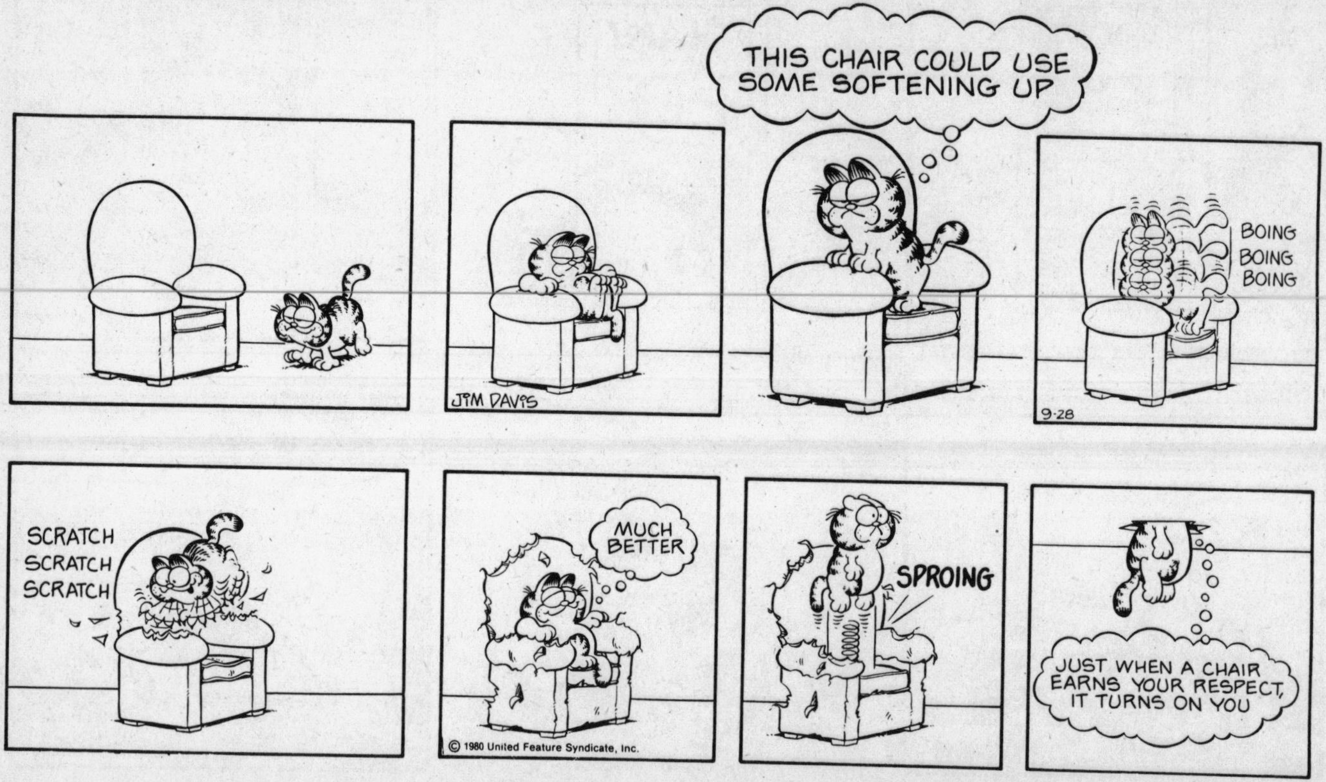
THIS CHAIR COULD USE SOME SOFTENING UP
BOING
BOING
BOING
JIM DAVIS
9-28
SCRATCH
SCRATCH
SCRATCH
MUCH BETTER
SPROING
JUST WHEN A CHAIR EARNS YOUR RESPECT, IT TURNS ON YOU
© 1980 United Feature Syndicate, Inc.

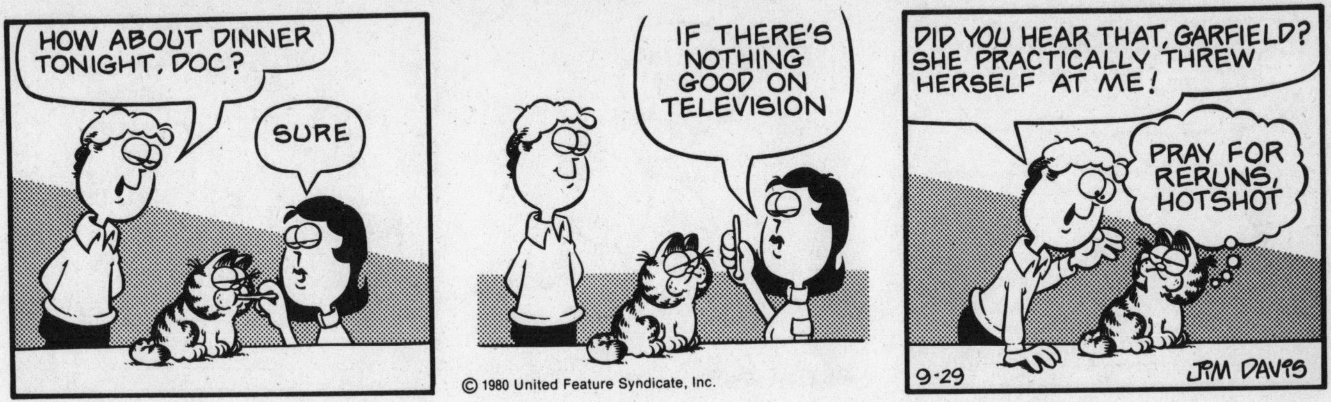
HOW ABOUT DINNER TONIGHT, DOC?
SURE
IF THERE'S NOTHING GOOD ON TELEVISION
DID YOU HEAR THAT, GARFIELD? SHE PRACTICALLY THREW HERSELF AT ME!
PRAY FOR RERUNS, HOTSHOT
9-29
JIM DAVIS

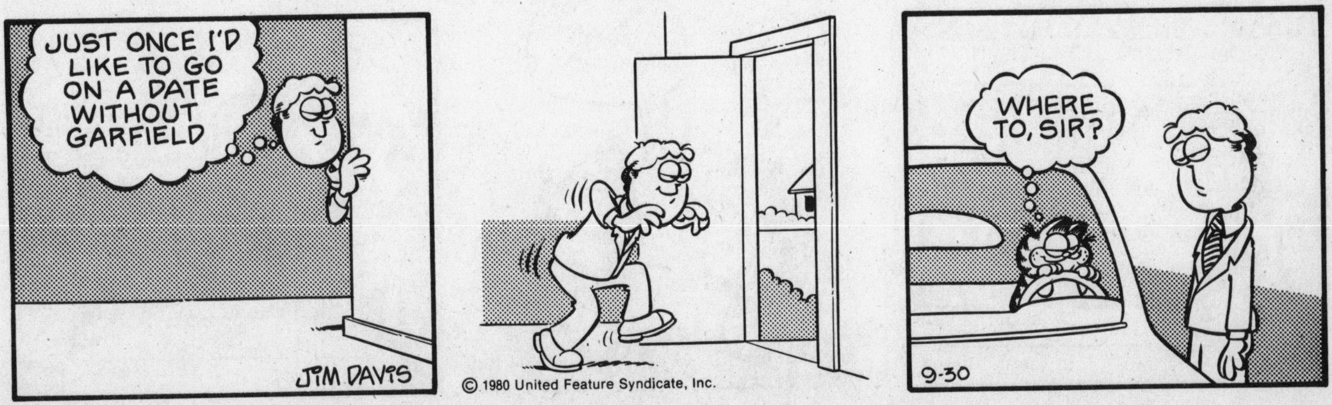
JUST ONCE I'D LIKE TO GO ON A DATE WITHOUT GARFIELD
JIM DAVIS
WHERE TO, SIR?
9-30

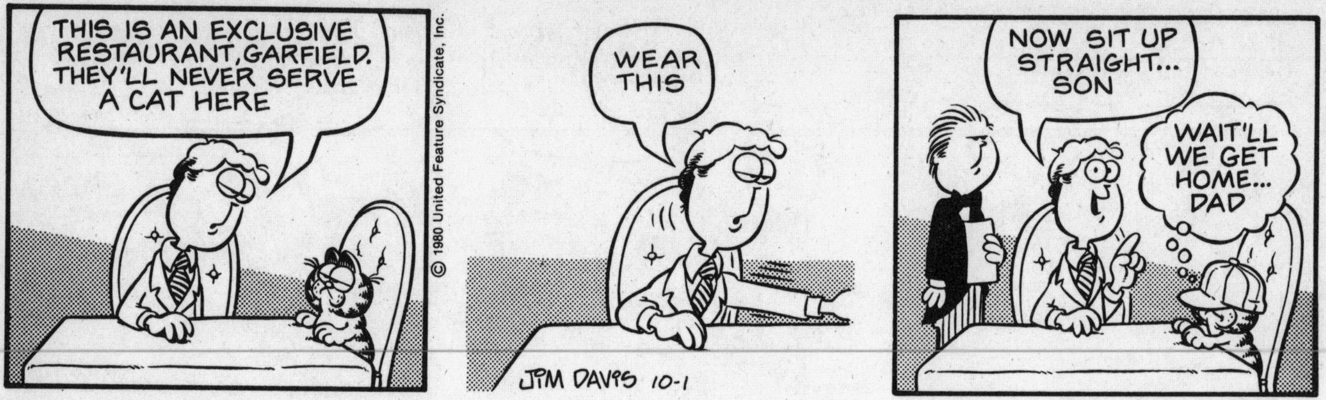
THIS IS AN EXCLUSIVE RESTAURANT, GARFIELD. THEY'LL NEVER SERVE A CAT HERE
© 1980 United Feature Syndicate, Inc.
WEAR THIS
JIM DAVIS 10-1
NOW SIT UP STRAIGHT... SON
WAIT'LL WE GET HOME... DAD

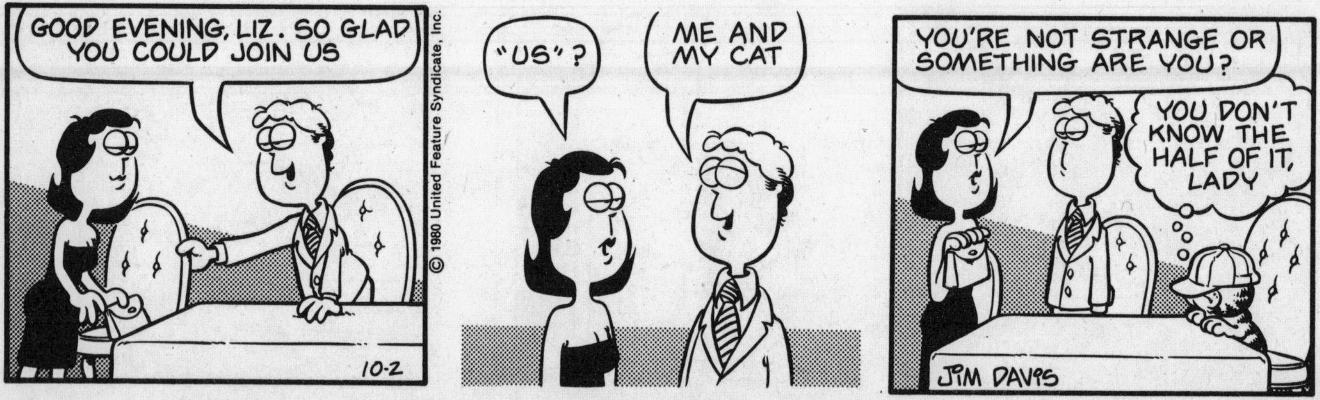
GOOD EVENING, LIZ. SO GLAD YOU COULD JOIN US
10-2
© 1980 United Feature Syndicate, Inc.
"US"?
ME AND MY CAT
YOU'RE NOT STRANGE OR SOMETHING ARE YOU?
YOU DON'T KNOW THE HALF OF IT, LADY
JIM DAVIS

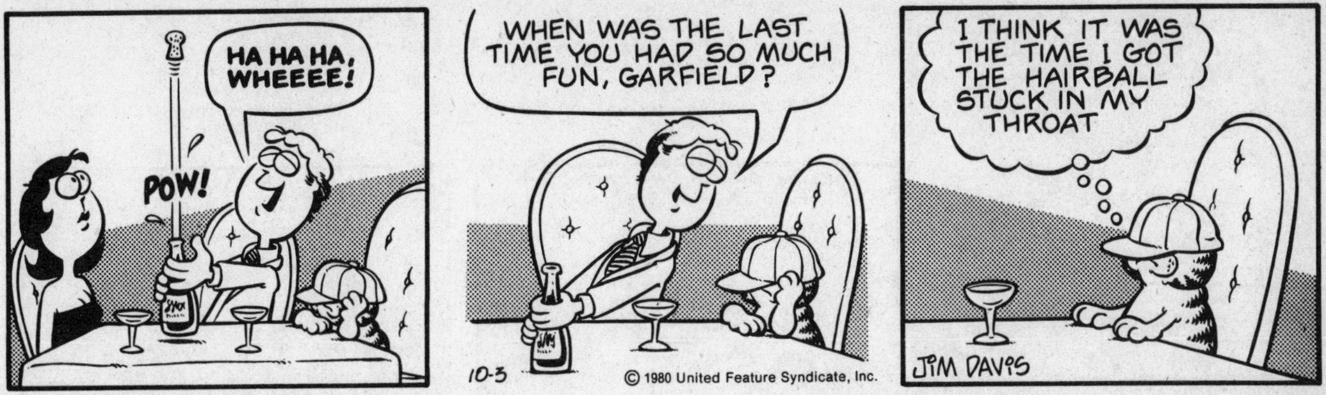
HA HA HA, WHEEEEE!
POW!
WHEN WAS THE LAST TIME YOU HAD SO MUCH FUN, GARFIELD?
I THINK IT WAS THE TIME I GOT THE HAIRBALL STUCK IN MY THROAT
10-3
© 1980 United Feature Syndicate, Inc.
JIM DAVIS

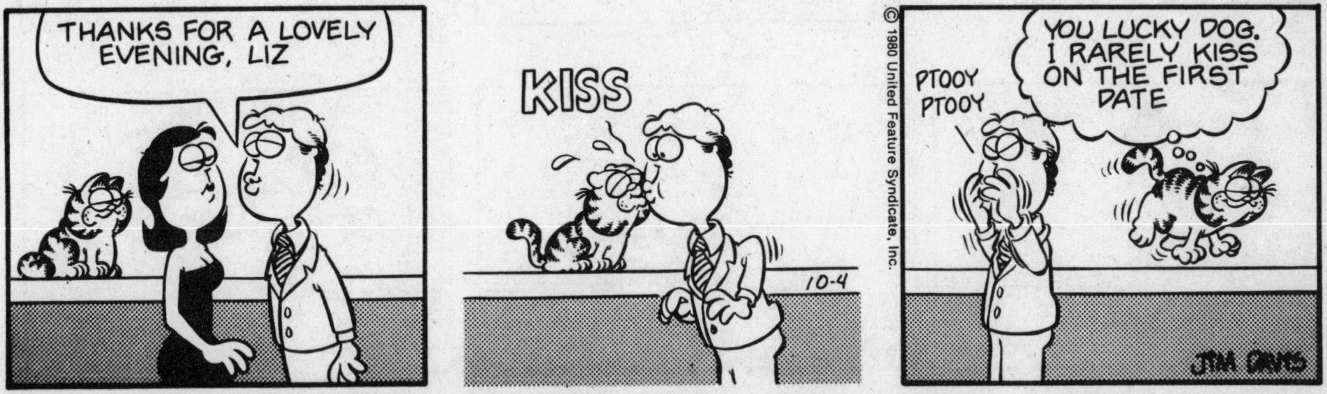
THANKS FOR A LOVELY EVENING, LIZ
KISS
10-4
PTOOY PTOOY
YOU LUCKY DOG. I RARELY KISS ON THE FIRST DATE
JIM DAVIS
© 1980 United Feature Syndicate, Inc.

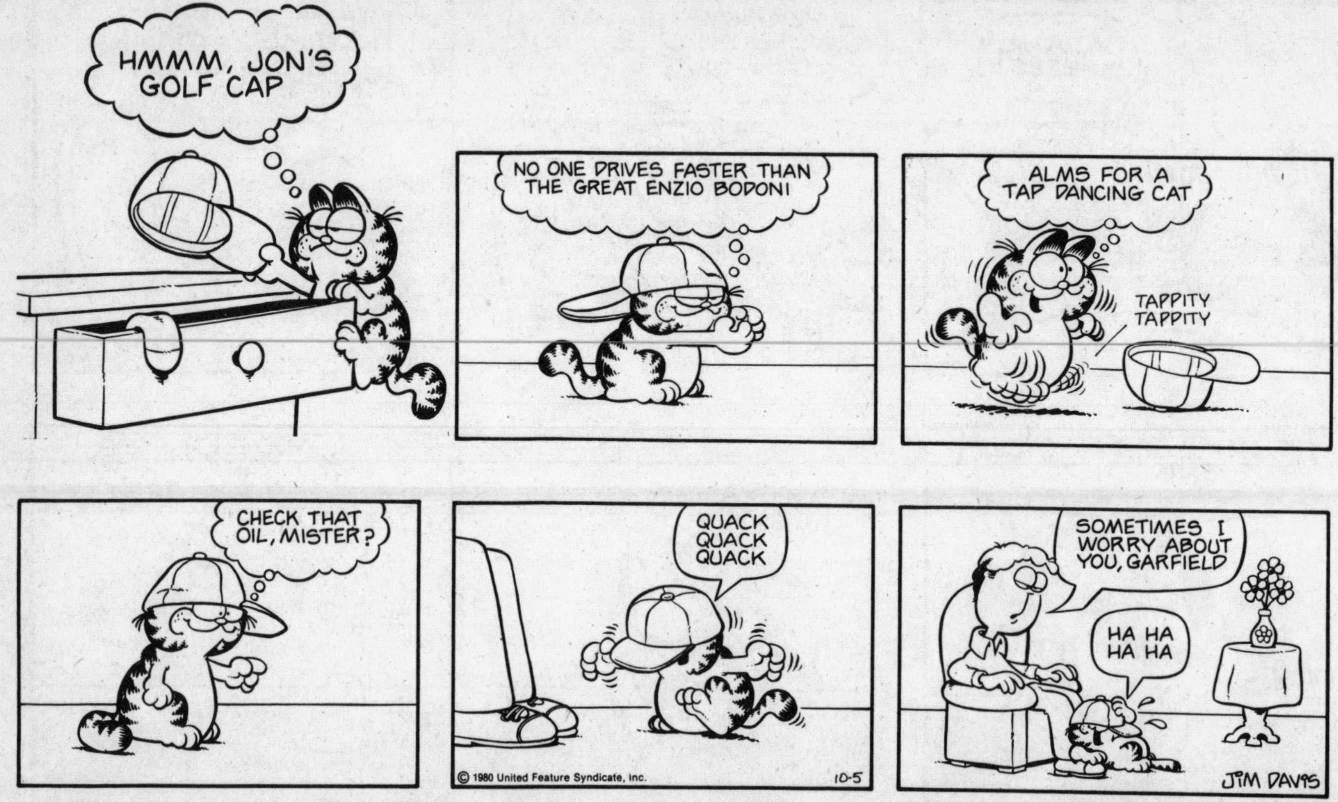
HMMM, JON'S GOLF CAP
NO ONE DRIVES FASTER THAN THE GREAT ENZIO BODONI
ALMS FOR A TAP DANCING CAT
TAPPITY TAPPITY
CHECK THAT OIL, MISTER?
QUACK QUACK QUACK
SOMETIMES I WORRY ABOUT YOU, GARFIELD
HA HA HA HA
© 1980 United Feature Syndicate, Inc.
10-5
JIM DAVIS

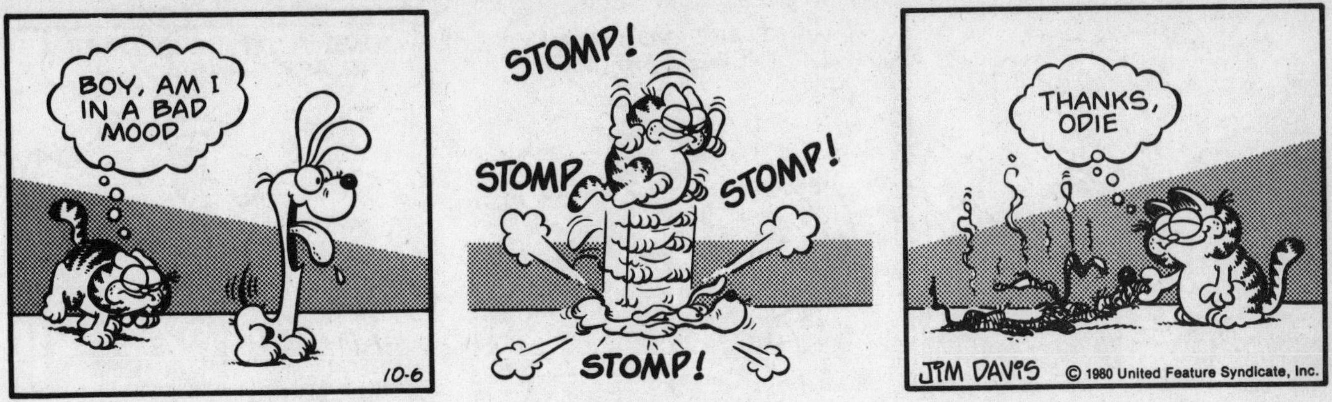
BOY, AM I IN A BAD MOOD
10-6
STOMP!
STOMP
STOMP!
STOMP!
THANKS, ODIE
JIM DAVIS
© 1980 United Feature Syndicate, Inc.

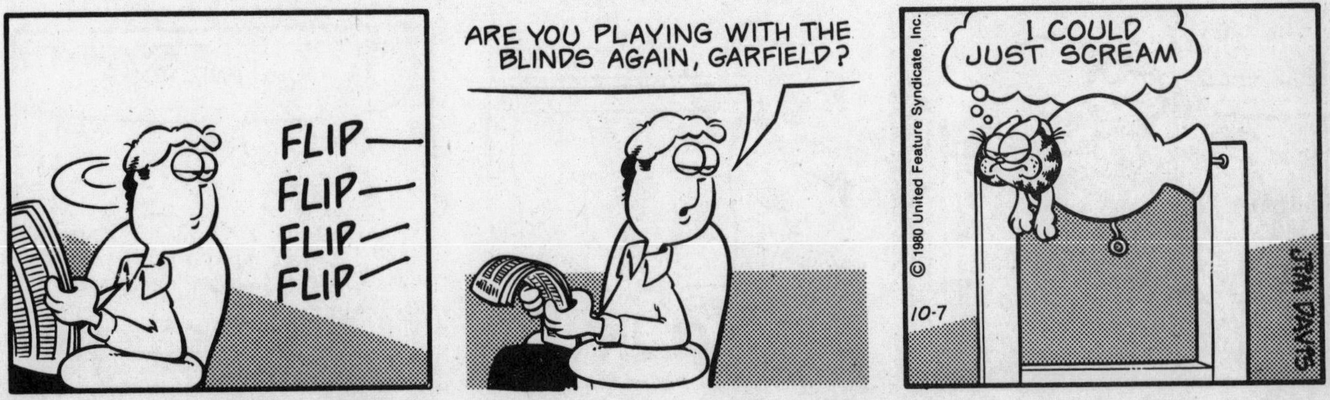
FLIP
FLIP
FLIP
FLIP
ARE YOU PLAYING WITH THE BLINDS AGAIN, GARFIELD?
© 1980 United Feature Syndicate, Inc.
I COULD JUST SCREAM
10-7
JIM DAVIS

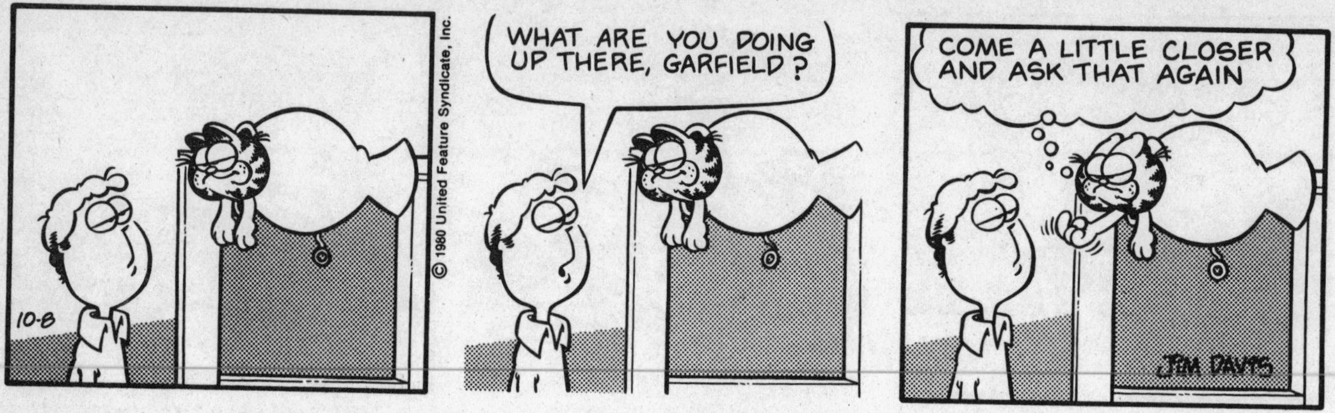
10-8
© 1980 United Feature Syndicate, Inc.
WHAT ARE YOU DOING UP THERE, GARFIELD?
COME A LITTLE CLOSER AND ASK THAT AGAIN
JIM DAVIS

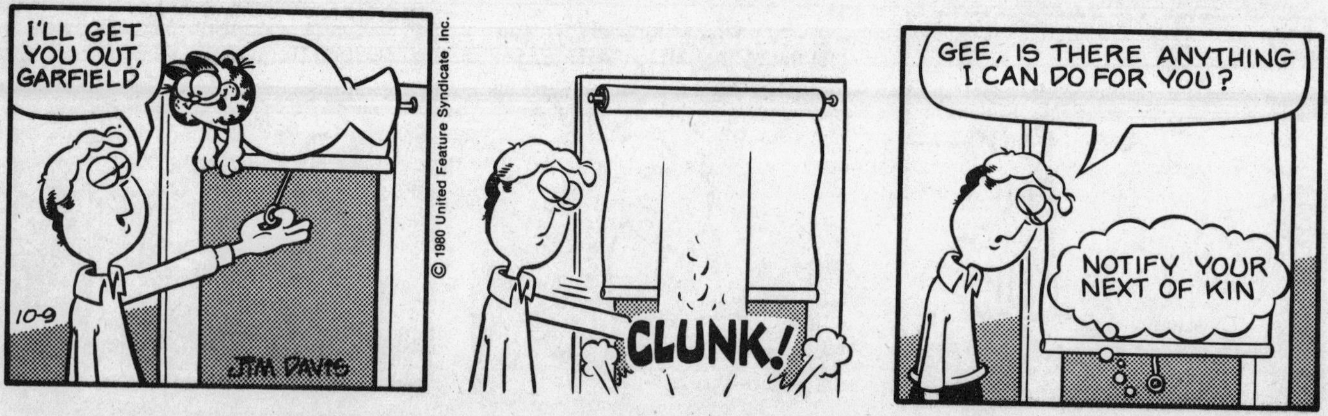
I'LL GET YOU OUT, GARFIELD
10-9
JIM DAVIS
© 1980 United Feature Syndicate, Inc.
CLUNK!
GEE, IS THERE ANYTHING I CAN DO FOR YOU?
NOTIFY YOUR NEXT OF KIN

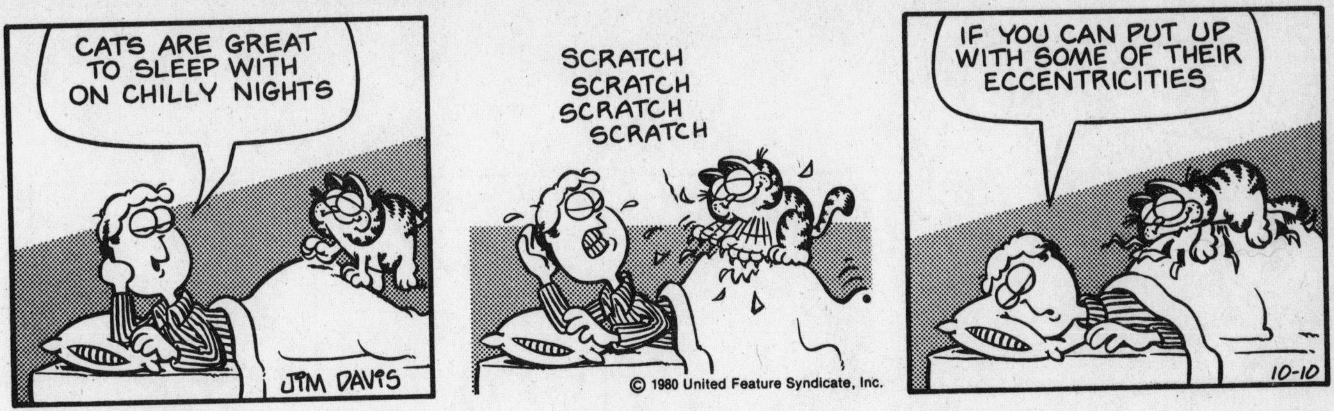
CATS ARE GREAT TO SLEEP WITH ON CHILLY NIGHTS
JIM DAVIS
SCRATCH SCRATCH SCRATCH SCRATCH
© 1980 United Feature Syndicate, Inc.
IF YOU CAN PUT UP WITH SOME OF THEIR ECCENTRICITIES
10-10

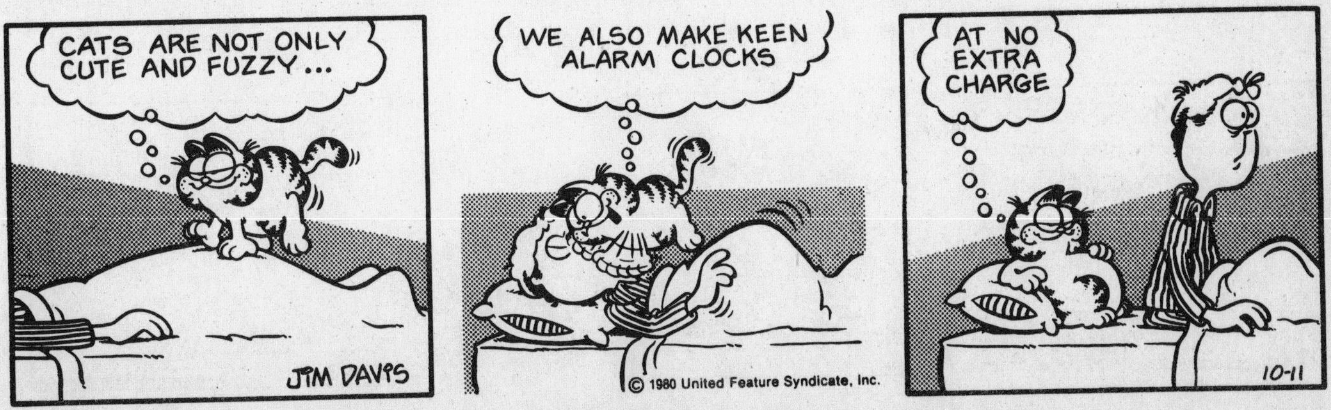
CATS ARE NOT ONLY CUTE AND FUZZY...
JIM DAVIS
WE ALSO MAKE KEEN ALARM CLOCKS
© 1980 United Feature Syndicate, Inc.
AT NO EXTRA CHARGE
10-11

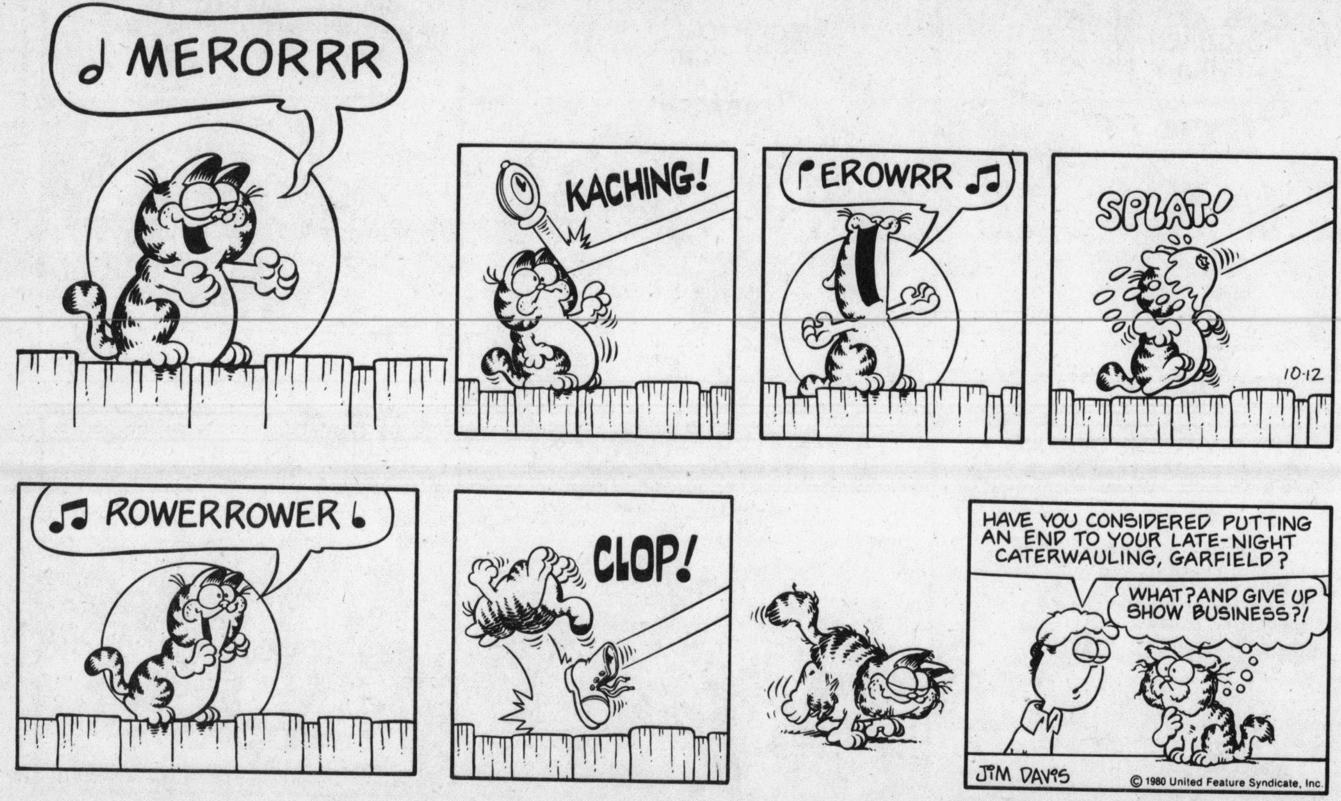
MERORRR
KACHING!
EROWRR
SPLAT!
10-12
ROWERROWER
CLOP!
HAVE YOU CONSIDERED PUTTING AN END TO YOUR LATE-NIGHT CATERWAULING, GARFIELD?
WHAT? AND GIVE UP SHOW BUSINESS?!
JIM DAVIS
© 1980 United Feature Syndicate, Inc.

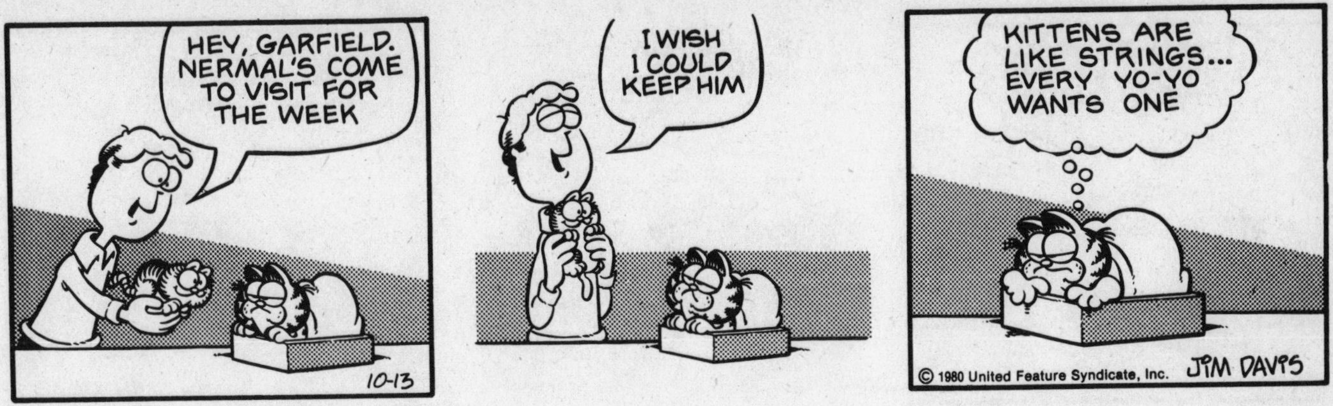
HEY, GARFIELD. NERMAL'S COME TO VISIT FOR THE WEEK
10-13
I WISH I COULD KEEP HIM
KITTENS ARE LIKE STRINGS... EVERY YO-YO WANTS ONE
© 1980 United Feature Syndicate, Inc.
JIM DAVIS

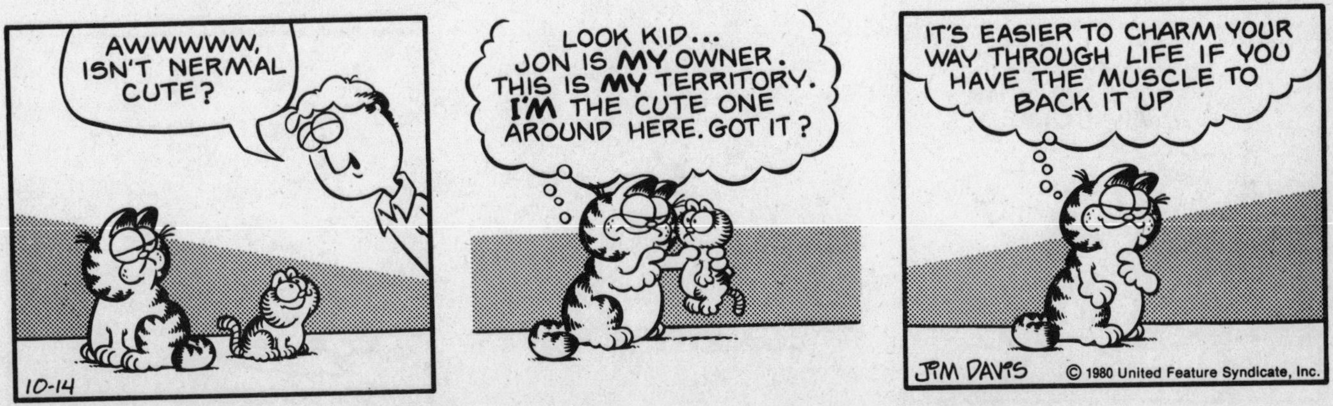
AWWWWW, ISN'T NERMAL CUTE?
10-14
LOOK KID... JON IS MY OWNER. THIS IS MY TERRITORY. I'M THE CUTE ONE AROUND HERE. GOT IT?
IT'S EASIER TO CHARM YOUR WAY THROUGH LIFE IF YOU HAVE THE MUSCLE TO BACK IT UP
JIM DAVIS
© 1980 United Feature Syndicate, Inc.

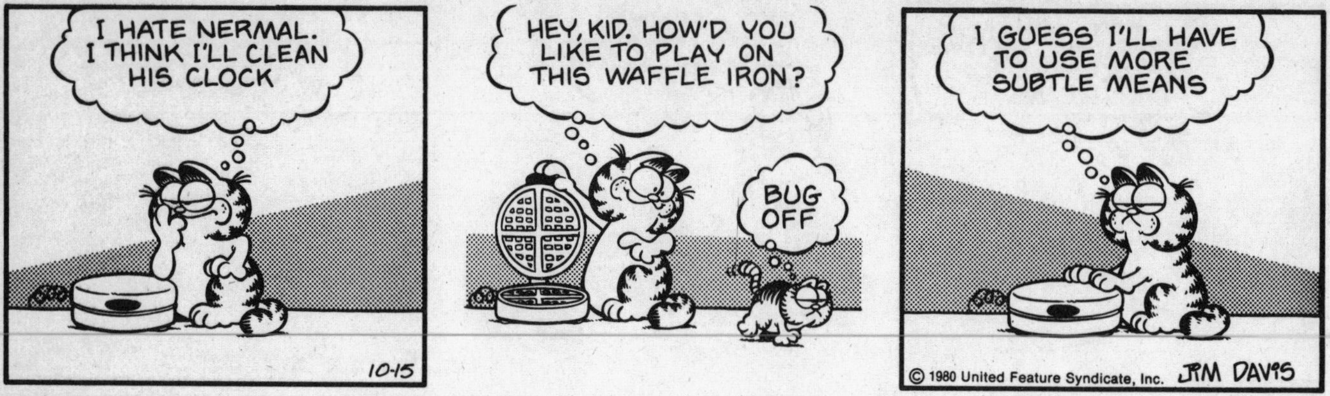
I HATE NERMAL. I THINK I'LL CLEAN HIS CLOCK
10-15
HEY, KID. HOW'D YOU LIKE TO PLAY ON THIS WAFFLE IRON?
BUG OFF
I GUESS I'LL HAVE TO USE MORE SUBTLE MEANS
© 1980 United Feature Syndicate, Inc.
JIM DAVIS

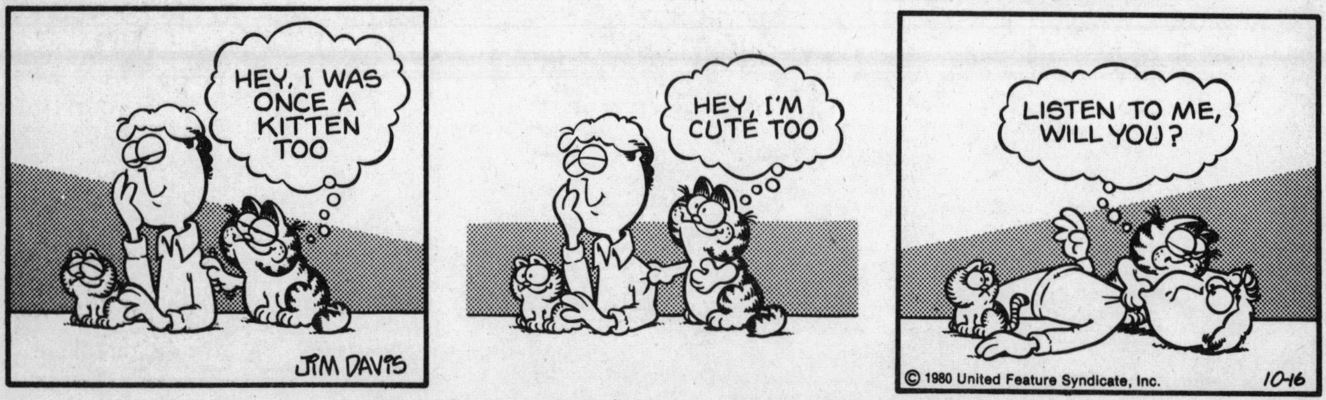
HEY, I WAS ONCE A KITTEN TOO
JIM DAVIS
HEY, I'M CUTE TOO
LISTEN TO ME, WILL YOU?
© 1980 United Feature Syndicate, Inc.
10-16

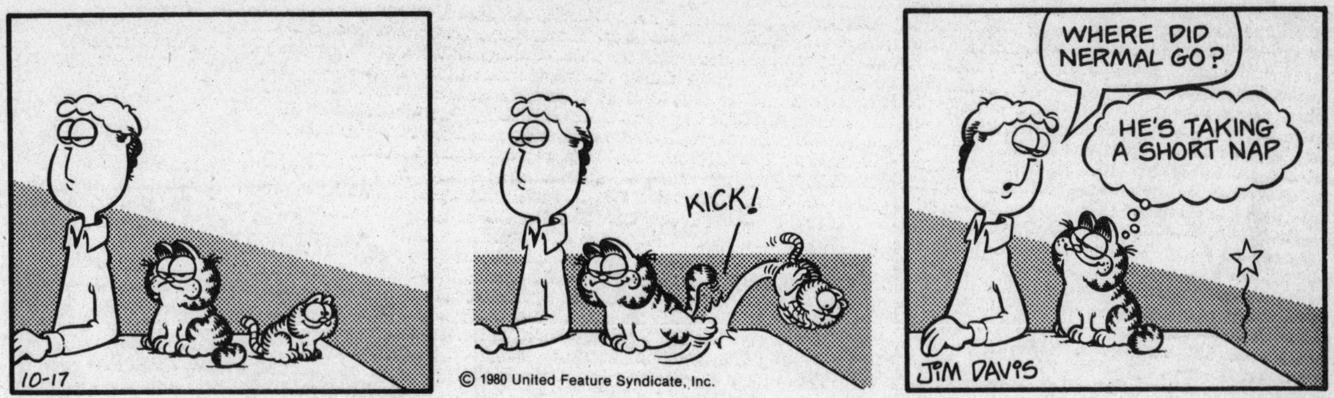
10-17
KICK!
© 1980 United Feature Syndicate, Inc.
WHERE DID NERMAL GO?
HE'S TAKING A SHORT NAP
JIM DAVIS

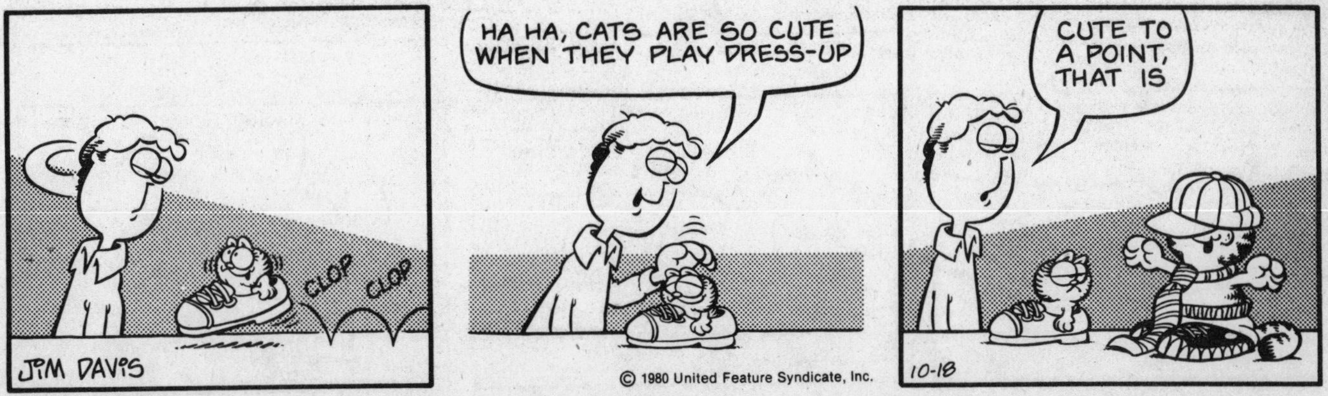
CLOP
CLOP
JIM DAVIS
HA HA, CATS ARE SO CUTE WHEN THEY PLAY DRESS-UP
© 1980 United Feature Syndicate, Inc.
CUTE TO A POINT, THAT IS
10-18

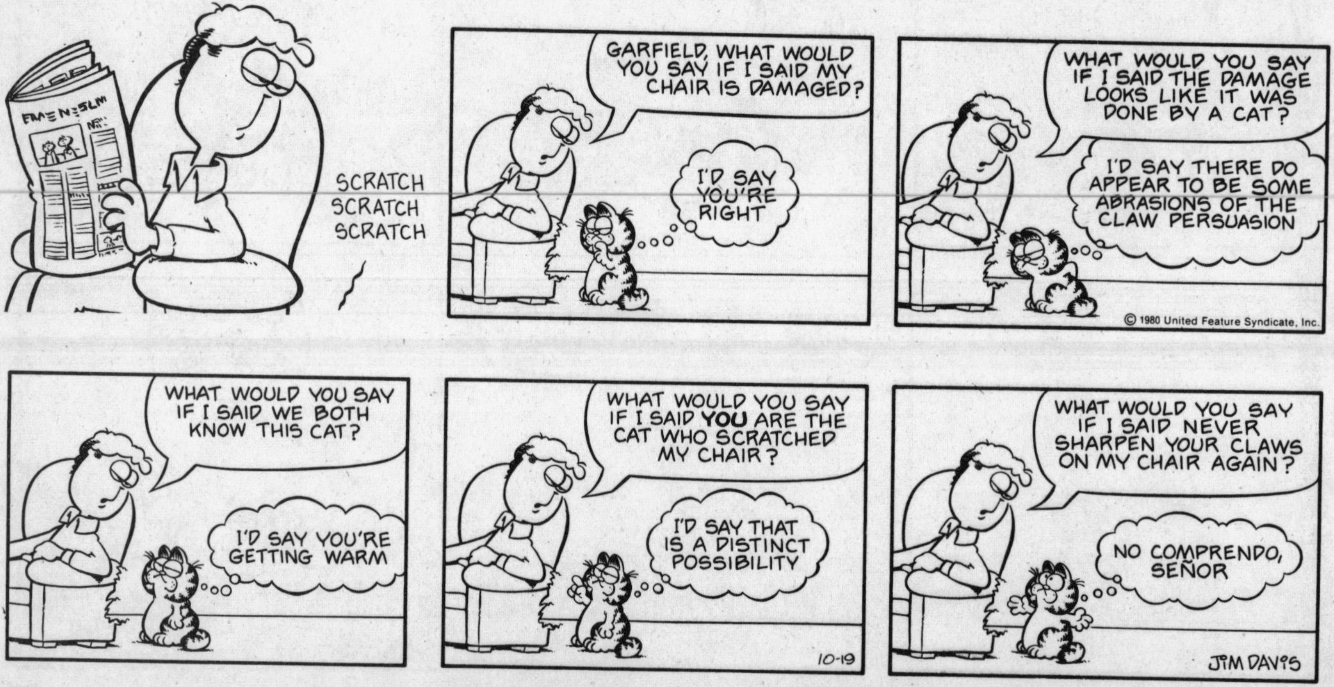
SCRATCH
SCRATCH
SCRATCH
GARFIELD, WHAT WOULD YOU SAY IF I SAID MY CHAIR IS DAMAGED?
I'D SAY YOU'RE RIGHT
WHAT WOULD YOU SAY IF I SAID THE DAMAGE LOOKS LIKE IT WAS DONE BY A CAT?
I'D SAY THERE DO APPEAR TO BE SOME ABRASIONS OF THE CLAW PERSUASION
© 1980 United Feature Syndicate, Inc.
WHAT WOULD YOU SAY IF I SAID WE BOTH KNOW THIS CAT?
I'D SAY YOU'RE GETTING WARM
WHAT WOULD YOU SAY IF I SAID **YOU** ARE THE CAT WHO SCRATCHED MY CHAIR?
I'D SAY THAT IS A DISTINCT POSSIBILITY
10-19
WHAT WOULD YOU SAY IF I SAID NEVER SHARPEN YOUR CLAWS ON MY CHAIR AGAIN?
NO COMPRENDO, SEÑOR
JIM DAVIS

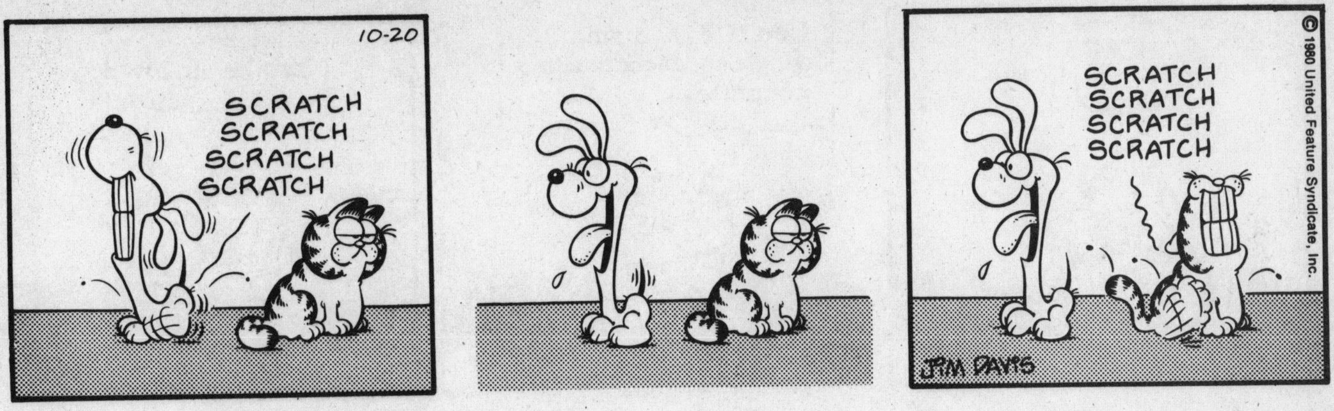
10-20
SCRATCH SCRATCH SCRATCH SCRATCH
SCRATCH SCRATCH SCRATCH SCRATCH
© 1980 United Feature Syndicate, Inc.
JIM DAVIS

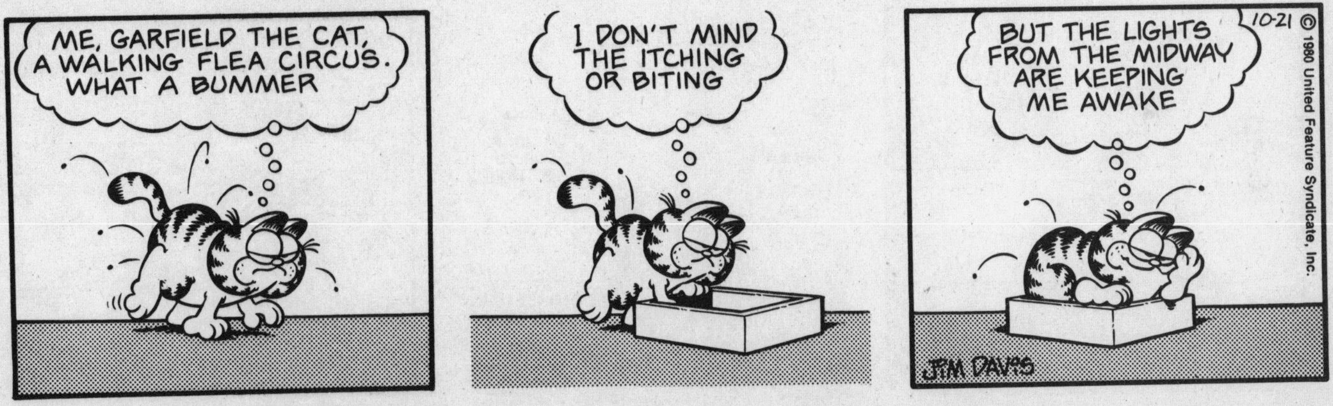
ME, GARFIELD THE CAT, A WALKING FLEA CIRCUS. WHAT A BUMMER
I DON'T MIND THE ITCHING OR BITING
10-21
BUT THE LIGHTS FROM THE MIDWAY ARE KEEPING ME AWAKE
© 1980 United Feature Syndicate, Inc.
JIM DAVIS

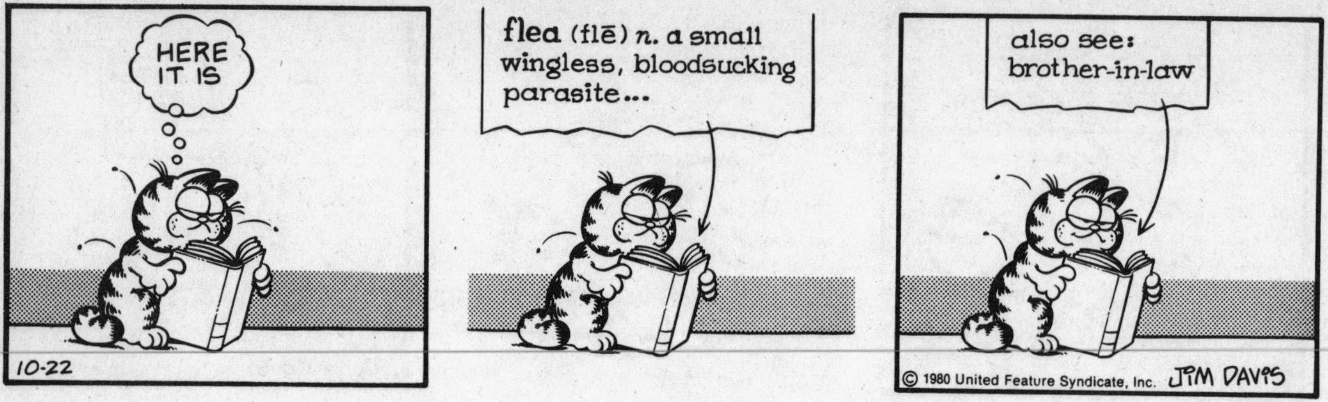
HERE IT IS
flea (flē) n. a small wingless, bloodsucking parasite...
also see: brother-in-law
10-22
© 1980 United Feature Syndicate, Inc.
JIM DAVIS

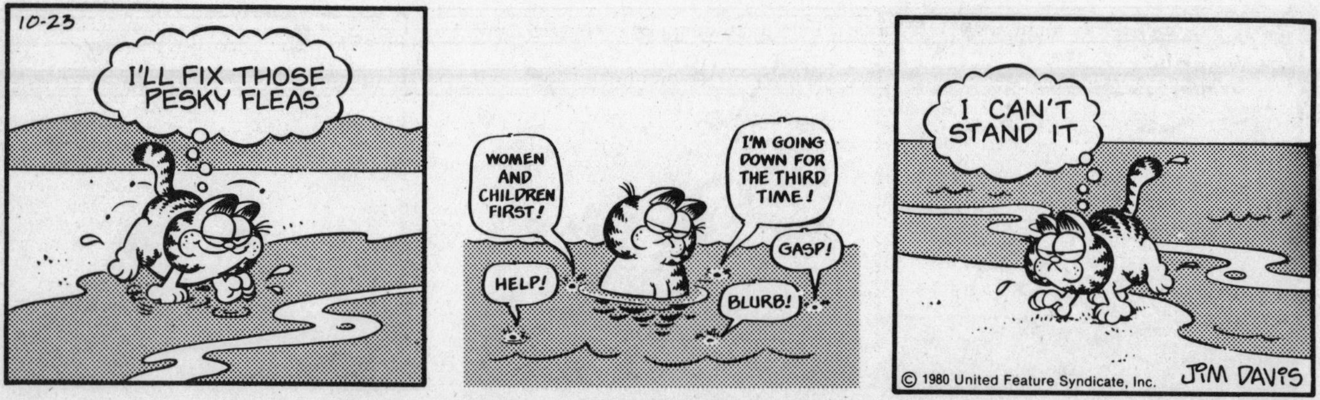
10-23
I'LL FIX THOSE PESKY FLEAS
WOMEN AND CHILDREN FIRST!
I'M GOING DOWN FOR THE THIRD TIME!
HELP!
GASP!
BLURB!
I CAN'T STAND IT
© 1980 United Feature Syndicate, Inc.
JIM DAVIS

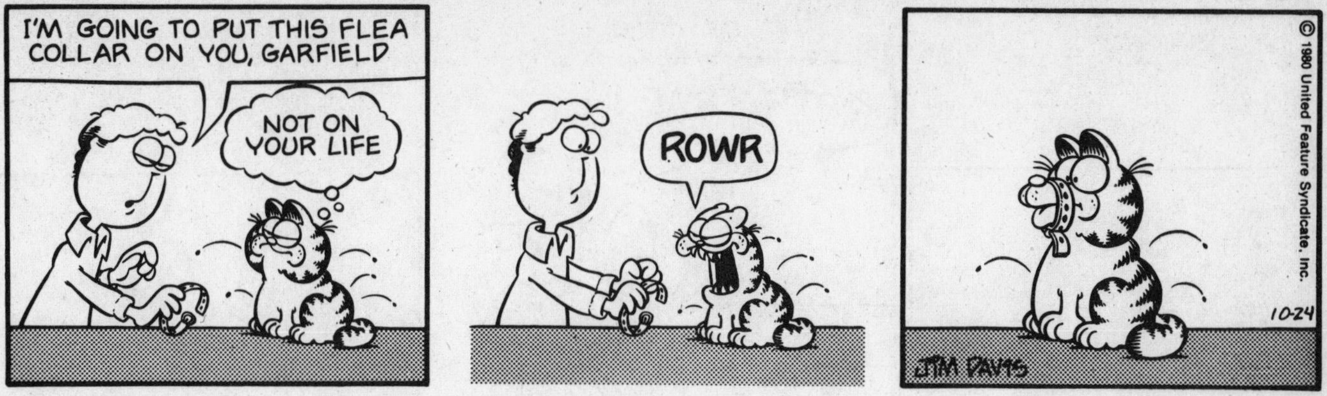
I'M GOING TO PUT THIS FLEA COLLAR ON YOU, GARFIELD
NOT ON YOUR LIFE
ROWR
© 1980 United Feature Syndicate, Inc.
10-24
JIM DAVIS

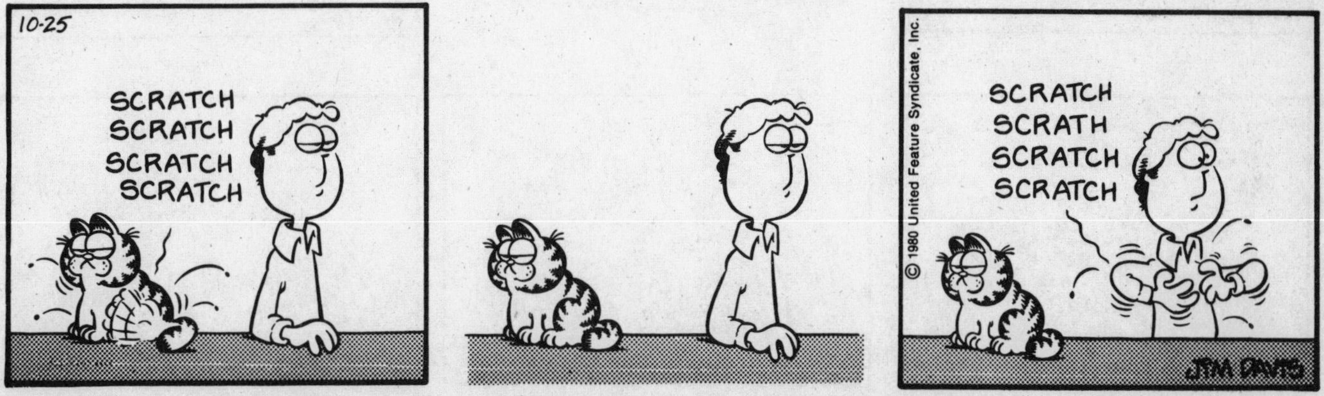
10-25
SCRATCH SCRATCH SCRATCH SCRATCH
© 1980 United Feature Syndicate, Inc.
SCRATCH SCRATH SCRATCH SCRATCH
JIM DAVIS

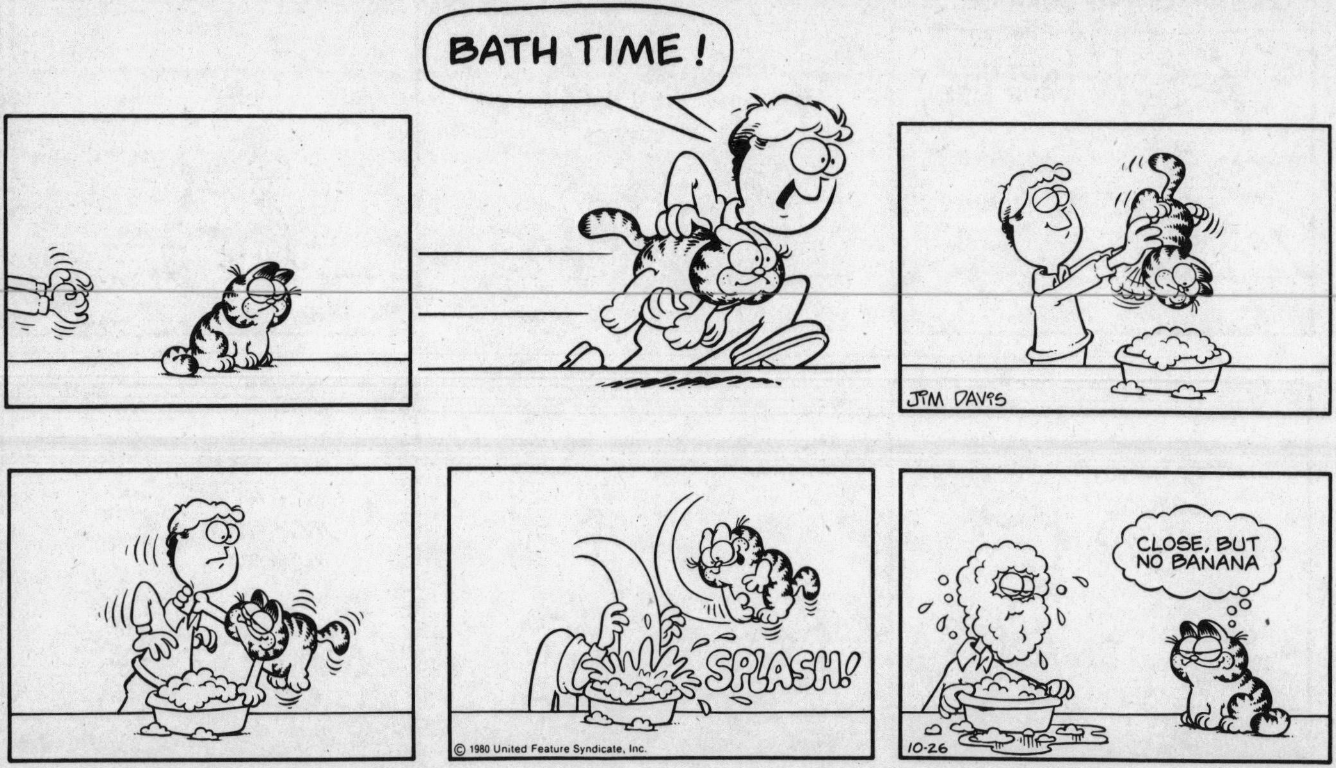
BATH TIME!
JIM DAVIS
SPLASH!
© 1980 United Feature Syndicate, Inc.
10-26
CLOSE, BUT NO BANANA

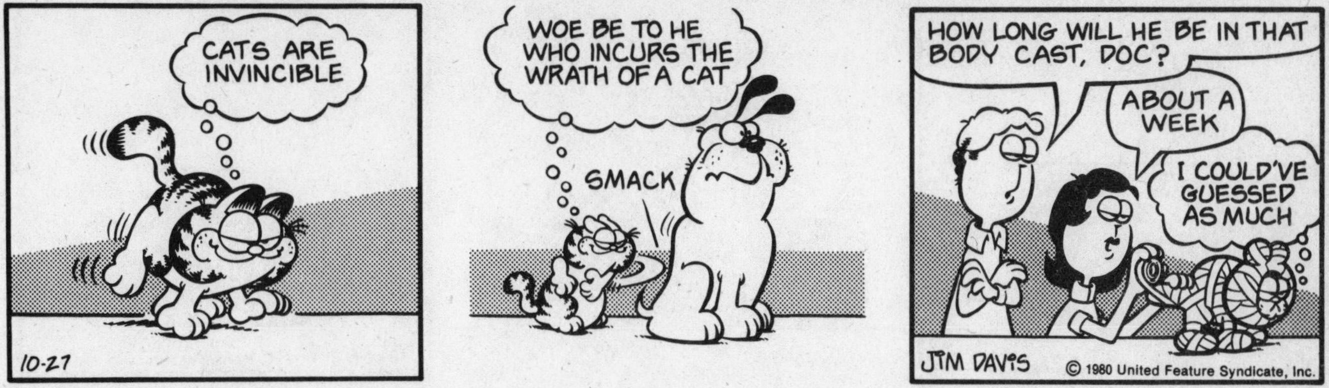
CATS ARE INVINCIBLE
10-27
WOE BE TO HE WHO INCURS THE WRATH OF A CAT
SMACK
HOW LONG WILL HE BE IN THAT BODY CAST, DOC?
ABOUT A WEEK
I COULD'VE GUESSED AS MUCH
JIM DAVIS
© 1980 United Feature Syndicate, Inc.

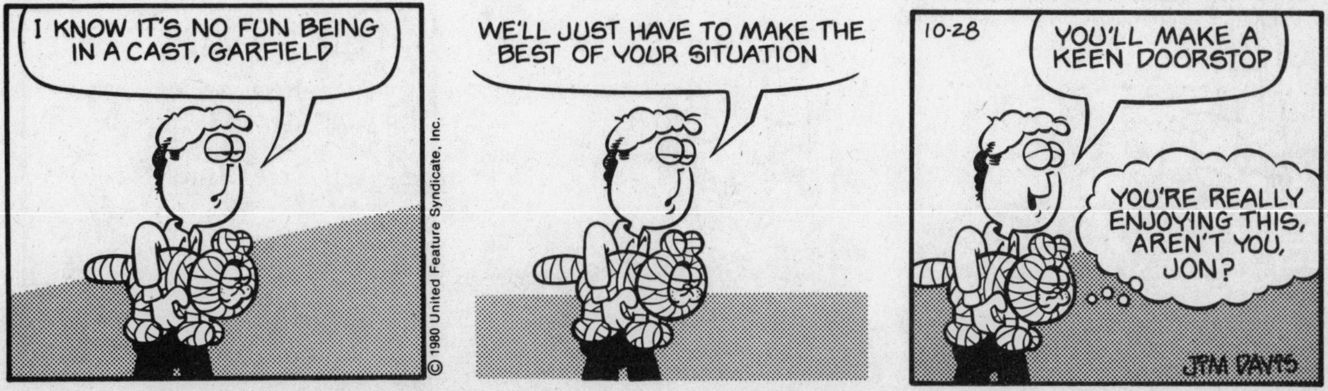
I KNOW IT'S NO FUN BEING IN A CAST, GARFIELD
© 1980 United Feature Syndicate, Inc.
WE'LL JUST HAVE TO MAKE THE BEST OF YOUR SITUATION
10-28
YOU'LL MAKE A KEEN DOORSTOP
YOU'RE REALLY ENJOYING THIS, AREN'T YOU, JON?
JIM DAVIS

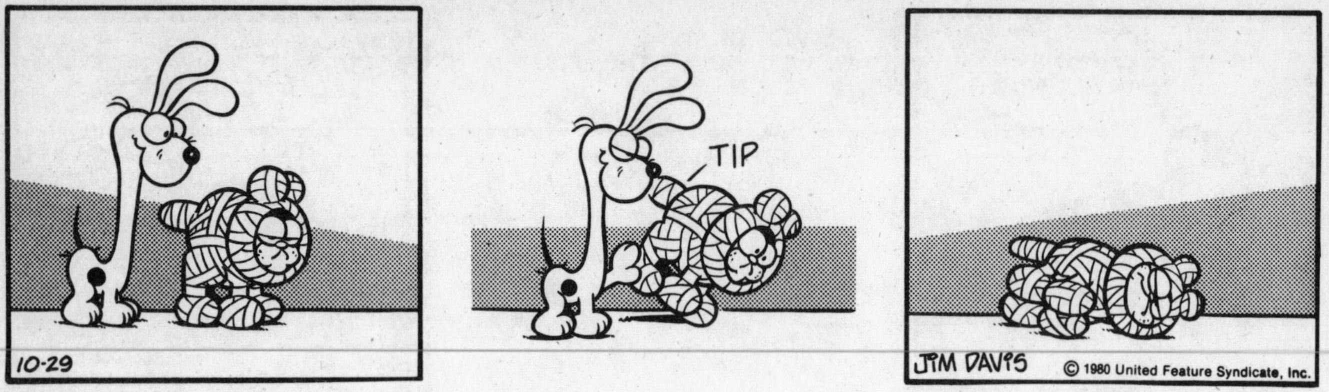
TIP
10-29
JIM DAVIS
© 1980 United Feature Syndicate, Inc.

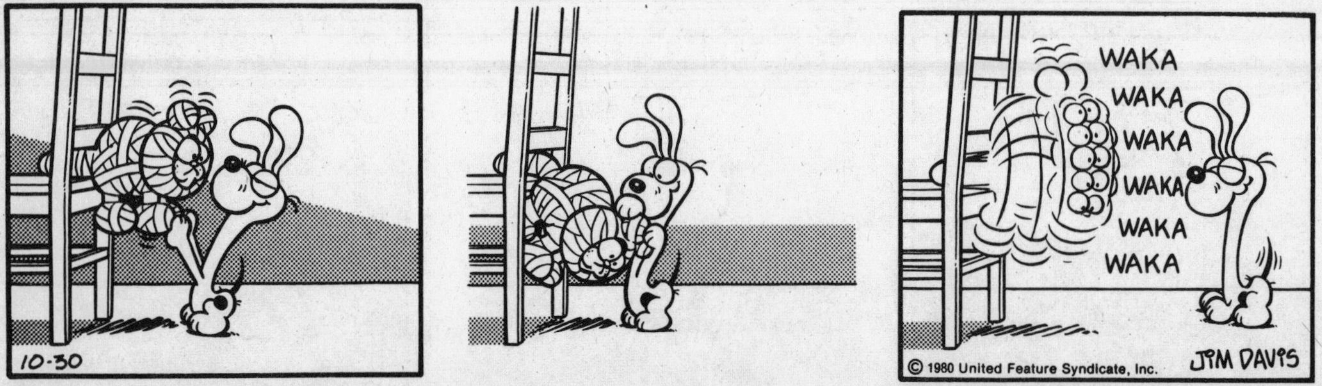
WAKA
WAKA
WAKA
WAKA
WAKA
WAKA
10-30
© 1980 United Feature Syndicate, Inc.
JIM DAVIS

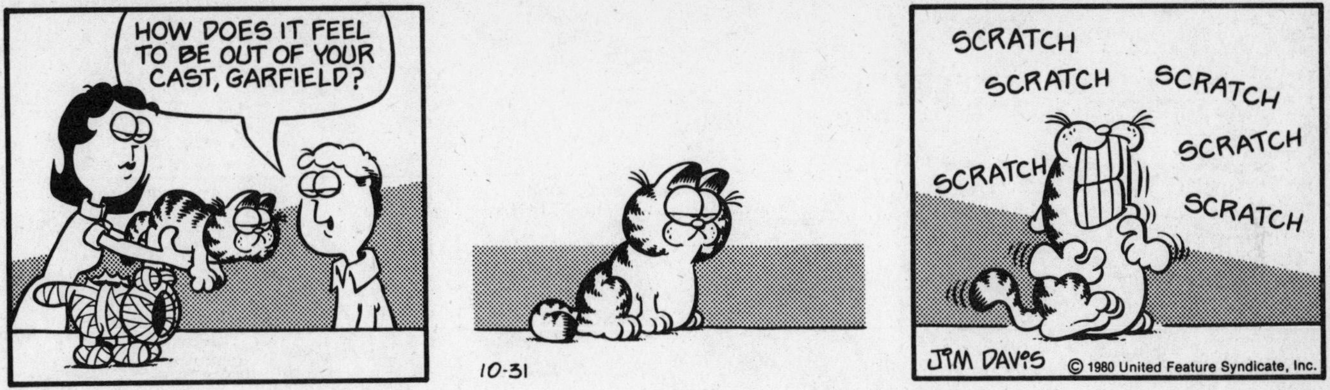
HOW DOES IT FEEL TO BE OUT OF YOUR CAST, GARFIELD?
10-31
SCRATCH
SCRATCH
SCRATCH
SCRATCH
SCRATCH
SCRATCH
JIM DAVIS
© 1980 United Feature Syndicate, Inc.

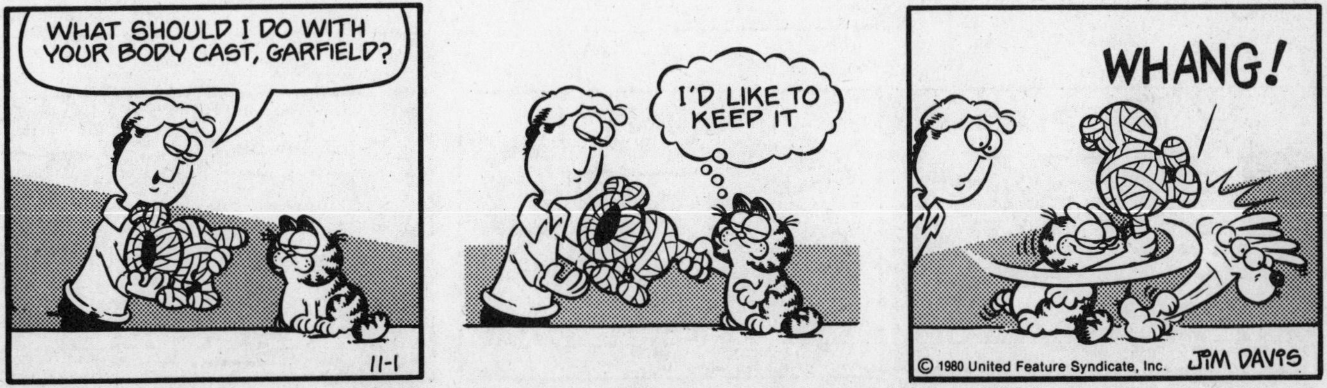
WHAT SHOULD I DO WITH YOUR BODY CAST, GARFIELD?
11-1
I'D LIKE TO KEEP IT
WHANG!
© 1980 United Feature Syndicate, Inc.
JIM DAVIS

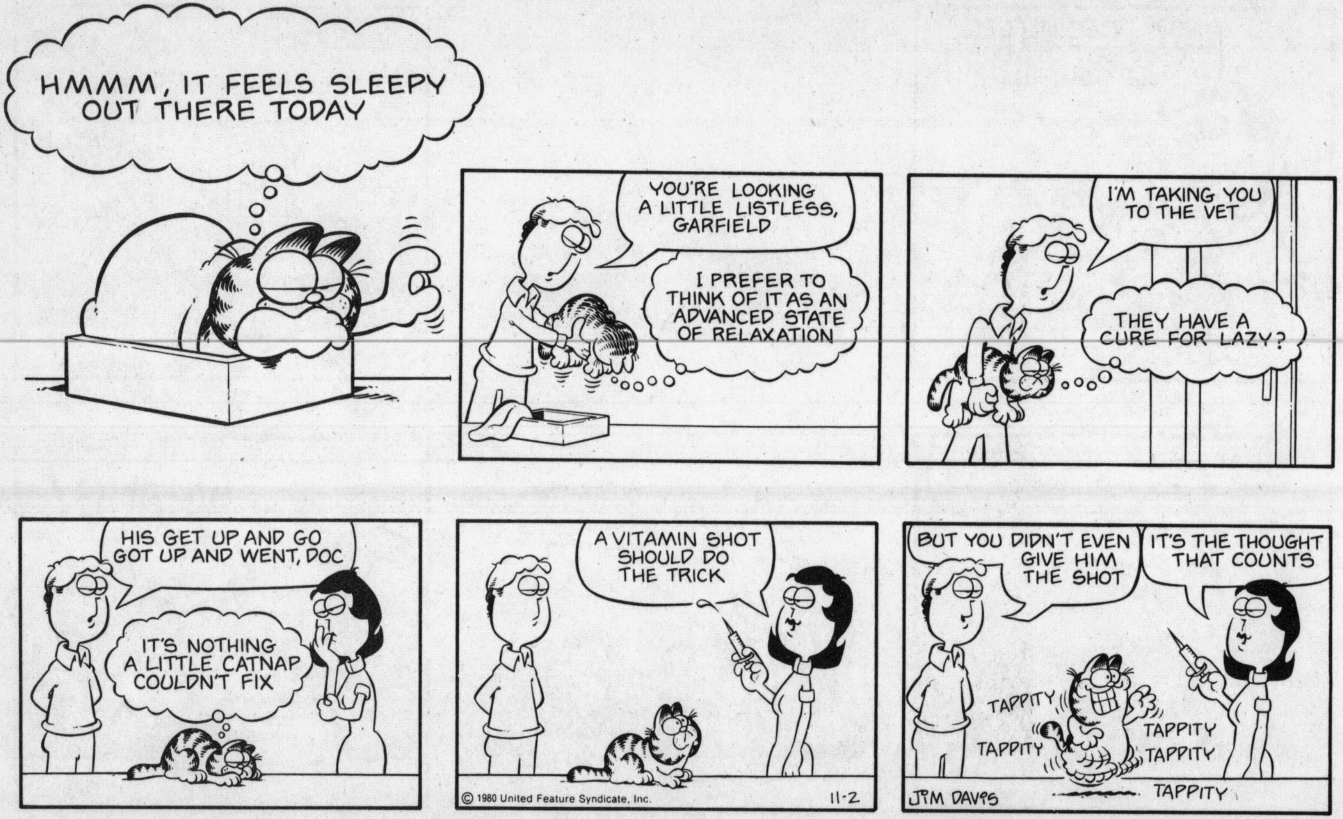
HMMM, IT FEELS SLEEPY OUT THERE TODAY
YOU'RE LOOKING A LITTLE LISTLESS, GARFIELD
I PREFER TO THINK OF IT AS AN ADVANCED STATE OF RELAXATION
I'M TAKING YOU TO THE VET
THEY HAVE A CURE FOR LAZY?
HIS GET UP AND GO GOT UP AND WENT, DOC
IT'S NOTHING A LITTLE CATNAP COULDN'T FIX
A VITAMIN SHOT SHOULD DO THE TRICK
© 1980 United Feature Syndicate, Inc.
11-2
BUT YOU DIDN'T EVEN GIVE HIM THE SHOT
IT'S THE THOUGHT THAT COUNTS
TAPPITY
TAPPITY
TAPPITY
TAPPITY
TAPPITY
JIM DAVIS

About Jim Davis, creator of GARFIELD

Jim Davis was born July 28, 1945, in Marion, Indiana. After growing up on a farm near Fairmount, Indiana, with about 25 cats, Jim attended Ball State University in Muncie. As an Art and Business major he distinguished himself by earning one of the lowest accumulative grade point averages in the history of the university.

During a two-year stint at a local advertising agency Jim met and married wife, Carolyn, a gifted singer and elementary school teacher.

In 1969 he became the assistant to Tom Ryan on the syndicated comic strip, TUMBLEWEEDS. In addition to cartooning, Jim maintained a career as a freelance commercial artist, copywriter, and radio-talent and political-campaign promoter.

His hobbies include chess, sandwiches, and good friends. A new pastime is playing with his two-year-old son, James Alexander.

In 1978 United Feature Syndicate gave the nod to GARFIELD.

Jim explains, "GARFIELD is strictly an entertainment strip built around the strong personality of a fat, lazy, cynical cat. It's the funniest strip I've ever seen. GARFIELD consciously avoids any social or political comment. My grasp of the world situation isn't that firm anyway. For years, I thought OPEC was a denture adhesive."

The strip is pumped out daily, in a cheerful atmosphere among friends. Valette Hildebrand is assistant cartoonist, Brian Strater is art director for merchandising, Neil Altekruse is production director, Jill Hahn is office manager, and Julie Hamilton is president of Paws, Incorporated, the company that handles the merchandising of the characters in the strip.

"To what do I attribute my cartooning ability?" Jim asks. "As a child I was asthmatic. I was stuck indoors with little more than my imagination and paper and pencil to play with. While asthma worked for me, I wouldn't recommend it for everyone.

"Do I like cartooning?...It's nice work if you can get it."

Garfield takes the cake

BY: JIM DAVIS

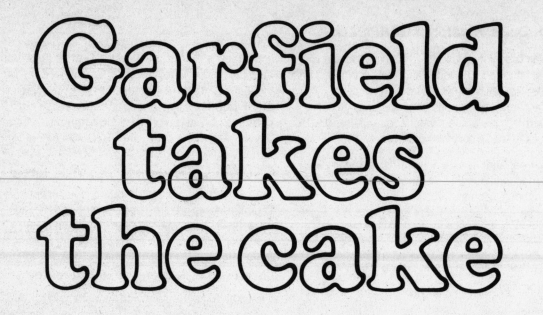

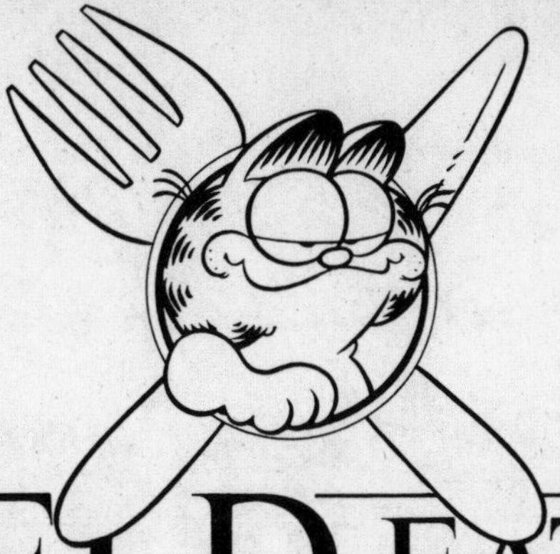

GARFIELD EATING TIPS

1. Never eat anything that's on fire.

2. Never leave your food dish under a bird cage.

3. Only play in your food if you've already eaten your toys.

4. Eat every meal as though it were your last.

5. Only snack between meals.

6. Chew your food at least once.

7. Avoid fruits and nuts: after all, you are what you eat.

8. Always dress up your leftovers: one clever way is with top hats and canes.

9. A handy breakfast tip: always check your Grape Nuts for squirrels.

10. Don't save your dessert for last. Eat it first.

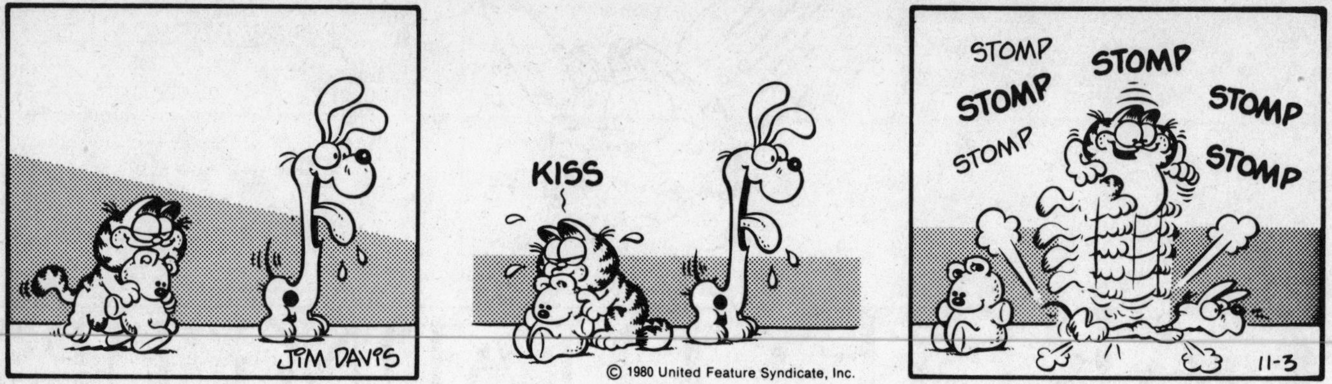
JIM DAVIS
KISS
© 1980 United Feature Syndicate, Inc.
STOMP
STOMP
STOMP
STOMP
STOMP
STOMP
11-3

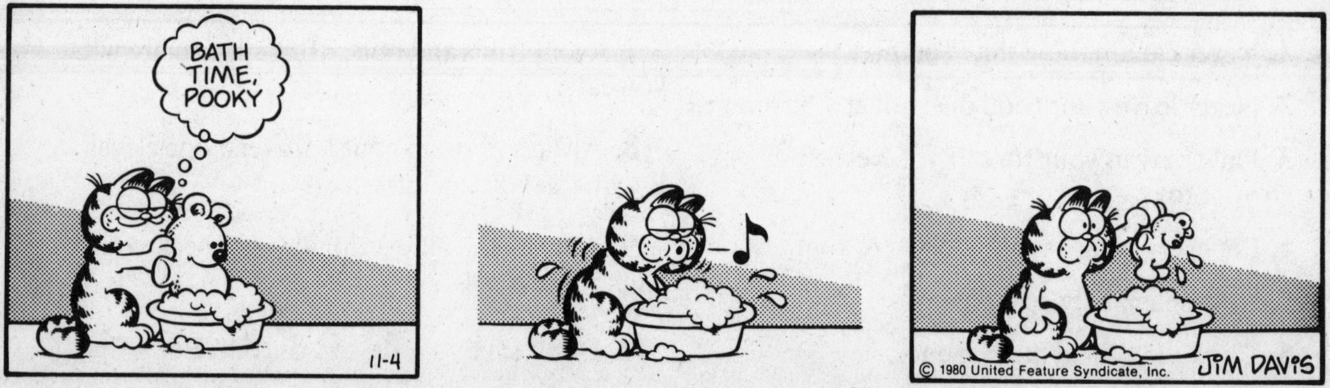
BATH TIME, POOKY
11-4
© 1980 United Feature Syndicate, Inc.
JIM DAVIS

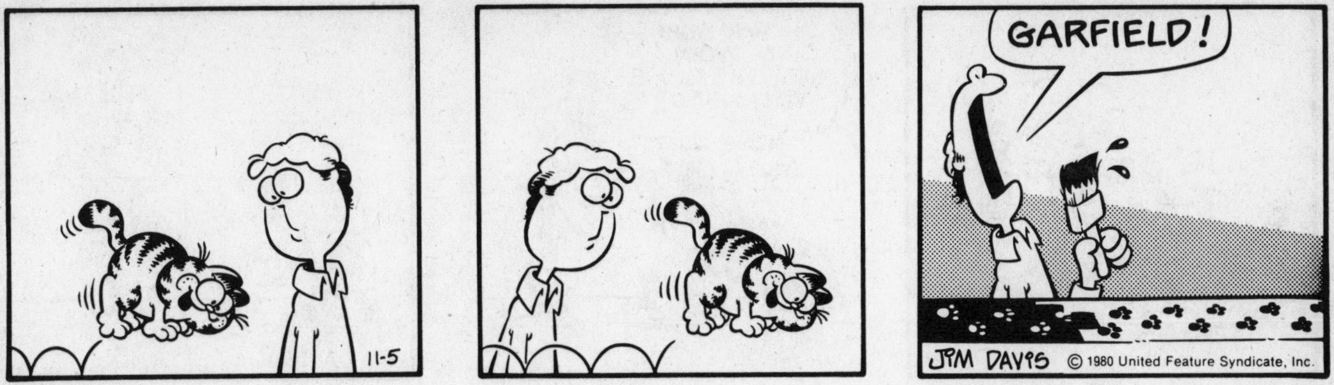
11-5
GARFIELD!
JIM DAVIS
© 1980 United Feature Syndicate, Inc.

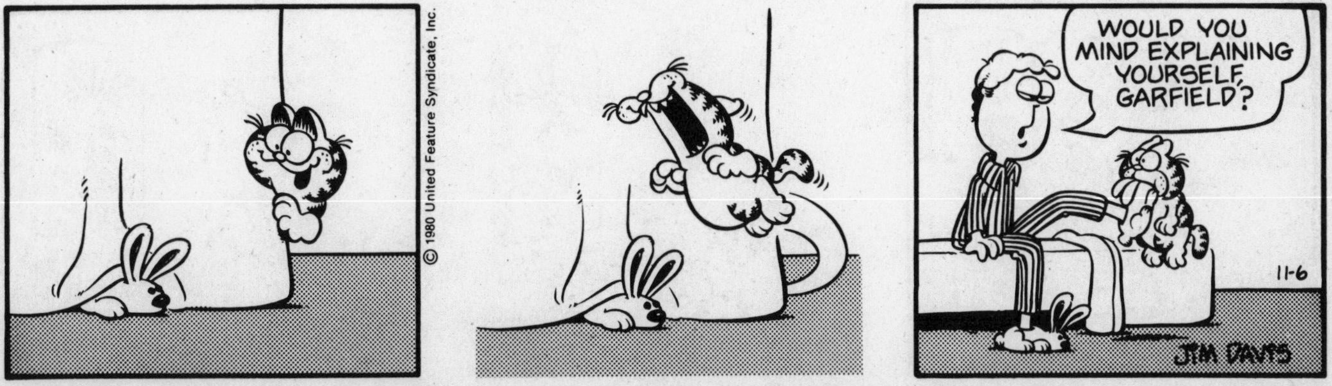
© 1980 United Feature Syndicate, Inc.
WOULD YOU MIND EXPLAINING YOURSELF, GARFIELD?
11-6
JIM DAVIS

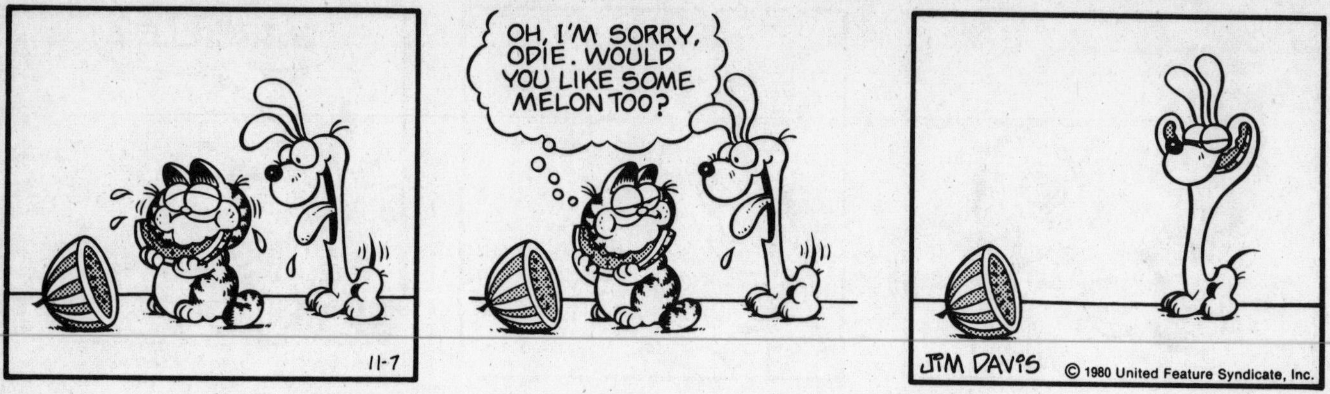
OH, I'M SORRY, ODIE. WOULD YOU LIKE SOME MELON TOO?
11-7
JIM DAVIS
© 1980 United Feature Syndicate, Inc.

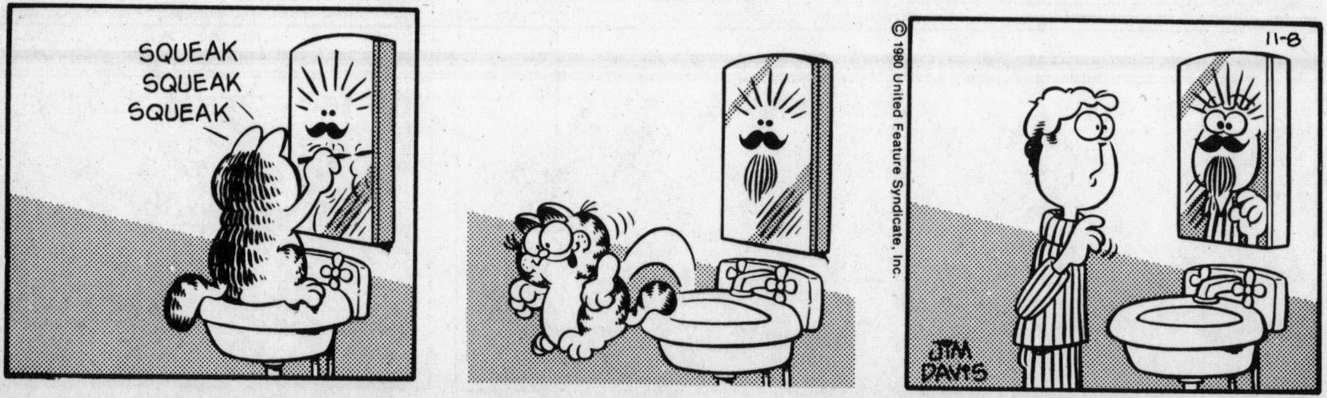
SQUEAK
SQUEAK
SQUEAK
© 1980 United Feature Syndicate, Inc.
11-8
JIM DAVIS

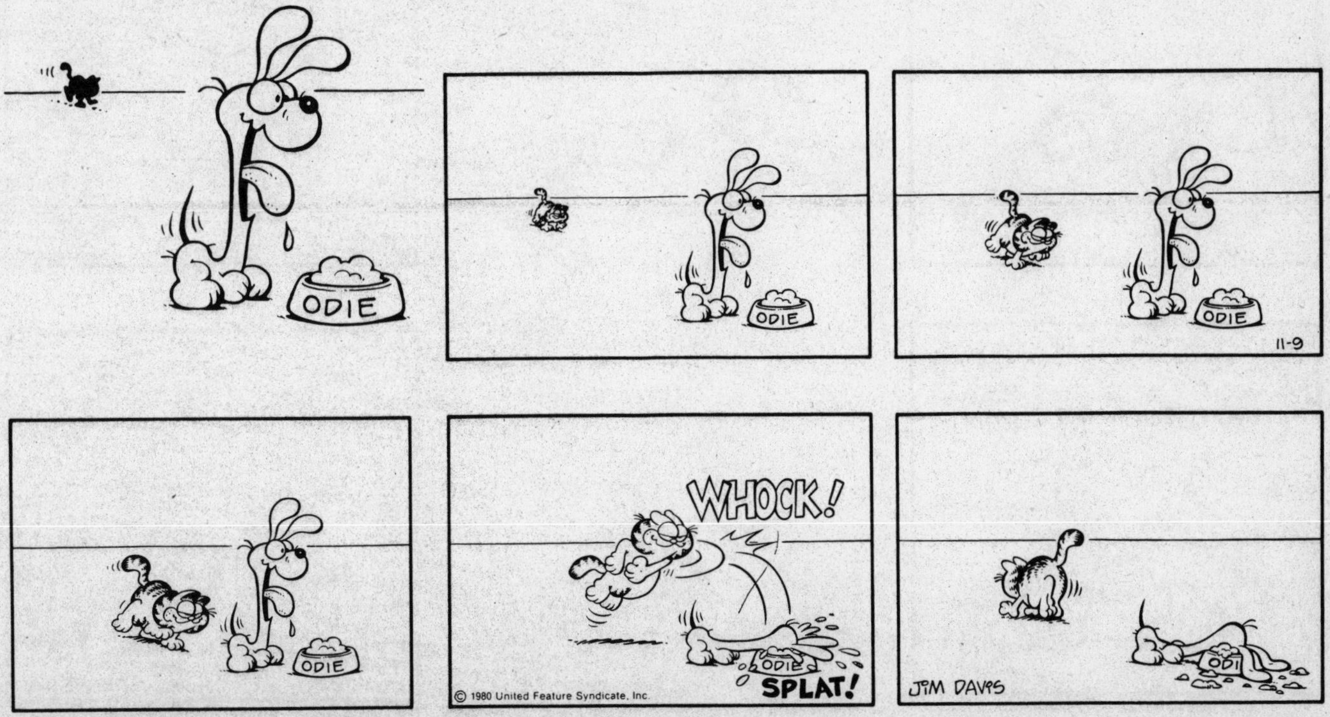

ODIE
ODIE
ODIE
11-9
ODIE
WHOCK!
ODIE
SPLAT!
© 1980 United Feature Syndicate, Inc.
ODI
JIM DAVIS

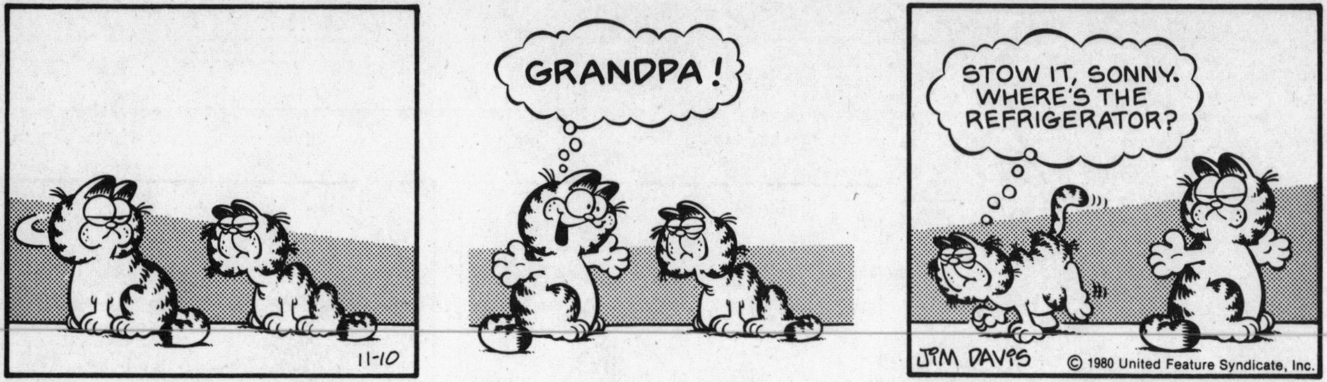
GRANDPA!
STOW IT, SONNY. WHERE'S THE REFRIGERATOR?
11-10
JIM DAVIS
© 1980 United Feature Syndicate, Inc.

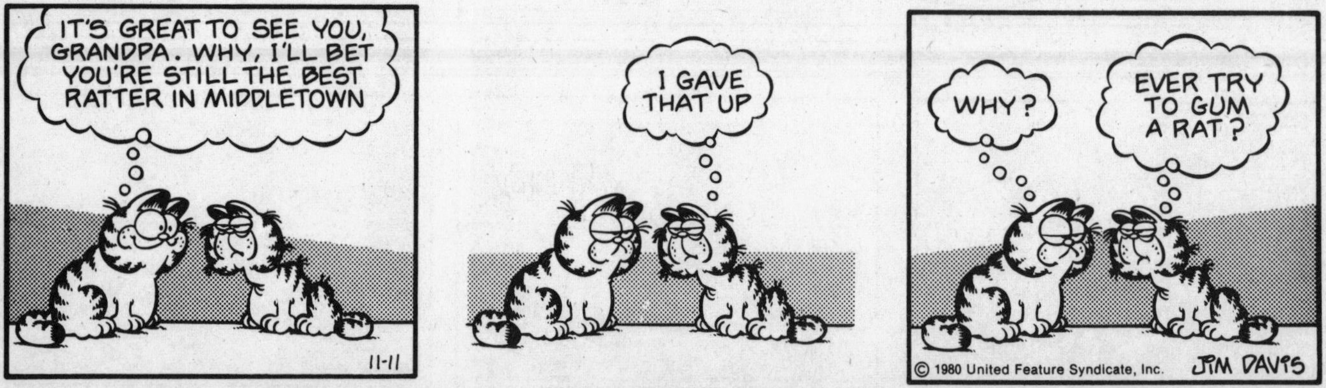
IT'S GREAT TO SEE YOU, GRANDPA. WHY, I'LL BET YOU'RE STILL THE BEST RATTER IN MIDDLETOWN
11-11
I GAVE THAT UP
WHY?
EVER TRY TO GUM A RAT?
© 1980 United Feature Syndicate, Inc.
JIM DAVIS

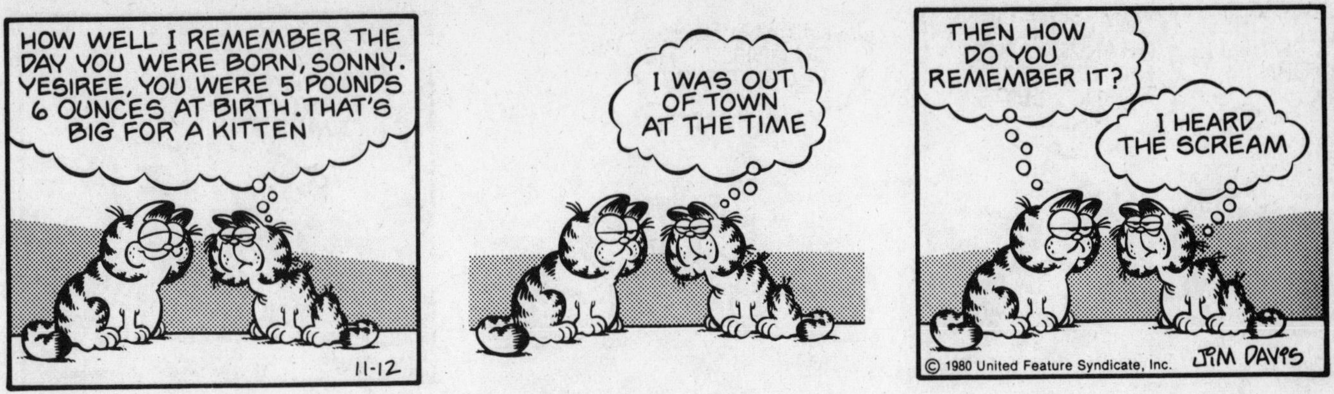
HOW WELL I REMEMBER THE DAY YOU WERE BORN, SONNY. YESIREE, YOU WERE 5 POUNDS 6 OUNCES AT BIRTH. THAT'S BIG FOR A KITTEN
11-12
I WAS OUT OF TOWN AT THE TIME
THEN HOW DO YOU REMEMBER IT?
I HEARD THE SCREAM
© 1980 United Feature Syndicate, Inc.
JIM DAVIS

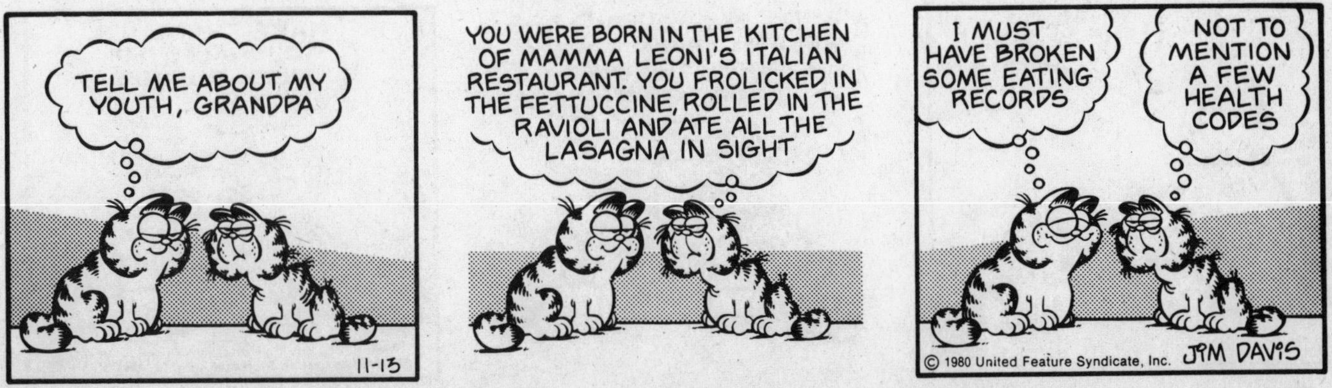
TELL ME ABOUT MY YOUTH, GRANDPA
11-13
YOU WERE BORN IN THE KITCHEN OF MAMMA LEONI'S ITALIAN RESTAURANT. YOU FROLICKED IN THE FETTUCCINE, ROLLED IN THE RAVIOLI AND ATE ALL THE LASAGNA IN SIGHT
I MUST HAVE BROKEN SOME EATING RECORDS
NOT TO MENTION A FEW HEALTH CODES
© 1980 United Feature Syndicate, Inc.
JIM DAVIS

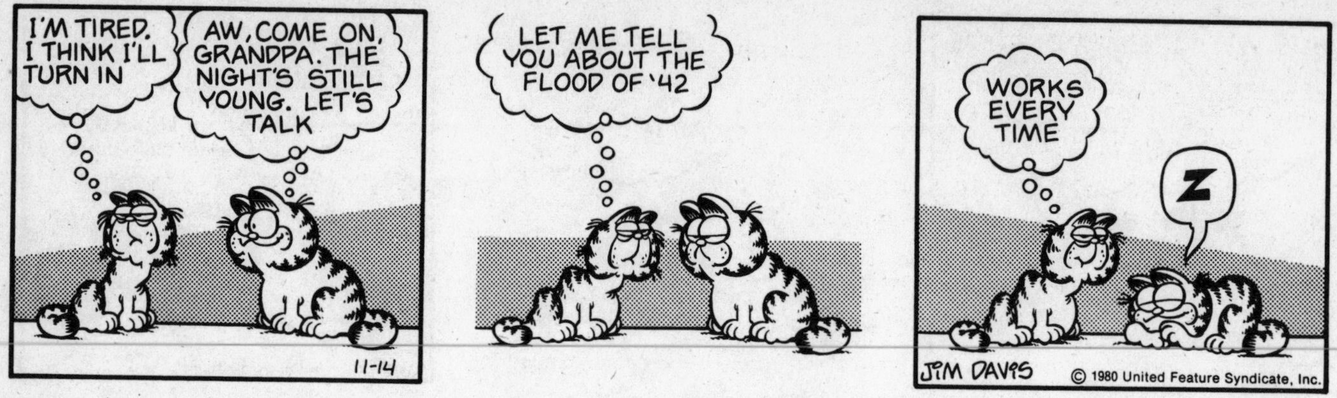
I'M TIRED. I THINK I'LL TURN IN
AW, COME ON, GRANDPA. THE NIGHT'S STILL YOUNG. LET'S TALK
11-14
LET ME TELL YOU ABOUT THE FLOOD OF '42
WORKS EVERY TIME
Z
JIM DAVIS
© 1980 United Feature Syndicate, Inc.

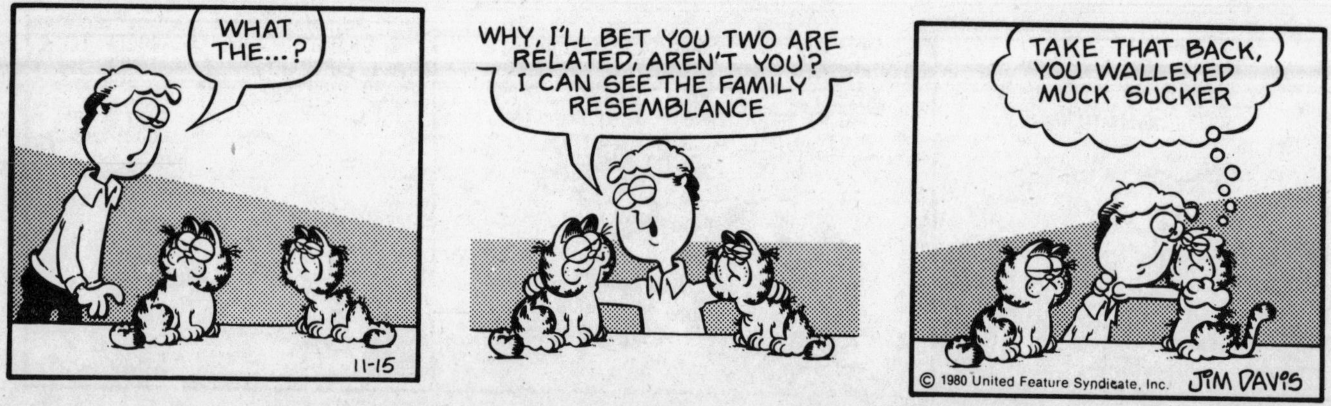
WHAT THE...?
11-15
WHY, I'LL BET YOU TWO ARE RELATED, AREN'T YOU? I CAN SEE THE FAMILY RESEMBLANCE
TAKE THAT BACK, YOU WALLEYED MUCK SUCKER
© 1980 United Feature Syndicate, Inc.
JIM DAVIS

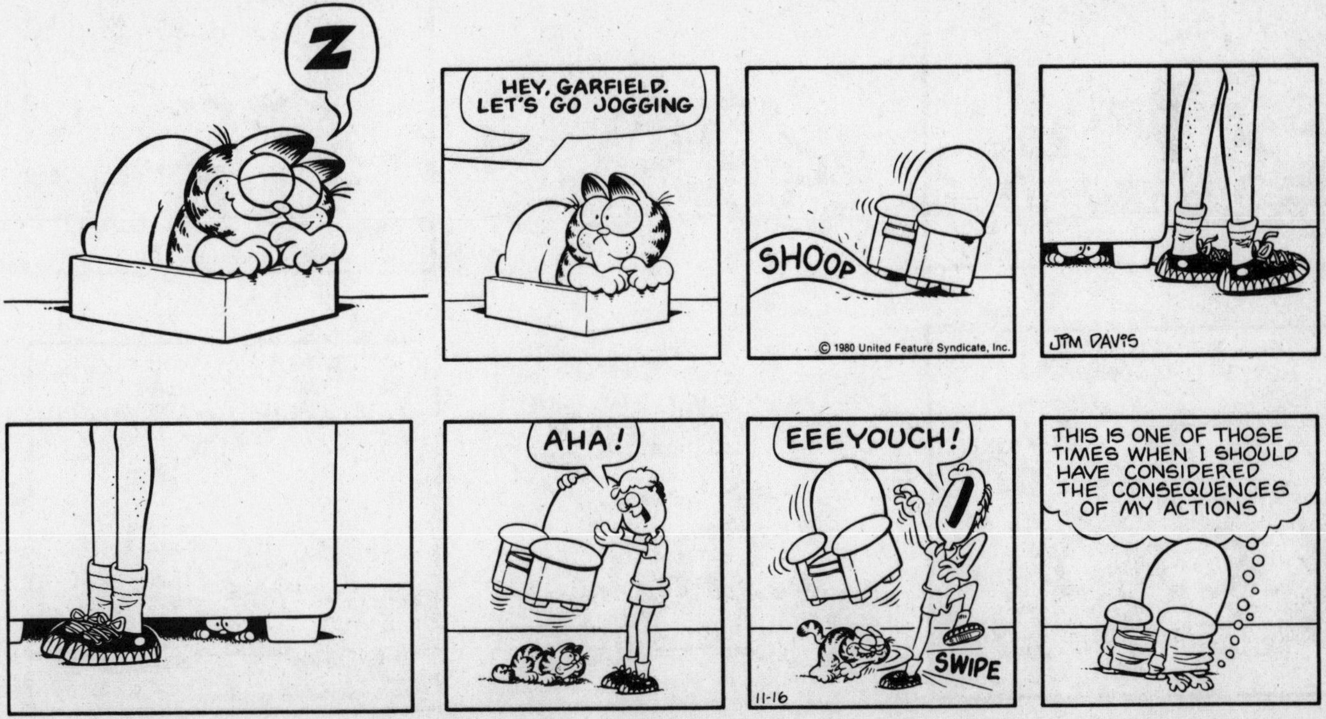
Z
HEY, GARFIELD. LET'S GO JOGGING
SHOOP
© 1980 United Feature Syndicate, Inc.
JIM DAVIS
AHA!
EEEYOUCH!
SWIPE
11-16
THIS IS ONE OF THOSE TIMES WHEN I SHOULD HAVE CONSIDERED THE CONSEQUENCES OF MY ACTIONS

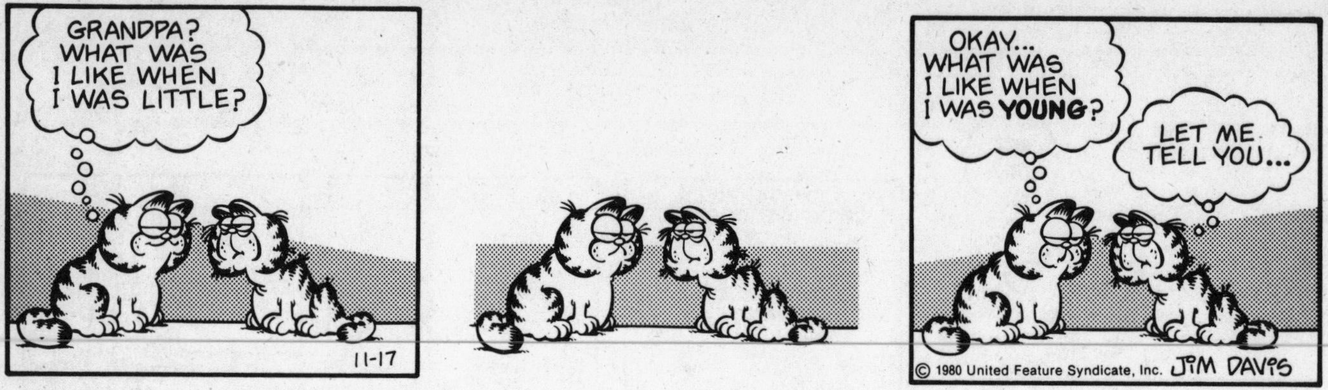
GRANDPA? WHAT WAS I LIKE WHEN I WAS LITTLE?
11-17
OKAY... WHAT WAS I LIKE WHEN I WAS YOUNG?
LET ME TELL YOU...
© 1980 United Feature Syndicate, Inc.
JIM DAVIS

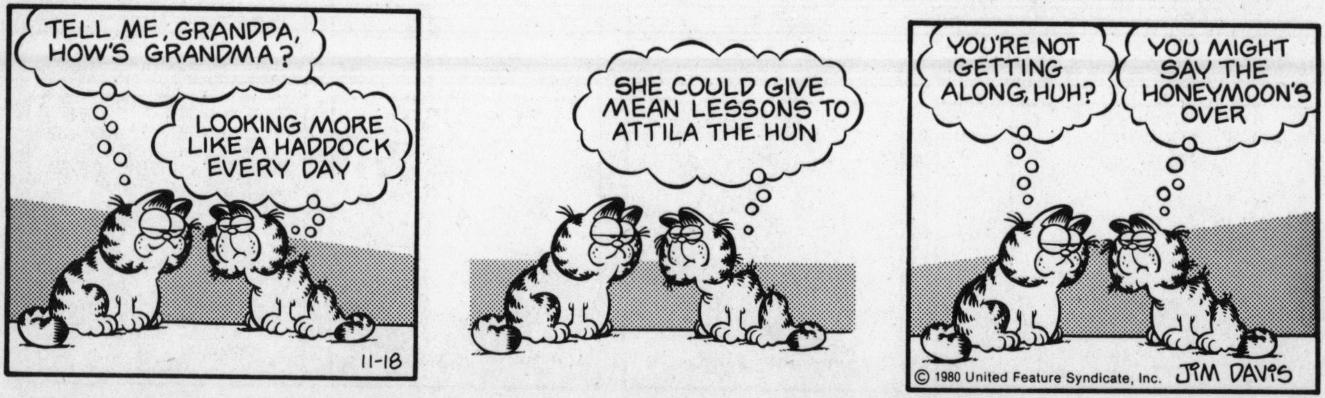
TELL ME, GRANDPA, HOW'S GRANDMA?
LOOKING MORE LIKE A HADDOCK EVERY DAY
11-18
SHE COULD GIVE MEAN LESSONS TO ATTILA THE HUN
YOU'RE NOT GETTING ALONG, HUH?
YOU MIGHT SAY THE HONEYMOON'S OVER
© 1980 United Feature Syndicate, Inc.
JIM DAVIS

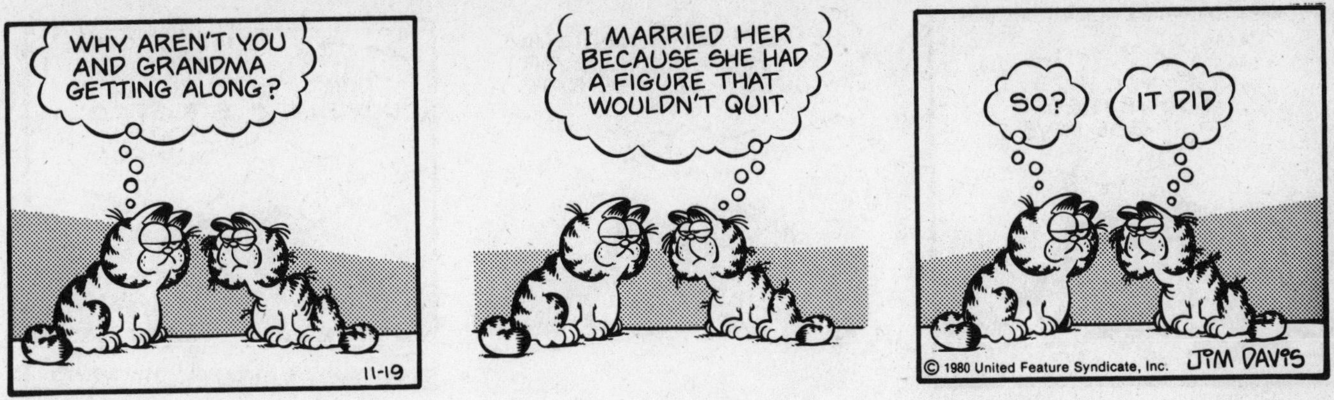
WHY AREN'T YOU AND GRANDMA GETTING ALONG?
11-19
I MARRIED HER BECAUSE SHE HAD A FIGURE THAT WOULDN'T QUIT
SO?
IT DID
© 1980 United Feature Syndicate, Inc.
JIM DAVIS

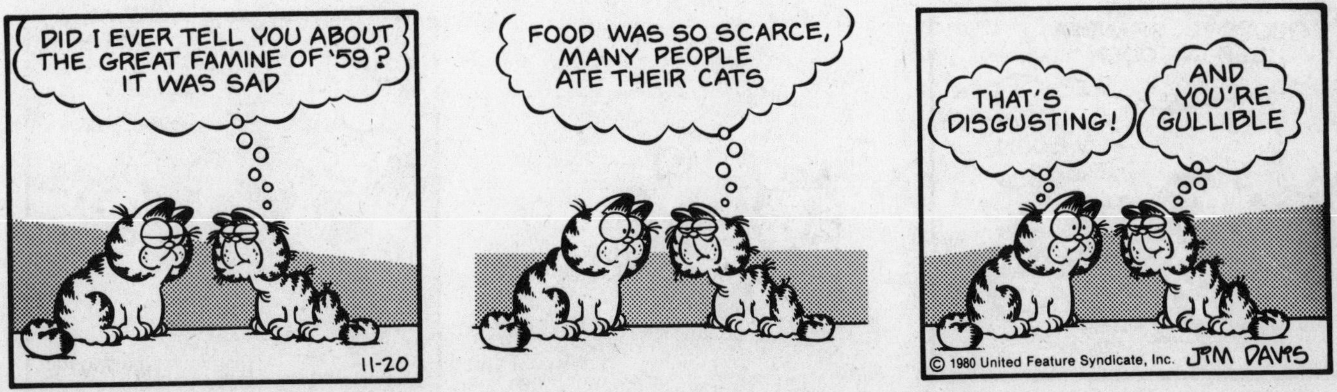
DID I EVER TELL YOU ABOUT THE GREAT FAMINE OF '59? IT WAS SAD
11-20
FOOD WAS SO SCARCE, MANY PEOPLE ATE THEIR CATS
THAT'S DISGUSTING!
AND YOU'RE GULLIBLE
© 1980 United Feature Syndicate, Inc.
JIM DAVIS

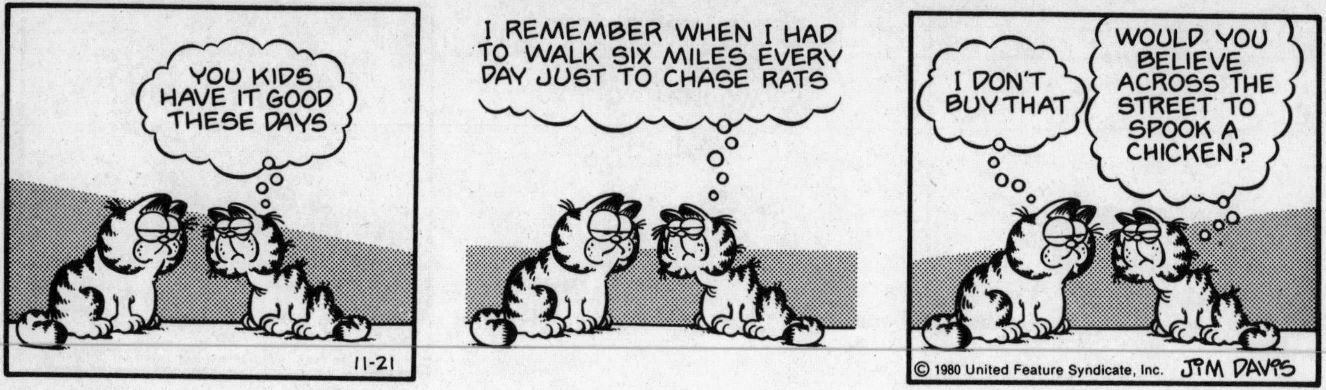
YOU KIDS HAVE IT GOOD THESE DAYS
I REMEMBER WHEN I HAD TO WALK SIX MILES EVERY DAY JUST TO CHASE RATS
I DON'T BUY THAT
WOULD YOU BELIEVE ACROSS THE STREET TO SPOOK A CHICKEN?
11-21
© 1980 United Feature Syndicate, Inc.
JIM DAVIS

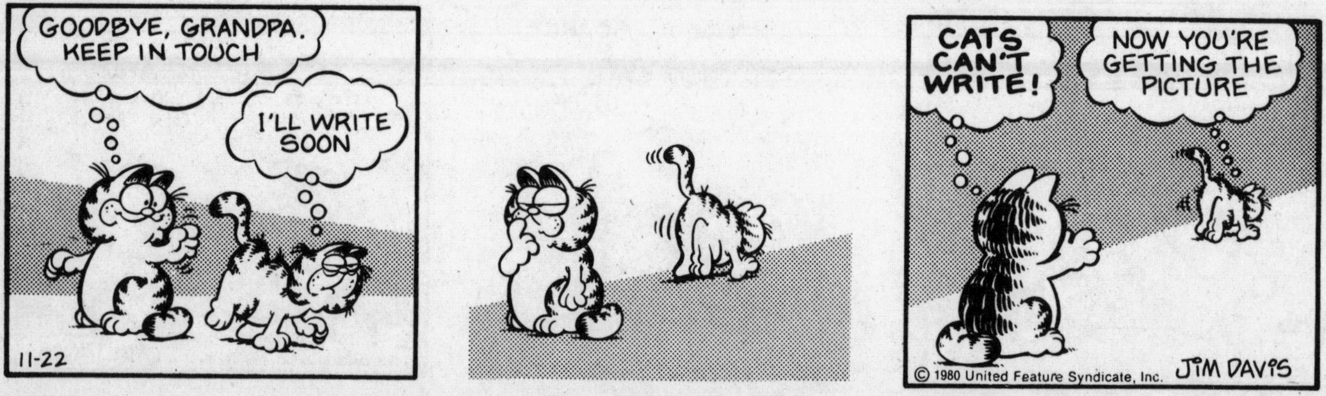
GOODBYE, GRANDPA. KEEP IN TOUCH
I'LL WRITE SOON
CATS CAN'T WRITE!
NOW YOU'RE GETTING THE PICTURE
11-22
© 1980 United Feature Syndicate, Inc.
JIM DAVIS

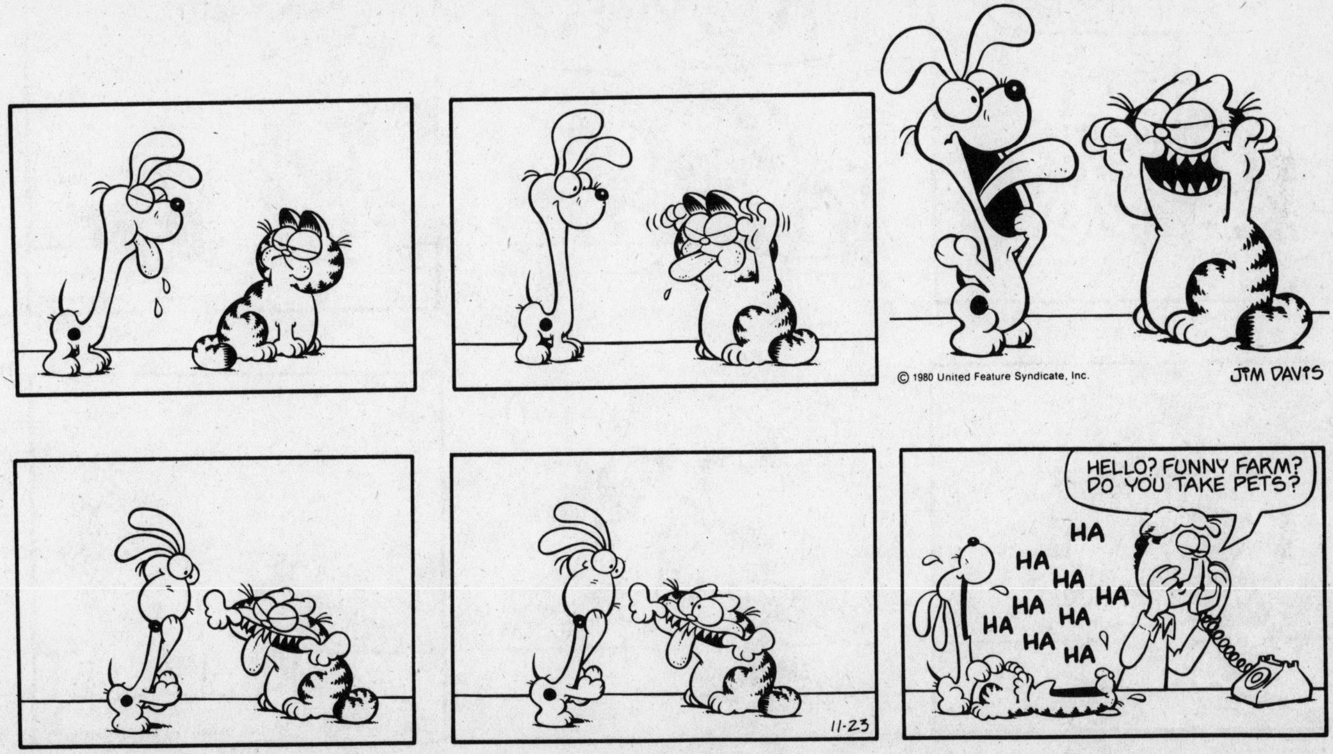

© 1980 United Feature Syndicate, Inc.
JIM DAVIS
11-23
HA HA HA HA HA HA HA HA HA HA
HELLO? FUNNY FARM? DO YOU TAKE PETS?

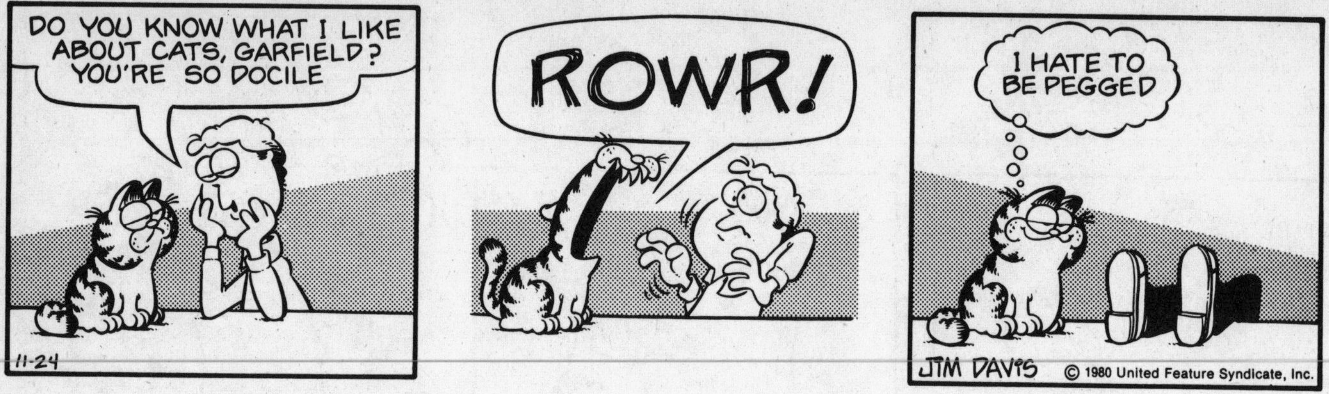
DO YOU KNOW WHAT I LIKE ABOUT CATS, GARFIELD? YOU'RE SO DOCILE
ROWR!
I HATE TO BE PEGGED
11-24
JIM DAVIS
© 1980 United Feature Syndicate, Inc.

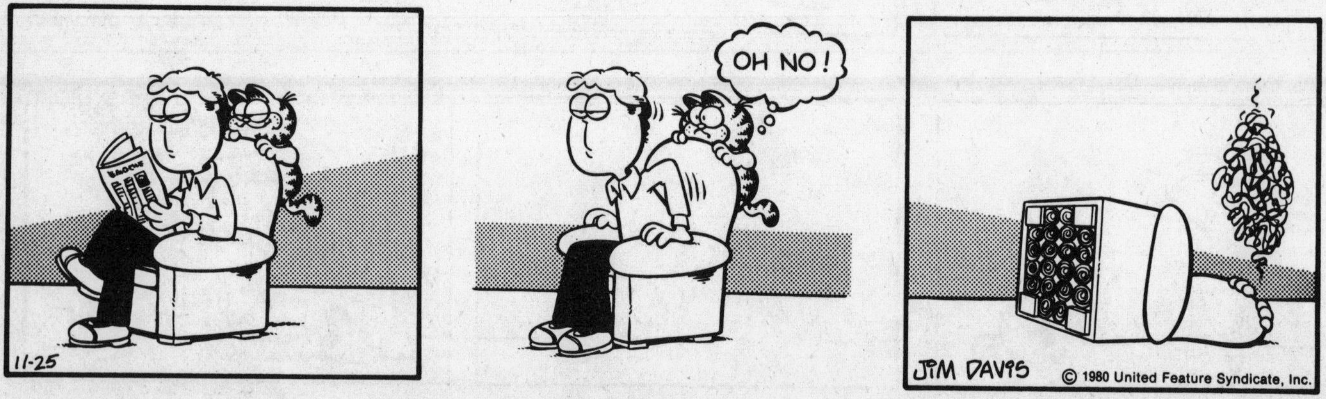
OH NO!
11-25
JIM DAVIS
© 1980 United Feature Syndicate, Inc.

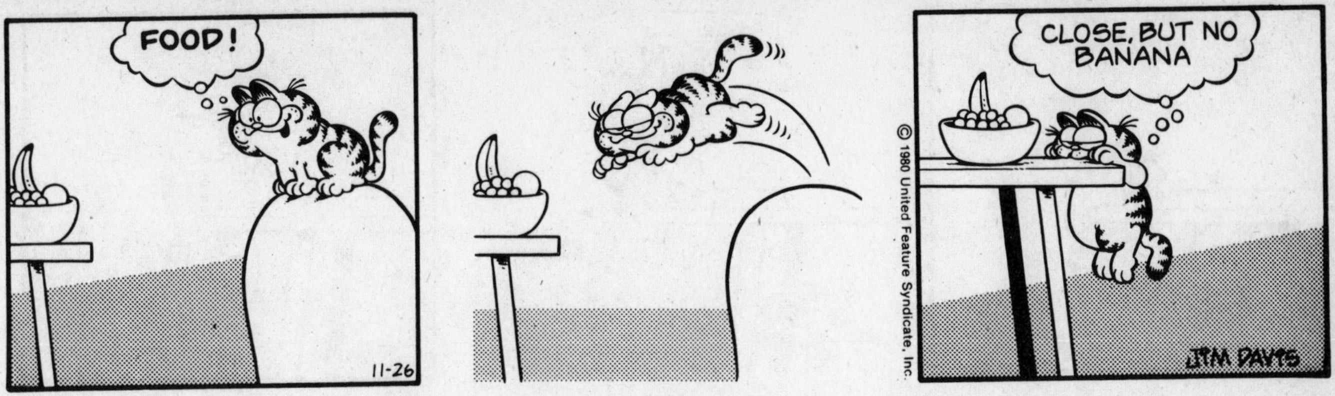
FOOD!
11-26
CLOSE, BUT NO BANANA
© 1980 United Feature Syndicate, Inc.
JIM DAVIS

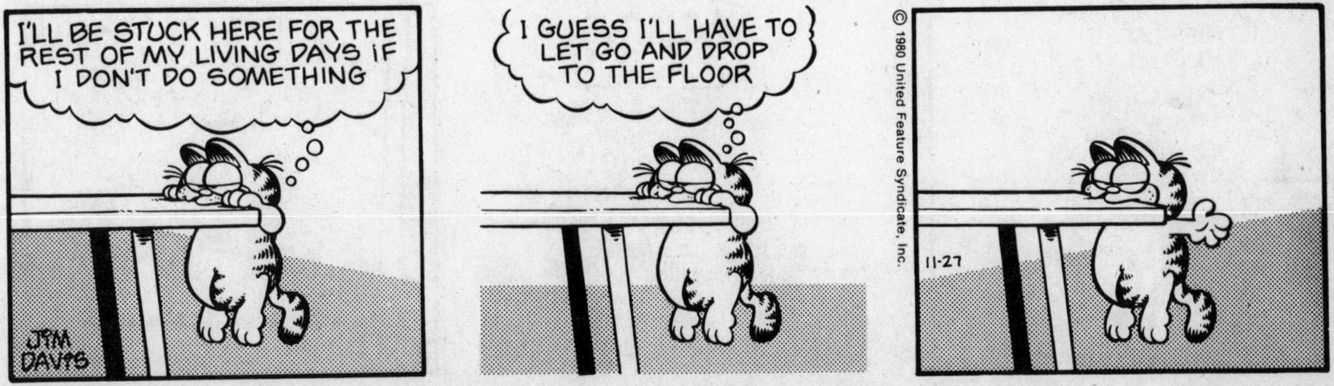
I'LL BE STUCK HERE FOR THE REST OF MY LIVING DAYS IF I DON'T DO SOMETHING
JIM DAVIS
I GUESS I'LL HAVE TO LET GO AND DROP TO THE FLOOR
© 1980 United Feature Syndicate, Inc.
11-27

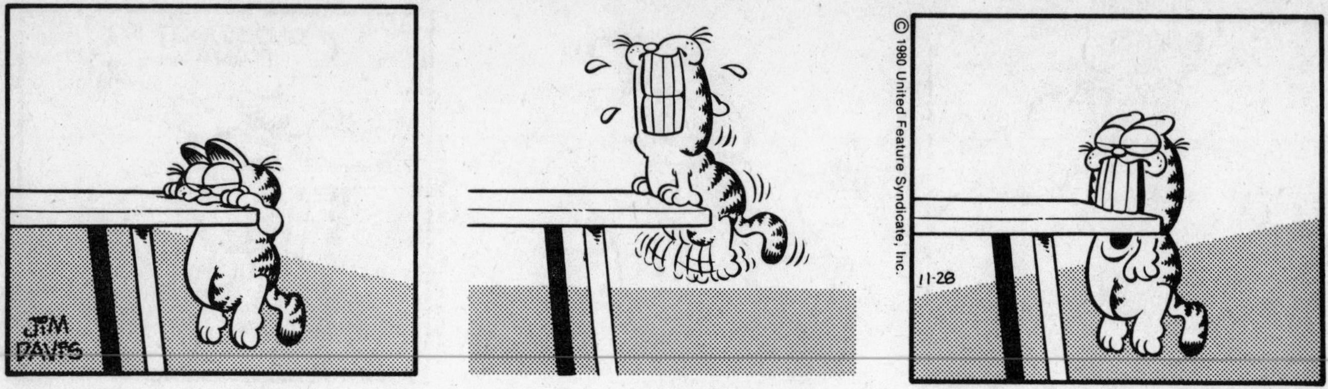
JIM DAVIS
© 1980 United Feature Syndicate, Inc.
11-28

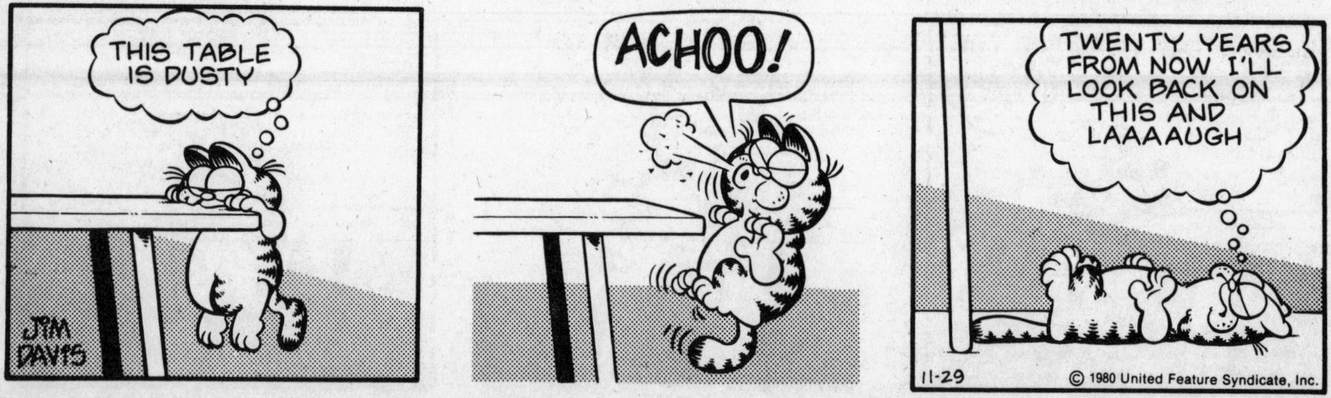
THIS TABLE IS DUSTY
JIM DAVIS
ACHOO!
TWENTY YEARS FROM NOW I'LL LOOK BACK ON THIS AND LAAAAUGH
11-29
© 1980 United Feature Syndicate, Inc.

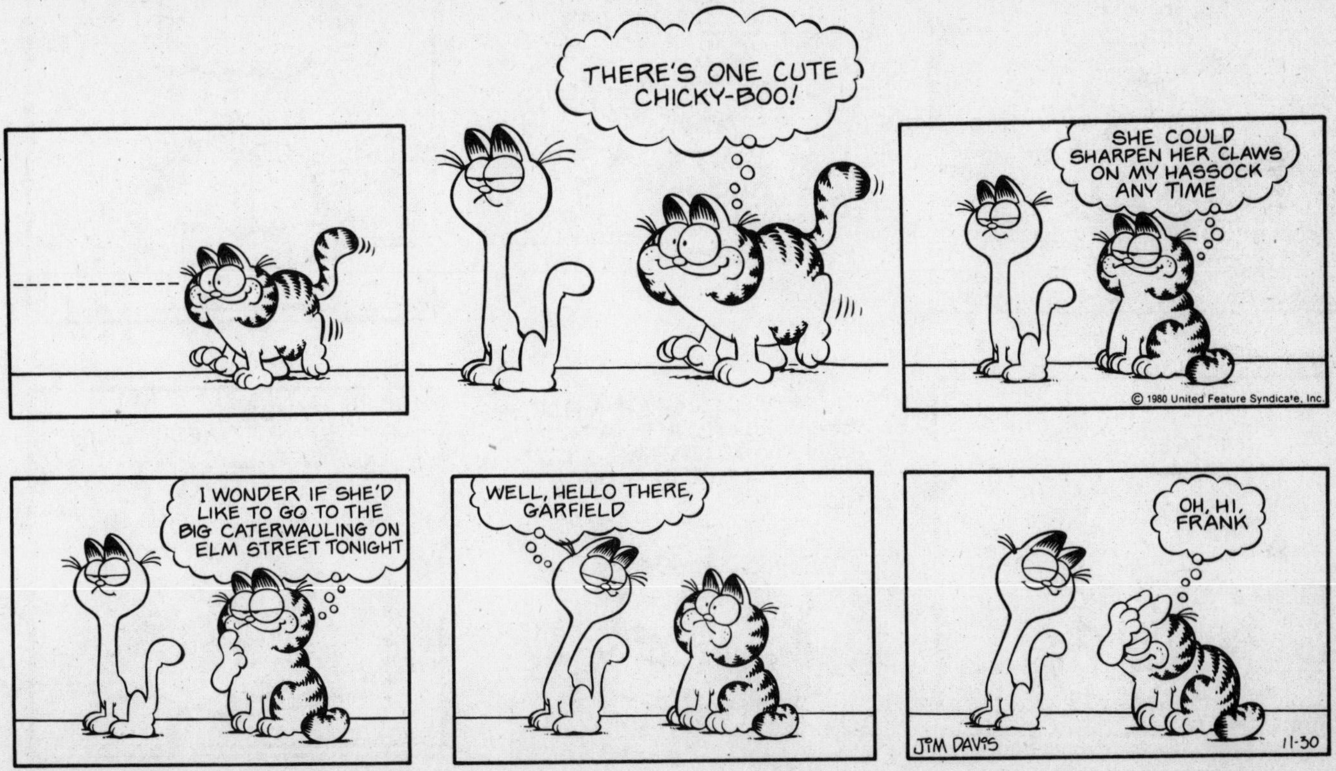
THERE'S ONE CUTE CHICKY-BOO!
SHE COULD SHARPEN HER CLAWS ON MY HASSOCK ANY TIME
© 1980 United Feature Syndicate, Inc.
I WONDER IF SHE'D LIKE TO GO TO THE BIG CATERWAULING ON ELM STREET TONIGHT
WELL, HELLO THERE, GARFIELD
OH, HI, FRANK
JIM DAVIS
11-30

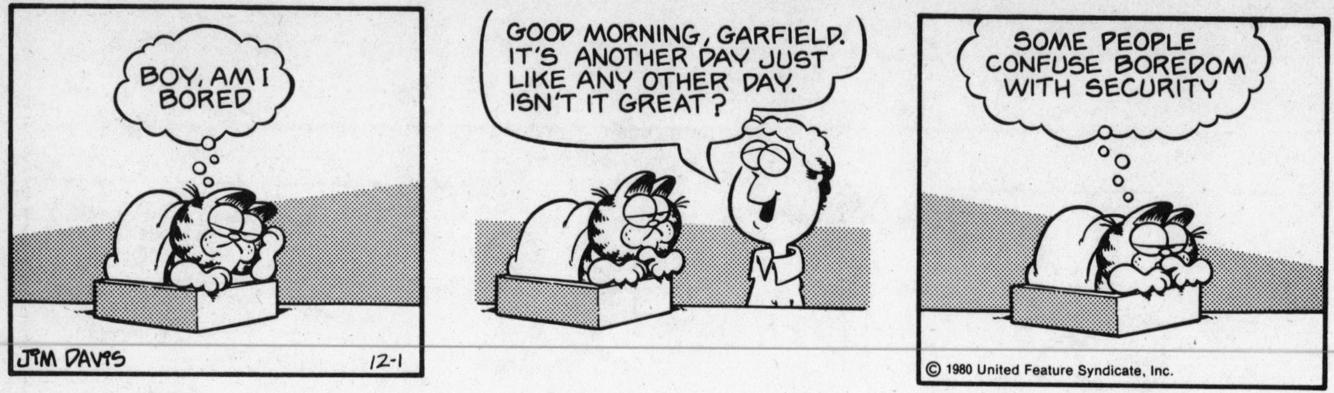
BOY, AM I BORED
GOOD MORNING, GARFIELD. IT'S ANOTHER DAY JUST LIKE ANY OTHER DAY. ISN'T IT GREAT?
SOME PEOPLE CONFUSE BOREDOM WITH SECURITY
JIM DAVIS
12-1
© 1980 United Feature Syndicate, Inc.

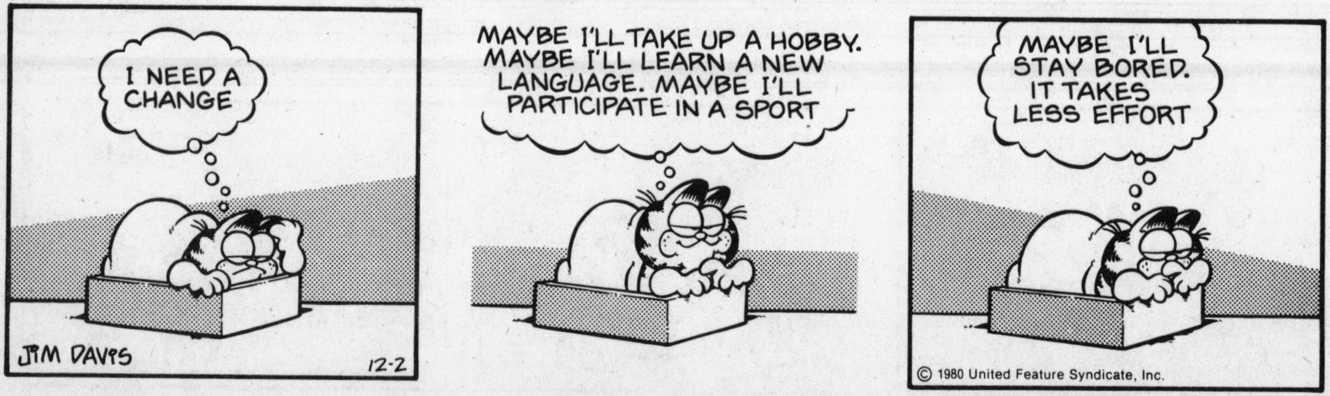
I NEED A CHANGE
MAYBE I'LL TAKE UP A HOBBY. MAYBE I'LL LEARN A NEW LANGUAGE. MAYBE I'LL PARTICIPATE IN A SPORT
MAYBE I'LL STAY BORED. IT TAKES LESS EFFORT
JIM DAVIS
12-2
© 1980 United Feature Syndicate, Inc.

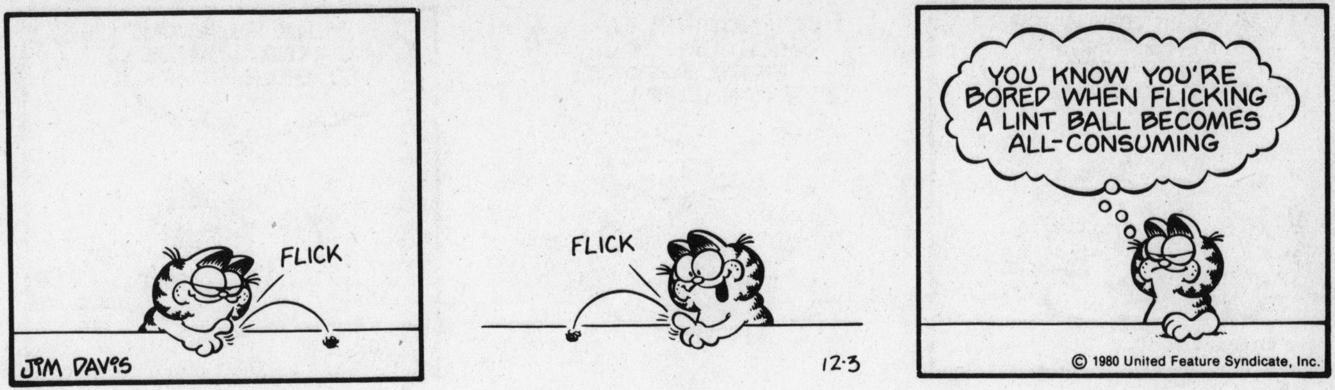
FLICK
JIM DAVIS
FLICK
12·3
YOU KNOW YOU'RE BORED WHEN FLICKING A LINT BALL BECOMES ALL-CONSUMING
© 1980 United Feature Syndicate, Inc.

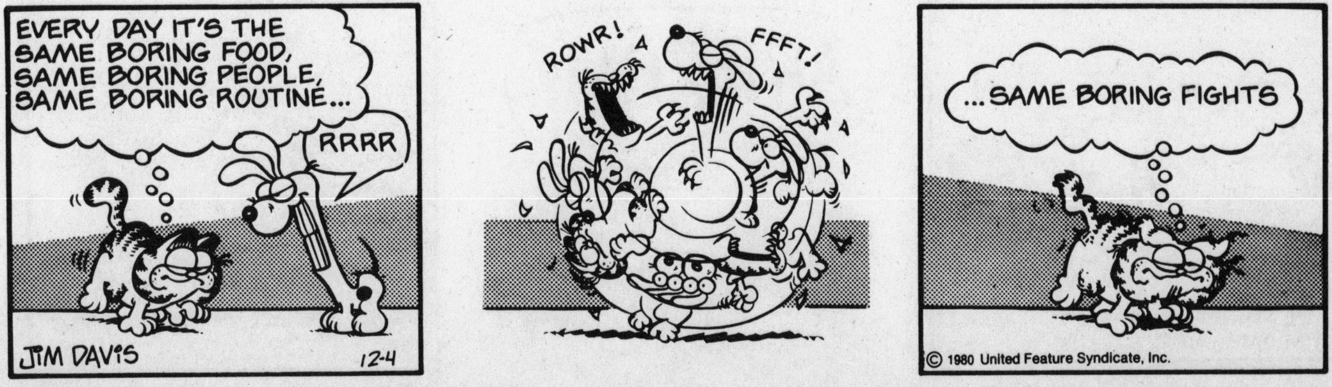
EVERY DAY IT'S THE SAME BORING FOOD, SAME BORING PEOPLE, SAME BORING ROUTINE...
RRRR
JIM DAVIS
12-4
ROWR!
FFFT!
...SAME BORING FIGHTS
© 1980 United Feature Syndicate, Inc.

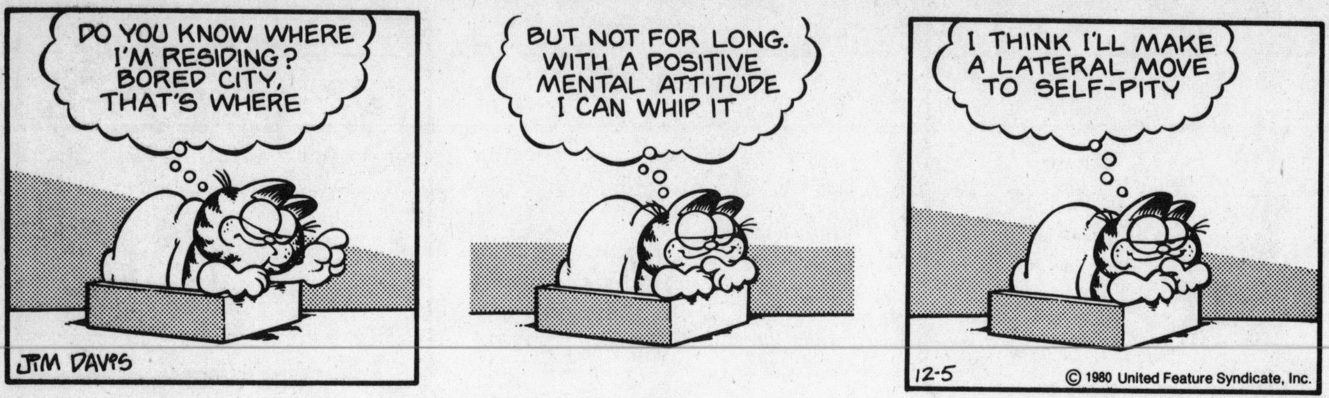
DO YOU KNOW WHERE I'M RESIDING? BORED CITY, THAT'S WHERE
JIM DAVIS
BUT NOT FOR LONG. WITH A POSITIVE MENTAL ATTITUDE I CAN WHIP IT
I THINK I'LL MAKE A LATERAL MOVE TO SELF-PITY
12-5
© 1980 United Feature Syndicate, Inc.

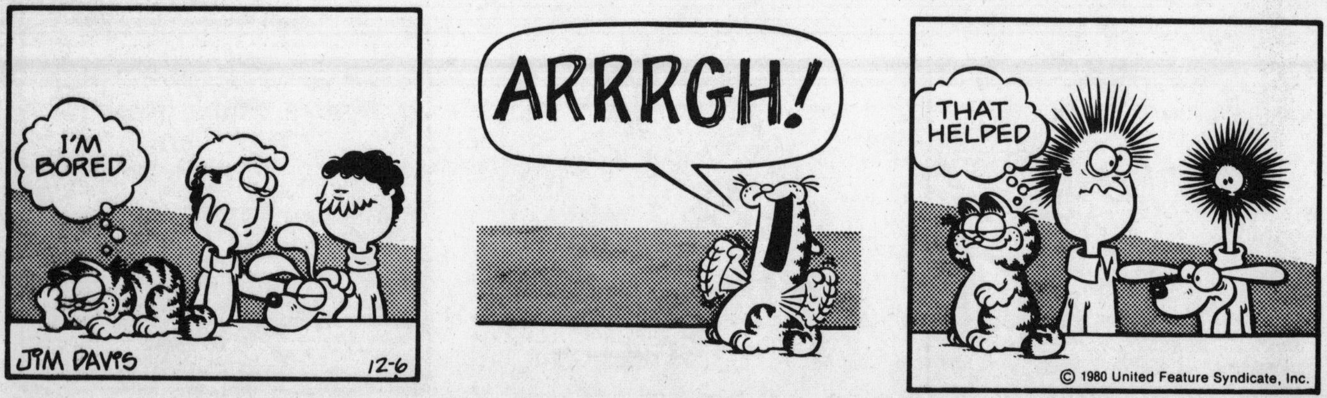
I'M BORED
JIM DAVIS
12-6
ARRRGH!
THAT HELPED
© 1980 United Feature Syndicate, Inc.

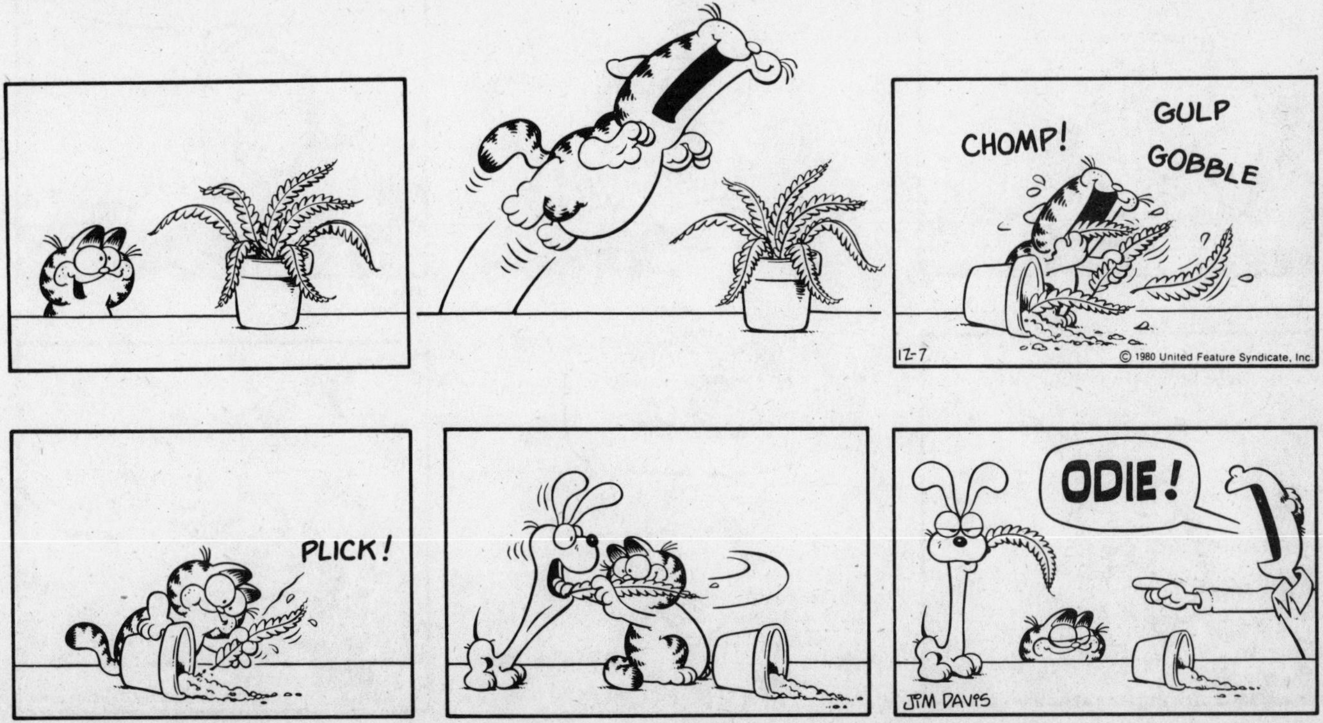
CHOMP!
GULP
GOBBLE
12-7
© 1980 United Feature Syndicate, Inc.
PLICK!
ODIE!
JIM DAVIS

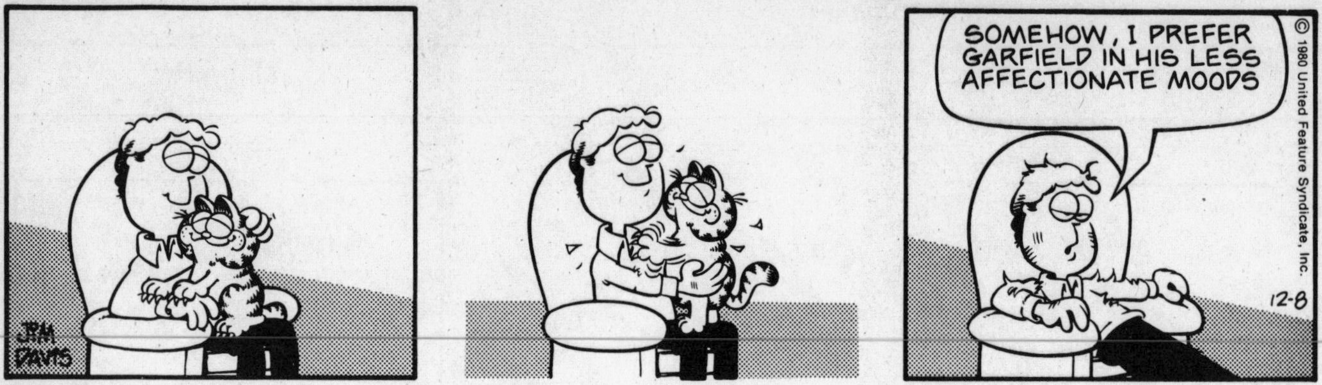
JIM DAVIS
SOMEHOW, I PREFER GARFIELD IN HIS LESS AFFECTIONATE MOODS
© 1980 United Feature Syndicate, Inc.
12-8

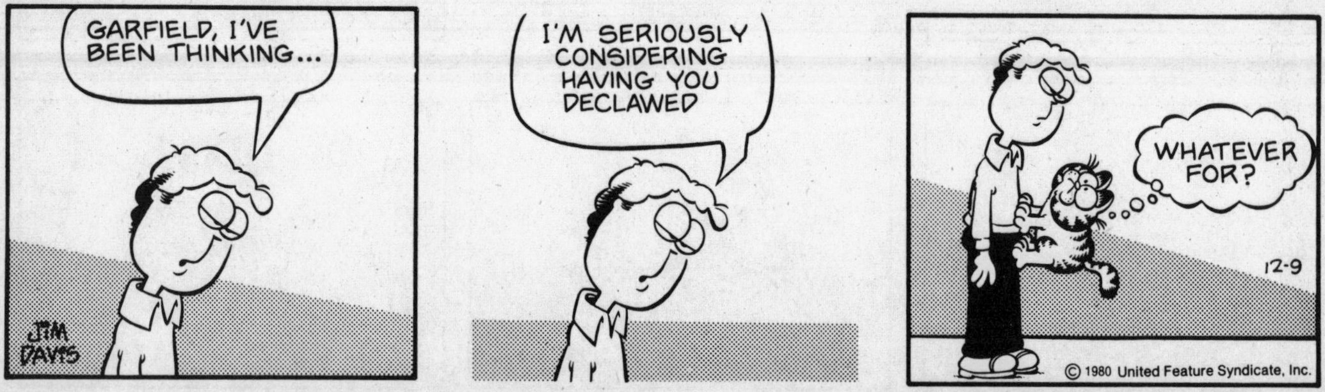
GARFIELD, I'VE BEEN THINKING...
JIM DAVIS
I'M SERIOUSLY CONSIDERING HAVING YOU DECLAWED
WHATEVER FOR?
12-9
© 1980 United Feature Syndicate, Inc.

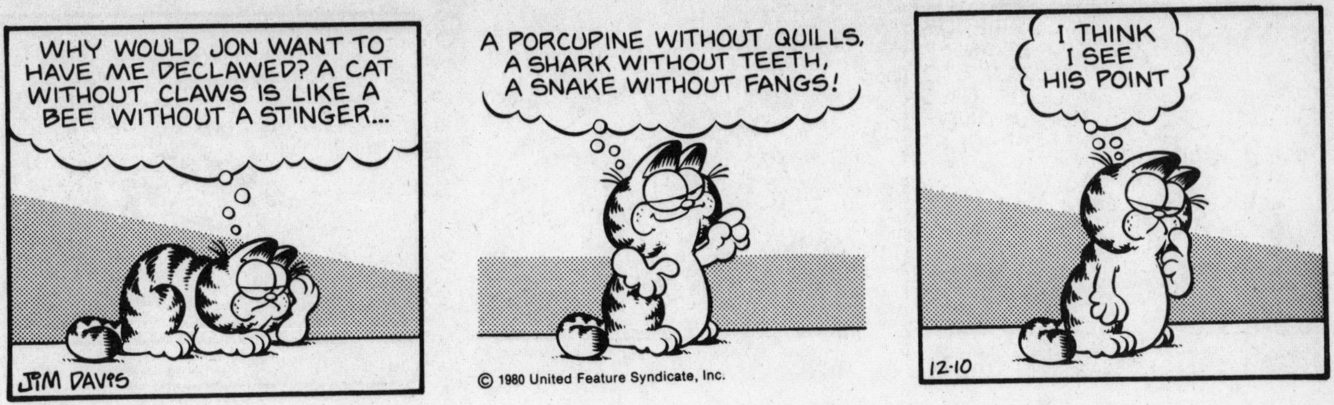
WHY WOULD JON WANT TO HAVE ME DECLAWED? A CAT WITHOUT CLAWS IS LIKE A BEE WITHOUT A STINGER...
JIM DAVIS
A PORCUPINE WITHOUT QUILLS, A SHARK WITHOUT TEETH, A SNAKE WITHOUT FANGS!
© 1980 United Feature Syndicate, Inc.
I THINK I SEE HIS POINT
12-10

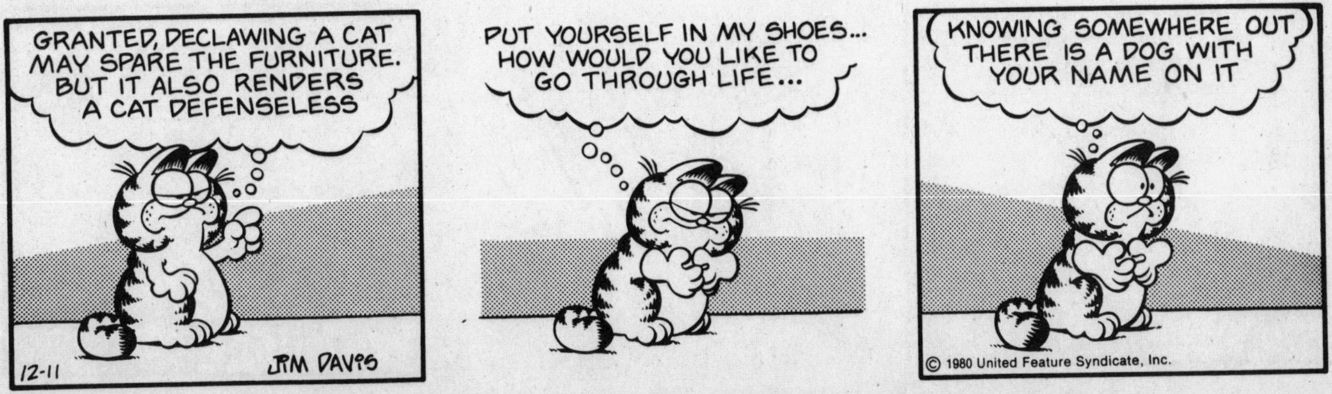
GRANTED, DECLAWING A CAT MAY SPARE THE FURNITURE. BUT IT ALSO RENDERS A CAT DEFENSELESS
12-11
JIM DAVIS
PUT YOURSELF IN MY SHOES... HOW WOULD YOU LIKE TO GO THROUGH LIFE...
KNOWING SOMEWHERE OUT THERE IS A DOG WITH YOUR NAME ON IT
© 1980 United Feature Syndicate, Inc.

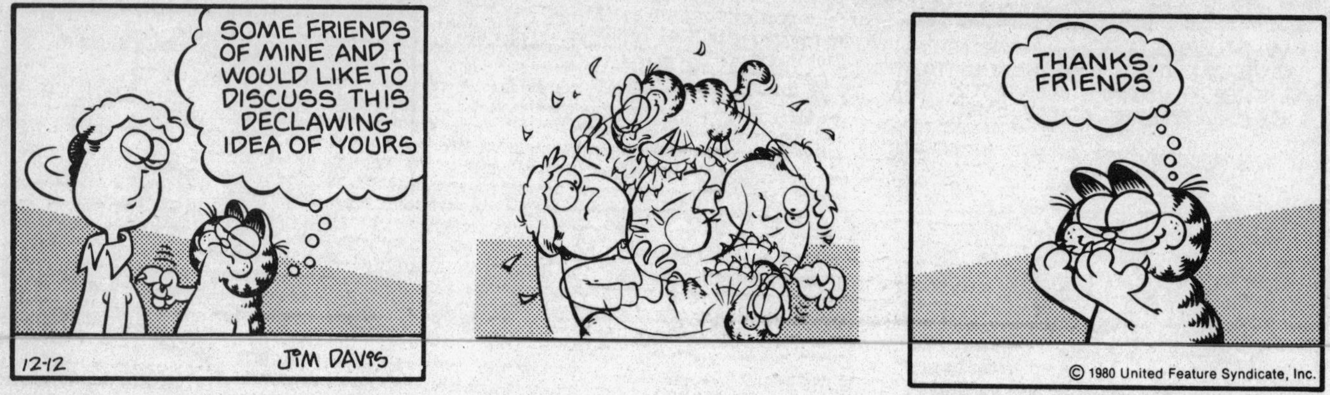
SOME FRIENDS OF MINE AND I WOULD LIKE TO DISCUSS THIS DECLAWING IDEA OF YOURS
12-12
JIM DAVIS
THANKS, FRIENDS
© 1980 United Feature Syndicate, Inc.

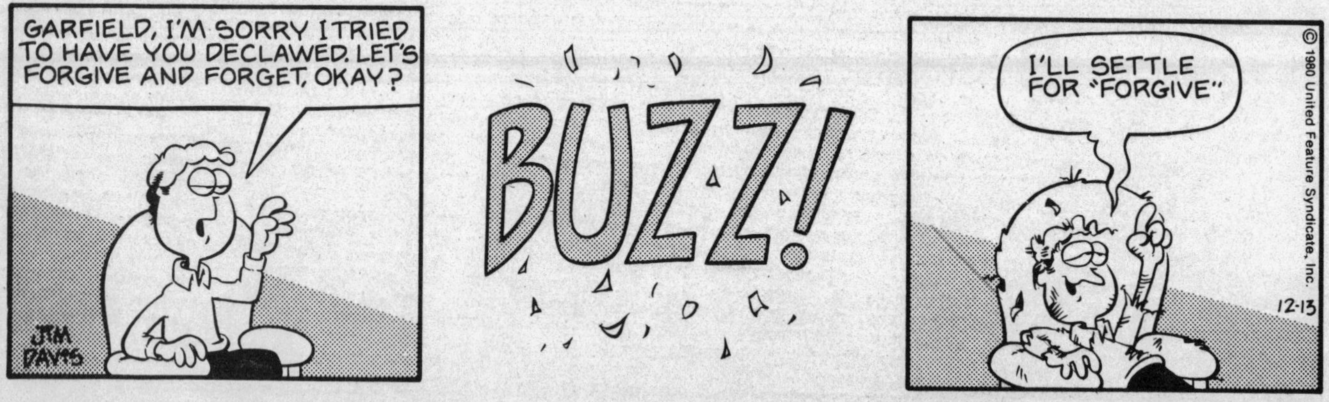
GARFIELD, I'M SORRY I TRIED TO HAVE YOU DECLAWED. LET'S FORGIVE AND FORGET, OKAY?
JIM DAVIS
BUZZ!
I'LL SETTLE FOR "FORGIVE"
© 1980 United Feature Syndicate, Inc.
12-13

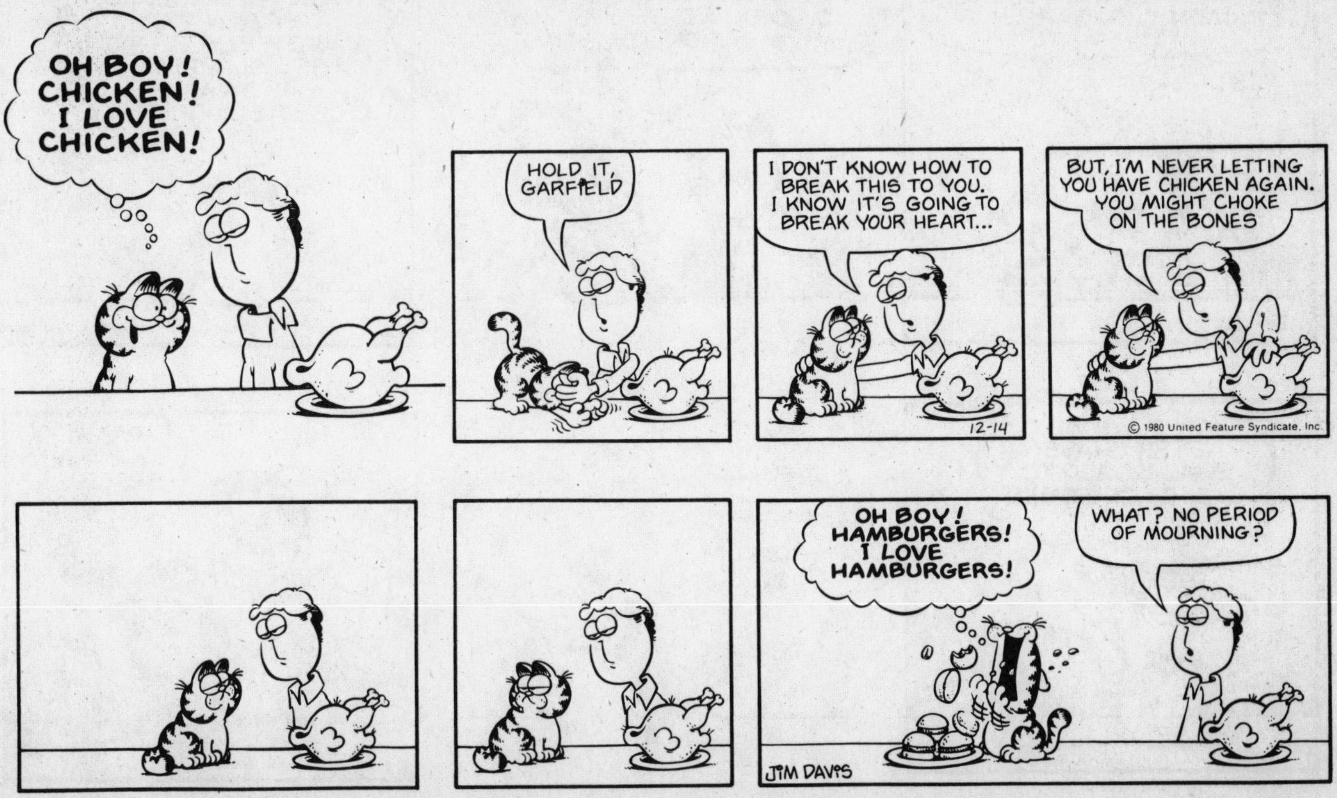
OH BOY! CHICKEN! I LOVE CHICKEN!
HOLD IT, GARFIELD
I DON'T KNOW HOW TO BREAK THIS TO YOU. I KNOW IT'S GOING TO BREAK YOUR HEART...
12-14
BUT, I'M NEVER LETTING YOU HAVE CHICKEN AGAIN. YOU MIGHT CHOKE ON THE BONES
© 1980 United Feature Syndicate, Inc.
OH BOY! HAMBURGERS! I LOVE HAMBURGERS!
WHAT? NO PERIOD OF MOURNING?
JIM DAVIS

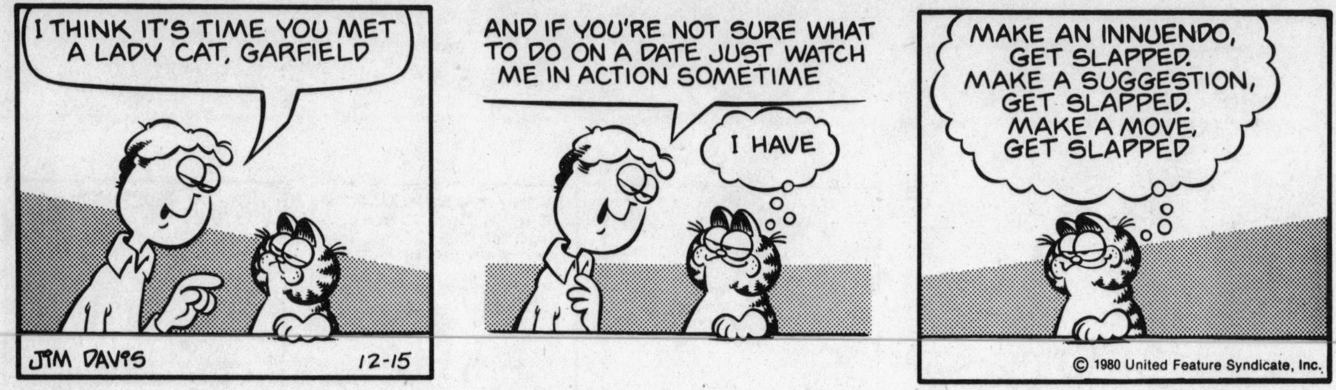
I THINK IT'S TIME YOU MET A LADY CAT, GARFIELD
JIM DAVIS
12-15
AND IF YOU'RE NOT SURE WHAT TO DO ON A DATE JUST WATCH ME IN ACTION SOMETIME
I HAVE
MAKE AN INNUENDO, GET SLAPPED. MAKE A SUGGESTION, GET SLAPPED. MAKE A MOVE, GET SLAPPED
© 1980 United Feature Syndicate, Inc.

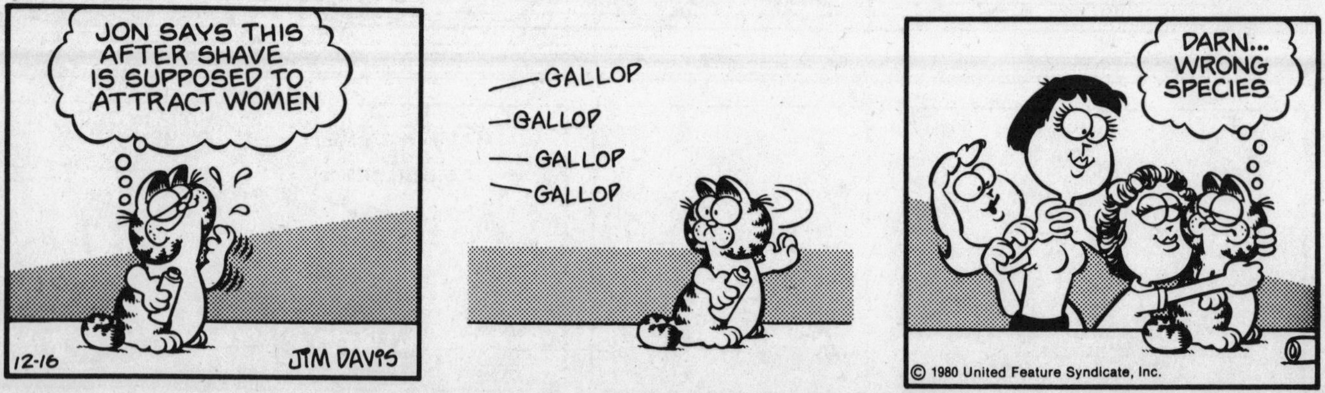
JON SAYS THIS AFTER SHAVE IS SUPPOSED TO ATTRACT WOMEN
12-16
JIM DAVIS
GALLOP
GALLOP
GALLOP
GALLOP
DARN... WRONG SPECIES
© 1980 United Feature Syndicate, Inc.

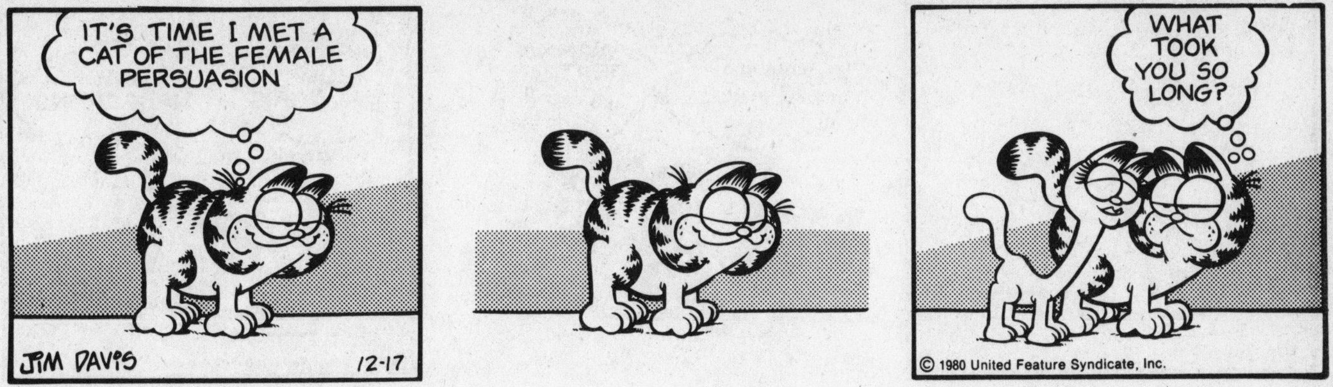
IT'S TIME I MET A CAT OF THE FEMALE PERSUASION
JIM DAVIS
12-17
WHAT TOOK YOU SO LONG?
© 1980 United Feature Syndicate, Inc.

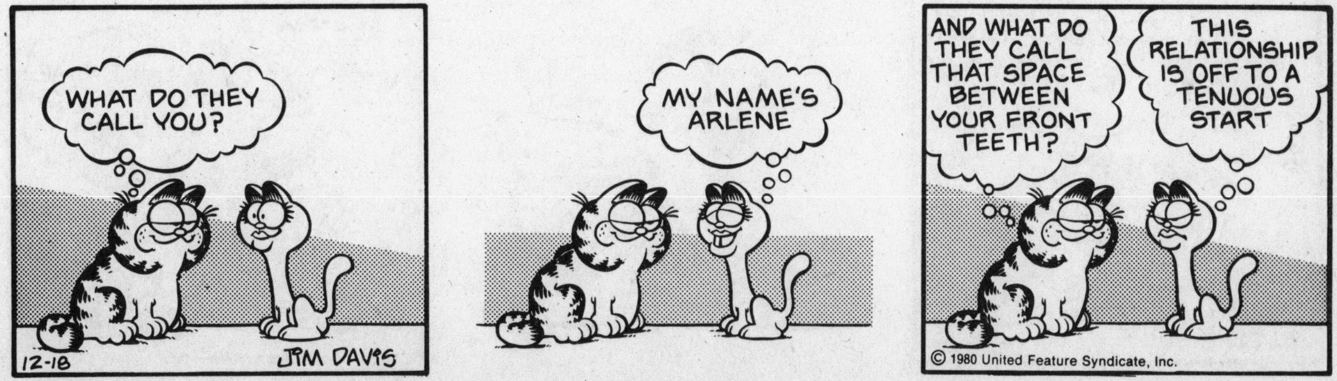
WHAT DO THEY CALL YOU?
12-18
JIM DAVIS
MY NAME'S ARLENE
AND WHAT DO THEY CALL THAT SPACE BETWEEN YOUR FRONT TEETH?
THIS RELATIONSHIP IS OFF TO A TENUOUS START
© 1980 United Feature Syndicate, Inc.

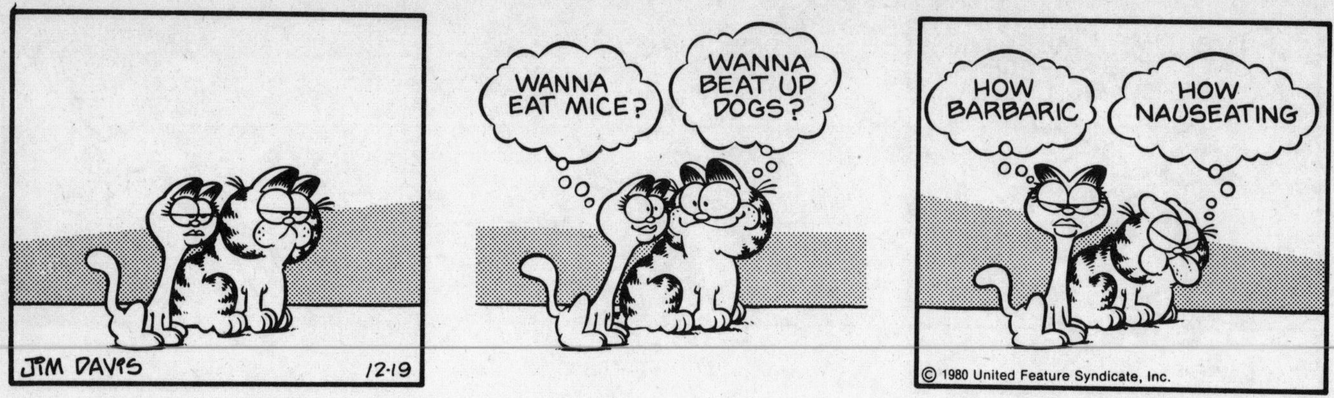
JIM DAVIS
12-19
WANNA EAT MICE?
WANNA BEAT UP DOGS?
HOW BARBARIC
HOW NAUSEATING
© 1980 United Feature Syndicate, Inc.

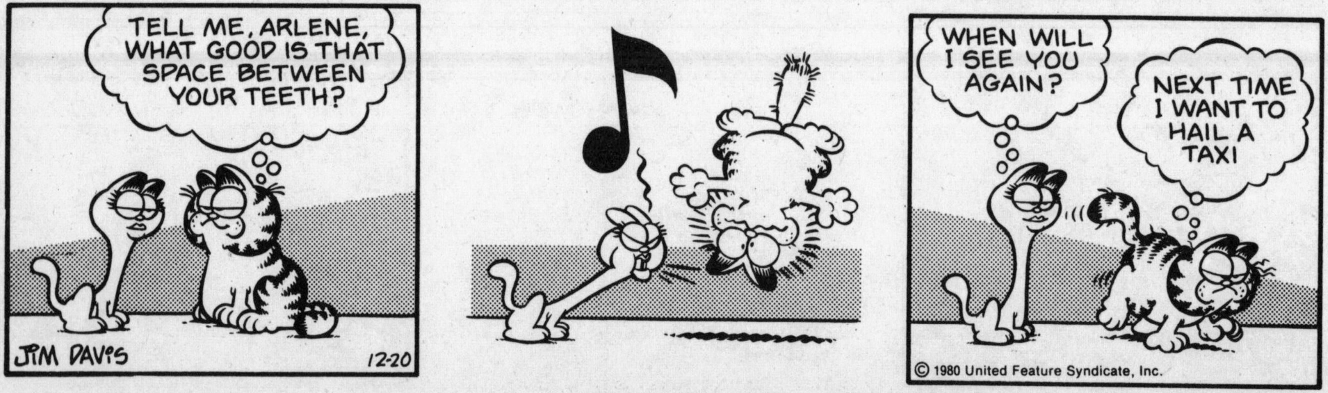
TELL ME, ARLENE, WHAT GOOD IS THAT SPACE BETWEEN YOUR TEETH?
JIM DAVIS
12-20
WHEN WILL I SEE YOU AGAIN?
NEXT TIME I WANT TO HAIL A TAXI
© 1980 United Feature Syndicate, Inc.

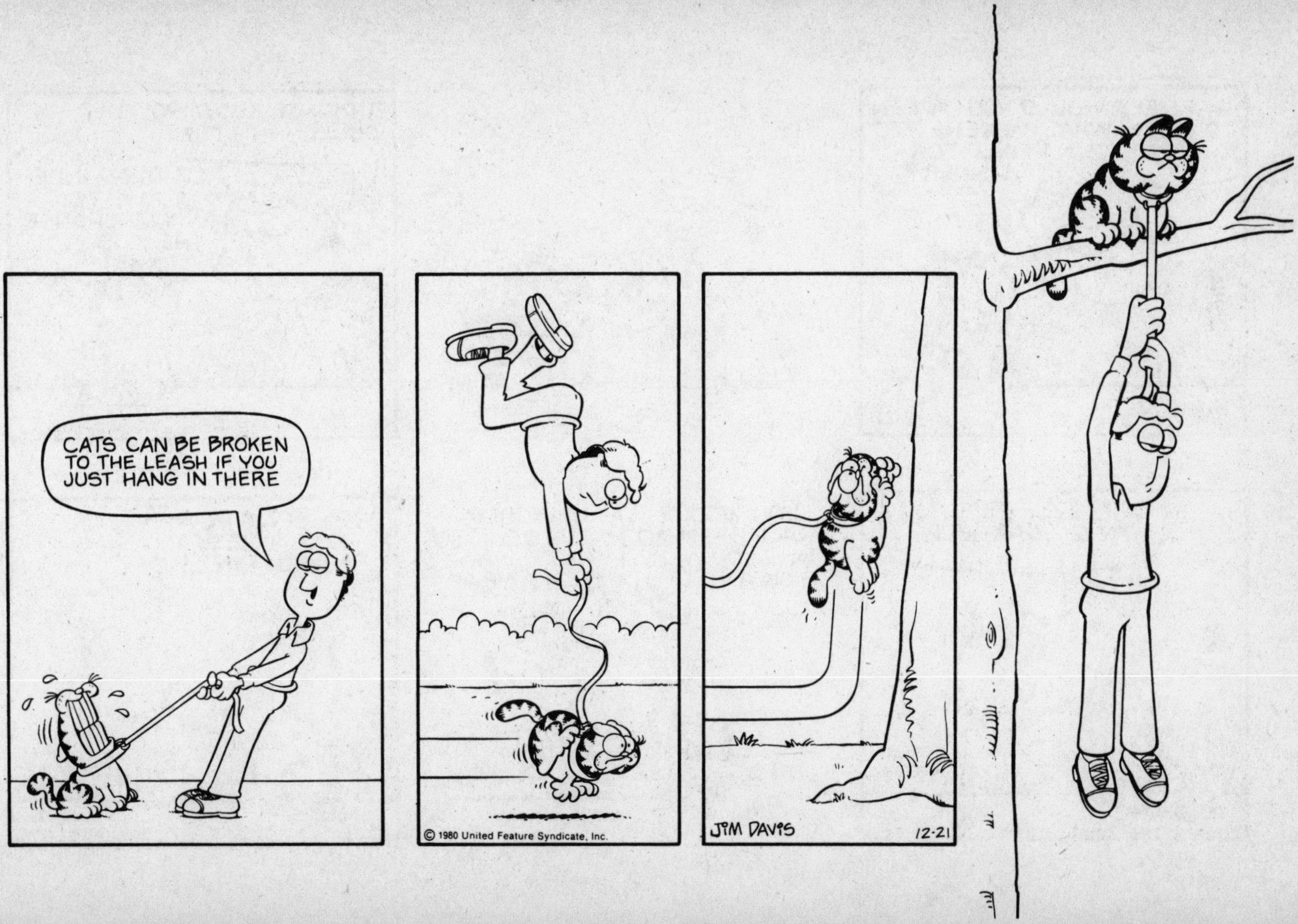
CATS CAN BE BROKEN TO THE LEASH IF YOU JUST HANG IN THERE
© 1980 United Feature Syndicate, Inc.
JIM DAVIS
12-21

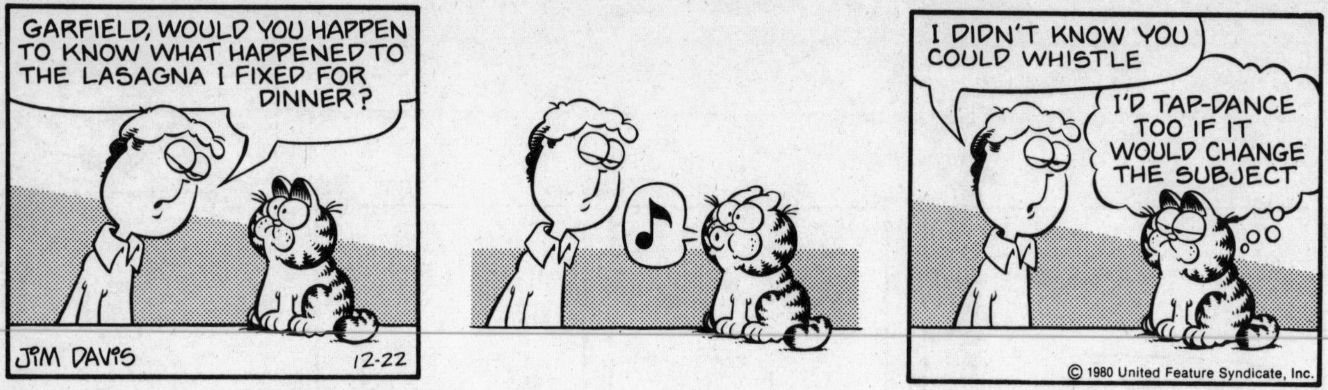
GARFIELD, WOULD YOU HAPPEN TO KNOW WHAT HAPPENED TO THE LASAGNA I FIXED FOR DINNER?
JIM DAVIS
12-22
♪
I DIDN'T KNOW YOU COULD WHISTLE
I'D TAP-DANCE TOO IF IT WOULD CHANGE THE SUBJECT
© 1980 United Feature Syndicate, Inc.

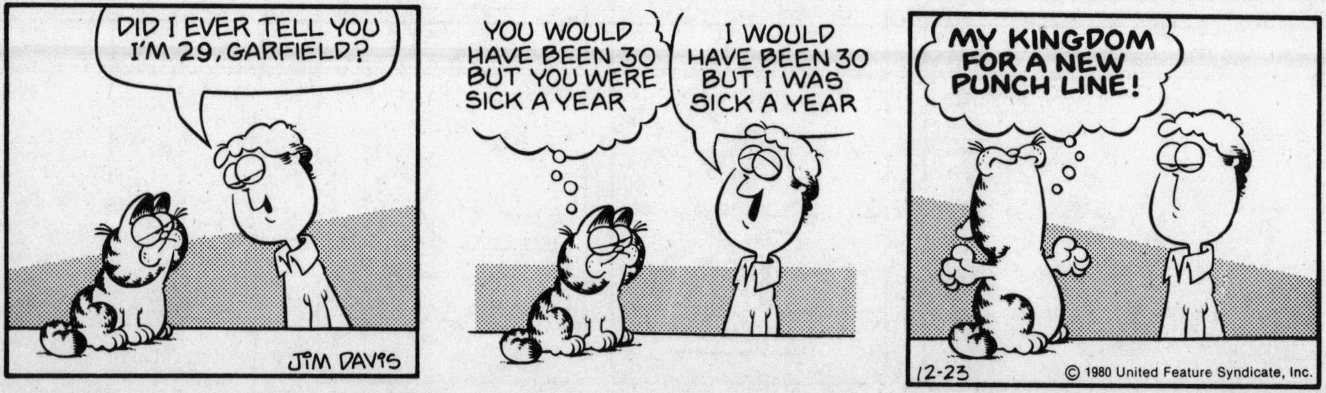
DID I EVER TELL YOU I'M 29, GARFIELD?
JIM DAVIS
YOU WOULD HAVE BEEN 30 BUT YOU WERE SICK A YEAR
I WOULD HAVE BEEN 30 BUT I WAS SICK A YEAR
MY KINGDOM FOR A NEW PUNCH LINE!
12-23
© 1980 United Feature Syndicate, Inc.

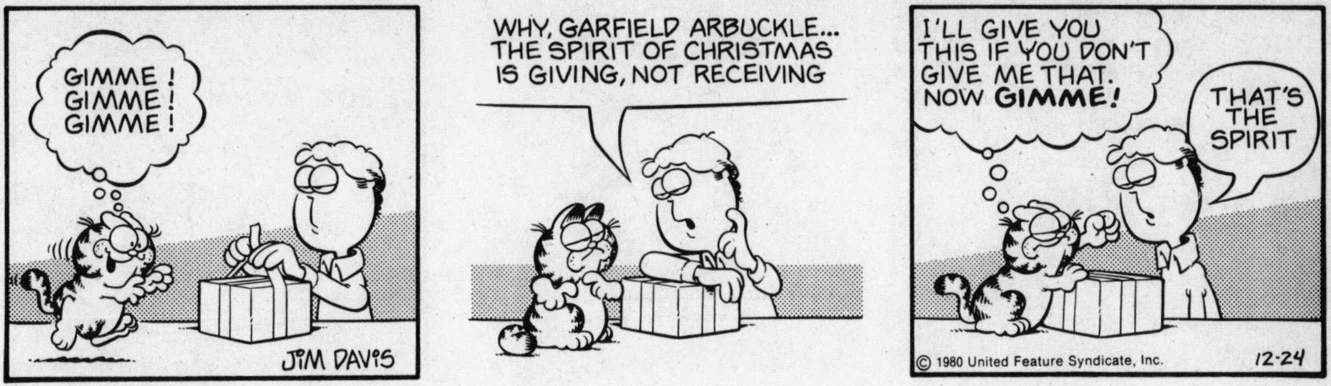
GIMME! GIMME! GIMME!
JIM DAVIS
WHY, GARFIELD ARBUCKLE... THE SPIRIT OF CHRISTMAS IS GIVING, NOT RECEIVING
I'LL GIVE YOU THIS IF YOU DON'T GIVE ME THAT. NOW **GIMME!**
THAT'S THE SPIRIT
© 1980 United Feature Syndicate, Inc.
12-24

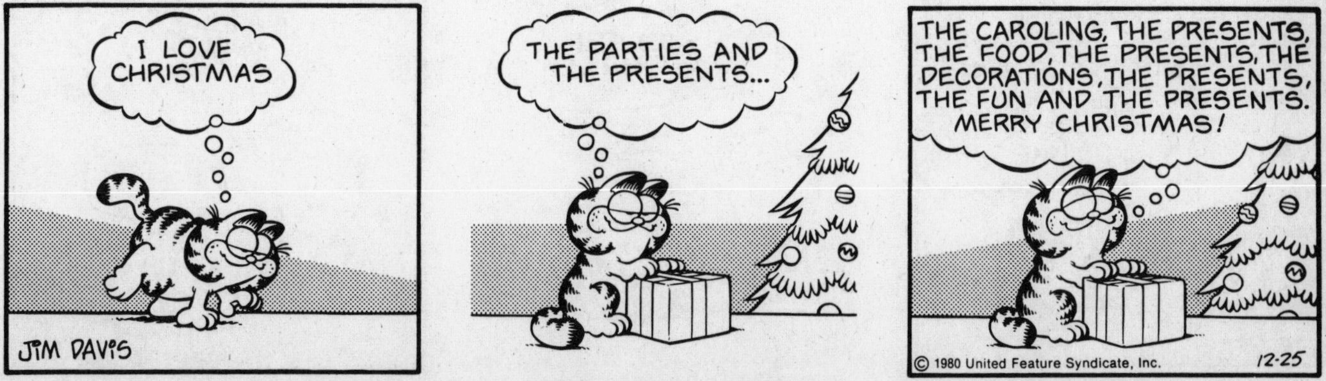
I LOVE CHRISTMAS
JIM DAVIS
THE PARTIES AND THE PRESENTS...
THE CAROLING, THE PRESENTS, THE FOOD, THE PRESENTS, THE DECORATIONS, THE PRESENTS, THE FUN AND THE PRESENTS. MERRY CHRISTMAS!
© 1980 United Feature Syndicate, Inc.
12-25

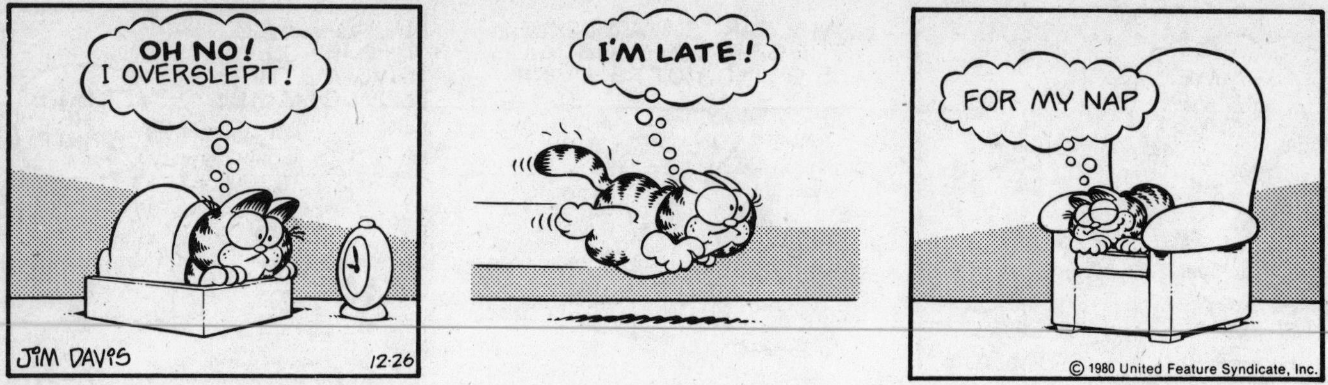
OH NO! I OVERSLEPT!
I'M LATE!
FOR MY NAP
JIM DAVIS
12·26
© 1980 United Feature Syndicate, Inc.

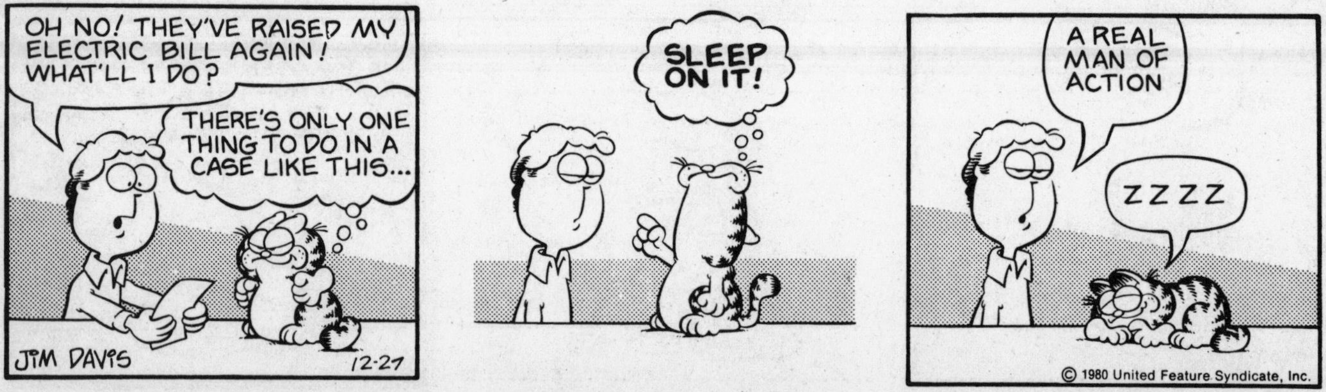
OH NO! THEY'VE RAISED MY ELECTRIC BILL AGAIN! WHAT'LL I DO?
THERE'S ONLY ONE THING TO DO IN A CASE LIKE THIS...
SLEEP ON IT!
A REAL MAN OF ACTION
ZZZZ
JIM DAVIS
12·27
© 1980 United Feature Syndicate, Inc.

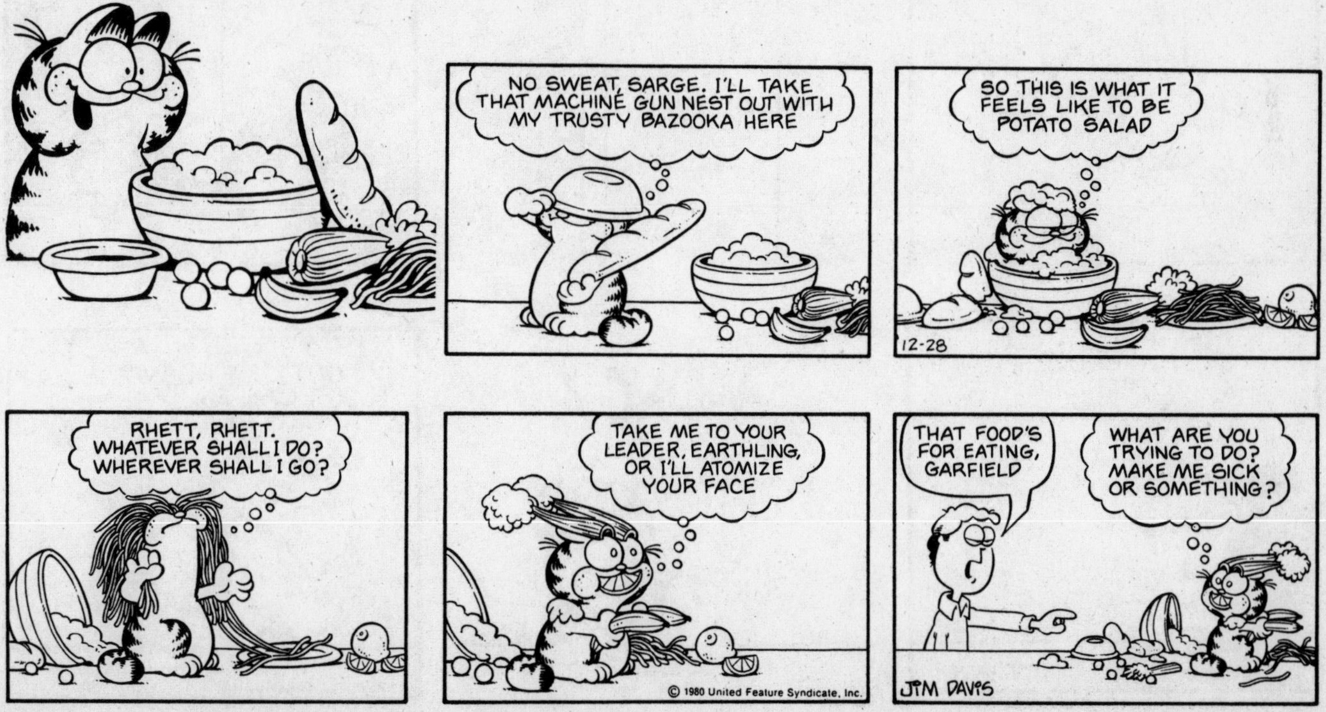

NO SWEAT, SARGE. I'LL TAKE THAT MACHINE GUN NEST OUT WITH MY TRUSTY BAZOOKA HERE
SO THIS IS WHAT IT FEELS LIKE TO BE POTATO SALAD
12-28
RHETT, RHETT. WHATEVER SHALL I DO? WHEREVER SHALL I GO?
TAKE ME TO YOUR LEADER, EARTHLING, OR I'LL ATOMIZE YOUR FACE
© 1980 United Feature Syndicate, Inc.
THAT FOOD'S FOR EATING, GARFIELD
WHAT ARE YOU TRYING TO DO? MAKE ME SICK OR SOMETHING?
JIM DAVIS

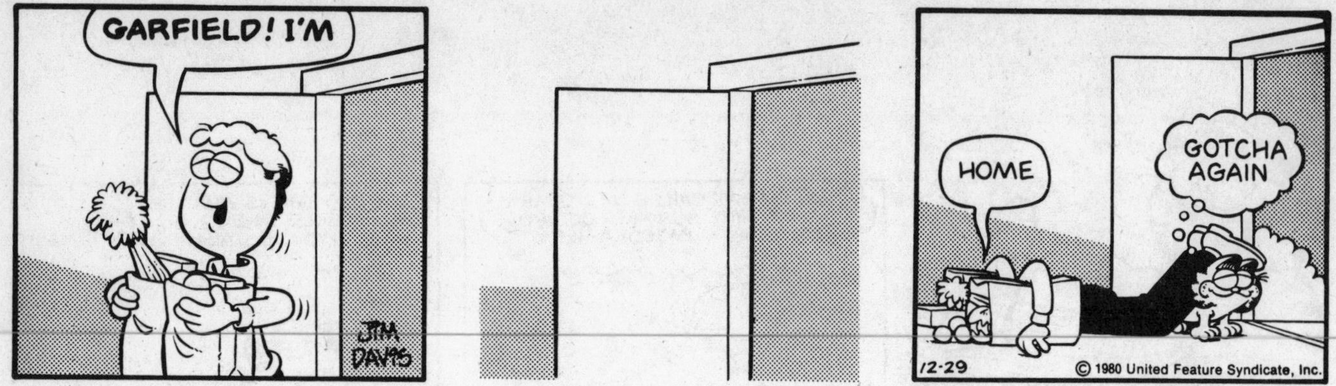
GARFIELD! I'M
JIM DAVIS
HOME
GOTCHA AGAIN
12-29
© 1980 United Feature Syndicate, Inc.

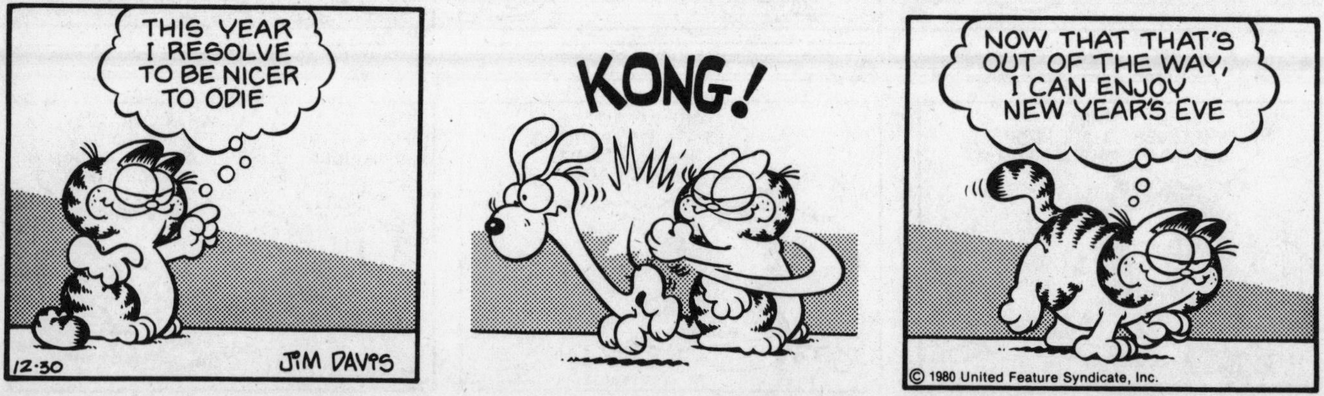
THIS YEAR I RESOLVE TO BE NICER TO ODIE
12-30
JIM DAVIS
KONG!
NOW THAT THAT'S OUT OF THE WAY, I CAN ENJOY NEW YEAR'S EVE
© 1980 United Feature Syndicate, Inc.

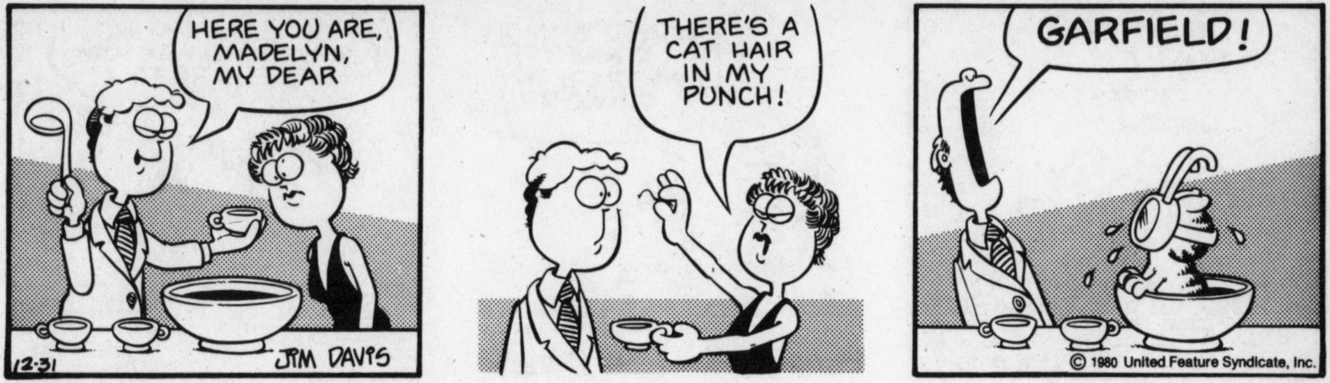
HERE YOU ARE, MADELYN, MY DEAR
12-31
JIM DAVIS
THERE'S A CAT HAIR IN MY PUNCH!
GARFIELD!
© 1980 United Feature Syndicate, Inc.

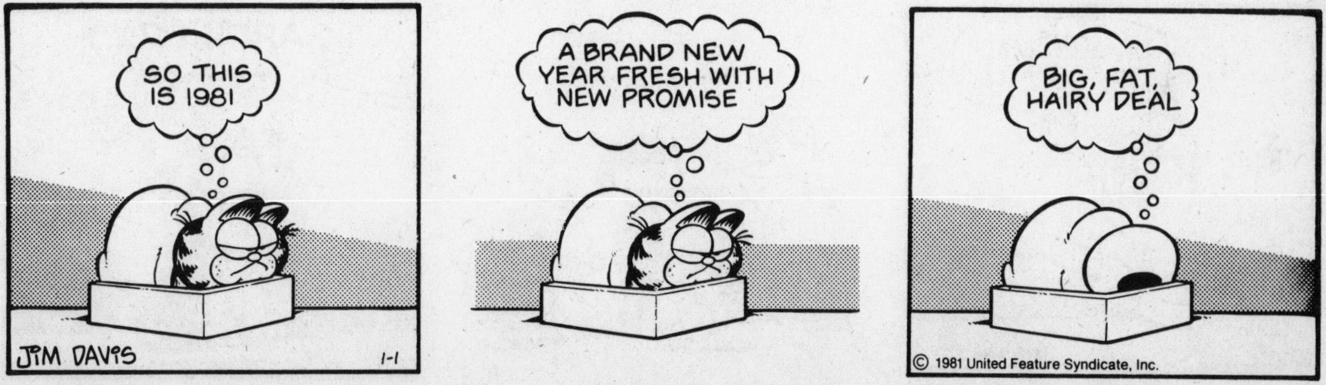
SO THIS IS 1981
JIM DAVIS
1-1
A BRAND NEW YEAR FRESH WITH NEW PROMISE
BIG, FAT, HAIRY DEAL
© 1981 United Feature Syndicate, Inc.

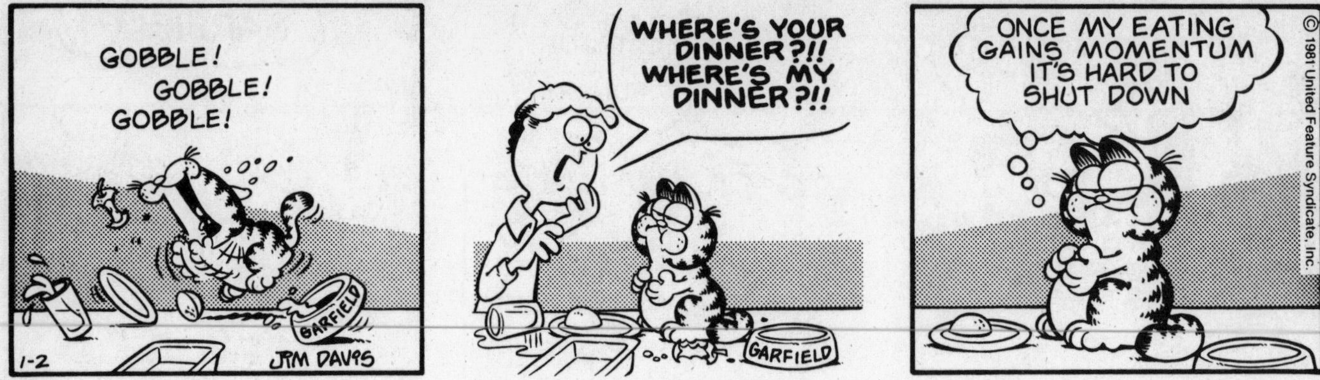
GOBBLE! GOBBLE! GOBBLE!
GARFIELD
1-2
JIM DAVIS
WHERE'S YOUR DINNER?!! WHERE'S MY DINNER?!!
GARFIELD
ONCE MY EATING GAINS MOMENTUM IT'S HARD TO SHUT DOWN
© 1981 United Feature Syndicate, Inc.

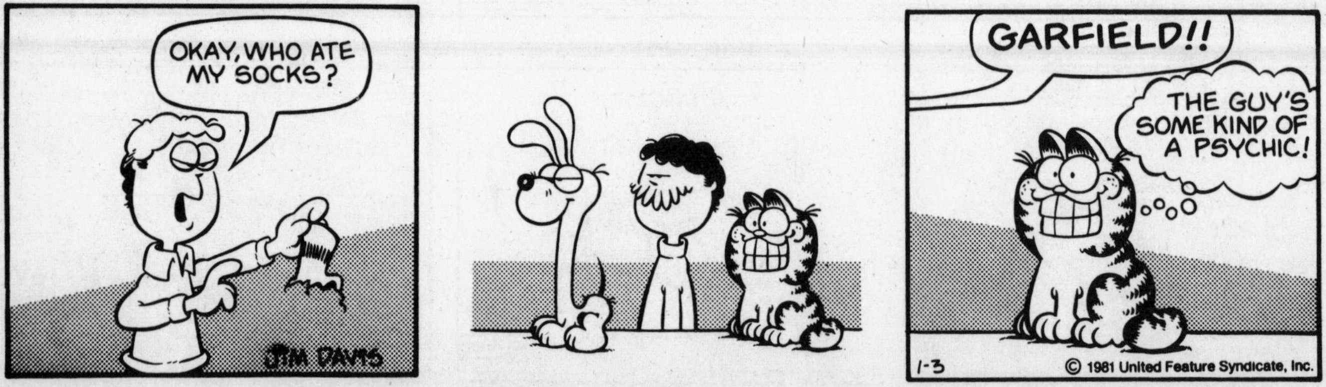
OKAY, WHO ATE MY SOCKS?
JIM DAVIS
GARFIELD!!
THE GUY'S SOME KIND OF A PSYCHIC!
1-3
© 1981 United Feature Syndicate, Inc.

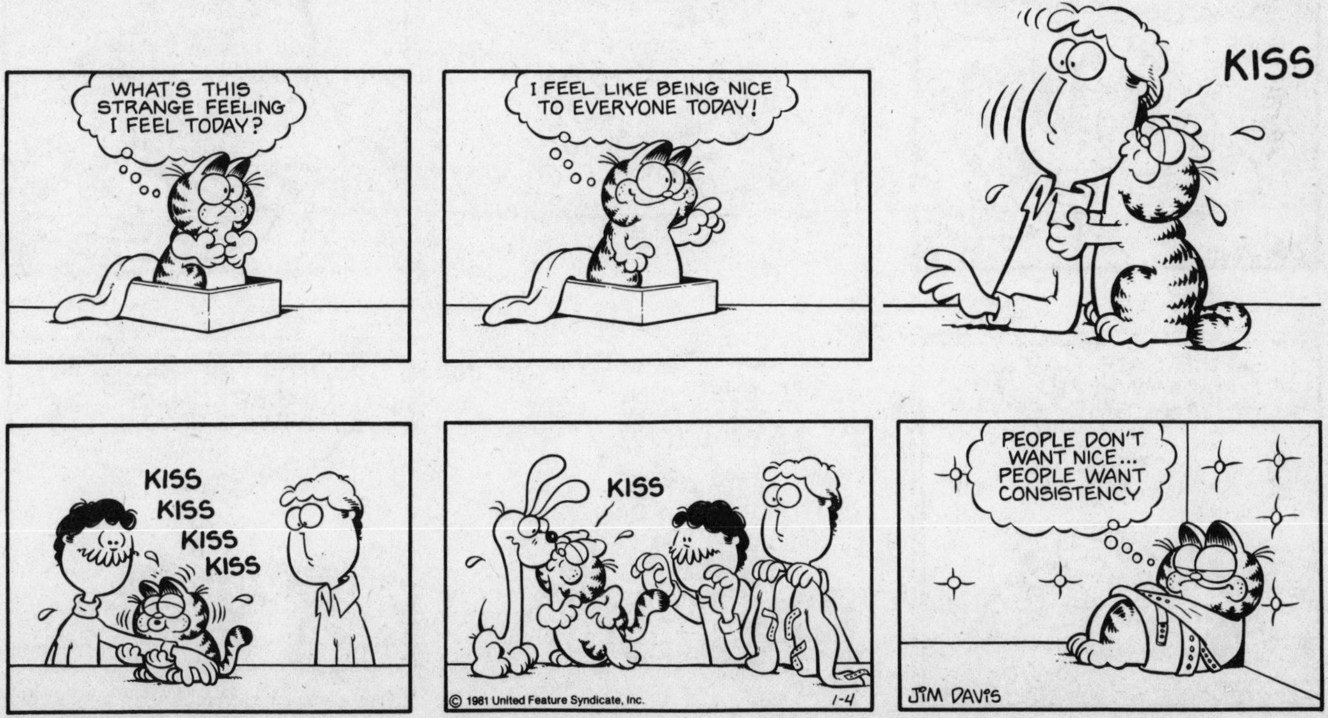
WHAT'S THIS STRANGE FEELING I FEEL TODAY?
I FEEL LIKE BEING NICE TO EVERYONE TODAY!
KISS
KISS
KISS
KISS
KISS
KISS
© 1981 United Feature Syndicate, Inc.
1-4
PEOPLE DON'T WANT NICE... PEOPLE WANT CONSISTENCY
JIM DAVIS

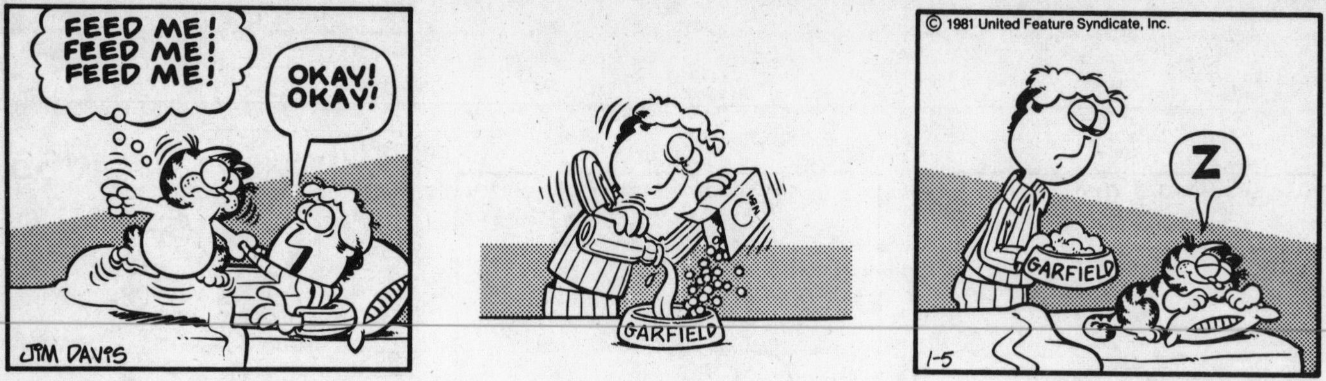
FEED ME! FEED ME! FEED ME!
OKAY! OKAY!
JIM DAVIS
GARFIELD
© 1981 United Feature Syndicate, Inc.
GARFIELD
Z
1-5

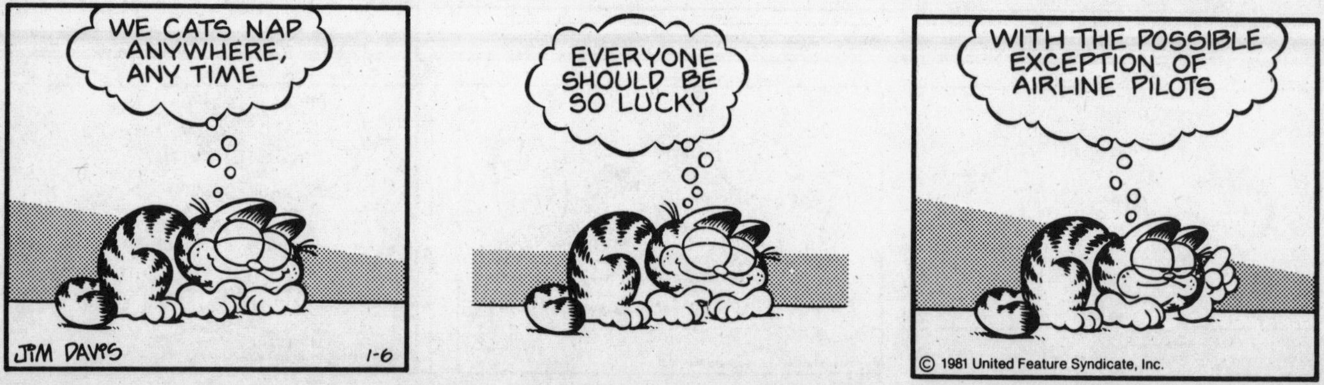
WE CATS NAP ANYWHERE, ANY TIME
JIM DAVIS
1-6
EVERYONE SHOULD BE SO LUCKY
WITH THE POSSIBLE EXCEPTION OF AIRLINE PILOTS
© 1981 United Feature Syndicate, Inc.

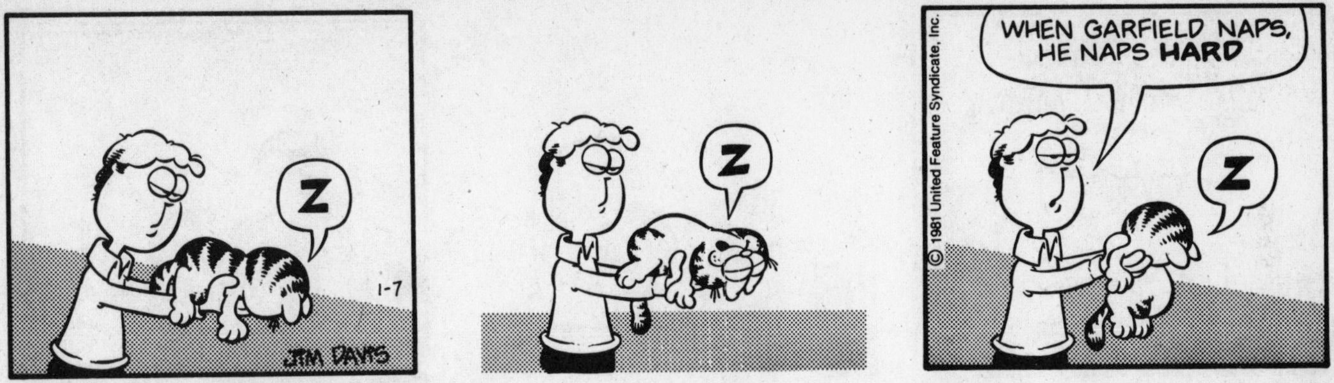
Z
1-7
JIM DAVIS
Z
© 1981 United Feature Syndicate, Inc.
WHEN GARFIELD NAPS, HE NAPS **HARD**
Z

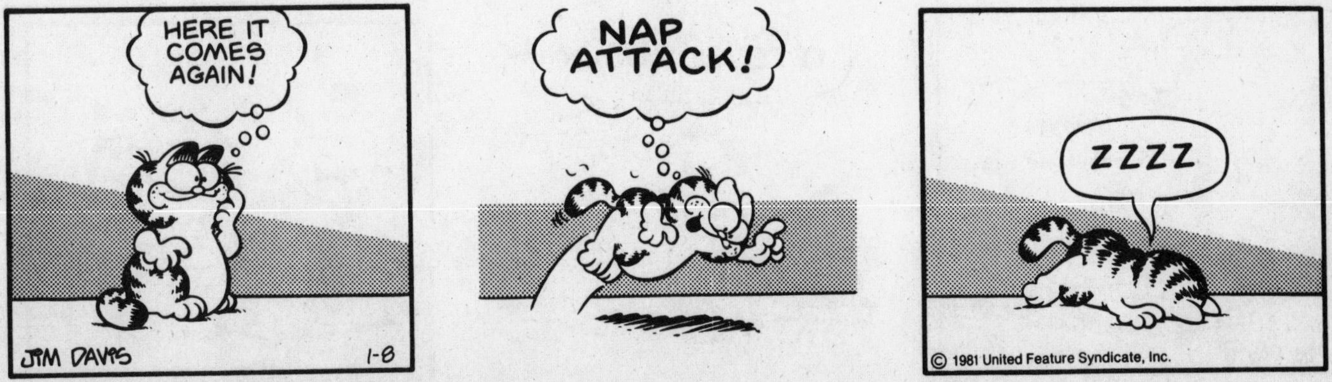
HERE IT COMES AGAIN!
JIM DAVIS
1-8
NAP ATTACK!
ZZZZ
© 1981 United Feature Syndicate, Inc.

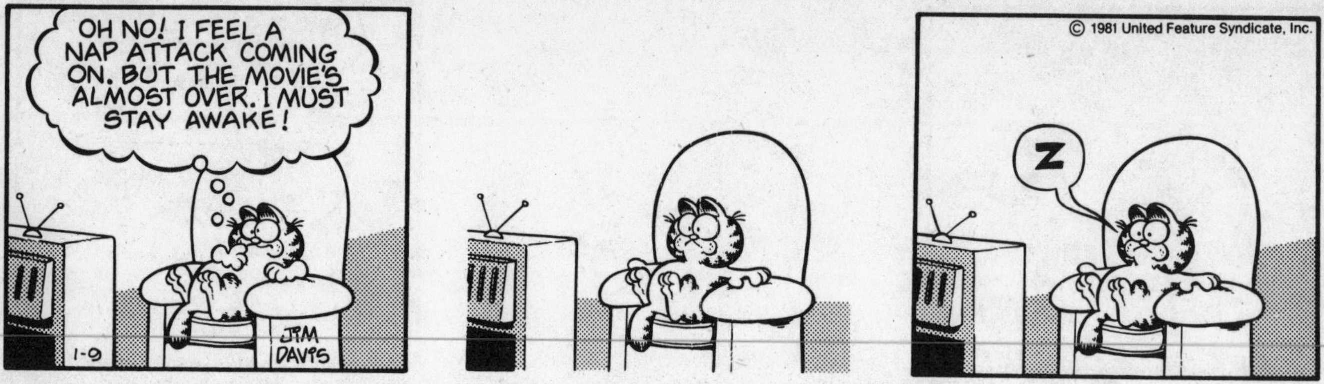
OH NO! I FEEL A NAP ATTACK COMING ON. BUT THE MOVIE'S ALMOST OVER. I MUST STAY AWAKE!
JIM DAVIS
1-9
Z
© 1981 United Feature Syndicate, Inc.

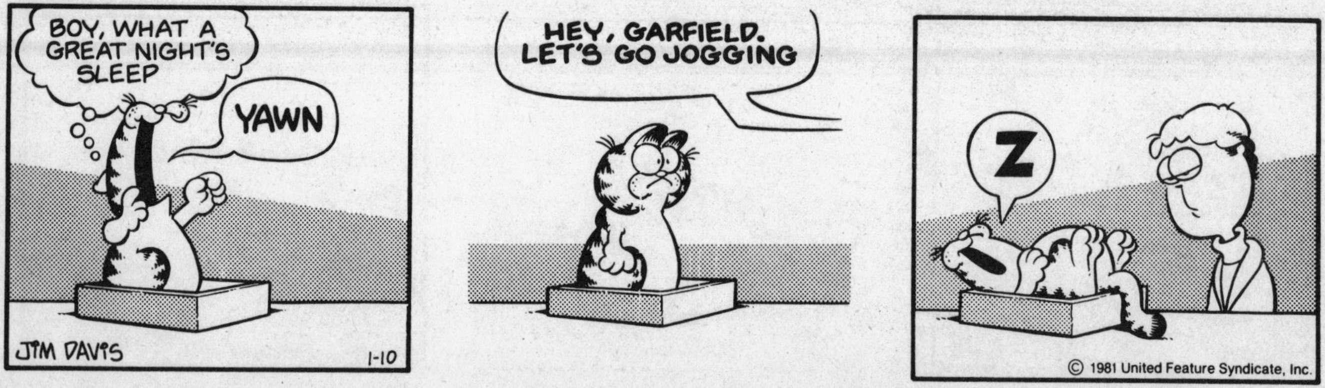
BOY, WHAT A GREAT NIGHT'S SLEEP
YAWN
JIM DAVIS
1-10
HEY, GARFIELD. LET'S GO JOGGING
Z
© 1981 United Feature Syndicate, Inc.

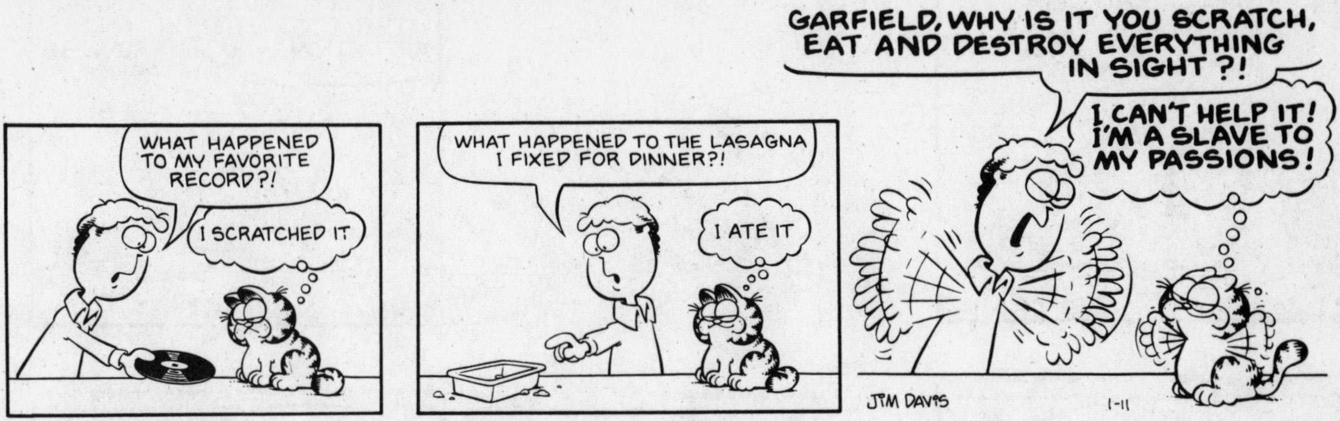
WHAT HAPPENED TO MY FAVORITE RECORD?!
I SCRATCHED IT
WHAT HAPPENED TO THE LASAGNA I FIXED FOR DINNER?!
I ATE IT
GARFIELD, WHY IS IT YOU SCRATCH, EAT AND DESTROY EVERYTHING IN SIGHT?!
I CAN'T HELP IT! I'M A SLAVE TO MY PASSIONS!
JIM DAVIS
1-11

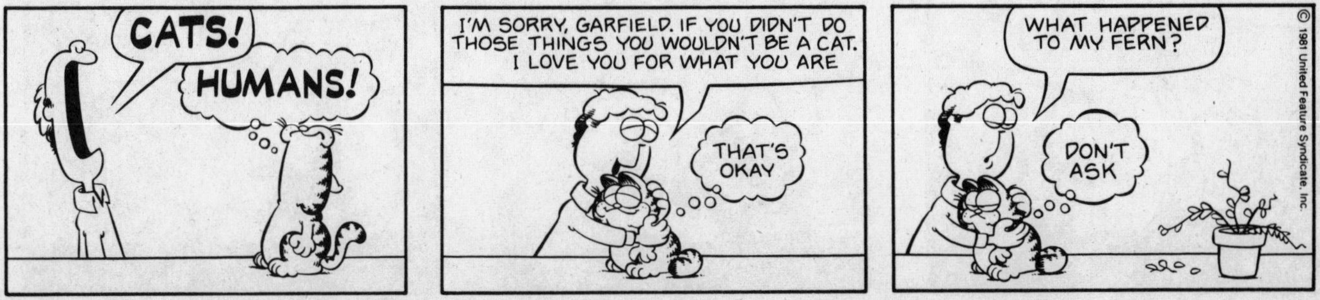
CATS!
HUMANS!
I'M SORRY, GARFIELD. IF YOU DIDN'T DO THOSE THINGS YOU WOULDN'T BE A CAT. I LOVE YOU FOR WHAT YOU ARE
THAT'S OKAY
WHAT HAPPENED TO MY FERN?
DON'T ASK
© 1981 United Feature Syndicate, Inc.

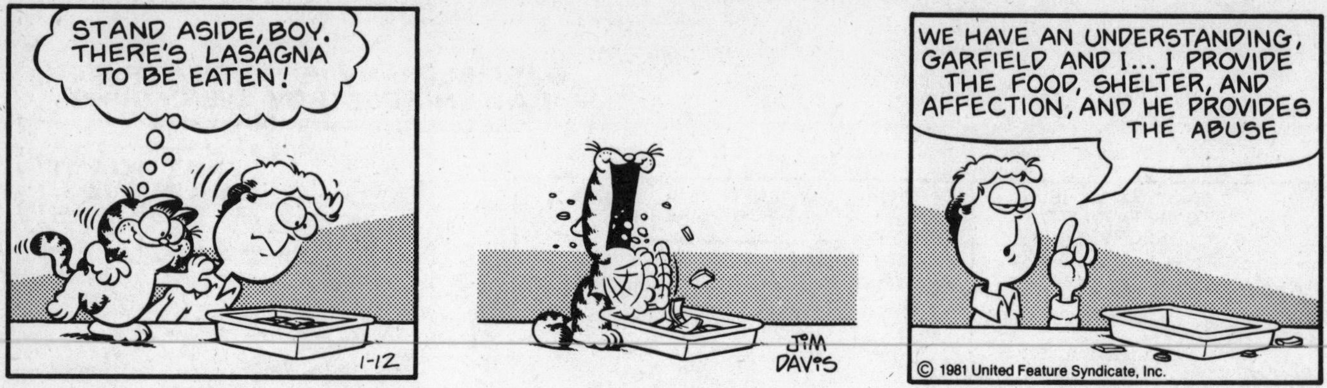
STAND ASIDE, BOY. THERE'S LASAGNA TO BE EATEN!
1-12
JIM DAVIS
WE HAVE AN UNDERSTANDING, GARFIELD AND I... I PROVIDE THE FOOD, SHELTER, AND AFFECTION, AND HE PROVIDES THE ABUSE
© 1981 United Feature Syndicate, Inc.

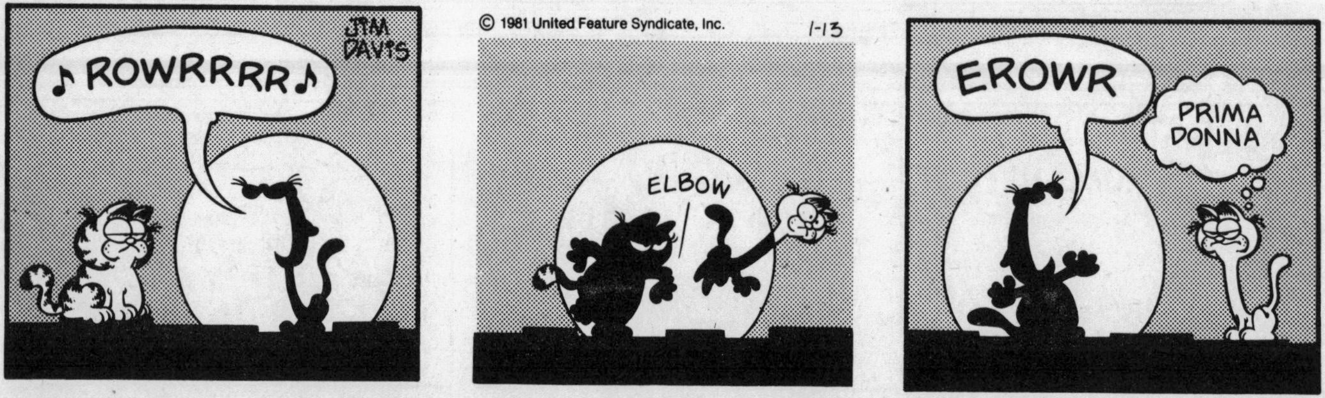
JIM DAVIS
♪ROWRRRRR♪
© 1981 United Feature Syndicate, Inc.
1-13
ELBOW
EROWR
PRIMA DONNA

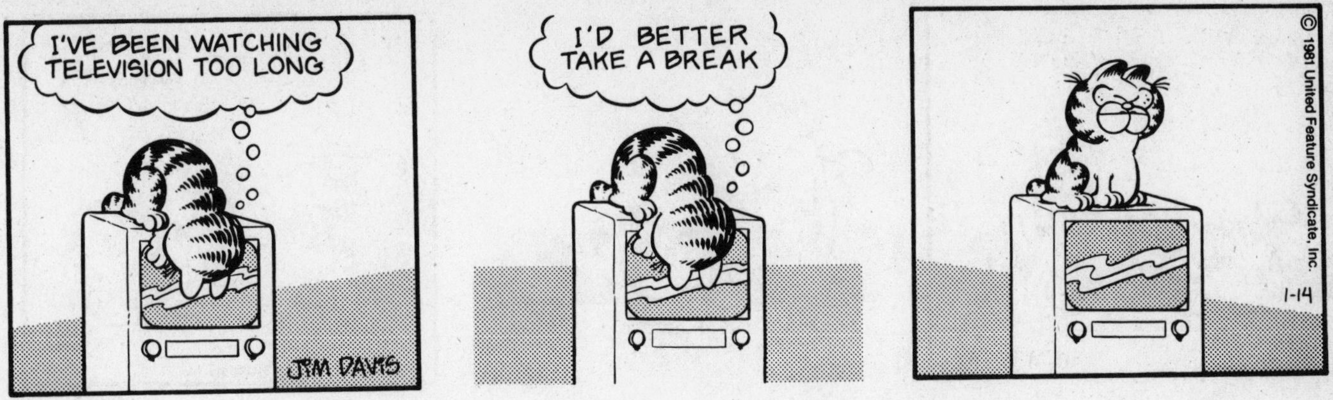
I'VE BEEN WATCHING TELEVISION TOO LONG
JIM DAVIS
I'D BETTER TAKE A BREAK
© 1981 United Feature Syndicate, Inc.
1-14

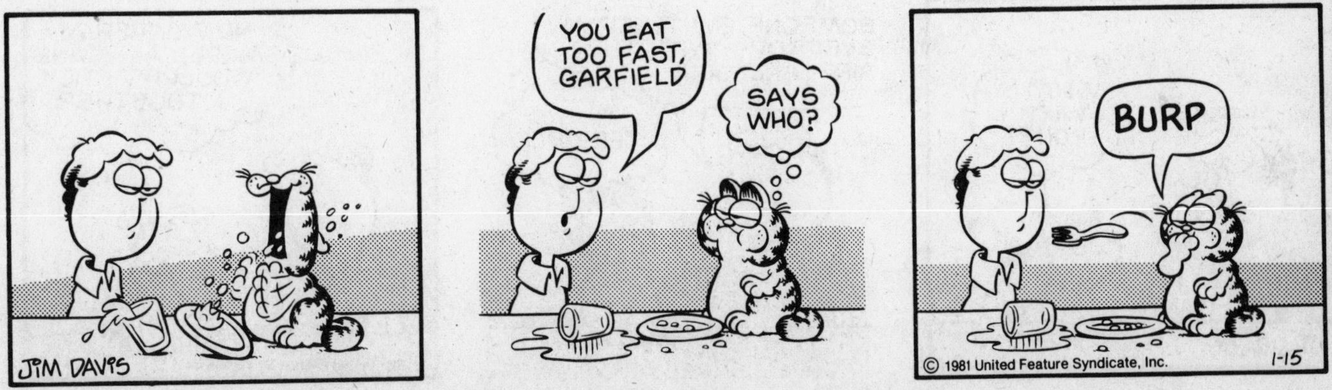
JIM DAVIS
YOU EAT TOO FAST, GARFIELD
SAYS WHO?
BURP
© 1981 United Feature Syndicate, Inc.
1-15

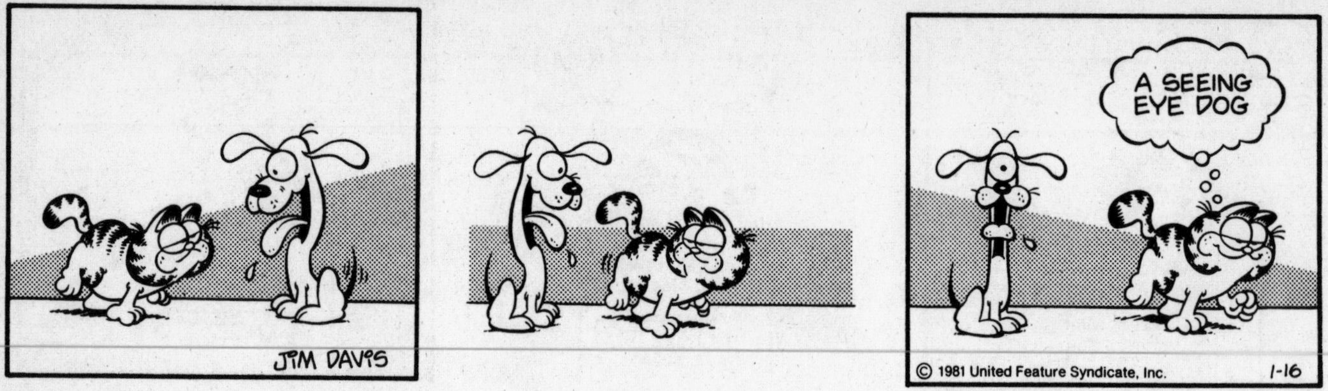
JIM DAVIS
A SEEING EYE DOG
© 1981 United Feature Syndicate, Inc.
1-16

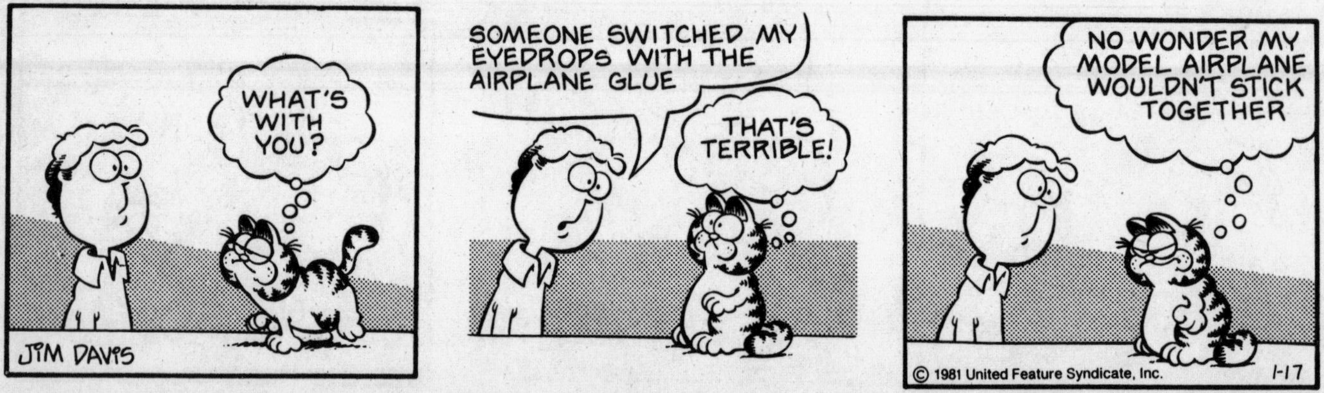
WHAT'S WITH YOU?
JIM DAVIS
SOMEONE SWITCHED MY EYEDROPS WITH THE AIRPLANE GLUE
THAT'S TERRIBLE!
NO WONDER MY MODEL AIRPLANE WOULDN'T STICK TOGETHER
© 1981 United Feature Syndicate, Inc.
1-17

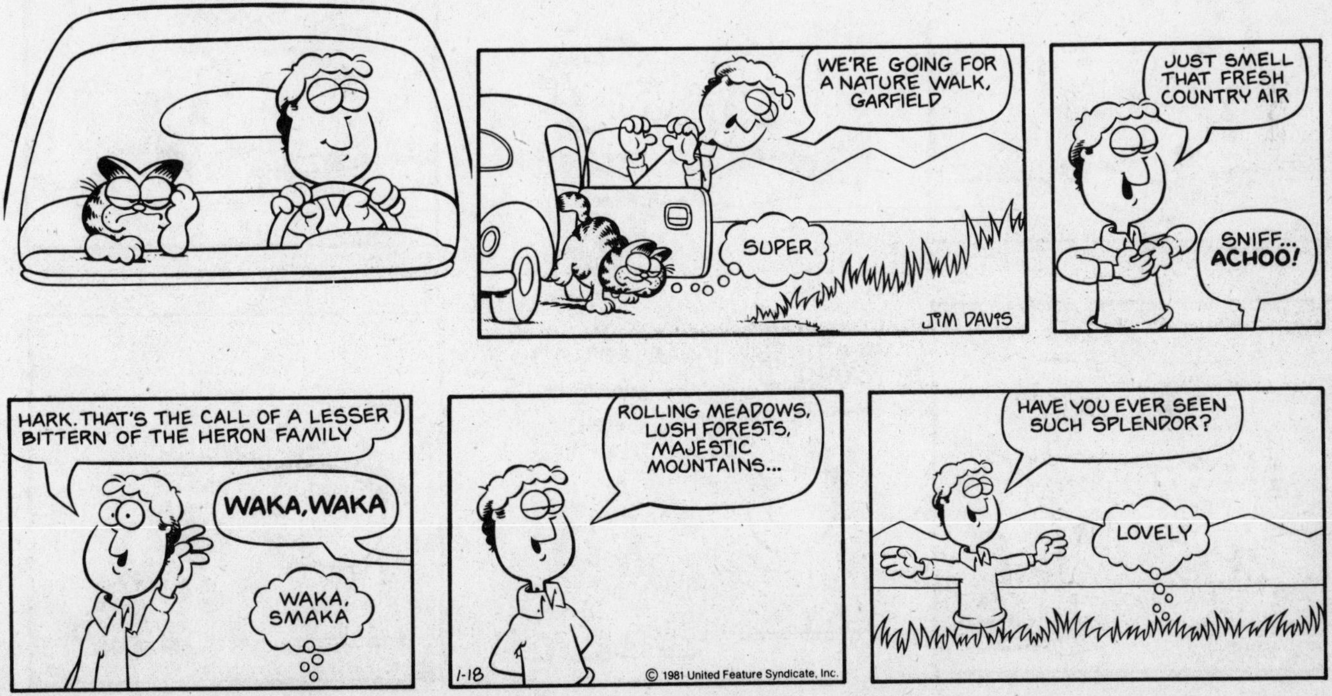
WE'RE GOING FOR A NATURE WALK, GARFIELD
SUPER
JIM DAVIS
JUST SMELL THAT FRESH COUNTRY AIR
SNIFF... ACHOO!
HARK. THAT'S THE CALL OF A LESSER BITTERN OF THE HERON FAMILY
WAKA, WAKA
WAKA, SMAKA
ROLLING MEADOWS, LUSH FORESTS, MAJESTIC MOUNTAINS...
1-18
© 1981 United Feature Syndicate, Inc.
HAVE YOU EVER SEEN SUCH SPLENDOR?
LOVELY

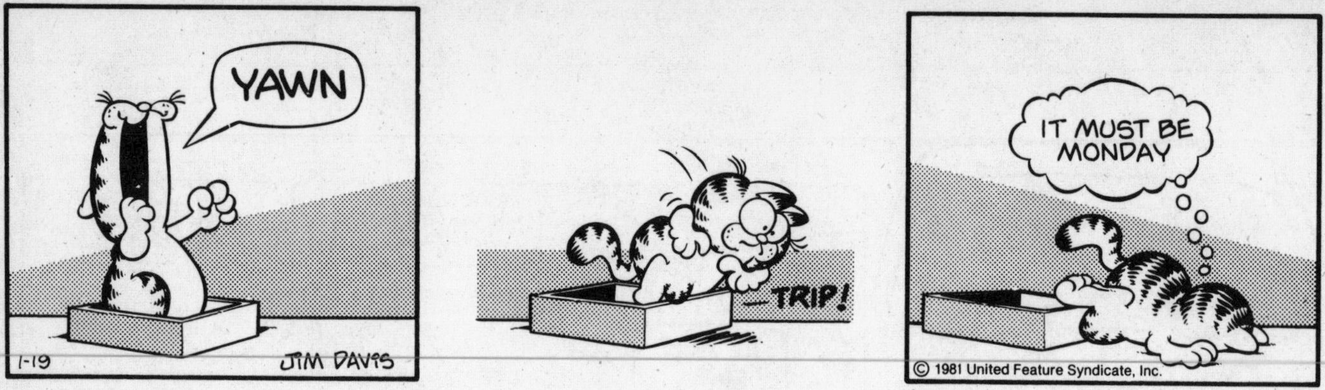
YAWN
1-19
JIM DAVIS
TRIP!
IT MUST BE MONDAY
© 1981 United Feature Syndicate, Inc.

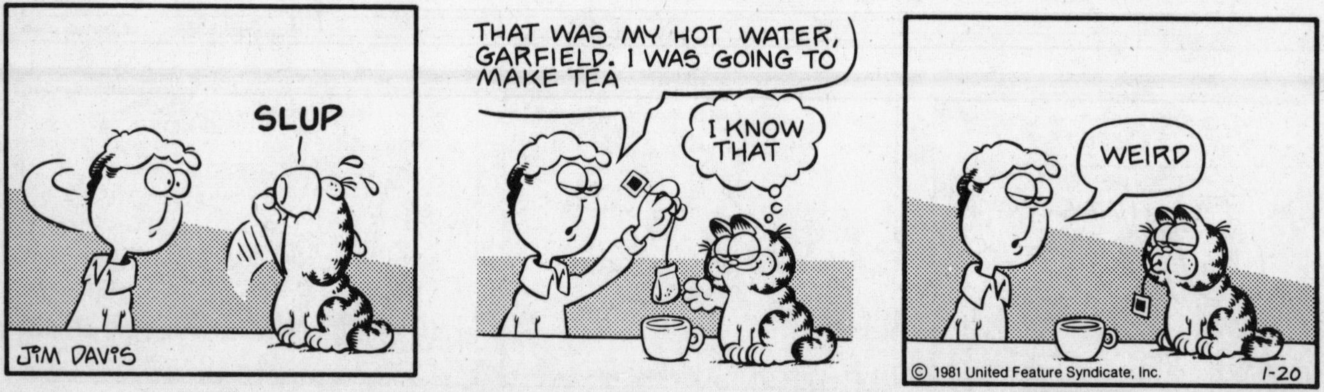
SLUP
JIM DAVIS
THAT WAS MY HOT WATER, GARFIELD. I WAS GOING TO MAKE TEA
I KNOW THAT
WEIRD
© 1981 United Feature Syndicate, Inc.
1-20

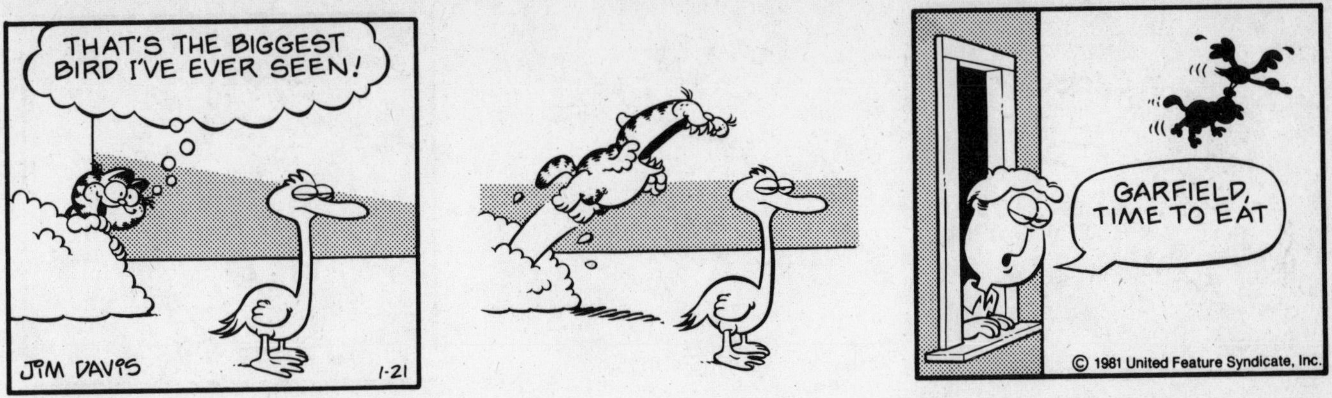
THAT'S THE BIGGEST BIRD I'VE EVER SEEN!
JIM DAVIS
1-21
GARFIELD, TIME TO EAT
© 1981 United Feature Syndicate, Inc.

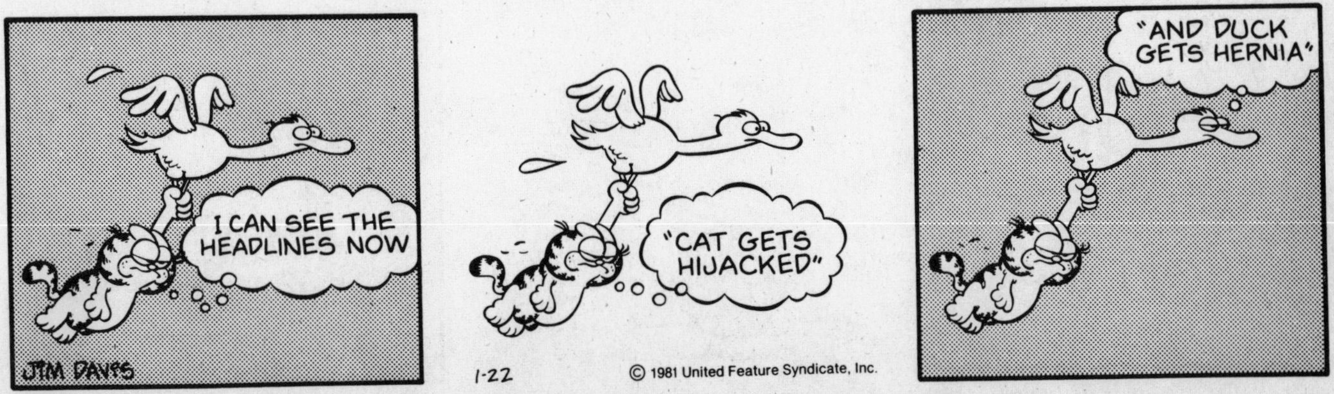
I CAN SEE THE HEADLINES NOW
JIM DAVIS
"CAT GETS HIJACKED"
1-22
© 1981 United Feature Syndicate, Inc.
"AND DUCK GETS HERNIA"

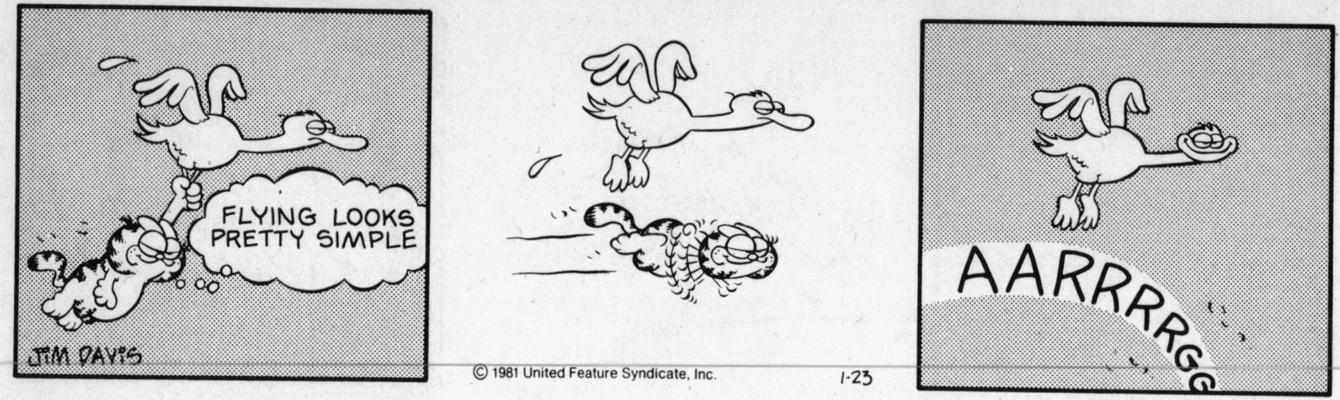
FLYING LOOKS PRETTY SIMPLE
JIM DAVIS
AARRRRGG
© 1981 United Feature Syndicate, Inc.
1-23

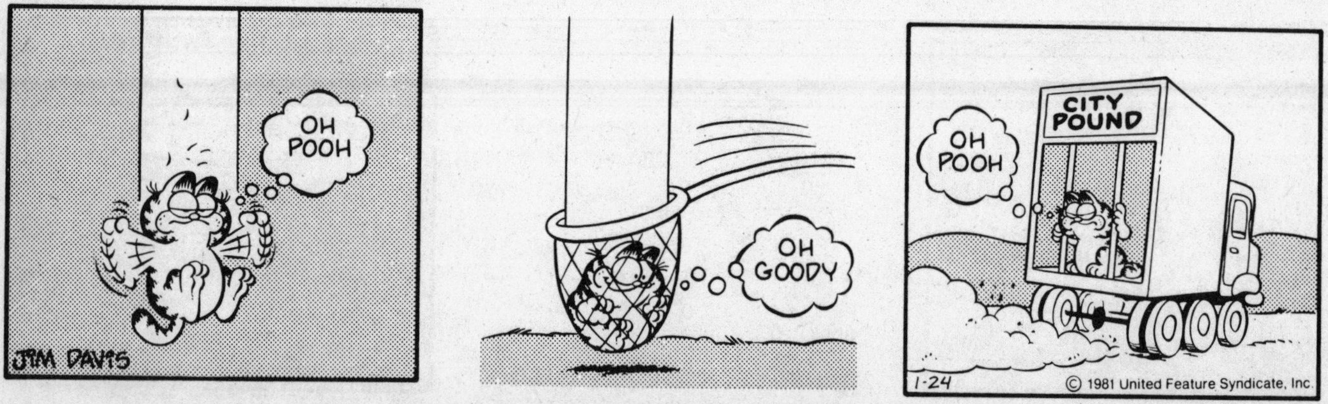
OH POOH
JIM DAVIS
OH GOODY
OH POOH
CITY POUND
1-24
© 1981 United Feature Syndicate, Inc.

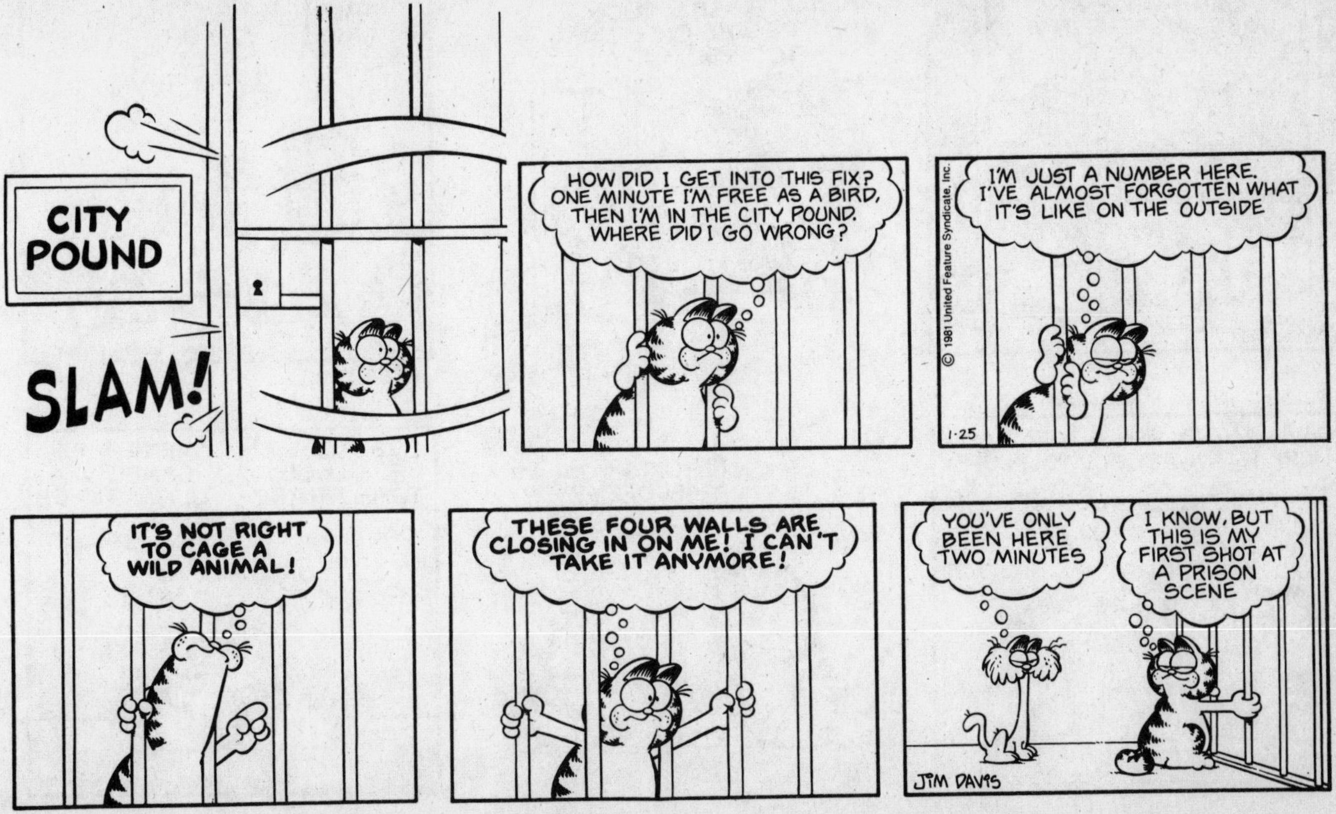
CITY POUND
SLAM!
HOW DID I GET INTO THIS FIX? ONE MINUTE I'M FREE AS A BIRD, THEN I'M IN THE CITY POUND. WHERE DID I GO WRONG?
© 1981 United Feature Syndicate, Inc.
1-25
I'M JUST A NUMBER HERE. I'VE ALMOST FORGOTTEN WHAT IT'S LIKE ON THE OUTSIDE
IT'S NOT RIGHT TO CAGE A WILD ANIMAL!
THESE FOUR WALLS ARE CLOSING IN ON ME! I CAN'T TAKE IT ANYMORE!
YOU'VE ONLY BEEN HERE TWO MINUTES
I KNOW, BUT THIS IS MY FIRST SHOT AT A PRISON SCENE
JIM DAVIS

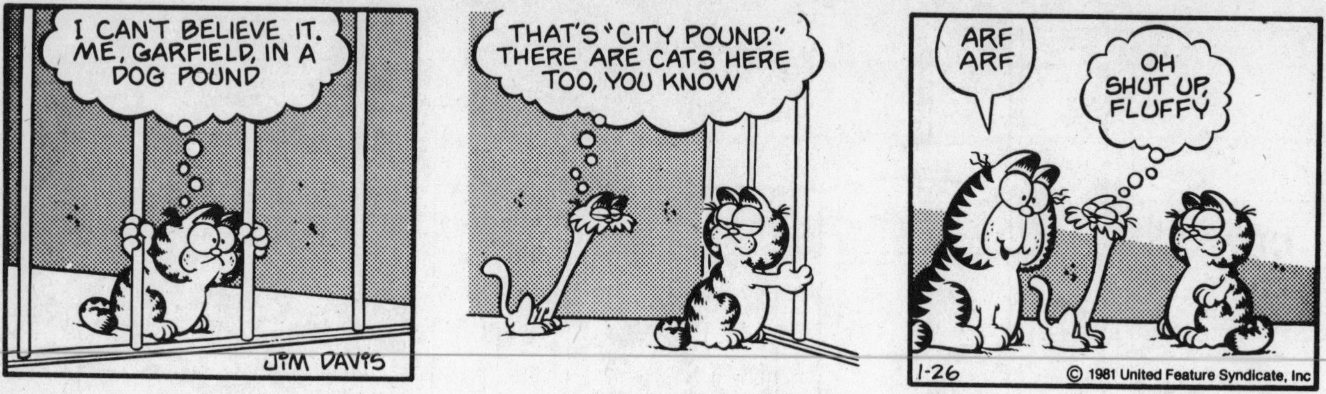
I CAN'T BELIEVE IT. ME, GARFIELD, IN A DOG POUND
THAT'S "CITY POUND." THERE ARE CATS HERE TOO, YOU KNOW
ARF ARF
OH SHUT UP, FLUFFY
JIM DAVIS
1-26
© 1981 United Feature Syndicate, Inc

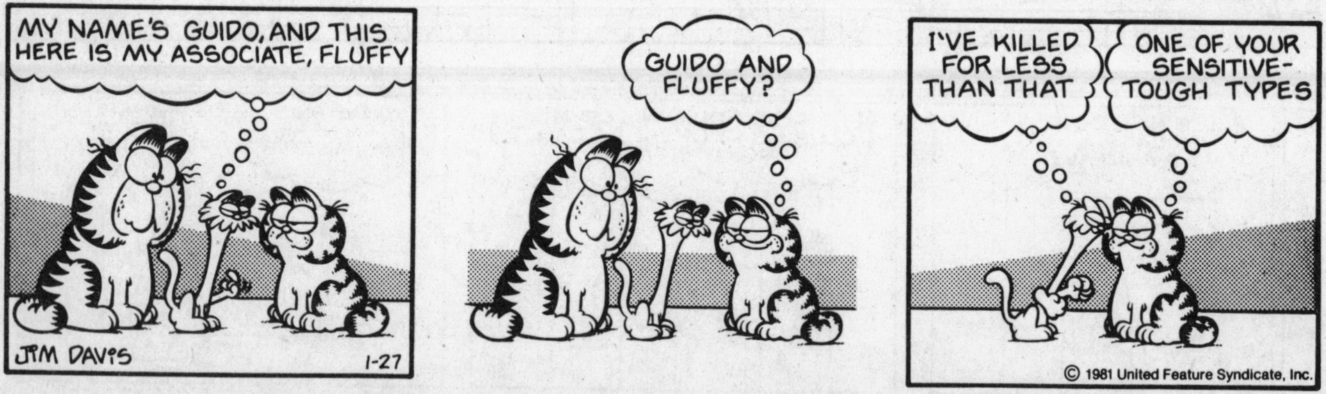
MY NAME'S GUIDO, AND THIS HERE IS MY ASSOCIATE, FLUFFY
GUIDO AND FLUFFY?
I'VE KILLED FOR LESS THAN THAT
ONE OF YOUR SENSITIVE-TOUGH TYPES
JIM DAVIS
1-27
© 1981 United Feature Syndicate, Inc.

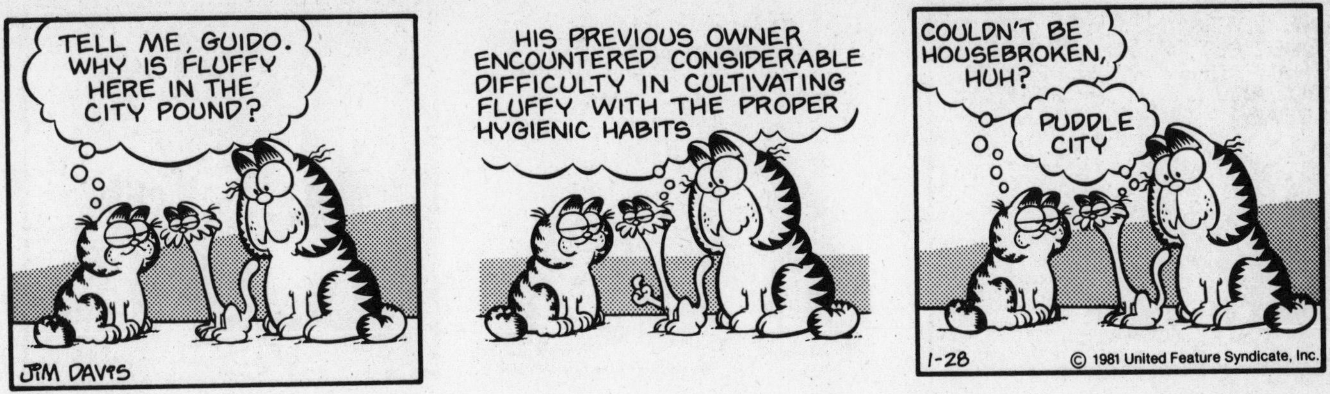
TELL ME, GUIDO. WHY IS FLUFFY HERE IN THE CITY POUND?
JIM DAVIS
HIS PREVIOUS OWNER ENCOUNTERED CONSIDERABLE DIFFICULTY IN CULTIVATING FLUFFY WITH THE PROPER HYGIENIC HABITS
COULDN'T BE HOUSEBROKEN, HUH?
PUDDLE CITY
1-28
© 1981 United Feature Syndicate, Inc.

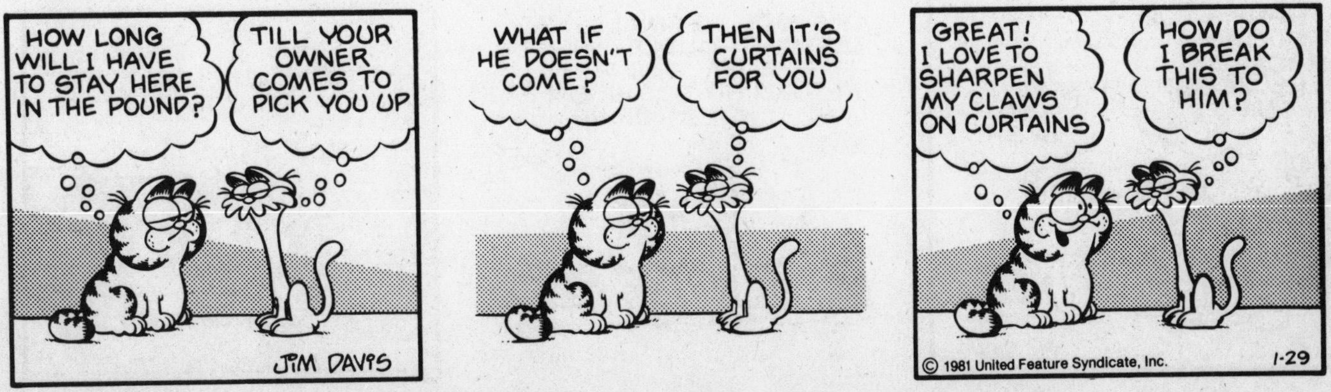
HOW LONG WILL I HAVE TO STAY HERE IN THE POUND?
TILL YOUR OWNER COMES TO PICK YOU UP
JIM DAVIS
WHAT IF HE DOESN'T COME?
THEN IT'S CURTAINS FOR YOU
GREAT! I LOVE TO SHARPEN MY CLAWS ON CURTAINS
HOW DO I BREAK THIS TO HIM?
© 1981 United Feature Syndicate, Inc.
1-29

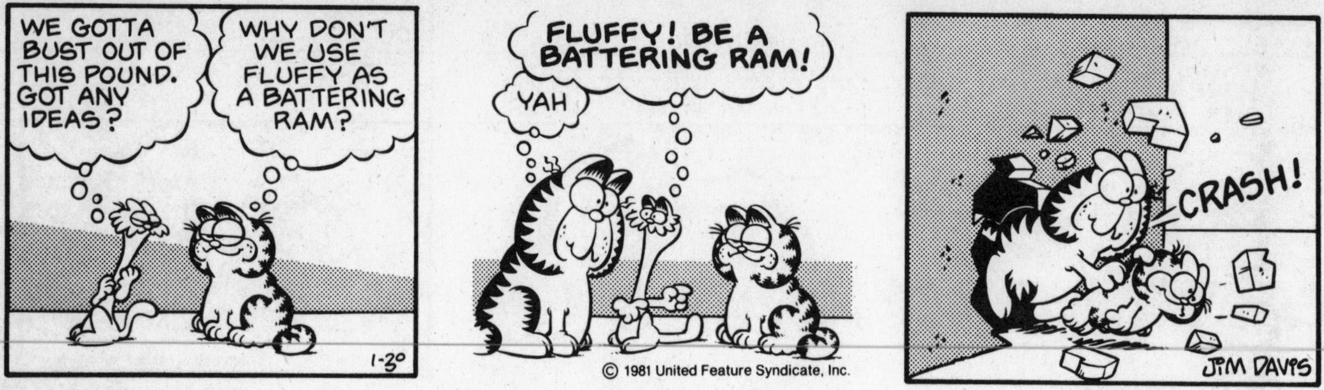
WE GOTTA BUST OUT OF THIS POUND. GOT ANY IDEAS?
WHY DON'T WE USE FLUFFY AS A BATTERING RAM?
1-30
YAH
FLUFFY! BE A BATTERING RAM!
© 1981 United Feature Syndicate, Inc.
CRASH!
JIM DAVIS

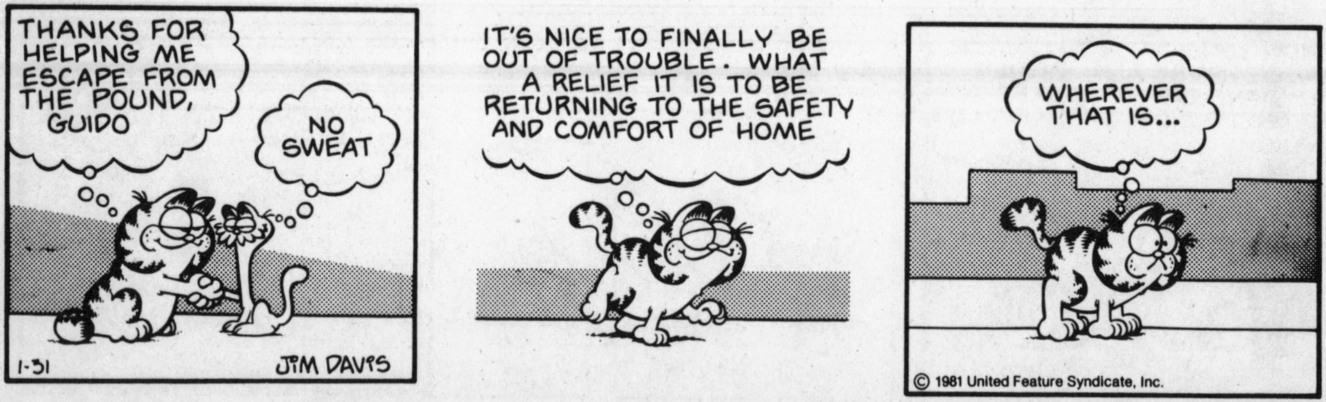
THANKS FOR HELPING ME ESCAPE FROM THE POUND, GUIDO
NO SWEAT
1-31
JIM DAVIS
IT'S NICE TO FINALLY BE OUT OF TROUBLE. WHAT A RELIEF IT IS TO BE RETURNING TO THE SAFETY AND COMFORT OF HOME
WHEREVER THAT IS...
© 1981 United Feature Syndicate, Inc.

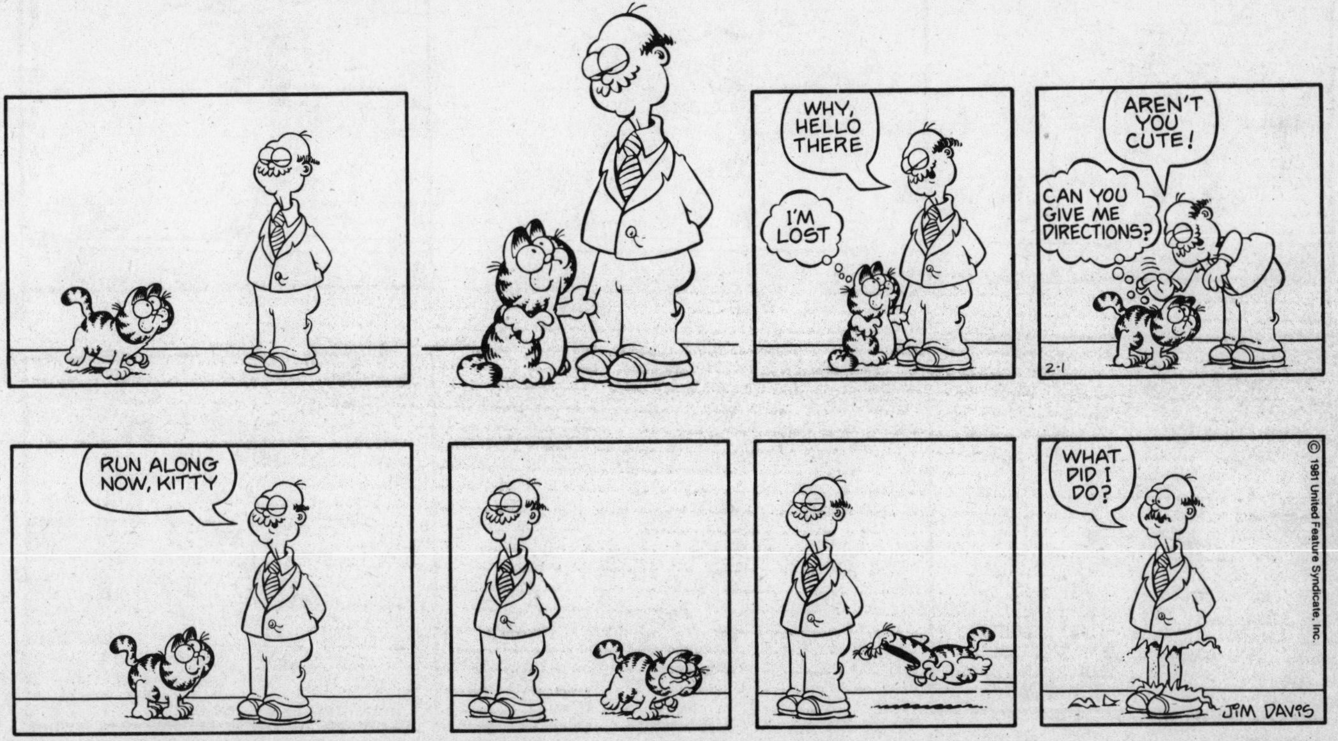
WHY, HELLO THERE
I'M LOST
AREN'T YOU CUTE!
CAN YOU GIVE ME DIRECTIONS?
2-1
RUN ALONG NOW, KITTY
WHAT DID I DO?
© 1981 United Feature Syndicate, Inc.
JIM DAVIS

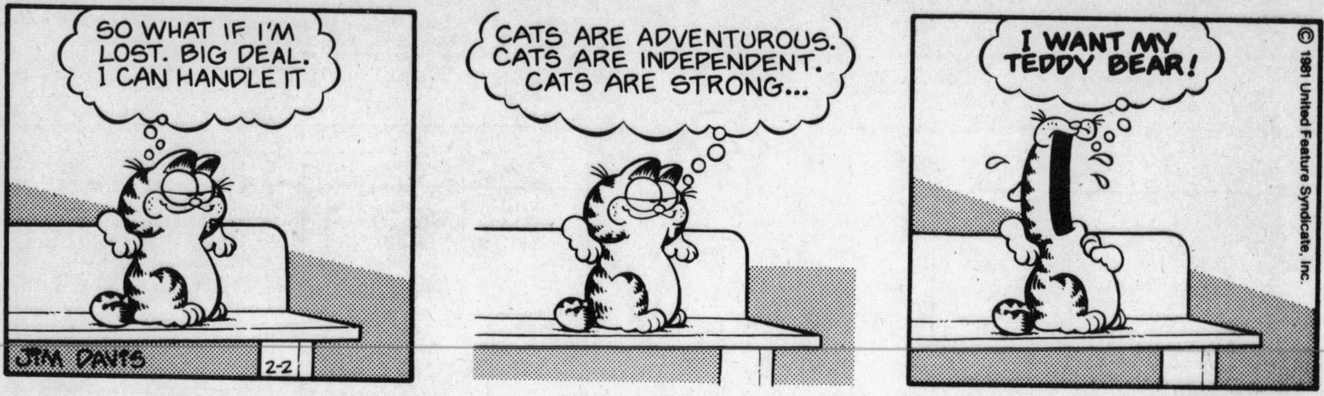
SO WHAT IF I'M LOST. BIG DEAL. I CAN HANDLE IT
JIM DAVIS
2-2
CATS ARE ADVENTUROUS. CATS ARE INDEPENDENT. CATS ARE STRONG...
I WANT MY TEDDY BEAR!
© 1981 United Feature Syndicate, Inc.

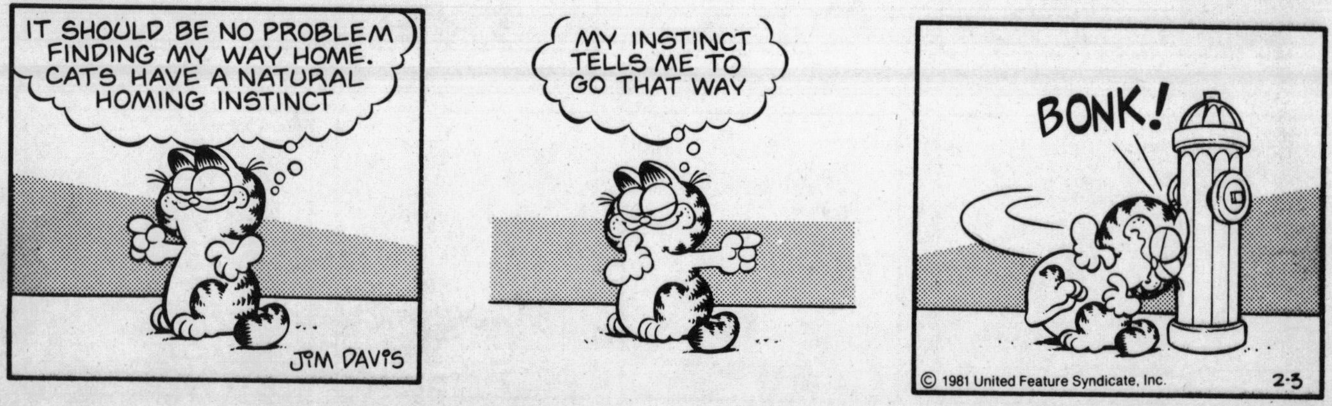
IT SHOULD BE NO PROBLEM FINDING MY WAY HOME. CATS HAVE A NATURAL HOMING INSTINCT
JIM DAVIS
MY INSTINCT TELLS ME TO GO THAT WAY
BONK!
© 1981 United Feature Syndicate, Inc.
2-3

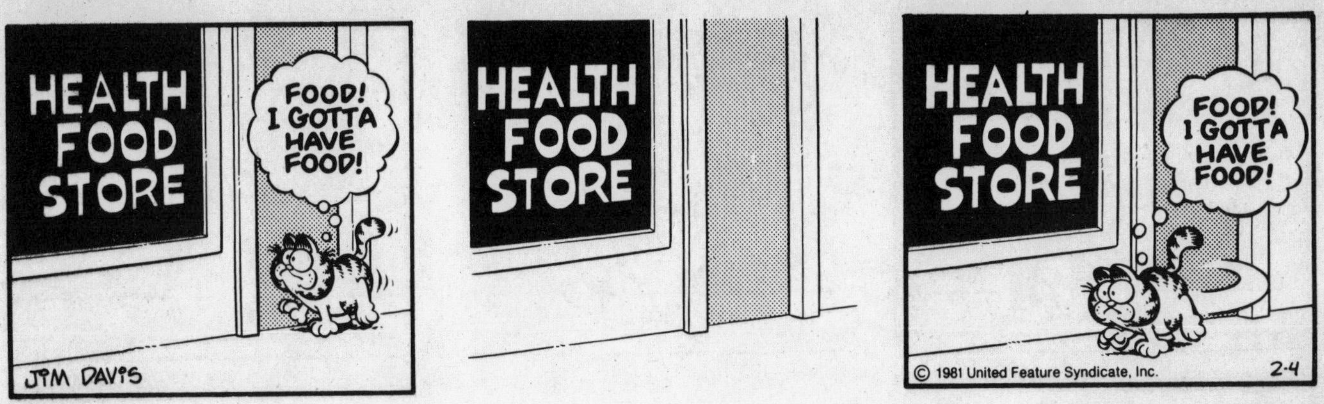
HEALTH FOOD STORE
FOOD! I GOTTA HAVE FOOD!
JIM DAVIS
HEALTH FOOD STORE
HEALTH FOOD STORE
FOOD! I GOTTA HAVE FOOD!
© 1981 United Feature Syndicate, Inc.
2-4

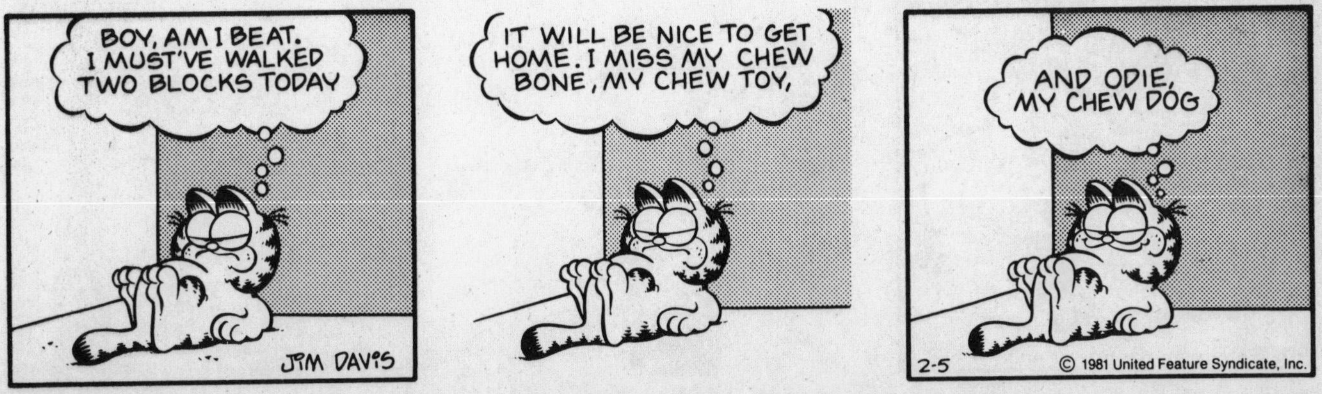
BOY, AM I BEAT. I MUST'VE WALKED TWO BLOCKS TODAY
JIM DAVIS
IT WILL BE NICE TO GET HOME. I MISS MY CHEW BONE, MY CHEW TOY,
AND ODIE, MY CHEW DOG
2-5
© 1981 United Feature Syndicate, Inc.

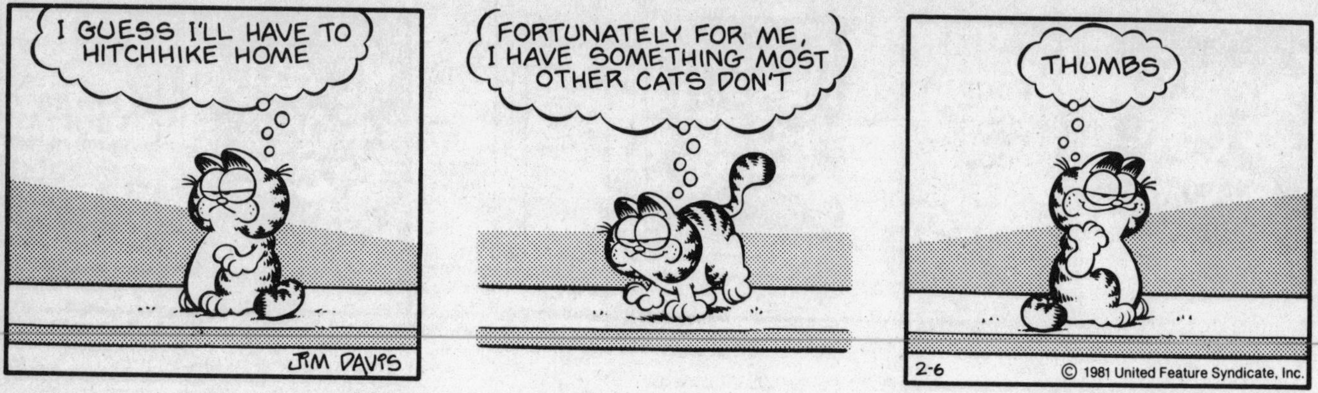
I GUESS I'LL HAVE TO HITCHHIKE HOME
JIM DAVIS
FORTUNATELY FOR ME, I HAVE SOMETHING MOST OTHER CATS DON'T
THUMBS
2-6
© 1981 United Feature Syndicate, Inc.

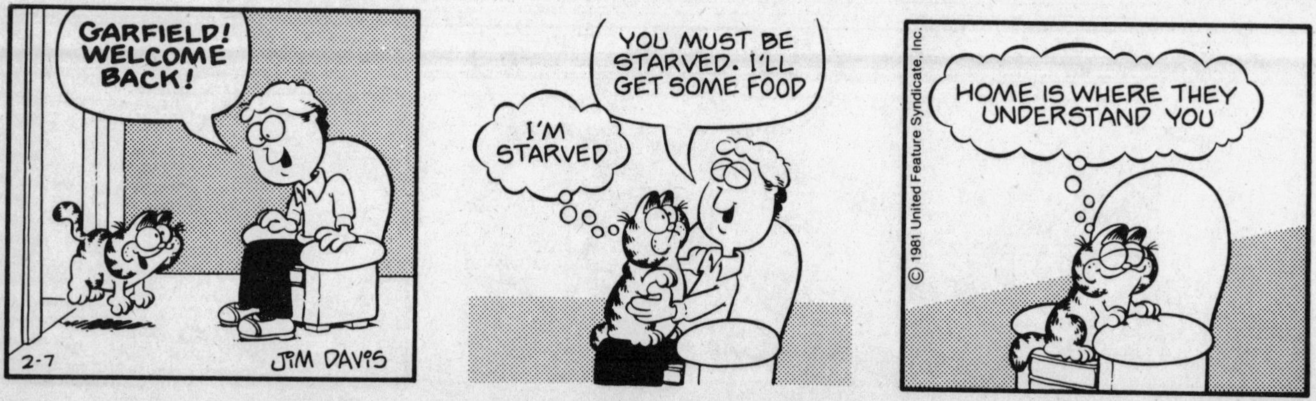
GARFIELD! WELCOME BACK!
2-7
JIM DAVIS
YOU MUST BE STARVED. I'LL GET SOME FOOD
I'M STARVED
© 1981 United Feature Syndicate, Inc.
HOME IS WHERE THEY UNDERSTAND YOU

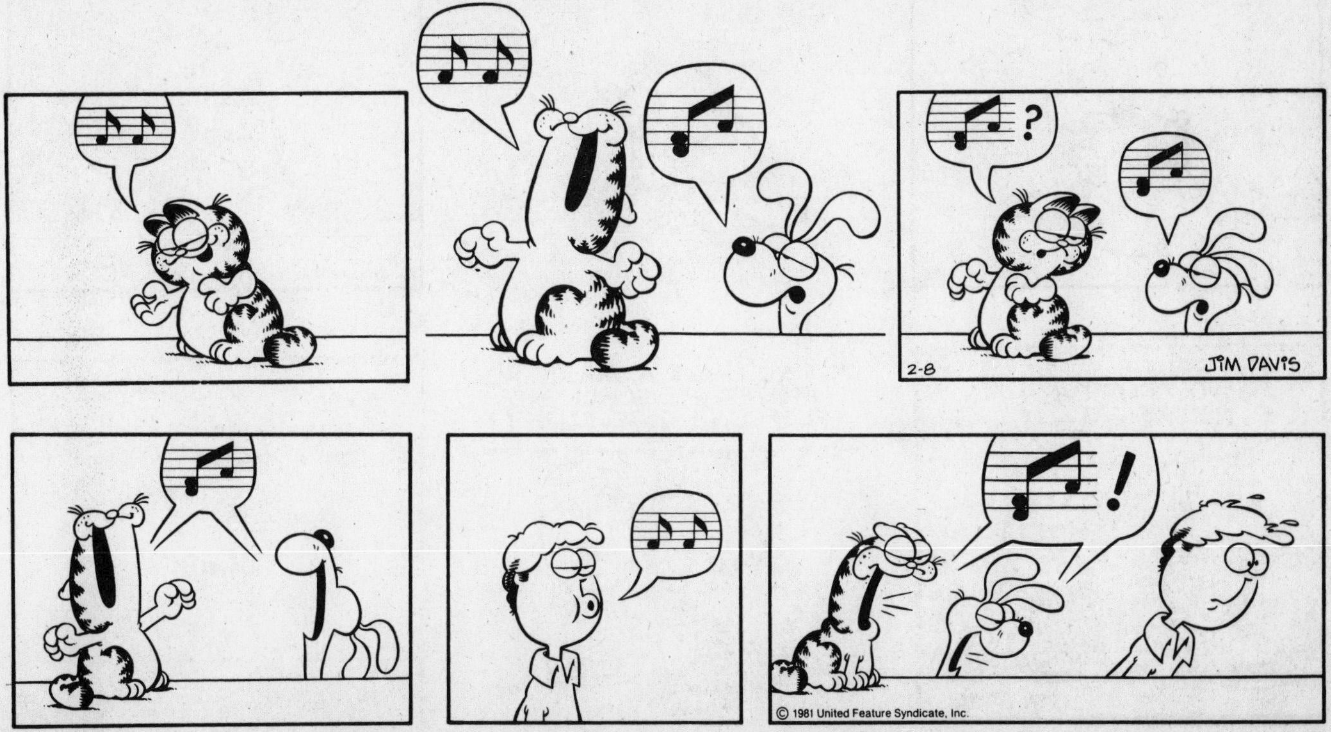

?
JIM DAVIS
2-8
!
© 1981 United Feature Syndicate, Inc.

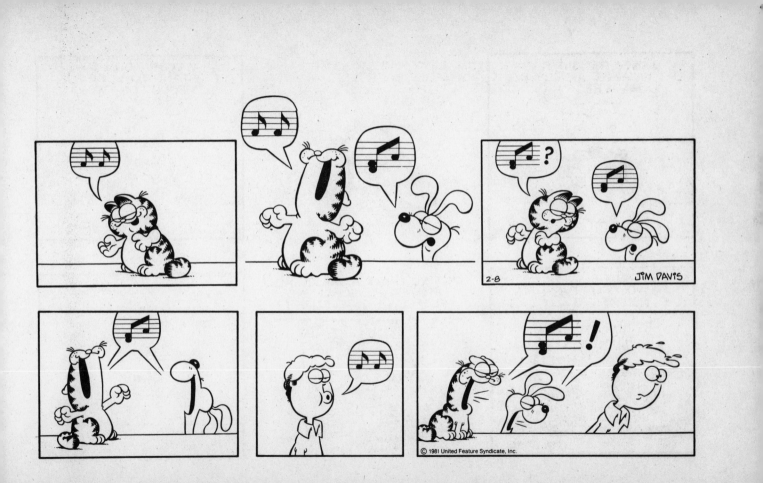

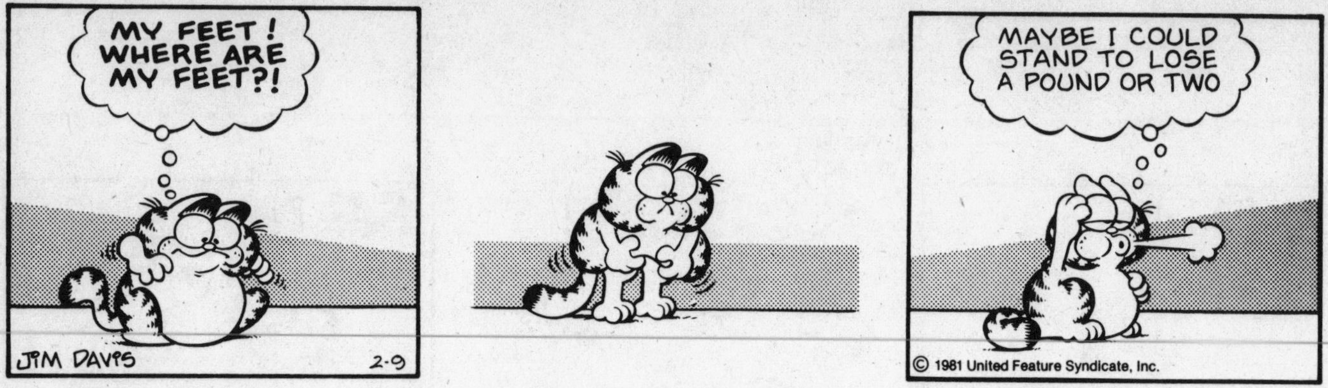
MY FEET! WHERE ARE MY FEET?!
JIM DAVIS
2-9
MAYBE I COULD STAND TO LOSE A POUND OR TWO
© 1981 United Feature Syndicate, Inc.

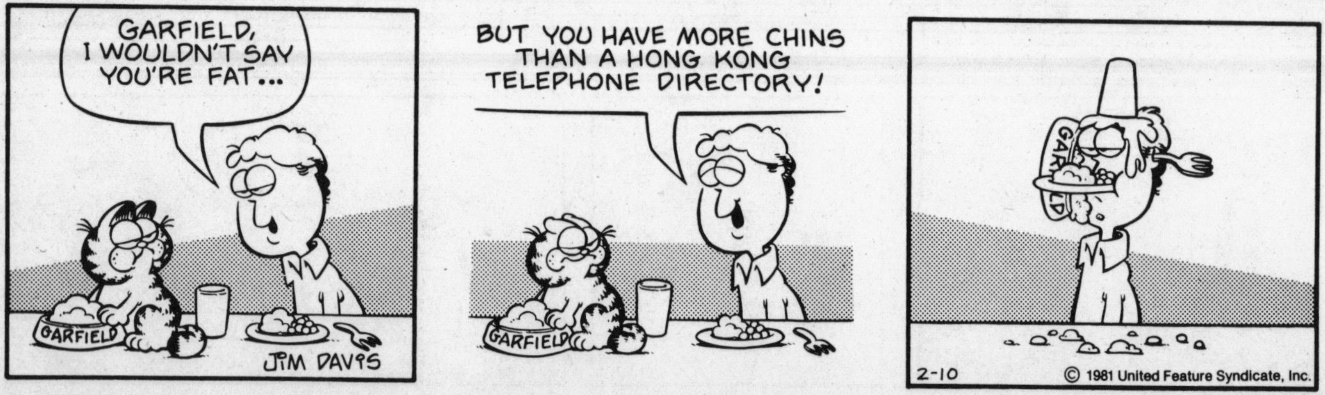
GARFIELD, I WOULDN'T SAY YOU'RE FAT...
GARFIELD
JIM DAVIS
BUT YOU HAVE MORE CHINS THAN A HONG KONG TELEPHONE DIRECTORY!
GARFIELD
2-10
© 1981 United Feature Syndicate, Inc.

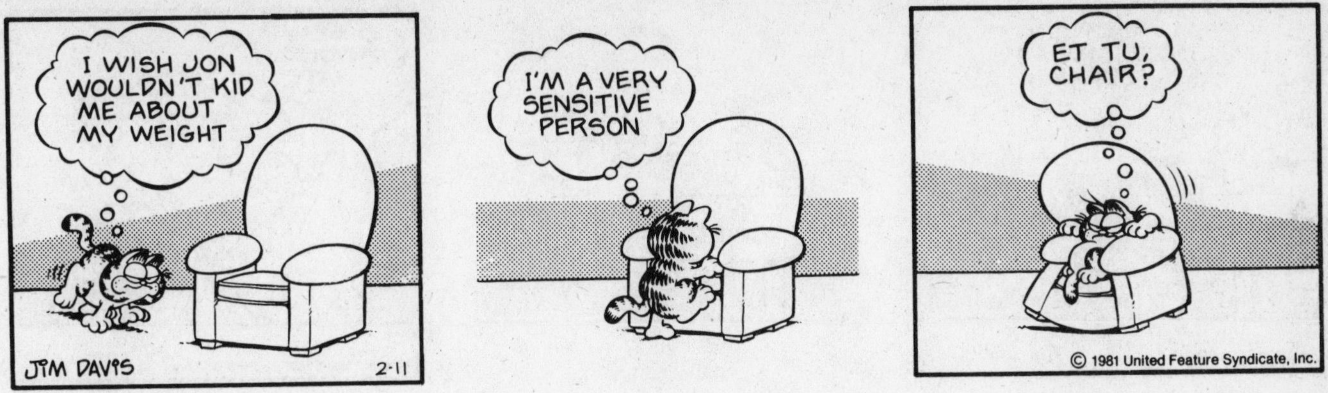
I WISH JON WOULDN'T KID ME ABOUT MY WEIGHT
JIM DAVIS
2-11
I'M A VERY SENSITIVE PERSON
ET TU, CHAIR?
© 1981 United Feature Syndicate, Inc.

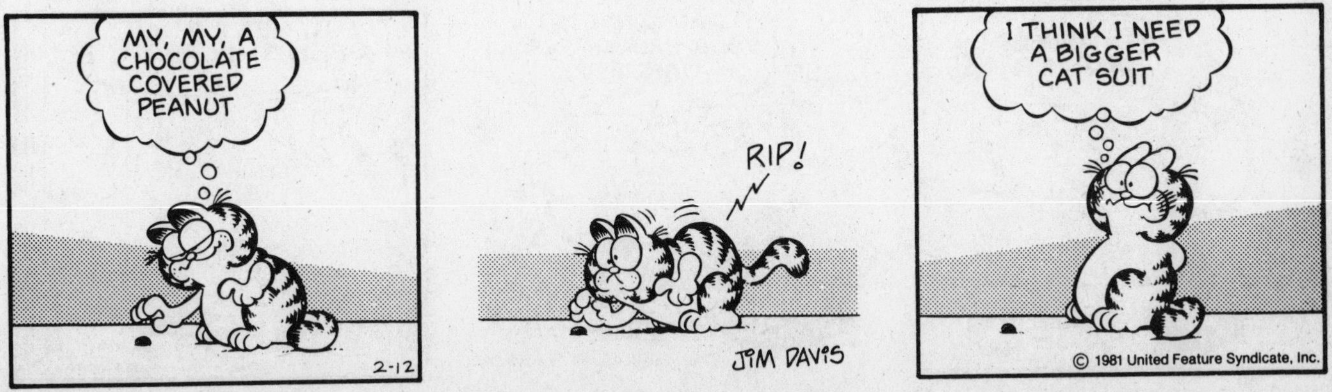
MY, MY, A CHOCOLATE COVERED PEANUT
2-12
RIP!
JIM DAVIS
I THINK I NEED A BIGGER CAT SUIT
© 1981 United Feature Syndicate, Inc.

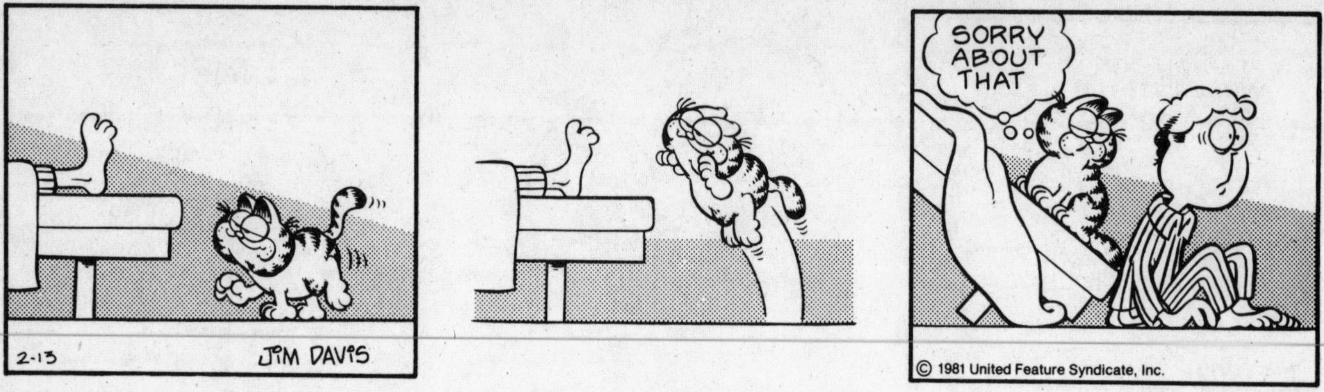
2-13
JIM DAVIS
SORRY ABOUT THAT
© 1981 United Feature Syndicate, Inc.

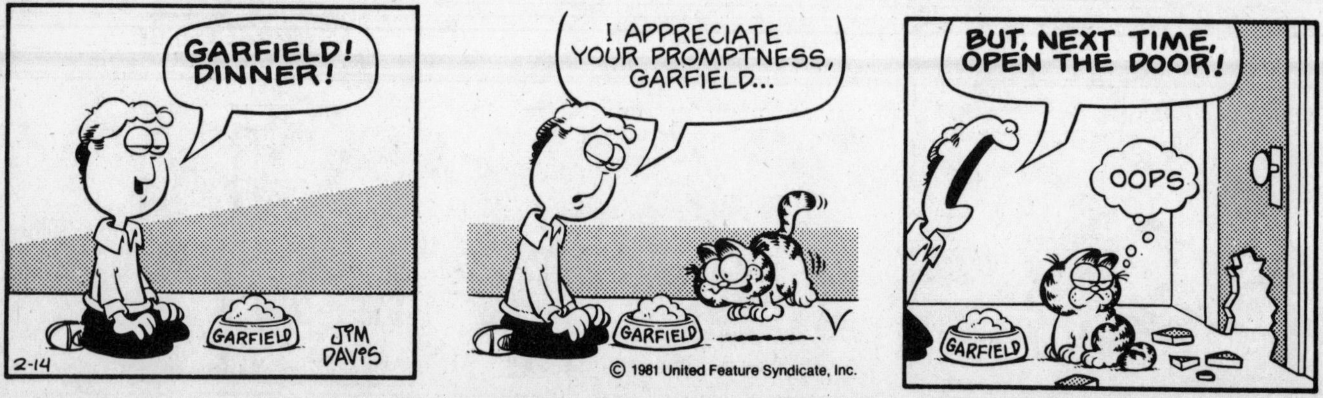
GARFIELD! DINNER!
GARFIELD
JIM DAVIS
2-14
I APPRECIATE YOUR PROMPTNESS, GARFIELD...
GARFIELD
© 1981 United Feature Syndicate, Inc.
BUT, NEXT TIME, OPEN THE DOOR!
OOPS
GARFIELD

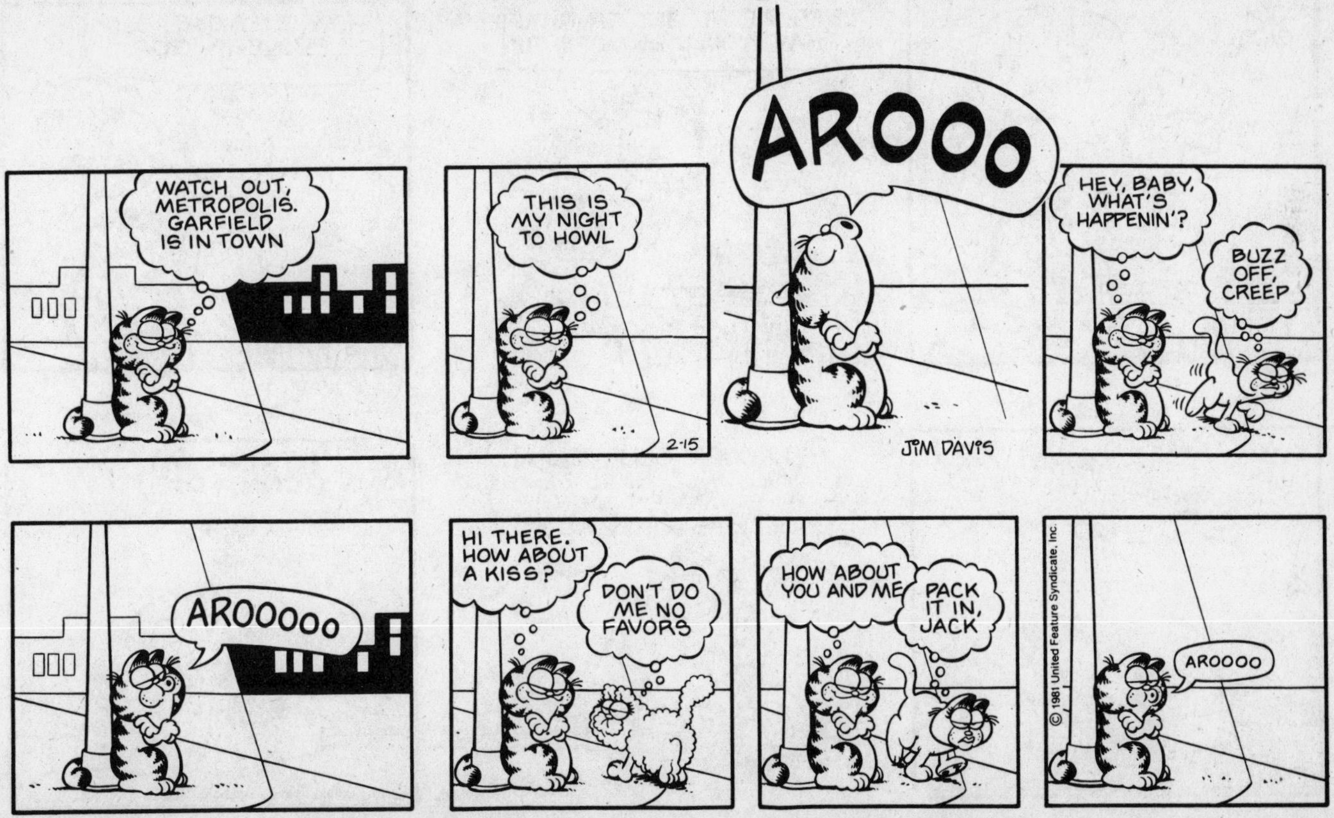
WATCH OUT, METROPOLIS. GARFIELD IS IN TOWN
THIS IS MY NIGHT TO HOWL
2-15
AROOO
JIM DAVIS
HEY, BABY, WHAT'S HAPPENIN'?
BUZZ OFF, CREEP
AROOOOO
HI THERE. HOW ABOUT A KISS?
DON'T DO ME NO FAVORS
HOW ABOUT YOU AND ME
PACK IT IN, JACK
© 1981 United Feature Syndicate, Inc.
AROOOO

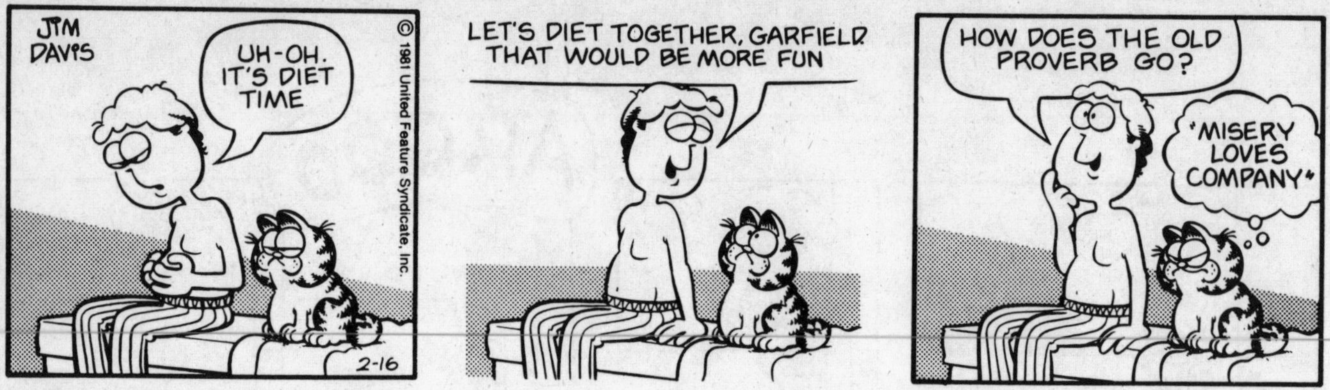
JIM DAVIS
UH-OH. IT'S DIET TIME
© 1981 United Feature Syndicate, Inc.
2-16
LET'S DIET TOGETHER, GARFIELD. THAT WOULD BE MORE FUN
HOW DOES THE OLD PROVERB GO?
"MISERY LOVES COMPANY"

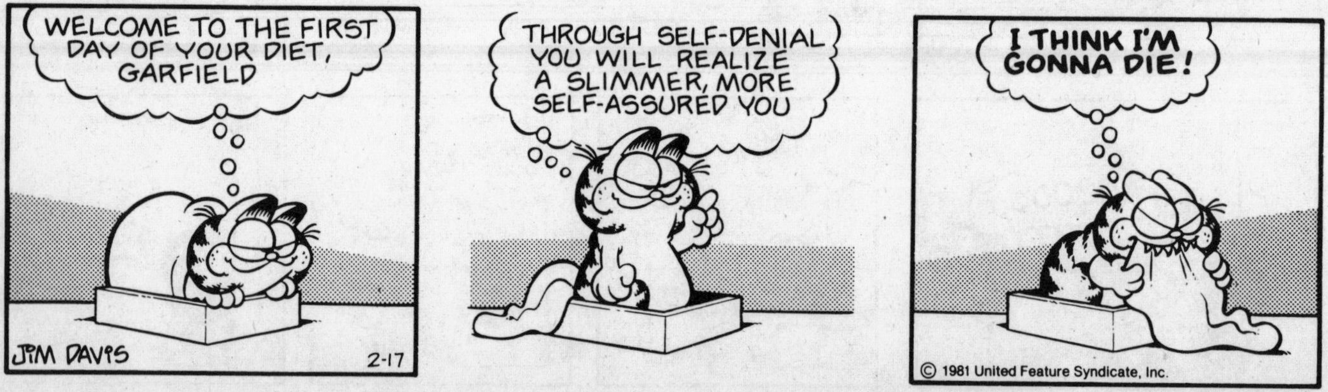
WELCOME TO THE FIRST DAY OF YOUR DIET, GARFIELD
JIM DAVIS
2-17
THROUGH SELF-DENIAL YOU WILL REALIZE A SLIMMER, MORE SELF-ASSURED YOU
I THINK I'M GONNA DIE!
© 1981 United Feature Syndicate, Inc.

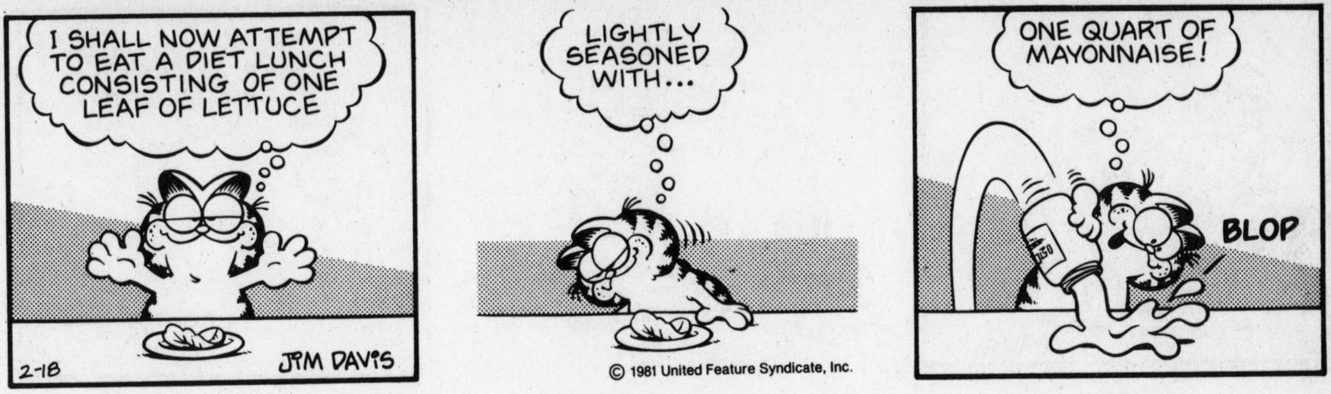
I SHALL NOW ATTEMPT TO EAT A DIET LUNCH CONSISTING OF ONE LEAF OF LETTUCE
2-18
JIM DAVIS
LIGHTLY SEASONED WITH...
© 1981 United Feature Syndicate, Inc.
ONE QUART OF MAYONNAISE!
BLOP

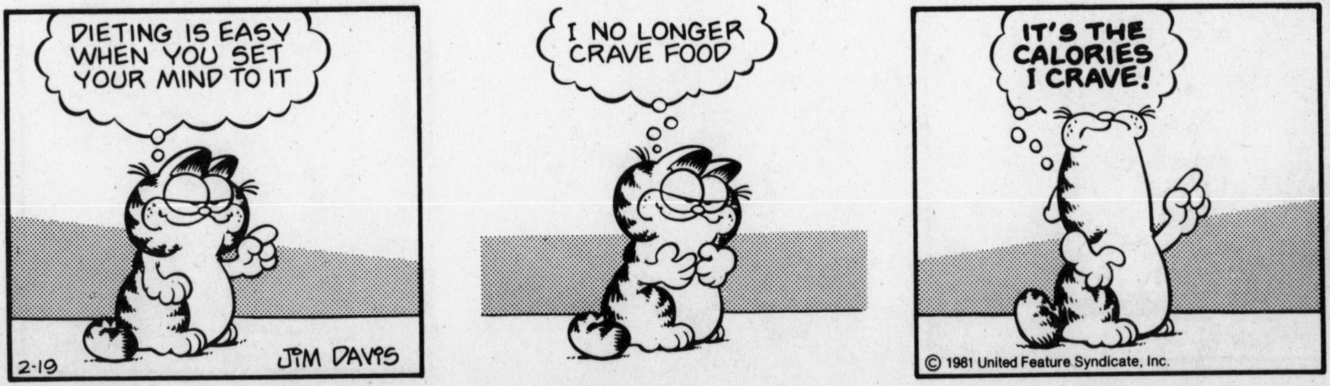
DIETING IS EASY WHEN YOU SET YOUR MIND TO IT
2-19
JIM DAVIS
I NO LONGER CRAVE FOOD
IT'S THE CALORIES I CRAVE!
© 1981 United Feature Syndicate, Inc.

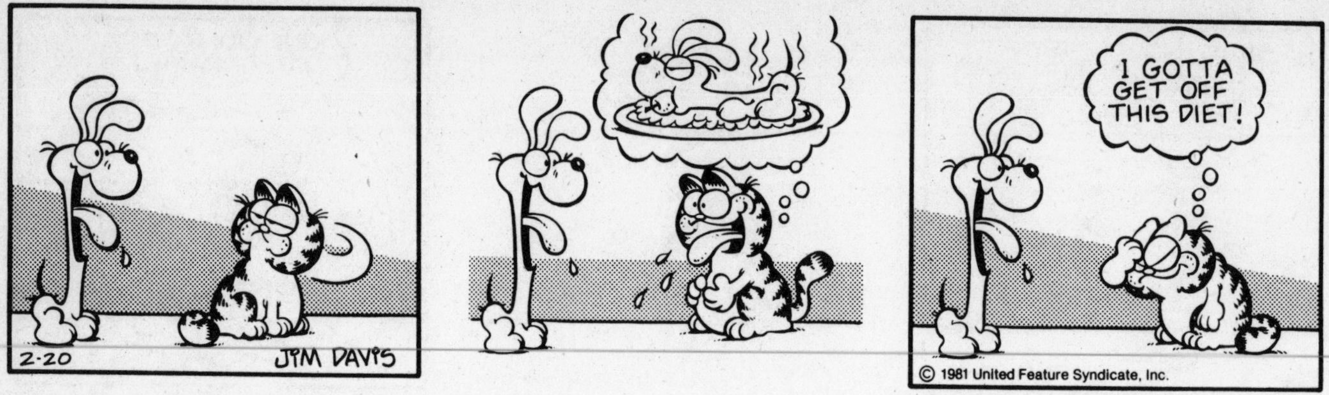
2-20
JIM DAVIS
I GOTTA GET OFF THIS DIET!
© 1981 United Feature Syndicate, Inc.

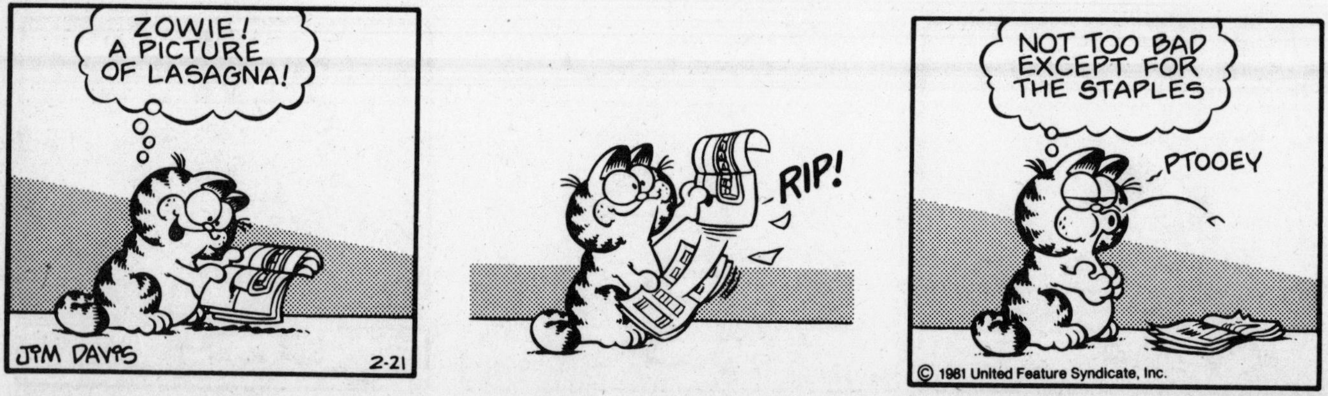
ZOWIE! A PICTURE OF LASAGNA!
JIM DAVIS
2-21
RIP!
NOT TOO BAD EXCEPT FOR THE STAPLES
PTOOEY
© 1981 United Feature Syndicate, Inc.

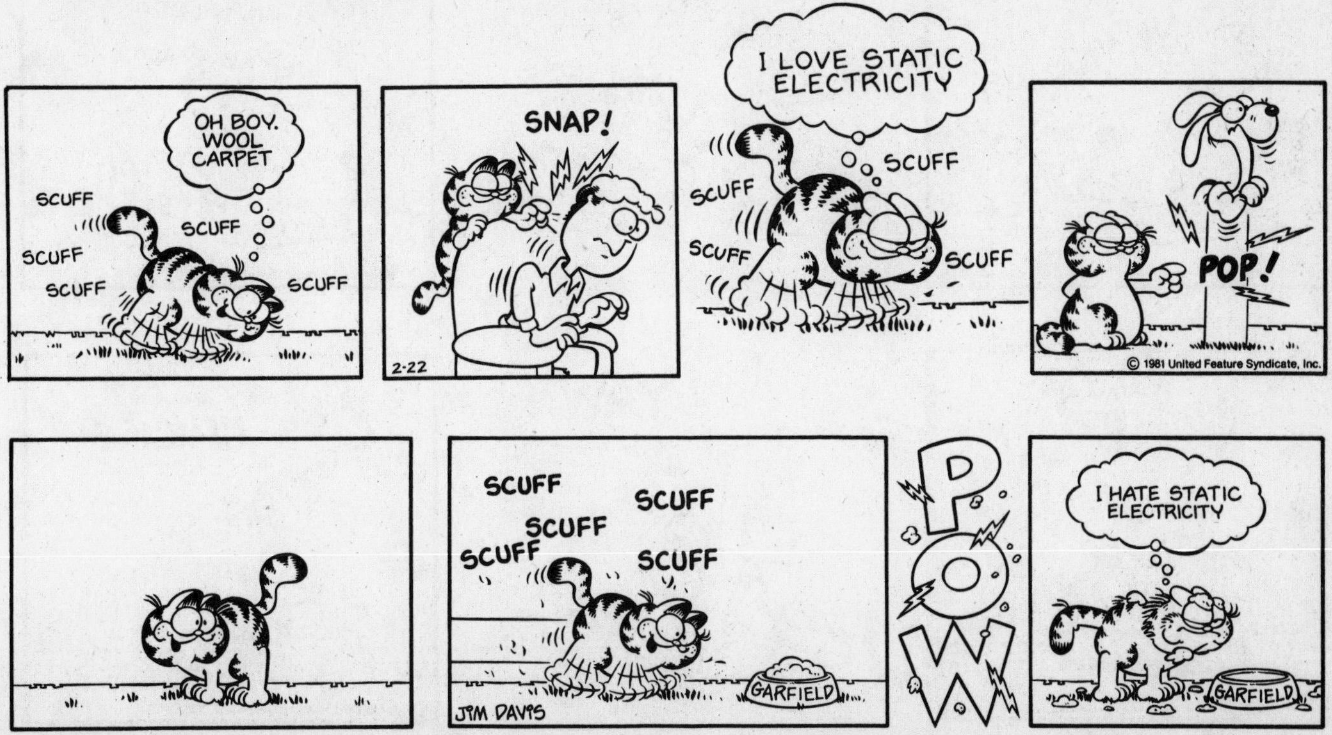
OH BOY. WOOL CARPET
SCUFF
SCUFF
SCUFF
SCUFF
SCUFF
SNAP!
2-22
I LOVE STATIC ELECTRICITY
SCUFF
SCUFF
SCUFF
SCUFF
POP!
© 1981 United Feature Syndicate, Inc.
SCUFF
SCUFF
SCUFF
SCUFF
SCUFF
GARFIELD
JIM DAVIS
POW
I HATE STATIC ELECTRICITY
GARFIELD

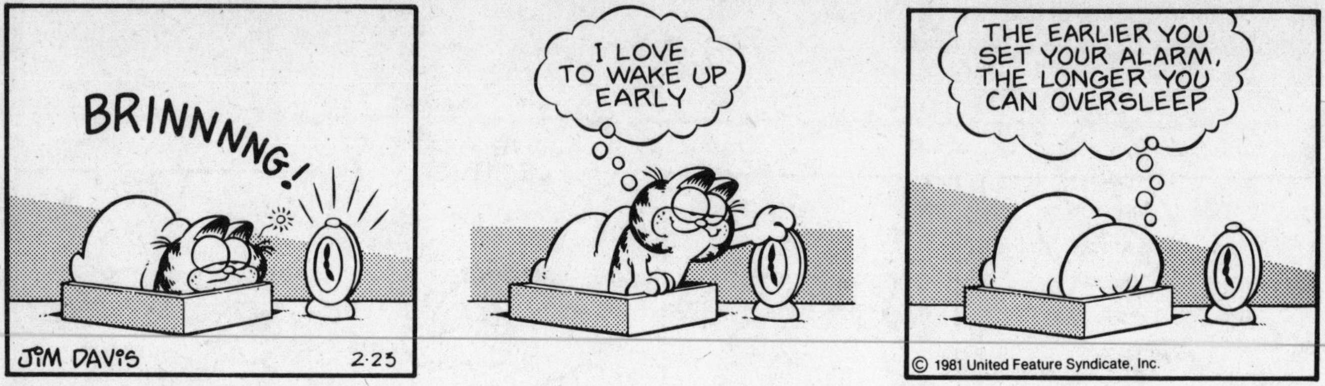
BRINNNNG!
I LOVE TO WAKE UP EARLY
THE EARLIER YOU SET YOUR ALARM, THE LONGER YOU CAN OVERSLEEP
JIM DAVIS
2-23
© 1981 United Feature Syndicate, Inc.

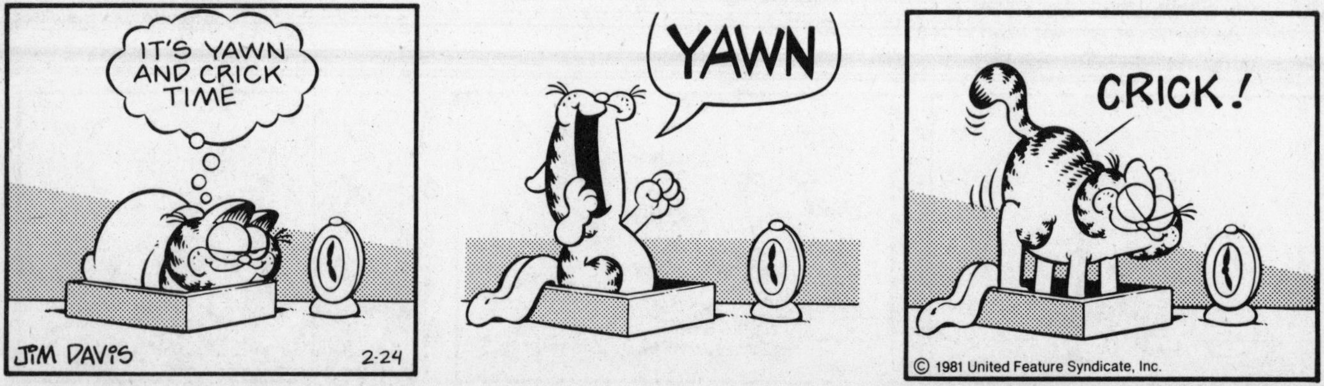
IT'S YAWN AND CRICK TIME
YAWN
CRICK!
JIM DAVIS
2-24
© 1981 United Feature Syndicate, Inc.

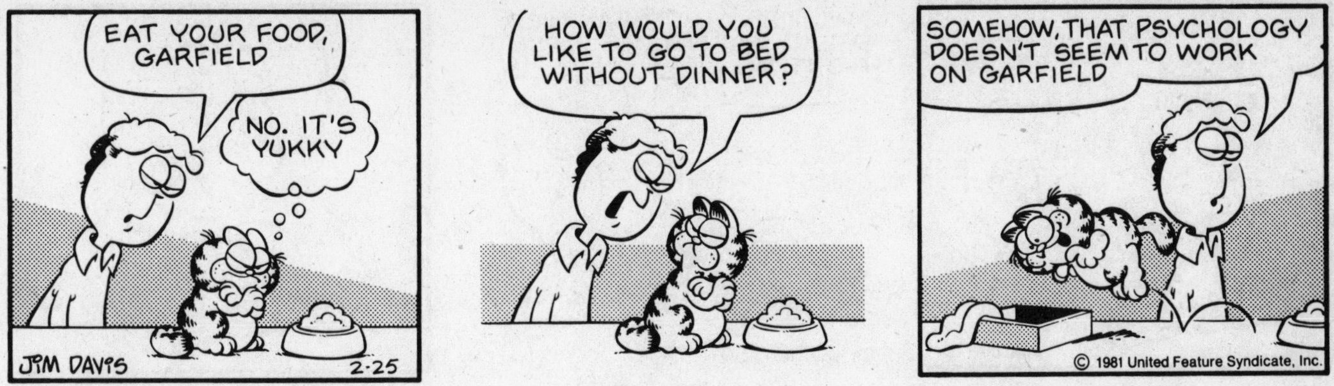
EAT YOUR FOOD, GARFIELD
NO. IT'S YUKKY
JIM DAVIS
2-25
HOW WOULD YOU LIKE TO GO TO BED WITHOUT DINNER?
SOMEHOW, THAT PSYCHOLOGY DOESN'T SEEM TO WORK ON GARFIELD
© 1981 United Feature Syndicate, Inc.

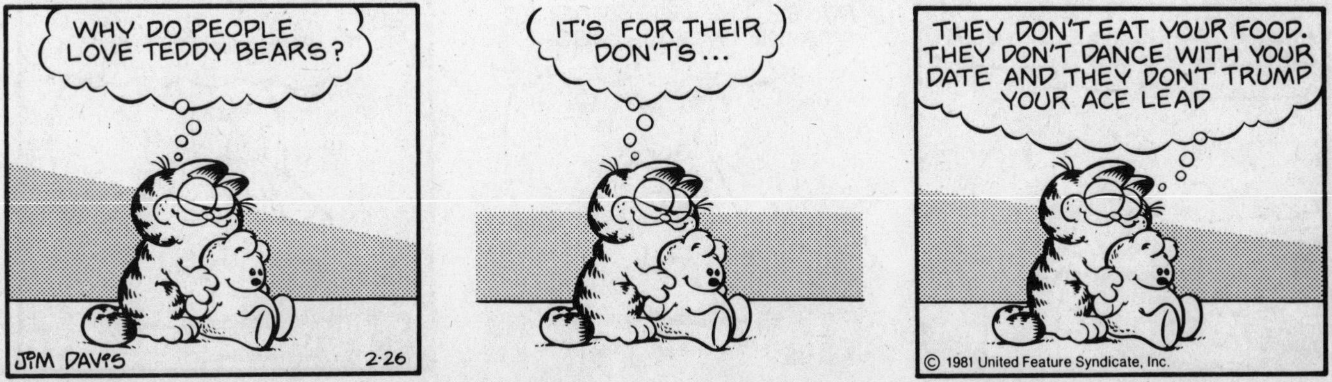
WHY DO PEOPLE LOVE TEDDY BEARS?
JIM DAVIS
2-26
IT'S FOR THEIR DON'TS...
THEY DON'T EAT YOUR FOOD. THEY DON'T DANCE WITH YOUR DATE AND THEY DON'T TRUMP YOUR ACE LEAD
© 1981 United Feature Syndicate, Inc.

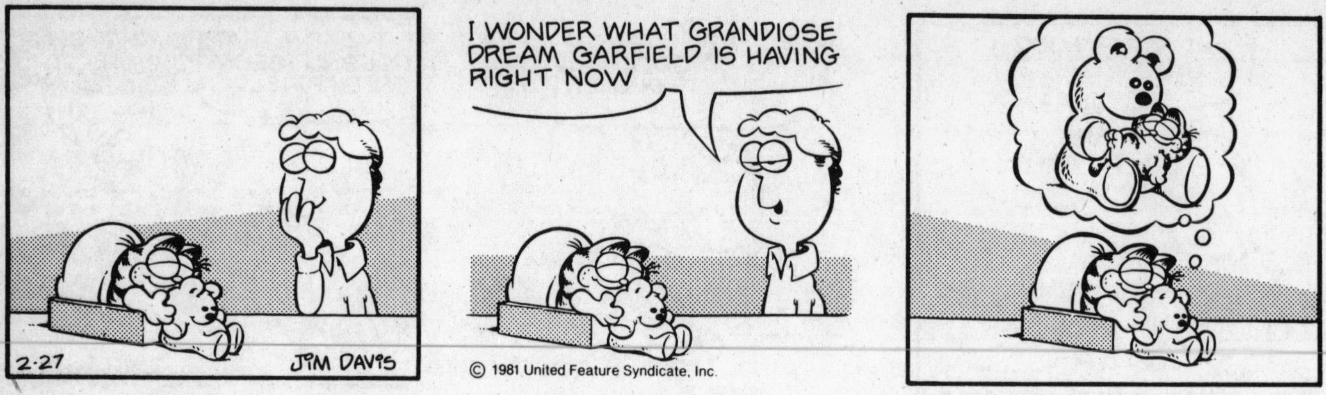
2·27
JIM DAVIS
I WONDER WHAT GRANDIOSE DREAM GARFIELD IS HAVING RIGHT NOW
© 1981 United Feature Syndicate, Inc.

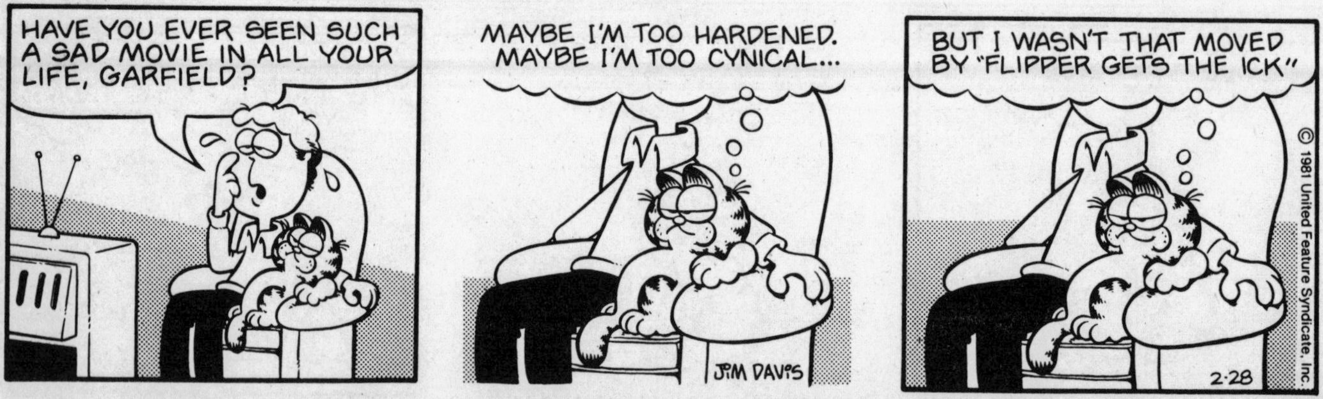
HAVE YOU EVER SEEN SUCH A SAD MOVIE IN ALL YOUR LIFE, GARFIELD?
MAYBE I'M TOO HARDENED. MAYBE I'M TOO CYNICAL...
JIM DAVIS
BUT I WASN'T THAT MOVED BY "FLIPPER GETS THE ICK"
2·28
© 1981 United Feature Syndicate, Inc.

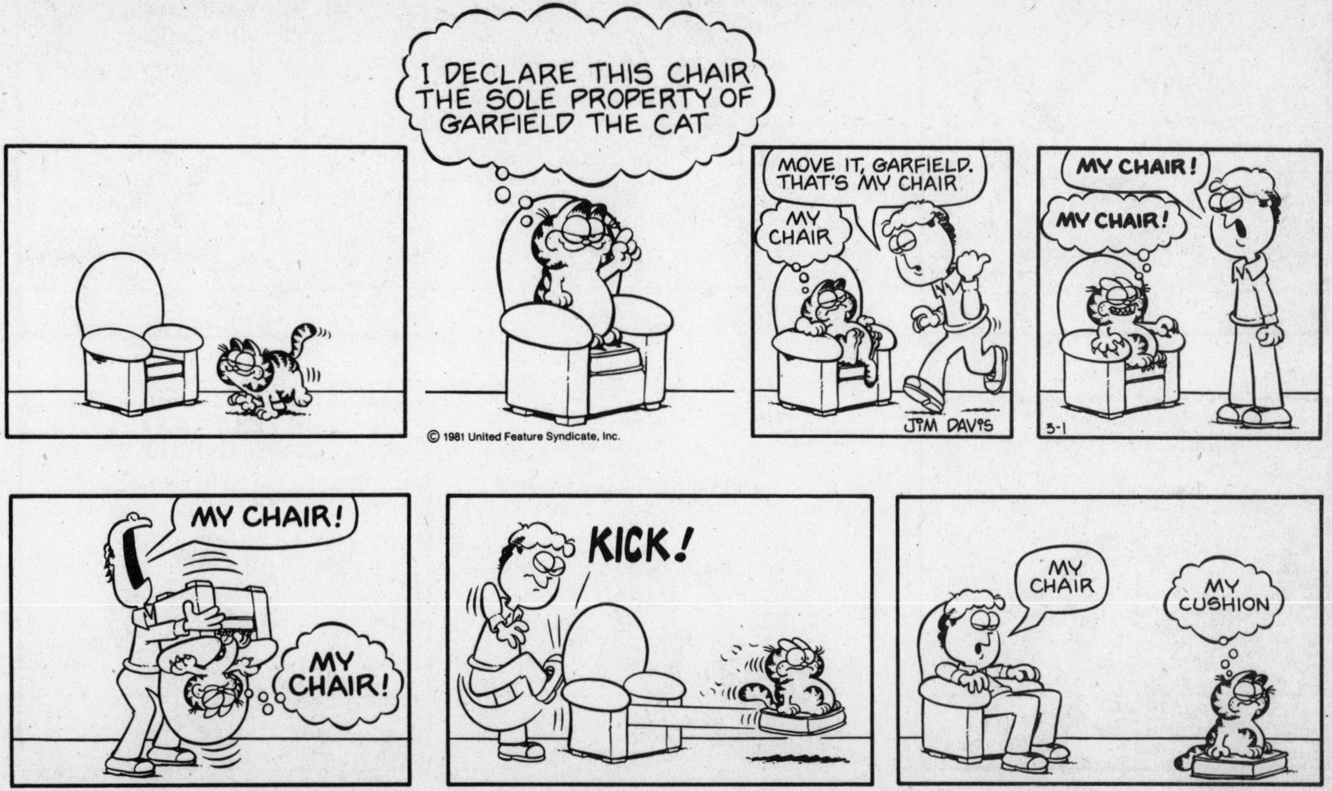
I DECLARE THIS CHAIR THE SOLE PROPERTY OF GARFIELD THE CAT
MOVE IT, GARFIELD. THAT'S MY CHAIR
MY CHAIR
MY CHAIR!
MY CHAIR!
MY CHAIR!
MY CHAIR!
KICK!
MY CHAIR
MY CUSHION
JIM DAVIS
3-1

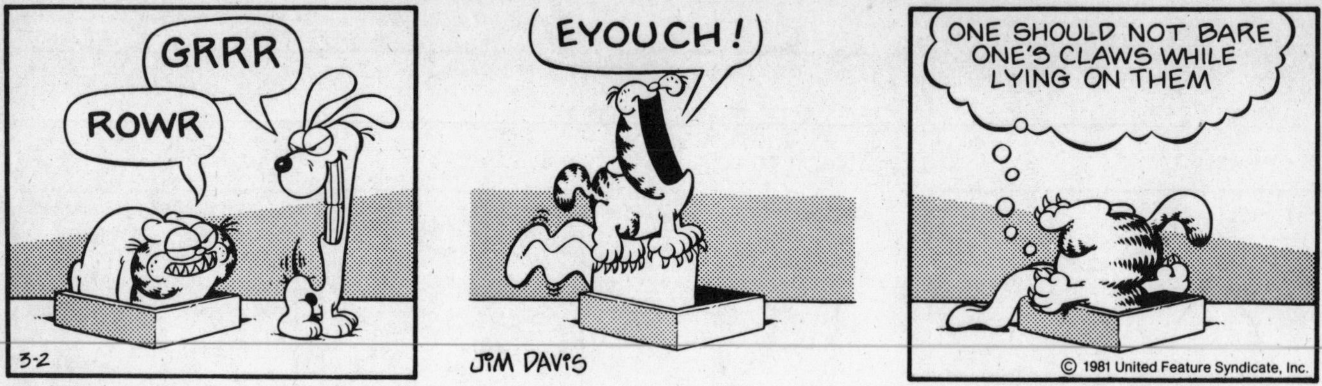
GRRR
ROWR
3-2
EYOUCH!
JIM DAVIS
ONE SHOULD NOT BARE ONE'S CLAWS WHILE LYING ON THEM
© 1981 United Feature Syndicate, Inc.

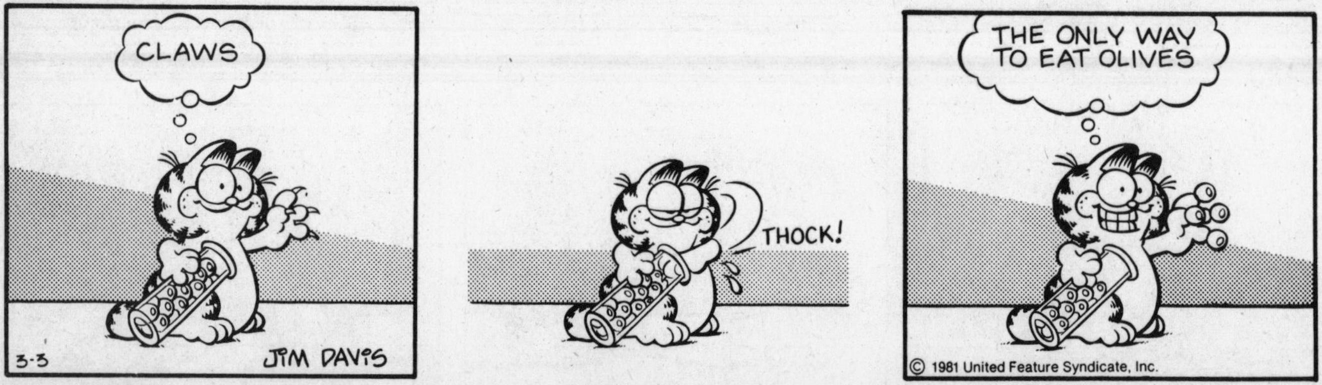
CLAWS
3-3
JIM DAVIS
THOCK!
THE ONLY WAY TO EAT OLIVES
© 1981 United Feature Syndicate, Inc.

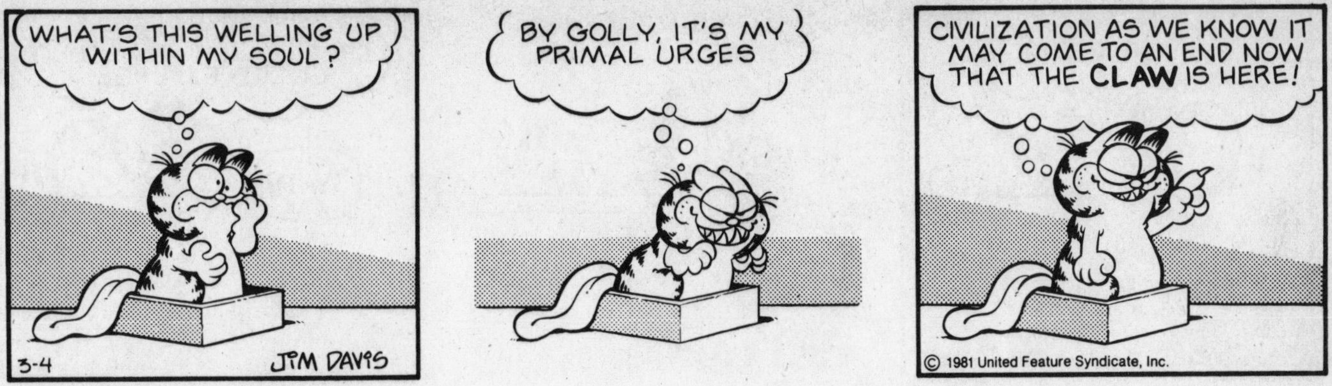
WHAT'S THIS WELLING UP WITHIN MY SOUL?
3-4
JIM DAVIS
BY GOLLY, IT'S MY PRIMAL URGES
CIVILIZATION AS WE KNOW IT MAY COME TO AN END NOW THAT THE **CLAW** IS HERE!
© 1981 United Feature Syndicate, Inc.

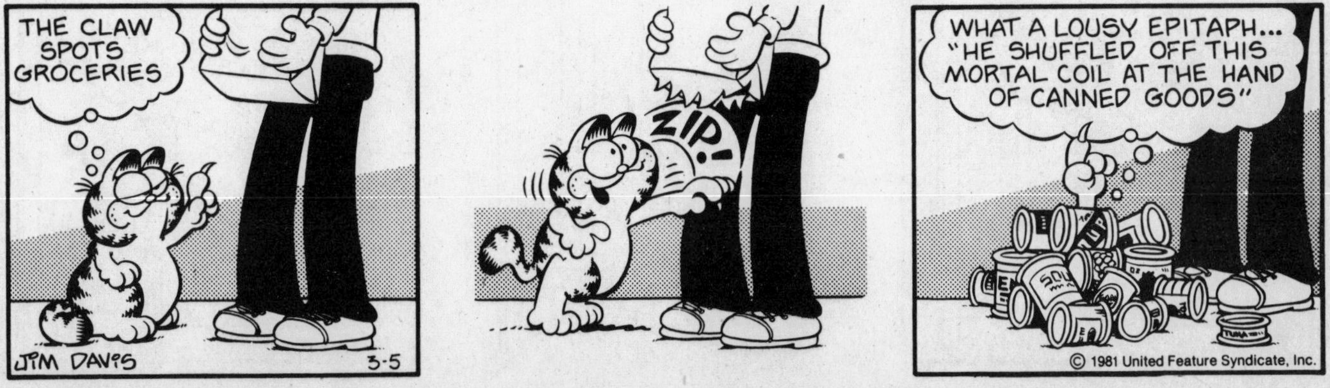
THE CLAW SPOTS GROCERIES
JIM DAVIS
3-5
ZIP!
WHAT A LOUSY EPITAPH... "HE SHUFFLED OFF THIS MORTAL COIL AT THE HAND OF CANNED GOODS"
© 1981 United Feature Syndicate, Inc.

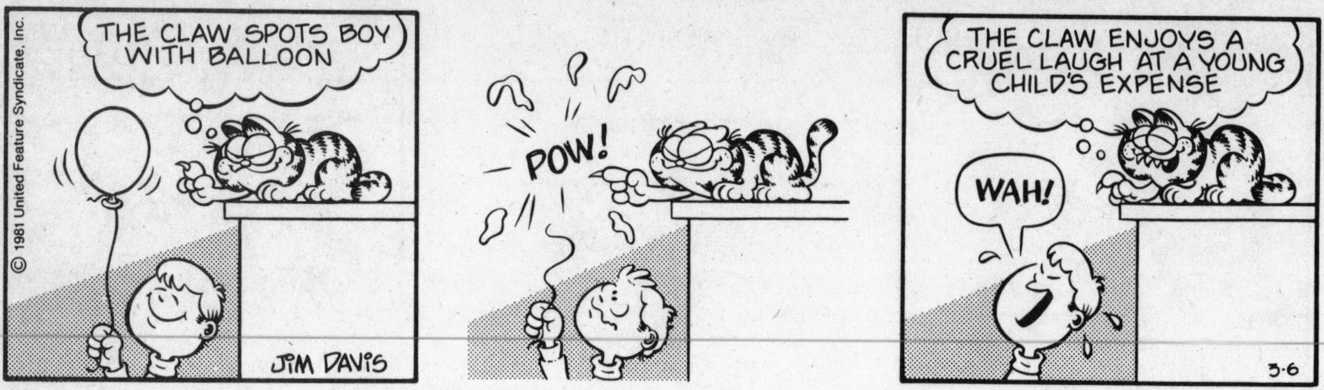

© 1981 United Feature Syndicate, Inc.
THE CLAW SPOTS BOY WITH BALLOON
JIM DAVIS
POW!
THE CLAW ENJOYS A CRUEL LAUGH AT A YOUNG CHILD'S EXPENSE
WAH!
3-6

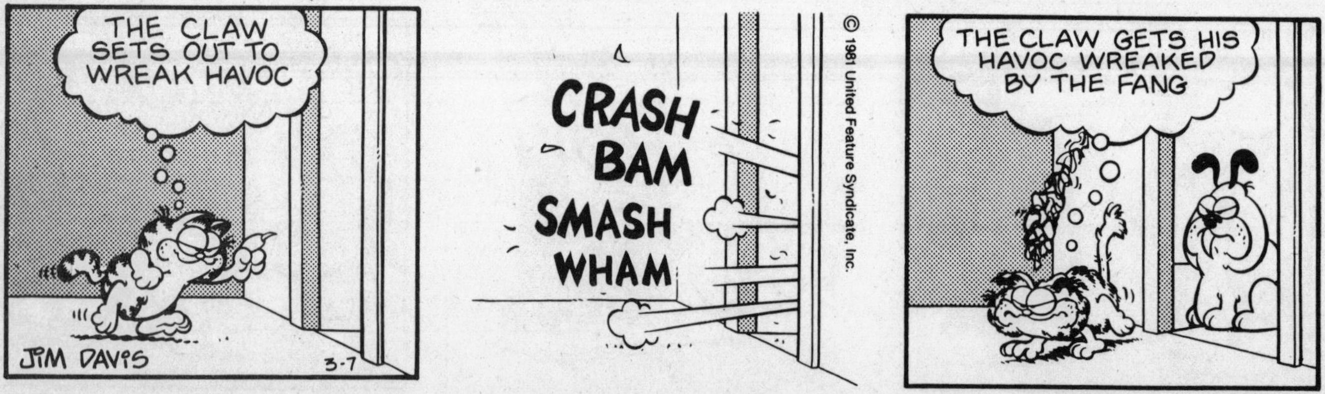

THE CLAW SETS OUT TO WREAK HAVOC
JIM DAVIS
3-7
CRASH
BAM
SMASH
WHAM
© 1981 United Feature Syndicate, Inc.
THE CLAW GETS HIS HAVOC WREAKED BY THE FANG

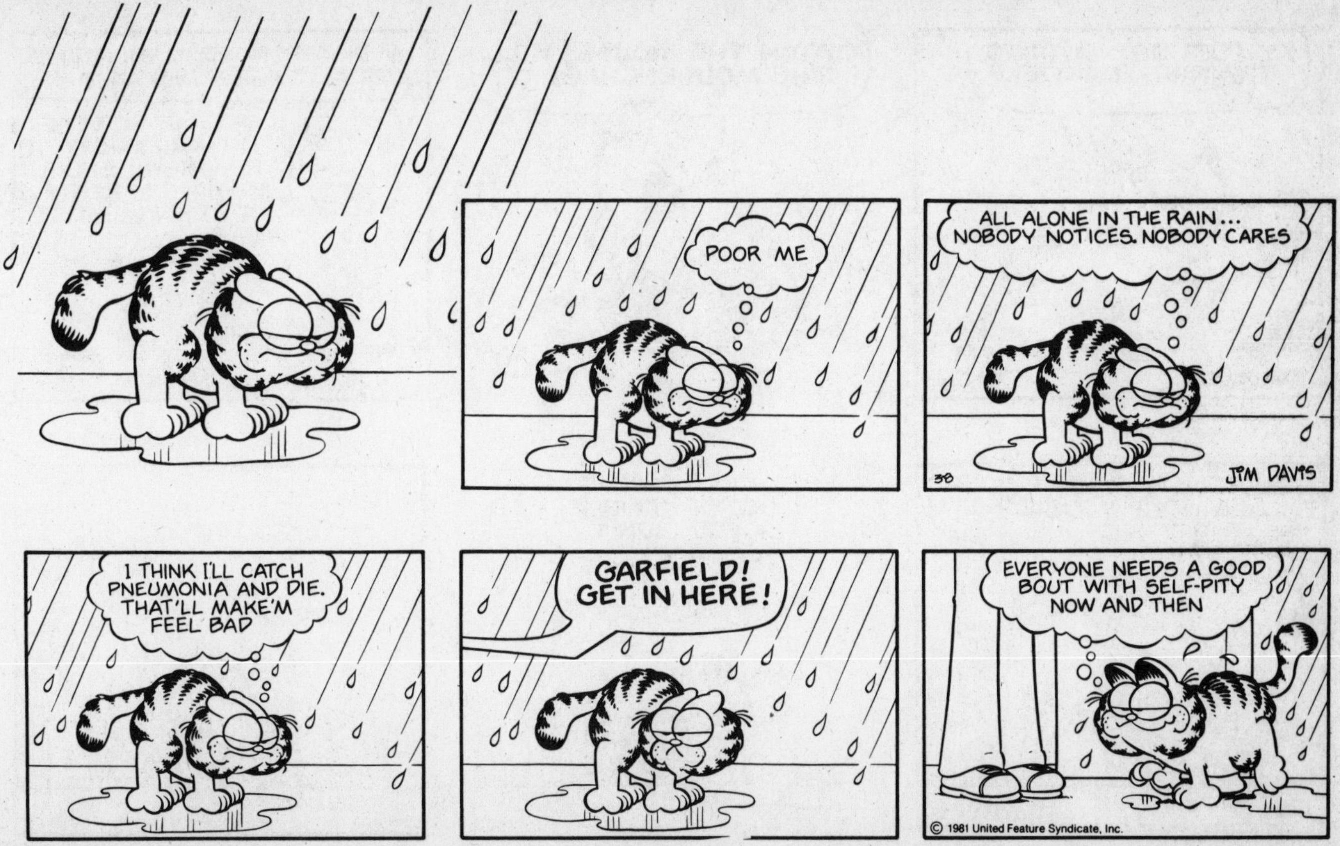
POOR ME
ALL ALONE IN THE RAIN... NOBODY NOTICES. NOBODY CARES
JIM DAVIS
I THINK I'LL CATCH PNEUMONIA AND DIE. THAT'LL MAKE'M FEEL BAD
GARFIELD! GET IN HERE!
EVERYONE NEEDS A GOOD BOUT WITH SELF-PITY NOW AND THEN
© 1981 United Feature Syndicate, Inc.

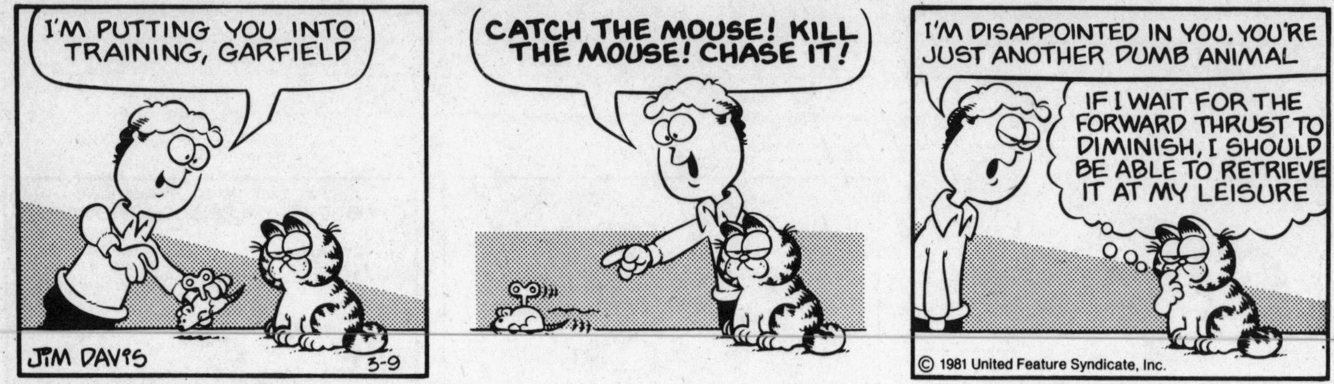
I'M PUTTING YOU INTO TRAINING, GARFIELD
JIM DAVIS
3-9
CATCH THE MOUSE! KILL THE MOUSE! CHASE IT!
I'M DISAPPOINTED IN YOU. YOU'RE JUST ANOTHER DUMB ANIMAL
IF I WAIT FOR THE FORWARD THRUST TO DIMINISH, I SHOULD BE ABLE TO RETRIEVE IT AT MY LEISURE
© 1981 United Feature Syndicate, Inc.

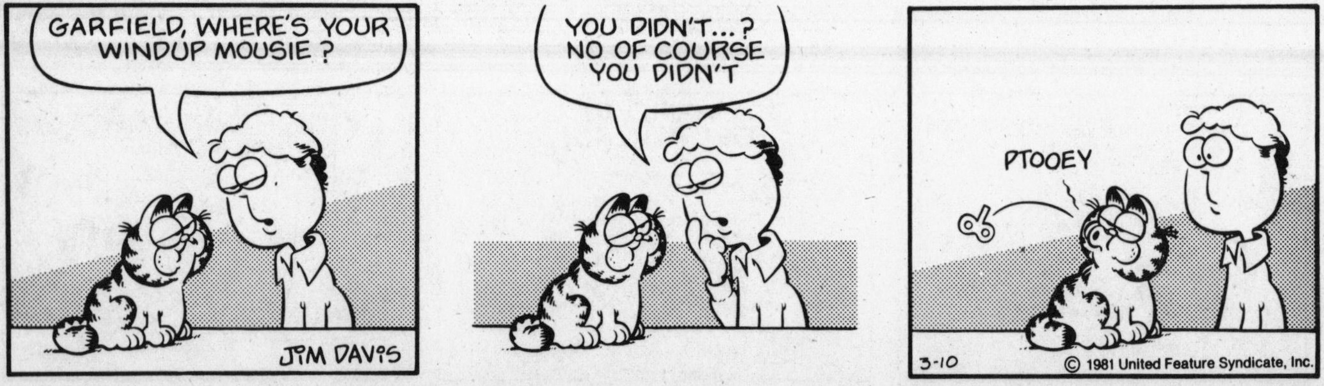
GARFIELD, WHERE'S YOUR WINDUP MOUSIE?
JIM DAVIS
YOU DIDN'T...? NO OF COURSE YOU DIDN'T
PTOOEY
3-10
© 1981 United Feature Syndicate, Inc.

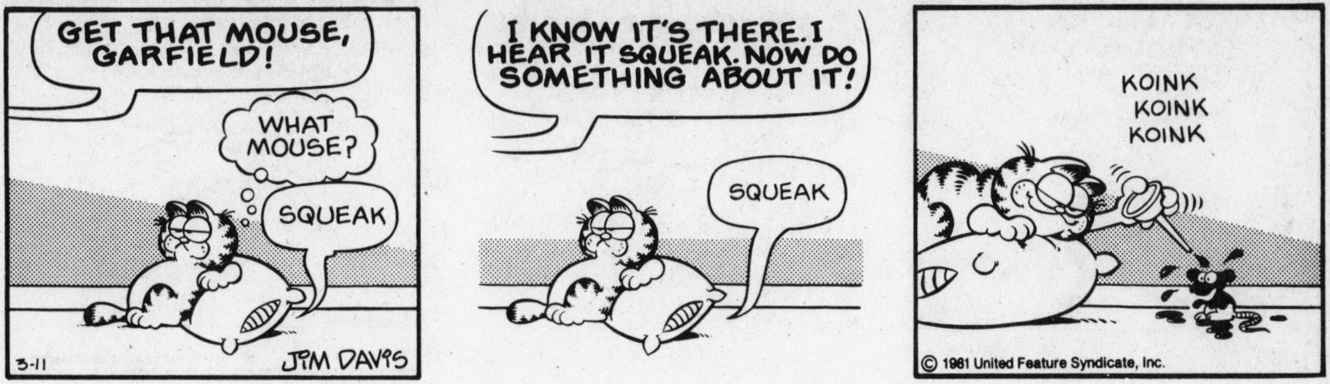
GET THAT MOUSE, GARFIELD!
WHAT MOUSE?
SQUEAK
3-11
JIM DAVIS
I KNOW IT'S THERE. I HEAR IT SQUEAK. NOW DO SOMETHING ABOUT IT!
SQUEAK
KOINK
KOINK
KOINK
© 1981 United Feature Syndicate, Inc.

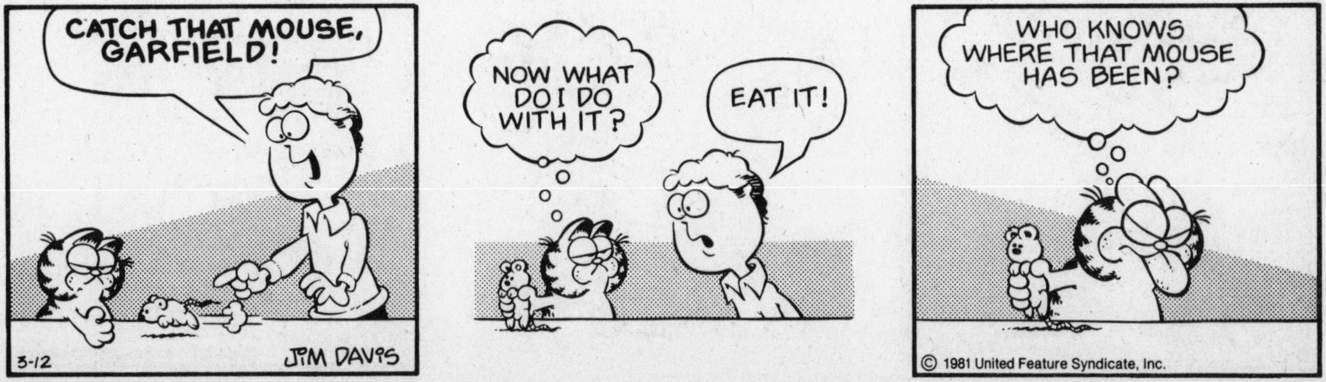
CATCH THAT MOUSE, GARFIELD!
3-12
JIM DAVIS
NOW WHAT DO I DO WITH IT?
EAT IT!
WHO KNOWS WHERE THAT MOUSE HAS BEEN?
© 1981 United Feature Syndicate, Inc.

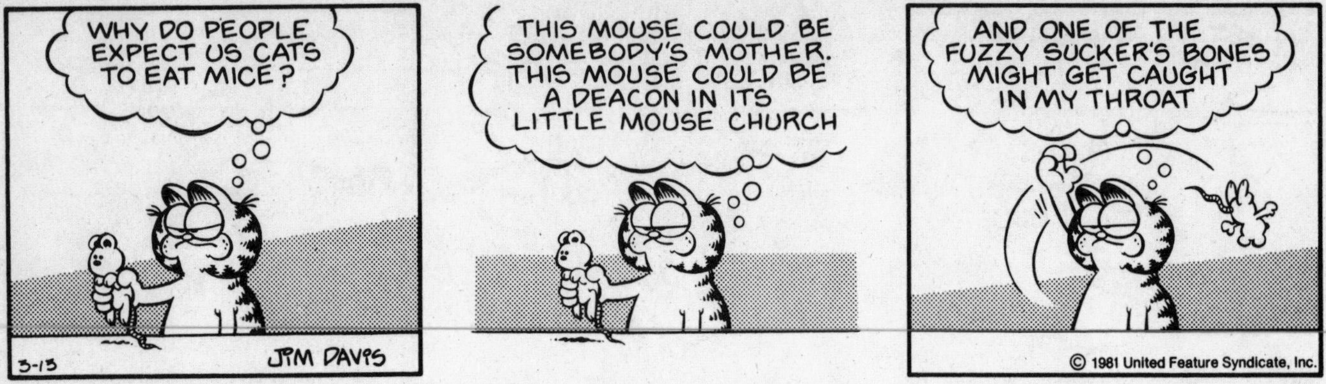
WHY DO PEOPLE EXPECT US CATS TO EAT MICE?
3-13
JIM DAVIS
THIS MOUSE COULD BE SOMEBODY'S MOTHER. THIS MOUSE COULD BE A DEACON IN ITS LITTLE MOUSE CHURCH
AND ONE OF THE FUZZY SUCKER'S BONES MIGHT GET CAUGHT IN MY THROAT
© 1981 United Feature Syndicate, Inc.

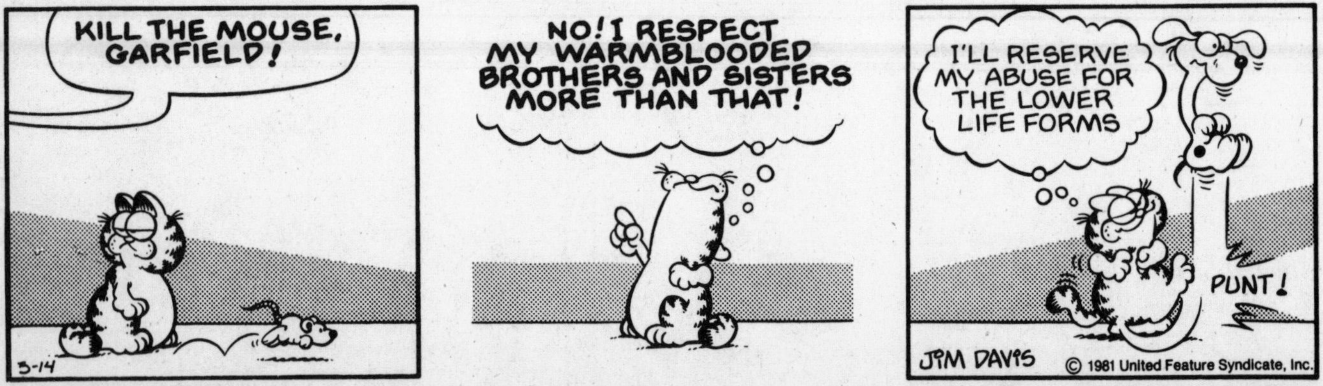
KILL THE MOUSE, GARFIELD!
3-14
NO! I RESPECT MY WARMBLOODED BROTHERS AND SISTERS MORE THAN THAT!
I'LL RESERVE MY ABUSE FOR THE LOWER LIFE FORMS
PUNT!
JIM DAVIS
© 1981 United Feature Syndicate, Inc.

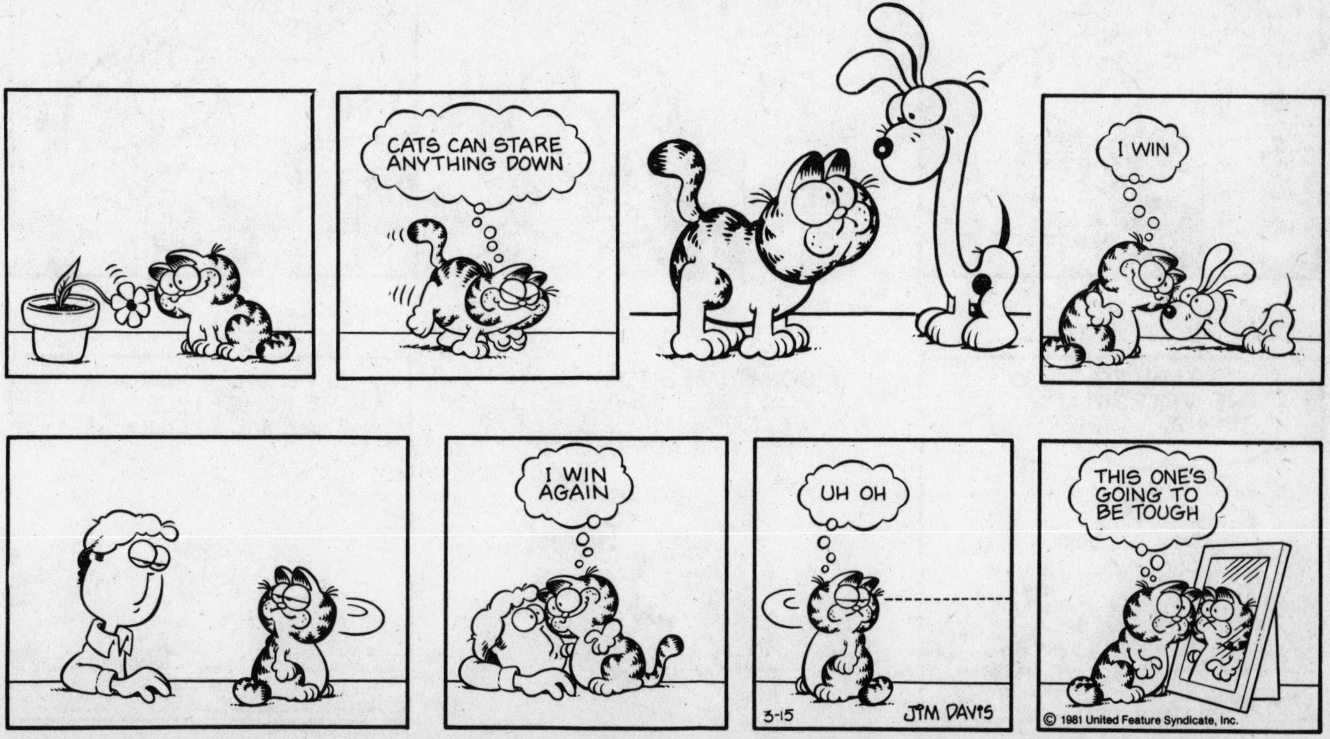
CATS CAN STARE ANYTHING DOWN
I WIN
I WIN AGAIN
UH OH
THIS ONE'S GOING TO BE TOUGH
3-15
JIM DAVIS
© 1981 United Feature Syndicate, Inc.

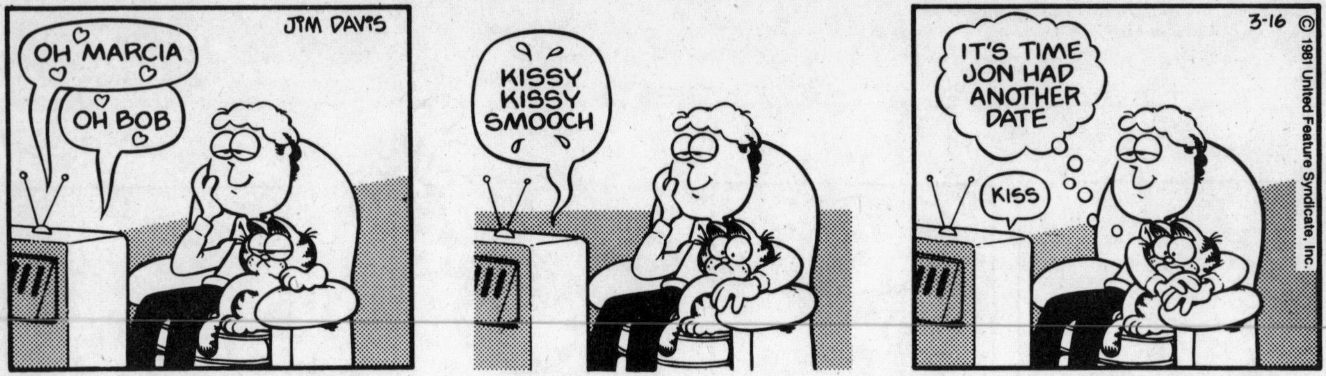
JIM DAVIS
OH MARCIA
OH BOB
KISSY KISSY SMOOCH
IT'S TIME JON HAD ANOTHER DATE
KISS
3-16
© 1981 United Feature Syndicate, Inc.

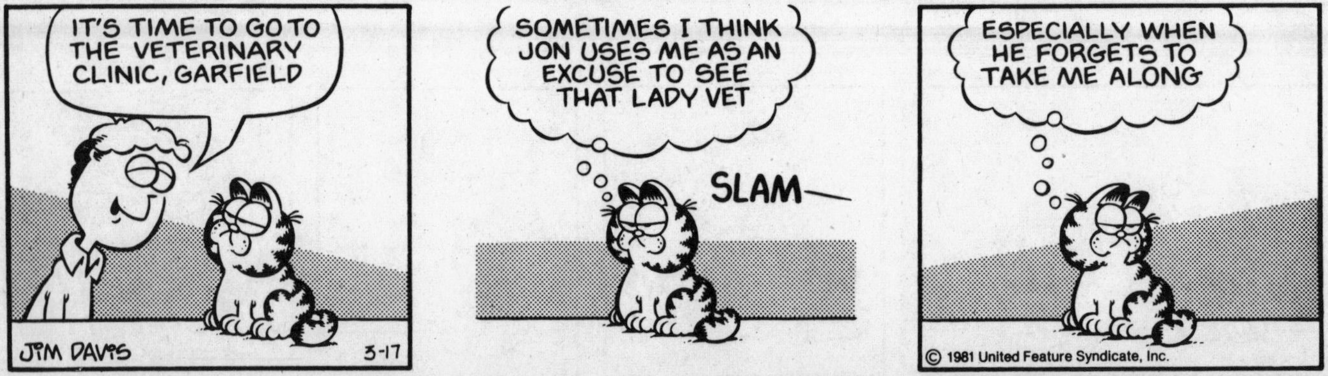
IT'S TIME TO GO TO THE VETERINARY CLINIC, GARFIELD
JIM DAVIS
3-17
SOMETIMES I THINK JON USES ME AS AN EXCUSE TO SEE THAT LADY VET
SLAM
ESPECIALLY WHEN HE FORGETS TO TAKE ME ALONG
© 1981 United Feature Syndicate, Inc.

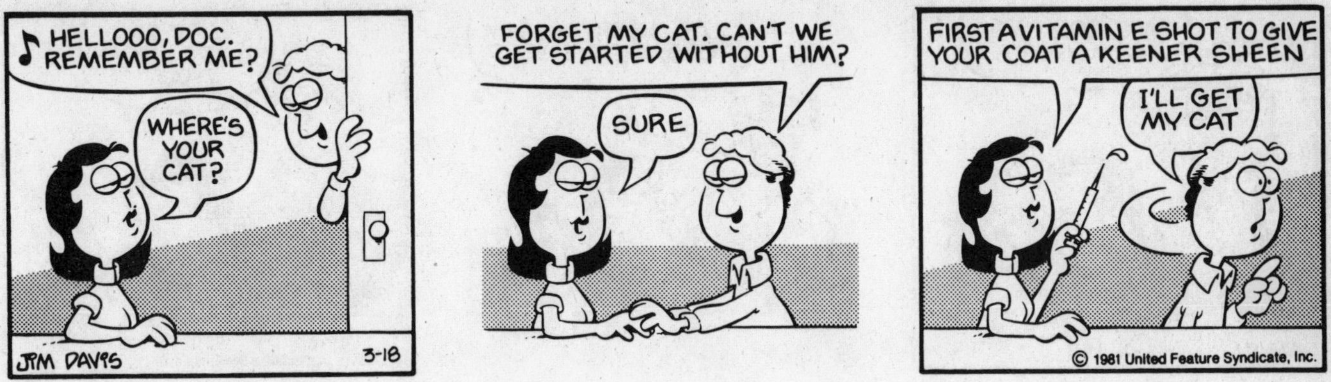
♪ HELLOOO, DOC. REMEMBER ME?
WHERE'S YOUR CAT?
JIM DAVIS
3-18
FORGET MY CAT. CAN'T WE GET STARTED WITHOUT HIM?
SURE
FIRST A VITAMIN E SHOT TO GIVE YOUR COAT A KEENER SHEEN
I'LL GET MY CAT
© 1981 United Feature Syndicate, Inc.

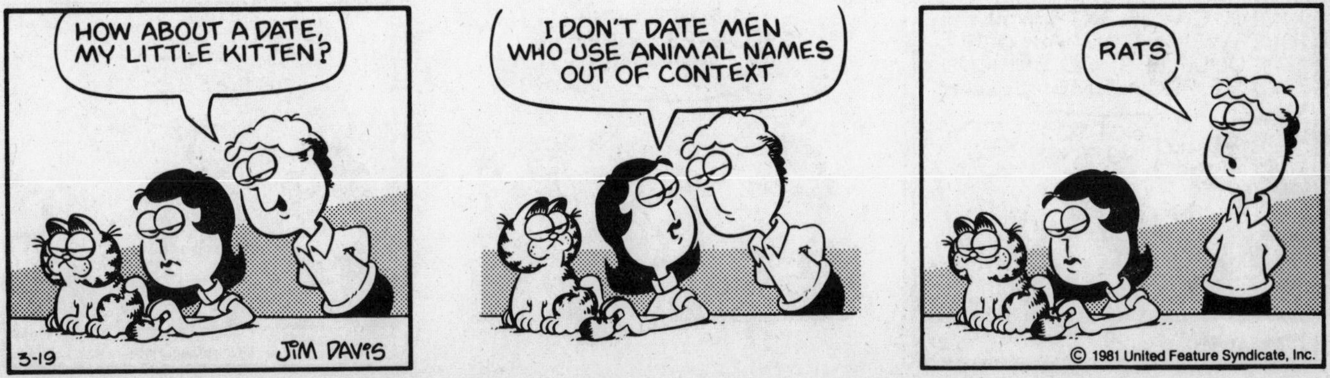
HOW ABOUT A DATE, MY LITTLE KITTEN?
3-19
JIM DAVIS
I DON'T DATE MEN WHO USE ANIMAL NAMES OUT OF CONTEXT
RATS
© 1981 United Feature Syndicate, Inc.

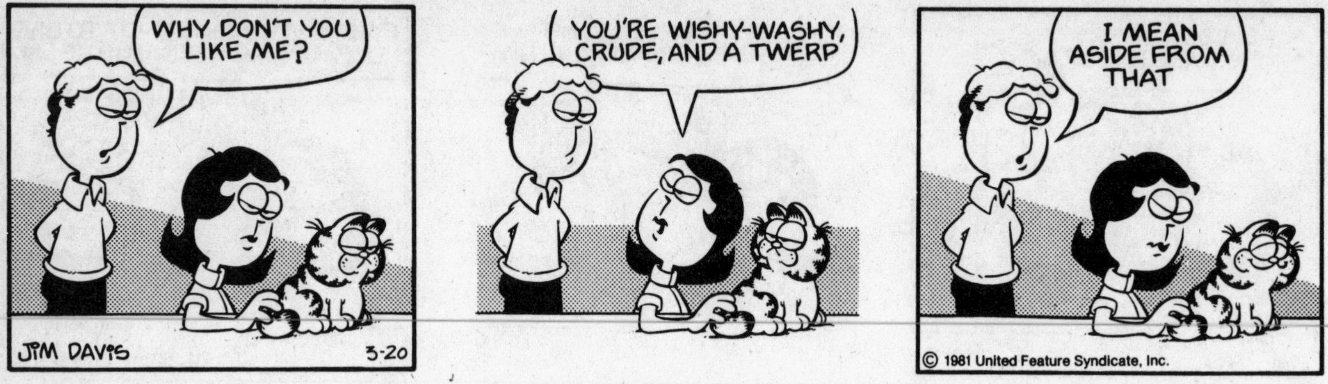
WHY DON'T YOU LIKE ME?
YOU'RE WISHY-WASHY, CRUDE, AND A TWERP
I MEAN ASIDE FROM THAT
JIM DAVIS
3-20
© 1981 United Feature Syndicate, Inc.

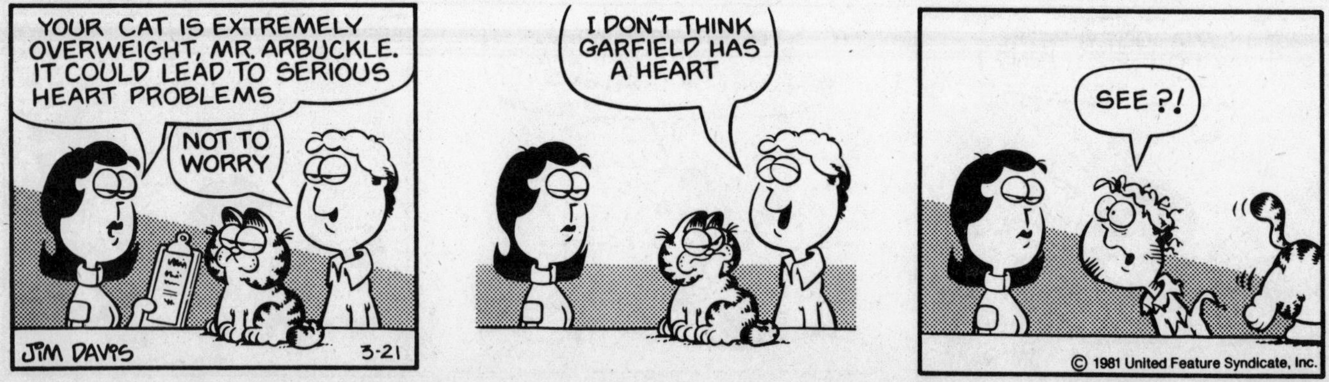
YOUR CAT IS EXTREMELY OVERWEIGHT, MR. ARBUCKLE. IT COULD LEAD TO SERIOUS HEART PROBLEMS
NOT TO WORRY
I DON'T THINK GARFIELD HAS A HEART
SEE ?!
JIM DAVIS
3-21
© 1981 United Feature Syndicate, Inc.

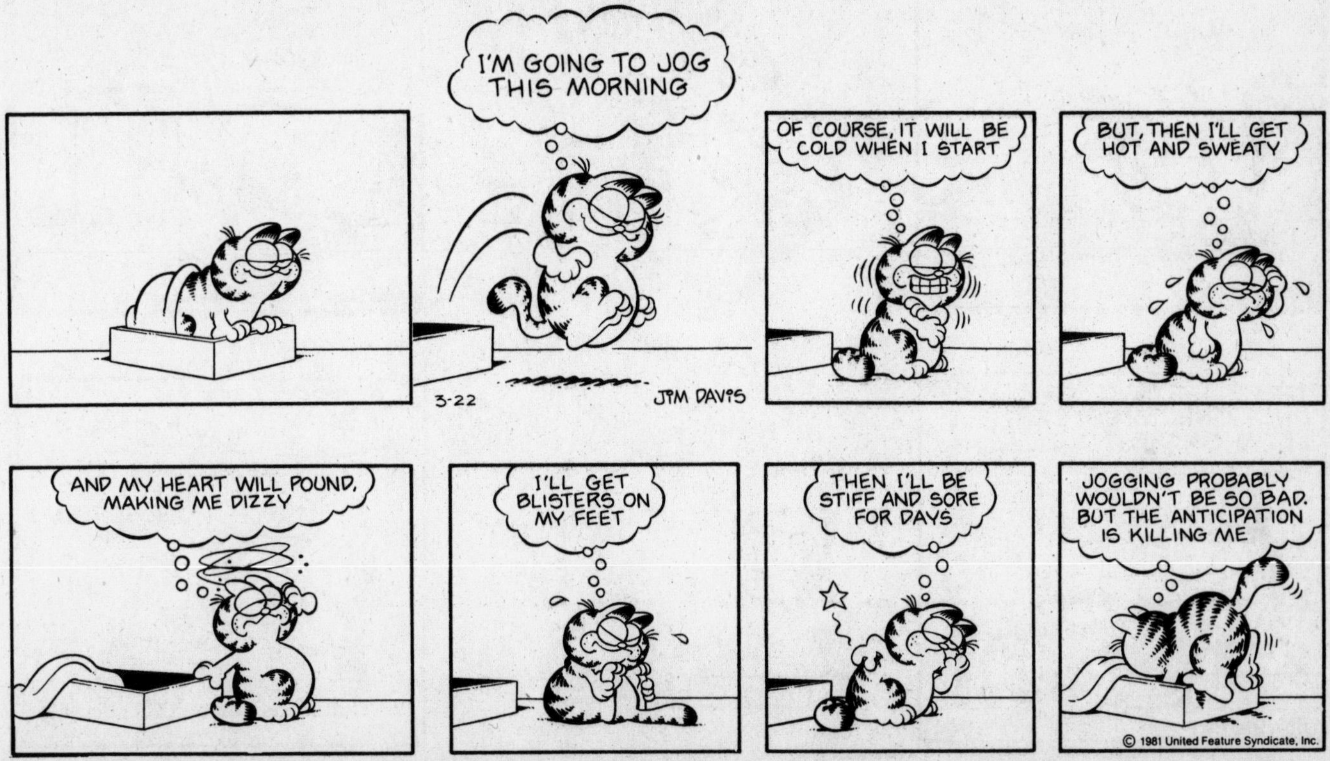
I'M GOING TO JOG THIS MORNING
3-22
JIM DAVIS
OF COURSE, IT WILL BE COLD WHEN I START
BUT, THEN I'LL GET HOT AND SWEATY
AND MY HEART WILL POUND, MAKING ME DIZZY
I'LL GET BLISTERS ON MY FEET
THEN I'LL BE STIFF AND SORE FOR DAYS
JOGGING PROBABLY WOULDN'T BE SO BAD. BUT THE ANTICIPATION IS KILLING ME
© 1981 United Feature Syndicate, Inc.

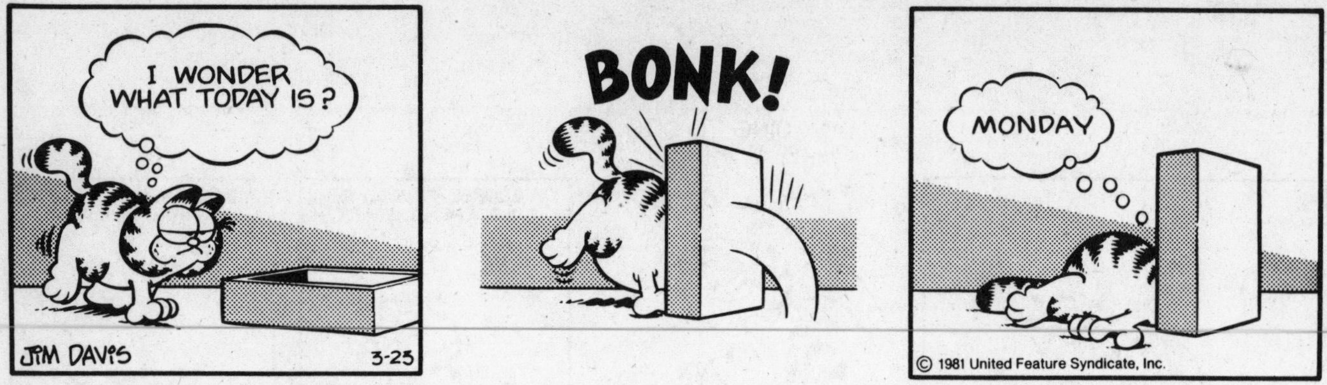
I WONDER WHAT TODAY IS?
JIM DAVIS
3-23
BONK!
MONDAY
© 1981 United Feature Syndicate, Inc.

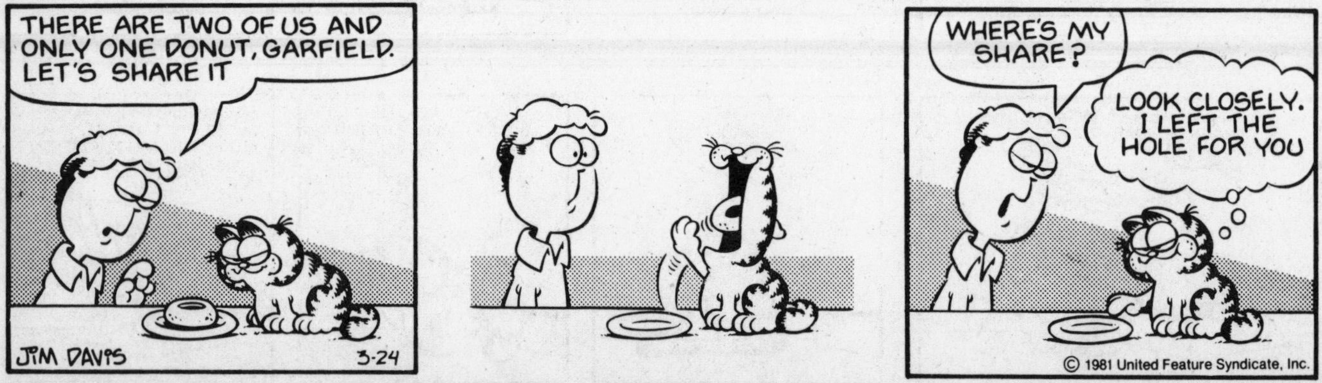
THERE ARE TWO OF US AND ONLY ONE DONUT, GARFIELD. LET'S SHARE IT
JIM DAVIS
3-24
WHERE'S MY SHARE?
LOOK CLOSELY. I LEFT THE HOLE FOR YOU
© 1981 United Feature Syndicate, Inc.

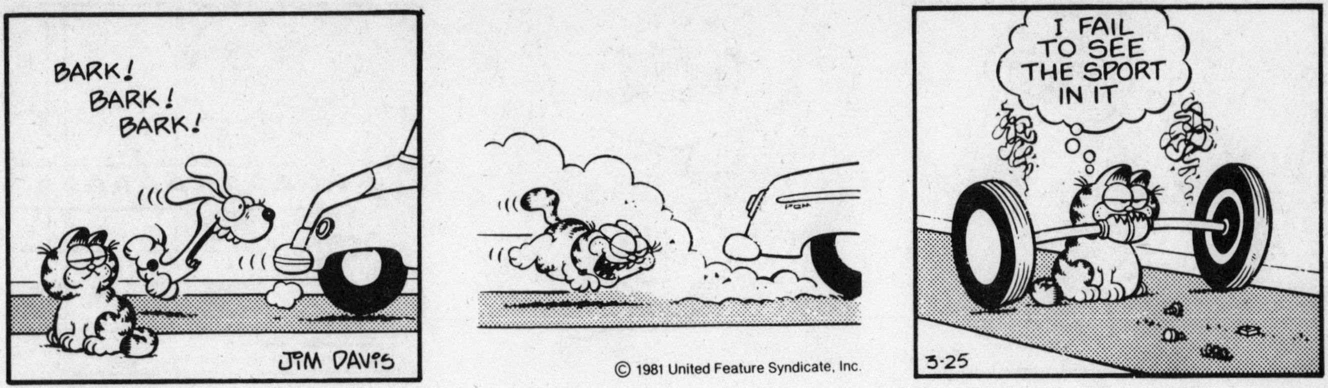
BARK! BARK! BARK!
JIM DAVIS
© 1981 United Feature Syndicate, Inc.
I FAIL TO SEE THE SPORT IN IT
3-25

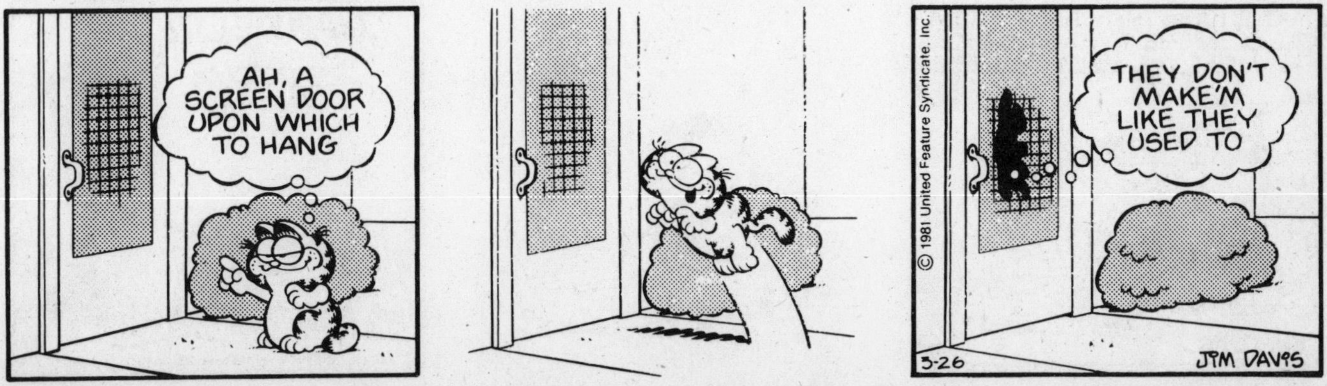
AH, A SCREEN DOOR UPON WHICH TO HANG
© 1981 United Feature Syndicate, Inc.
THEY DON'T MAKE'M LIKE THEY USED TO
3-26
JIM DAVIS

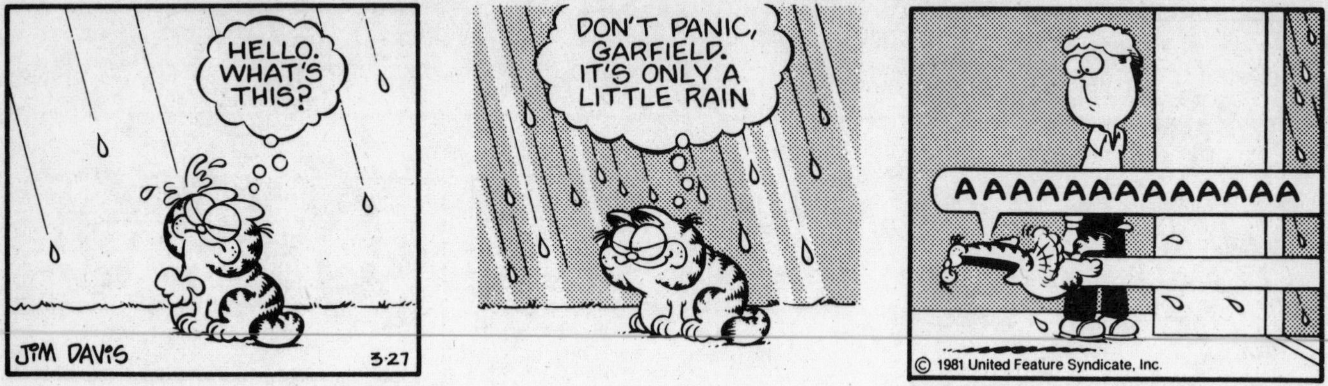
HELLO. WHAT'S THIS?
JIM DAVIS
3-27
DON'T PANIC, GARFIELD. IT'S ONLY A LITTLE RAIN
AAAAAAAAAAAAAA
© 1981 United Feature Syndicate, Inc.

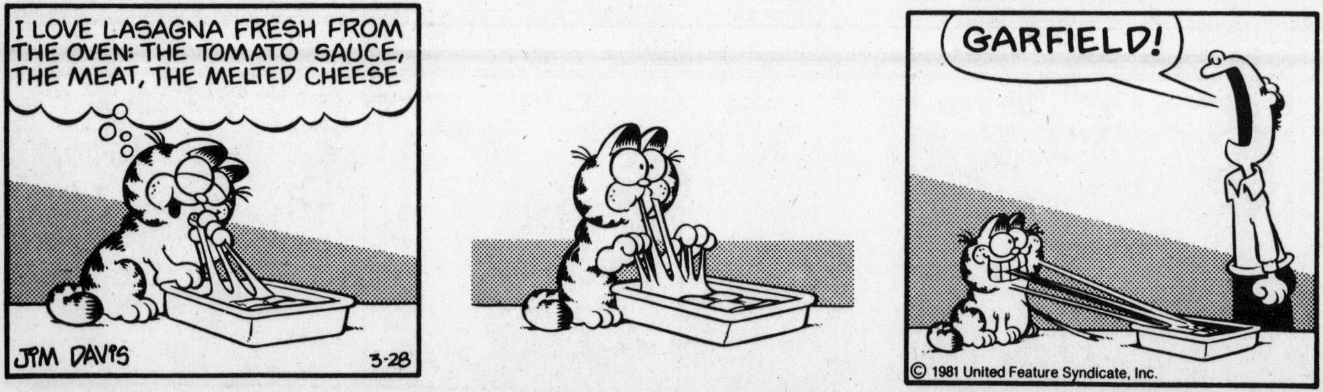
I LOVE LASAGNA FRESH FROM THE OVEN: THE TOMATO SAUCE, THE MEAT, THE MELTED CHEESE
JIM DAVIS
3-28
GARFIELD!
© 1981 United Feature Syndicate, Inc.

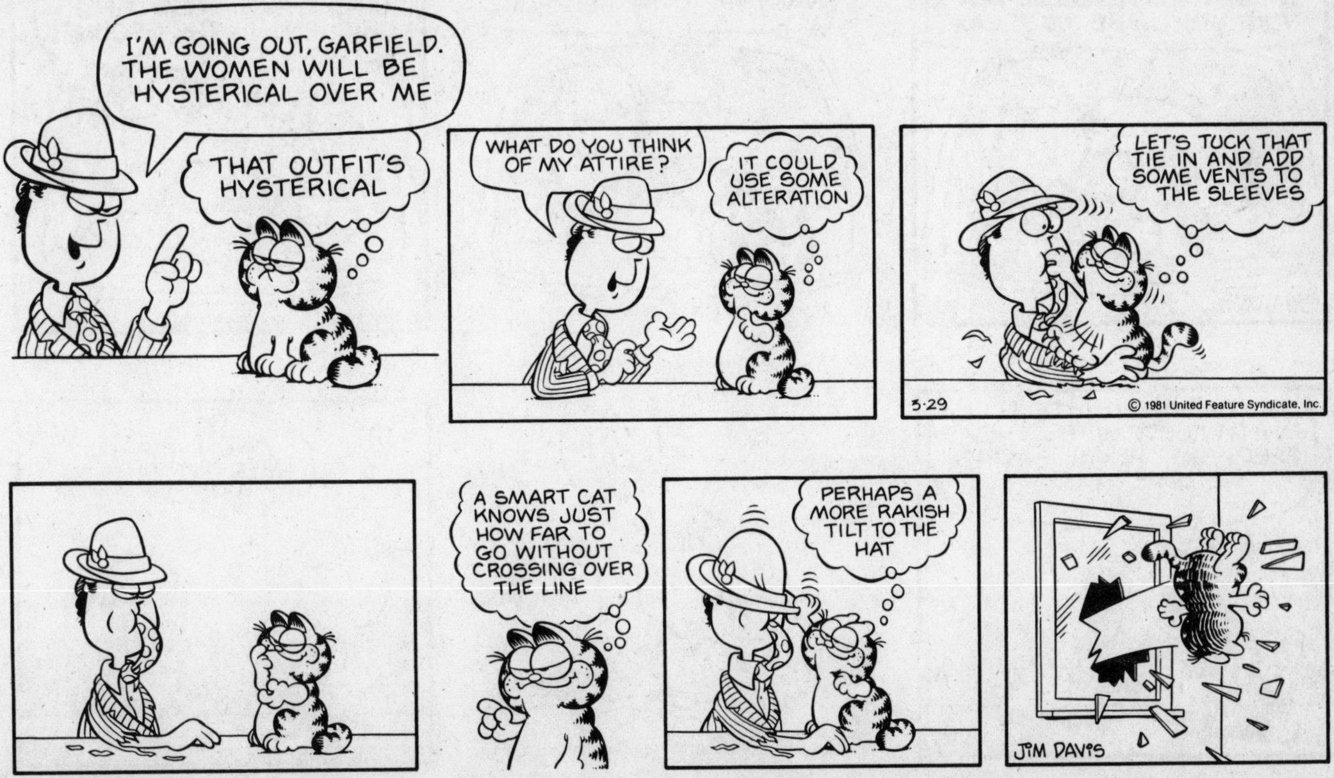
I'M GOING OUT, GARFIELD. THE WOMEN WILL BE HYSTERICAL OVER ME
THAT OUTFIT'S HYSTERICAL
WHAT DO YOU THINK OF MY ATTIRE?
IT COULD USE SOME ALTERATION
LET'S TUCK THAT TIE IN AND ADD SOME VENTS TO THE SLEEVES
3-29
© 1981 United Feature Syndicate, Inc.
A SMART CAT KNOWS JUST HOW FAR TO GO WITHOUT CROSSING OVER THE LINE
PERHAPS A MORE RAKISH TILT TO THE HAT
JIM DAVIS

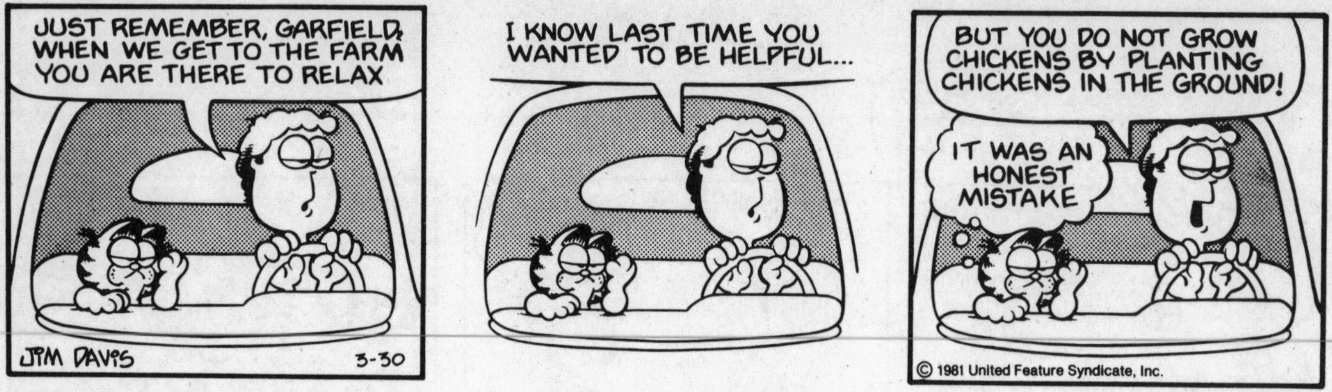
JUST REMEMBER, GARFIELD, WHEN WE GET TO THE FARM YOU ARE THERE TO RELAX
JIM DAVIS
3-30
I KNOW LAST TIME YOU WANTED TO BE HELPFUL...
BUT YOU DO NOT GROW CHICKENS BY PLANTING CHICKENS IN THE GROUND!
IT WAS AN HONEST MISTAKE
© 1981 United Feature Syndicate, Inc.

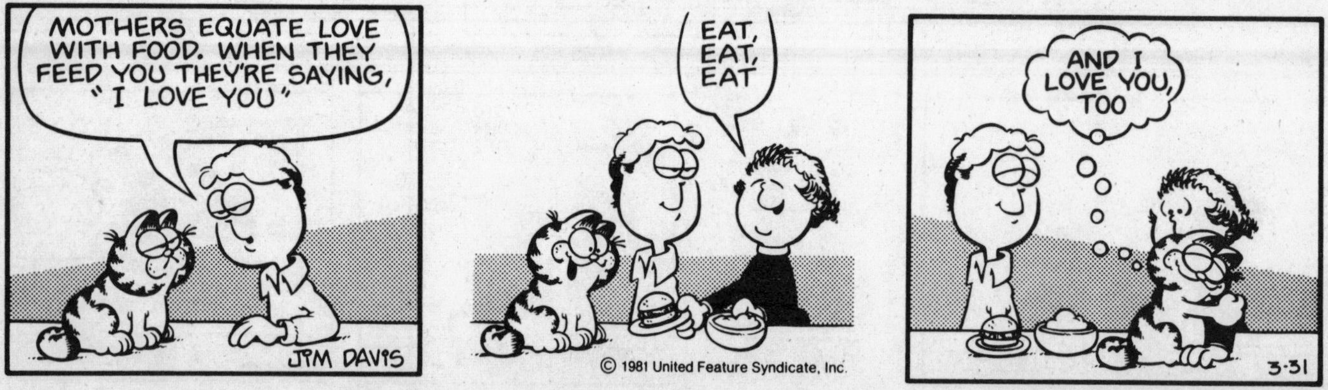
MOTHERS EQUATE LOVE WITH FOOD. WHEN THEY FEED YOU THEY'RE SAYING, "I LOVE YOU"
JIM DAVIS
EAT, EAT, EAT
© 1981 United Feature Syndicate, Inc.
AND I LOVE YOU, TOO
3-31

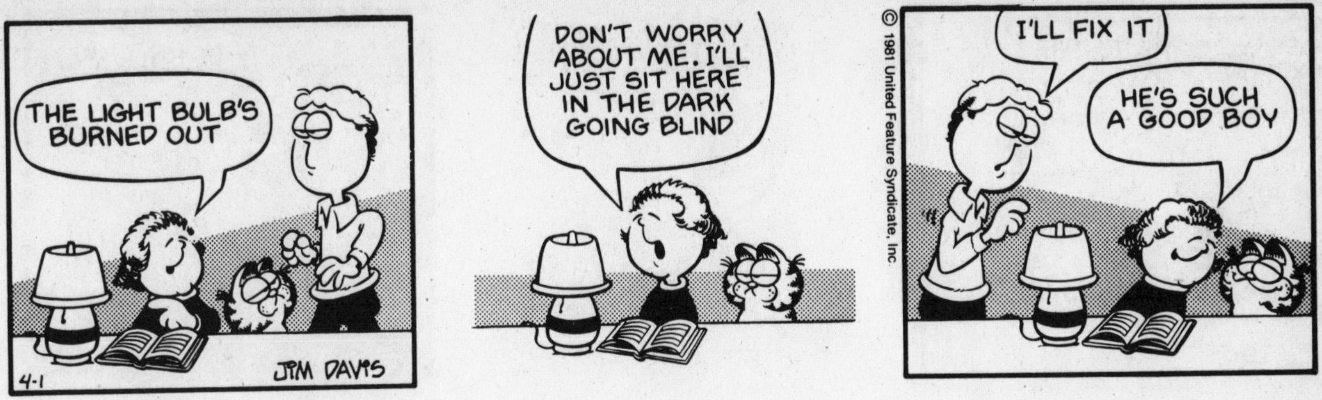
THE LIGHT BULB'S BURNED OUT
JIM DAVIS
4-1
DON'T WORRY ABOUT ME. I'LL JUST SIT HERE IN THE DARK GOING BLIND
I'LL FIX IT
HE'S SUCH A GOOD BOY

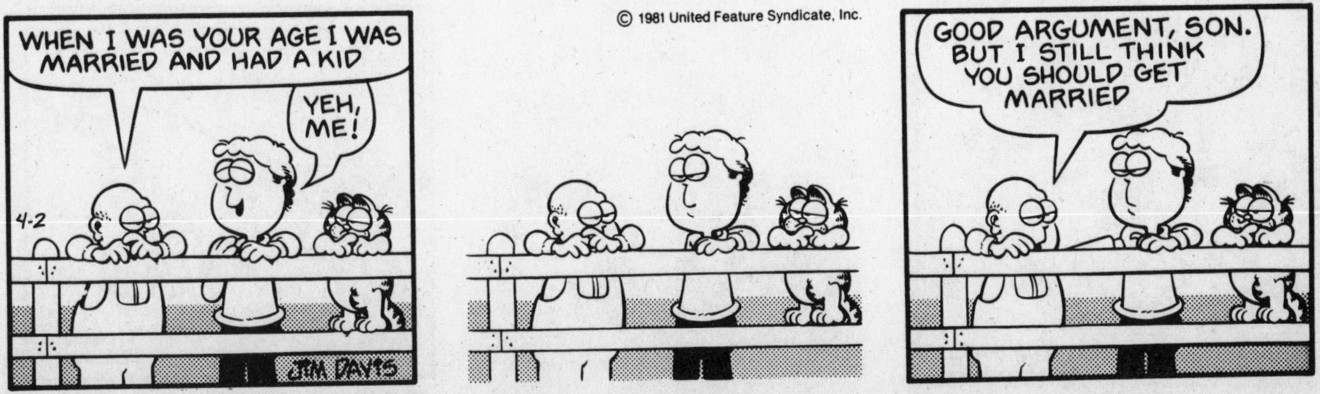
WHEN I WAS YOUR AGE I WAS MARRIED AND HAD A KID
YEH, ME!
4-2
JIM DAVIS
GOOD ARGUMENT, SON. BUT I STILL THINK YOU SHOULD GET MARRIED

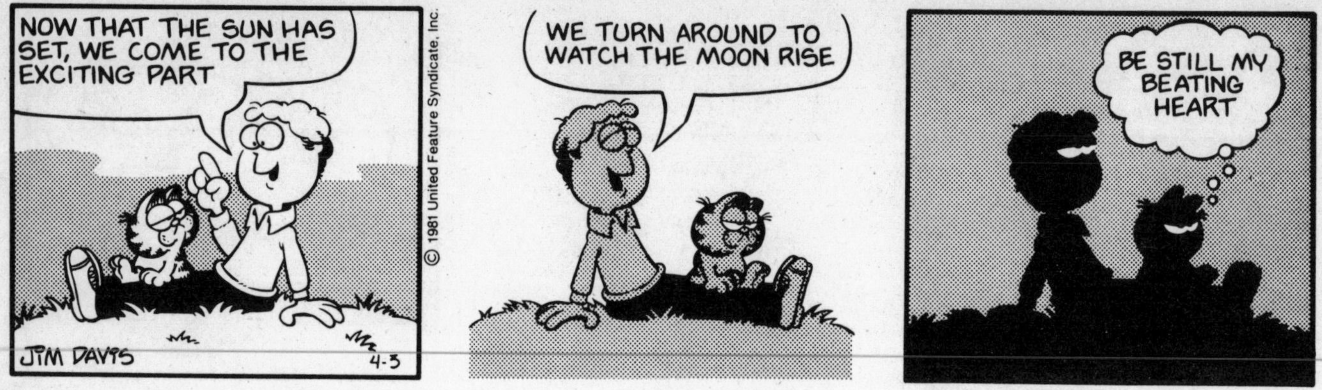
NOW THAT THE SUN HAS SET, WE COME TO THE EXCITING PART
JIM DAVIS
4-3
© 1981 United Feature Syndicate, Inc.
WE TURN AROUND TO WATCH THE MOON RISE
BE STILL MY BEATING HEART

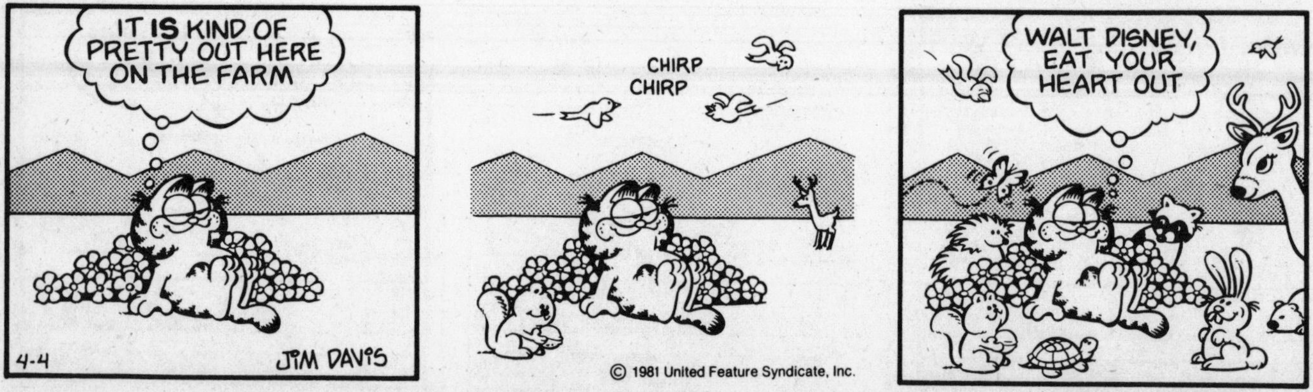
IT **IS** KIND OF PRETTY OUT HERE ON THE FARM
4-4
JIM DAVIS
CHIRP
CHIRP
© 1981 United Feature Syndicate, Inc.
WALT DISNEY, EAT YOUR HEART OUT

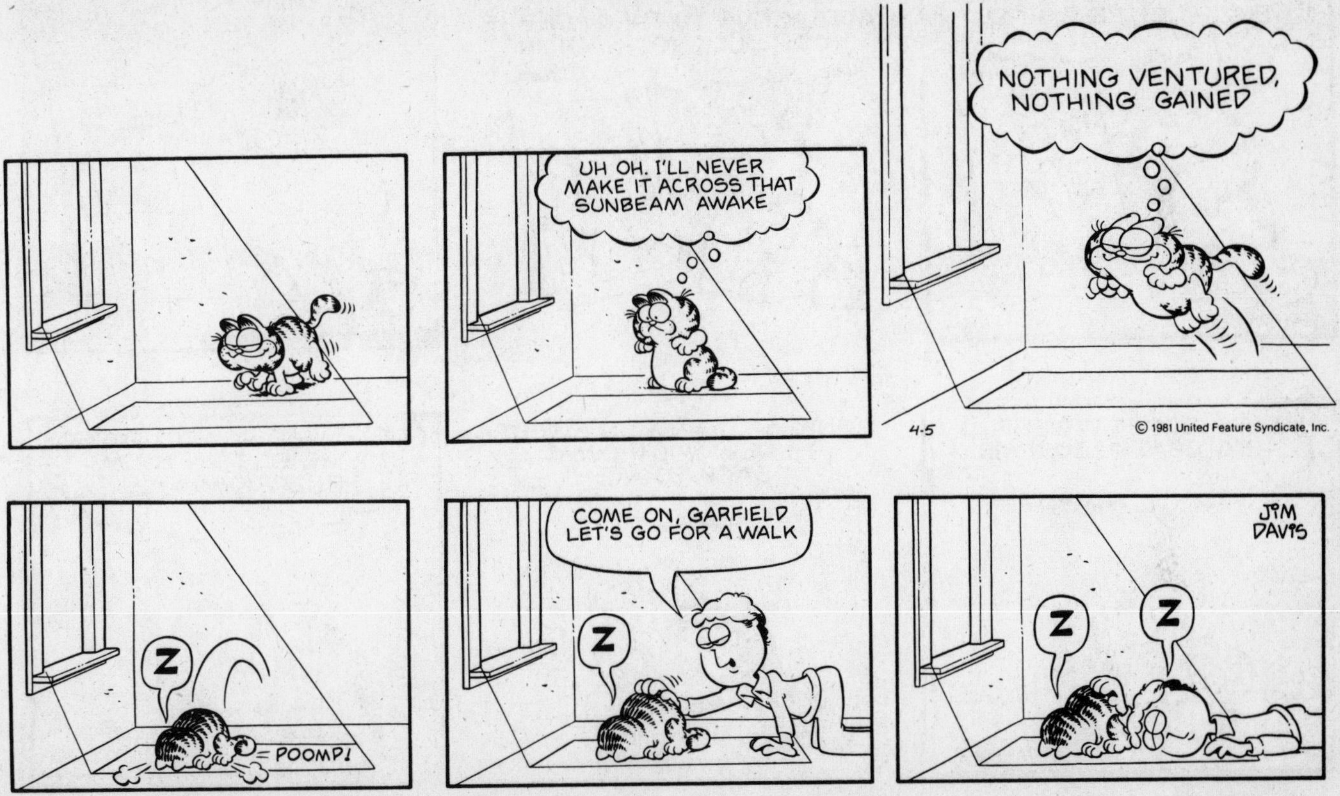
UH OH. I'LL NEVER MAKE IT ACROSS THAT SUNBEAM AWAKE
NOTHING VENTURED, NOTHING GAINED
4-5
© 1981 United Feature Syndicate, Inc.
Z
POOMP!
COME ON, GARFIELD LET'S GO FOR A WALK
Z
JIM DAVIS
Z
Z

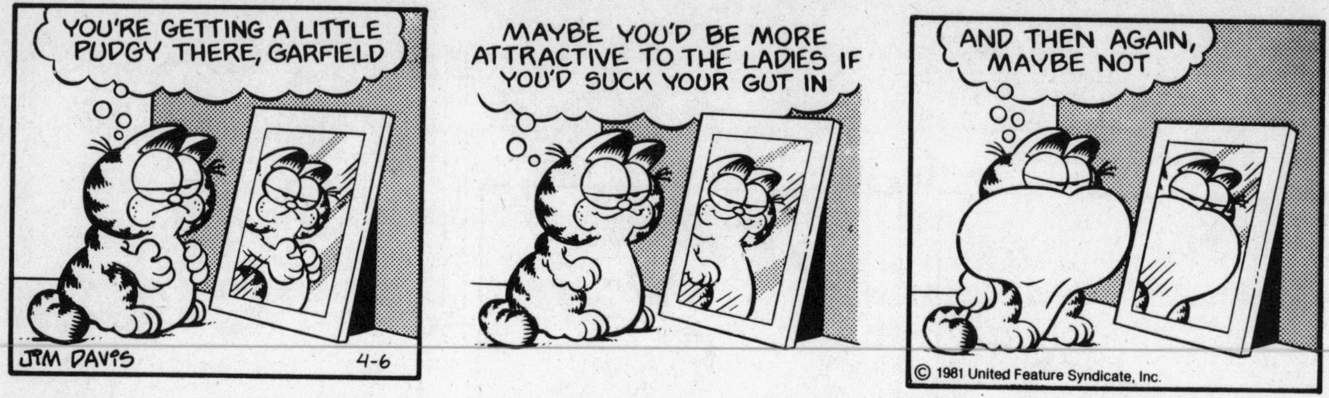
YOU'RE GETTING A LITTLE PUDGY THERE, GARFIELD
JIM DAVIS
4-6
MAYBE YOU'D BE MORE ATTRACTIVE TO THE LADIES IF YOU'D SUCK YOUR GUT IN
AND THEN AGAIN, MAYBE NOT
© 1981 United Feature Syndicate, Inc.

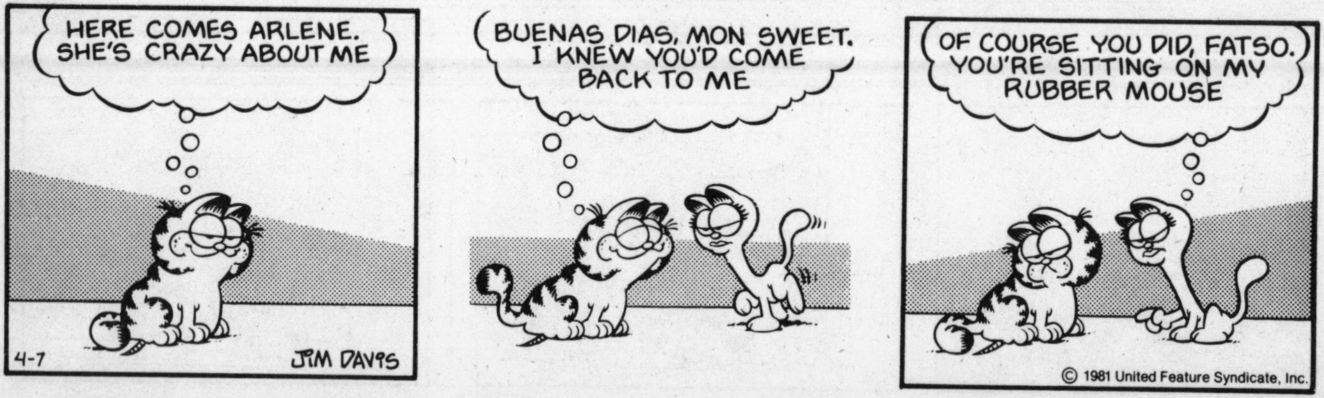
HERE COMES ARLENE. SHE'S CRAZY ABOUT ME
4-7
JIM DAVIS
BUENAS DIAS, MON SWEET. I KNEW YOU'D COME BACK TO ME
OF COURSE YOU DID, FATSO. YOU'RE SITTING ON MY RUBBER MOUSE
© 1981 United Feature Syndicate, Inc.

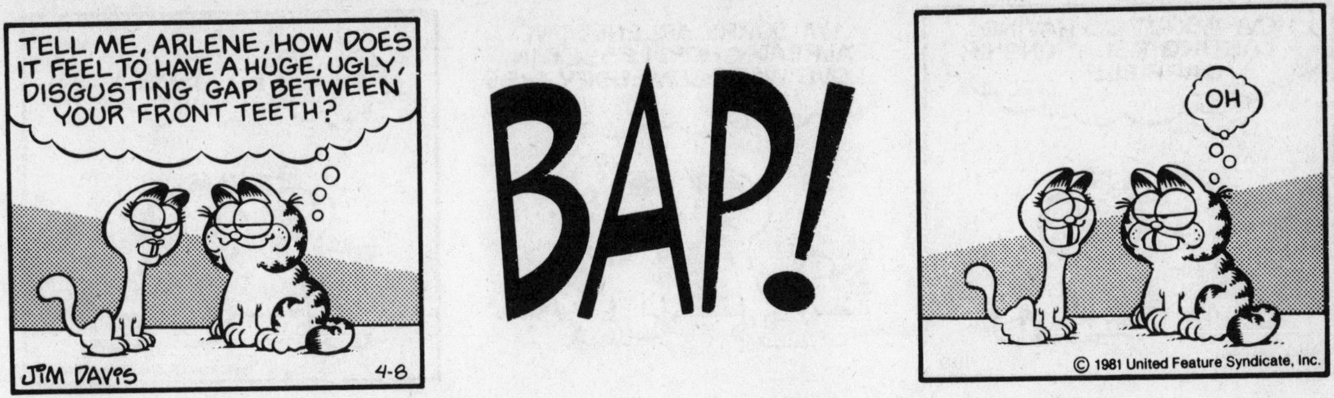
TELL ME, ARLENE, HOW DOES IT FEEL TO HAVE A HUGE, UGLY, DISGUSTING GAP BETWEEN YOUR FRONT TEETH?
JIM DAVIS
4-8
BAP!
OH
© 1981 United Feature Syndicate, Inc.

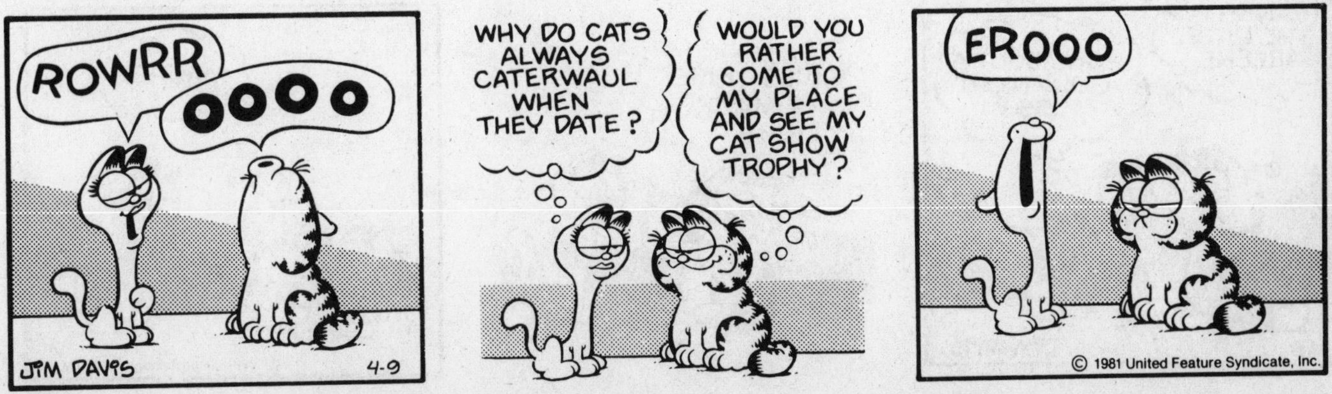
ROWRR
OOOO
JIM DAVIS
4-9
WHY DO CATS ALWAYS CATERWAUL WHEN THEY DATE?
WOULD YOU RATHER COME TO MY PLACE AND SEE MY CAT SHOW TROPHY?
EROOO
© 1981 United Feature Syndicate, Inc.

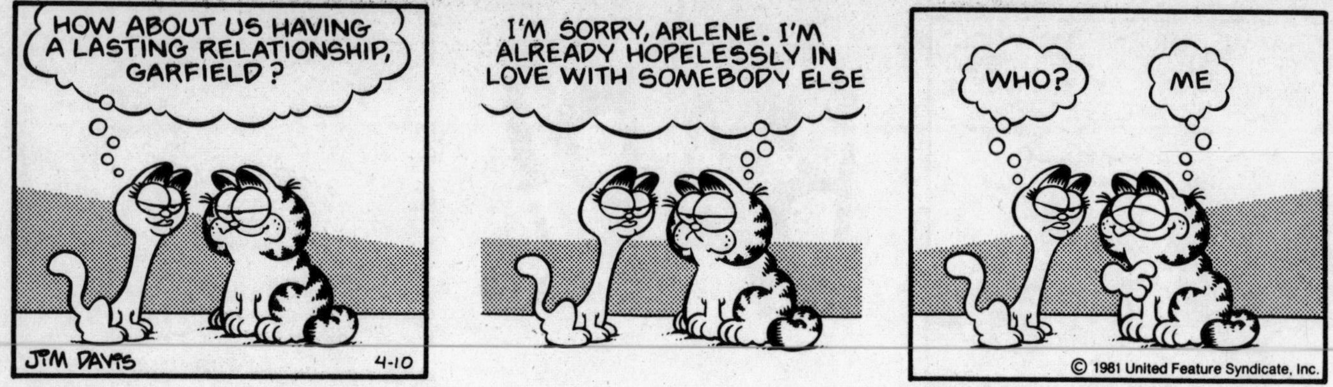
HOW ABOUT US HAVING A LASTING RELATIONSHIP, GARFIELD?
JIM DAVIS
4-10
I'M SORRY, ARLENE. I'M ALREADY HOPELESSLY IN LOVE WITH SOMEBODY ELSE
WHO?
ME
© 1981 United Feature Syndicate, Inc.

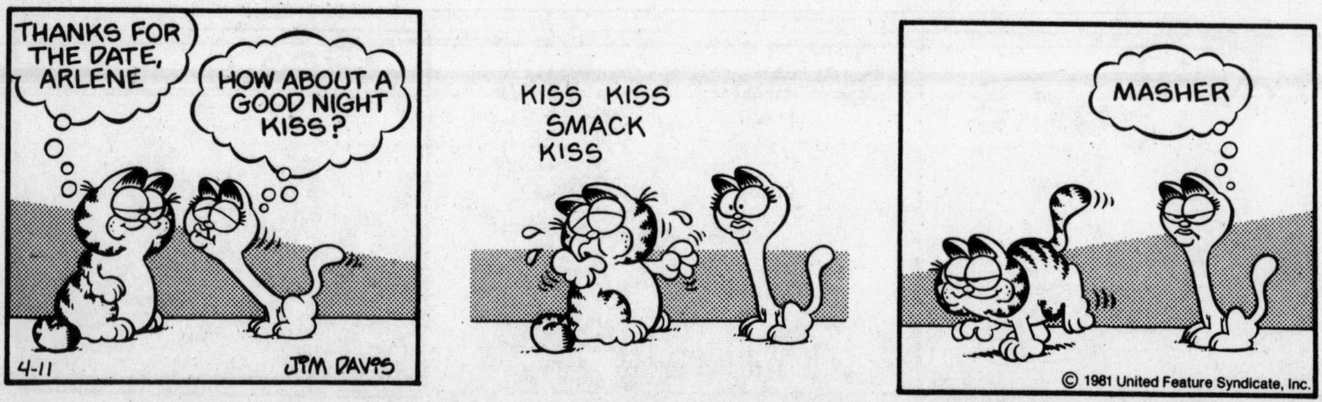
THANKS FOR THE DATE, ARLENE
HOW ABOUT A GOOD NIGHT KISS?
4-11
JIM DAVIS
KISS KISS SMACK KISS
MASHER
© 1981 United Feature Syndicate, Inc.

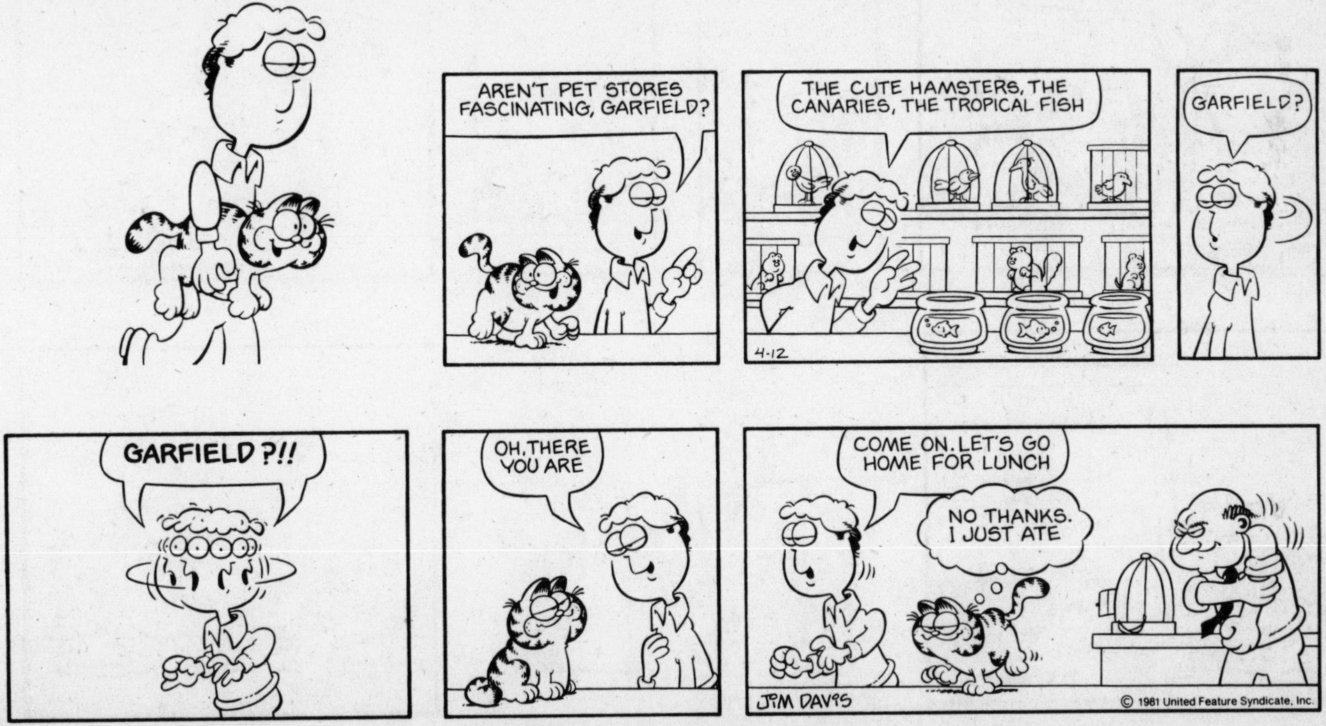

AREN'T PET STORES FASCINATING, GARFIELD?
THE CUTE HAMSTERS, THE CANARIES, THE TROPICAL FISH
4-12
GARFIELD?
GARFIELD?!!
OH, THERE YOU ARE
COME ON. LET'S GO HOME FOR LUNCH
NO THANKS. I JUST ATE
JIM DAVIS
© 1981 United Feature Syndicate, Inc.

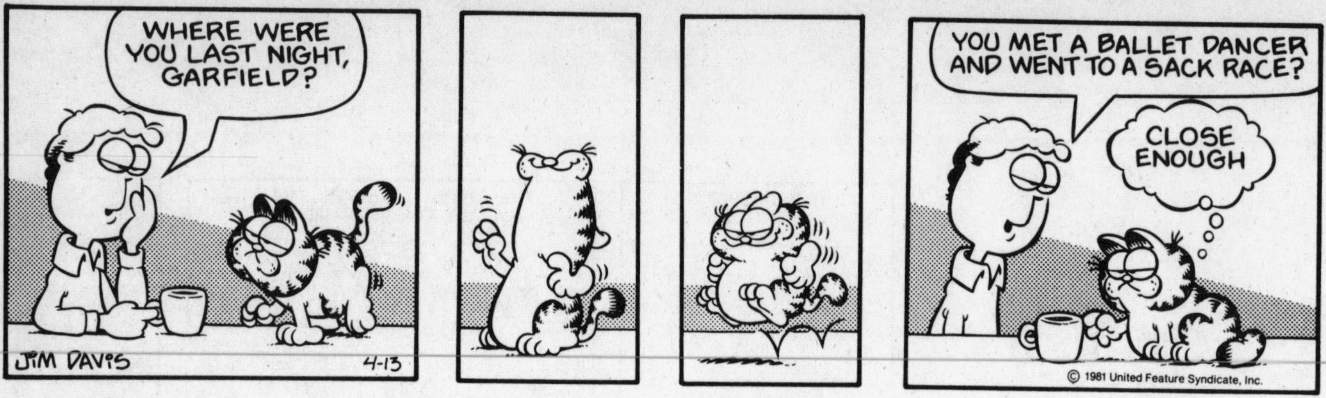
WHERE WERE YOU LAST NIGHT, GARFIELD?
JIM DAVIS
4-13
YOU MET A BALLET DANCER AND WENT TO A SACK RACE?
CLOSE ENOUGH
© 1981 United Feature Syndicate, Inc.

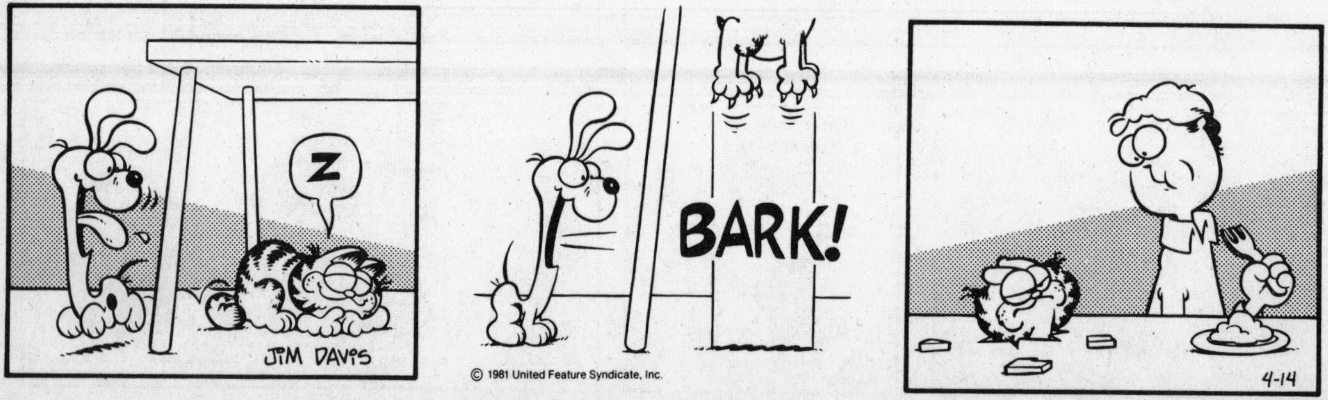
Z
JIM DAVIS
BARK!
© 1981 United Feature Syndicate, Inc.
4-14

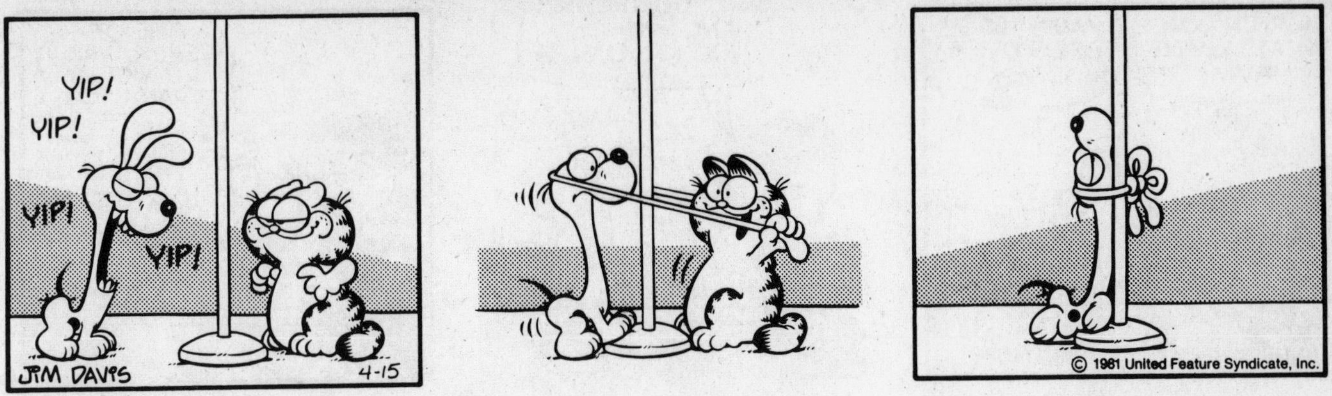
YIP!
YIP!
YIP!
YIP!
JIM DAVIS
4-15
© 1981 United Feature Syndicate, Inc.

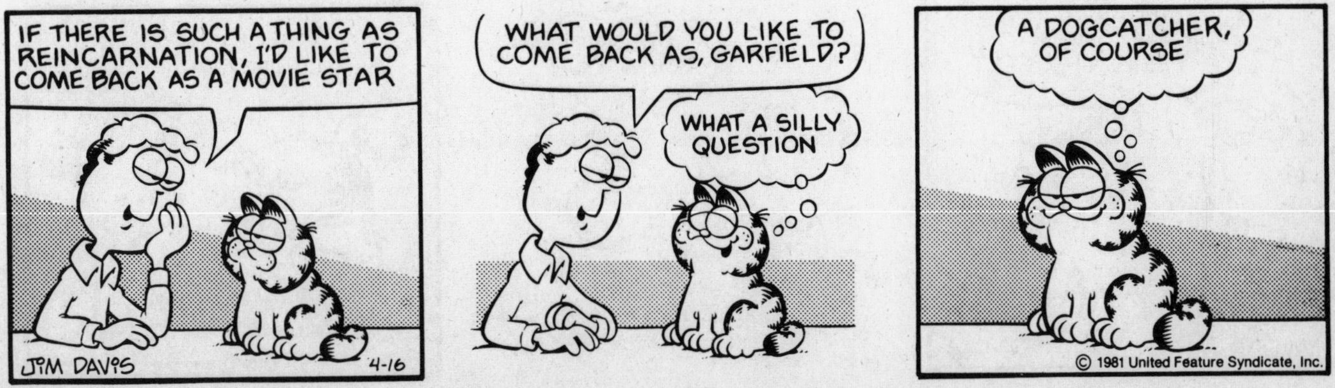
IF THERE IS SUCH A THING AS REINCARNATION, I'D LIKE TO COME BACK AS A MOVIE STAR
JIM DAVIS
4-16
WHAT WOULD YOU LIKE TO COME BACK AS, GARFIELD?
WHAT A SILLY QUESTION
A DOGCATCHER, OF COURSE
© 1981 United Feature Syndicate, Inc.

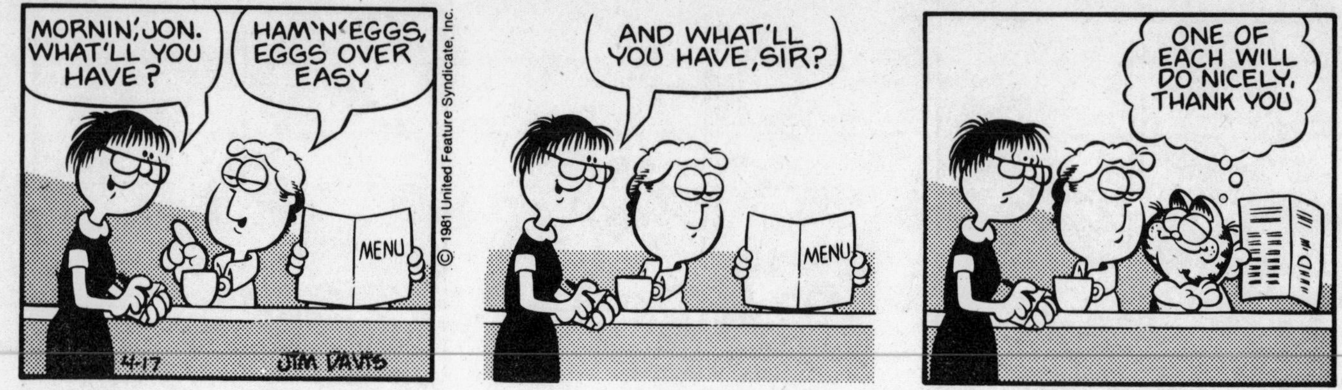
MORNIN', JON. WHAT'LL YOU HAVE?
HAM'N'EGGS, EGGS OVER EASY
MENU
4-17
JIM DAVIS
© 1981 United Feature Syndicate, Inc.
AND WHAT'LL YOU HAVE, SIR?
MENU
ONE OF EACH WILL DO NICELY, THANK YOU

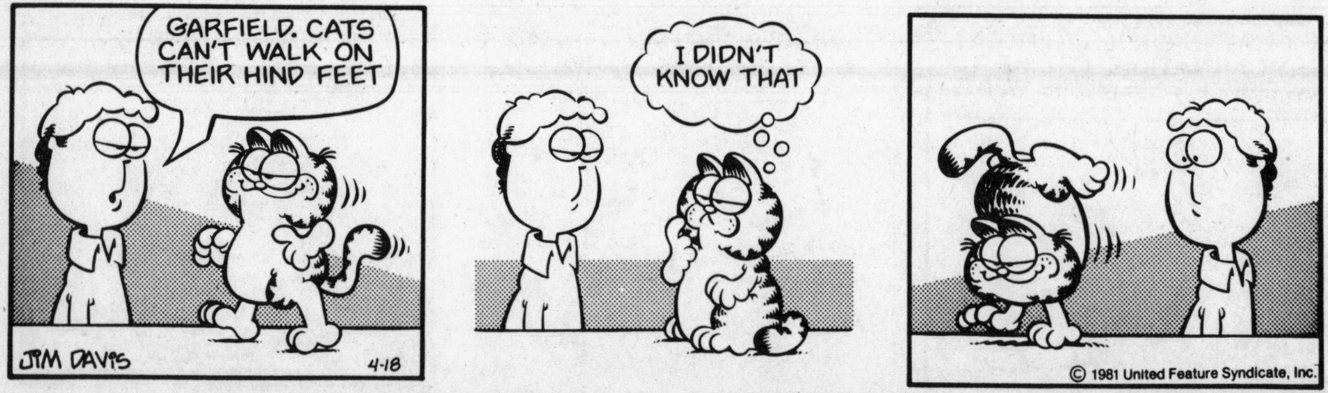
GARFIELD. CATS CAN'T WALK ON THEIR HIND FEET
JIM DAVIS
4-18
I DIDN'T KNOW THAT
© 1981 United Feature Syndicate, Inc.

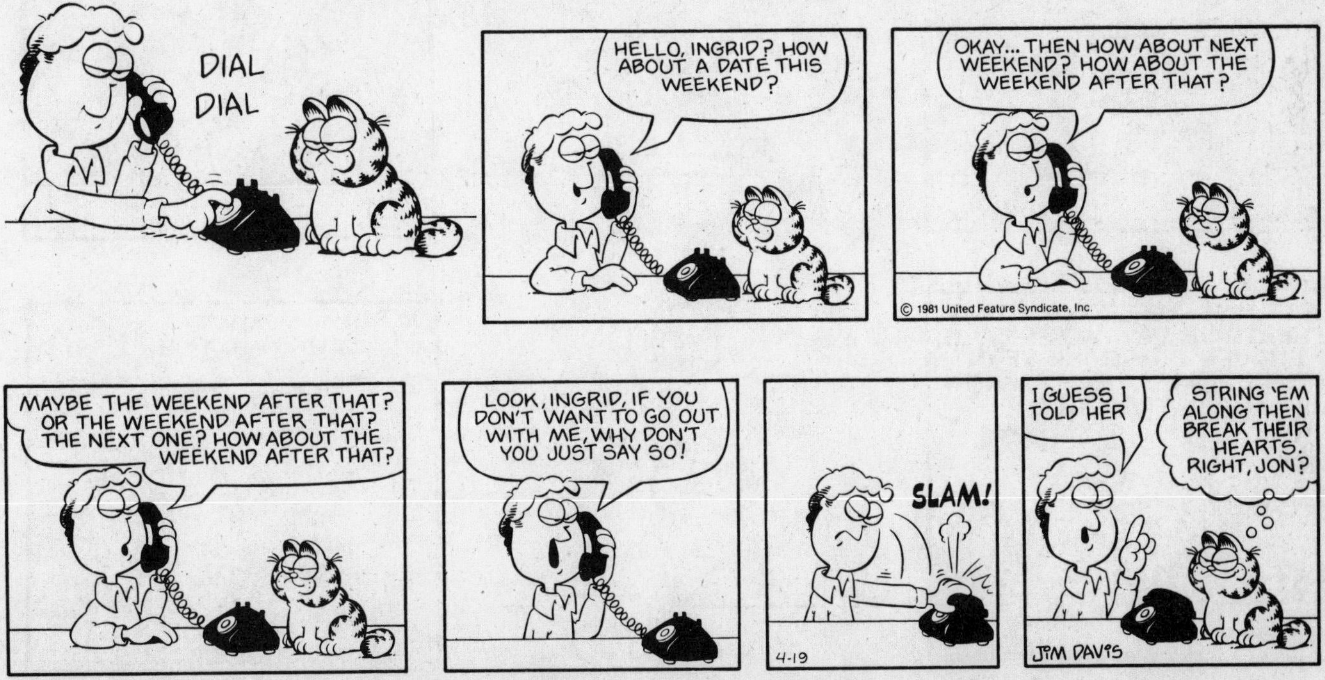
DIAL
DIAL
HELLO, INGRID? HOW ABOUT A DATE THIS WEEKEND?
OKAY... THEN HOW ABOUT NEXT WEEKEND? HOW ABOUT THE WEEKEND AFTER THAT?
© 1981 United Feature Syndicate, Inc.
MAYBE THE WEEKEND AFTER THAT? OR THE WEEKEND AFTER THAT? THE NEXT ONE? HOW ABOUT THE WEEKEND AFTER THAT?
LOOK, INGRID, IF YOU DON'T WANT TO GO OUT WITH ME, WHY DON'T YOU JUST SAY SO!
SLAM!
4-19
I GUESS I TOLD HER
STRING 'EM ALONG THEN BREAK THEIR HEARTS. RIGHT, JON?
JIM DAVIS

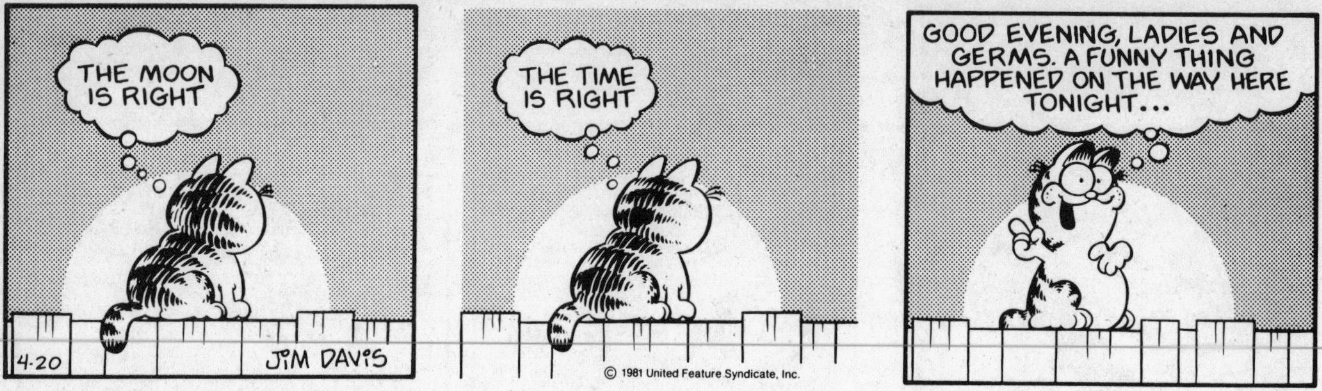
THE MOON IS RIGHT
4-20
JIM DAVIS
THE TIME IS RIGHT
© 1981 United Feature Syndicate, Inc.
GOOD EVENING, LADIES AND GERMS. A FUNNY THING HAPPENED ON THE WAY HERE TONIGHT...

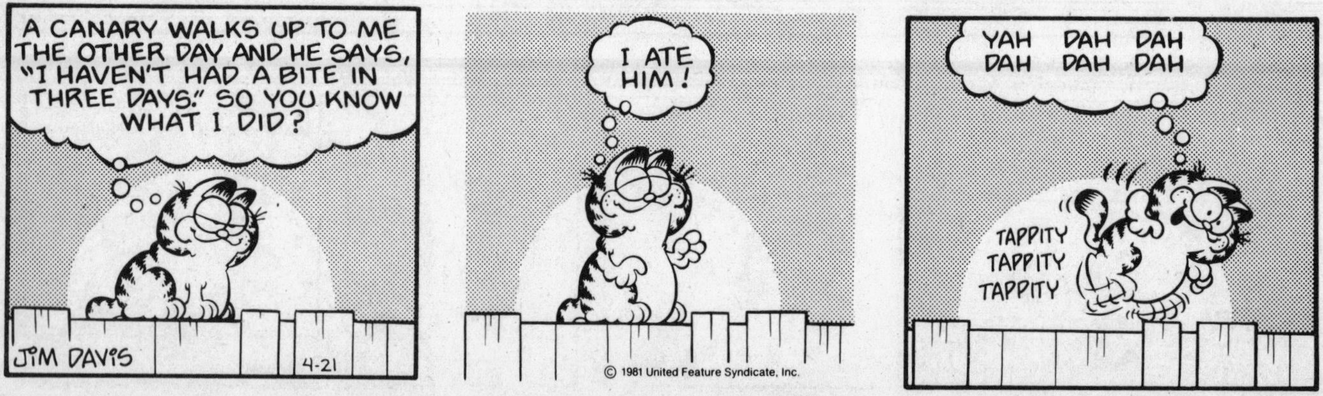
A CANARY WALKS UP TO ME THE OTHER DAY AND HE SAYS, "I HAVEN'T HAD A BITE IN THREE DAYS." SO YOU KNOW WHAT I DID?
JIM DAVIS
4-21
I ATE HIM!
© 1981 United Feature Syndicate, Inc.
YAH DAH DAH DAH DAH DAH
TAPPITY TAPPITY TAPPITY

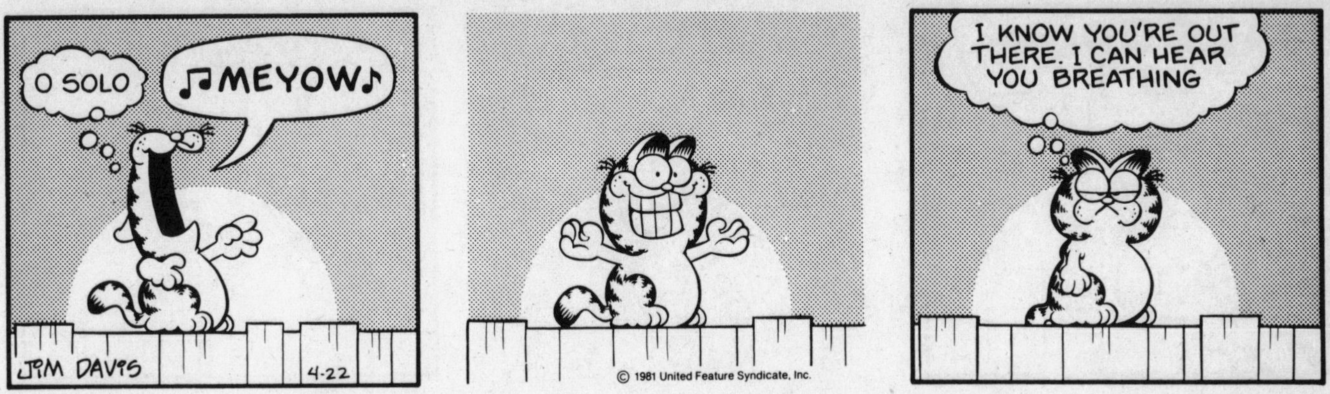
O SOLO
♫MEYOW♪
JIM DAVIS
4-22
© 1981 United Feature Syndicate, Inc.
I KNOW YOU'RE OUT THERE. I CAN HEAR YOU BREATHING

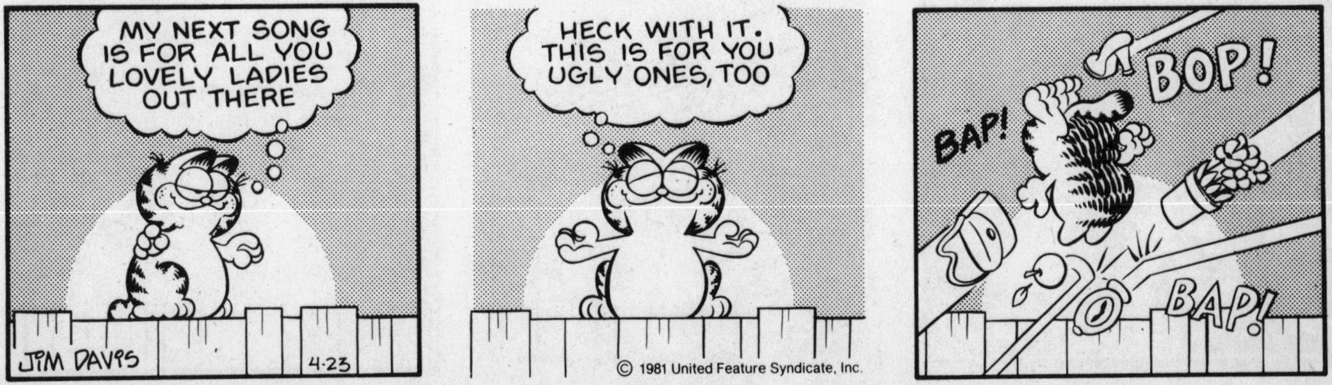
MY NEXT SONG IS FOR ALL YOU LOVELY LADIES OUT THERE
JIM DAVIS
4-23
HECK WITH IT. THIS IS FOR YOU UGLY ONES, TOO
© 1981 United Feature Syndicate, Inc.
BOP!
BAP!
BAP!

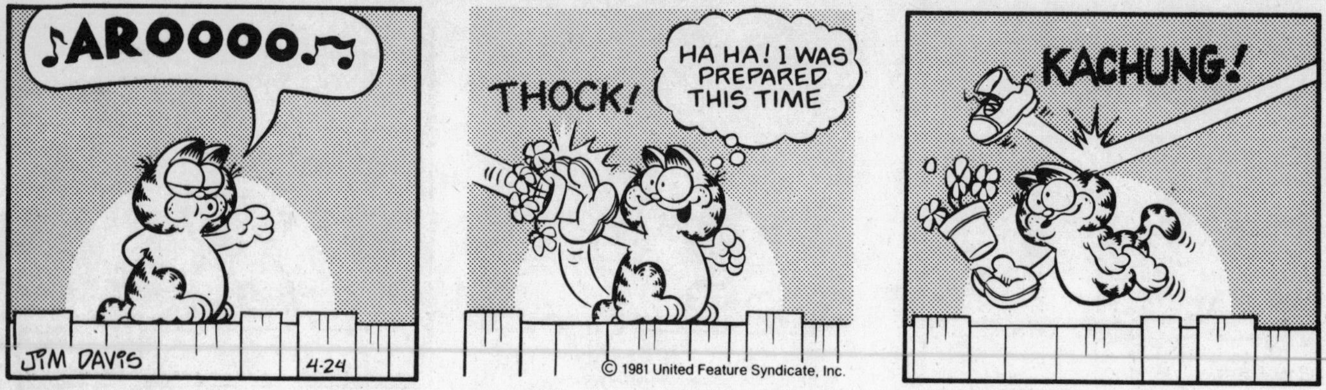
♪AROOOO.♪
JIM DAVIS
4-24
THOCK!
HA HA! I WAS PREPARED THIS TIME
© 1981 United Feature Syndicate, Inc.
KACHUNG!

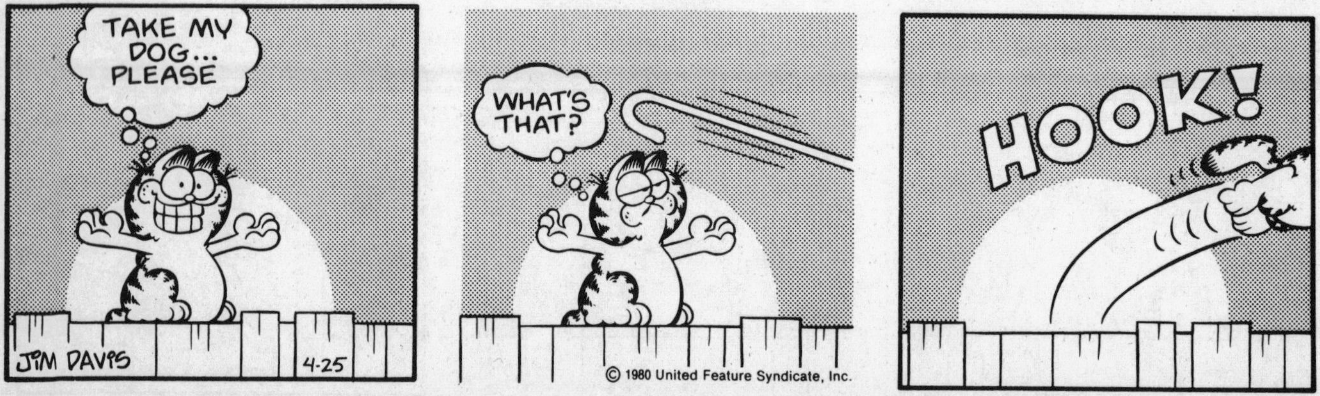
TAKE MY DOG... PLEASE
JIM DAVIS
4-25
WHAT'S THAT?
© 1980 United Feature Syndicate, Inc.
HOOK!

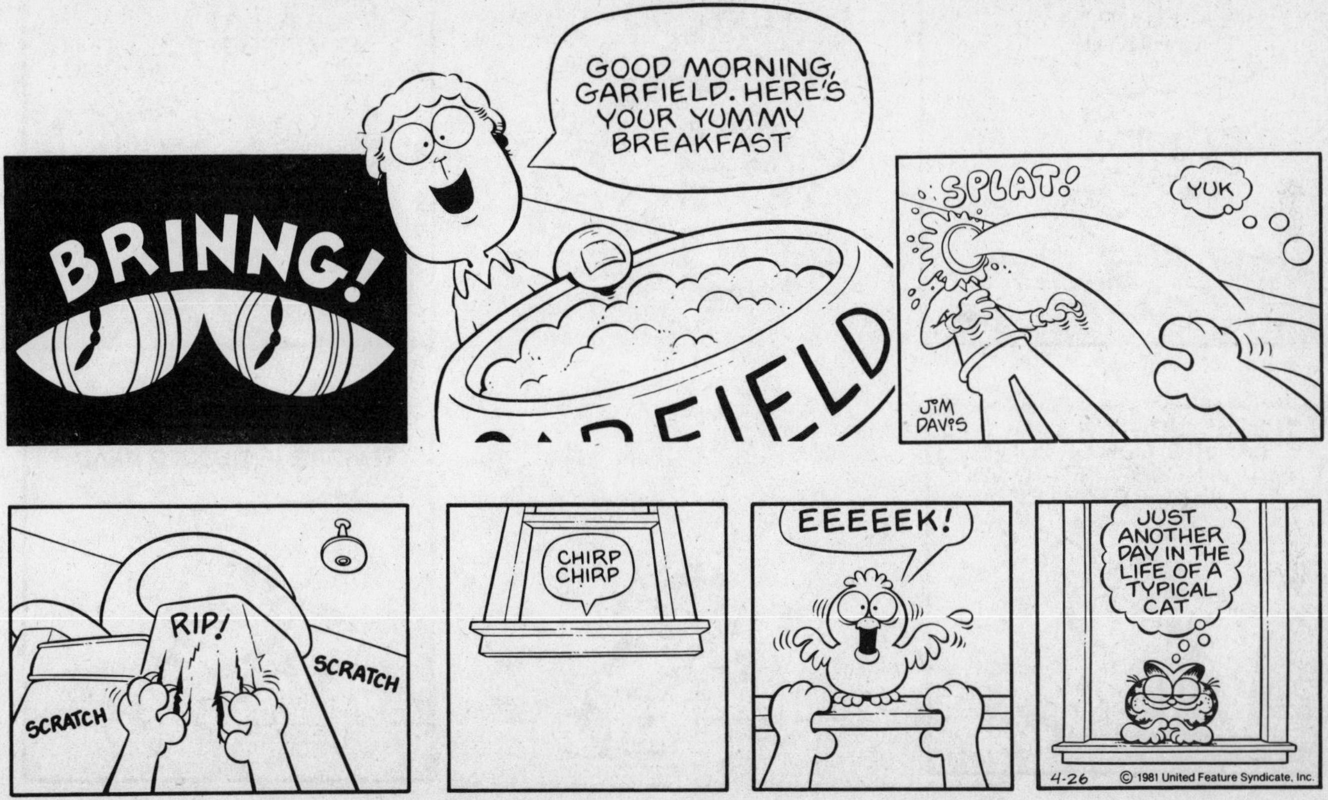

BRINNG!
GOOD MORNING, GARFIELD. HERE'S YOUR YUMMY BREAKFAST
GARFIELD
SPLAT!
YUK
JIM DAVIS
RIP!
SCRATCH
SCRATCH
CHIRP CHIRP
EEEEEK!
JUST ANOTHER DAY IN THE LIFE OF A TYPICAL CAT
4-26
© 1981 United Feature Syndicate, Inc.

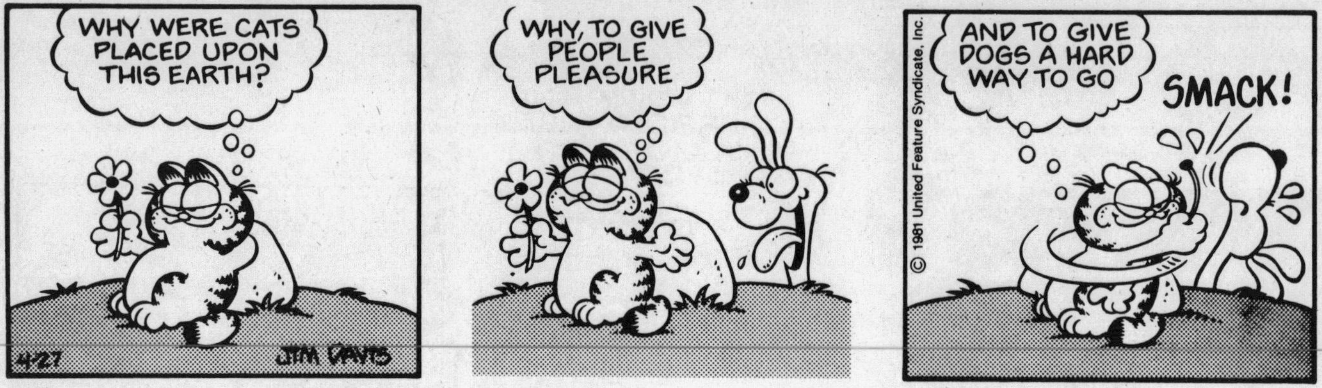
WHY WERE CATS PLACED UPON THIS EARTH?
WHY, TO GIVE PEOPLE PLEASURE
AND TO GIVE DOGS A HARD WAY TO GO
SMACK!
4-27
JIM DAVIS
© 1981 United Feature Syndicate, Inc.

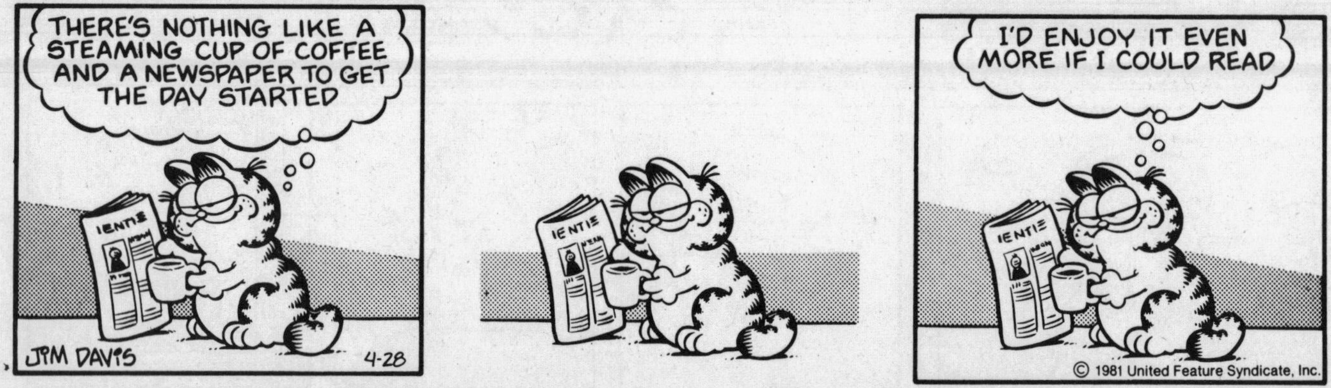
THERE'S NOTHING LIKE A STEAMING CUP OF COFFEE AND A NEWSPAPER TO GET THE DAY STARTED
I'D ENJOY IT EVEN MORE IF I COULD READ
JIM DAVIS
4-28
© 1981 United Feature Syndicate, Inc.

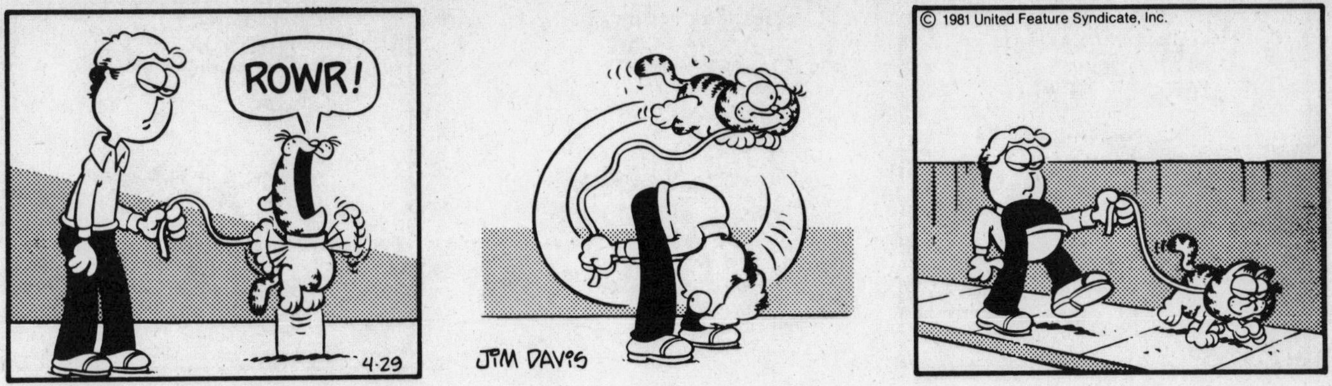
ROWR!
4-29
JIM DAVIS
© 1981 United Feature Syndicate, Inc.

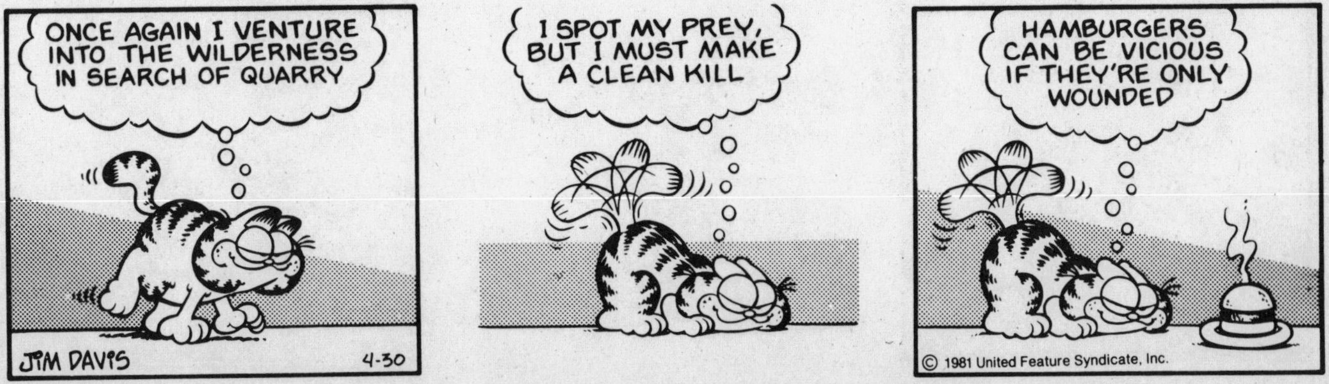
ONCE AGAIN I VENTURE INTO THE WILDERNESS IN SEARCH OF QUARRY
JIM DAVIS
4-30
I SPOT MY PREY, BUT I MUST MAKE A CLEAN KILL
HAMBURGERS CAN BE VICIOUS IF THEY'RE ONLY WOUNDED
© 1981 United Feature Syndicate, Inc.

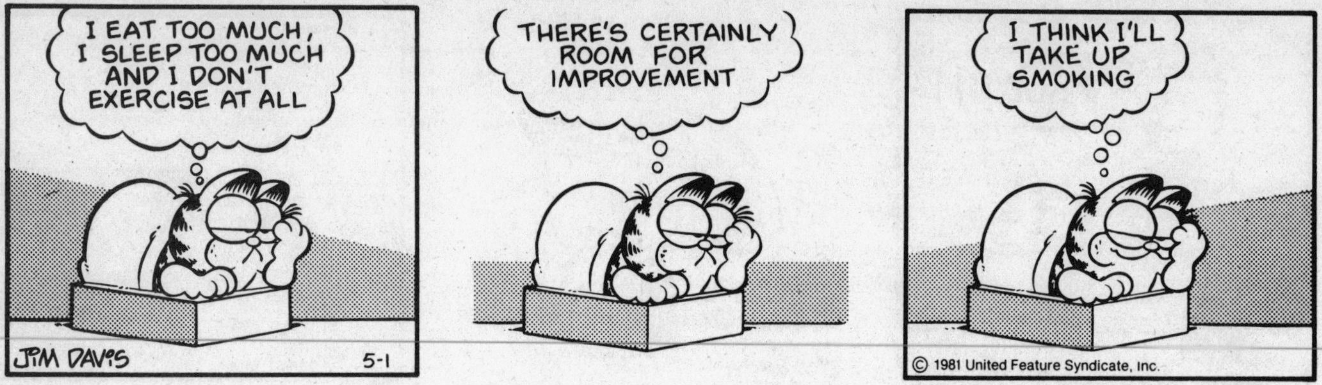
I EAT TOO MUCH, I SLEEP TOO MUCH AND I DON'T EXERCISE AT ALL
JIM DAVIS
5-1
THERE'S CERTAINLY ROOM FOR IMPROVEMENT
I THINK I'LL TAKE UP SMOKING
© 1981 United Feature Syndicate, Inc.

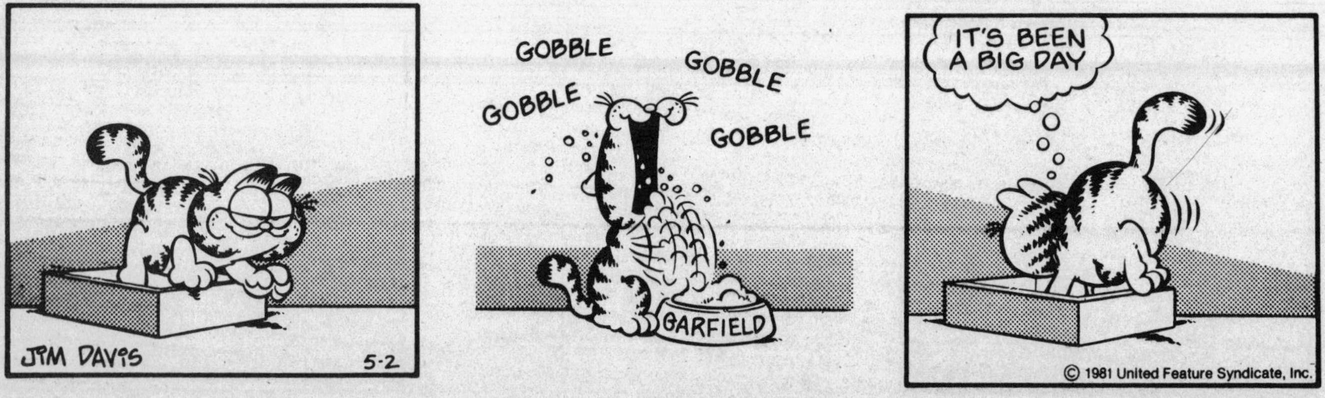
JIM DAVIS
5-2
GOBBLE
GOBBLE
GOBBLE
GOBBLE
GARFIELD
IT'S BEEN A BIG DAY
© 1981 United Feature Syndicate, Inc.

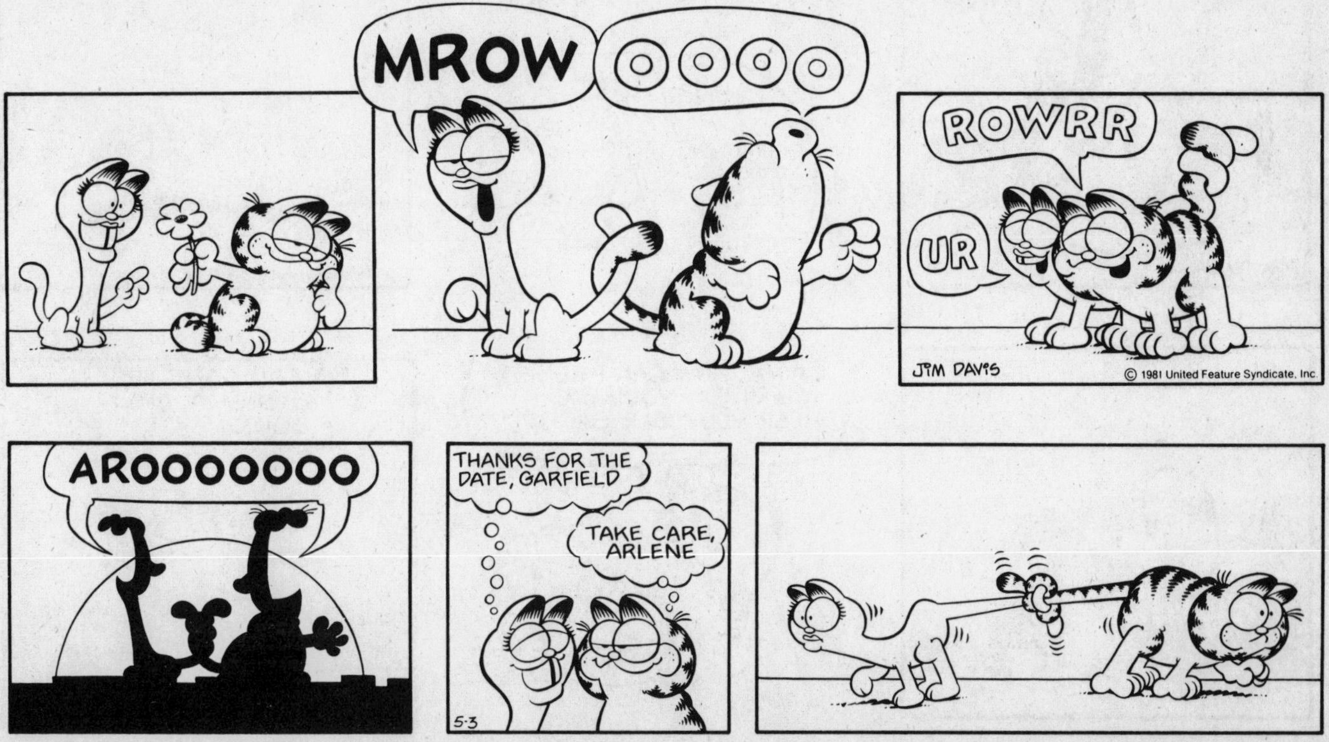

MROW
OOOO
ROWRR
UR
JIM DAVIS
© 1981 United Feature Syndicate, Inc.
AROOOOOOO
THANKS FOR THE DATE, GARFIELD
TAKE CARE, ARLENE
5-3

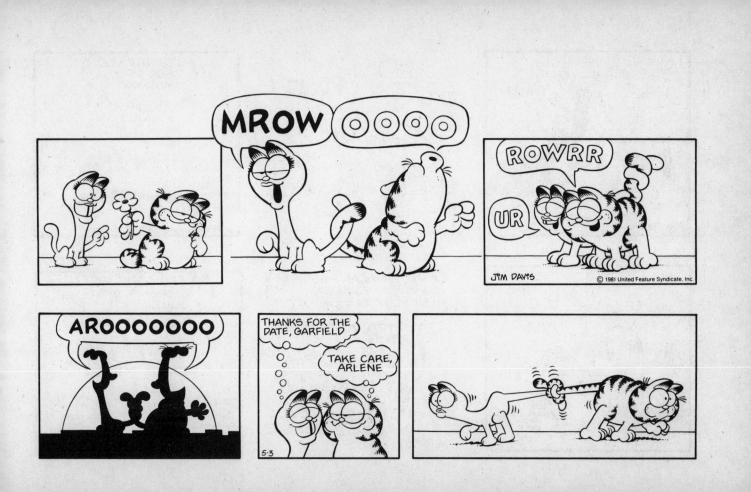

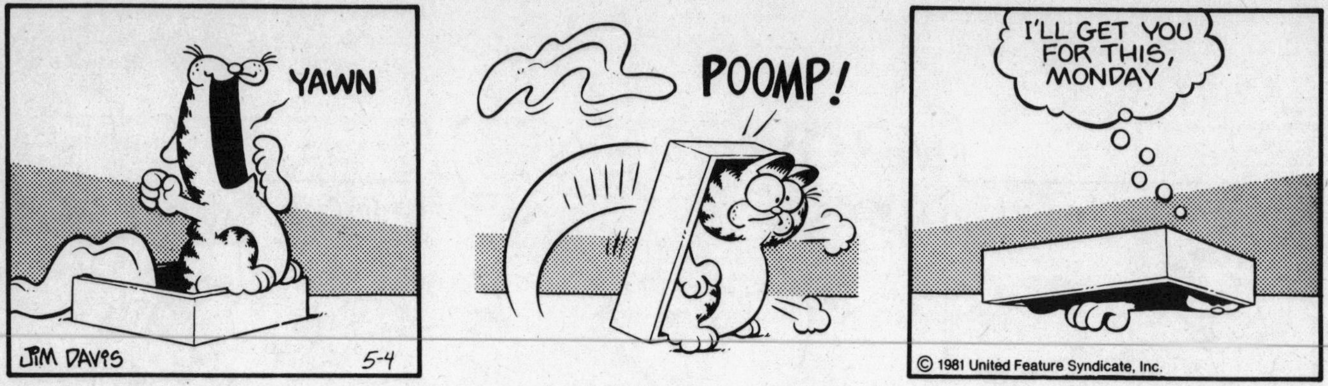
YAWN
JIM DAVIS
5-4
POOMP!
I'LL GET YOU FOR THIS, MONDAY
© 1981 United Feature Syndicate, Inc.

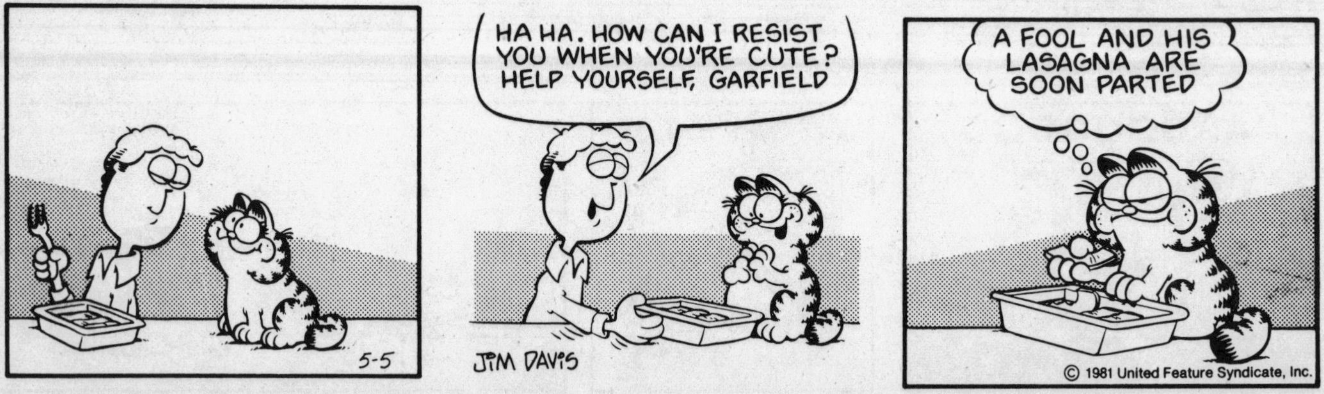
5-5
HA HA. HOW CAN I RESIST YOU WHEN YOU'RE CUTE? HELP YOURSELF, GARFIELD
JIM DAVIS
A FOOL AND HIS LASAGNA ARE SOON PARTED
© 1981 United Feature Syndicate, Inc.

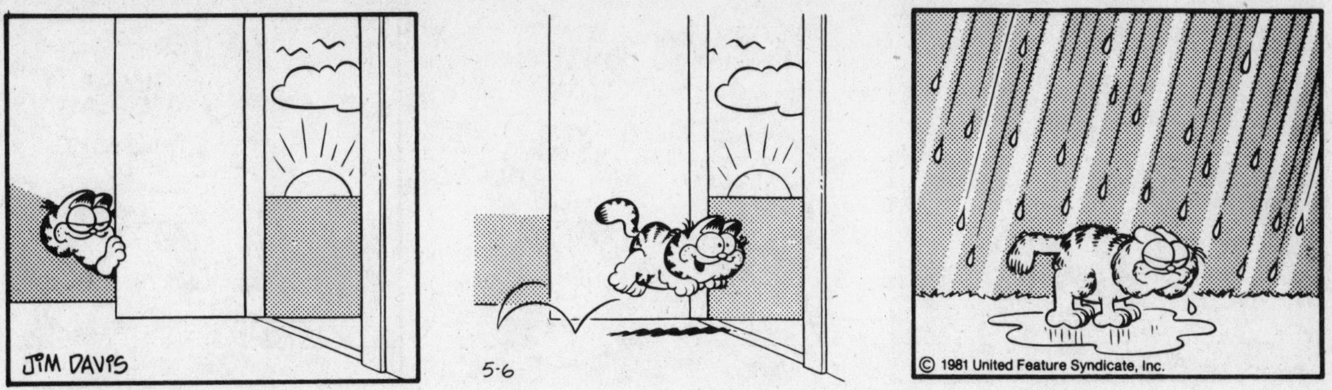
JIM DAVIS
5-6
© 1981 United Feature Syndicate, Inc.

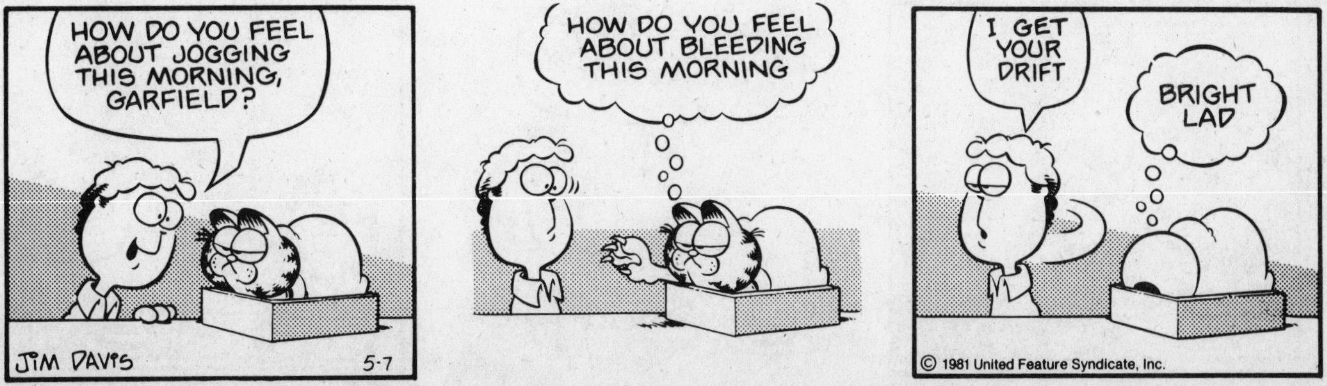
HOW DO YOU FEEL ABOUT JOGGING THIS MORNING, GARFIELD?
JIM DAVIS
5-7
HOW DO YOU FEEL ABOUT BLEEDING THIS MORNING
I GET YOUR DRIFT
BRIGHT LAD
© 1981 United Feature Syndicate, Inc.

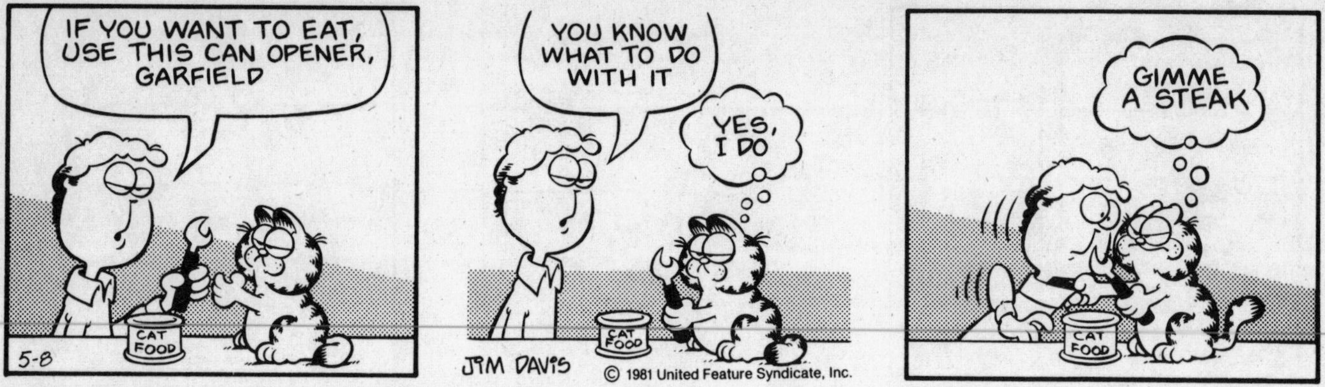
IF YOU WANT TO EAT, USE THIS CAN OPENER, GARFIELD
CAT FOOD
5-8
YOU KNOW WHAT TO DO WITH IT
YES, I DO
JIM DAVIS
GIMME A STEAK

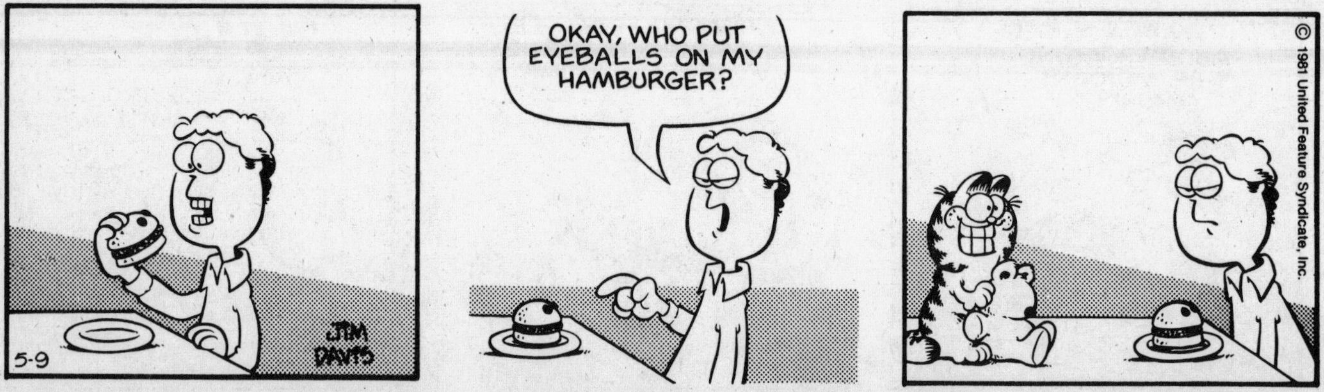
5-9
JIM DAVIS
OKAY, WHO PUT EYEBALLS ON MY HAMBURGER?

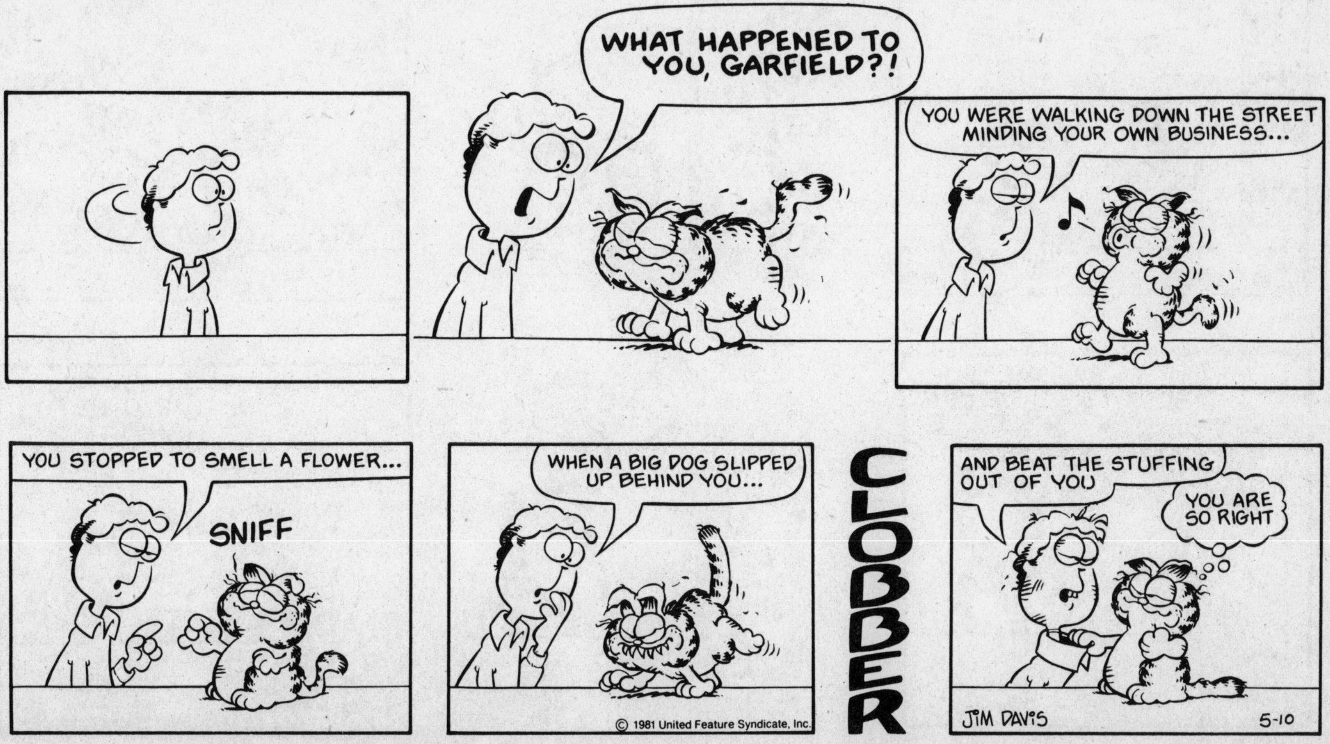
WHAT HAPPENED TO YOU, GARFIELD?!
YOU WERE WALKING DOWN THE STREET MINDING YOUR OWN BUSINESS...
YOU STOPPED TO SMELL A FLOWER...
SNIFF
WHEN A BIG DOG SLIPPED UP BEHIND YOU...
© 1981 United Feature Syndicate, Inc.
CLOBBER
AND BEAT THE STUFFING OUT OF YOU
YOU ARE SO RIGHT
JIM DAVIS
5-10

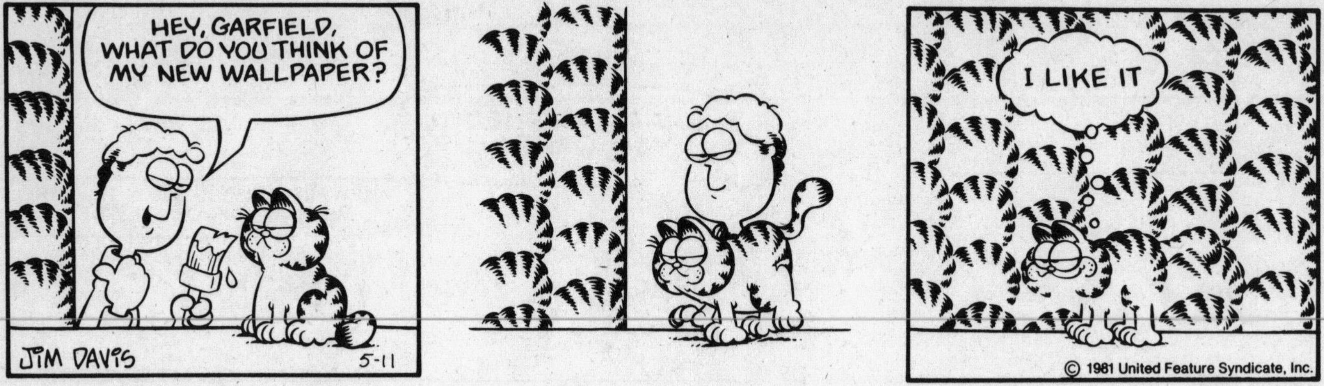
HEY, GARFIELD, WHAT DO YOU THINK OF MY NEW WALLPAPER?
JIM DAVIS
5-11
I LIKE IT
© 1981 United Feature Syndicate, Inc.

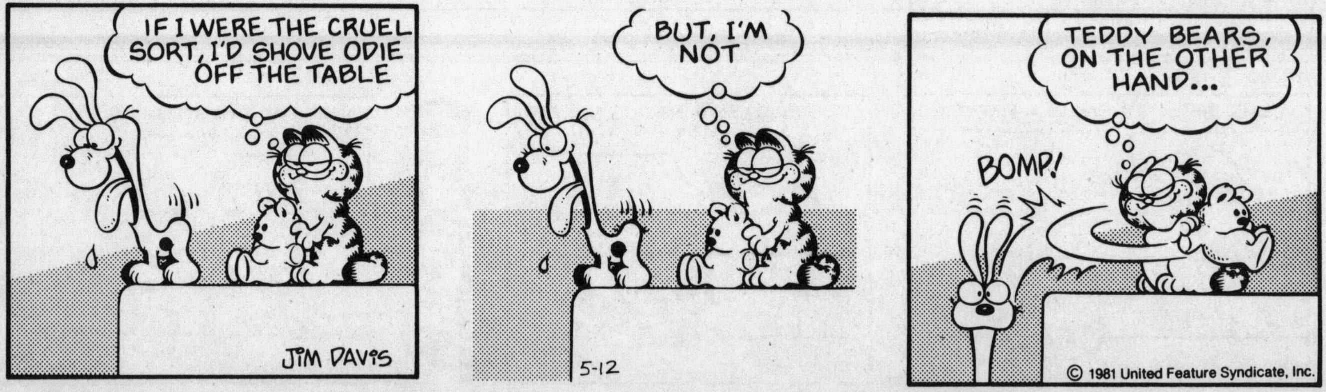
IF I WERE THE CRUEL SORT, I'D SHOVE ODIE OFF THE TABLE
JIM DAVIS
BUT, I'M NOT
5-12
TEDDY BEARS, ON THE OTHER HAND...
BOMP!
© 1981 United Feature Syndicate, Inc.

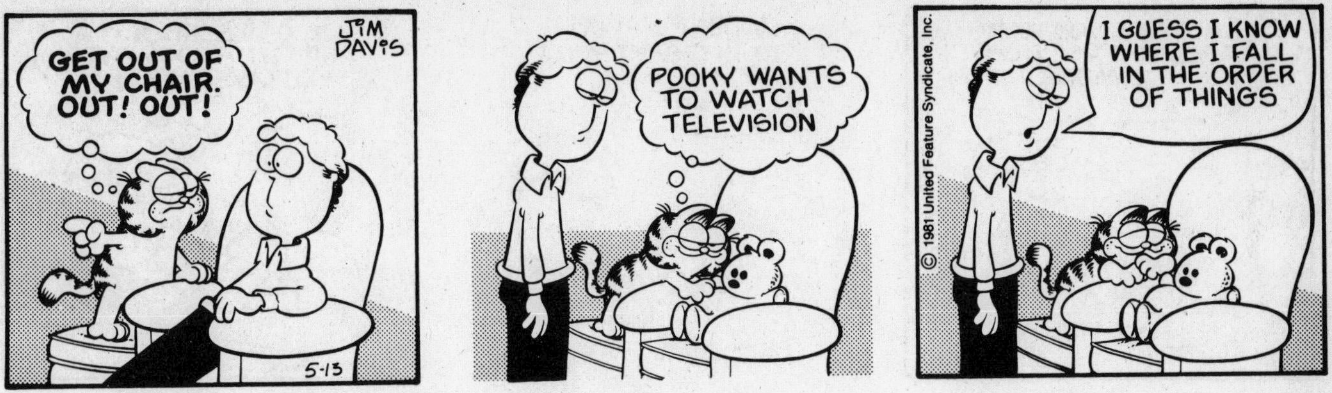
JIM DAVIS
GET OUT OF MY CHAIR. OUT! OUT!
5-13
POOKY WANTS TO WATCH TELEVISION
I GUESS I KNOW WHERE I FALL IN THE ORDER OF THINGS
© 1981 United Feature Syndicate, Inc.

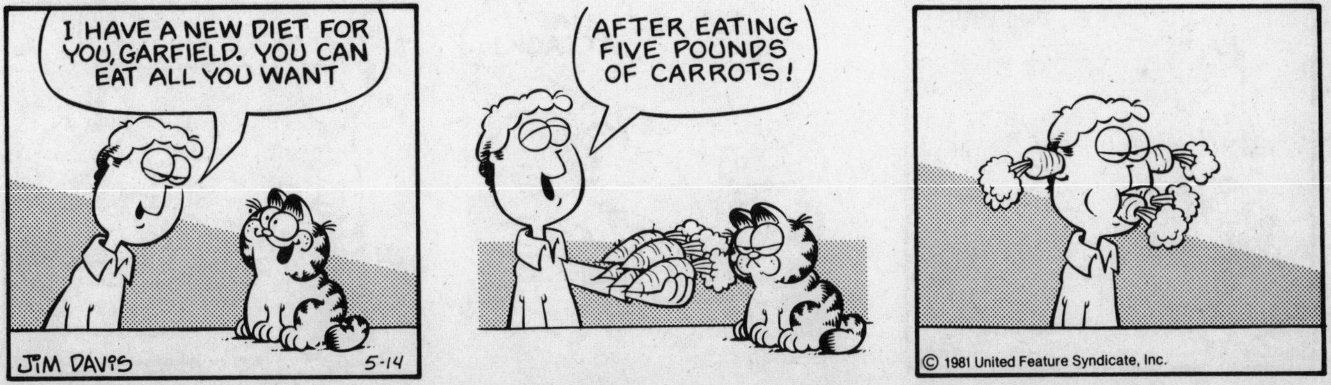
I HAVE A NEW DIET FOR YOU, GARFIELD. YOU CAN EAT ALL YOU WANT
JIM DAVIS
5-14
AFTER EATING FIVE POUNDS OF CARROTS!
© 1981 United Feature Syndicate, Inc.

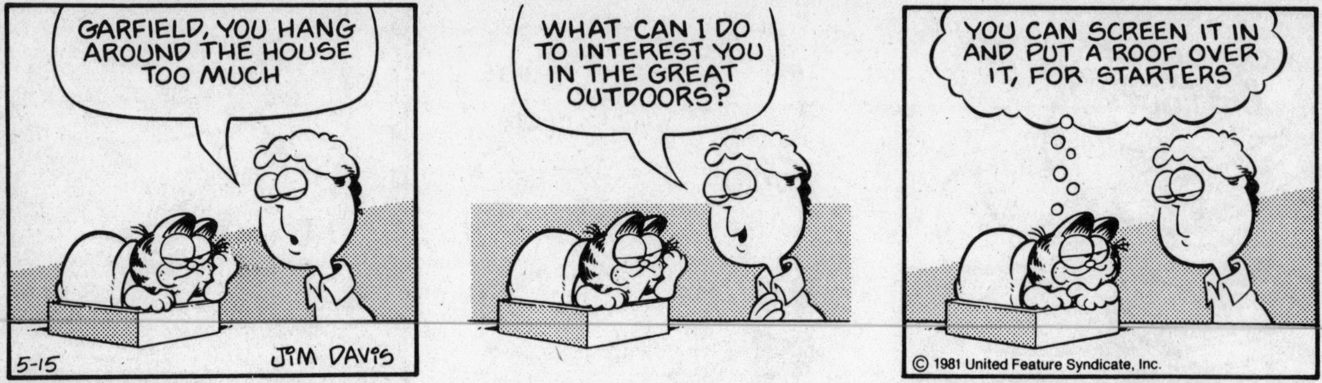
GARFIELD, YOU HANG AROUND THE HOUSE TOO MUCH
5-15
JIM DAVIS
WHAT CAN I DO TO INTEREST YOU IN THE GREAT OUTDOORS?
YOU CAN SCREEN IT IN AND PUT A ROOF OVER IT, FOR STARTERS
© 1981 United Feature Syndicate, Inc.

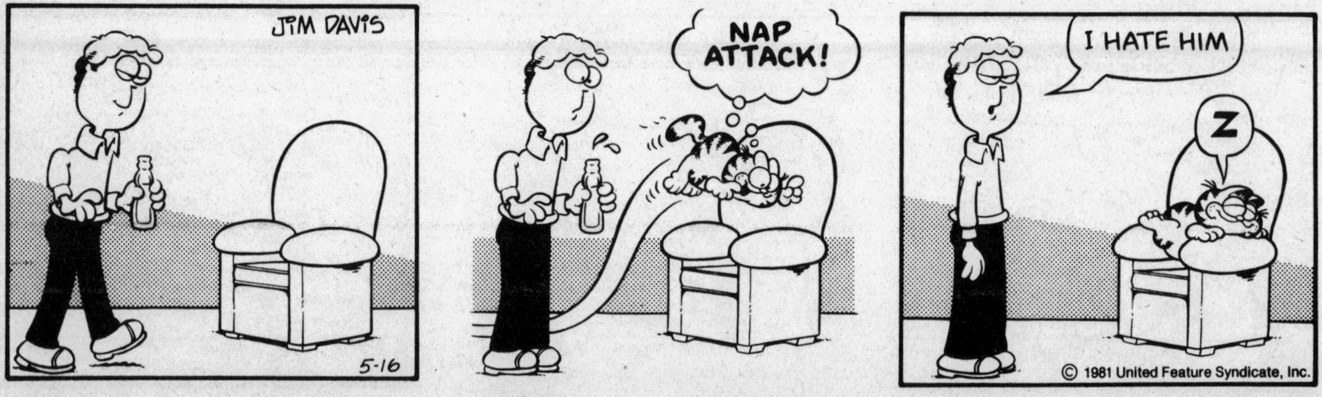
JIM DAVIS
5-16
NAP ATTACK!
I HATE HIM
Z
© 1981 United Feature Syndicate, Inc.

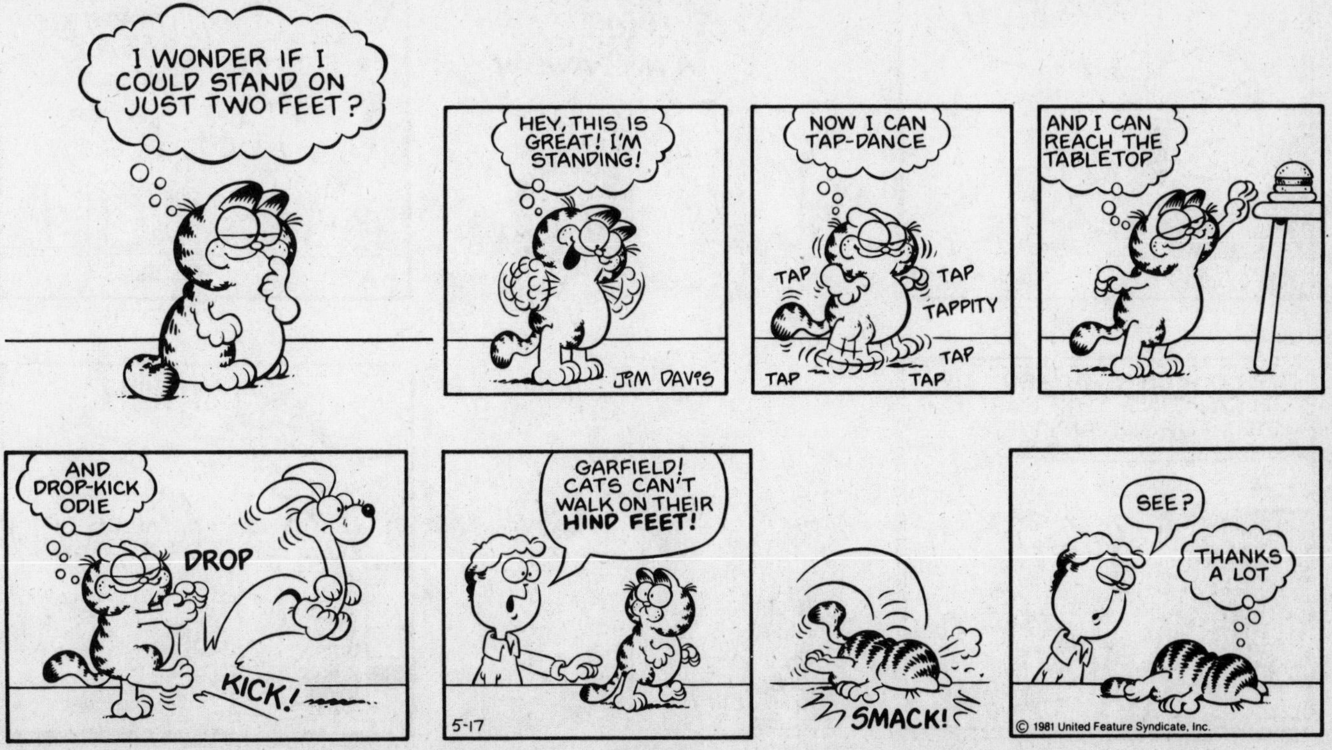
I WONDER IF I COULD STAND ON JUST TWO FEET?
HEY, THIS IS GREAT! I'M STANDING!
JIM DAVIS
NOW I CAN TAP-DANCE
TAP
TAP
TAPPITY
TAP
TAP
TAP
AND I CAN REACH THE TABLETOP
AND DROP-KICK ODIE
DROP
KICK!
GARFIELD! CATS CAN'T WALK ON THEIR **HIND FEET!**
5-17
SMACK!
SEE?
THANKS A LOT
© 1981 United Feature Syndicate, Inc.

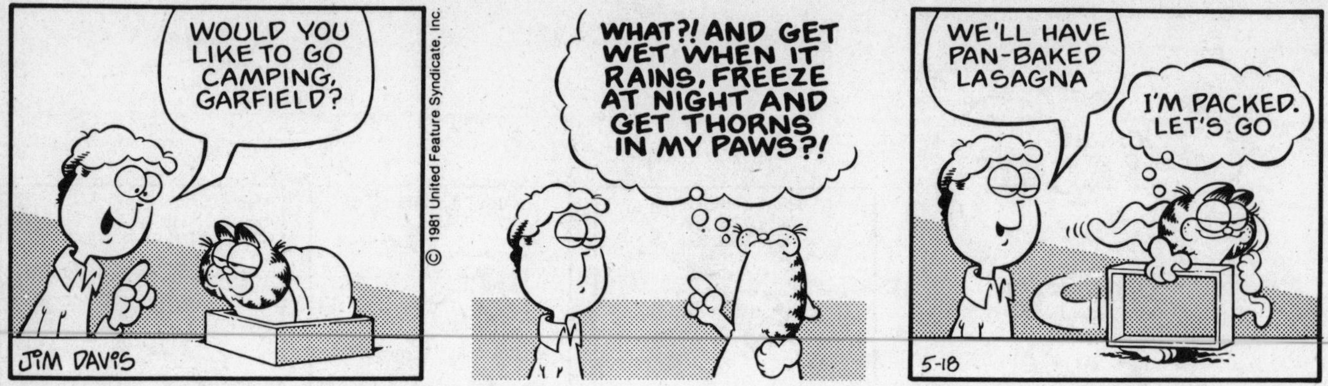
WOULD YOU LIKE TO GO CAMPING, GARFIELD?
JIM DAVIS
© 1981 United Feature Syndicate, Inc.
WHAT?! AND GET WET WHEN IT RAINS, FREEZE AT NIGHT AND GET THORNS IN MY PAWS?!
WE'LL HAVE PAN-BAKED LASAGNA
I'M PACKED. LET'S GO
5-18

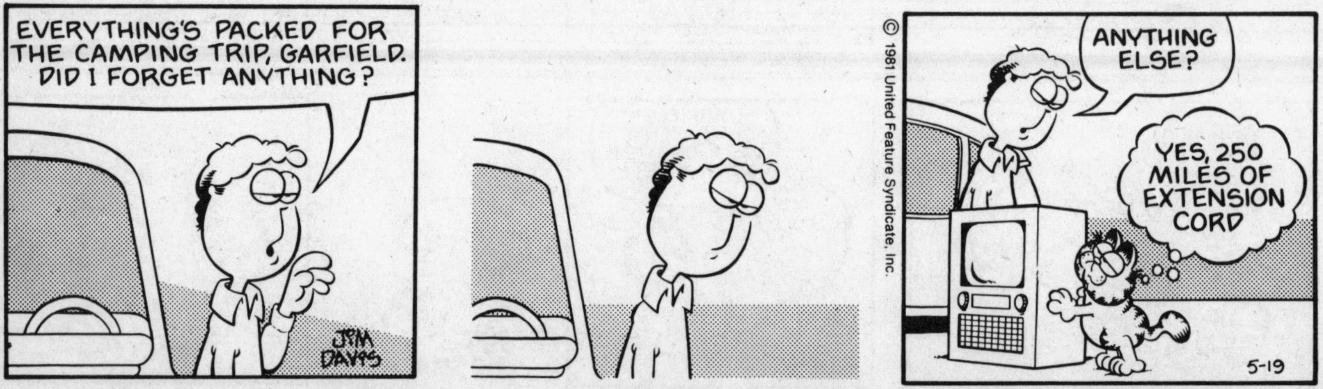
EVERYTHING'S PACKED FOR THE CAMPING TRIP, GARFIELD. DID I FORGET ANYTHING?
JIM DAVIS
© 1981 United Feature Syndicate, Inc.
ANYTHING ELSE?
YES, 250 MILES OF EXTENSION CORD
5-19

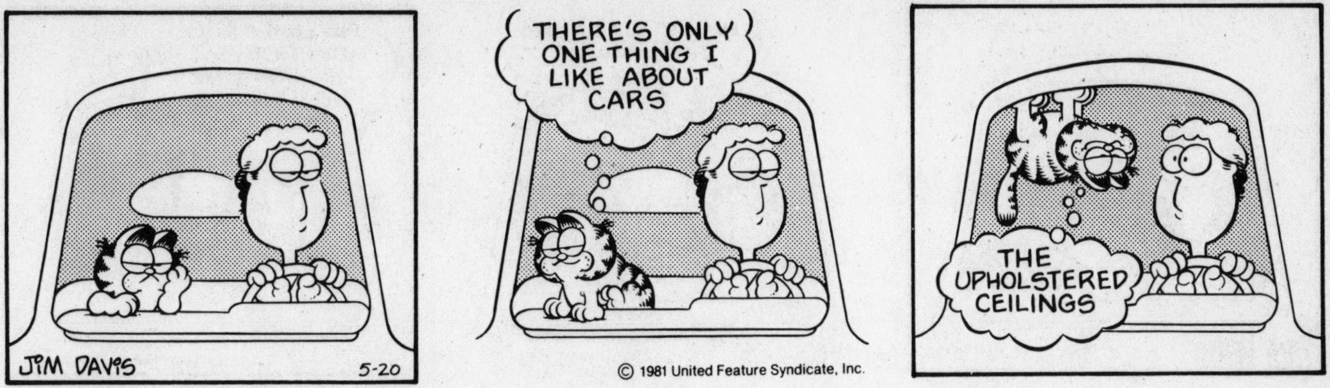
JIM DAVIS 5-20
THERE'S ONLY ONE THING I LIKE ABOUT CARS
THE UPHOLSTERED CEILINGS
© 1981 United Feature Syndicate, Inc.

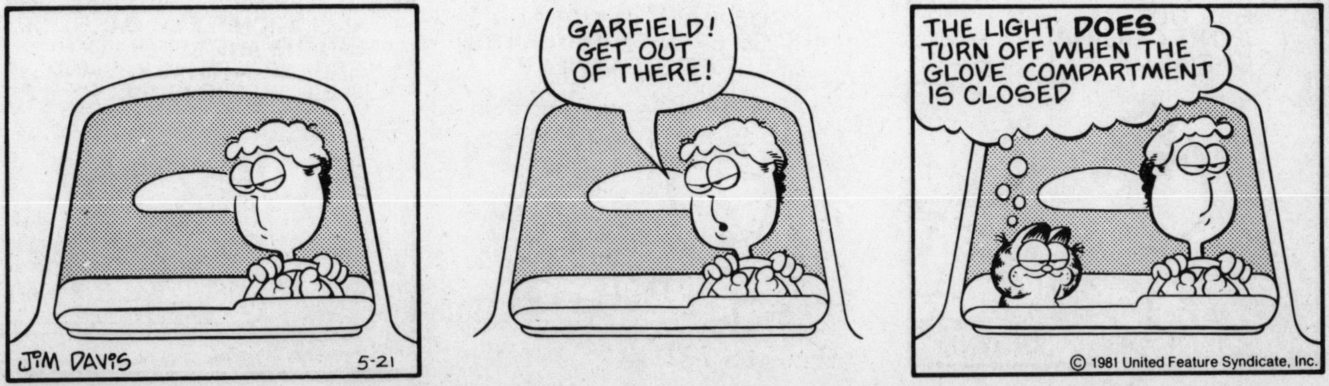
JIM DAVIS 5-21
GARFIELD! GET OUT OF THERE!
THE LIGHT **DOES** TURN OFF WHEN THE GLOVE COMPARTMENT IS CLOSED
© 1981 United Feature Syndicate, Inc.

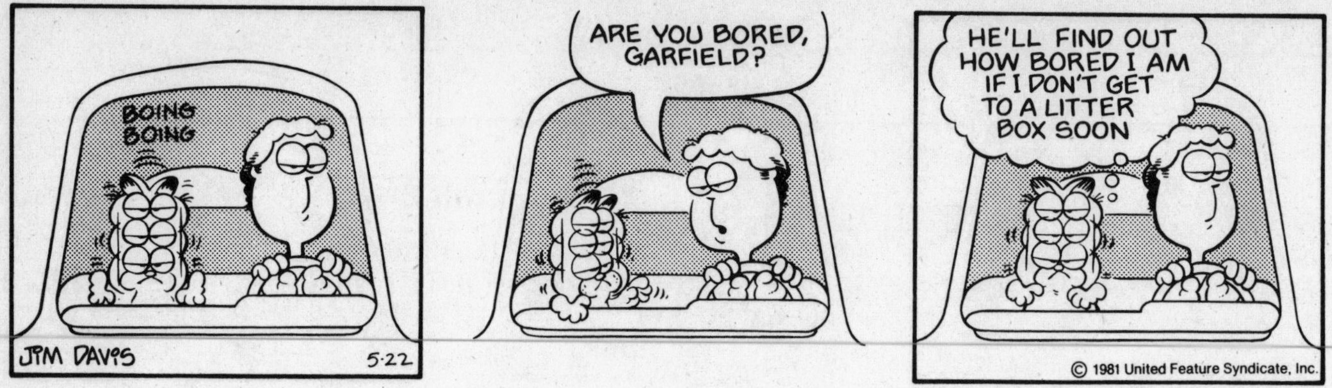
BOING
BOING
ARE YOU BORED, GARFIELD?
HE'LL FIND OUT HOW BORED I AM IF I DON'T GET TO A LITTER BOX SOON
JIM DAVIS
5·22
© 1981 United Feature Syndicate, Inc.

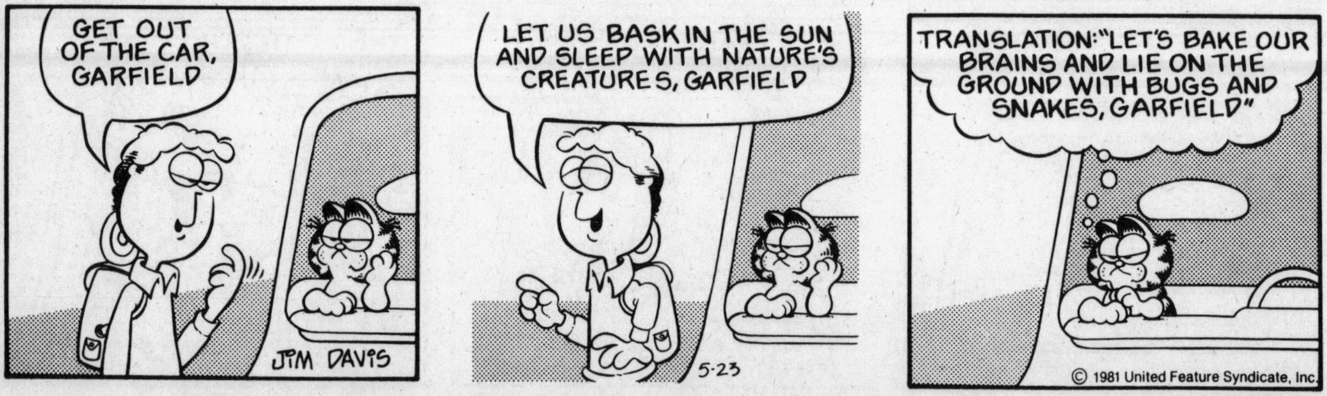
GET OUT OF THE CAR, GARFIELD
JIM DAVIS
LET US BASK IN THE SUN AND SLEEP WITH NATURE'S CREATURES, GARFIELD
5·23
TRANSLATION: "LET'S BAKE OUR BRAINS AND LIE ON THE GROUND WITH BUGS AND SNAKES, GARFIELD"
© 1981 United Feature Syndicate, Inc.

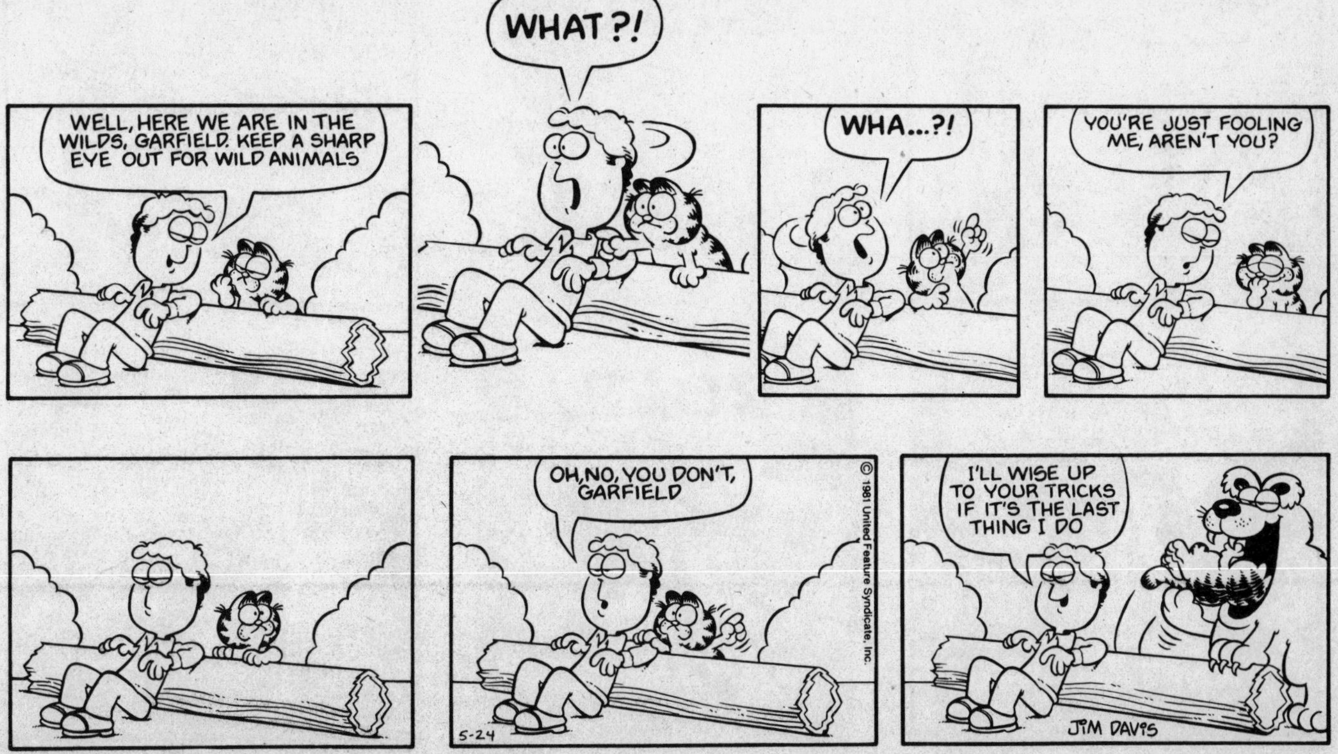

WELL, HERE WE ARE IN THE WILDS, GARFIELD. KEEP A SHARP EYE OUT FOR WILD ANIMALS
WHAT?!
WHA...?!
YOU'RE JUST FOOLING ME, AREN'T YOU?
OH, NO, YOU DON'T, GARFIELD
5-24
© 1981 United Feature Syndicate, Inc.
I'LL WISE UP TO YOUR TRICKS IF IT'S THE LAST THING I DO
JIM DAVIS

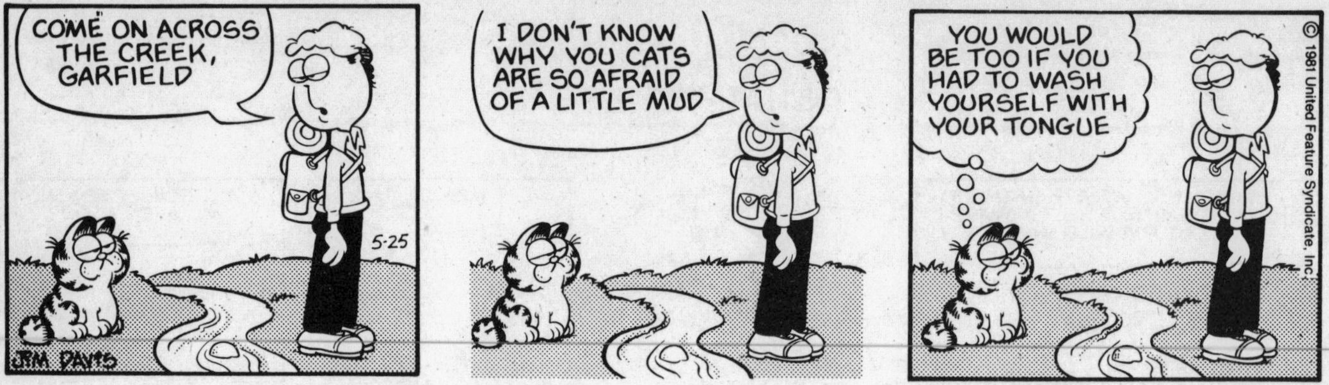
COME ON ACROSS THE CREEK, GARFIELD
5-25
JIM DAVIS
I DON'T KNOW WHY YOU CATS ARE SO AFRAID OF A LITTLE MUD
YOU WOULD BE TOO IF YOU HAD TO WASH YOURSELF WITH YOUR TONGUE
© 1981 United Feature Syndicate, Inc.

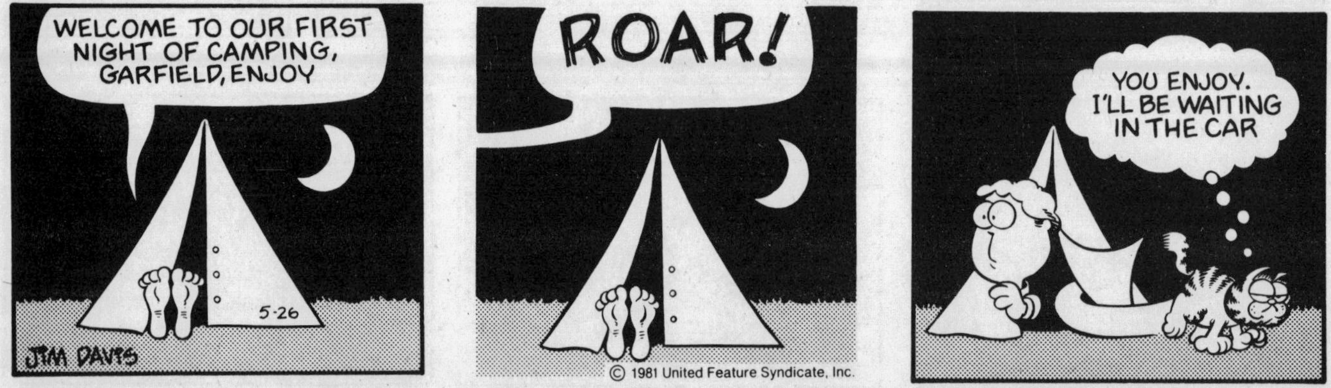
WELCOME TO OUR FIRST NIGHT OF CAMPING, GARFIELD, ENJOY
5-26
JIM DAVIS
ROAR!
YOU ENJOY. I'LL BE WAITING IN THE CAR
© 1981 United Feature Syndicate, Inc.

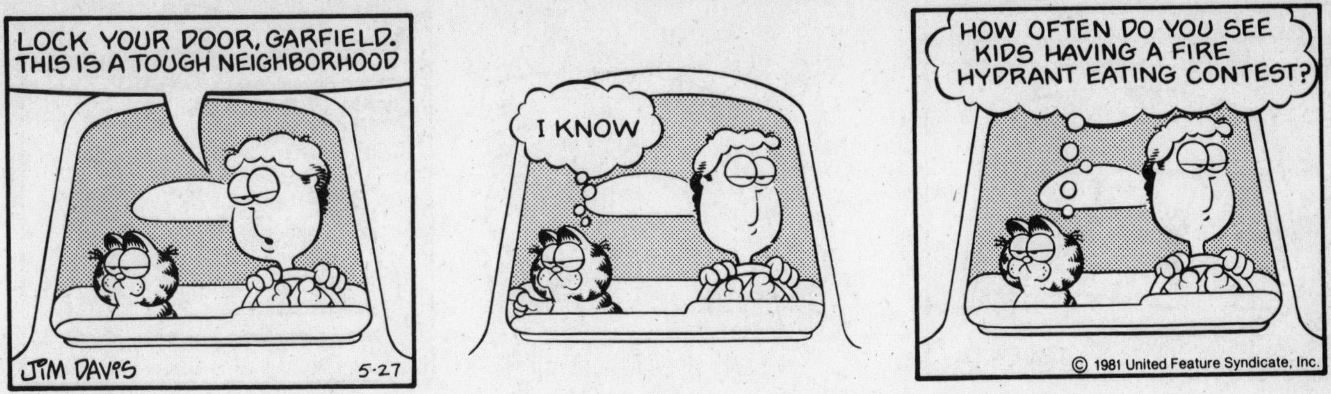
LOCK YOUR DOOR, GARFIELD. THIS IS A TOUGH NEIGHBORHOOD
I KNOW
HOW OFTEN DO YOU SEE KIDS HAVING A FIRE HYDRANT EATING CONTEST?
JIM DAVIS
5-27
© 1981 United Feature Syndicate, Inc.

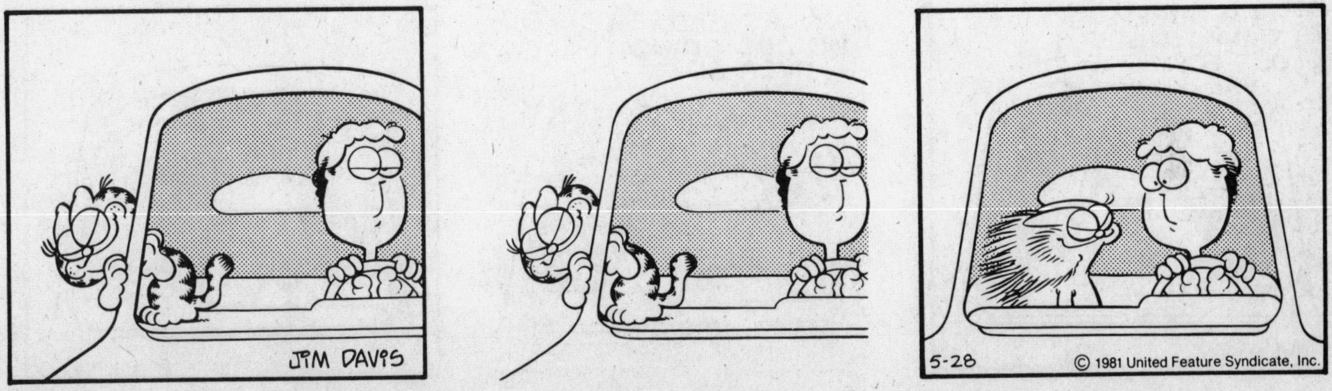
JIM DAVIS
5-28
© 1981 United Feature Syndicate, Inc.

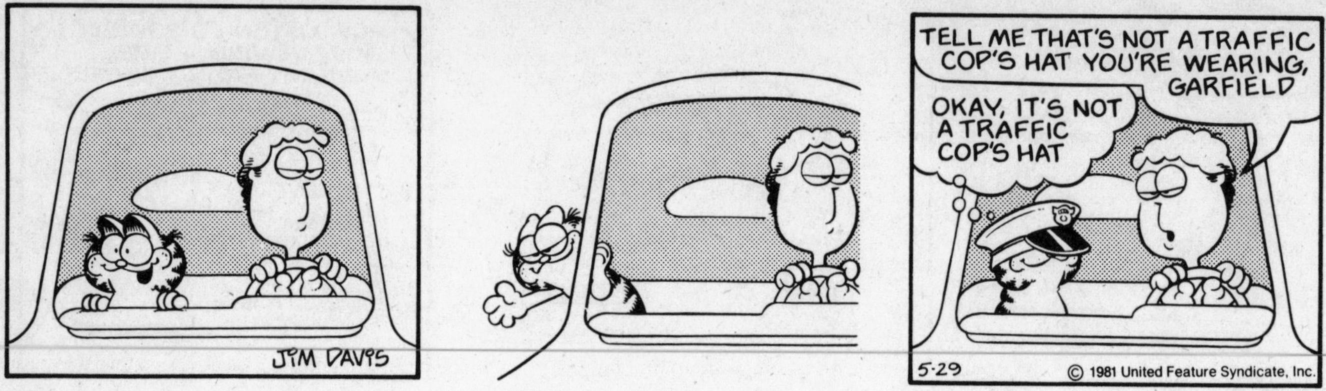
JIM DAVIS
TELL ME THAT'S NOT A TRAFFIC COP'S HAT YOU'RE WEARING, GARFIELD
OKAY, IT'S NOT A TRAFFIC COP'S HAT
5-29
© 1981 United Feature Syndicate, Inc.

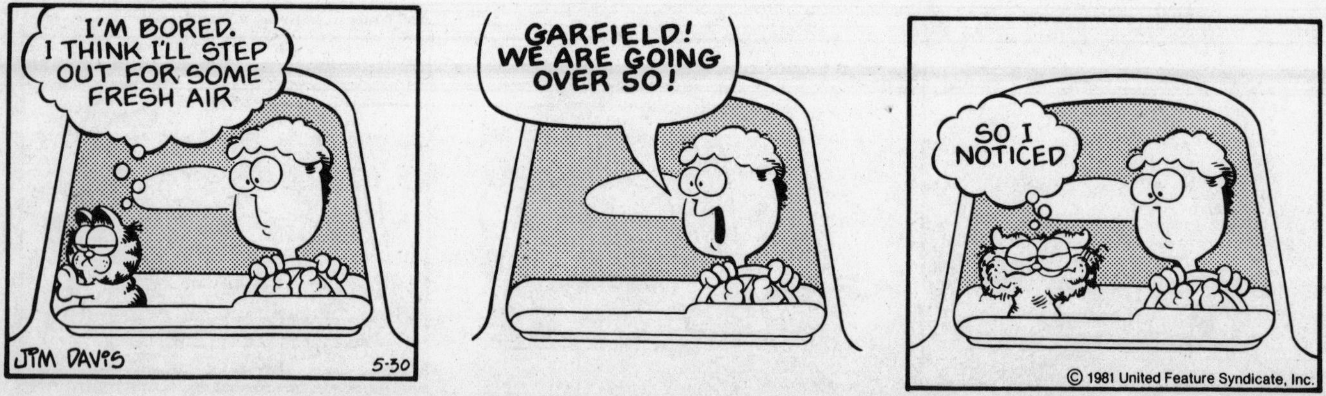
I'M BORED. I THINK I'LL STEP OUT FOR SOME FRESH AIR
JIM DAVIS
5-30
GARFIELD! WE ARE GOING OVER 50!
SO I NOTICED
© 1981 United Feature Syndicate, Inc.

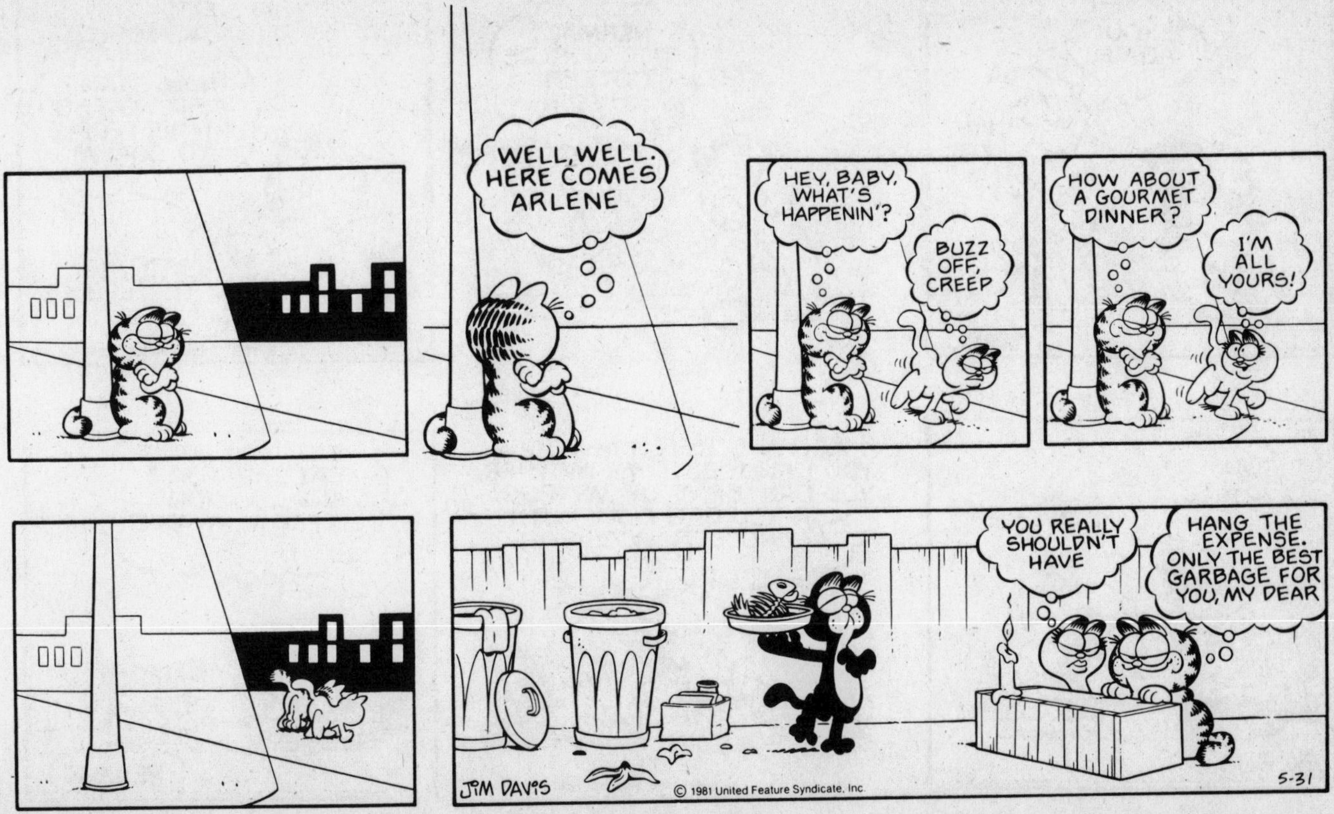
WELL, WELL. HERE COMES ARLENE
HEY, BABY, WHAT'S HAPPENIN'?
BUZZ OFF, CREEP
HOW ABOUT A GOURMET DINNER?
I'M ALL YOURS!
YOU REALLY SHOULDN'T HAVE
HANG THE EXPENSE. ONLY THE BEST GARBAGE FOR YOU, MY DEAR
JIM DAVIS
© 1981 United Feature Syndicate, Inc.
5-31

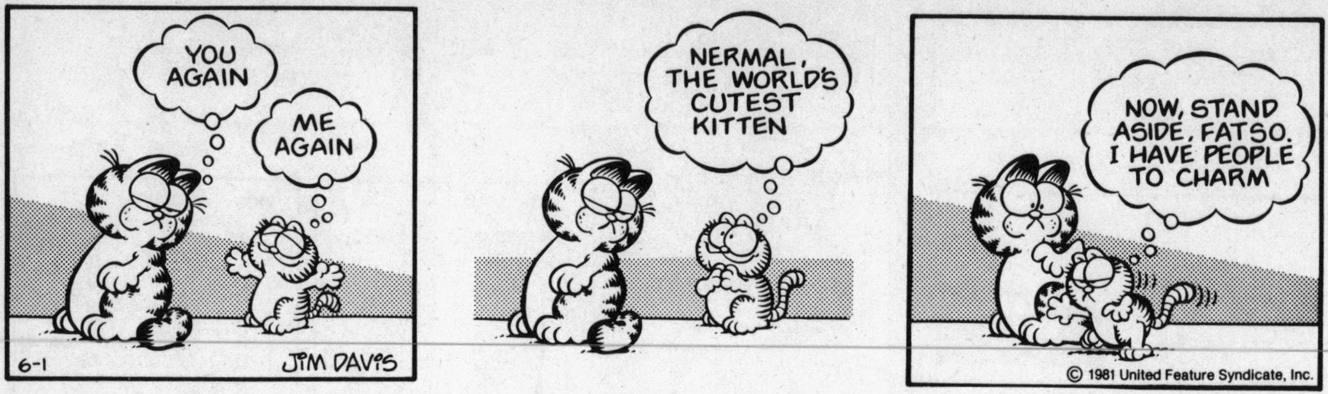
YOU AGAIN
ME AGAIN
NERMAL, THE WORLD'S CUTEST KITTEN
NOW, STAND ASIDE, FATSO. I HAVE PEOPLE TO CHARM
6-1
JIM DAVIS

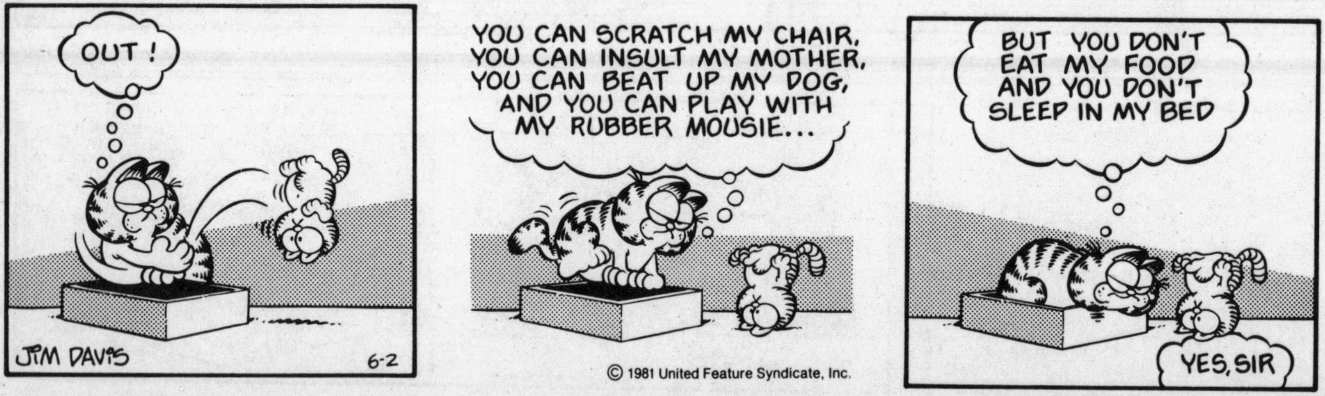
OUT!
YOU CAN SCRATCH MY CHAIR, YOU CAN INSULT MY MOTHER, YOU CAN BEAT UP MY DOG, AND YOU CAN PLAY WITH MY RUBBER MOUSIE...
BUT YOU DON'T EAT MY FOOD AND YOU DON'T SLEEP IN MY BED
YES, SIR
JIM DAVIS
6-2

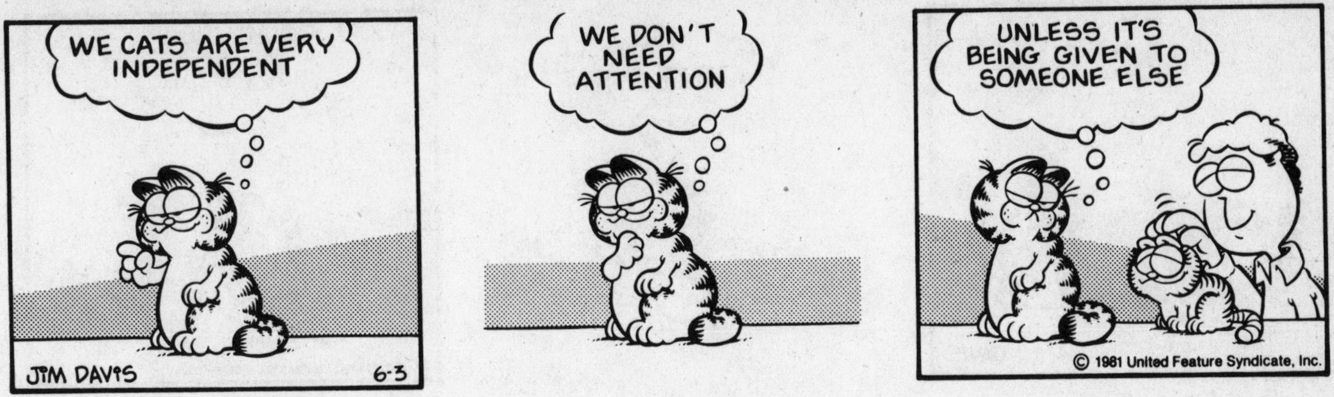
WE CATS ARE VERY INDEPENDENT
JIM DAVIS
6-3
WE DON'T NEED ATTENTION
UNLESS IT'S BEING GIVEN TO SOMEONE ELSE
© 1981 United Feature Syndicate, Inc.

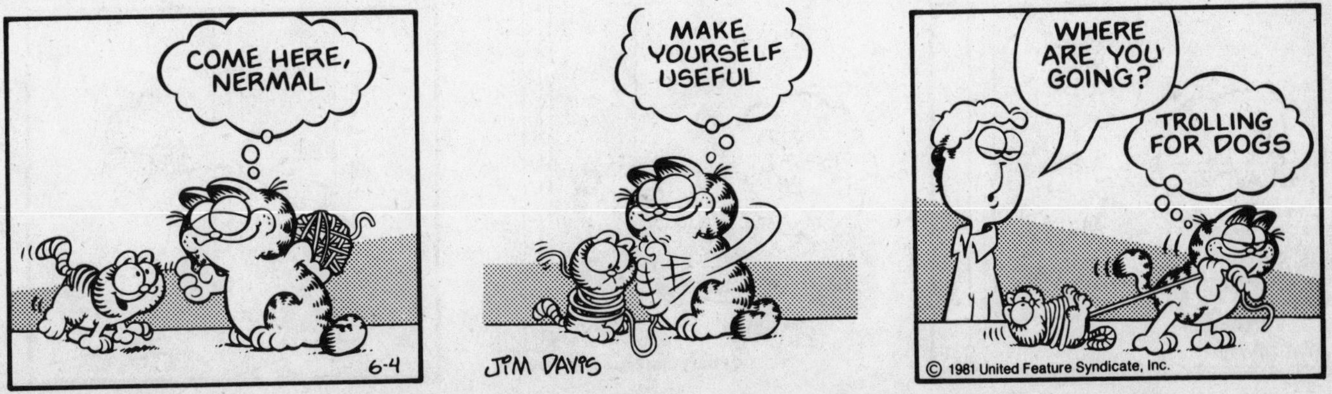
COME HERE, NERMAL
6-4
MAKE YOURSELF USEFUL
JIM DAVIS
WHERE ARE YOU GOING?
TROLLING FOR DOGS
© 1981 United Feature Syndicate, Inc.

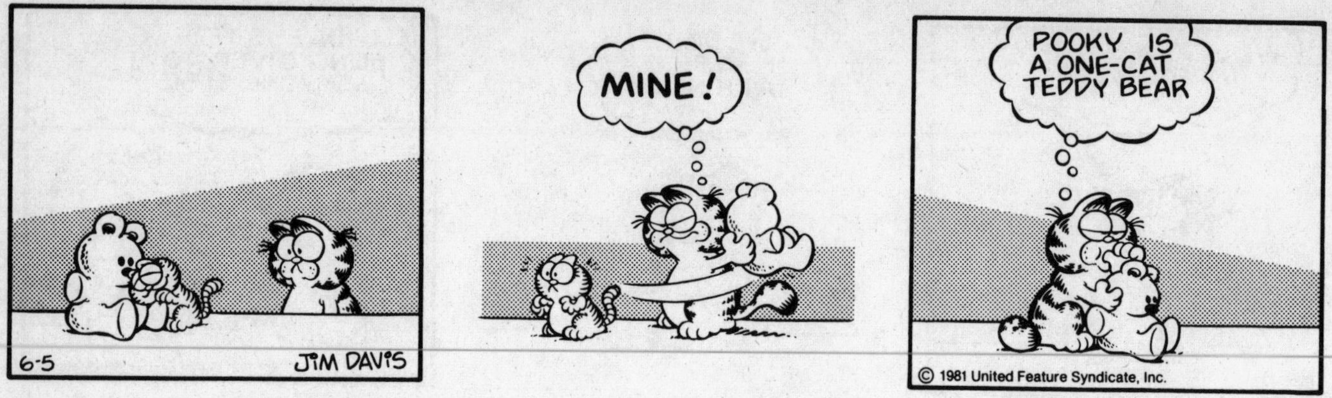
6-5
JIM DAVIS
MINE!
POOKY IS A ONE-CAT TEDDY BEAR
© 1981 United Feature Syndicate, Inc.

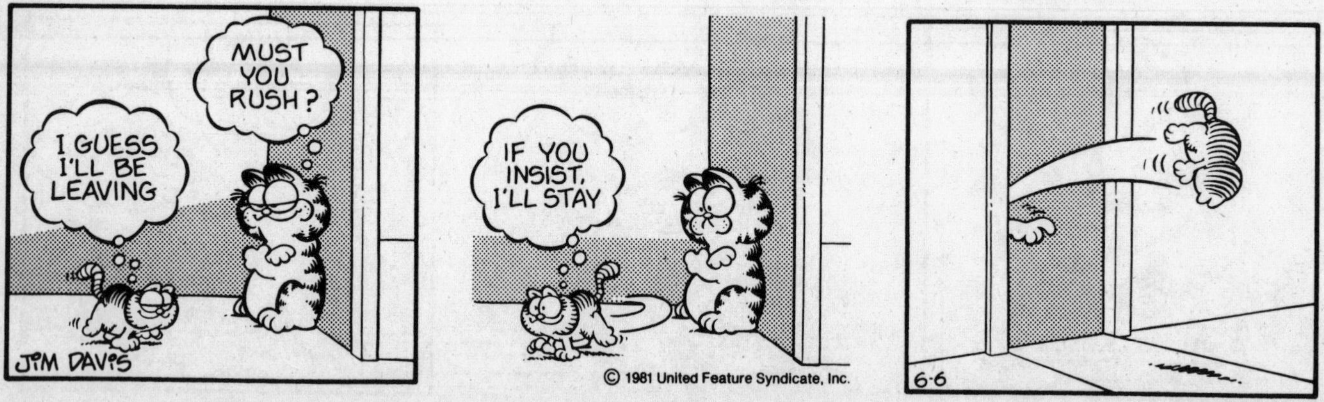
I GUESS I'LL BE LEAVING
MUST YOU RUSH?
JIM DAVIS
IF YOU INSIST, I'LL STAY
© 1981 United Feature Syndicate, Inc.
6-6

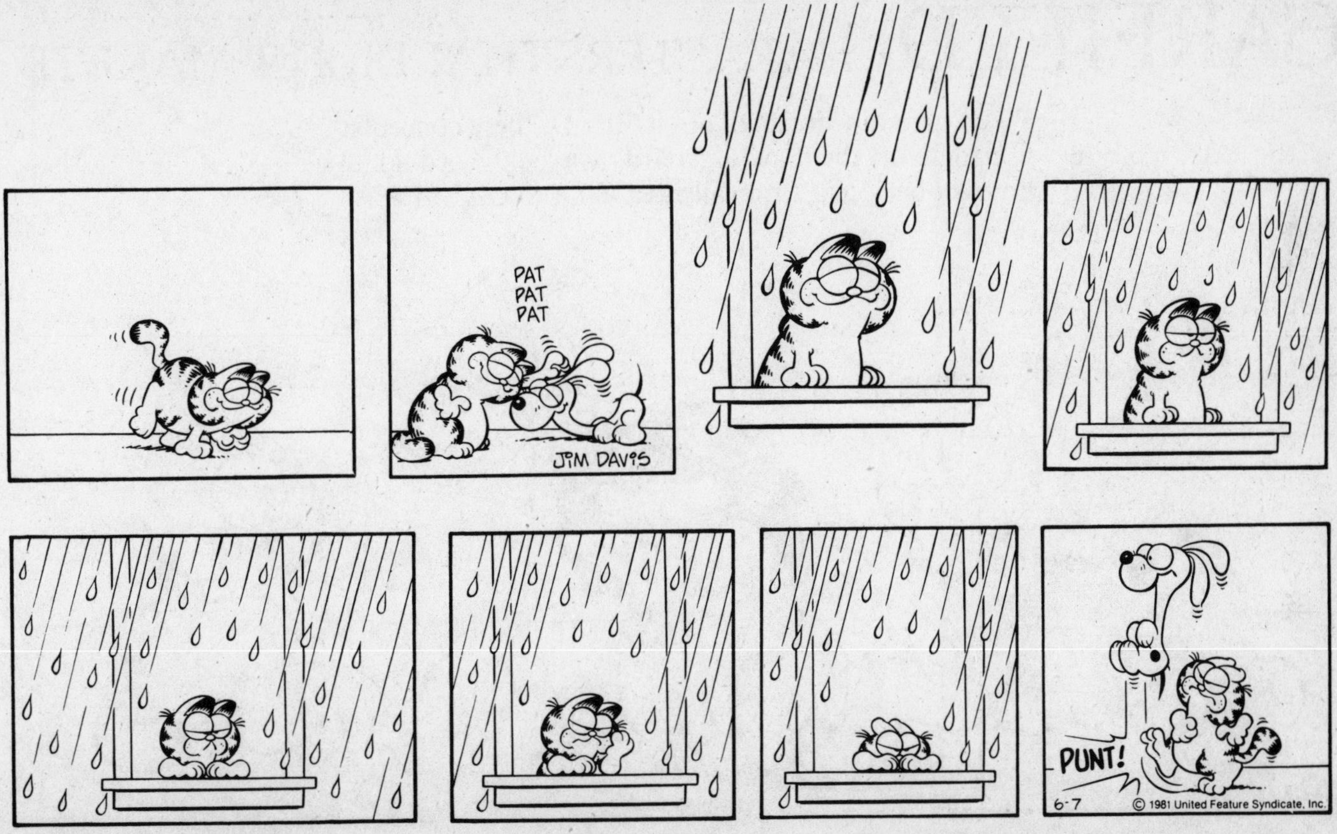
PAT
PAT
PAT
JIM DAVIS
PUNT!
6-7
© 1981 United Feature Syndicate, Inc.

GARFIELD CHARACTERS THAT DIDN'T MAKE IT

When I initially designed GARFIELD, these concepts
never made it off the drawing board. Maybe they could all be
brought back in a strip called ROGUES' GALLERY.

JIM DAVIS

Garfield eats his heart out

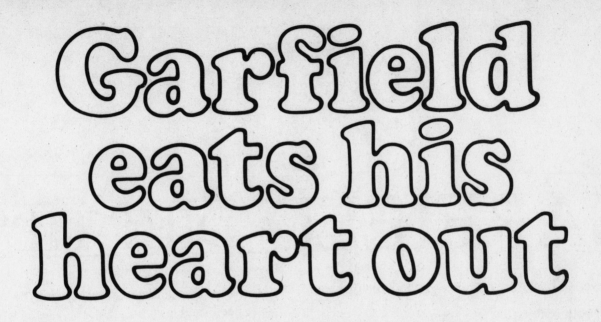

BY: JIM DAVIS

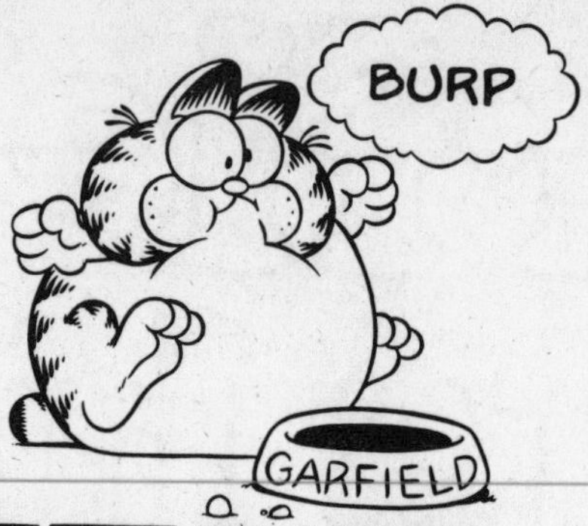
BURP
GARFIELD

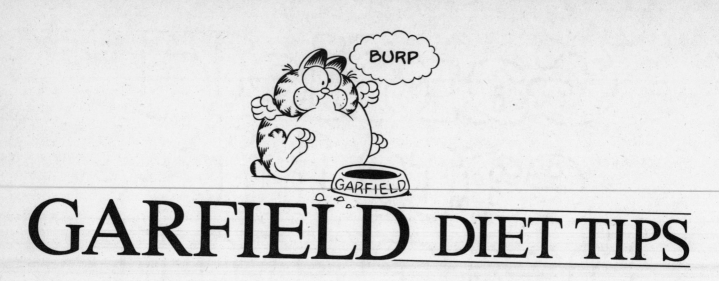

GARFIELD DIET TIPS

1. Never go back for seconds—get it all the first time.

2. Set your scales back five pounds.

3. Never accept a candygram.

4. Don't date Sara Lee.

5. Vegetables are a must on a diet. I suggest carrot cake, zucchini bread and pumpkin pie.

6. Never start a diet cold turkey (maybe cold roast beef, cold lasagna...).

7. Try to cut back. Leave the cherry off your ice cream sundae.

8. Hang around people fatter than you.

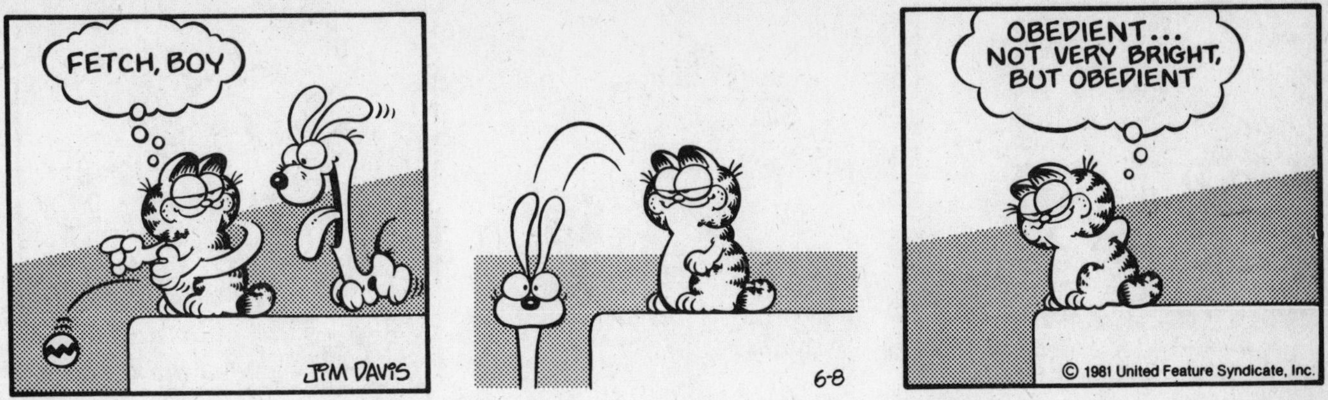
FETCH, BOY
OBEDIENT... NOT VERY BRIGHT, BUT OBEDIENT
JIM DAVIS
6-8
© 1981 United Feature Syndicate, Inc.

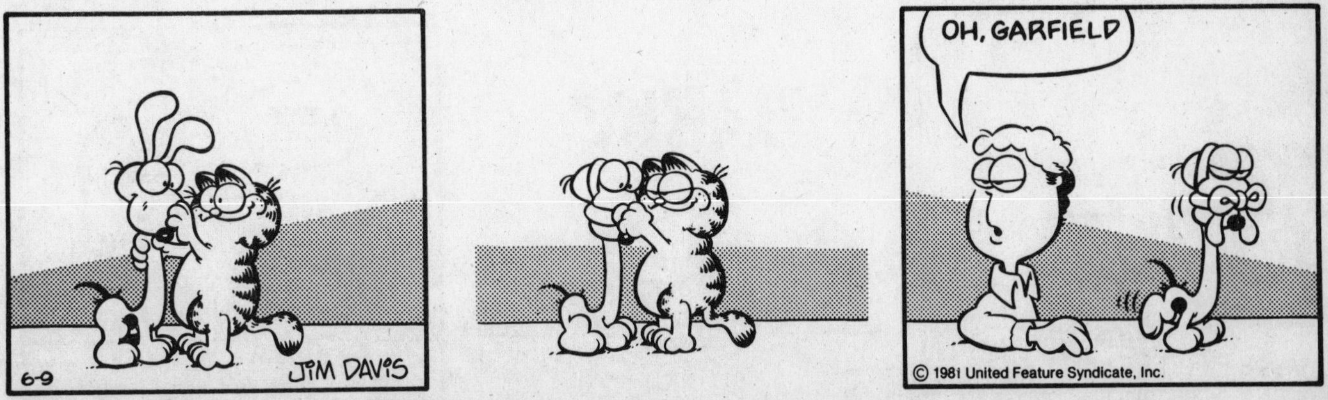
OH, GARFIELD
JIM DAVIS
6-9
© 1981 United Feature Syndicate, Inc.

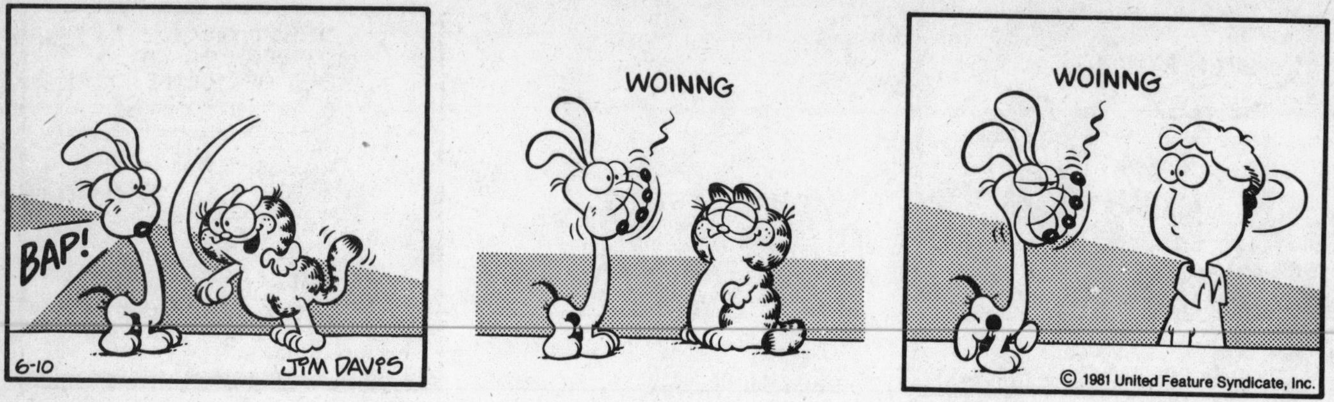
BAP!
6-10
JIM DAVIS
WOINNG
WOINNG
© 1981 United Feature Syndicate, Inc.

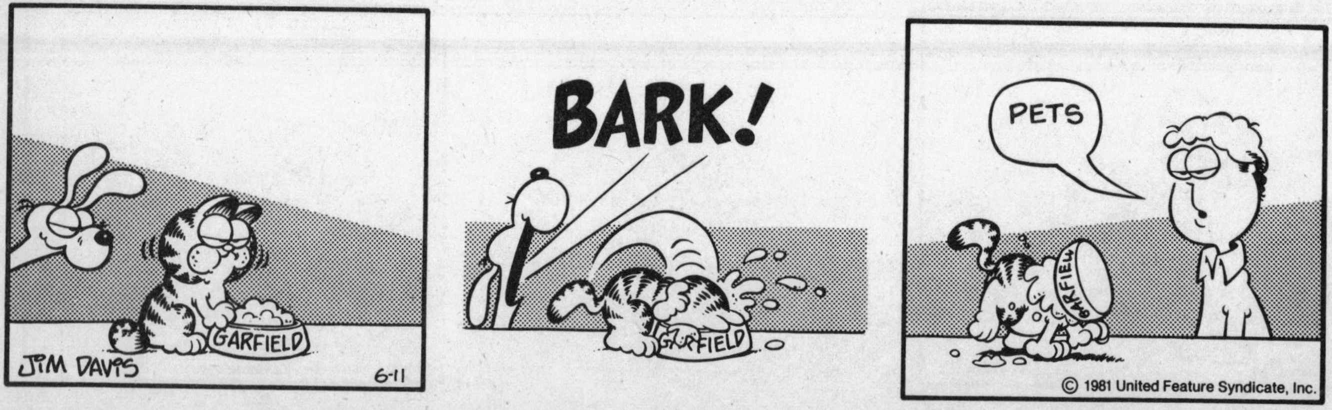
GARFIELD
JIM DAVIS
6-11
BARK!
GARFIELD
PETS
GARFIELD
© 1981 United Feature Syndicate, Inc.

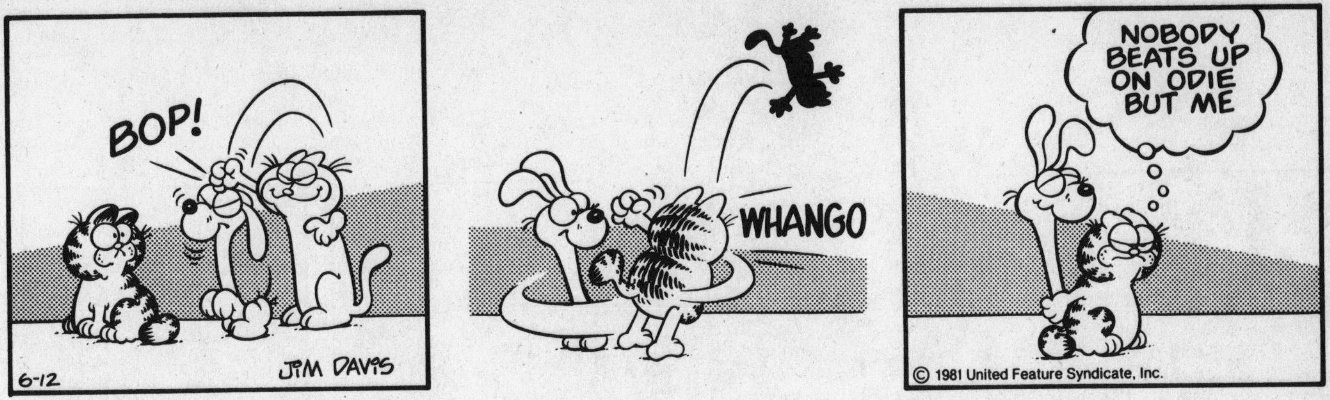
BOP!
JIM DAVIS
6-12
WHANGO
NOBODY BEATS UP ON ODIE BUT ME
© 1981 United Feature Syndicate, Inc.

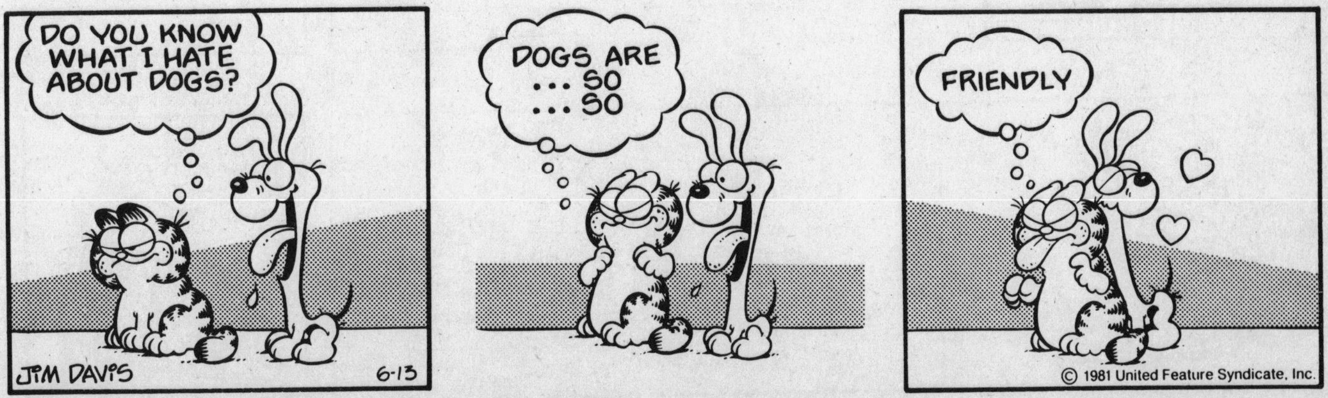
DO YOU KNOW WHAT I HATE ABOUT DOGS?
JIM DAVIS
6-13
DOGS ARE ... SO ... SO
FRIENDLY
© 1981 United Feature Syndicate, Inc.

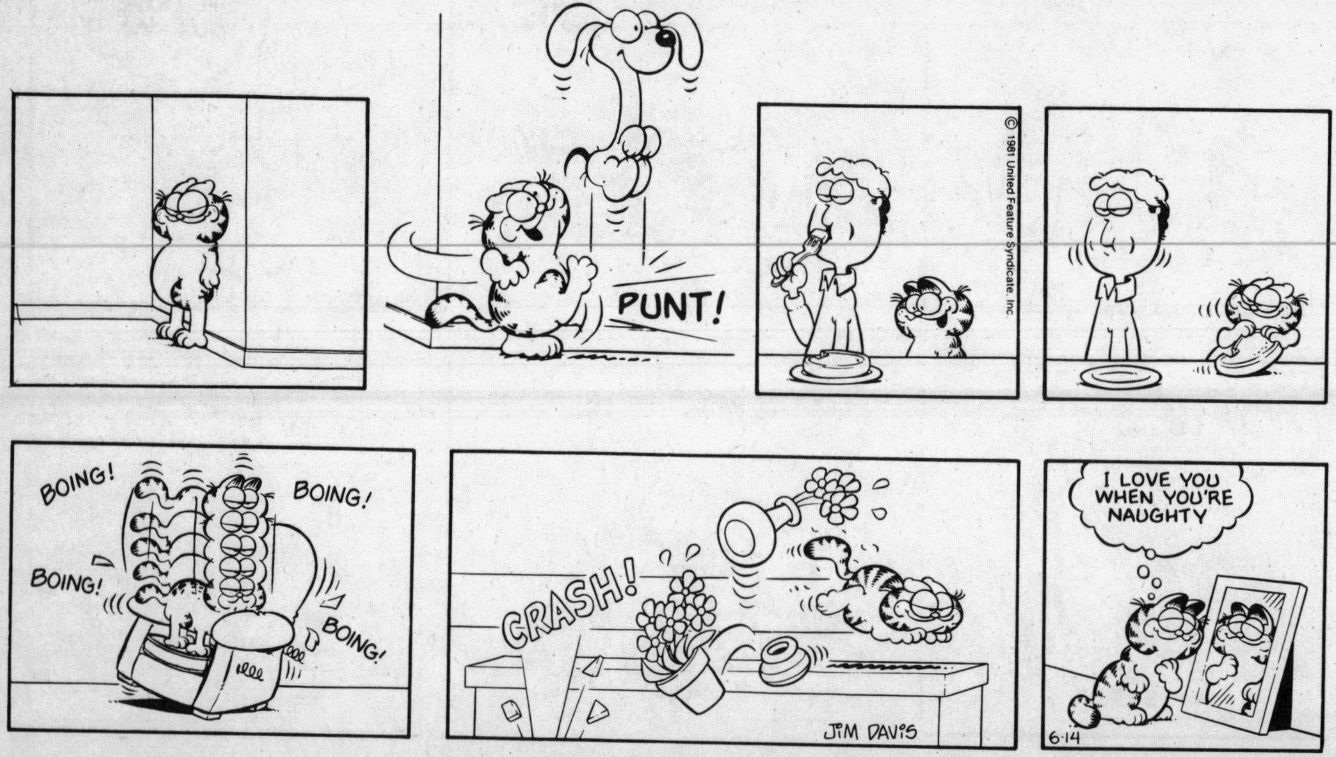

PUNT!
© 1981 United Feature Syndicate, Inc.
BOING!
BOING!
BOING!
BOING!
CRASH!
JIM DAVIS
I LOVE YOU WHEN YOU'RE NAUGHTY
6·14

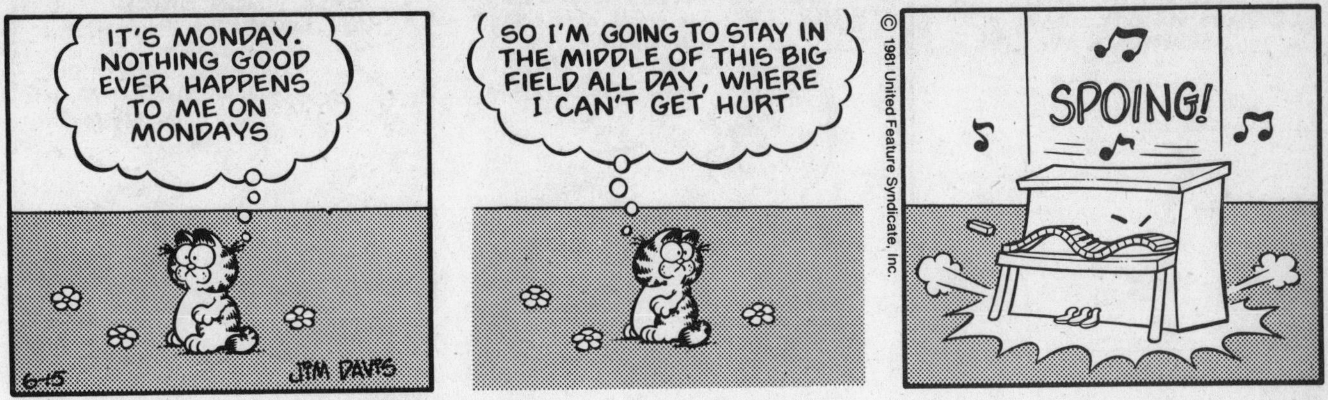
IT'S MONDAY. NOTHING GOOD EVER HAPPENS TO ME ON MONDAYS
6-15
JIM DAVIS
SO I'M GOING TO STAY IN THE MIDDLE OF THIS BIG FIELD ALL DAY, WHERE I CAN'T GET HURT
SPOING!
© 1981 United Feature Syndicate, Inc.

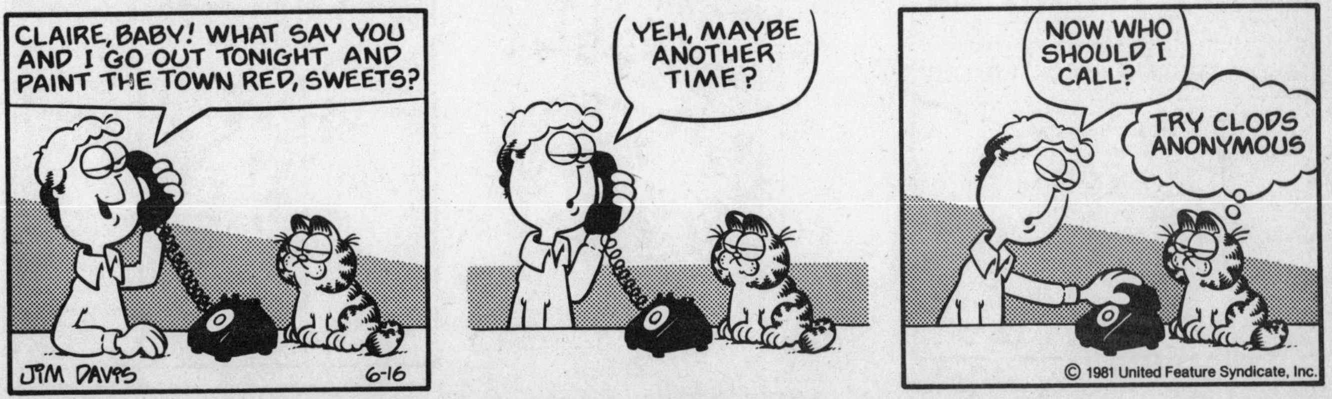
CLAIRE, BABY! WHAT SAY YOU AND I GO OUT TONIGHT AND PAINT THE TOWN RED, SWEETS?
JIM DAVIS
6-16
YEH, MAYBE ANOTHER TIME?
NOW WHO SHOULD I CALL?
TRY CLODS ANONYMOUS
© 1981 United Feature Syndicate, Inc.

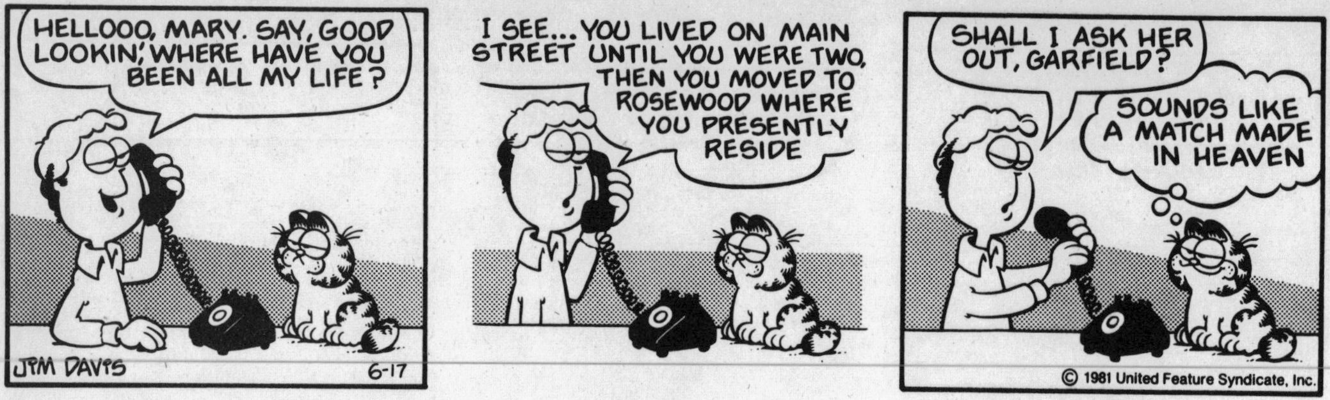
HELLOOO, MARY. SAY, GOOD LOOKIN,' WHERE HAVE YOU BEEN ALL MY LIFE?
JIM DAVIS
6-17
I SEE... YOU LIVED ON MAIN STREET UNTIL YOU WERE TWO, THEN YOU MOVED TO ROSEWOOD WHERE YOU PRESENTLY RESIDE
SHALL I ASK HER OUT, GARFIELD?
SOUNDS LIKE A MATCH MADE IN HEAVEN
© 1981 United Feature Syndicate, Inc.

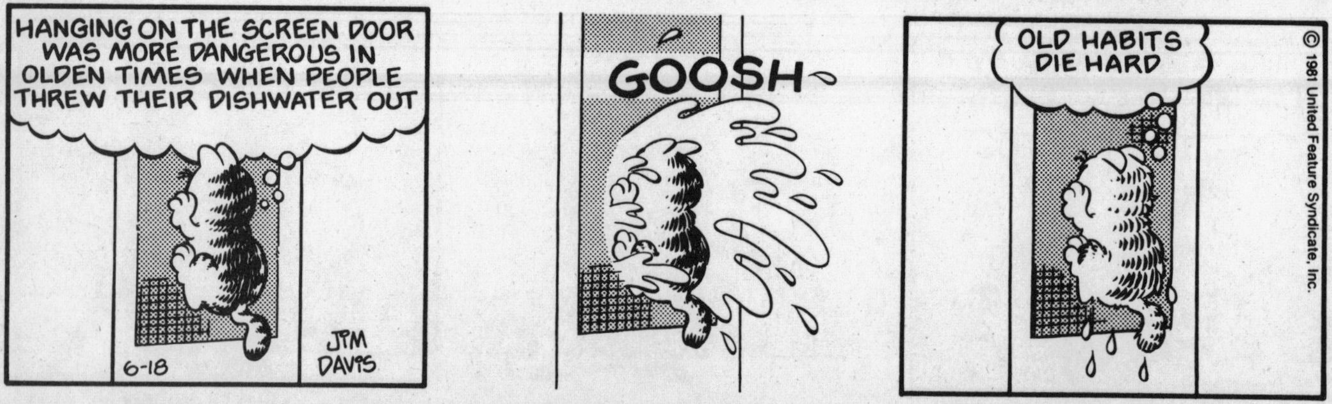
HANGING ON THE SCREEN DOOR WAS MORE DANGEROUS IN OLDEN TIMES WHEN PEOPLE THREW THEIR DISHWATER OUT
6-18
JIM DAVIS
GOOSH
OLD HABITS DIE HARD
© 1981 United Feature Syndicate, Inc.

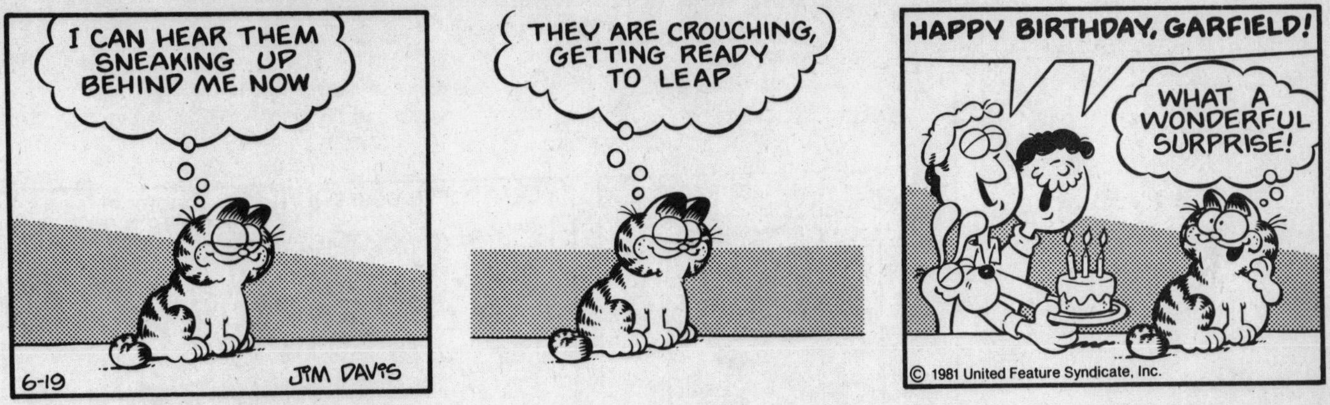
I CAN HEAR THEM SNEAKING UP BEHIND ME NOW
6-19
JIM DAVIS
THEY ARE CROUCHING, GETTING READY TO LEAP
HAPPY BIRTHDAY, GARFIELD!
WHAT A WONDERFUL SURPRISE!
© 1981 United Feature Syndicate, Inc.

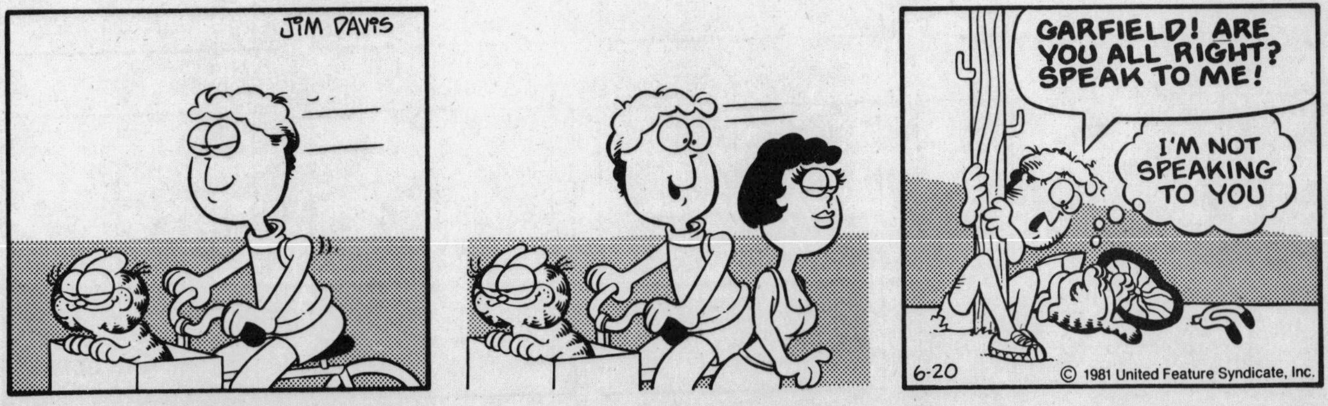
JIM DAVIS
GARFIELD! ARE YOU ALL RIGHT? SPEAK TO ME!
I'M NOT SPEAKING TO YOU
6-20
© 1981 United Feature Syndicate, Inc.

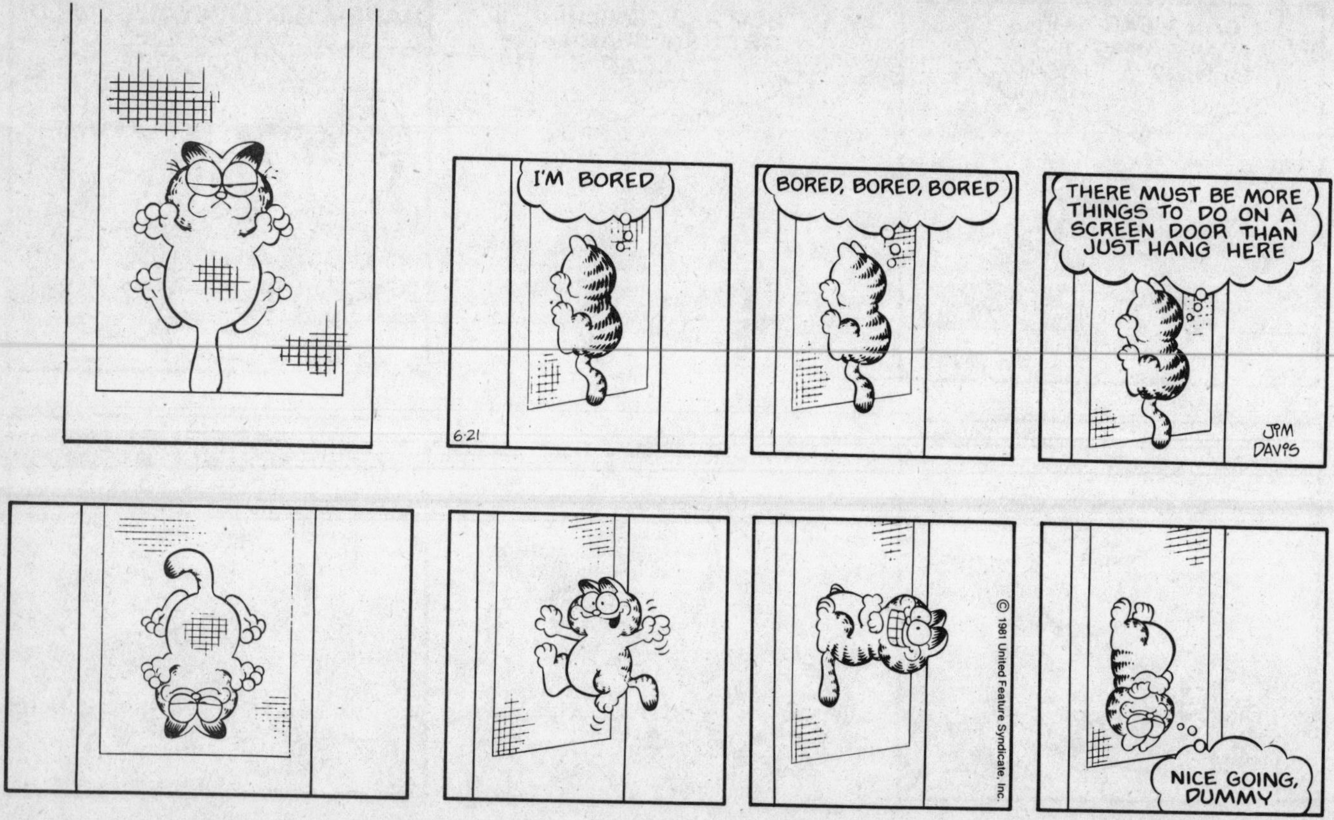
I'M BORED
BOREDBORED, BORED, BORED
THERE MUST BE MORE THINGS TO DO ON A SCREEN DOOR THAN JUST HANG HERE
JIM DAVIS
6-21
© 1981 United Feature Syndicate, Inc.
NICE GOING, DUMMY

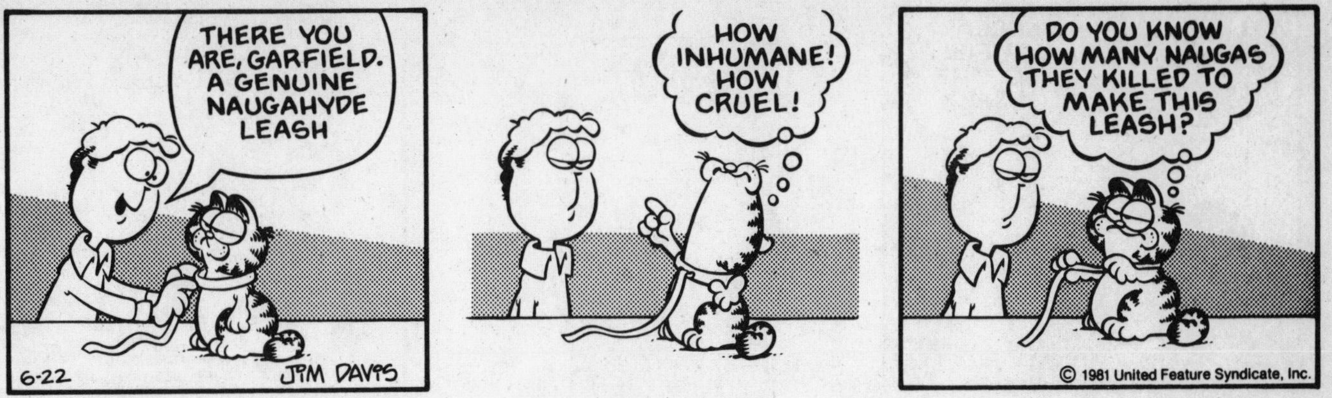
THERE YOU ARE, GARFIELD. A GENUINE NAUGAHYDE LEASH
6-22
JIM DAVIS
HOW INHUMANE! HOW CRUEL!
DO YOU KNOW HOW MANY NAUGAS THEY KILLED TO MAKE THIS LEASH?
© 1981 United Feature Syndicate, Inc.

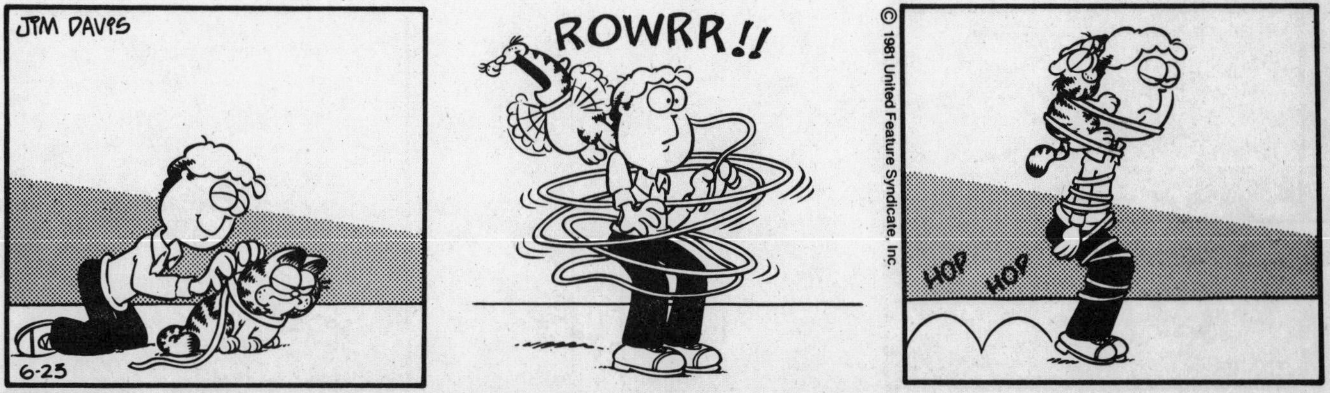
JIM DAVIS
6-23
ROWRR!!
© 1981 United Feature Syndicate, Inc.
HOP
HOP

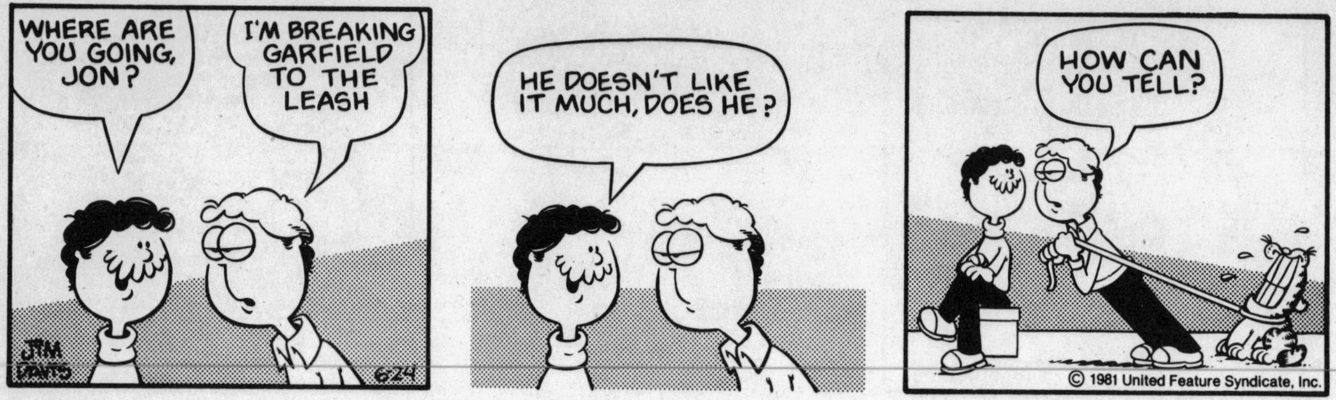
WHERE ARE YOU GOING, JON?
I'M BREAKING GARFIELD TO THE LEASH
JIM DAVIS
6-24
HE DOESN'T LIKE IT MUCH, DOES HE?
HOW CAN YOU TELL?
© 1981 United Feature Syndicate, Inc.

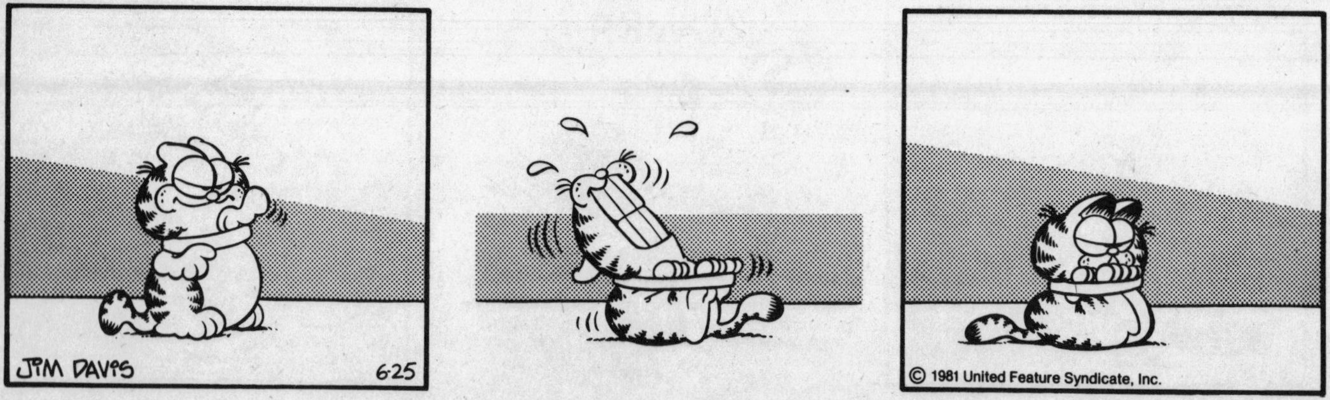
JIM DAVIS
6-25
© 1981 United Feature Syndicate, Inc.

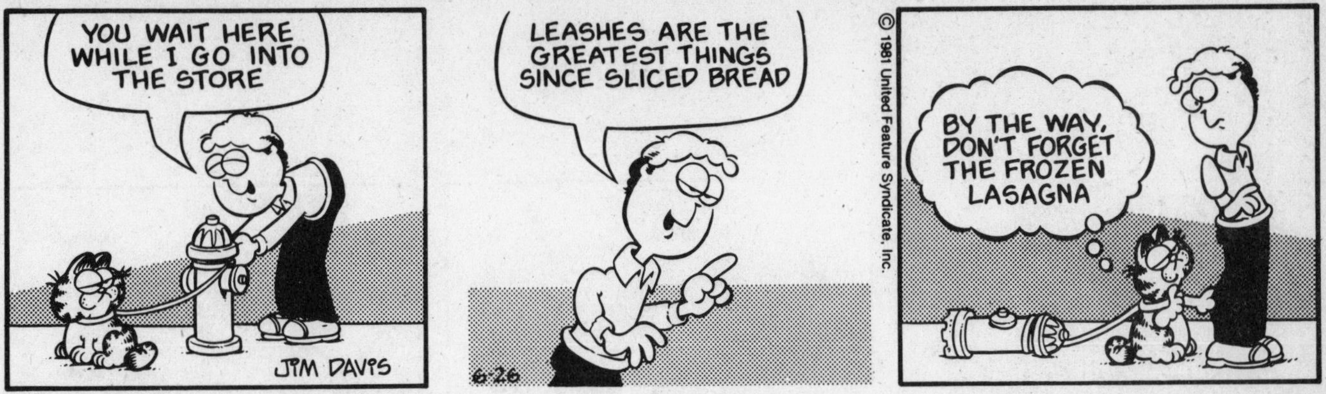
YOU WAIT HERE WHILE I GO INTO THE STORE
JIM DAVIS
LEASHES ARE THE GREATEST THINGS SINCE SLICED BREAD
6-26
© 1981 United Feature Syndicate, Inc.
BY THE WAY, DON'T FORGET THE FROZEN LASAGNA

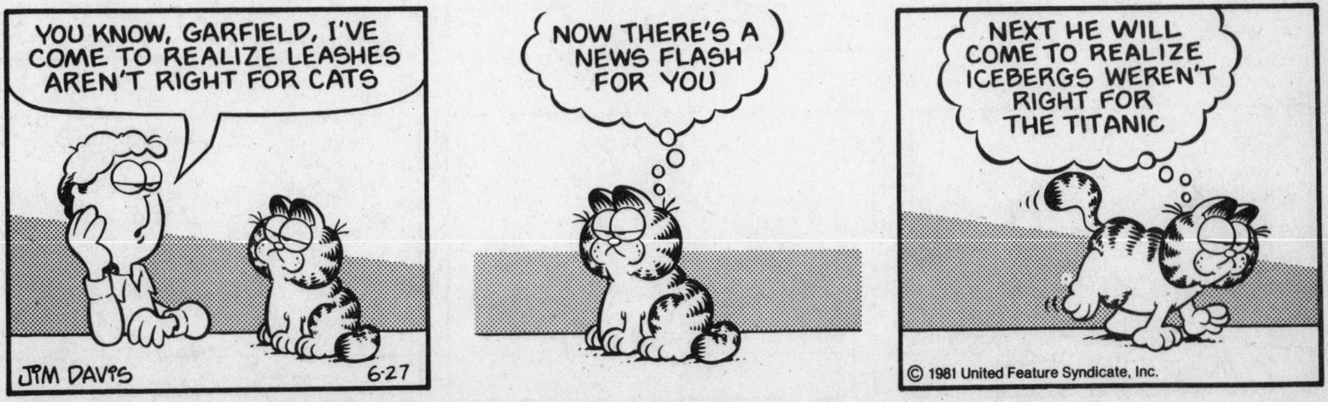
YOU KNOW, GARFIELD, I'VE COME TO REALIZE LEASHES AREN'T RIGHT FOR CATS
JIM DAVIS
6-27
NOW THERE'S A NEWS FLASH FOR YOU
NEXT HE WILL COME TO REALIZE ICEBERGS WEREN'T RIGHT FOR THE TITANIC
© 1981 United Feature Syndicate, Inc.

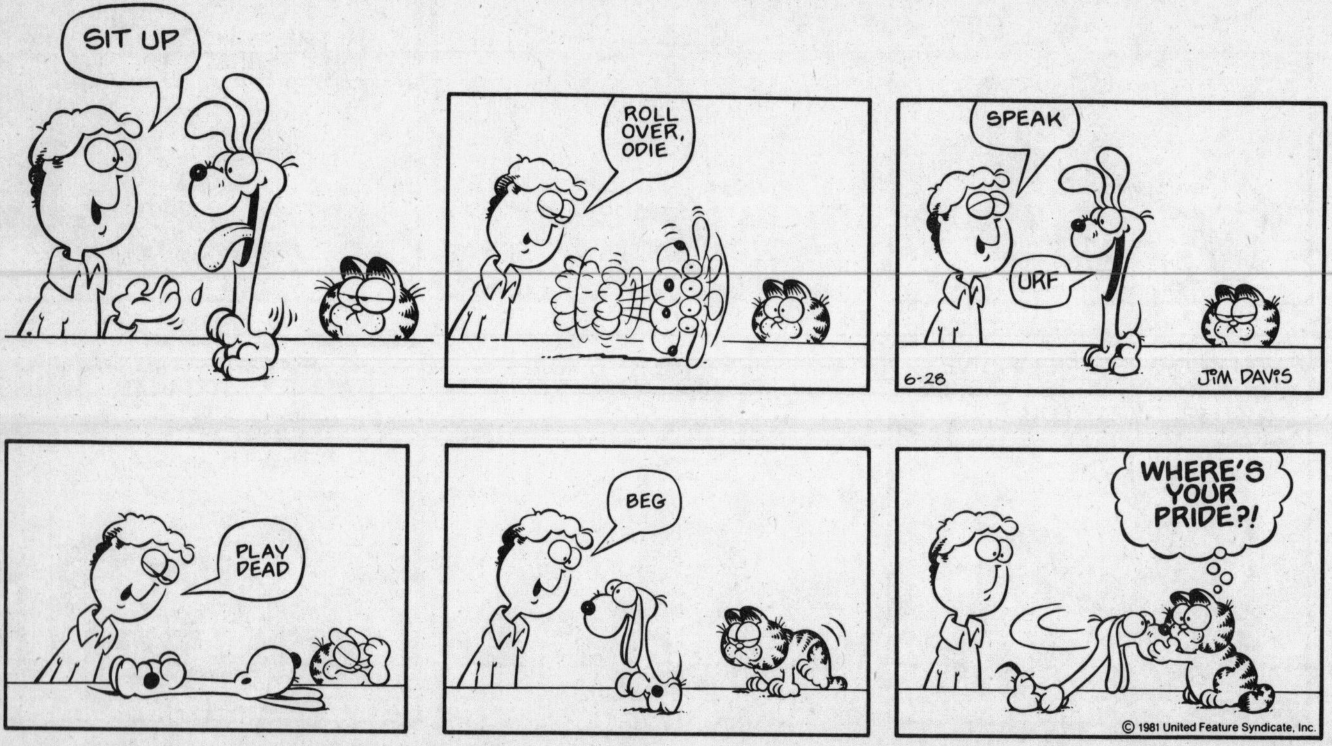
SIT UP
ROLL OVER, ODIE
SPEAK
URF
6-28
JIM DAVIS
PLAY DEAD
BEG
WHERE'S YOUR PRIDE?!
© 1981 United Feature Syndicate, Inc.

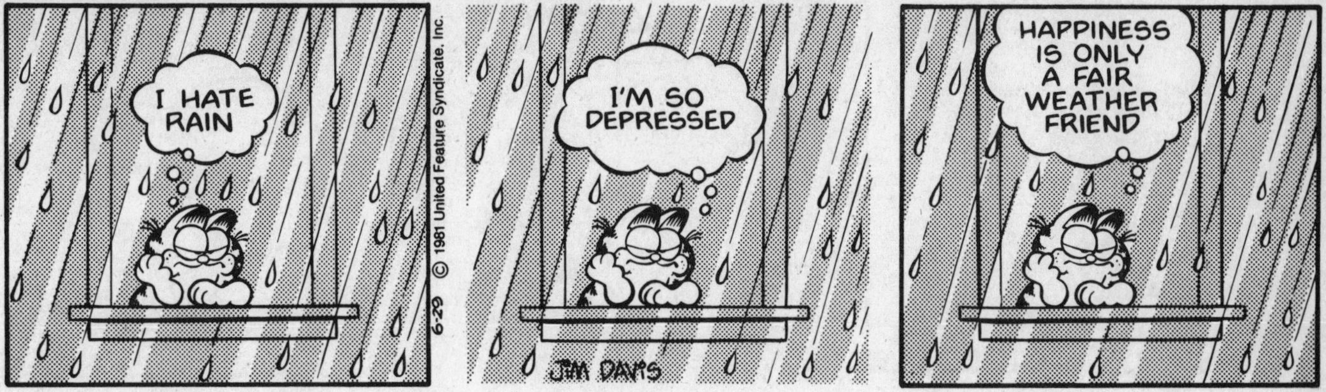
I HATE RAIN
6-29
© 1981 United Feature Syndicate, Inc.
I'M SO DEPRESSED
JIM DAVIS
HAPPINESS IS ONLY A FAIR WEATHER FRIEND

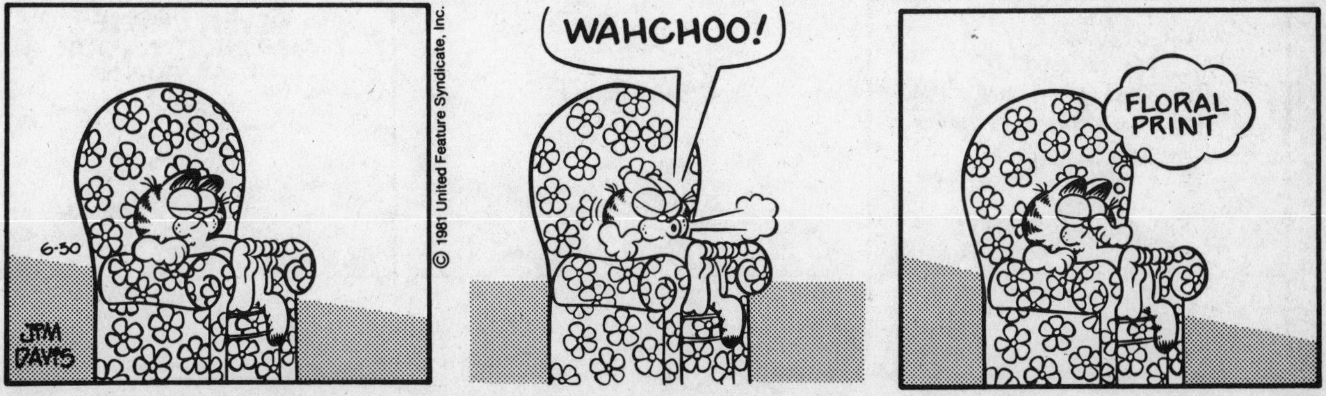
6-30
JIM DAVIS
© 1981 United Feature Syndicate, Inc.
WAHCHOO!
FLORAL PRINT

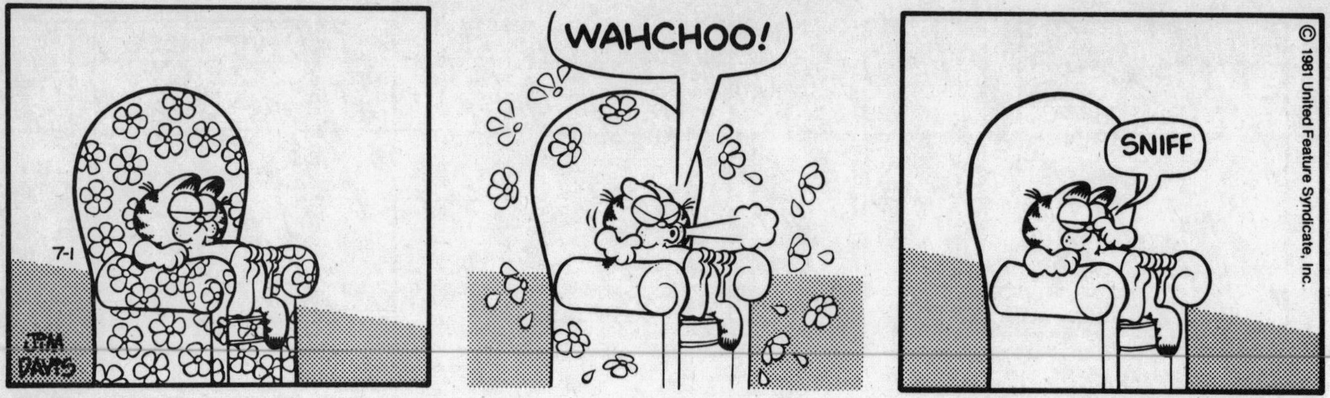
7-1
JIM DAVIS
WAHCHOO!
SNIFF
© 1981 United Feature Syndicate, Inc.

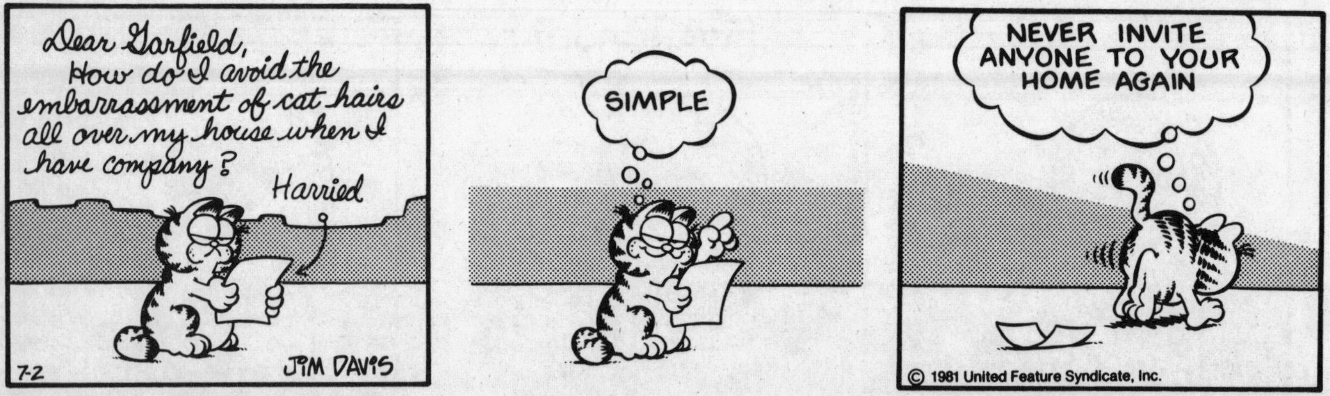
Dear Garfield,
How do I avoid the embarrassment of cat hairs all over my house when I have company?
Harried
7-2
JIM DAVIS
SIMPLE
NEVER INVITE ANYONE TO YOUR HOME AGAIN
© 1981 United Feature Syndicate, Inc.

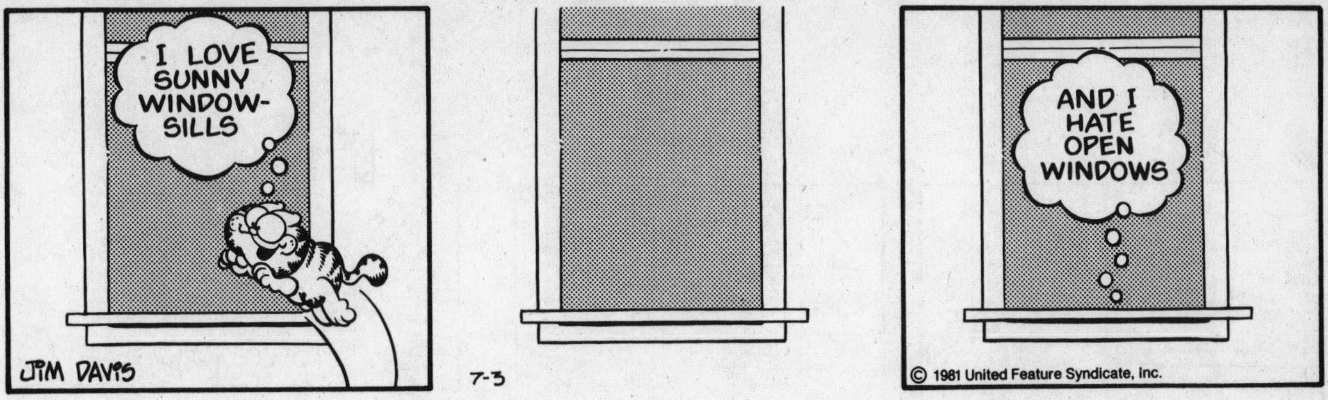
I LOVE SUNNY WINDOW-SILLS
JIM DAVIS
7-3
AND I HATE OPEN WINDOWS
© 1981 United Feature Syndicate, Inc.

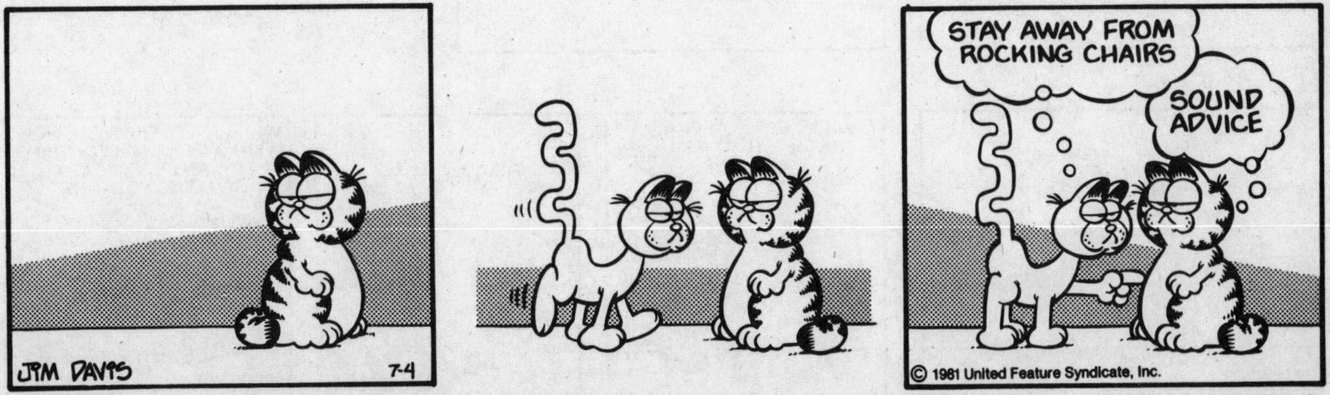
JIM DAVIS
7-4
STAY AWAY FROM ROCKING CHAIRS
SOUND ADVICE
© 1981 United Feature Syndicate, Inc.

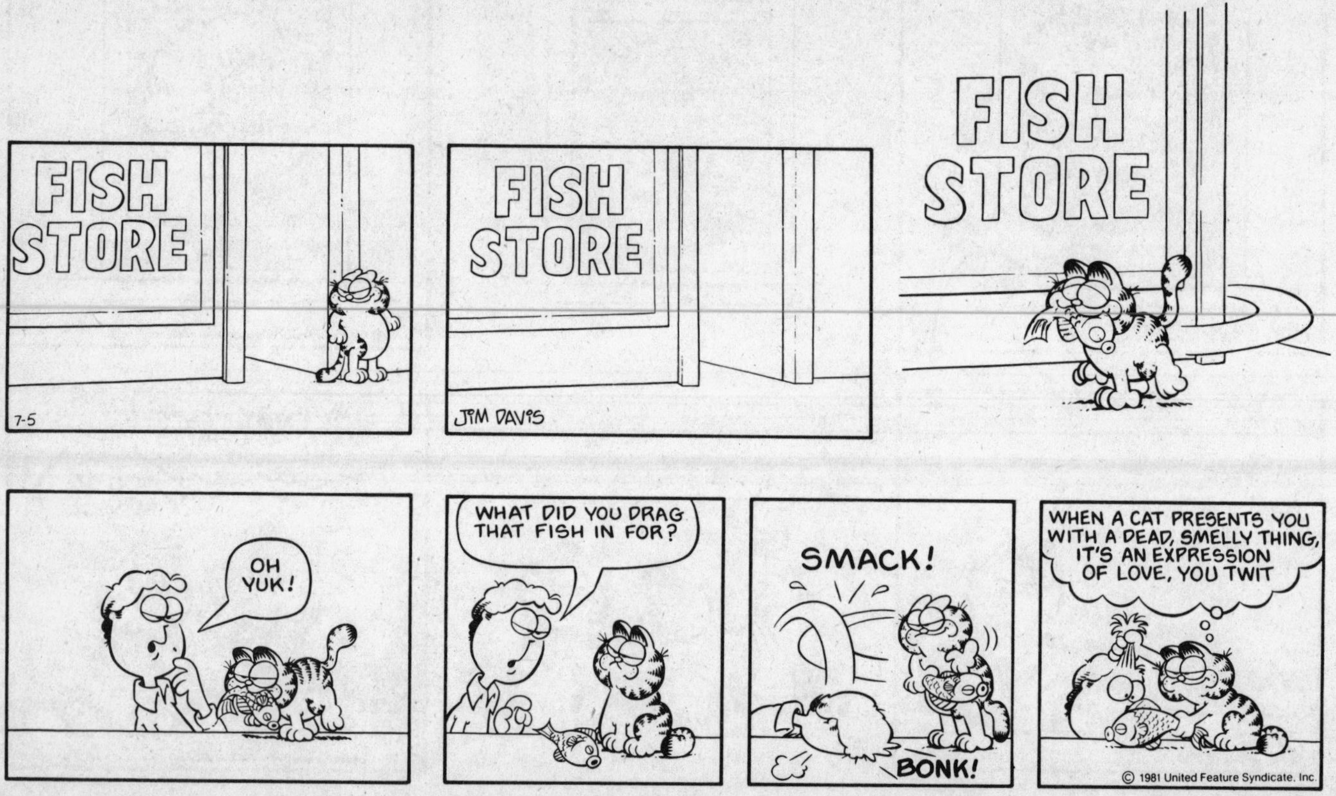
FISH STORE
7-5
FISH STORE
JIM DAVIS
FISH STORE
OH YUK!
WHAT DID YOU DRAG THAT FISH IN FOR?
SMACK!
BONK!
WHEN A CAT PRESENTS YOU WITH A DEAD, SMELLY THING, IT'S AN EXPRESSION OF LOVE, YOU TWIT
© 1981 United Feature Syndicate, Inc.

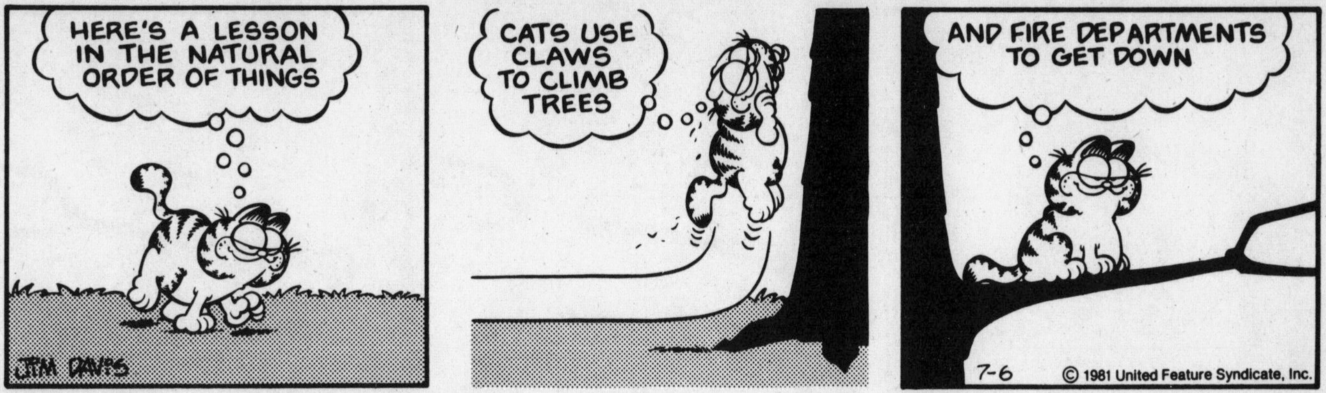
HERE'S A LESSON IN THE NATURAL ORDER OF THINGS
JIM DAVIS
CATS USE CLAWS TO CLIMB TREES
AND FIRE DEPARTMENTS TO GET DOWN
7-6
© 1981 United Feature Syndicate, Inc.

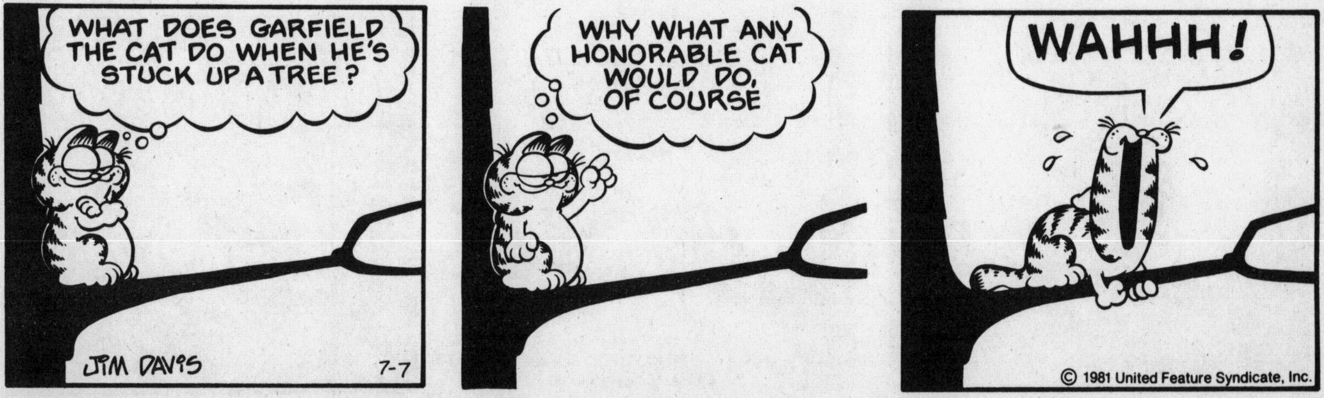
WHAT DOES GARFIELD THE CAT DO WHEN HE'S STUCK UP A TREE?
JIM DAVIS
7-7
WHY WHAT ANY HONORABLE CAT WOULD DO, OF COURSE
WAHHH!
© 1981 United Feature Syndicate, Inc.

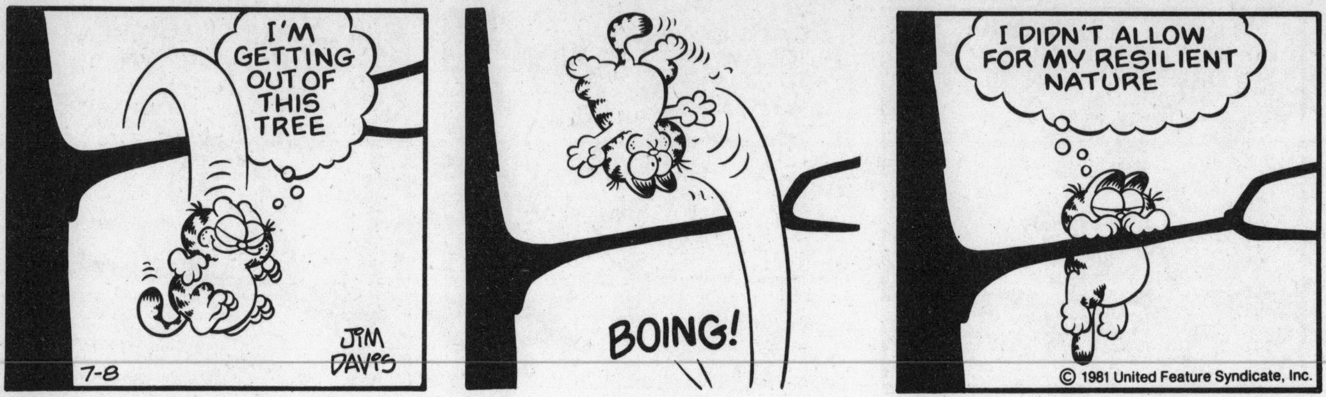
I'M GETTING OUT OF THIS TREE
JIM DAVIS
7-8
BOING!
I DIDN'T ALLOW FOR MY RESILIENT NATURE
© 1981 United Feature Syndicate, Inc.

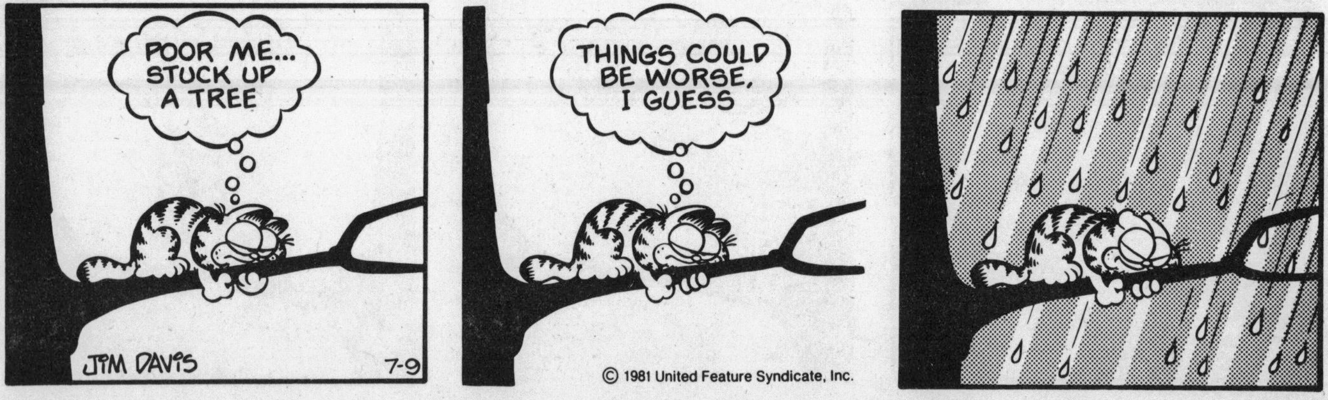
POOR ME... STUCK UP A TREE
JIM DAVIS
7-9
THINGS COULD BE WORSE, I GUESS
© 1981 United Feature Syndicate, Inc.

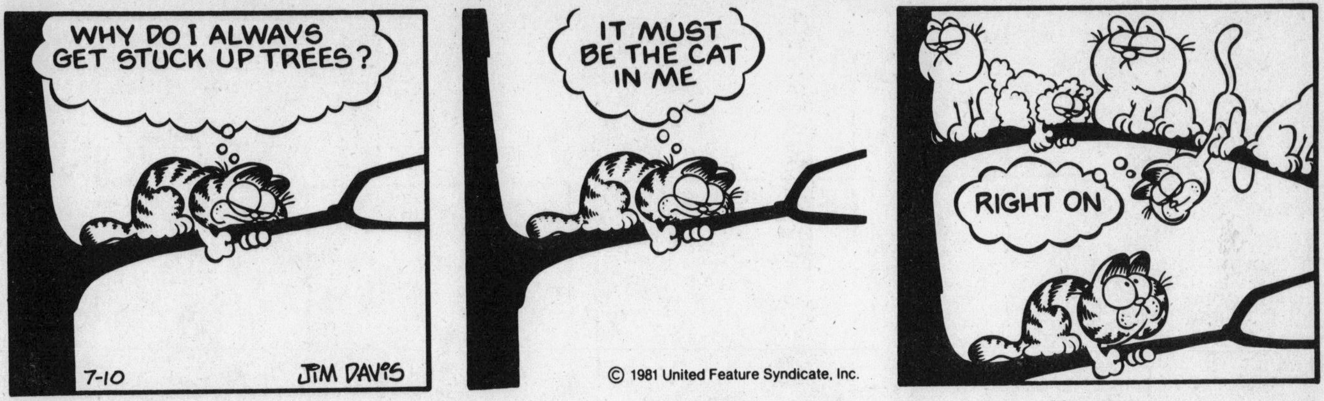
WHY DO I ALWAYS GET STUCK UP TREES?
7-10
JIM DAVIS
IT MUST BE THE CAT IN ME
© 1981 United Feature Syndicate, Inc.
RIGHT ON

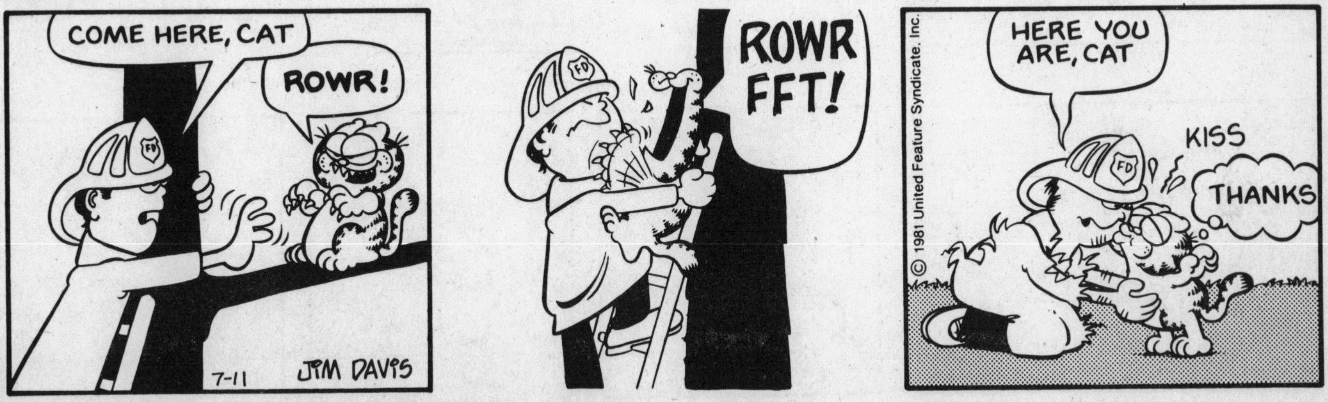
COME HERE, CAT
ROWR!
7-11
JIM DAVIS
ROWR FFT!
© 1981 United Feature Syndicate, Inc.
HERE YOU ARE, CAT
KISS
THANKS

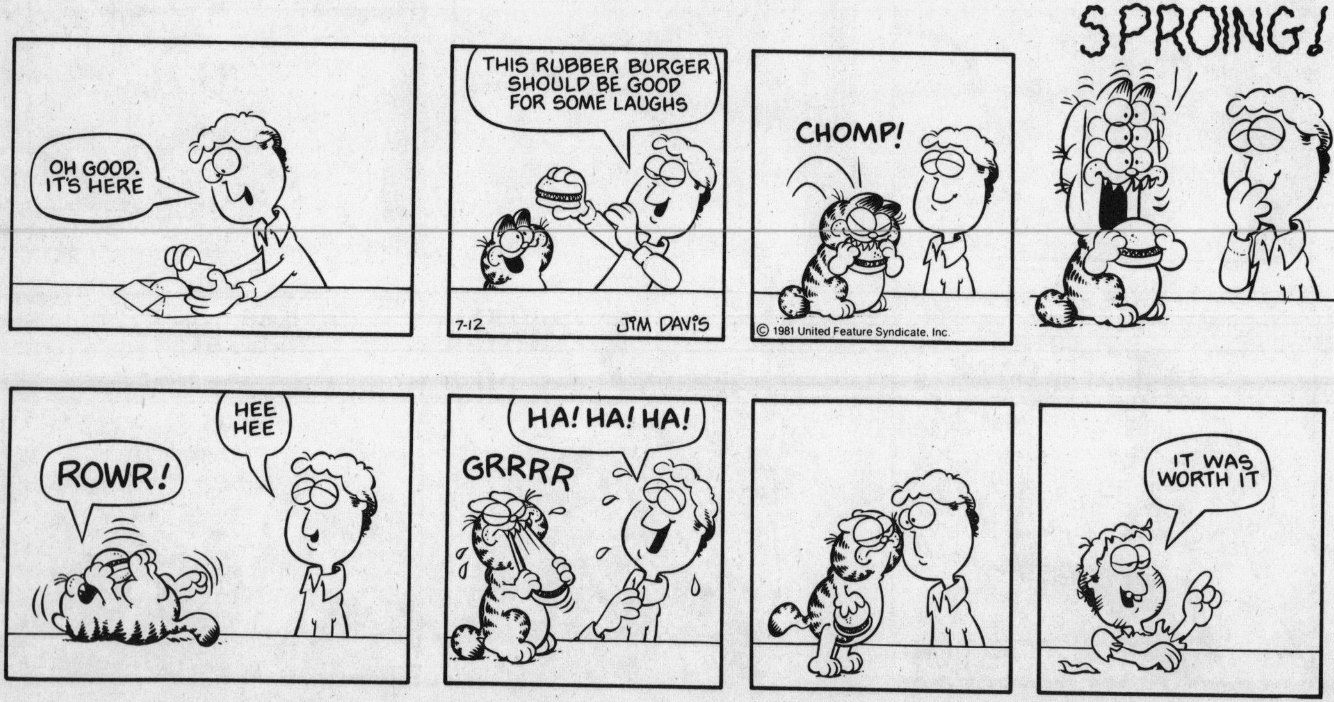
OH GOOD. IT'S HERE
THIS RUBBER BURGER SHOULD BE GOOD FOR SOME LAUGHS
7-12
JIM DAVIS
CHOMP!
© 1981 United Feature Syndicate, Inc.
SPROING!
ROWR!
HEE HEE
HA! HA! HA!
GRRRR
IT WAS WORTH IT

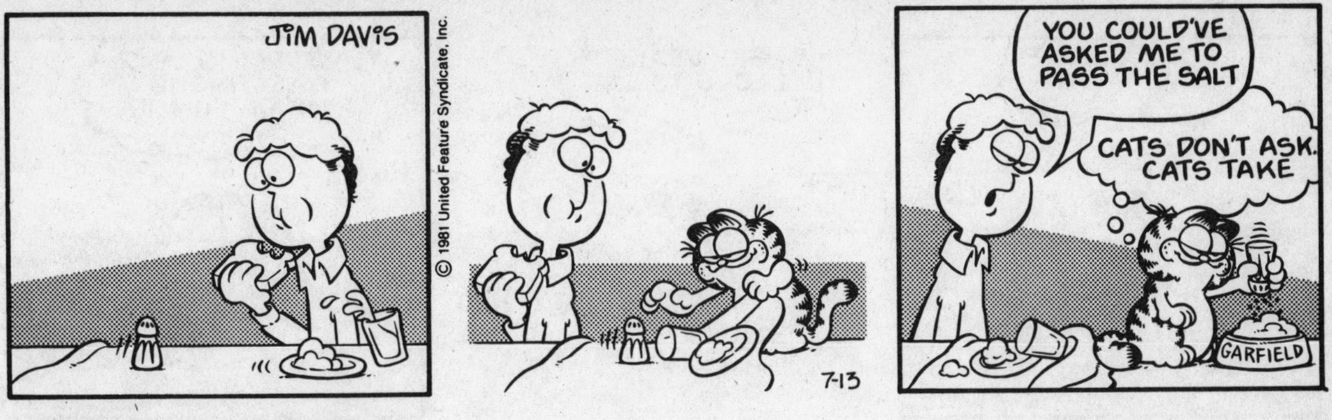
JIM DAVIS
© 1981 United Feature Syndicate, Inc.
7-13
YOU COULD'VE ASKED ME TO PASS THE SALT
CATS DON'T ASK. CATS TAKE
GARFIELD

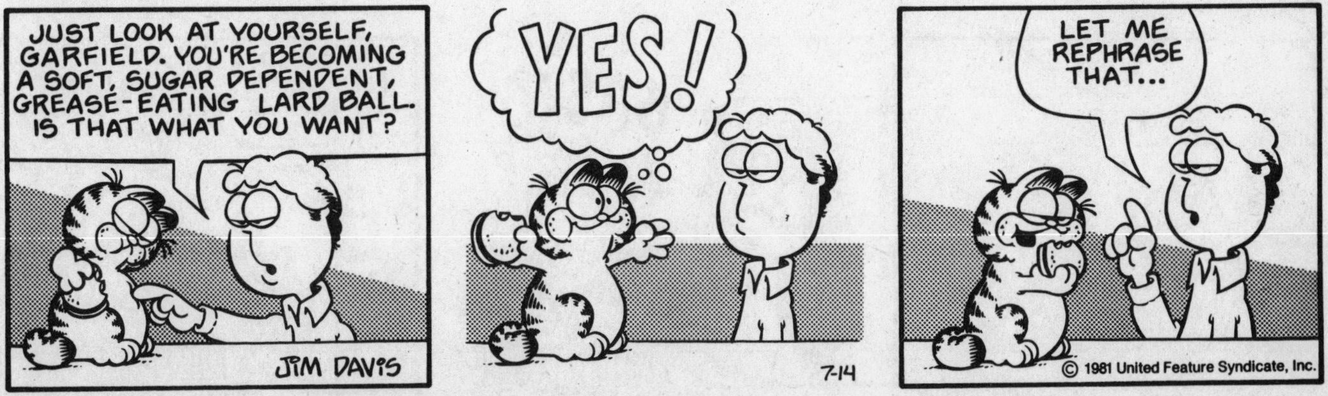
JUST LOOK AT YOURSELF, GARFIELD. YOU'RE BECOMING A SOFT, SUGAR DEPENDENT, GREASE-EATING LARD BALL. IS THAT WHAT YOU WANT?
JIM DAVIS
YES!
7-14
LET ME REPHRASE THAT...
© 1981 United Feature Syndicate, Inc.

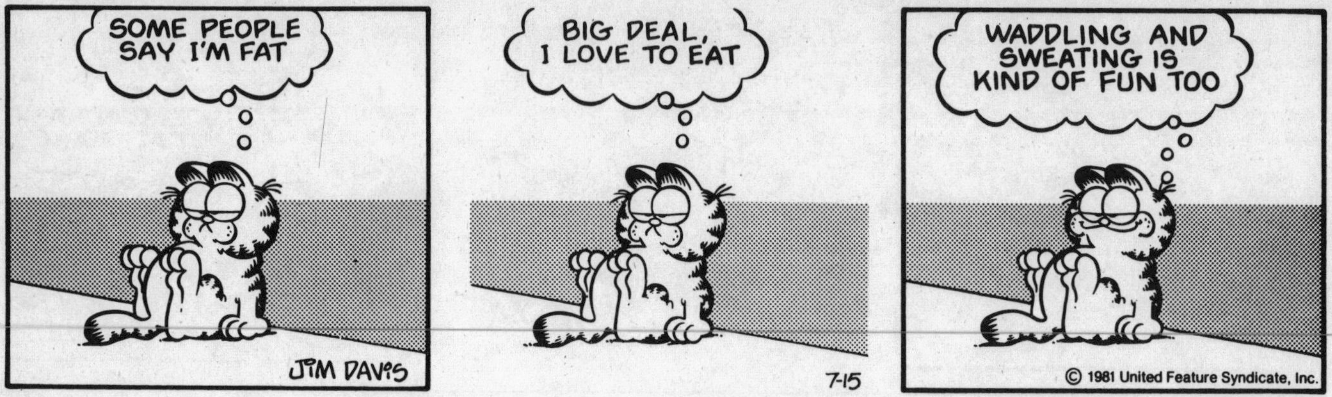
SOME PEOPLE SAY I'M FAT
BIG DEAL, I LOVE TO EAT
WADDLING AND SWEATING IS KIND OF FUN TOO
JIM DAVIS
7-15
© 1981 United Feature Syndicate, Inc.

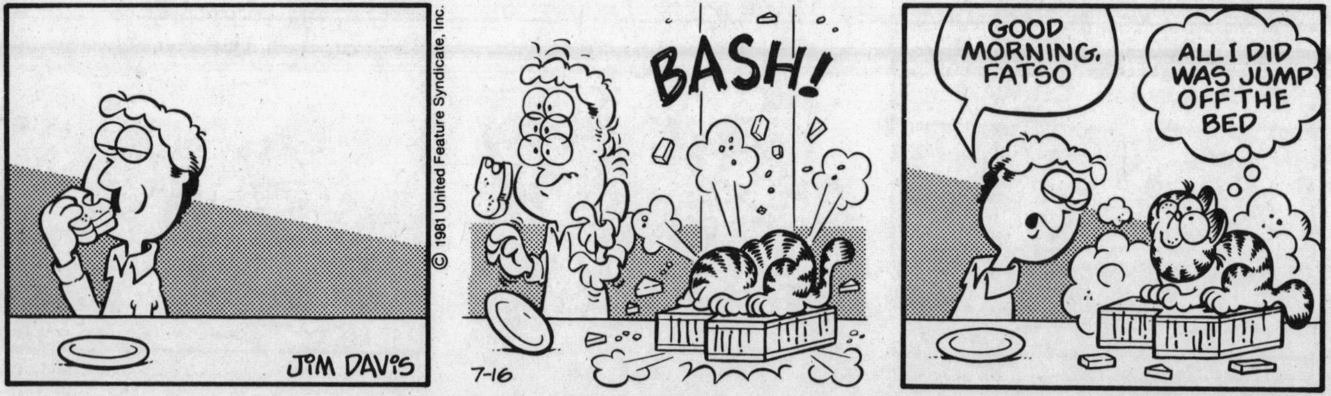
JIM DAVIS
© 1981 United Feature Syndicate, Inc.
BASH!
7-16
GOOD MORNING, FATSO
ALL I DID WAS JUMP OFF THE BED

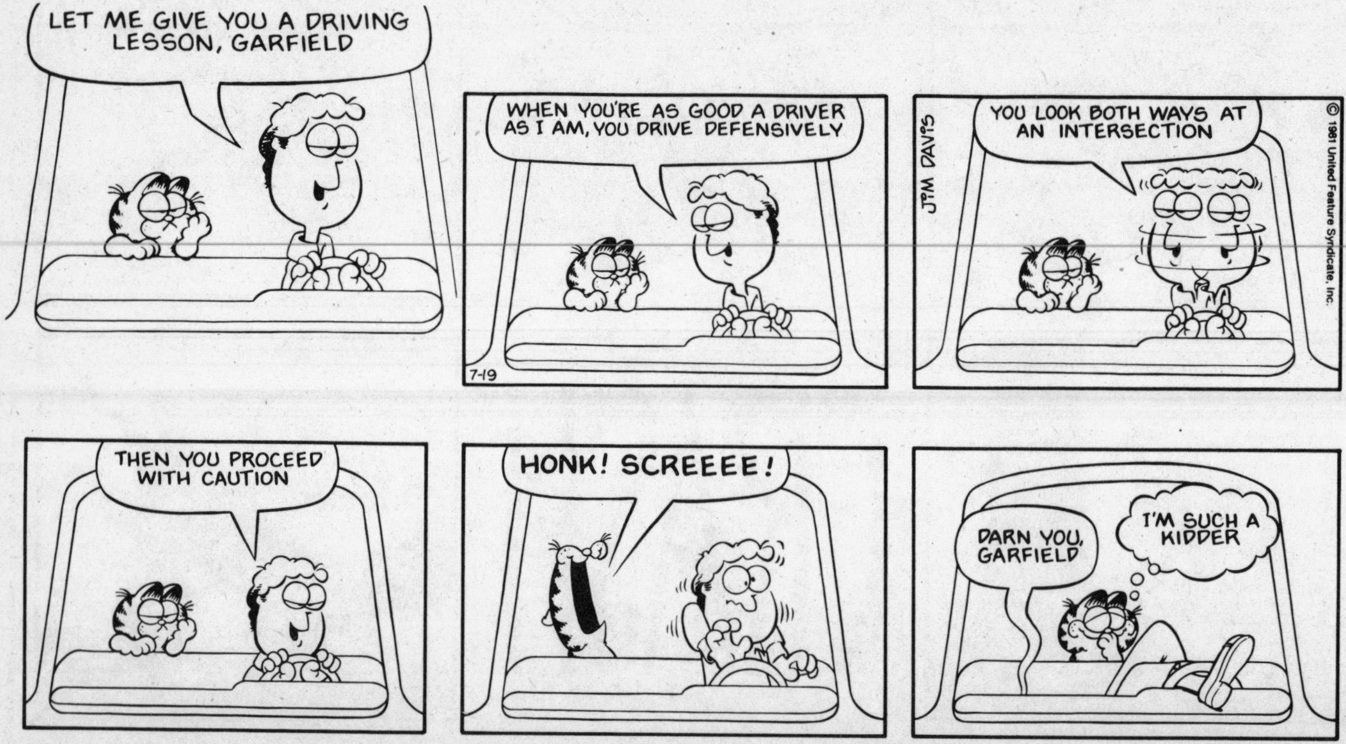
LET ME GIVE YOU A DRIVING LESSON, GARFIELD
WHEN YOU'RE AS GOOD A DRIVER AS I AM, YOU DRIVE DEFENSIVELY
7-19
JIM DAVIS
YOU LOOK BOTH WAYS AT AN INTERSECTION
© 1981 United Feature Syndicate, Inc.
THEN YOU PROCEED WITH CAUTION
HONK! SCREEEE!
DARN YOU, GARFIELD
I'M SUCH A KIDDER

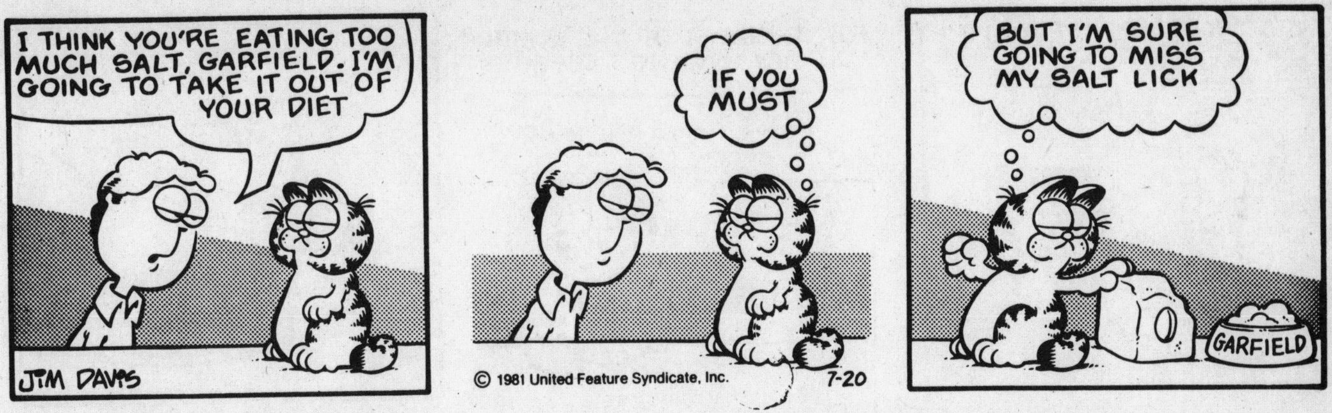
I THINK YOU'RE EATING TOO MUCH SALT, GARFIELD. I'M GOING TO TAKE IT OUT OF YOUR DIET
JIM DAVIS
IF YOU MUST
© 1981 United Feature Syndicate, Inc.
7-20
BUT I'M SURE GOING TO MISS MY SALT LICK
GARFIELD

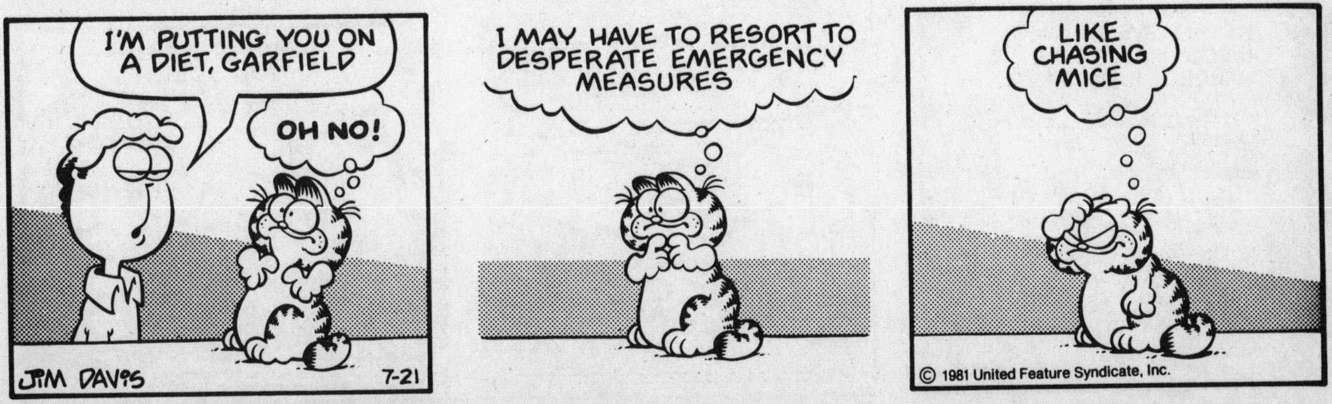
I'M PUTTING YOU ON A DIET, GARFIELD
OH NO!
JIM DAVIS
7-21
I MAY HAVE TO RESORT TO DESPERATE EMERGENCY MEASURES
LIKE CHASING MICE
© 1981 United Feature Syndicate, Inc.

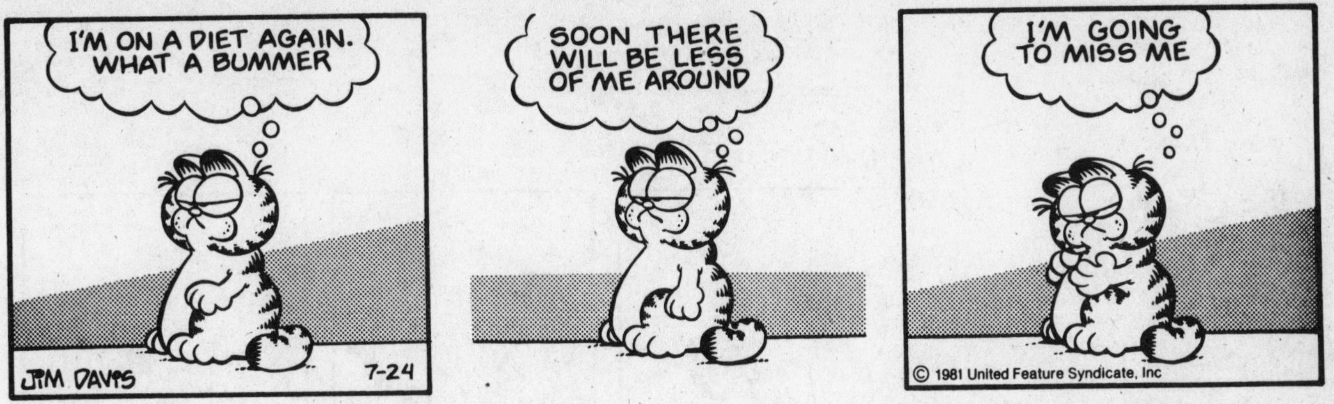
I'M ON A DIET AGAIN. WHAT A BUMMER
JIM DAVIS
7-24
SOON THERE WILL BE LESS OF ME AROUND
I'M GOING TO MISS ME
© 1981 United Feature Syndicate, Inc

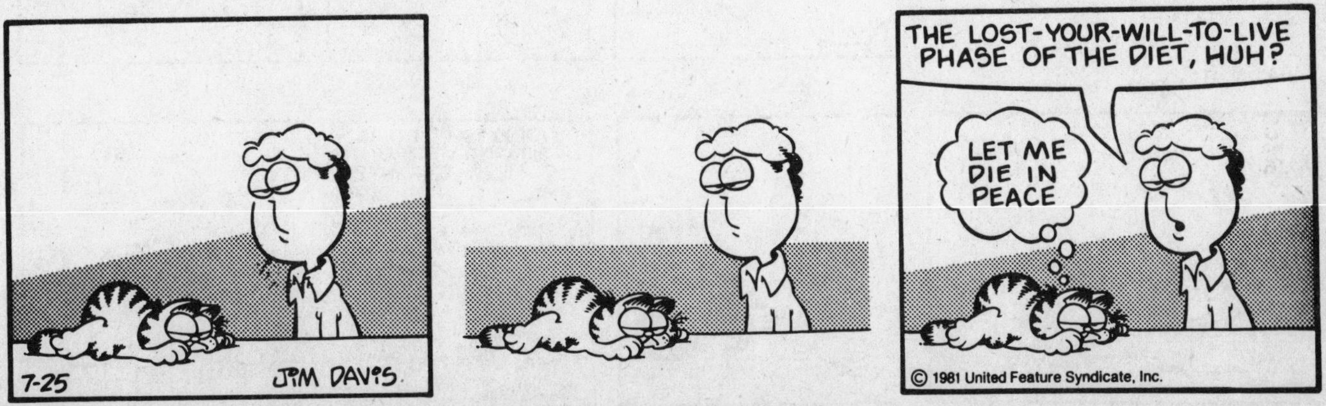
7-25
JIM DAVIS
THE LOST-YOUR-WILL-TO-LIVE PHASE OF THE DIET, HUH?
LET ME DIE IN PEACE
© 1981 United Feature Syndicate, Inc.

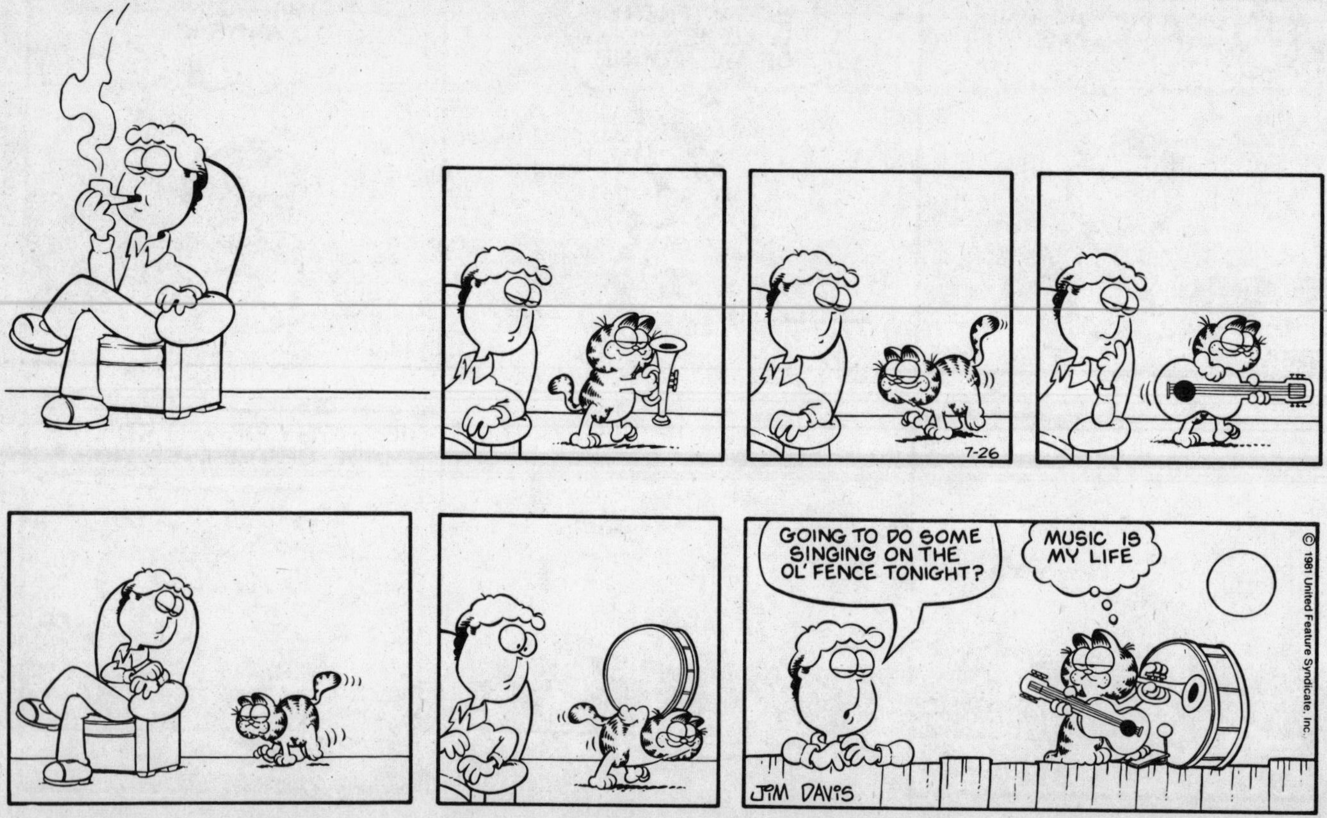
7-26
GOING TO DO SOME SINGING ON THE OL' FENCE TONIGHT?
MUSIC IS MY LIFE
JIM DAVIS
© 1981 United Feature Syndicate, Inc.

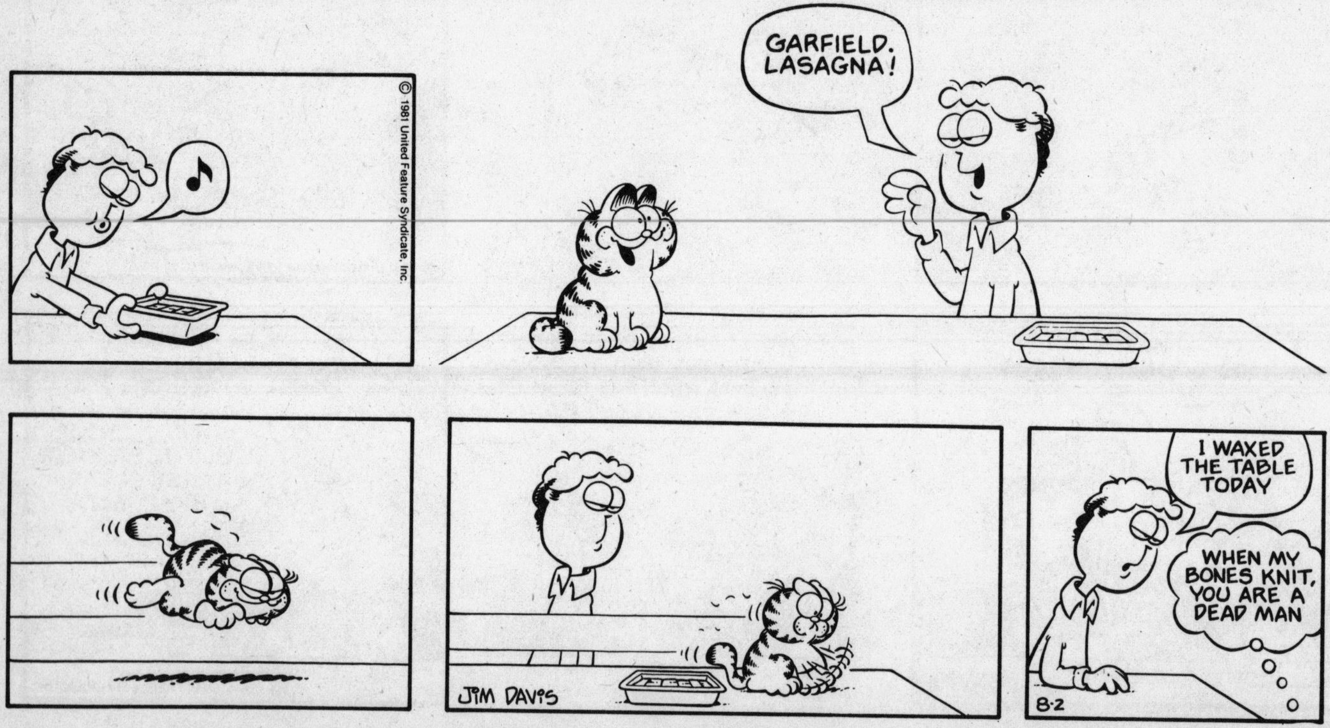
© 1981 United Feature Syndicate, Inc.
♪
GARFIELD. LASAGNA!
JIM DAVIS
I WAXED THE TABLE TODAY
WHEN MY BONES KNIT, YOU ARE A DEAD MAN
8·2

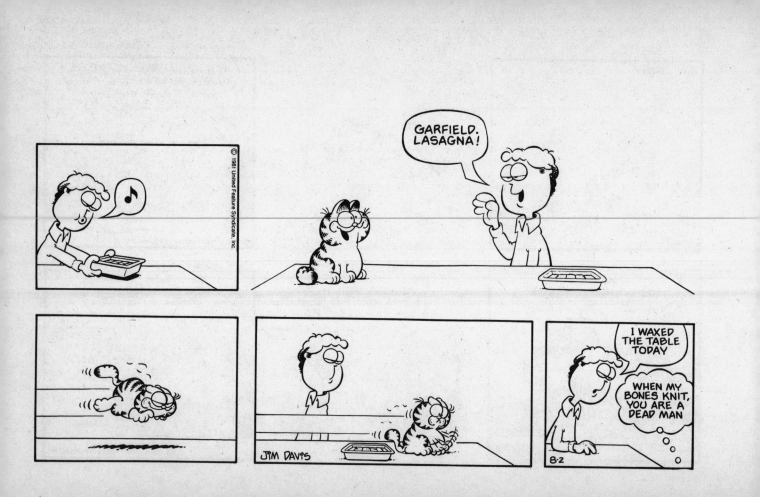

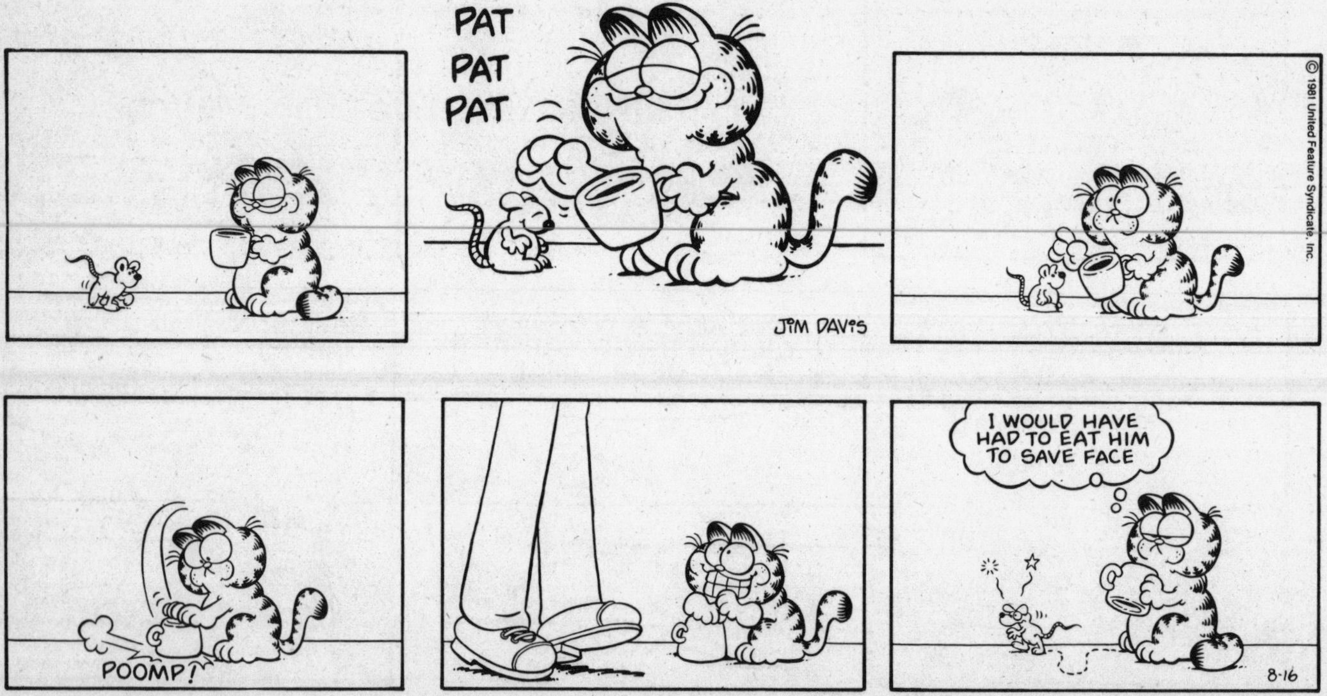

PAT
PAT
PAT
JIM DAVIS
© 1981 United Feature Syndicate, Inc.
POOMP!
I WOULD HAVE HAD TO EAT HIM TO SAVE FACE
8-16

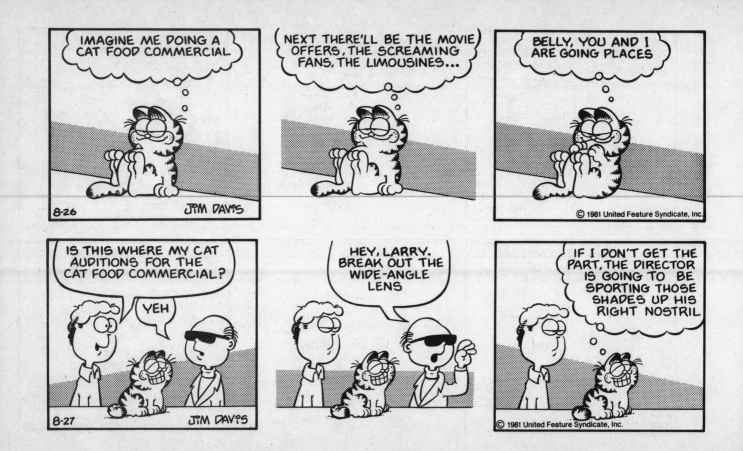

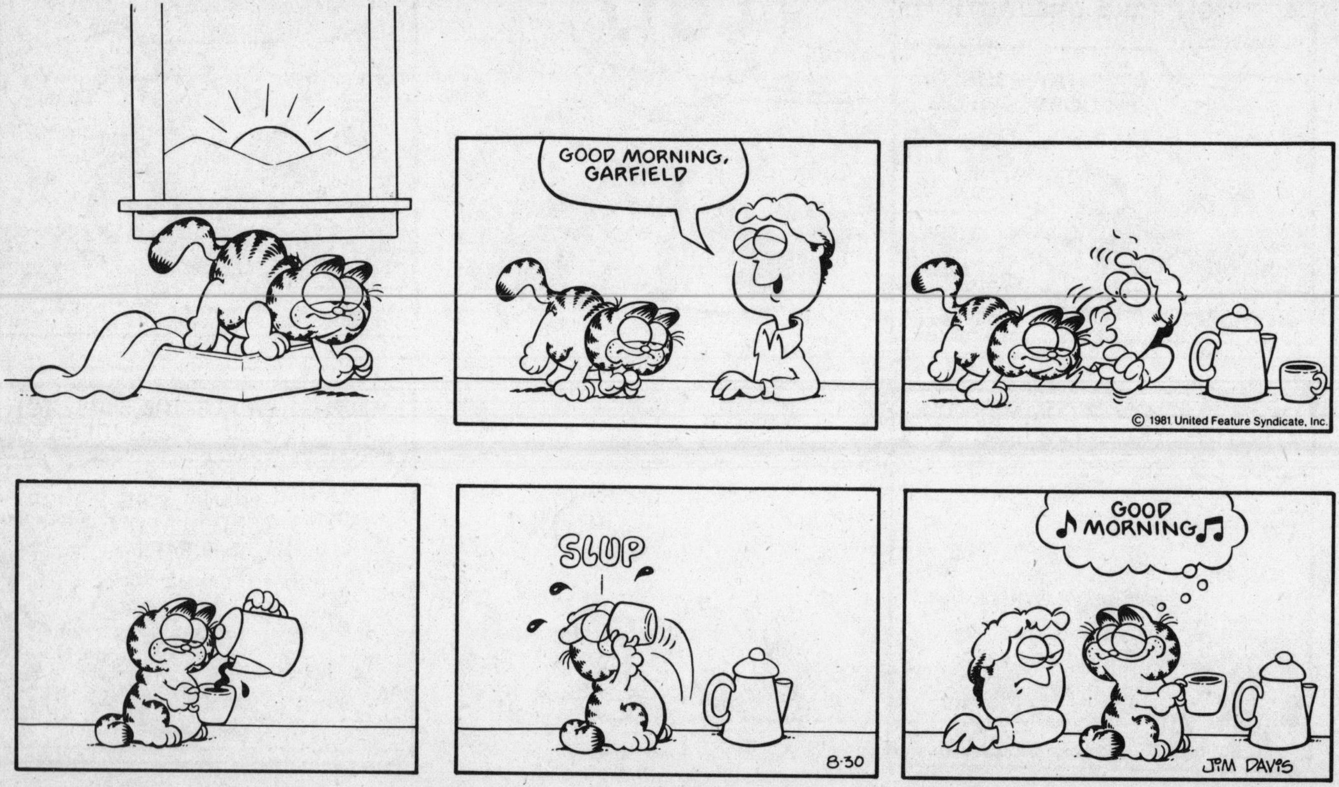
GOOD MORNING, GARFIELD
© 1981 United Feature Syndicate, Inc.
SLUP
8·30
GOOD MORNING
JIM DAVIS

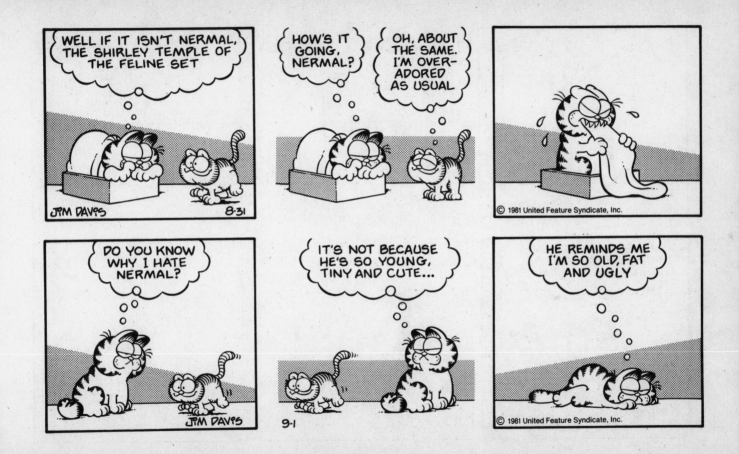

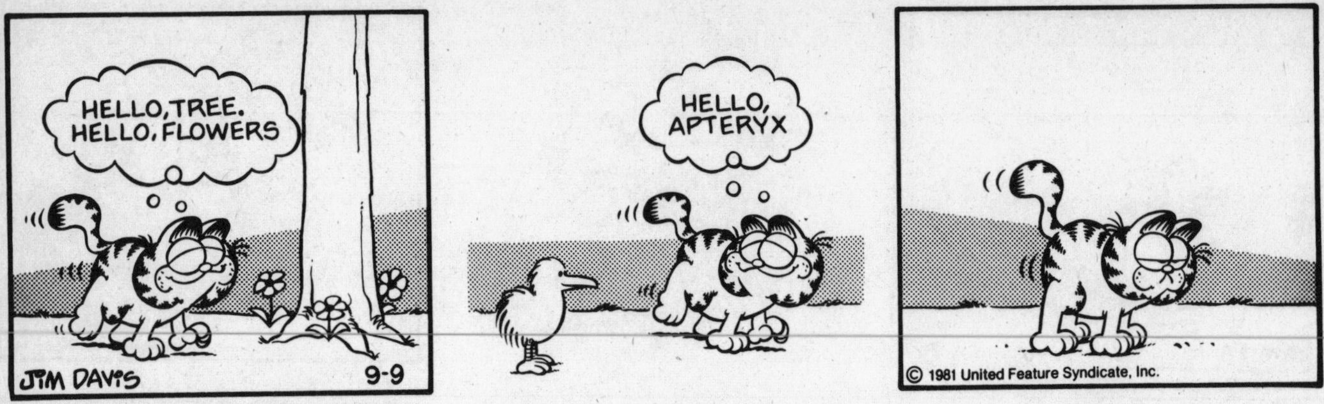
HELLO, TREE. HELLO, FLOWERS
HELLO, APTERYX
JIM DAVIS 9-9
© 1981 United Feature Syndicate, Inc.

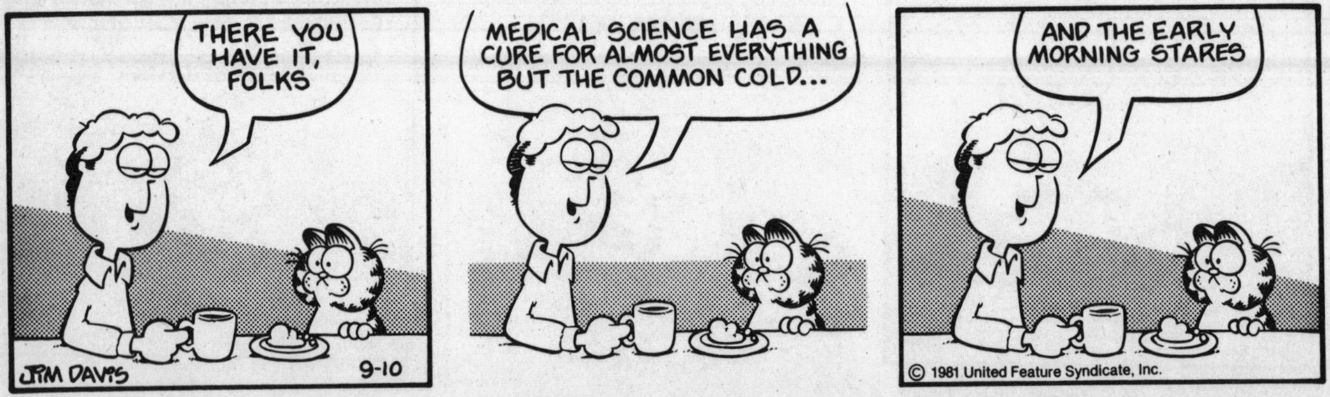
THERE YOU HAVE IT, FOLKS
MEDICAL SCIENCE HAS A CURE FOR ALMOST EVERYTHING BUT THE COMMON COLD...
AND THE EARLY MORNING STARES
JIM DAVIS 9-10
© 1981 United Feature Syndicate, Inc.

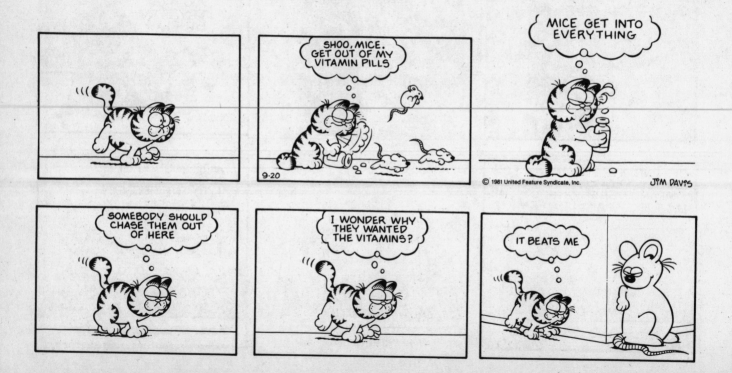

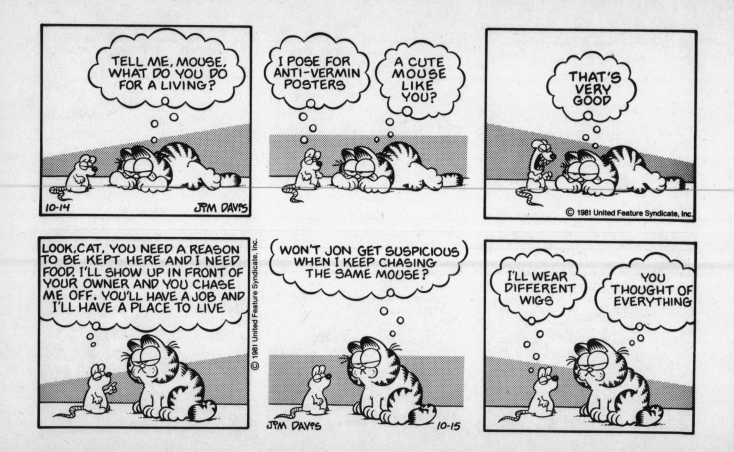

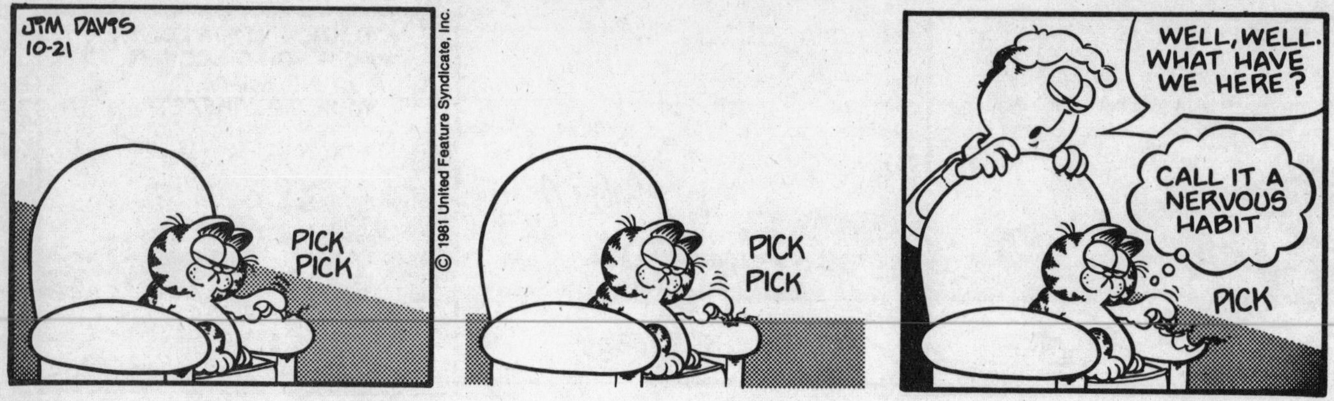
JIM DAVIS
10-21
PICK PICK
© 1981 United Feature Syndicate, Inc.
PICK PICK
WELL, WELL. WHAT HAVE WE HERE?
CALL IT A NERVOUS HABIT
PICK

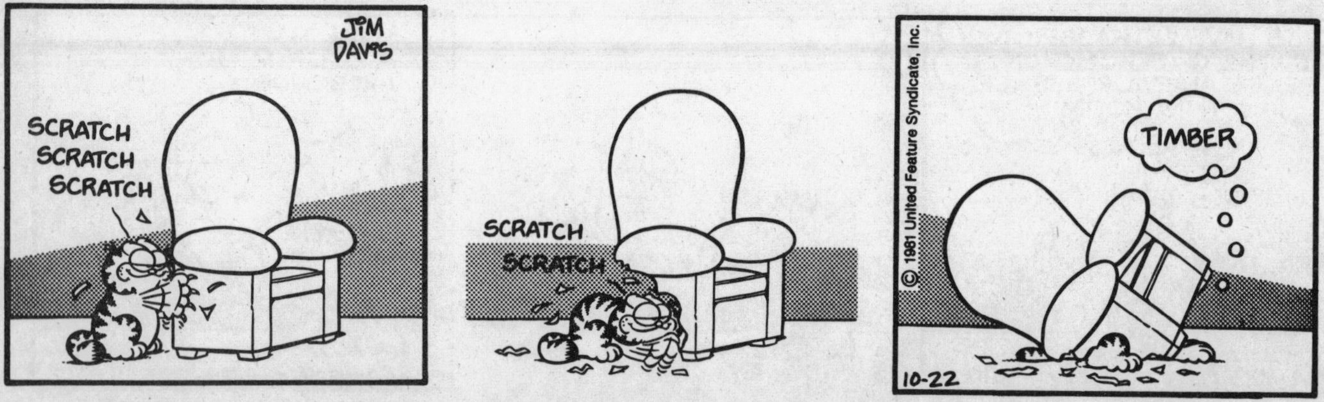
JIM DAVIS
SCRATCH SCRATCH SCRATCH
SCRATCH SCRATCH
© 1981 United Feature Syndicate, Inc.
TIMBER
10-22

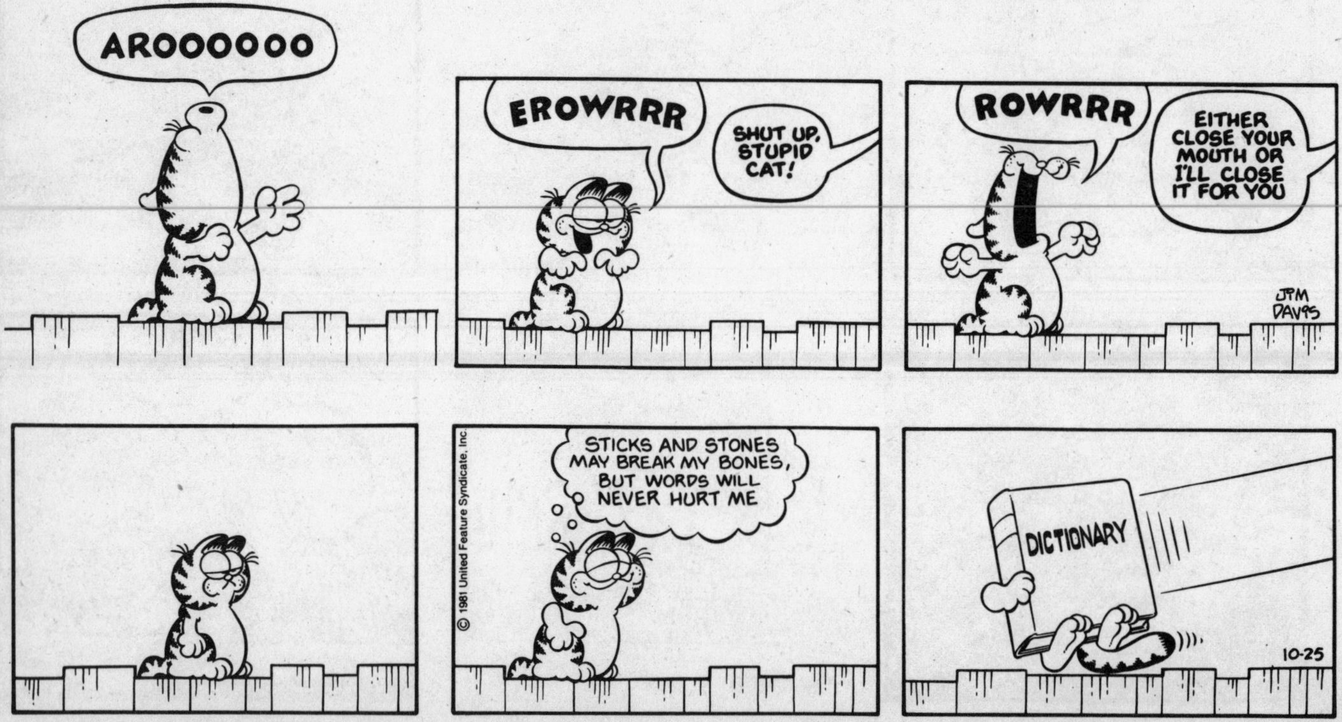
AROOOOOO
EROWRRR
SHUT UP, STUPID CAT!
ROWRRR
EITHER CLOSE YOUR MOUTH OR I'LL CLOSE IT FOR YOU
JIM DAVIS
© 1981 United Feature Syndicate, Inc.
STICKS AND STONES MAY BREAK MY BONES, BUT WORDS WILL NEVER HURT ME
DICTIONARY
10-25

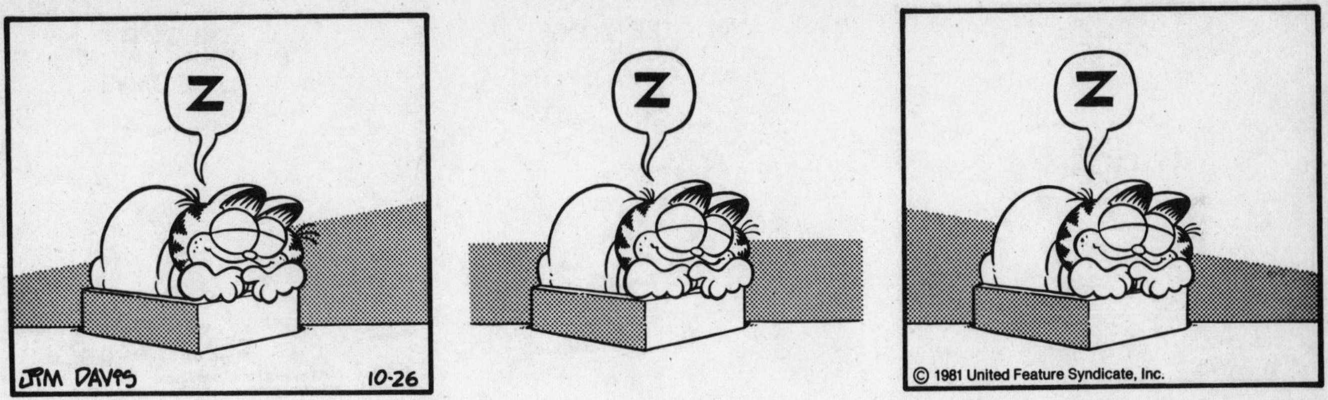
Z
Z
Z
JIM DAVIS
10-26
© 1981 United Feature Syndicate, Inc.

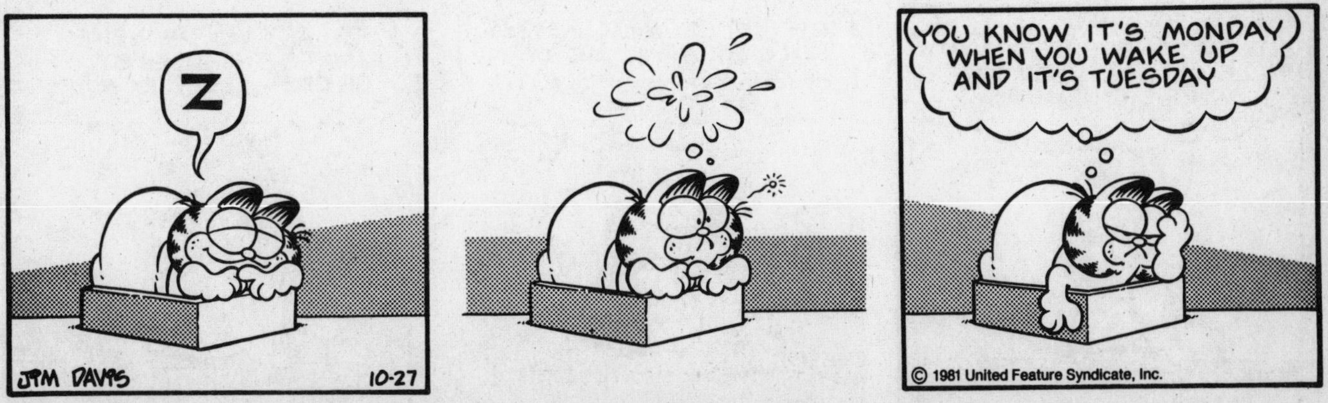
Z
JIM DAVIS
10-27
YOU KNOW IT'S MONDAY WHEN YOU WAKE UP AND IT'S TUESDAY
© 1981 United Feature Syndicate, Inc.

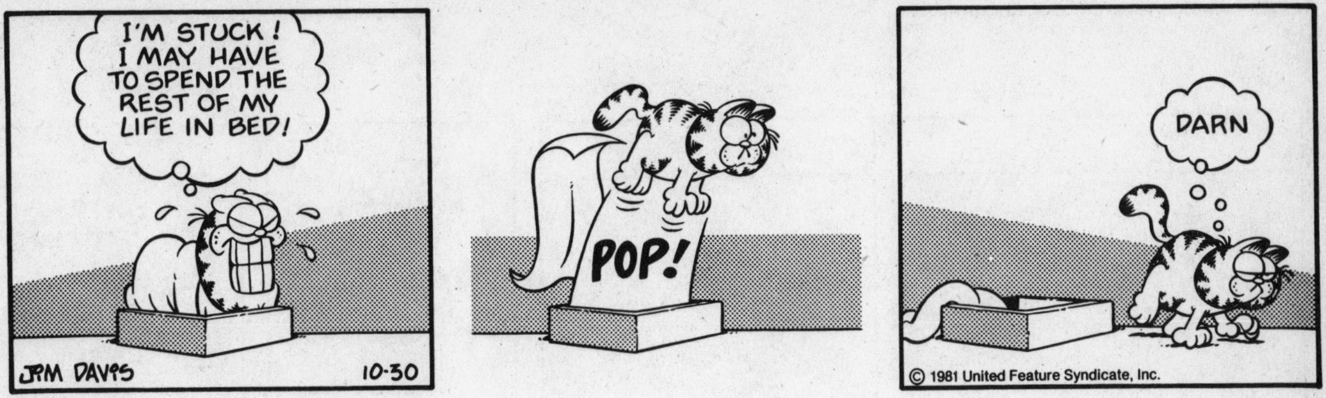
I'M STUCK ! I MAY HAVE TO SPEND THE REST OF MY LIFE IN BED!
JIM DAVIS
10-30
POP!
DARN
© 1981 United Feature Syndicate, Inc.

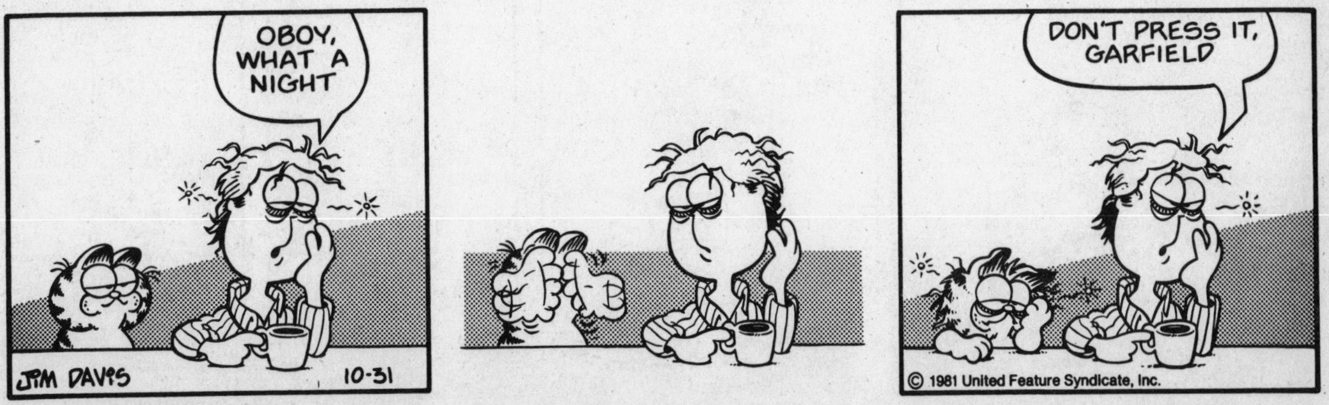
OBOY, WHAT A NIGHT
JIM DAVIS
10-31
DON'T PRESS IT, GARFIELD
© 1981 United Feature Syndicate, Inc.

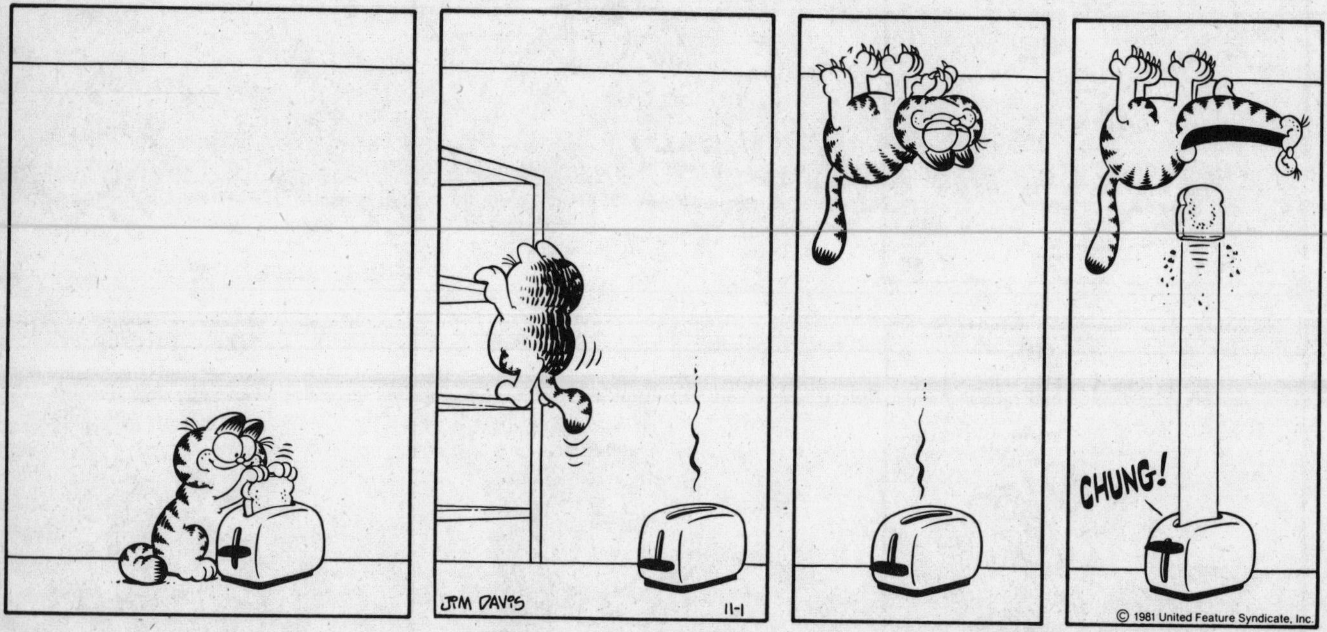
JIM DAVIS
11-1
CHUNG!
© 1981 United Feature Syndicate, Inc.

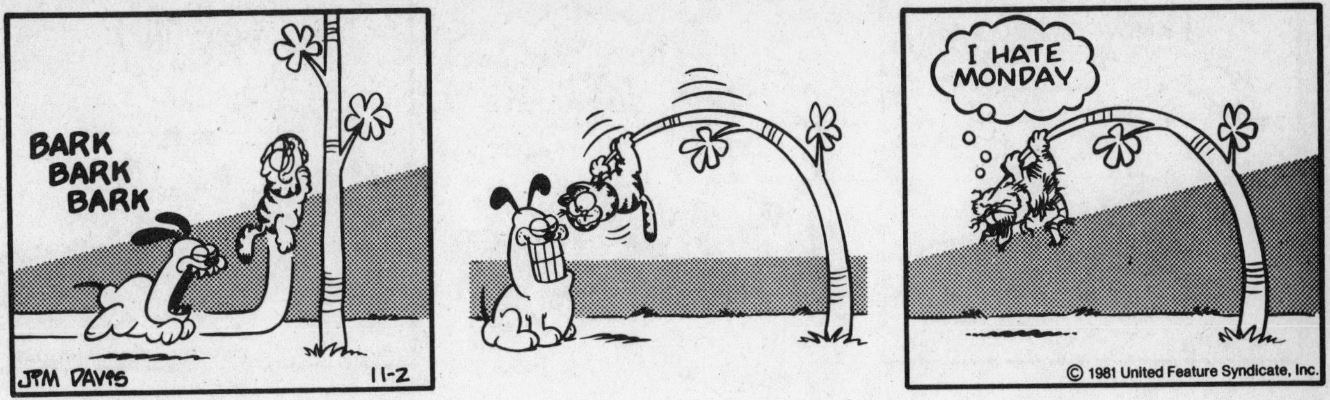
BARK
BARK
BARK
I HATE MONDAY
JIM DAVIS
11-2
© 1981 United Feature Syndicate, Inc.

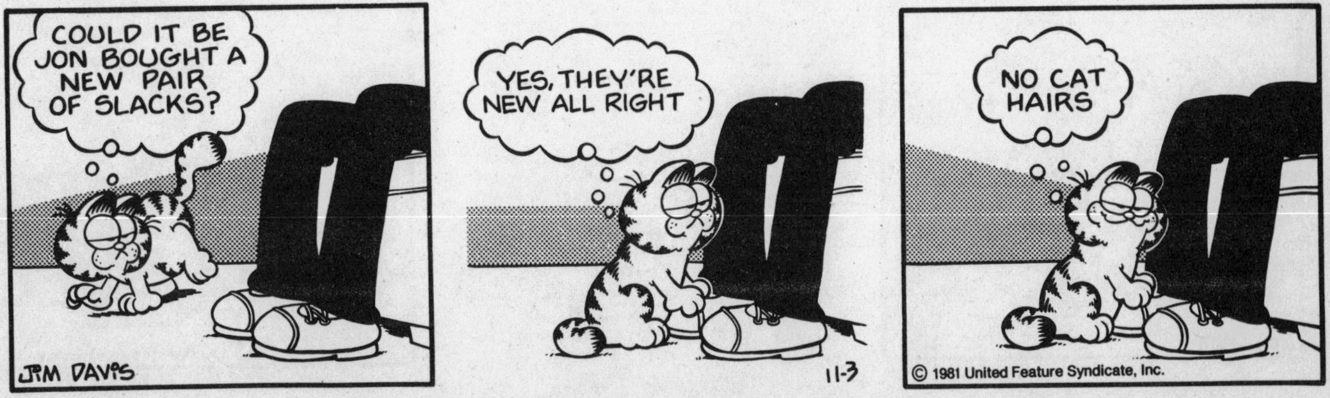
COULD IT BE JON BOUGHT A NEW PAIR OF SLACKS?
YES, THEY'RE NEW ALL RIGHT
NO CAT HAIRS
JIM DAVIS
11-3
© 1981 United Feature Syndicate, Inc.

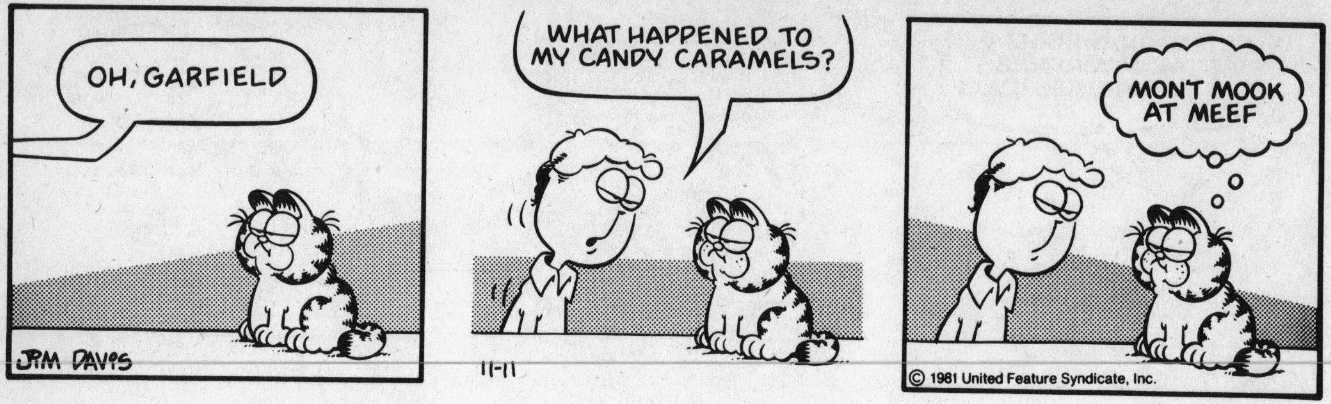
OH, GARFIELD
WHAT HAPPENED TO MY CANDY CARAMELS?
MON'T MOOK AT MEEF
JIM DAVIS
11-11
© 1981 United Feature Syndicate, Inc.

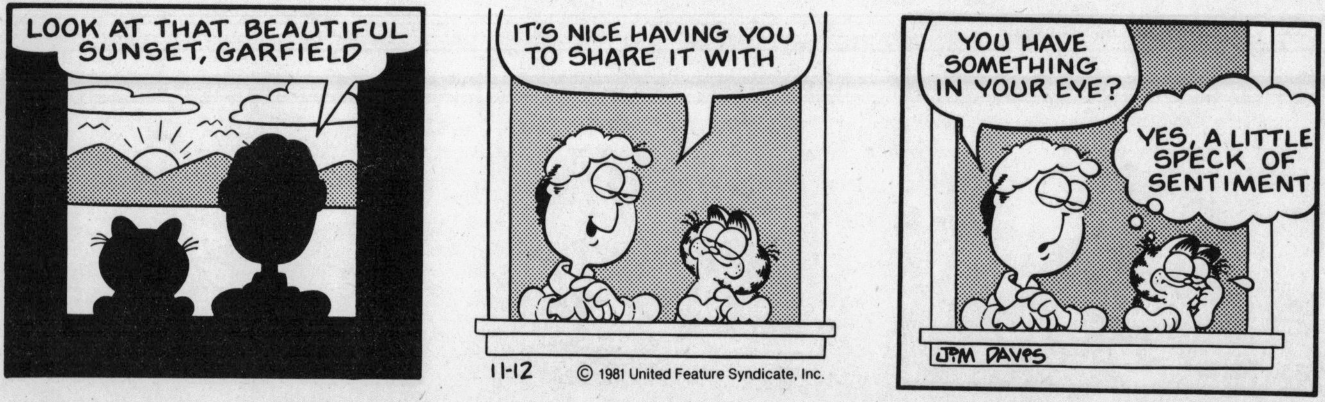
LOOK AT THAT BEAUTIFUL SUNSET, GARFIELD
IT'S NICE HAVING YOU TO SHARE IT WITH
YOU HAVE SOMETHING IN YOUR EYE?
YES, A LITTLE SPECK OF SENTIMENT
JIM DAVIS
11-12
© 1981 United Feature Syndicate, Inc.

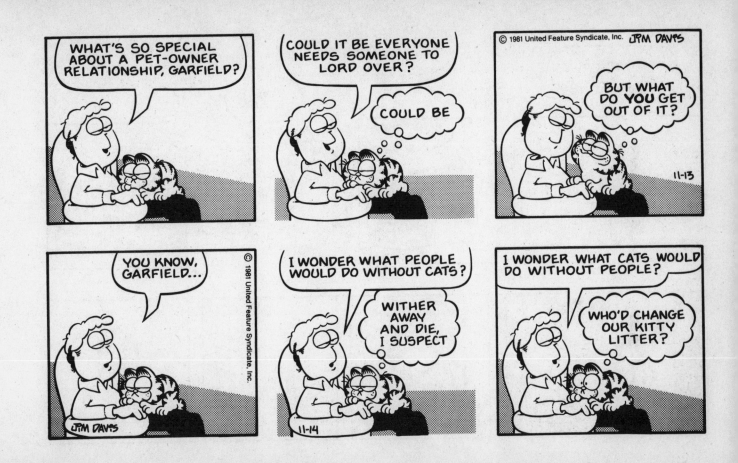

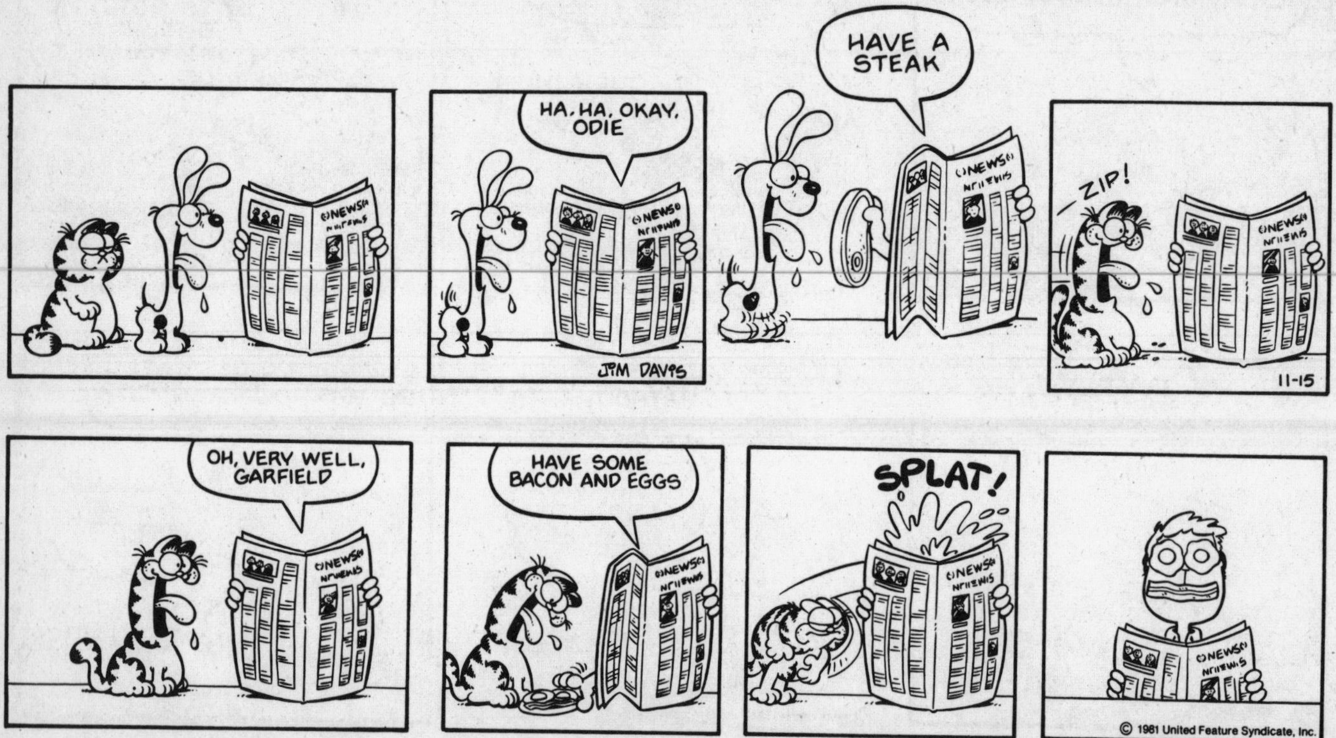
HA, HA, OKAY, ODIE
JIM DAVIS
HAVE A STEAK
ZIP!
11-15
OH, VERY WELL, GARFIELD
HAVE SOME BACON AND EGGS
SPLAT!
© 1981 United Feature Syndicate, Inc.

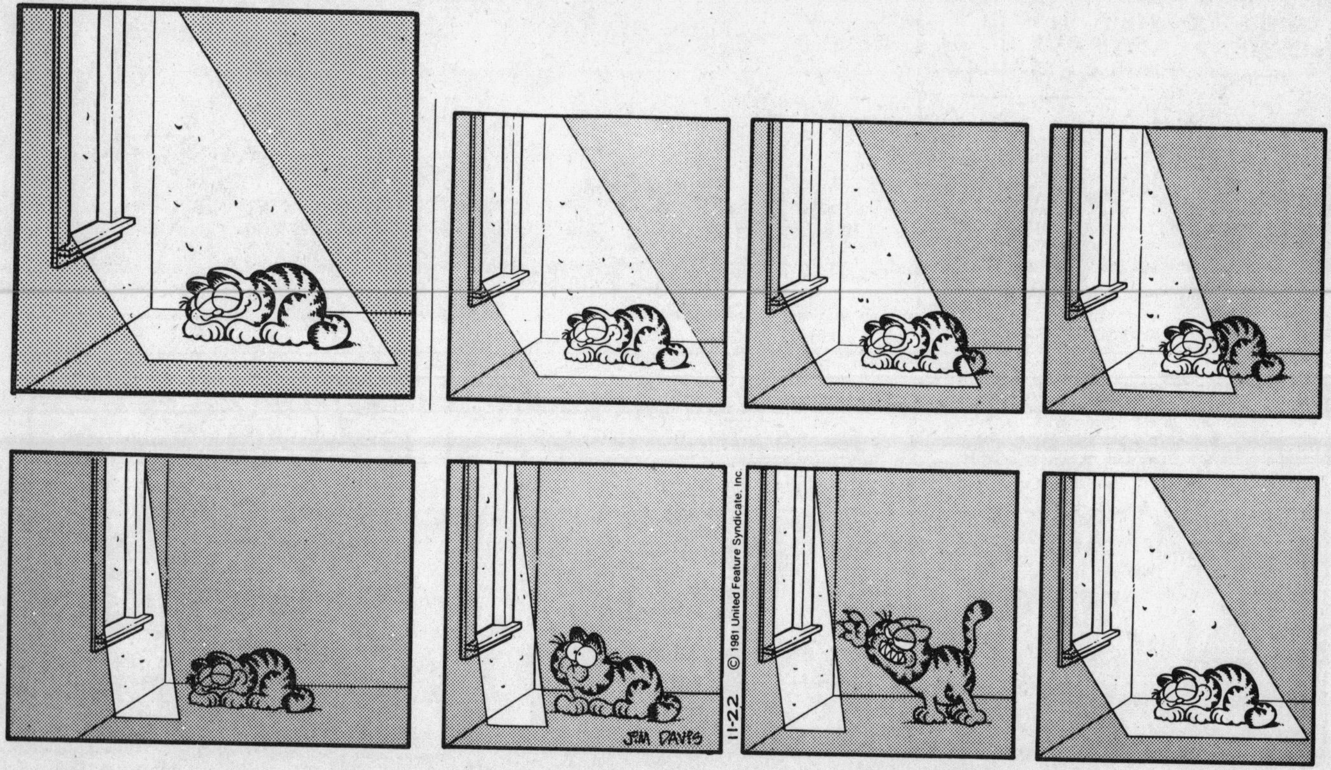
JIM DAVIS
11-22
© 1981 United Feature Syndicate, Inc.

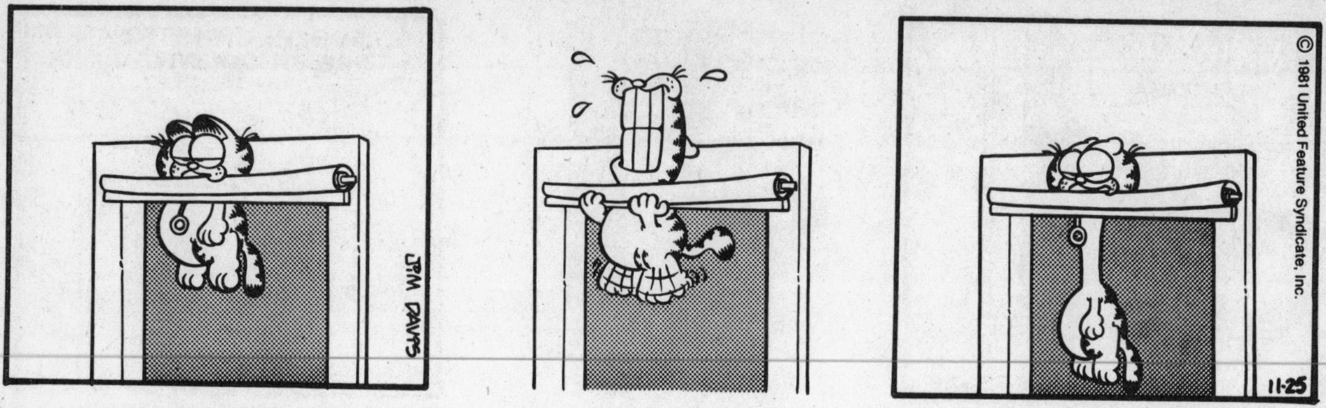
JIM DAVIS
11-25
© 1981 United Feature Syndicate, Inc.

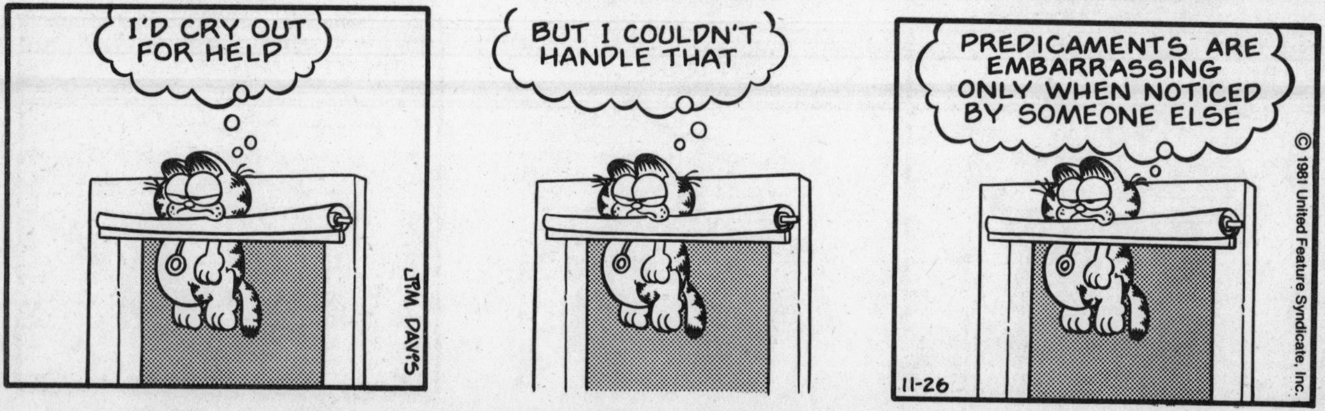
I'D CRY OUT FOR HELP
BUT I COULDN'T HANDLE THAT
PREDICAMENTS ARE EMBARRASSING ONLY WHEN NOTICED BY SOMEONE ELSE
JIM DAVIS
11-26
© 1981 United Feature Syndicate, Inc.

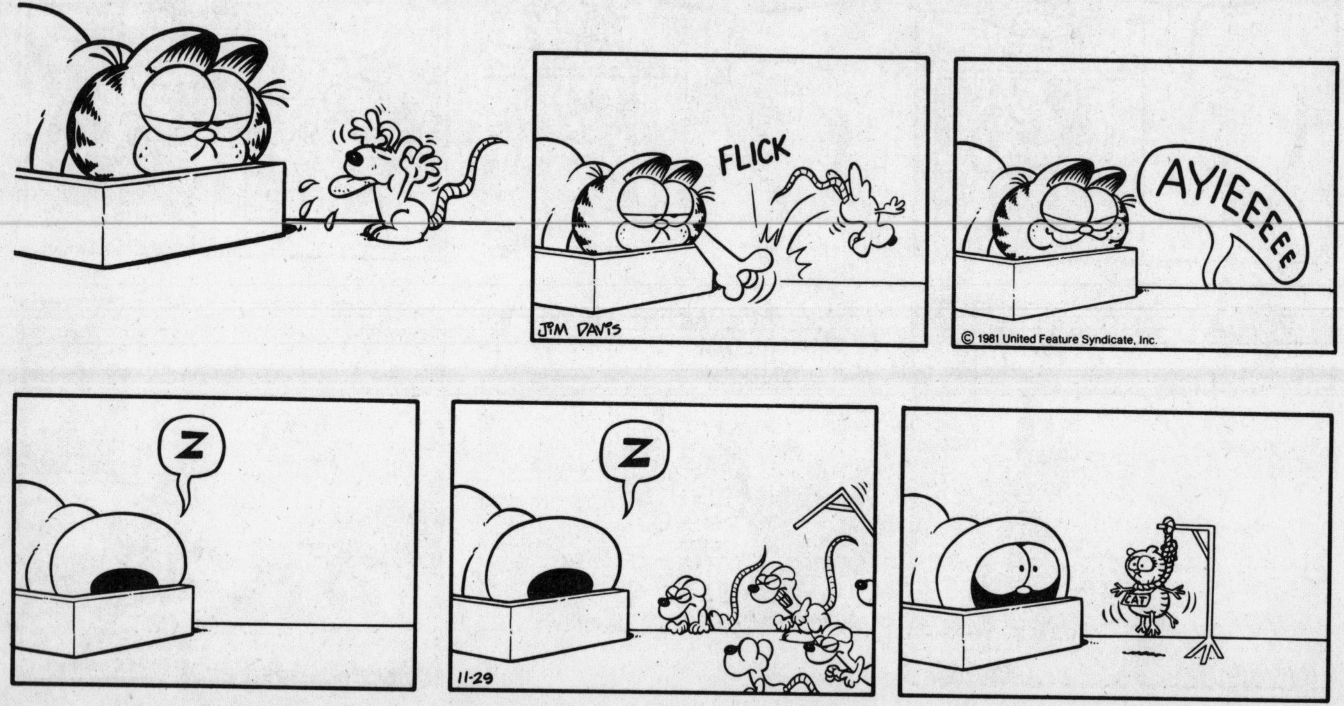
FLICK
JIM DAVIS
AYIEEEEEE
© 1981 United Feature Syndicate, Inc.
Z
Z
11-29
CAT

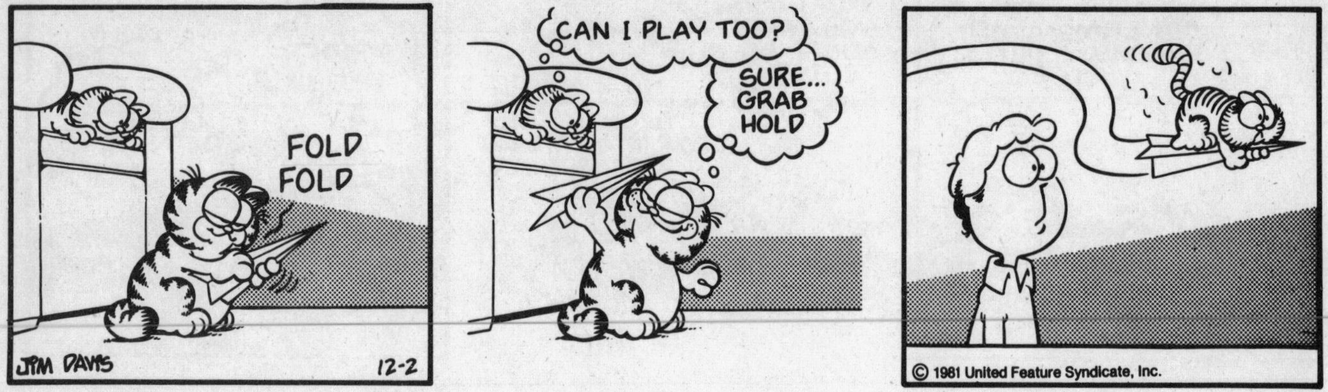
FOLD
FOLD
JIM DAVIS
12-2
CAN I PLAY TOO?
SURE... GRAB HOLD
© 1981 United Feature Syndicate, Inc.

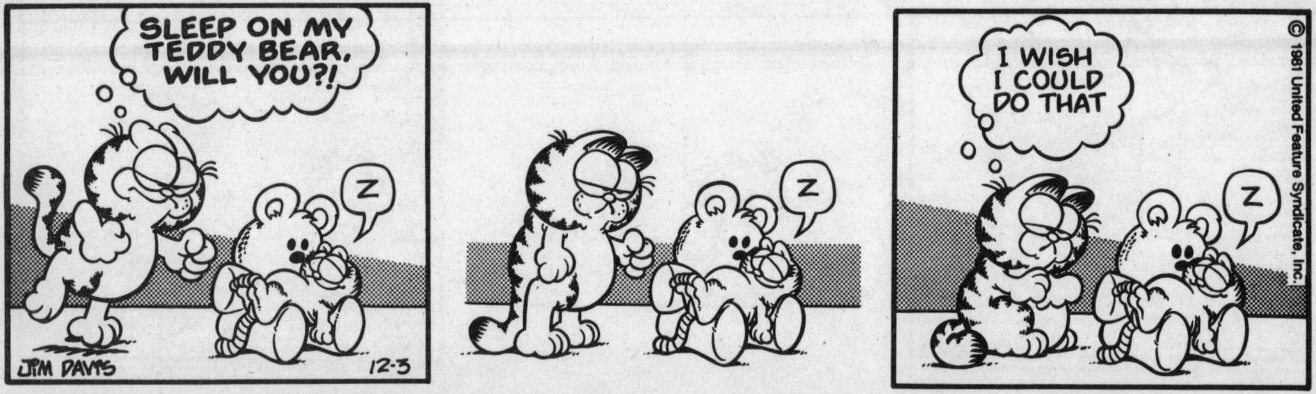
SLEEP ON MY TEDDY BEAR, WILL YOU?!
Z
JIM DAVIS
12-3
Z
I WISH I COULD DO THAT
Z
© 1981 United Feature Syndicate, Inc.

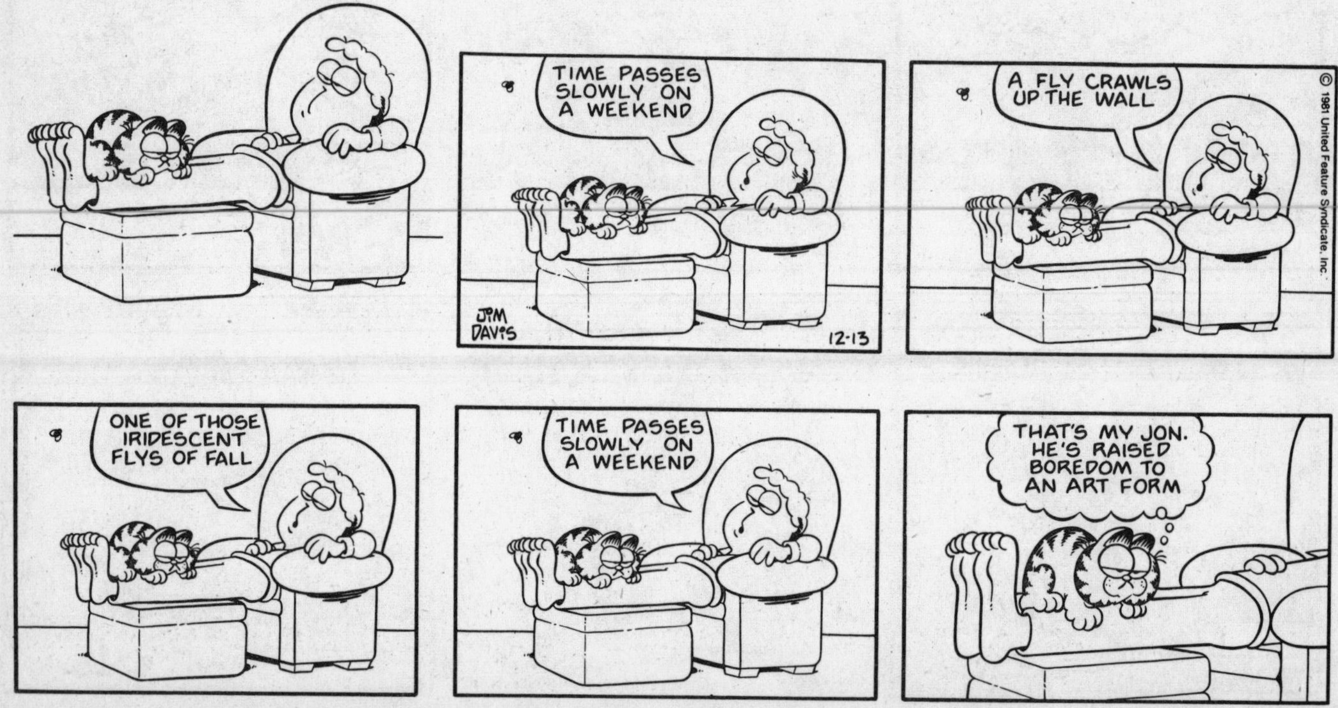
TIME PASSES SLOWLY ON A WEEKEND
A FLY CRAWLS UP THE WALL
ONE OF THOSE IRIDESCENT FLYS OF FALL
TIME PASSES SLOWLY ON A WEEKEND
THAT'S MY JON. HE'S RAISED BOREDOM TO AN ART FORM
JIM DAVIS
12-13
© 1981 United Feature Syndicate, Inc.

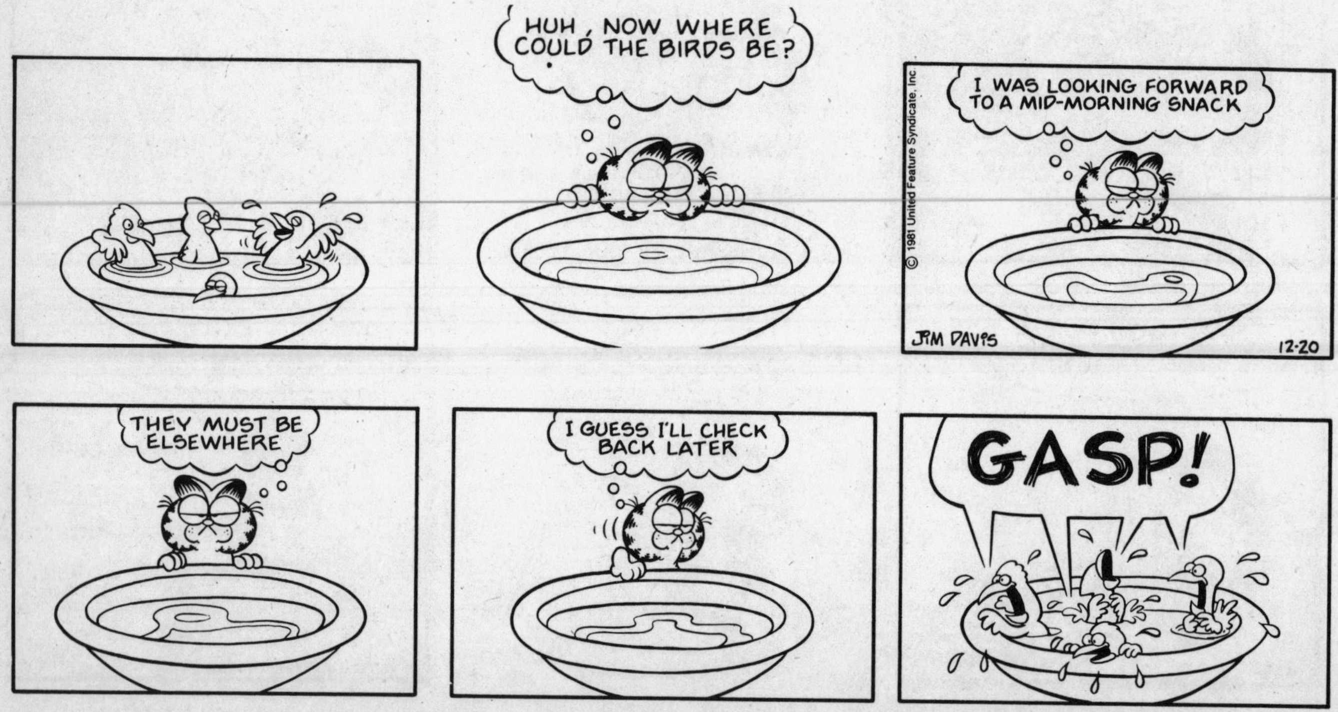
HUH, NOW WHERE COULD THE BIRDS BE?
I WAS LOOKING FORWARD TO A MID-MORNING SNACK
© 1981 United Feature Syndicate, Inc.
JIM DAVIS
12-20
THEY MUST BE ELSEWHERE
I GUESS I'LL CHECK BACK LATER
GASP!

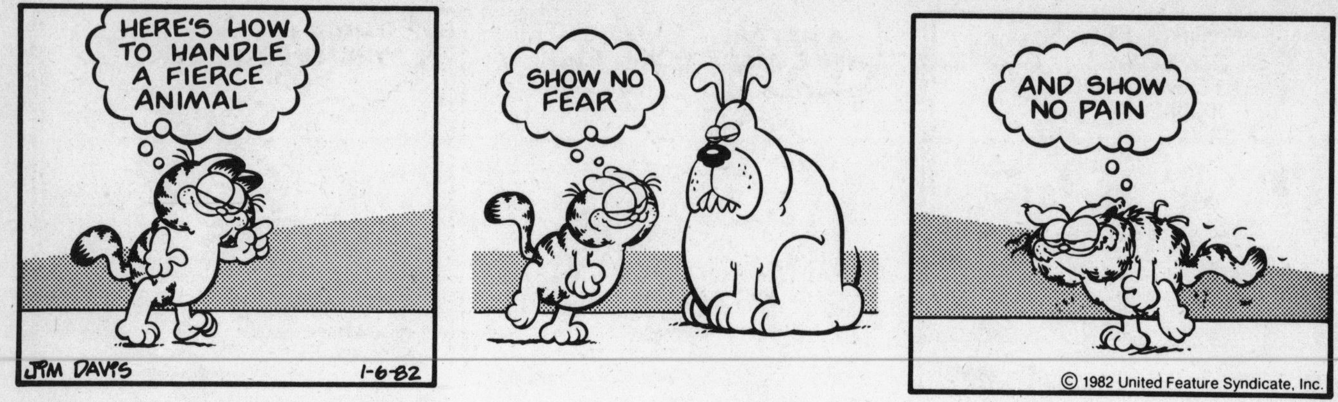
HERE'S HOW TO HANDLE A FIERCE ANIMAL
SHOW NO FEAR
AND SHOW NO PAIN
JIM DAVIS
1-6-82
© 1982 United Feature Syndicate, Inc.

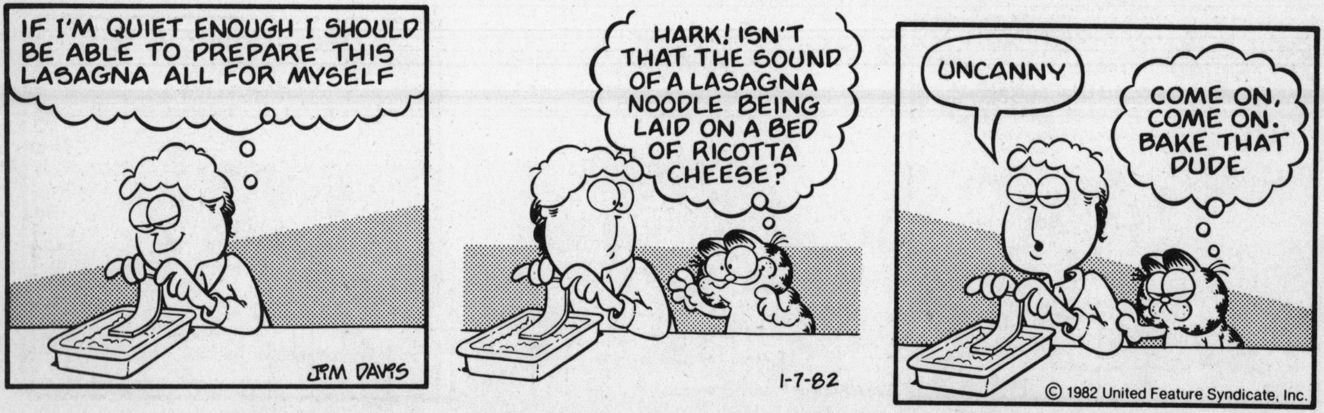
IF I'M QUIET ENOUGH I SHOULD BE ABLE TO PREPARE THIS LASAGNA ALL FOR MYSELF
HARK! ISN'T THAT THE SOUND OF A LASAGNA NOODLE BEING LAID ON A BED OF RICOTTA CHEESE?
UNCANNY
COME ON, COME ON. BAKE THAT DUDE
JIM DAVIS
1-7-82
© 1982 United Feature Syndicate, Inc.

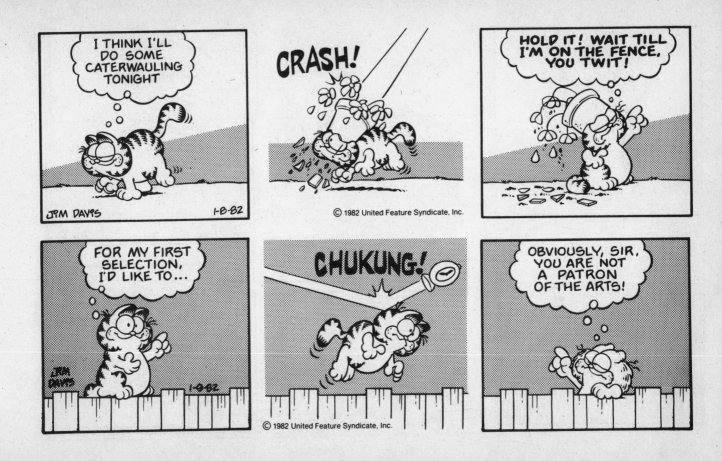

Garfield Goes Globetrotting

The GARFIELD strip appears worldwide.

GARFIELD! DINNER!
I APPRECIATE YOUR PROMPTNESS, GARFIELD...
BUT, NEXT TIME, OPEN THE DOOR!
OOPS
GARFIELD
JIM DAVIS
2-14
© 1981 United Feature Syndicate, Inc.

Here's GARFIELD in English...

¡GARFIELD! LA COMIDA!
ME ALEGRO QUE HAYAS RESPONDI-DO PRONTO
PERO, ABRE LA PUER-TA LA PRÓXIMA VEZ
¡OH!
GARFIELD
JIM DAVIS
© 1981 United Feature Syndicate, Inc.

Spanish...

GARFIELD ! A TABLE !
CONTENT QUE TU OBEISSES SI VITE, GARFIELD...
...MAIS LA PROCHAINE FOIS, OUVRE LA PORTE!
AIE!
GARFIELD
JIM DAVIS
© 1981 United Feature Syndicate, Inc.

French...

GARFIELD! ESSEN!
ICH FREUE MICH ÜBER DEIN PROMPTES ER-SCHEINEN, GARFIELD
ABER MACH NÄCHSTES MAL DIE TÜR AUF!
UPPS
GARFIELD
JIM DAVIS
© 1981 United Feature Syndicate, Inc.

German...

GARFIELD.. SÅ ER DER MAD!
JEG SÆTTER STOR PRIS PÅ DU KOMMER, NÅR JEG KALDER, GARFIELD...
...MEN ÅBN DØREN FØRST !!!
HOVSA!
GARFIELD
© 1981 United Feature Syndicate, Inc.

Danish...

STRIPS, SPECIALS OR BESTSELLING BOOKS . . .
GARFIELD'S ON EVERYONE'S MENU
Don't miss even one episode in the Tubby Tabby's hilarious series!

___GARFIELD AT LARGE (#1) 32013/$6.95
___GARFIELD GAINS WEIGHT (#2) 32008/$6.95
___GARFIELD BIGGER THAN LIFE (#3) 32007/$6.95
___GARFIELD WEIGHS IN (#4) 32010/$6.95
___GARFIELD TAKES THE CAKE (#5) 32009/$6.95
___GARFIELD EATS HIS HEART OUT (#6) 32018/$6.95
___GARFIELD SITS AROUND THE HOUSE (#7) 32011/$6.95
___GARFIELD TIPS THE SCALES (#8) 33580/$6.95
___GARFIELD LOSES HIS FEET (#9) 31805/$6.95
___GARFIELD MAKES IT BIG (#10) 31928/$6.95
___GARFIELD ROLLS ON (#11) 32634/$6.95
___GARFIELD OUT TO LUNCH (#12) 33118/$6.95
___GARFIELD FOOD FOR THOUGHT (#13) 34129/$6.95

___GARFIELD SWALLOWS HIS PRIDE (#14) 34725/$6.95
___GARFIELD WORLDWIDE (#15) 35158/$6.95
___GARFIELD ROUNDS OUT (#16) 35388/$6.95
___GARFIELD CHEWS THE FAT (#17) 35956/$6.95
___GARFIELD GOES TO WAIST (#18) 36430/$6.95
___GARFIELD HANGS OUT (#19) 36835/$6.95
___GARFIELD TAKES UP SPACE (#20) 37029/$6.95
___GARFIELD SAYS A MOUTHFUL (#21) 37368/$6.95
___GARFIELD BY THE POUND (#22) 37579/$6.95
___GARFIELD KEEPS HIS CHINS UP (#23) 37959/$6.95
___GARFIELD TAKES HIS LICKS (#24) 38170/$6.95
___GARFIELD HITS THE BIG TIME (#25) 38332/$6.95

GARFIELD AT HIS SUNDAY BEST!
___GARFIELD TREASURY 32106/$11.95
___THE SECOND GARFIELD TREASURY 33276/$10.95
___THE THIRD GARFIELD TREASURY 32635/$11.00
___THE FOURTH GARFIELD TREASURY 34726/$10.95
___THE FIFTH GARFIELD TREASURY 36268/$12.00
___THE SIXTH GARFIELD TREASURY 37367/$10.95
___THE SEVENTH GARFIELD TREASURY 38427/$10.95

Please send me the BALLANTINE BOOKS I have checked above. I am enclosing $_____. (Please add $2.00 for the first book and $.50 for each additional book for postage and handling and include the appropriate state sales tax.) Send check or money order (no cash or C.O.D.'s) to Ballantine Mail Sales Dept. TA, 400 Hahn Road, Westminster, MD 21157.

To order by phone, call 1-800-733-3000 and use your major credit card.

Prices and numbers are subject to change without notice. Valid in the U.S. only. All orders are subject to availability.

Name_____

Address_____

City_____ State_____ Zip_____

Allow at least 4 weeks for delivery   7/93